CCIE Professional Development
Cisco LAN Switching

Kennedy Clark, CCIE #2175, CCSI
Kevin Hamilton, CCSI

Cisco Press

Cisco Press
201 West 103rd Street
Indianapolis, IN 46290 USA

Cisco LAN Switching

Kennedy Clark, Kevin Hamilton

Copyright© 1999 Cisco Press

Cisco Press logo is a trademark of Cisco Systems, Inc.

Published by:
Cisco Press
201 West 103rd Street
Indianapolis, IN 46290 USA

Printed in the United States of America   3 4 5 6 7 8 9 0

Library of Congress Cataloging-in-Publication Number: 99-61692

ISBN: 1-57870-094-9

Warning and Disclaimer

This book is designed to provide information about Cisco LAN switching. Every effort has been made to make this book as complete and as accurate as possible, but no warranty or fitness is implied.

The information is provided on an "as is" basis. The authors, Cisco Press, and Cisco Systems, Inc., shall have neither liability nor responsibility to any person or entity with respect to any loss or damages arising from the information contained in this book or from the use of the discs or programs that may accompany it.

The opinions expressed in this book belong to the author and are not necessarily those of Cisco Systems, Inc.

Trademark Acknowledgments

All terms mentioned in this book that are known to be trademarks or service marks have been appropriately capitalized. Cisco Press or Cisco Systems, Inc. cannot attest to the accuracy of this information. Use of a term in this book should not be regarded as affecting the validity of any trademark or service mark.

Feedback Information

At Cisco Press, our goal is to create in-depth technical books of the highest quality and value. Each book is crafted with care and precision, undergoing rigorous development that involves the unique expertise of members from the professional technical community.

Readers' feedback is a natural continuation of this process. If you have any comments regarding how we could improve the quality of this book, or otherwise alter it to better suit your needs, you can contact us through e-mail at ciscopress@mcp.com. Please make sure to include the book title and ISBN in your message.

We greatly appreciate your assistance.

Publisher	John Wait
Executive Editor	John Kane
Cisco Systems Program Manager	Jim LeValley
Managing Editor	Patrick Kanouse
Acquisitions Editor	Brett Bartow
Development Editor	Christopher Cleveland
Project Editor	Caroline Wise
Copy Editor	Kelli Brooks
Technical Editors	Tom Nosella, Jennifer DeHaven Carroll, Phil Bourgeois, Merwyn Andrade, Stuart Hamilton
Team Coordinator	Amy Lewis
Book Designer	Gina Rexrode
Cover Designer	Aren Howell
Production Team	Steve Gifford
Indexer	Tim Wright

CISCO SYSTEMS

CISCO PRESS

Corporate Headquarters
Cisco Systems, Inc.
170 West Tasman Drive
San Jose, CA 95134-1706
USA
http://www.cisco.com
Tel: 408 526-4000
      800 553-NETS (6387)
Fax: 408 526-4100

European Headquarters
Cisco Systems Europe s.a.r.l.
Parc Evolic, Batiment L1/L2
16 Avenue du Quebec
Villebon, BP 706
91961 Courtaboeuf Cedex
France
http://www-europe.cisco.com
Tel: 33 1 69 18 61 00
Fax: 33 1 69 28 83 26

Americas Headquarters
Cisco Systems, Inc.
170 West Tasman Drive
San Jose, CA 95134-1706
USA
http://www.cisco.com
Tel: 408 526-7660
Fax: 408 527-0883

Asia Headquarters
Nihon Cisco Systems K.K.
Fuji Building, 9th Floor
3-2-3 Marunouchi
Chiyoda-ku, Tokyo 100
Japan
http://www.cisco.com
Tel: 81 3 5219 6250
Fax: 81 3 5219 6001

Cisco Systems has more than 200 offices in the following countries. Addresses, phone numbers, and fax numbers are listed on the Cisco Connection Online Web site at http://www.cisco.com/offices.

Argentina • Australia • Austria • Belgium • Brazil • Canada • Chile • China • Colombia • Costa Rica • Croatia • Czech Republic • Denmark • Dubai, UAE Finland • France • Germany • Greece • Hong Kong • Hungary • India • Indonesia • Ireland • Israel • Italy • Japan • Korea • Luxembourg • Malaysia Mexico • The Netherlands • New Zealand • Norway • Peru • Philippines • Poland • Portugal • Puerto Rico • Romania • Russia • Saudi Arabia • Singapore Slovakia • Slovenia • South Africa • Spain • Sweden • Switzerland • Taiwan • Thailand • Turkey • Ukraine • United Kingdom • United States • Venezuela

About the Authors

Kennedy Clark is a CCIE instructor and consultant for Chesapeake Computer Consultants, Inc. (CCCI), a Cisco training partner. As a Cisco Certified Systems Instructor (CCSI), Kennedy was one of the original Catalyst instructors for Cisco. Having focused on Catalyst and ATM switching since 1996, he has taught a wide variety of switching classes. As a consultant for CCCI, Kennedy has been involved in the design and implementation of many large, switched backbones.

Kevin Hamilton is also an instructor and consultant for Chesapeake. As a CCSI, Kevin spends most of his instructional time teaching the Cisco Catalyst and ATM courses. Prior to joining Chesapeake, Kevin worked for 11 years at Litton-FiberCom, where he designed and deployed numerous analog and digital communications systems worldwide, including Ethernet, Token-Ring, FDDI, and ATM. Kevin obtained a degree in Electrical Engineering from Pennsylvania State University.

About the Technical Reviewers

Merwyn Andrade works as a Senior Technical Marketing Engineer for Cisco Systems, Inc. in San Jose, California. Merwyn works closely with Cisco engineering and customers on features running across Cisco switches as well as enhancements to minimizing downtime and convergence and improving network availability. Merwyn also has a patent in progress in this area. Prior to Cisco, Merwyn worked with the Bombay Stock Exchange and as a Network Consultant with HCL-Hewlett Packard in India. He is an Industrial Electronics Engineer from Bombay, India.

Philip B. Bourgeois has been in the computer industry for fifteen years, spending seven years as a networking specialist with IBM and the past five years as a Senior Systems Engineer with Cisco Systems. Phil is experienced in the design and implementation of large IP and multiprotocol networks, encompassing complex wide area network designs and campus local area networks. Phil is a networking consultant to the largest commercial enterprises in the northeast area, including insurance, the health care industry, aerospace, pharmaceuticals, casino/gaming industry, state government agencies, and higher education. His current position is as a Consulting Systems Engineer with a specialty focus in high-speed LAN switching and ATM network design projects.

Jennifer DeHaven Carroll is a Principal Consultant for International Network Services. She is CCIE number 1402. She earned her Bachelor of Science degree in Computer Science from University of California, Santa Barbara. In the past 11 years, Jennifer has planned, designed, and implemented many networks, utilizing both Layer 2 and Layer 3 techniques. She has also developed and taught many theory and Cisco implementation classes on various networking technologies.

Stuart Hamilton is the Senior Manager of Enterprise Network Design at Cisco Systems where he leads a team of engineers focused on the design requirements of enterprise customers. Stuart is a CCIE and joined Cisco in 1992 where, as a System Engineer and Consulting Engineer, worked closely in the field with numerous customers on large scale network designs and implementations. Early in Stuart's 14 years of experience he held various technical design and engineering roles at Bell Northern Research, Northern Telecom (now Nortel Networks), and Cognos Incorporated.

Tom Nosella is Manager of Network Design Engineering for Cisco's Enterprise Line of Business. Tom and his team of network design engineers provide direction and expertise in enterprise network design for both Cisco's worldwide systems engineers and Cisco's enterprise customer base. Tom is a CCIE and has six years of experience in managing and designing large data networks for customers within the enterprise and service provider area. Tom joined Cisco Systems from Bell Canada where he led a team of network engineers providing outsourced network management services for large enterprise customers.

Dedications

To my wife, Debbie, for being the most supportive, understanding, patient, and loving partner a person could ever ask for. And, to God, for giving me the ability, gifts, and privilege to work in such an exciting and fulfilling career.

-Kennedy

To my wife, Emily, the true author in our family, who taught me the joy of communication through the printed page and who now has many romantic evenings due in appreciation for the ones neglected. And to my four boys, Jay, Scott, Alex and Caleb, who endured with exceeding patience the hours dad locked himself in a quiet room instead of playing ball and camping.

-Kevin

Acknowledgments

Kennedy Clark: An avid reader of all things nerdy, I have always taken acknowledgements and dedications fairly lightly. Having now been through the book-writing process myself, I can assure you that this will never be the case again. Writing a book (especially one on technology that is as fast-moving as switching) is an incredibly demanding process that warrants a huge number of "thank yous." In the brief space I have here, I would like to express appreciation to a small number of the people involved in this project. First, I would like to thank Kevin Hamilton, my co-author. Kevin was willing to jump into a project that had almost been left for dead because I was feeling completely overwhelmed by the staggering amount of work it involved. I would like to thank Radia Perlman for reading the e-mails and Spanning Tree chapters of an "unknown author." Also, the people at Cisco Press have been wonderful to work with (I would encourage other authors to check them out). Chris Cleveland and Brett Bartow deserve special mention. There are many people at Cisco to thank... Jon Crawfurd for giving a young NetWare guy a chance with router technology. Stuart Hamilton for taking this project under his wing. Merwyn Andrade for being the switching genius I someday hope to be. Tom Nosella for sticking with the project through its entirety. I owe many thanks to the people at Chesapeake Computer Consultants. I would especially like to thank Tim Brown for teaching me one of my first network courses and remaining a faithful friend and mentor. Also, Tom Van Meter for showing me the ropes with ATM. Finally, a very special thanks to my wife for her never-ending love and encouragement.

And, to God, for giving me the ability, gifts, and privilege to work in such an exciting and fulfilling career.

Kevin Hamilton: A project of this magnitude reflects the hard work of many individuals beyond myself. Most notably, Kennedy. He repeatedly amazes me with his ability to not only understand minute details for a vast array of subjects (many of which are Catalyst related), but to reiterate them without reference to written materials months and even years past the time when he is exposed to the point. His keen insights to networking and unique methods of communicating them consistently challenge me to greater professional depths. I, therefore, thank Kennedy for the opportunity to join him in this endeavor, and for the knowledge I gained as a result of sharing ink with him. I also must thank the staff and instructors at Chesapeake Computer Consultants for their continuous inspiration and support as we at times felt discouraged thinking we would never write the last page. And Tim Brown, who taught me that technology can be funny. And lastly, the staff at Cisco Press. Brett Bartow and Chris Cleveland must especially be commended for their direction and vision in this project. They worked hard at keeping us focused and motivated. I truly believe that without their guidance, we could never have produced this book on our own.

Contents at a Glance

Contents

Icons Used in This Book

Throughout the book, you will see the following icons used for the varying types of switches:

ATM Switch

Catalyst 5000

Layer 3 (MLS) Routing Switch

Layer 3 (8500) Switching Router

In addition, you will see the usual battery of network device, peripheral, topology, and connection icons associated with Cisco Systems documentation. These icons are as follows:

Router

Bridge

Repeater

Hub

PBX/SWITCH

MAU

Modem

File Server

Printer

Phone

Terminal

Workstation

PC

Sun Workstation

Macintosh

Telecommuter

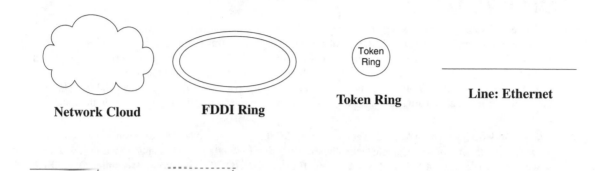

Network Cloud   **FDDI Ring**   **Token Ring**   **Line: Ethernet**

Line: Serial   **Line: Circuit Switched**

Foreword

With the advent of switching technology and specifically the enormously successful Catalyst Switching products from Cisco Systems, corporations all over the world are upgrading their infrastructures to enable their networks for high bandwidth applications. Although the original goal of most switched network design was primarily increased bandwidth, the networks of today require much more with the advent of mission critical applications and IP Voice emerging as mainstream networking requirements. It is therefore important not only to reap the bandwidth benefits of Catalyst switching but also learn sound network design principles leveraging all of the features in the Catalyst software suite.

One thing network designers have learned over the years is that things never get any easier when it comes to understanding and evaluating all of the available technologies that appear in standards bodies and are written about in trade magazines. We read about MPOA, LANE, Gigabit Ethernet, 802.1Q, 802.1p, Layer 3 switching, OSPF, BGP, VPN, MPLS, and many others. The key, however, to building and operating a successful network is understanding the basic fundamentals of the relevant technologies, knowing where and how to apply them most effectively in a network, and most importantly leveraging the successes of others to streamline the deployment of the network. Internetworking design is part art and part science mostly due to the fact that the applications that ride on top of the network have widely varying traffic characteristics. This represents another challenge when designing a network because you might well optimize it to perform for a certain application only to find that a few months later a brand new application places entirely differing demands on the network.

The science part of campus network design relies on a few basic principles. First, every user connects to a port on a switch and so wiring closets are provisioned with Catalyst switches such as the Catalyst 5000 family to connect end users either at 10 megabit Ethernet or increasingly 100 megabit Ethernet. The base level of switching capability here is called Layer 2 switching.

There are typically tens to hundreds of wiring closets that need to be connected somehow. Although there are many ways to do this, experience has taught us that a structured approach with some hierarchy is the best technique for a stable and easily expandable network. Wiring closets then are typically consolidated into a network layer called the distribution layer that is characterized by a combination of Layer 2 and Layer 3 switching.

If the network is large in size, there can still be a large number of distribution layer switches, and so in keeping with the structured methodology, another layer is used to network the distribution layer together. Often called the core of the network, a number of technologies can be used, typified by ATM, Gigabit Ethernet, and Layer 3 switching.

This probably sounds rather simple at this point, however as you can see from the thickness of this book, there is plenty of art (and a lot more science) toward making your design into a highly available, easy to manage, expandable, easy to troubleshoot network and preparing you with a solid foundation for new emerging applications.

This book not only covers the science part of networking in great detail in the early chapters, but more importantly deals with real-world experience in the implementation of networks using Catalyst products. The book's authors not only teach this material in training classes but also have to prove that they can make the network work at customer sites. This invaluable experience is captured throughout the book. Reading these tips carefully can save you countless hours of time experimenting on finding the best way to fine tune your particular network. In addition, as part of the CCIE Professional Development series of Cisco Press, you can use the experience gained from reading and understanding this book to prepare for one of the most sought after professional certifications in the industry.

Stuart Hamilton, CCIE #1282

Senior Manager, Enterprise Network Design

Cisco Systems Inc.

Introduction

Driven by a myriad of factors, LAN switching technology has literally taken the world by storm. The Internet, Web technology, new applications, and the convergence of voice, video, and data have all placed unprecedented levels of traffic on campus networks. In response, network engineers have had to look past traditional network solutions and rapidly embrace switching. Cisco, *the* router company, has jumped heavily into the LAN switching arena and quickly established a leadership position. The Catalyst series of switches has set a new standard for performance and features, not to mention sales.

Despite the popularity of campus switching equipment, it has been very difficult to obtain detailed and clear information on how it should be designed, utilized, and deployed. Although many books have been published in the last several years on routing technology, virtually no books have been published on LAN switching. The few that have been published are vague, out-of-date, and absent of real-world advice. Important topics such as the Spanning-Tree Protocol and Layer 3 switching have either been ignored or received inadequate coverage. Furthermore, most have contained virtually no useful information on the subject of campus design.

This book was written to change that. It has the most in-depth coverage of LAN switching technology in print to date. Not only does it have expansive coverage of foundational issues, but it is also full of practical suggestions. Proven design models, technologies, and strategies are thoroughly discussed and analyzed.

Both authors have drawn on their extensive experience with campus switching technology. As two of the first certified Catalyst instructors, they have first-hand knowledge of how to effectively communicate switching concepts. Through design and implementation experience, they have a detailed understanding of what works, as well as what doesn't work.

Objectives

Cisco LAN Switching is designed to help people move forward with their knowledge of the exciting field of campus switching. CCIE candidates will receive broad and comprehensive instruction on a wide variety of switching-related technologies. Other network professionals will also benefit from hard-to-find information on subjects such as Layer 3 switching and campus design best practices.

Audience

Cisco LAN Switching should appeal to a wide variety of people working in the network field. It is designed for any network administrator, engineer, designer, or manager who requires a detailed knowledge of LAN switching technology.

Obviously, the book is designed to be an authoritative source for network engineers preparing for the switching portion of the CCIE exams and Cisco Career Certifications. *Cisco LAN Switching* is not a "quick fix" guide that helps you cram (such books are virtually worthless when it comes to taking the CCIE practical exams). Instead, it focuses extensively on theory and building practical knowledge. When allied with hands-on experience, this can be a potent combination.

However, this book is designed to go far beyond test preparation. It is designed to be both a tutorial and a reference tool for a wide range of network professionals, including the following:

- People with less switching experience will benefit extensively from the foundational material discussed in Part I. This material then transitions smoothly into the more advanced subject matter discussed in later chapters.
- Network professionals with a detailed understanding of routing but new to campus switching will find that *Cisco LAN Switching* can open up a whole new world of technology.

- Network engineers with extensive switching experience will find *Cisco LAN Switching* taking them farther into the field. For example, much of the Spanning-Tree Protocol information in Part II and the real-world design information in Part V has never been published before. The Catalyst 6000 material discussed in Part VI is also completely new.

- Network designers will benefit from the state-of-the-art coverage of campus design models and the detailed discussions of opposing design strategies.

- Engineers who have already obtained their CCIE will value *Cisco LAN Switching* as a reference tool and for design information.

Organization

The eighteen chapters and one appendix of this book fall into seven parts:

- **Part I: Foundational Issues**—This section takes you through technologies that underlie the material covered in the rest of the book. Important issues such as Fast Ethernet, Gigabit Ethernet, routing versus switching, the types of Layer 2 switching, the Catalyst command-line environment, and VLANs are discussed. Although advanced readers might want to skip some of this material, they are encouraged to at least skim the sections on Gigabit Ethernet and VLANs.

- **Part II: Spanning Tree**—The Spanning-Tree Protocol can make or break a campus network. Despite the ubiquitous deployment of this protocol, very little detailed information about its internals has been published. This section is designed to be the most comprehensive source available on this important protocol. It presents a detailed analysis of common problems and Spanning Tree troubleshooting. This chapter also discusses important enhancements such Port-Fast, UplinkFast, BackboneFast, and PVST+.

- **Part III: Trunking**—Part III examines the critical issue of trunk connections, the links used to carry multiple VLANs throughout a campus network. Chapter 8 begins with a detailed discussion of trunking concepts and covers Ethernet-based forms of trunking, ISL, and 802.1Q. Chapters 9 and 10 look at LAN Emulation (LANE) and MPOA (Multiprotocol over ATM), two forms of trunking that utilize Asynchronous Transfer Mode (ATM).

- **Part IV: Advanced Features**—This section begins with an in-depth discussion of the important topic of Layer 3 switching, a technology that has created a whole switching paradigm. Both MLS (routing switch) and hardware-based (switching router) routing are examined. The next two chapters examine the VLAN Trunking Protocol (VTP) and multicast-related topics such as Cisco Group Management Protocol (CGMP) and Internet Group Membership Protocol (IGMP) Snooping.

- **Part V: Real-World Campus Design and Implementation**—Part V focuses on real-world issues such as design, implementation, and troubleshooting. These chapters are oriented toward helping you benefit from the collective advice of many LAN switching experts.

- **Part VI: Catalyst 6000 Technology**—This section includes a chapter that analyzes the Catalyst 6000 and 6500 models. Focusing primarily on Layer 3 switching, it discusses the important "Native IOS Mode" of operation.

- **Part VII: Appendix**—The single appendix in this section provides answers and solutions to the Review Questions and Hands-On Labs from the book.

Features and Conventions

Where applicable, each chapter includes a variety of questions and exercises to further your knowledge of the material covered in that chapter. Many of the questions probe at the theoretical issues that indicate your mastery of the subject matter. Other questions and exercises provide an opportunity to build switching scenarios yourself. By utilizing extra equipment you might have available, you can build your own laboratory to explore campus switching. For those not fortunate enough to have racks of idle switching gear, the authors will be working with MentorLabs (http://www.mentorlabs.com) to provide value-added labs via the Internet.

Two conventions are used to draw your attention to sidebar, important, or useful information:

TIP	Tips are used to highlight important points or useful shortcuts.

NOTE	Notes are used for sidebar information related to the main text.

Various elements of Catalyst and Cisco router command syntax are presented in the course of each chapter. This book uses the same conventions as the Cisco documentation:

- Vertical bars (|) separate alternative, mutually exclusive, elements.
- Square brackets [] indicate optional elements.
- Braces { } indicate a required choice.
- Braces within square brackets [{ }] indicate a required choice within an optional element.
- **Boldface** indicates commands and keywords that are entered literally as shown.
- *Italics* indicate arguments for which you supply values.

Feedback

If you have questions, comments, or feedback, please contact the authors at the following e-mail addresses. By letting us know of any errors, we can fix them for the benefit of future generations. Moreover, being technical geeks in the true sense of the word, we are always up for a challenging technical discussion.

Kennedy Clark   KClark@iname.com
Kevin Hamilton   KHamilton@ccci.com

Foundational Issues

This chapter covers the following key topics:

- **Legacy Ethernet**—This section explains the operations and implementation rules of legacy 10 Mbps CSMA/CD systems.

- **LAN Frames**—This section presents various common formats for transporting packets over Ethernet.

- **Fast Ethernet**—A now popular desktop Ethernet migration, this uses 100 Mbps technology. This section describes its characteristics and some of the common media options.

- **Gigabit Ethernet**—As the highest speed Ethernet available today, this technology finds immediate utility for trunking Catalysts and connecting high performance servers. This section describes media options and characteristics.

- **Token Ring**—Token Ring, the other popular LAN alternative, operates very differently from Ethernet. This section provides a brief overview of Token Ring.

CHAPTER 1

Desktop Technologies

Since the inception of local-area networks (LANs) in the 1970s, numerous LAN technologies graced the planet at one point or another. Some technologies became legends: ArcNet and StarLAN, for example. Others became legacies: Ethernet, Token Ring, and FDDI. ArcNet was the basis for some of the earliest office networks in the 1980s, because Radio Shack sold it for its personal computer line, Model II. A simple coaxial-based network, it was easy to deploy by office administrators for a few workstations. StarLAN, one of the earliest twisted-pair network technologies, became the basis for the Institute of Electrical and Electronic Engineers (IEEE) 10BaseT network. Running at 1 Mbps, StarLAN demonstrated that networking over twisted pair was feasible. Both ArcNet and StarLAN enjoyed limited success in the market because higher speed technologies such as 10 Mbps Ethernet and 4 Mbps Token Ring were introduced soon afterwards. With the higher bandwidth capacity of newer network technologies and the rapid development of higher speed workstations demanding more network bandwidth, ArcNet (now fondly referred to as ArchaicNet) and StarLAN were doomed to limited market presence.

The legacy networks continue to find utility as distribution and backbone technologies for both manufacturing and office environments. But like ArcNet and StarLAN, even these technologies see higher speed networks such as Fast Ethernet, High Speed Token Ring, and ATM crowding into the network arena. However, the legacy systems will remain for many more years due to the existence of such a large installed base. Users will replace Ethernet and Token Ring in phases as applications demand more bandwidth.

This chapter discusses the legacy network technologies, Ethernet and Token Ring, as well as Fast Ethernet and Gigabit Ethernet. Although Gigabit Ethernet is not yet a popular desktop technology, it is discussed here because of its relationship to Ethernet and its use in Catalyst networks for trunking Catalysts together. This chapter also describes how the access methods operate, some of the physical characteristics of each, and various frame formats and address types.

Legacy Ethernet

When mainframe computers dominated the industry, user terminals attached either directly to ports on the computer or to a controller that gave the appearance of a direct connection. Each wire connection was dedicated to an individual terminal. Users entered data, and the terminal immediately transmitted signals to the host. Performance was driven by the horsepower in the hosts. If the host became overworked, users experienced delays in responses. Note, though, that the connection between the host and terminal was not the cause in the delay. The users had full media bandwidth on the link regardless of the workload of the host device.

Facility managers installing the connections between the terminal and the host experienced distance constraints imposed by the host's terminal line technology. The technology limited users to locations that were a relatively short radius from the host. Further, labor to install the cables created inflated installation and maintenance expenses. Local-area networks (LANs) mitigated these issues to a large degree. One of the immediate benefits of a LAN was to reduce the installation and maintenance costs by eliminating the need to install dedicated wires to each user. Instead, a single cable pulled from user to user allowed users to share a common infrastructure instead of having dedicated infrastructures for each station.

A technology problem arises when users share a cable, though. Specifically, how does the network control who uses the cable and when? Broadband technologies like cable television (CATV) support multiple users by multiplexing data on different channels (frequencies). For example, think of each video signal on a CATV system as a data stream. Each data stream is transported over its own channel. A CATV system carries multiple channels on a single cable and can, therefore, carry multiple data streams concurrently. This is an example of frequency-division multiplexing (FDM). The initial LANs were conceived as *baseband* technologies, however, which do not have multiple channels. Baseband technologies do not transmit using FDM. Rather, they use bandwidth-sharing, which simply means that users take turns transmitting.

Ethernet and Token Ring define sets of rules known as *access methods* for sharing the cable. The access methods approach media sharing differently, but have essentially the same end goal in mind.

Carrier Sense with Multiple Access with Collision Detection (CSMA/CD)

Carrier sense multiple access collision detect (CSMA/CD) describes the Ethernet access method. CSMA/CD follows rules similar to those in a meeting. In a meeting, all individuals have the right to speak. The unspoken rule that all follows, though, is "Only one person can talk at a time." If you have something to say, you need to listen to see if someone is speaking. If someone is already speaking, you must wait until they are finished. When you start to speak, you need to continue to listen in case someone else decides to speak at the same time. If this happens, both parties must stop talking and wait a random amount of time. Only then do they have the right to start the process again. If individuals fail to observe the protocol of only one speaker at a time, the meeting quickly degenerates and no effective communication occurs. (Unfortunately, this happens all too often.)

In Ethernet, *multiple access* is the terminology for many stations attaching to the same cable and having the opportunity to transmit. No station has any priority over any other station. However, they do need to take turns per the access algorithm.

Carrier sense refers to the process of listening before speaking. The Ethernet device wishing to communicate looks for energy on the media (an electrical carrier). If a carrier exists, the cable is in use and the device must wait to transmit. Many Ethernet devices maintain a counter of how often they need to wait before they can transmit. Some devices call the counter a deferral or back-off counter. If the deferral counter exceeds a threshold value of 15 retries, the device attempting to transmit assumes that it will never get access to the cable to transmit the packet. In this situation, the source device discards the frame. This might happen if there are too many devices on the network, implying that there is not enough bandwidth available. When this situation becomes chronic, you should segment the network into smaller segments. Chapter 2, "Segmenting LANs," discusses various approaches to segmentation. If the power level exceeds a certain threshold, that implies to the system that a collision occurred. When stations detect that a collision occurs, the participants generate a *collision enforcement signal*. The enforcement signal lasts as long as the smallest frame size. In the case of Ethernet, that equates to 64 bytes. This ensures that all stations know about the collision and that no other station attempts to transmit during the collision event. If a station experiences too many consecutive collisions, the station stops transmitting the frame. Some workstations display an error message stating **Media not available**. The exact message differs from implementation to implementation, but every workstation attempts to convey to the user that it was unable to send data for one reason or another.

Addressing in Ethernet

How do stations identify each other? In a meeting, you identify the intended recipient by name. You can choose to address the entire group, a set of individuals, or a specific person. Speaking to the group equates to a broadcast; a set of individuals is a multicast; and addressing one person by name is a unicast. Most traffic in a network is unicast in nature, characterized as traffic from a specific station to another specific device. Some applications generate multicast traffic. Examples include multimedia services over LANs. These applications intend for more than one station to receive the traffic, but not necessarily all for all stations. Video conferencing applications frequently implement multicast addressing to specify a group of recipients. Networking protocols create broadcast traffic, whereas IP creates broadcast packets for ARP and other processes. Routers often transmit routing updates as broadcast frames, and AppleTalk, DecNet, Novell IPX, and many other protocols create broadcasts for various reasons.

Figure 1-1 shows a simple legacy Ethernet system with several devices attached. Each device's Ethernet adapter card has a 48-bit (6 octet) address built in to the module that uniquely identifies the station. This is called the Media Access Control (MAC) address, or the hardware address. All of the devices in a LAN must have a unique MAC address. Devices express MAC addresses as hexadecimal values. Sometimes MAC address octets are separated by hyphens (-) sometimes by colons (:) and sometimes periods (.). The three formats of **00-60-97-8F-4F-86**, **00:60:97:8F:4F:86**, and **0060.978F.4F86** all specify the same host. This book usually uses the first format because most of the Catalyst displays use this convention; however, there are a couple of exceptions where you might see the second or third format. Do not let this confuse you. They all represent MAC addresses.

Figure 1-1 *A Simple Ethernet Network*

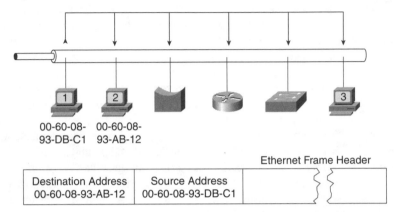

To help ensure uniqueness, the first three octets indicate the vendor who manufactured the interface card. This is known as the Organizational Unique Identifier (OUI). Each manufacturer has a unique OUI value that it acquired from IEEE, the global administrator for OUI values. Cisco has several OUI values: **00000C, 00067C, 0006C1, 001007, 00100B, 00100D, 001011, 001014, 00101F, 001029, 00102F, 001054, 001079, 00107B, 0010A6, 0010F6, 0010FF, 00400B** (formerly Crescendo), **00500F, 005014, 00502A, 00503E, 005050, 005053, 005054, 005073, 005080, 0050A2, 0050A7, 0050BD, 0050E2, 006009, 00602F, 00603E, 006047, 00605C, 006070, 006083, 00900C, 009021, 00902B, 00905F, 00906D, 00906F, 009086, 009092, 0090A6, 0090AB, 0090B1, 0090BF, 0090D9, 0090F2, 00D006, 00D058, 00D0BB, 00D0C0, 00E014, 00E01E, 00E034, 00E04F, 00E08F, 00E0A3, 00E0B0, 00E0F7, 00E0F9,** and **00E0FE.**

The last three octets of the MAC address equate to a host identifier for the device. They are locally assigned by the vendor. The combination of OUI and host number creates a unique address for that device. Each vendor is responsible to ensure that the devices it manufactures have a unique combination of 6 octets.

Unicast Frames

In a LAN, stations must use the MAC address for the Layer 2 address in a frame to identify the source and destination. When Station 1 transmits to Station 2 in Figure 1-1, Station 1 generates a frame that includes Station 2's MAC address (00-60-08-93-AB-12) for the destination and Station 1's address (00-60-08-93-DB-C1) for the source. This is a *unicast* frame. Because the LAN is a shared media, all stations on the network receive a copy of the frame. Only Station 2 performs any processing on the frame, though. All stations compare the destination MAC address with their own MAC address. If they do not match, the station's interface module discards (ignores) the frame. This prevents the packet from consuming CPU cycles in the device. Station 2, however, sees a match and sends the packet to the CPU for further analysis. The CPU examines the network protocol and the intended application and decides whether to drop or use the packet.

Broadcast Frames

Not all frames contain unicast destination addresses. Some have broadcast or multicast destination addresses. Stations treat broadcast and multicast frames differently than they do unicast frames. Stations view broadcast frames as public service announcements. When a station receives a broadcast, it means, "Pay attention! I might have an important message for you!" A broadcast frame has a destination MAC address of FF-FF-FF-FF-FF-FF (all binary 1s). Like unicast frames, all stations receive a frame with a broadcast destination address. When the interface compares its own MAC address against the destination address, they don't match. Normally, a station discards the frame because the destination address does not match its own hardware address. But broadcast frames are treated differently. Even though the destination and built-in address don't match, the interface module is designed so that it still passes the broadcast frame to the processor. This is intentional because designers and users want to receive the broadcast frame as it might have an important request or information. Unfortunately, probably only one or at most a few stations really need to receive the broadcast message. For example, an IP ARP request creates a broadcast frame even though it intends for only one station to respond. The source sends the request as a broadcast because it does not know the destination MAC address and is attempting to acquire it. The only thing the source knows for sure when it creates the ARP request is the destination's IP address. That is not enough, however, to address the station on a LAN. The frame must also contain the MAC address.

Routing protocols sometimes use broadcast MAC addresses when they announce their routing tables. For example, by default, routers send IP RIP updates every 30 seconds. The router transmits the update in a broadcast frame. The router does not necessarily know all of the routers on the network. By sending a broadcast message, the router is sure that all routers attached to the network will receive the message. There is a downside to this, however. All devices on the LAN receive and process the broadcast frame, even though only a few devices really needed the updates. This consumes CPU cycles in every device. If the number of broadcasts in the network becomes excessive, workstations cannot do the things they need to do, such as run word processors or flight simulators. The station is too busy processing useless (for them) broadcast frames.

Multicast Frames

Multicast frames differ from broadcast frames in a subtle way. Multicast frames address a group of devices with a common interest and allow the source to send only one copy of the frame on the network, even though it intends for several stations to receive it. When a station receives a multicast frame, it compares the multicast address with its own address. Unless the card is previously configured to accept multicast frames, the multicast is discarded on the interface and does not consume CPU cycles. (This behaves just like a unicast frame.)

For example, Cisco devices running the Cisco Discovery Protocol (CDP) make periodic announcements to other locally attached Cisco devices. The information contained in the announcement is only interesting to other Cisco devices (and the network administrator). To transfer the announcement, the Cisco source could send a unicast to each and every

Cisco device. That, however, means multiple transmissions on the segment and consumes network bandwidth with redundant information. Further, the source might not know about all of the local Cisco devices and could, therefore, choose to send one broadcast frame. All Cisco devices would receive the frame. Unfortunately, so would all non-Cisco devices. The last alternative is a multicast address. Cisco has a special multicast address reserved, 01-00-0C-CC-CC-CC, which enables Cisco devices to transmit to all other Cisco devices on the segment. All non-Cisco devices ignore this multicast message.

Open Shortest Path First (OSPF), an IP routing protocol, makes routing update announcements on a specially reserved multicast address. The reserved multicast OSPF IP addresses 224.0.0.5 and 224.0.0.6 translate to MAC multicast addresses of 01-00-5E-00-00-05 and 01-00-5E-00-00-06. Chapter 13, "Multicast and Broadcast Services," discusses how these MAC addresses are derived. Only routers interested in receiving the OSPF announcement configure their interface to receive the message. All other devices filter the frame.

LAN Frames

When stations transmit to each other on a LAN, they format the data in a structured manner so that devices know what octets signify what information. Various frame formats are available. When you configure a device, you must define what format your station will use, realizing that more than one format might be configured, as is true for a router.

Figure 1-2 illustrates four common frame formats for Ethernet. Some users interchange the terms *packets* and *frames* rather loosely. According to RFC 1122, a subtle difference exists. Frames refer to the entire message, from the data link layer (Layer 2) header information through and including the user data. Packets exclude Layer 2 headers and only include the IP header (Layer 3 protocol header) through and including user data.

Figure 1-2   *Four Ethernet Frame Formats*

Frame Format	Layer 2 Header Field 14-octets			Data Field 1500-octets						
Ethernet v2 (ARPA)	MAC DA 6-octets	MAC SA 6-octets	Type 2-octets	Data						F C S
802.3	MAC DA 6-octets	MAC SA 6-octets	Length 2-octets	Data						
802.3/802.2	MAC DA 6-octets	MAC SA 6-octets	Length 2-octets	DSAP 1-octet	SSAP 1-octet	Control 1-octet	Data			
802.3/802.2 SNAP	MAC DA 6-octets	MAC SA 6-octets	Length 2-octets	0xAA 1-octet	0xAA 1-octet	0x03 1-octet	Org Code 3-octets	Type 2-octets	Data	4-octets

The frame formats developed as the LAN industry evolved and differing requirements arose for protocols. When XEROX developed the original Ethernet (which was later adopted by the industry), a frame format like the Ethernet frame in Figure 1-2 was defined. The first 6 octets contain the destination's MAC address, whereas the next field of 6 octets contain the source's MAC address. Two bytes follow that indicate to the receiver the correct Layer 3 protocol to which the packet belongs. For example, if the packet belongs to IP, then the type field value is **0x0800**. Table 1-1 lists several common protocols and their associated type values.

Table 1-1   *Common Routed Protocols and Their Hex Type Values*

Protocol	Hex Type Value
IP	0800
ARP	0806
Novell IPX	8137
AppleTalk	809B
Banyan Vines	0BAD
802.3	0000-05DC

Following the type value, the receiver expects to see additional protocol headers. For example, if the type value indicates that the packet is IP, the receiver expects to decode IP headers next. If the value is 8137, the receiver tries to decode the packet as a Novell packet.

IEEE defined an alternative frame format. In the IEEE 802.3 formats, the source and destination MAC addresses remain, but instead of a type field value, the packet length is indicated. Three derivatives to this format are used in the industry: raw 802.3, 802.3 with 802.2 LLC, and 802.3 with 802.2 and SNAP. A receiver recognizes that a packet follows 802.3 formats rather than Ethernet formats by the value of the two-byte field following the source MAC address. If the value falls within the range of 0x0000 and 0x05DC (1500 decimal), the value indicates length; protocol type values begin after 0x05DC.

Ethernet SlotTimes

Ethernet's rules govern how stations operate in a CSMA/CD environment. The rules constantly keep in mind the need to detect collisions and to report them to the participants. Ethernet defines a slotTime wherein a frame travels from one network extreme to the other. In Figure 1-3, assume that Station 1, located at one extreme of the network, transmits a frame. Just before the frame reaches Station 2, located at the other extreme of the network, Station 2 transmits. Station 2 transmits because it has something to send, and because Station 1's frame hasn't arrived yet, Station 2 detects silence on the line. This demonstrates a prime example of a collision event between devices at opposite extremes of the network. Because they are at opposite ends of the network, the timing involves worst case values for detecting and reporting collisions.

Figure 1-3 *A Worst Case Collision Example*

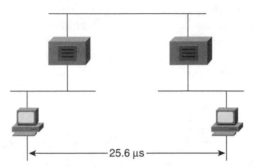

Ethernet rules state that a station must detect and report collisions between the furthest points in the network before the source completes its frame transmission. Specifically, for a legacy 10 Mbps Ethernet, this must all occur within 51.2 microseconds. Why 51.2 microseconds? The time is based on the smallest frame size for Ethernet, which corresponds to the smallest time window to detect and report collisions. The minimum frame size for Ethernet is 64 bytes, which has 512 bits. Each bit time is 0.1 microseconds in length, which is calculated from one over Ethernet's data rate ($1/10^6$). Therefore, the slot time for Ethernet is 0.1 microseconds/bit $\times$ 512 bits or 51.2 microseconds.

Next, the Ethernet specification translates the slotTime into distance. As the Ethernet signal propagates through the various components of the collision domain, time delays are introduced. Time delay values are calculated for copper cables, optical fibers, and repeaters. The amount of delay contributed by each component varies based upon the media characteristics. A correctly designed network topology totals the delay contribution for each component between the network extremes and ensures that the total is less than one half of 51.2 microseconds. This guarantees that Station 2 can detect the collision and report it to Station 1 before Station 1 completes the transmission of the smallest frame.

A network that violates the slotTime rules by extending the network to distances that require more than 51.2 microseconds experience late collisions, which can cause the network to malfunction. When a station transmits, it retains the frame in a local buffer until it either transmits the frame successfully (that is, without a collision) or the deferral counter threshold is exceeded. We previously discussed the deferral counter situation. Assume that a network administrator overextends the network in Figure 1-3 by inserting too many repeaters or by deploying segments that are too long. When Station 1 transmits, it assumes that the frame successfully transmitted if it experiences no collision by the time that it transmits 64 octets. Once the frame believes that it was successfully transmitted, the frame is eliminated from buffers leaving no opportunity to retry. When the network overextends the slotTime, the source might learn of a collision after it transmits the first 64 octets. But no frame is in the buffer at this point to resend, because the source thought that the transmission was successful!

Ethernet Frame Rates/Performance

Debates rage over Ethernet performance. Specifically, network administrators focus on the question, "What is the average loading that should be supported on a network?" Some administrators claim that the network load should not exceed about 30 percent of the available bandwidth. Some state as high as 50 percent. The answer really depends upon your users' application needs. At what point do users complain? When it is most inconvenient for you to do anything about it, of course! Networks rarely support a sustained loading over 50 percent due to bandwidth loss from collisions. Collisions consume bandwidth and force stations to retransmit, consuming even more bandwidth. If the network were collisionless, up to 100 percent utilization could be achieved. This is not likely.

To provide some guidelines though, consider the theoretical frame rates for Ethernet. Frame rates depend upon the size of the frame. To calculate the packets per second for various frame sizes, use the following formula:

Packets/second = 1 second/(IFG + PreambleTime + FrameTime)

where:

- Inter Frame Gap (IFG) is equal to the amount of time required between each frame. This is specified as 9.6 microseconds.

- PreambleTime is equal to the number of microseconds to transmit the 64-bit preamble. This is 6.4 microseconds.

- FrameTime is equal to the number of microseconds to transmit the frame. For a 64-octet frame, this is 51.2 microseconds.

The packet per second (pps) rate for a 64-octet frame is, therefore, as follows:

1 second/(9.6 + 6.4 + 51.2) microseconds per packet = 14,880 pps

At the other extreme, consider the pps rate for the largest frame size, 1,518 octets:

1 second/(9.6 + 6.4 + 1,214.4) microseconds per packet = 812 pps

A 30 percent average loading implies that a network analyzer measures about 3 Mbps of sustained traffic on the system. This in and of itself is not enough to determine how well or how poorly the network is functioning. What size packets are creating the load? Usually numerous packet sizes are involved. How many collisions are there on the network? If there are few, only some of the stations are transmitting. This might provide a clue for you that more transmitters can be supported on the network. In any event, a good measurement is needed of your network and what users perceive the current network response to be.

Fast Ethernet

When Ethernet technology availed itself to users, the 10 Mbps bandwidth seemed like an unlimited resource. (Almost like when we had 640k of PC RAM…it seemed we would never need more!) Yet workstations have developed rapidly since then, and applications demand more data in shorter amounts of time. When the data comes from remote sources rather than from a local storage device, this amounts to the application needing more network bandwidth. New applications find 10 Mbps to be too slow. Consider a surgeon downloading an image from a server over a 10 Mbps shared media network. He needs to wait for the image to download so that he can begin/continue the surgery. If the image is a high resolution image, not unusually on the order of 100 MB, it could take a while to receive the image. What if the shared network makes the available user bandwidth about 500 kbps (a generous number for most networks) on the average? It could take the physician 26 minutes to download the image:

$$100 \text{ MB} \times 8/500 \text{ kbps} = 26 \text{ minutes}$$

If that were you on the operating table waiting for the image to download, you would not be very happy! If you are the hospital administration, you are exposing yourself to surgical complications at worst and idle physician time at best. Obviously, this is not a good situation. Sadly, many hospital networks function like this and consider it normal. Clearly, more bandwidth is needed to support this application.

Recognizing the growing demand for higher speed networks, the IEEE formed the 802.3u committee to begin work on a 100 Mbps technology that works over twisted-pair cables. In June of 1995, IEEE approved the 802.3u specification defining a system that offered vendor interoperability at 100 Mbps.

Like 10 Mbps systems such as 10BaseT, the 100 Mbps systems use CSMA/CD, but provide a tenfold improvement over legacy 10 Mbps networks. Because they operate at 10 times the speed of 10 Mbps Ethernet, all timing factors reduce by a factor of 10. For example, the slotTime for 100 Mbps Ethernet is 5.12 microseconds rather than 51.2 microseconds. The IFG is .96 microseconds. And because timing is one tenth that of 10 Mbps Ethernet, the network diameter must also shrink to avoid late collisions.

An objective of the 100BaseX standard was to maintain a common frame format with legacy Ethernet. Therefore, 100BaseX uses the same frame sizes and formats as 10BaseX. Everything else scales by one tenth due to the higher data rate. When passing frames from a 10BaseX to a 100BaseX system, the interconnecting device does not need to re-create the frame's Layer 2 header because they are identical on the two systems.

10BaseT, the original Ethernet over twisted-pair cable standard, supports Category 3, 4, and 5 cables up to 100 meters in length. 10BaseT uses a single encoding technique, *Manchester*, and signals at 20 MHz well within the bandwidth capability of all three cable types. Because of the higher signaling rate of 100BaseT, creating a single method to work over all cable types was not likely. The encoding technologies that were available at the time forced IEEE to create variants of the standard to support Category 3 and 5 cables. A fiber optic version was created as well.

Full-Duplex and Half-Duplex Support

This chapter began with discussions on legacy Ethernet and CSMA/CD. Legacy Ethernet uses CSMA/CD because it operates on a shared media where only one device can talk at a time. When a station talks, all other devices must listen or else the system experiences a collision. In a 10 Mbps system, the total bandwidth available is dedicated to transmitting or receiving depending upon whether the station is the source or the recipient. This describes *half duplex*.

The original LAN standards operate in half-duplex mode allowing only one station to transmit at a time. This was a side effect of the bus topology of 10Base5 and 10Base2 where all stations attached to the same cable. With the introduction of 10BaseT, networks deployed hubs and attached stations to the hub on dedicated point-to-point links. Stations do not share the wire in this topology. 100BaseX uses hubs with dedicated point-to-point links. Because each link is not shared, a new operational mode becomes feasible. Rather than running in half-duplex mode, the systems can operate in *full-duplex mode*, which allows stations to transmit and receive at the same time, eliminating the need for collision detection. What advantage does this provide? The tremendous asset of the precious network commodity—bandwidth. When a station operates in full-duplex mode, the station transmits and receives at full bandwidth in each direction.

The most bandwidth that a legacy Ethernet device can expect to enjoy is 10 Mbps. It either listens at 10 Mbps or transmits at 10 Mbps. In contrast, a 100BaseX device operating in full-duplex mode sees 200 Mbps of bandwidth—100 Mbps for transmitting and 100 Mbps for receiving. Users upgraded from 10BaseT to 100BaseX have the potential to immediately enjoy a twentyfold, or more, bandwidth improvement. If the user previously attached to a shared 10 Mbps system, they might only practically enjoy a couple megabits per second of effective bandwidth. Upgrading to a full duplex 100 Mbps system might provide a perceived one hundredfold improvement. If your users are unappreciative of the additional bandwidth, you have an unenviable group of colleagues with which to work. Put them back on 10BaseT!

NOTE   Be aware, however: Just because an interface card runs 100BaseX full duplex, you cannot assume that the device where you install it supports full-duplex mode. In fact, some devices might actually experience worse throughput when in full-duplex mode than when in half-duplex mode. For example, Windows NT 4.0 does not support full-duplex operations because of driver limitations. Some SUN workstations can also experience this, especially with Gigabit Ethernet.

The IEEE 802.3x committee designed a standard for full-duplex operations that covers 10BaseT, 100BaseX, and 1000BaseX. (1000BaseX is Gigabit Ethernet discussed in a later section, "Gigabit Ethernet.") 802.3x also defined a *flow control* mechanism. This allows a receiver to send a special frame back to the source whenever the receiver's buffers overflow. The receiver sends a special packet called a *pause frame*. In the frame, the receiver can request the source to stop sending for a specified period of time. If the receiver can handle incoming traffic again before the timer value in the pause frame expires, the receiver can send another pause frame with the timer set to zero. This tells the receiver that it can start sending again.

Although 100BaseX supports both full- and half-duplex modes, you can deploy 100 Mbps hubs that operate in half-duplex mode. That means the devices attached to the hub share the bandwidth just like the legacy Ethernet systems. In this case, the station must run in half-duplex mode. To run in full-duplex mode, the device and the hub (switch) must both support and be configured for full duplex. Note that you cannot have a full duplex for a shared hub. If the hub is shared, it must operate in half-duplex mode.

Autonegotiation

With the multiple combinations of network modes available, configuring devices gets confusing. You need to determine if the device needs to operate at 10 or 100 Mbps, whether it needs to run in half- or full-duplex mode, and what media type to use. The device configuration must match the hub configuration to which it attaches.

Autonegotiation attempts to simplify manual configuration requirements by enabling the device and hub to automatically agree upon the highest common operational level. The 802.3u committee defined Fast Link Pulse (FLP) to support the autonegotiation process. FLP, an enhanced version of 10BaseT's Link Integrity Test, sends a series of pulses on the link announcing its capabilities. The other end also transmits FLP announcements, and the two ends settle on whatever method has highest priority in common between them. Table 1-2 illustrates the priority scheme.

Table 1-2   *Autonegotiation Prioritization*

Priority	Method
1	100BaseT2 full duplex
2	100BaseT2 half duplex
3	100BaseTX full duplex
4	100BaseT4 (Only half duplex)
5	100BaseTX half duplex
6	10BaseT full duplex
7	10BaseT half duplex

According to Table 1-2, 100BaseT2 full-duplex mode has highest priority, whereas the slowest method, 10BaseT half-duplex, has lowest priority. Priority is determined by speed, cable types supported, and duplex mode. A system always prefers 100 Mbps over 10 Mbps, and always prefers full duplex over half duplex. Note that 100BaseT2 has higher priority than 100BaseTX. This is not a direct result of 100BaseT2 being a more recent medium. Rather, 100BaseT2 has higher priority because it supports more cable types than does 100BaseTX. 100BaseTX only supports Category 5 type cable, whereas 100BaseT2 supports Category 3, 4, and 5 cables.

TIP	Not all devices perform autonegotiation. We have observed at several customer locations failure of the autonegotiation process—either because of equipment not supporting the feature or poor implementations. We recommend that critical devices such as routers, switches, bridges, and servers be manually configured at both ends of the link to ensure that, upon reboot, the equipment operates in a common mode with its hub/switch port.

100BaseTX

Many existing 10 Mbps twisted-pair systems use a cabling infrastructure based upon Category 5 (unshielded twisted-pair) UTP and (shielded twisted-pair) STP. The devices use two pairs of the cable: one pair on pins 1 and 2 for transmit and one pair on pins 3 and 6 for receive and collision detection. 100BaseTX also uses this infrastructure. Your existing Category 5 cabling for 10BaseT should support 100BaseTX, which also implies that 100BaseTX works up to 100 meters, the same as 10BaseT.

100BaseTX uses an encoding scheme like Fiber Distributed Data Interface (FDDI) of 4B/5B. This encoding scheme adds a fifth bit for every four bits of user data. That means there is a 25 percent overhead in the transmission to support the encoding. Although 100BaseTX carries 100 Mbps of user data, it actually operates at 125 Megabaud. (We try not to tell this to marketing folks so that they do not put on their data sheets 125 Mbps throughput!)

100BaseT4

Not all building infrastructures use Category 5 cable. Some use Category 3. Category 3 cable was installed in many locations to support voice transmission and is frequently referred to as *voice grade cable*. It is tested for voice and low speed data applications up to 16 MHz. Category 5 cable, on the other hand, is intended for data applications and is tested at 100 MHz. Because Category 3 cable exists in so many installations, and because many 10BaseT installations are on Category 3 cable, the IEEE 802.3u committee included this as an option. As with 10BaseT, 100BaseT4 links work up to 100 meters. To support the higher data rates, though, 100BaseT4 uses more cable pairs. Three pairs support transmission and one pair supports collision detection. Another technology aspect to support the high data rates over a lower bandwidth cable comes from the encoding technique used for 100BaseT4. 100BaseT4 uses an encoding method of 8B/6T (8 bits/6 ternary signals) which significantly lowers the signaling frequency, making it suitable for voice-grade wire.

100BaseT2

Although 100BaseT4 provides a solution for Category 3 cable, it needs four pairs to support operations. Most Category 3 cable installations intend for the cable to support voice communications. By consuming all the pairs in the cable for data transmissions, no pairs remain to support voice communications. 100BaseT2, completed by IEEE in 1997 and called 802.3y, operates on Category 3, 4, and 5 cables and only requires two cable pairs. A new addition to the 100BaseT standards, 100BaseT2 relies upon advanced digital signal processing chips and encoding methods called PAM 5x5 (4 bits point to one of 25 possible values) to function over the lower bandwidth cable type. 100BaseT2 works on link lengths up to 100 meters.

100BaseFX

802.3u specifies a variant for single-mode and multimode fiber optic cables. 100BaseFX uses two strands (one pair) of fiber optic cables—one for transmitting and one for receiving. Like 100BaseTx, 100BaseFX uses a 4B/5B encoding signaling at 125 MHz on the optical fiber. When should you use the fiber optic version? One clear situation arises when you need to support distances greater than 100 meters. Multimode supports up to 2,000 meters in full-duplex mode, 412 meters in half-duplex mode. Single-mode works up to 10 kms—a significant distance advantage. Other advantages of fiber include its electrical isolation properties. For example, if you need to install the cable in areas where there are high levels of radiated electrical noise (near high voltage power lines or transformers), fiber optic cable is best. The cable's immunity to electrical noise makes it ideal for this environment. If you are installing the system in an environment where lightning frequently damages equipment, or where you suffer from ground loops between buildings on a campus, use fiber. Fiber optic cable carries no electrical signals to damage your equipment.

Table 1-3   *100BaseX Media Comparisons*

Standard	Cable Type	Mode	Pairs Required	Distance (meters)
10BaseT	Category 3,4,5	Half Duplex	2	100
100BaseTX	Category 5	Half Duplex, Full Duplex	2	100
100BaseT4	Category 3	Half Duplex	4	100
100BaseT2	Category 3,4,5	Half Duplex, Full Duplex	2	100
100BaseFX	Multimode	Half Duplex, Full Duplex	1	412(Half-Duplex) 2000(Full-Duplex)
100BaseFX	Single-mode	Half Duplex, Full Duplex	1	10 kms

Note that the multimode fiber form of 100BaseFX specifies two distances. If you run the equipment in half-duplex mode, you can only transmit 412 meters. Full-duplex mode reaches up to 2 kms.

Media-Independent Interface (MII)

When you order networking equipment, you usually order the system with a specific interface type. For example, you can purchase a router with a 100BaseTX connection. When you buy it with this kind of interface, the 100BaseTX transceiver is built in to the unit. This connection is fine, as long as you only attach it to another 100BaseTX device such as another workstation, hub, or switch. What if you decide at a later time that you need to move the router to another location, but the distance demands that you need to connect over fiber optics rather than over copper? You need to buy another module to replace the 100BaseTX that you previously installed. This can be costly.

An alternative is the MII connector. This is a 40-pin connector that allows you to connect an external transceiver that has an MII connection on one side and a 100BaseX interface on the other side. Functionally, it is similar to the AUI connector for 10 Mbps Ethernet and allows you to change the media type without having to replace any modules. Rather, you can change a less expensive media adapter (transceiver). For Fast Ethernet, if you decide to change the interface type, all you need to do is change the MII transceiver. This is potentially a much less expensive option than replacing an entire router module.

Network Diameter (Designing with Repeaters in a 100BaseX Network)

In a legacy Ethernet system, repeaters extend cable distances, allowing networks to reach further than the segment length. For example, a 10Base2 segment only reaches 185 meters in length. If an administrator desires to attach devices beyond this reach, the administrator can use repeaters to connect a second section of 10Base2 cable to the first. In a 10BaseT network, hubs perform the repeater functions allowing two 100 meter segments to connect together. Legacy repeaters are discussed in more detail in Chapter 2, "Segmenting LANs."

802.3u defines two classes of repeaters for 100BaseX systems. The two repeater classes differ in their latency which affects the network diameter supported. A Class I repeater latency is 0.7 microseconds or less, whereas a Class II repeater latency is 0.46 microseconds or less. Only one Class I repeater is allowed in a 100BaseX system, whereas two hops are permitted for Class II repeaters. Why are there two repeater classes?

Class I repeaters operate by converting the incoming signal from a port into an internal digital signal. It then converts the frame back into an analog signal when it sends it out the other ports. This allows a Class I repeater to have a mix of ports that are 100BaseTX, 100BaseT4, 100BaseT2 or 100BaseFX. Remember that the line encoding scheme for these methods differ. The only ones with a common encoding scheme, 4B/5B, are 100BaseTX and 100BaseFX. A Class I repeater can translate the line encoding to support the differing media types.

Class II repeaters, on the other hand, are not as sophisticated. They can only support ports with a same line encoding method. Therefore, if you are using 100BaseT4 cabling, all ports in a Class II repeater must be 100BaseT4. Similarly, if you are using 100BaseT2, all ports of your

Class II repeater must be 100BaseT2. The only exception to mixing is for 100BaseTX and 100BaseFX, because these both use 4B/5B and no encoding translation is necessary.

The lower latency value for a Class II repeater enables it to support a slightly larger network diameter than a Class I based network. Converting the signal from analog to digital and performing line encoding translation consumes bit times. A Class I repeater therefore introduces more latency than a Class II repeater reducing the network diameter.

Figure 1-4 illustrates interconnecting stations directly together without the use of a repeater. Each station is referred to as a DTE (data terminal equipment) device. Transceivers and hubs are DCE (data communication equipment) devices. Use a straight through cable when connecting a DTE to a DCE device. Use a cross-over when connecting a DTE to DTE or a DCE to DCE. Either copper or fiber can be used. Be sure, however, that you use a cross-over cable in this configuration. A cross-over cable attaches the transmitter pins at one end to the receiver pins at the other end. If you use a straight through cable, you connect "transmit" at one end to "transmit" at the other end and fail to communicate. (The Link Status light does not illuminate!)

Figure 1-4   *Interconnecting DTE to DTE*

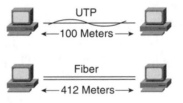

NOTE   There is an exception to this where you can, in fact, connect two DTE or two DCE devices directly together with a straight through cable. Some devices have MDI (medial interface) and MDIX ports. The MDIX is a media interface cross-over port. Most ports on devices are MDI. You can use a straight through cable when connecting from an MDI to an MDIX port.

Using a Class I repeater as in Figure 1-5 enables you to extend the distance between workstations. Note that with a Class I repeater you can mix the types of media attaching to the repeater. Any mix of 100BaseTX, 100BaseT4, 100BaseT2, or 100BaseFX works. Only one Class I repeater is allowed in the network. To connect Class I repeaters together, a bridge, switch, or router must connect between them.

Figure 1-5   *Networking with Class I Repeaters*

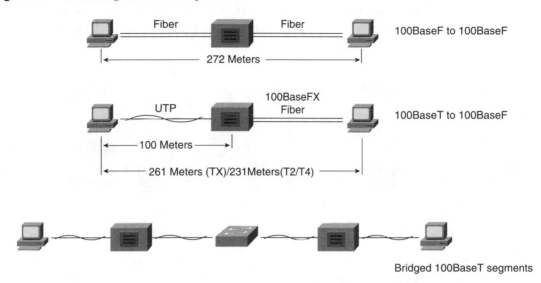

Figure 1-6   *Networking with one Class II Repeater*

Class II repeaters demand homogenous cabling to be attached to them. If you use 100BaseT4, all ports must be 100BaseT4. The only mix permitted uses 100BaseTX and 100BaseFX. Figure 1-6 illustrates a network with only one Class II repeater.

Figure 1-6   *Networking with one Class II Repeater*

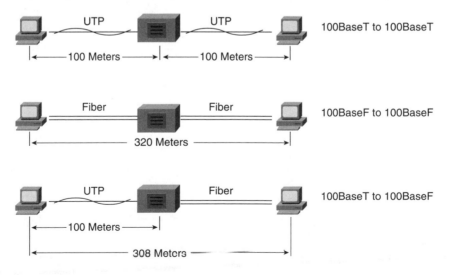

Unlike Class I repeaters, two Class II repeaters are permitted as in Figure 1-7. The connection between the repeaters must be less than or equal to five meters. Why daisy chain the repeaters if it only gains five meters of distance? Simply because it increases the number of ports available in the system.

Figure 1-7   *Networking with Two Class II Repeaters*

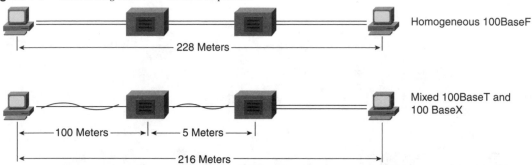

The networks in Figure 1-5 through Figure 1-7 illustrate networks with repeaters operating in half-duplex mode. The network diameter constraints arise from a need to honor the slotTime window for 100BaseX half-duplex networks. Extending the network beyond this diameter without using bridges, switches, or routers violates the maximum extent of the network and makes the network susceptible to late collisions. This is a bad situation. The network in Figure 1-8 demonstrates a proper use of Catalyst switches to extend a network.

Figure 1-8 *An Extended 100BaseX Network with Catalyst Switches*

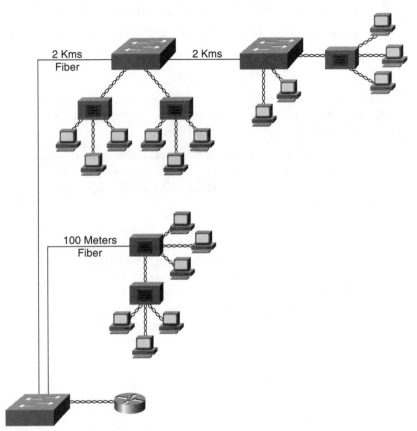

Practical Considerations

100BaseX networks offer at least a tenfold increase in network bandwidth over shared legacy Ethernet systems. In a full-duplex network, the bandwidth increases by twentyfold. Is all this bandwidth really needed? After all, many desktop systems cannot generate anywhere near 100 Mbps of traffic. Most network systems are best served by a hybrid of network technologies. Some users are content on a shared 10 Mbps system. These users normally do little more than e-mail, Telnet, and simple Web browsing. The interactive applications they use demand little network bandwidth and so the user rarely notices delays in usage. Of the applications mentioned for this user, Web browsing is most susceptible because many pages incorporate graphic images that can take some time to download if the available network bandwidth is low.

If the user does experience delays that affect work performance (as opposed to non-work-related activities), you can increase the users bandwidth by doing the following:

- Upgrading the user to 10BaseT full duplex and immediately double the bandwidth.
- Upgrading the user to 100BaseX half duplex.
- Upgrading the user to 100BaseX full duplex.

Which of these is most reasonable? It depends upon the user's application needs and the workstation capability. If the user's applications are mostly interactive in nature, either of the first two options can suffice to create bandwidth.

However, if the user transfers large files, as in the case of a physician retrieving medical images, or if the user frequently needs to access a file server, 100BaseX full duplex might be most appropriate. Option 3 should normally be reserved for specific user needs, file servers, and routers.

Another appropriate use of Fast Ethernet is for backbone segments. A corporate network often has an invisible hierarchy where distribution networks to the users are lower speed systems, whereas the networks interconnecting the distribution systems operate at higher rates. This is where Fast Ethernet might fit in well as part of the infrastructure. The decision to deploy Fast Ethernet as part of the infrastructure is driven by corporate network needs as opposed to individual user needs, as previously considered. Chapter 8, "Trunking Technologies and Applications," considers the use of Fast Ethernet to interconnect Catalyst switches together as a backbone.

Gigabit Ethernet

As if 100 Mbps is not enough, yet another higher bandwidth technology was unleashed on the industry in June of 1998. Gigabit Ethernet (IEEE 802.3z) specifies operations at 1000 Mbps, another tenfold bandwidth improvement. We discussed earlier how stations are hard-pressed to fully utilize 100 Mbps Ethernet. Why then do we need a Gigabit bandwidth technology? Gigabit Ethernet proponents expect to find it as either a backbone technology or as a pipe into very high speed file servers. This contrasts with Fast Ethernet in that Fast Ethernet network administrators can deploy Fast Ethernet to clients, servers, or use it as a backbone technology. Gigabit Ethernet will not be used to connect directly to clients any time soon. Some initial studies of Gigabit Ethernet indicate that installing 1000 Mbps interfaces in a Pentium class workstation will actually *slow down* its performance due to software interrupts. On the other hand, high performance UNIX stations functioning as file servers can indeed benefit from a larger pipe to the network.

In a Catalyst network, Gigabit Ethernet interconnects Catalysts to form a high-speed backbone. The Catalysts in Figure 1-9 have low speed stations connecting to them (10 and 100 Mbps), but have 1000 Mbps to pass traffic between workstations. A file server in the network also benefits from a 1000 Mbps connection supporting more concurrent client accesses.

Figure 1-9   *Gigabit Ethernet Backbone Between Catalysts*

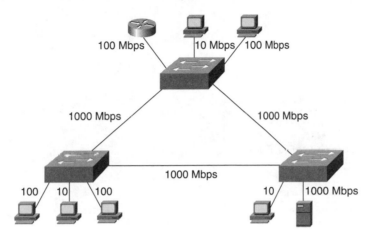

Gigabit Architecture

Gigabit Ethernet merges aspects of 802.3 Ethernet and Fiber Channel, a Gigabit technology intended for high-speed interconnections between file servers as a LAN replacement. The Fiber Channel standard details a layered network model capable of scaling to bandwidths of 4 Gbps and to extend to distances of 10 kms. Gigabit Ethernet borrows the bottom two layers of the standard: FC-1 for encoding/decoding and FC-0, the interface and media layer. FC-0 and FC-1 replace the physical layer of the legacy 802.3 model. The 802.3 MAC and LLC layers contribute to the higher levels of Gigabit Ethernet. Figure 1-10 illustrates the merger of the standards to form Gigabit Ethernet.

Figure 1-10   *The Formation of the Gigabit Ethernet Standard*

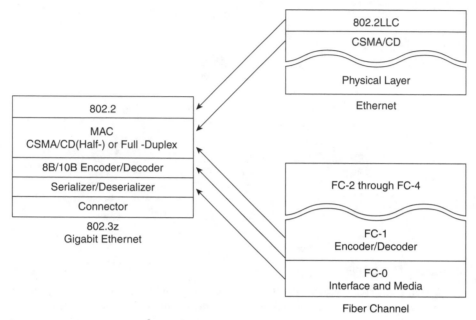

The Fiber Channel standard incorporated by Gigabit Ethernet transmits at 1.062 MHz over fiber optics and supports 800 Mbps data throughput. Gigabit Ethernet increases the signaling rate to 1.25 GHz. Further, Gigabit Ethernet uses 8B/10B encoding which means that 1 Gbps is available for data. 8B/10B is similar to 4B/5B discussed for 100BaseTX, except that for every 8 bits of data, 2 bits are added creating a 10-bit symbol. This encoding technique simplifies fiber optic designs at this high data rate. The optical connector used by Fiber Channel, and therefore by Gigabit Ethernet, is the SC style connector. This is the push-in/pull-out, or snap and click, connector used by manufacturers to overcome deficiencies with the ST style connector. The ST, or snap and twist, style connectors previously preferred were a bayonet type connector and required finger space on the front panel to twist the connector into place. The finger space requirement reduced the number of ports that could be built in to a module.

NOTE   A new connector type, the MT-RJ, is now finding popularity in the fiber industry. The MT-RJ uses a form factor and latch like the RJ-45 connectors, supports full duplex, has lower cost than ST or SC connectors, and is easier to terminate and install than ST or SC. Further, its smaller size allows twice the port density on a face plate than ST or SC connectors.

Full-Duplex and Half-Duplex Support

Like Fast Ethernet, Gigabit Ethernet supports both full- and half-duplex modes with flow control. In half-duplex mode, though, the system operates using CSMA/CD and must consider the reduced slotTime even more than Fast Ethernet. The slotTimes for 10BaseX and 100BaseX networks are 51.2 microseconds and 5.12 microseconds, respectively. These are derived from the smallest frame size of 64 octets. In the 100BaseX network, the slot-time translates into a network diameter of about 200 meters. If the same frame size is used in Gigabit Ethernet, the slotTime reduces to .512 microseconds and about 20 meters in diameter. This is close to unreasonable. Therefore, 802.3z developed a carrier extension that enables the network distance to extend further in half-duplex mode and still support the smallest 802.3 packets.

The *carrier extension* process increases the slotTime value to 4096 bits or 4.096 microseconds. The transmitting station expands the size of the transmitted frame to ensure that it meets the minimal slotTime requirements by adding non-data symbols after the FCS field of the frame. Not all frame sizes require carrier extension. This is left as an exercise in the review questions. The 8B10B encoding scheme used in Gigabit Ethernet defines various combinations of bits called symbols. Some symbols signal real data, whereas the rest indicate non-data. The station appends these non-data symbols to the frame. The receiving station identifies the non-data symbols, strips off the carrier extension bytes, and recovers the original message. Figure 1-11 shows the anatomy of an extended frame.

Figure 1-11 *An Extended Gigabit Ethernet Frame*

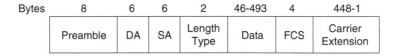

The addition of the carrier extension bits does not change the actual Gigabit Ethernet frame size. The receiving station still expects to see no fewer than 64 octets and no more than 1518 octets.

Gigabit Media Options

IEEE 802.3z specified several media options to support different grades of fiber optic cable and a version to support a new copper cable type. The fiber optic options vary for the size of the fiber and the modal bandwidth. Table 1-4 summarizes the options and the distances supported by each.

Table 1-4   *Gigabit Ethernet Media Option*

Standard	Cable Size (Micrometers)	Cable Bandwidth (MHz-Kms)	Distance* (Meters)
1000BaseSX	62.5	160	220
1000BaseSX	62.5	200	275
1000BaseSX	50	400	500
1000BaseSX	50	500	550
1000BaseLX	62.5	500	550
1000BaseLX	50	400	550
1000BaseLX	50	500	550
1000BaseLX	9/10	N/A	5,000
1000BaseLH**	9/10	N/A	10,000
1000BaseZX**	9/10	N/A	90,000

*Note that the minimum distance in each case is 2 meters

**Cisco capabilities that support distances greater than the 5,000 meters specified by the IEEE 802.3z standard.

1000BaseSX

1000BaseSX uses the short wavelength of 850 nms. Although this is a LASER-based system, the distances supported are generally shorter than for 1000BaseLX. This results from the interaction of the light with the fiber cable at this wavelength. Why use 1000BaseSX then? Because the components are less expensive than for 1000BaseLX. Use this less expensive method for short link distances (for example, within an equipment rack).

1000BaseLX

In fiber optic systems, light sources differ in the type of device (LED or LASER) generating the optical signal and in the wavelength they generate. Wavelength correlates to the frequency of RF systems. In the case of optics, we specify the wavelength rather than frequency. In practical terms, this corresponds to the color of the light. Typical wavelengths are 850 nanometers (nms) and 1300 nms. 850 nm light is visible to the human eye as red, whereas 1300 is invisible. 1000BaseLX uses 1300 nm optical sources. In fact, the L of LX stands for *long* wavelength. 1000BaseLX uses LASER sources. Be careful when using fiber optic systems. Do not look into the port or the end of a fiber! It can be hazardous to the health of your eye.

Use the LX option for longer distance requirements. If you need to use single mode, you must use the LX.

1000BaseCX

Not included in Table 1-4 is a copper media option. 1000BaseCX uses a 150-Ohm balanced shielded copper cable. This new cable type is not well-known in the industry, but is necessary to support the high-bandwidth data over copper. 1000BaseCX supports transmissions up to 25 meters. It is intended to be used to interconnect devices collocated within an equipment rack very short distances apart. This is appropriate when Catalysts are stacked in a rack and you want a high speed link between them, but you do not want to spend the money for fiber optic interfaces.

1000BaseT

One final copper version is the 1000BaseT standard which uses Category 5 twisted-pair cable. It supports up to 100 meters, but uses all four pairs in the cable. This offers another low cost alternative to 1000BaseSX and 1000BaseLX and does not depend upon the special cable used by 1000BaseCX. This standard is under the purview of the IEEE 802.3ab committee.

Gigabit Ethernet Interface Converter

A Gigabit Ethernet Interface Converter (GBIC) is similar to an MII connector described in the Fast Ethernet section and allows a network administrator to configure an interface with external components rather than purchasing modules with a built-in interface type. With a GBIC interface, the administrator has flexibility to change the interface depending upon his needs. GBIC transceivers have a common connector type that attaches to the Gigabit device, and the appropriate media connector for the media selected: 1000BaseSX, 1000BaseLX, or 1000BaseCX.

Token Ring

This chapter began with an overview of LAN access methods. To this point, you should be familiar with the various options using the CSMA/CD method. This section briefly examines Token Ring, the other popular form of LAN access.

Token Ring systems, like Ethernet, use a shared media technology. Multiple stations attach to a network and share the bandwidth. Token Ring supports two bandwidth options: 4 Mbps and 16 Mbps. The 4 Mbps version represents the original technology released by IBM. 16 Mbps, a version released after 4 Mbps, essentially works the same as 4 Mbps Token Ring and introduces a couple of optional new features to further improve the system.

Token Ring Operations

To control access onto the system, Token Ring passes a token on the network that authorizes the current holder to transmit onto the cable. Figure 1-12 illustrates a logical representation of a Token Ring system.

Figure 1-12 *A Simple Token Ring Network*

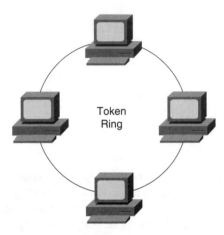

Each station in the network creates a break in the ring. A token passes around the ring from station to station. If a station desires to send information, it holds onto the token and starts to transmit onto the cable. Assume Station 1 wants to transmit to Station 3. Station 1, when it receives a token, possesses the token and transmits the frame with Station 3's MAC address as the destination and Station 1's MAC address as the source. The frame circulates around the ring from station to station. Each station locally copies the frame and passes it to the next station. Each station compares the destination MAC address against its own hardware address and either discards the frame if they don't match, or sends the frame to the processor. When Station 2 receives the frame, it too copies the frame and sends it on to the next station. All stations receive a copy of the frame because, just like Ethernet, Token Ring is a broadcast network. The frame eventually returns to the source. The source is responsible for removing the frame and introducing a new token onto the network.

In this model, only one station at a time transmits because only one station can possess the token at a time. Some network inefficiencies result, however, when a station retains the token until it removes the frame it transmitted from the ring. Depending upon the length of the ring, a station can complete transmission of a frame before the frame returns back to the source. During the time between the completion of transmission and the removal of the frame, the network remains idle—no other station can transmit. This amounts to wasted bandwidth on the network. *Early token release*, an optional feature introduced with 16 Mbps Token Ring, permits the source to create a new token after it completes transmission, and before it removes its frame from the network. This increases the Token Ring utilization to a much higher degree than for systems without early token release.

Occasionally, a source might not be online whenever the frame it transmitted returns to it. This prevents the source from removing the frame and causes it to circulate around the network—possibly indefinitely. This consumes bandwidth on the network and prevents other stations from generating traffic. To prevent this, one of the stations on the ring is elected to be the *ring monitor*. Whenever a packet circulates around the ring, the ring monitor marks a particular bit in the frame indicating, "I already saw this frame once." If the ring monitor sees any frame with this bit set, the ring monitor assumes that the source cannot remove the frame and removes it.

Token Ring Components

Token Ring systems use a hub architecture to interconnect stations. The hub, called a multistation access unit (MAU), creates a logical ring from the star attached stations as shown in Figure 1-13.

Figure 1-13 *Token Ring Stations Attached to an MAU*

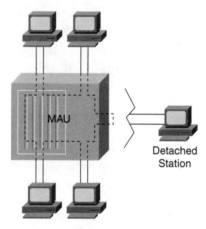

Internal to the MAU, the transmit from one station connects to the receive of another station. This continues between all attached stations until the ring is completed. What happens if a user detaches a station? When this occurs, the MAU bypasses the unused port to maintain ring integrity.

A network administrator can daisy-chain MAUs together to extend the distance and to introduce more ports in the network. Figure 1-14 illustrates how MAUs usually have ring-in (RI) and ring-out (RO) ports to attach to other MAUs.

Figure 1-14 *Cascading Token Ring MAUs*

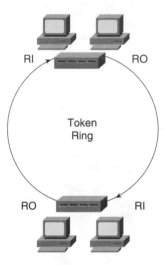

Summary

Although many of you use a number of different LAN technologies, the market still has a preponderance of legacy Ethernet deployed. A lot of 10 Mbps systems still exist with varied media options such as copper and fiber. You should expect to encounter this type of connection method for at least another few years. This chapter covered the basics of how legacy Ethernet functions.

Because of the limitations that legacy Ethernet can cause some applications, higher speed network technologies had to be developed. The IEEE created Fast Ethernet to meet this need. With the capability to run in full-duplex modes, Fast Ethernet offers significant bandwidth leaps to meet the needs of many users. This chapter discussed the media options available for Fast Ethernet and some of the operational characteristics of it.

And for real bandwidth consumers, Gigabit Ethernet offers even more capacity to meet the needs of trunking switches together and to feed high performance file servers. This chapter covered some of the attributes of Gigabit Ethernet and choices available to you for media.

Review Questions

1   What is the pps rate for a 100BaseX network? Calculate it for the minimum and maximum frame sizes.

2   What are the implications of mixing half-duplex and full-duplex devices? How do you do it?

3   In the opening section on Fast Ethernet, we discussed the download time for a typical medical image over a shared legacy Ethernet system. What is an approximate download time for the image over a half-duplex 100BaseX system? Over a full-duplex 100BaseX system?

4   What disadvantages are there in having an entire network running in 100BaseX full-duplex mode?

5   Can a Class II repeater ever attach to a Class I repeater? Why or why not?

6   What is the smallest Gigabit Ethernet frame size that does not need carrier extension?

This chapter covers the following key topics:

- **Why Segment LANs?**—Discusses motivations for segmenting LANs and the disadvantages of not segmenting.

- **Segmenting LANS with Repeaters**—Discusses the purpose, benefits, and limitations of repeaters in LANs.

- **Segmenting LANS with Bridges**—Discusses how bridges create collision domains and extend networks. As the foundational technology for LAN switches, this section describes the benefits and limitations of bridges.

- **Segmenting LANS with Routers**—Discusses how routers create broadcast domains by limiting the distribution of broadcast frames.

- **Segmenting LANS with Switches**—Discusses the differences between bridges and switches, and how switches create broadcast domains differently from routers.

CHAPTER 2

Segmenting LANs

As corporations grow, network administrators find themselves deep in frustration. Management wants more users on the network, whereas users want more bandwidth. To further confuse the issue, finances often conflict with the two objectives, effectively limiting options. Although this book cannot help with the last issue, it can help clarify what technology options exist to increase the number of users served while enhancing the available bandwidth in the system. Network engineers building LAN infrastructures can choose from many internetworking devices to extend networks: repeaters, bridges, routers, and switches. Each component serves specific roles and has utility when properly deployed. Engineers often exhibit some confusion about which component to use for various network configurations. A good understanding of how these devices manipulate collision and broadcast domains helps the network engineer to make intelligent choices. Further, by understanding these elements, discussions in later chapters about collision and broadcast domains have a clearer context.

This chapter, therefore, defines broadcast and collision domains and discusses the role of repeaters, bridges, routers, and switches in manipulating the domains. It also describes why network administrators segment LANs, and how these devices facilitate segmentation.

Why Segment LANs?

Network designers often face a need to extend the distance of a network, the number of users on the system, or the bandwidth available to users. From a corporate point of view, this is a good thing, because it might indicate growth. From a network administrator's point of view, this is often a bad thing, implying sleepless nights and no weekends. Even so, how does an administrator keep everyone happy while maintaining personal sanity?

A straightforward technology answer might include the deployment of a higher speed network. If users currently attach to a legacy 10 Mbps network, you could deploy a Fast Ethernet network and provide an immediate tenfold improvement in bandwidth. Changing the network infrastructure in this way means replacing workstation adapter cards with ones capable of 100 Mbps. It also means replacing the hubs to which the stations connect. The new hubs must also support the new network bandwidth. Although effective, a wholesale upgrade might be cost prohibitive.

Segmenting LANs is another approach to provide users additional bandwidth without replacing all user equipment. By segmenting LANs, the administrator breaks a network into smaller portions and connects them with some type of internetworking equipment. Figure 2-1 illustrates a before-and-after situation for segmenting networks.

Figure 2-1 *A Network Before and After Segmentation*

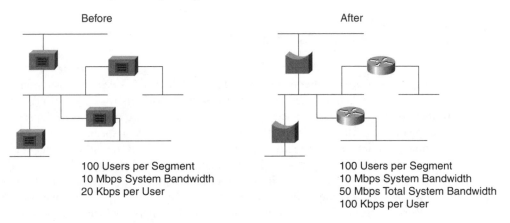

100 Users per Segment
10 Mbps System Bandwidth
20 Kbps per User

100 Users per Segment
10 Mbps System Bandwidth
50 Mbps Total System Bandwidth
100 Kbps per User

Before segmentation, all 500 users share the network's 10 Mbps bandwidth because the segments interconnect with repeaters. (The next section in this chapter describes how repeaters work and why this is true.) The after network replaces the repeaters with bridges and routers isolating segments and providing more bandwidth for users. Bridges and routers generate bandwidth by creating new collision and broadcast domains as summarized in Table 2-1. (The sections on LAN segmentation with bridges and routers later in this chapter define collision and broadcast domains and describe why this is so.)

Table 2-1 *A Comparison of Collision and Broadcast Domain*

Device	Collision Domains	Broadcast Domains
Repeater	One	One
Bridge	Many	One
Router	Many	Many
Switch	Many	Configurable

Each segment can further divide with additional bridges, routers, and switches providing even more user bandwidth. By reducing the number of users on each segment, more bandwidth avails itself to users. The extreme case dedicates one user to each segment providing full media bandwidth to each user. This is exactly what switches allow the administrator to build.

The question remains, though, "What should you use to segment the network? Should you use a repeater, bridge, router, or LAN switch?" Repeaters do not really segment a network and do not create more bandwidth. They simply allow you to extend the network distance to some degree. Bridges, routers, and switches are more suitable for LAN segmentation. The sections that follow describe the various options. The repeater is included in the discussion because you might attach a repeater-based network to your segmented network. Therefore, you need to know how repeaters interact with segmentation devices.

Segmenting LANs with Repeaters

Legacy Ethernet systems such as 10Base5, 10Base2, and 10BaseT have distance limitations for segments as described in Chapter 1, "Desktop Technologies." Whenever you desire to extend the distance, you can use an internetworking device like a repeater. Repeaters operate at Layer 1 of the OSI model and appear as an extension to the cable segment. Workstations have no knowledge of the presence of a repeater which is completely transparent to the attached devices. A repeater attaches wire segments together as shown in Figure 2-2.

Figure 2-2   *Interconnecting LAN Segments with a Repeater*

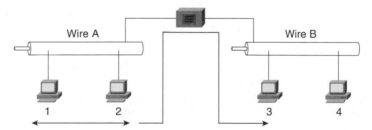

Repeaters regenerate the signal from one wire on to the other. When Station 1 transmits to Station 2, the frame also appears on Wire B, even though the source and destination device coexist on Wire A. Repeaters are unintelligent devices and have no insight to the data content. They blindly perform their responsibility of forwarding signals from one wire to all other wires. If the frame contains errors, the repeater forwards it. If the frame violates the minimum or maximum frame sizes specified by Ethernet, the repeater forwards it. If a collision occurs on Wire A, Wire B also sees it. Repeaters truly act like an extension of the cable.

Although Figure 2-2 shows the interconnection of two segments, repeaters can have many ports to attach multiple segments as shown in Figure 2-3.

Figure 2-3 *A Multiport Repeater*

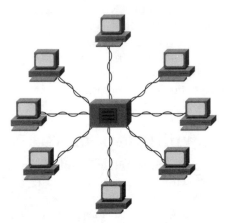

A 10BaseT network is comprised of hubs and twisted-pair cables to interconnect workstations. Hubs are multiport repeaters and forward signals from one interface to all other interfaces. As in Figure 2-2, all stations attached to the hub in Figure 2-3 see all traffic, both the good and the bad.

Repeaters perform several duties associated with signal propagation. For example, repeaters regenerate and retime the signal and create a new preamble. Preamble bits precede the frame destination MAC address and help receivers to synchronize. The 8-byte preamble has an alternating binary 1010 pattern except for the last byte. The last byte of the preamble, which ends in a binary pattern of 10101011, is called the start of frame delimiter (SFD). The last two bits indicate to the receiver that data follows. Repeaters strip all eight preamble bytes from the incoming frame, then generate and prepend a new preamble on the frame before transmission through the outbound interface.

Repeaters also ensure that collisions are signaled on all ports. If Stations 1 and 2 in Figure 2-2 participate in a collision, the collision is enforced through the repeater so that the stations on Wire B also know of the collision. Stations on Wire B must wait for the collision to clear before transmitting. If Stations 3 and 4 do not know of the collision, they might attempt a transmission during Station 1 and 2's collision event. They become additional participants in the collision.

Limitations exist in a repeater-based network. They arise from different causes and must be considered when extending a network with repeaters. The limitations include the following:

- Shared bandwidth between devices
- Specification constraints on the number of stations per segment
- End-to-end distance capability

Shared Bandwidth

A repeater extends not just the distance of the cable, but it also extends the *collision domain*. Collisions on one segment affect stations on another repeater-connected segment. Collisions extend through a repeater and consume bandwidth on all interconnected segments. Another side effect of a collision domain is the propagation of frames through the network. If the network uses shared network technology, all stations in the repeater-based network share the bandwidth. This is true whether the source frame is unicast, multicast, or broadcast. All stations see all frames. Adding more stations to the repeater network potentially divides the bandwidth even further. Legacy Ethernet systems have a shared 10 Mbps bandwidth. The stations take turns using the bandwidth. As the number of transmitting workstations increases, the amount of available bandwidth decreases.

NOTE   Bandwidth is actually divided by the number of *transmitting* stations. Simply attaching a station does not consume bandwidth until the device transmits. As a theoretical extreme, a network can be constructed of 1,000 devices with only one device transmitting and the other 999 only listening. In this case, the bandwidth is dedicated to the single transmitting station by virtue of the fact that no other device is transmitting. Therefore, the transmitter never experiences collisions and can transmit whenever it desires at full media rates.

It behooves the network administrator to determine bandwidth requirements for user applications and to compare them against the theoretical bandwidth available in the network, as well as actual bandwidth available. Use a network analyzer to measure the average and peak bandwidth consumed by the applications. This helps to determine by how much you need to increase the network's capacity to support the applications.

Number of Stations per Segment

Further, Ethernet imposes limits on how many workstations can attach to a cable. These constraints arise from electrical considerations. As the number of transceivers attached to a cable increases, the cable impedance changes and creates electrical reflections in the system. If the impedance changes too much, the collision detection process fails. Limits for legacy systems, for example, include no more than 100 attached devices per segment for a 10Base5 network. A 10Base2 system cannot exceed 30 stations. Repeaters cannot increase the number of stations supported per segment. The limitation is inherent in the bus architectures of 10Base2 and 10Base5 networks.

End-to-End Distance

Another limitation on extending networks with repeaters focuses on distance. An Ethernet link can extend only so far before the media slotTime specified by Ethernet standards is violated. As described in Chapter 1, the slotTime is a function of the network data rate. A 10 Mbps network such as 10BaseT has a slotTime of 51.2 microseconds. A 100 Mbps network slotTime is one tenth that of 10BaseT. The calculated network extent takes into account the slotTime size, latency through various media such as copper and fiber, and the number of repeaters in a network. In a 10 Mbps Ethernet, the number of repeaters in a network must follow the 5/3/1 rule illustrated in Figure 2-4. This rule states that up to *five* segments can be interconnected with repeaters. But only *three* of the segments can have devices attached. The other two segments interconnect segments and only allow repeaters to attach at the ends. When following the 5/3/1 rule, an administrator creates *one* collision domain. A collision in the network propagates through all repeaters to all other segments.

Figure 2-4   *Interconnecting with the 5/3/1 Rule*

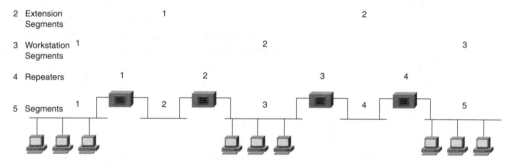

Repeaters, when correctly used, extend the collision domain by interconnecting segments at OSI Layer 1. Any transmission in the collision domain propagates to all other stations in the network. A network administrator must, however, take into account the 5/3/1 rule. If the network needs to extend beyond these limits, other internetworking device types must be used. For example, the administrator could use a bridge or a router.

Repeaters extend the bounds of broadcast and collision domains, but only to the extent allowed by media repeater rules. The maximum geographical extent, constrained by the media slotTime value, defines the collision domain extent. If you extend the collision domain beyond the bounds defined by the media, the network cannot function correctly. In the case of Ethernet, it experiences *late collisions* if the network extends too far. Late collision events occur whenever a station experiences a collision outside of the 51.2 µs slotTime.

Figure 2-5 illustrates the boundaries of a collision domain defined by the media slotTime. All segments connected together by repeaters belong to the same collision domain. Figure 2-5 also illustrates the boundaries of a broadcast domain in a repeater-based network. Broadcast domains define the extent that a broadcast propagates throughout a network.

Figure 2-5   *Broadcast and Collision Domains in a Repeater Network*

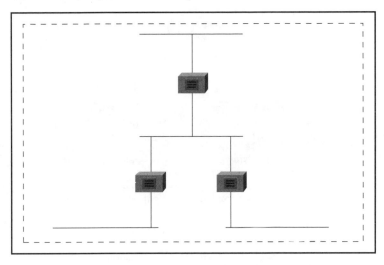

– – – – – – – – – = Collision Domain
———————————— = Broadcast Domain

To demonstrate a collision domain, consider IP's Address Resolution Protocol (ARP) process as in Figure 2-6 when IP Station 1 desires to communicate with Station 2. The stations must belong to the same subnetwork as there is no router in the network. Station 1 first ARPs the destination to determine the destination's MAC address. The ARP frame is a broadcast that traverses the entire segment and transparently passes through all repeaters in the network. All stations receive the broadcast and therefore belong to the same broadcast domain. Station 2 sends a unicast reply to Station 1. All stations receive the reply because they all belong to the same collision domain (although it is handled by the NIC hardware as discussed in Chapter 1).

Figure 2-6 *ARP Operation in a Repeater Network*

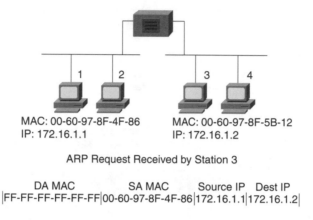

MAC: 00-60-97-8F-4F-86   MAC: 00-60-97-8F-5B-12
IP: 172.16.1.1   IP: 172.16.1.2

ARP Request Received by Station 3

DA MAC   SA MAC   Source IP   Dest IP
|FF-FF-FF-FF-FF-FF|00-60-97-8F-4F-86|172.16.1.1|172.16.1.2|

ARP Reply Received by Station 1

DA MAC   SA MAC   Source IP   Dest IP
|00-60-97-8F-4F-86|00-60-97-8F-5B-12|172.16.1.2|172.16.1.1|

Segmenting LANs with Bridges

As discussed in the previous section, Ethernet rules limit the overall distance a network segment extends and the number of stations attached to a cable segment. What do you do if you need to go further or add more devices? Bridges provide a possible solution. When connecting networks as in Figure 2-7, significant differences exist when compared to repeater-connected networks. For example, whenever stations on the same segment transmit to each other in a repeated network, the frame appears on all other segments in the repeated network. But this does not normally happen in a bridged network. Bridges use a filter process to determine whether or not to forward a frame to other interfaces.

Figure 2-7 *Interconnecting Segments with a Bridge*

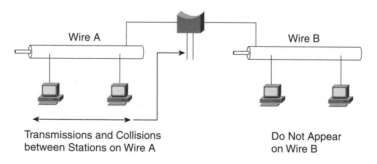

Wire A   Wire B

Transmissions and Collisions   Do Not Appear
between Stations on Wire A   on Wire B

The filter process differs for access methods such as Ethernet and Token Ring. For example, Ethernet employs a process called *transparent bridging* that examines the destination MAC address and determines if a frame should be forwarded, filtered, or flooded. Bridges operate at Layer 2 of the OSI model, the data link layer. By functioning at this layer, bridges have the capability to examine the MAC headers of frames. They can, therefore, make forwarding decisions based on information in the header such as the MAC address. Token Ring can also use source-route bridging which determines frame flow differently from transparent bridges. These methods, and others, are discussed in more detail in Chapter 3, "Bridging Technologies."

More importantly, though, bridges interconnect collision domains allowing independent collision domains to appear as if they were connected, without propagating collisions between them. Figure 2-8 shows the same network as in Figure 2-5, but with bridges interconnecting the segments. In the repeater-based network, all the segments belong to the same collision domain. The network bandwidth was divided between the four segments. In Figure 2-8, however, each segment belongs to a different collision domain. If this were a 10 Mbps legacy network, each segment would have its own 10 Mbps of bandwidth for a collective bandwidth of 40 Mbps.

Figure 2-8   *Bridges Create Multiple Collision Domains and One Broadcast Domain*

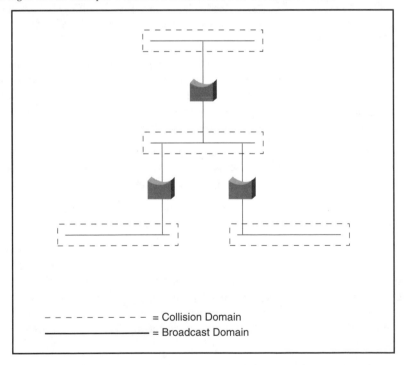

This significant improvement in bandwidth demonstrates why segmenting a LAN benefits users. The same number of users in the network in Figure 2-8 now have more available bandwidth than they did in the network in Figure 2-5. Although switching is discussed later in the chapter, it is valid to comment now that the ultimate bandwidth distribution occurs when you dedicate one user for each bridge interface. Each user then has all of the local bandwidth to himself; only one station and the bridge port belong to the collision domain. This is, in effect, what switching technology does.

Another advantage of bridges stems from their Layer 2 operation. In the repeater-based network, an end-to-end distance limitation prevents the network from extending indefinitely. Bridges allow each segment to extend a full distance. Each segment has its own slotTime value. Bridges do not forward collisions between segments. Rather, bridges isolate collision domains and reestablish slotTimes. Bridges can, in theory, extend networks indefinitely. Practical considerations prevent this, however.

Bridges filter traffic when the source and destination reside on the same interface. Broadcast and multicast frames are the exception to this. Whenever a bridge receives a broadcast or multicast, it floods the broadcast message out all interfaces. Again, consider ARP as in the repeater-based network. When a station in a bridged network wants to communicate with another IP station in the same bridged network, the source sends a broadcast ARP request. The request, a broadcast frame, passes through all bridges and out all bridge interfaces. All segments attached to a bridge belong to the same broadcast domain. Because they belong to the same broadcast domain, all stations should also belong to the same IP subnetwork.

A bridged network can easily become overwhelmed with broadcast and multicast traffic if applications generate this kind of traffic. For example, multimedia applications such as video conferencing over IP networks create multicast traffic. Frames from all participants propagate to every segment. In effect, this reduces the network to appear as one giant shared network. The bandwidth becomes shared bandwidth.

In most networks, the majority of frames are not broadcast frames. Some protocols generate more than others, but the bandwidth consumed by these protocol broadcast frames is a relatively small percentage of the LAN media bandwidth.

When should you use bridges? Are there any advantages of bridges over repeaters? What about stations communicating with unicast frames? How do bridges treat this traffic?

When a source and destination device are on the same interface, the bridge filters the frames and does not forward the traffic to any other interface. (Unless the frame is a broadcast or multicast.) If the source and destination reside on different ports relative to the bridge, the bridge forwards the frame to the appropriate interface to reach the destination. The processes of filtering and selective forwarding preserve bandwidth on other segments. This is a significant advantage of bridges over repeaters that offers no frame discrimination capabilities.

When a bridge forwards traffic, it does not change the frame. Like a repeater, a bridge does nothing more to the frame than to clean up the signal before it sends it to another port. Layer 2 and Layer 3 addresses remain unchanged as frames transit a bridge. In contrast, routers change the Layer 2 address. (This is shown in the following section on routers.)

A rule of thumb when designing networks with bridges is the 80/20 rule. This rule states that bridges are most efficient when 80 percent of the segment traffic is local and only 20 percent needs to cross a bridge to another segment. This rule originated from traditional network design where server resources resided on the same segments with the client devices they served, as in Figure 2-9.

Figure 2-9   *The 80/20 Rule Demonstrated in a Traditional Network*

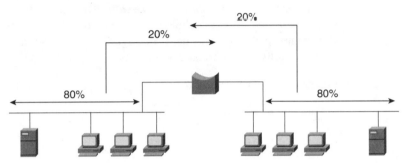

The clients only infrequently needed to access devices on the other side of a bridge. Bridged networks are considered to be well designed when the 80/20 rule is observed. As long as this traffic balance is maintained, each segment in the network appears to have full media bandwidth. If however, the flow balance shifts such that more traffic gets forwarded through the bridge rather than filtered, the network behaves as if all segments operate on the same shared network. The bridge in this case provides nothing more than the capability to daisy-chain collision domains to extend distance, but without any bandwidth improvements.

Consider the worst case for traffic flow in a bridged network: 0/100 where none of the traffic remains local and all sources transmit to destinations on other segments. In the case of a two-port bridge, the entire system has shared bandwidth rather than isolated bandwidth. The bridge only extends the geographical extent of the network and offers no bandwidth gains. Unfortunately, many intranets see similar traffic patterns, with typical ratios of 20/80 rather than 80/20. This results from many users attempting to communicate with and through the Internet. Much of the traffic flows from a local segment to the WAN connection and crosses broadcast domain boundaries. Chapter 14, "Campus Design Models," discusses the current traffic trends and the demise of the 80/20 rule of thumb in modern networks.

One other advantage of bridges is that they prevent errored frames from transiting to another segment. If the bridge sees that a frame has errors or that it violates the media access method size rules, the bridge drops the frame. This protects the destination network from bad frames that do nothing more than consume bandwidth for the destination device discards the frame anyway. Collisions on a shared legacy network often create frame fragments that are sometimes called runt frames. These frames violate the Ethernet minimum frame size rule of 64 bytes. Chapter 3, "Bridging Technologies," shows the frame size rules in Table 3-5. Whereas a repeater forwards runts to the other segments, a bridge blocks them.

Segmenting LANs with Routers

Bridges, operating at a layer higher than repeaters, add functionality to the network, which is not present in repeaters. Bridges perform all repeater functions, and more, by creating new collision domains. Likewise, routers, which operate at Layer 3, add functionality beyond bridges. Routers extend networks like bridges, but they create both collision and broadcast domains. Routers prevent broadcasts from propagating across networks. This broadcast isolation creates individual *broadcast domains* not found in bridges. The router behavior of blocking broadcast frames defines broadcast domain boundaries—the extent to which a broadcast frame propagates in a network. Figure 2-10 shows a network built with routers and identifies collision and broadcast domains.

Figure 2-10 *Broadcast and Collision Domains in a Routed Network*

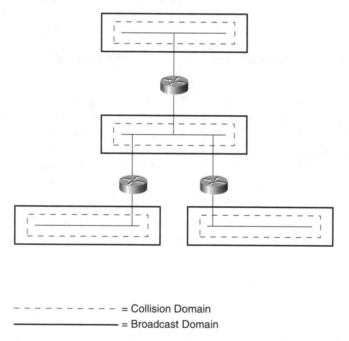

— — — — — — — — — — = Collision Domain
————————————— = Broadcast Domain

A side effect of separate broadcast domains demonstrates itself in the behavior of routers. In a repeater- or bridge-based network, all stations belong to the same subnetwork because they all belong to the same broadcast domain. In a router-based network, however, which creates multiple broadcast domains, each segment belongs to a different subnetwork. This forces workstations to behave differently than they did in the bridged network. Refer to Figure 2-11 and Table 2-2 for a description of the ARP process in a routed network. Although the world does not need another description of ARP, it does in this case serve to illustrate how frames flow through a router in contrast to bridges and repeaters. Further, it serves as an example of how workstations must behave differently with the presence of a router. In a bridge- or repeater-based network, the workstations transmit as if the source and destination are in the collision domain, even though it is possible in a bridged network for them to be in different domains. The aspect that allows them to behave this way in the bridged network is that they are in the same broadcast domain. However, when they are in different broadcast domains, as with the introduction of a router, the source and destination must be aware of the router and must address their traffic to the router.

Figure 2-11   *Frame Header Changes through a Router*

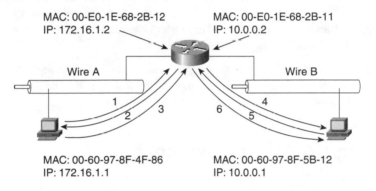

Wire A   Wire B

MAC: 00-E0-1E-68-2B-12   MAC: 00-E0-1E-68-2B-11
IP: 172.16.1.2   IP: 10.0.0.2

MAC: 00-60-97-8F-4F-86   MAC: 00-60-97-8F-5B-12
IP: 172.16.1.1   IP: 10.0.0.1

Table 2-2   *Frame Exchange in a Routed Network*

	Layer 2 Header (Modified)		Layer 3 Header (Unmodified)	
Frame	Destination MAC	Source MAC	Source IP	Destination IP
1*	FF-FF-FF-FF-FF-FF	00-60-97-8F-4F-86	172.16.1.1	172.16.1.2
2**	00-60-97-8F-4F-86	00-E0-1E-68-2B-12	172.16.1.2	172.16.1.1
3***	00-E0-1E-68-2B-12	00-60-97-8F-4F-86	172.16.1.1	10.0.0.1
4*	FF-FF-FF-FF-FF-FF	00-E0-1E-68-2B-11	10.0.0.2	10.0.0.1
5**	00-E0-1E-68-2B-11	00-60-97-8F-5B-12	10.0.0.1	10.0.0.2
6***	00-60-97-8F-5B-12	00-E0-1E-68-2B-11	172.16.1.1	10.0.0.1

*ARP Request

**ARP Reply

***User Data Frame

When Station 1 wants to talk to Station 2, Station 1 realizes that the destination is on a different network by comparing the destination's logical address to its own. Knowing that they are on different networks forces the source to communicate through a router. The router is identified through the default router or default gateway setting on the workstation.

To communicate with the router, the source must address the router at Layer 2 using the router's MAC address. To obtain the router's MAC address, the source first ARPs the router (see frames 1 and 2 in Figure 2-11). The source then creates a frame with the router's MAC address as the destination MAC address and with Station 2's logical address for the destination Layer 3 address (see frame 3 in Figure 2-11). When the frame enters the router, the router determines how to get to the destination network. In this example, the destination directly attaches to the router. The router ARPs for Station 2 (frames 4 and 5 in Figure 2-11) and creates a frame with station 2's MAC address for the L2 destination and router's MAC for the L2 source (see frame 6 in Figure 2-11). The router uses L3 addresses for Stations 1 and 2. The data link layer header changes as the frame moves through a router, while the L3 header remains the same.

In contrast, remember that as the frame transits a repeater or bridge, the frame remains the same. Neither repeaters nor bridges modify the frame. Like a bridge, routers prevent errored frames from entering the destination network.

Segmenting LANs with Switches

So far, this chapter reviewed three legacy internetworking devices. These devices interconnected networks and segments together. During the early 1990s, a bridge derivative found a place in the market. Kalpana introduced a LAN switching device, called the EtherSwitch. EtherSwitch was a glorified bridge in that it offered many ports to attach directly to devices rather than to segments. Each port defined a separate collision domain providing maximum media bandwidth for the attached user. Such an innovative application of a well-known technology, bridging, quickly found favor among network administrators. It provided immediate bandwidth increase for users without needing to implement a complete infrastructure renovation. Recognizing the technology value, Cisco Systems purchased Kalpana in December of 1994. This complemented the Catalyst product line acquired in September 1993 from Crescendo Communications. The Catalyst product line consisted of the Catalyst 1200 and, in March of 1995, the Catalyst 5000. Yet another acquisition in September 1995 of Grand Junction Networks further expanded the product line by introducing the Catalyst 1900 and 2820 products. This growing product line deeply penetrated and frontiered the switching market.

What exactly is a LAN switch? A LAN switch is a multiport bridge that allows workstations to attach directly to the switch to experience full media bandwidth and enables many workstations to transmit concurrently. For example, Figure 2-12 shows four workstations communicating at the same time, something impossible in a shared network environment.

Figure 2-12 *Multiple Concurrent Sessions through a LAN Switch*

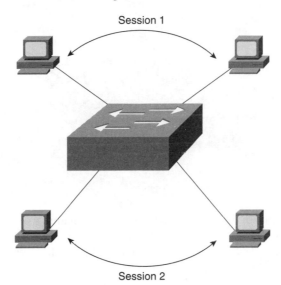

Because a switch is nothing more than a complex bridge with multiple interfaces, all of the ports on a switch belong to one broadcast domain. If Station 1 sends a broadcast frame, all devices attached to the switch receive it. The switch floods broadcast transmissions to all other ports. Unfortunately, this makes the switch no more efficient than a shared media interconnected with repeaters or bridges when dealing with broadcast or multicast frames.

It is possible to design the switch so that ports can belong to different broadcast domains as assigned by a network administrator, thus providing broadcast isolation. In Figure 2-13, some ports belong to Broadcast Domain 1 (BD1), some ports to Broadcast Domain 2 (BD2), and still others to Broadcast Domain 3 (BD3). If a station attached to an interface in BD1 transmits a broadcast frame, the switch forwards the broadcast only to the interfaces belonging to the same domain. The other broadcast domains do not experience any bandwidth consumption resulting from BD1's broadcast. In fact, it is impossible for *any* frame to cross from one broadcast domain to another without the introduction of another external device, such as a router, to interconnect the domains.

Figure 2-13 *A Multibroadcast Domain Capable Switch*

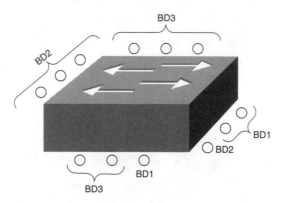

Switches capable of defining multiple broadcast domains actually define *virtual LANs* (VLANs). Each broadcast domain equates to a VLAN. Chapter 5, "VLANs," discusses VLANs in more detail. For now, think of a VLAN capable switch as a device that creates multiple isolated bridges as shown in Figure 2-14.

Figure 2-14 *A Logical Internal Representation of a VLAN Capable Switch*

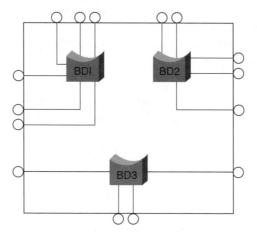

If you create five VLANs, you create five virtual bridge functions within the switch. Each bridge function is logically isolated from the others.

Summary

What is the difference between a bridge and a switch? Marketing. A switch uses bridge technology but positions itself as a device to interconnect individual devices rather than networks. Both devices create collision domains on each port. Both have the potential to create multiple broadcast domains depending upon the vendor implementation and the user configuration.

Review Questions

Refer to the network setup in Figure 2-15 to answer Questions 1 and 2.

Figure 2-15 *Graphic for Review Questions 1 and 2*

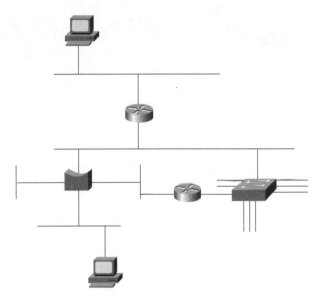

1 Examine Figure 2-15. How many broadcast and collision domains are there?

2 In Figure 2-15, how many Layer 2 and Layer 3 address pairs are used to transmit between Stations 1 and 2?

Refer to the network setup in Figure 2-16 to answer Question 3.

Figure 2-16 *Graphic for Review Question 3*

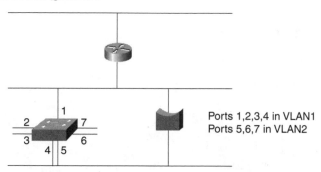

Ports 1,2,3,4 in VLAN1
Ports 5,6,7 in VLAN2

3 What is the problem with the network in Figure 2-16?

4 If you attach a multiport repeater (hub) to a bridge port, how many broadcast domains are seen on the hub?

5 Can a legacy bridge belong to more than one broadcast domain?

This chapter covers the following key topics:

- **Transparent Bridging**—This section explains the five main processes of transparent bridging. These include Forwarding, Flooding, Filtering, Learning and Aging.

- **Switching Modes**—Various switching modes such as store-and-forward, cut through and others are compared and contrasted.

- **Token Ring Bridging**—Different methods exist for bridging Token Ring. This section describes your options.

- **Token Ring Switching**—Token Ring switching provides many of the benefits found in Ethernet switching. This section discusses rules for Token Ring switching in a Catalyst environment

- **Ethernet or Token Ring**—Some users are installing new network systems and do not know which to use. This section provides some thoughts for making the selection

- **Migrating Token Ring to Ethernet**—Administrators frequently elect to replace legacy Token Ring systems with Fast Ethernet switched solutions. This section offers suggestions of things to consider in such an upgrade.

CHAPTER 3

Bridging Technologies

Although various internetworking devices exist for segmenting networks, Layer 2 LAN switches use bridge internetworking technology to create smaller collision domains. Chapter 2, "Segmenting LANs," discussed how bridges segment collision domains. But bridges do far more than segment collision domains: they protect networks from unwanted unicast traffic and eliminate active loops which otherwise inhibit network operations. How they do this differs for Ethernet and Token Ring networks. Ethernet employs transparent bridging to forward traffic and Spanning Tree to control loops. Token Ring typically uses a process called source-route bridging. This chapter describes transparent bridging, source-route bridging (along with some variations), and Layer 2 LAN switching. Chapter 6 covers Spanning Tree for Ethernet.

Transparent Bridging

As discussed in Chapter 2, networks are segmented to provide more bandwidth per user. Bridges provide more user bandwidth by reducing the number of devices contending for the segment bandwidth. But bridges also provide additional bandwidth by controlling data flow in a network. Bridges forward traffic only to the interface(s) that need to receive the traffic. In the case of known unicast traffic, bridges forward the traffic to a single port rather than to all ports. Why consume bandwidth on a segment where the intended destination does not exist?

Transparent bridging, defined in IEEE 802.1d documents, describes five bridging processes for determining what to do with a frame. The processes are as follows:

1 Learning

2 Flooding

3 Filtering

4 Forwarding

5 Aging

Figure 3-1 illustrates the five processes involved in transparent bridging.

Figure 3-1 *Transparent Bridge Flow Chart*

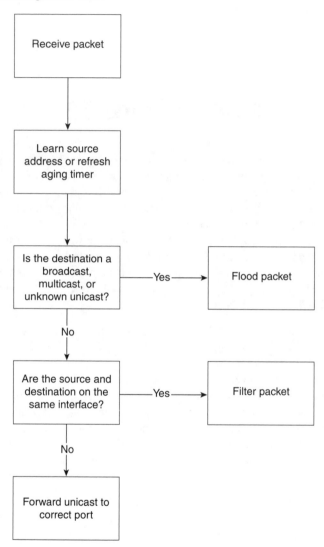

When a frame enters the transparent bridge, the bridge adds the source Ethernet MAC address (SA) and source port to its bridging table. If the source address already exists in the table, the bridge updates the aging timer. The bridge examines the destination MAC address (DA). If the DA is a broadcast, multicast, or unknown unicast, the bridge floods the frame out all bridge ports in the Spanning Tree forwarding state, except for the source port. If the destination address and source address are on the same interface, the bridge discards (filters) the frame. Otherwise, the bridge forwards the frame out the interface where the destination is known in its bridging table.

The sections that follow address in greater detail each of the five transparent bridging processes.

Learning

Each bridge has a table that records all of the workstations that the bridge knows about on every interface. Specifically, the bridge records the source MAC address and the source port in the table whenever the bridge sees a frame from a device. This is the bridge *learning process*. Bridges learn only unicast source addresses. A station never generates a frame with a broadcast or multicast source address. Bridges learn source MAC addresses in order to intelligently send data to appropriate destination segments. When the bridge receives a frame, it references the table to determine on what port the destination MAC address exists. The bridge uses the information in the table to either filter the traffic (if the source and destination are on the same interface) or to send the frame out of the appropriate interface(s).

But when a bridge is first turned on, the table contains no entries. Assume that the bridges in Figure 3-2 were all recently powered "ON," and no station had yet transmitted. Therefore, the tables in all four bridges are empty. Now assume that Station 1 transmits a unicast frame to Station 2. All the stations on that segment, including the bridge, receive the frame because of the shared media nature of the segment. Bridge A learns that Station 1 exists off of port A.1 by looking at the source address in the data link frame header. Bridge A enters the source MAC address and bridge port in the table.

Figure 3-2   *Sample Bridged Network*

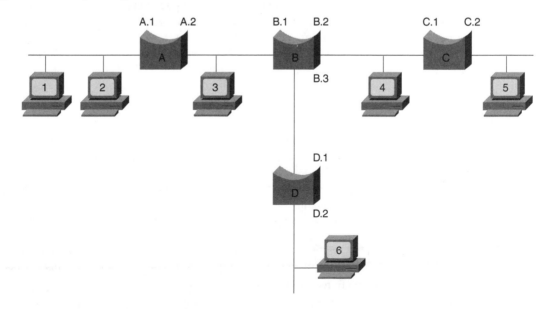

Flooding

Continuing with Figure 3-2, when Station 1 transmits, Bridge A also looks at the destination address in the data link header to see if it has an entry in the table. At this point, Bridge A only knows about Station 1. When a bridge receives a unicast frame (a frame targeting a single destination), no table entry exists for the DA, the bridge receives an *unknown unicast frame*. The bridging rules state that a bridge must send an unknown unicast frame out all forwarding interfaces except for the source interface. This is known as flooding. Therefore, Bridge A floods the frame out all interfaces, even though Stations 1 and 2 are on the same interface. Bridge B receives the frame and goes through the same process as Bridge A of learning and flooding. Bridge B floods the frame to Bridges C and D, and they learn and flood. Now the bridging tables look like Table 3-1. The bridges do not know about Station 2 because it did not yet transmit.

Table 3-1 *Bridging Table after Flooding*

Bridge Port	A.1	A.2	B.1	B.2	B.3	C.1	C.2	D.1
MAC Address	1		1			1		1

Still considering Figure 3-2, all the bridges in the network have an entry for Station 1 associated with an interface, pointing toward Station 1. The bridge tables indicate the *relative* location of a station to the port. Examining Bridge C's table, an entry for Station 1 is associated with port C.1. This does not mean Station 1 directly attaches to C.1. It merely reflects that Bridge C *heard* from Station 1 on this port.

In addition to flooding unknown unicast frames, legacy bridges flood two other frame types: broadcast and multicast. Many multimedia network applications generate broadcast or multicast frames that propagate throughout a bridged network (broadcast domain). As the number of participants in multimedia services increases, more broadcast/multicast frames consume network bandwidth. Chapter 13, "Multicast and Broadcast Services," discusses ways of controlling multicast and broadcast traffic flows in a Catalyst-based network.

Filtering

What happens when Station 2 in Figure 3-2 responds to Station 1? All stations on the segment off port A.1, including Bridge A, receive the frame. Bridge A learns about the presence of Station 2 and adds its MAC address to the bridge table along with the port identifier (A.1). Bridge A also looks at the destination MAC address to determine where to send the frame. Bridge A knows Station 1 and Station 2 exist on the same port. It concludes that it does not need to send the frame anywhere. Therefore, Bridge A *filters the frame*. Filtering occurs when the source and destination reside on the same interface. Bridge A could send the frame out other interfaces, but because this wastes bandwidth on the other segments, the bridging algorithm specifies to discard the frame. Note that only Bridge A knows about the existence of Station 2 because no frame from this station ever crossed the bridge.

Forwarding

If in Figure 3-2, Station 2 sends a frame to Station 6, the bridges flood the frame because no entry exists for Station 6. All the bridges learn Station 2's MAC address and relative location. When Station 6 responds to Station 2, Bridge D examines its bridging table and sees that to reach Station 2, it must forward the frame out interface D.1. A bridge *forwards* a frame when the destination address is a known unicast address (it has an entry in the bridging table) and the source and destination are on different interfaces. The frame reaches Bridge B, which forwards it out interface B.1. Bridge A receives the frame and forwards it out A.1. Only Bridges A, B, and D learn about Station 6. Table 3-2 shows the current bridge tables.

Table 3-2   *Bridging Table after Forwarding*

Bridge Port	A.1	A.2	B.1	B.2	B.3	C.1	C.2	D.1	D.2
MAC Address	1		1			1		1	
		2	2^*				2^*	2^*	
			6			6			6

*.   B.1, C.1, and D.1 did not learn about Station 2 until Station 2 transmitted to Station 6.

Aging

When a bridge learns a source address, it time stamps the entry. Every time the bridge sees a frame from that source, the bridge updates the timestamp. If the bridge does not hear from that source before an *aging timer* expires, the bridge removes the entry from the table. The network administrator can modify the aging timer from the default of five minutes.

Why remove an entry? Bridges have a finite amount of memory, limiting the number of addresses it can remember in its bridging tables. For example, higher end bridges can remember upwards of 16,000 addresses, while some of the lower-end units may remember as few as 4,096. But what happens if all 16,000 spaces are full in a bridge, but there are 16,001 devices? The bridge floods all frames from station 16,001 until an opening in the bridge table allows the bridge to learn about the station. Entries become available whenever the aging timer expires for an address. The aging timer helps to limit flooding by remembering the most active stations in the network. If you have fewer devices than the bridge table size, you could increase the aging timer. This causes the bridge to remember the station longer and reduces flooding.

Bridges also use aging to accommodate station moves. In Table 3-2, the bridges know the location of Stations 1, 2, and 6. If you move Station 6 to another location, devices may not be able to reach Station 6. For example, if Station 6 relocates to C.2 and Station 1 transmits to Station 6, the frame never reaches Station 6. Bridge A forwards the frame to Bridge B, but Bridge B still thinks Station 6 is located on port B.3. Aging allows the bridges to "forget" Station 6's entry. After Bridge B ages the Station 6 entry, Bridge B floods the frames destined to Station 6 until Bridge B learns the new location. On the other hand, if

Station 6 initiates the transmission to Station 1, then the bridges immediately learn the new location of Station 6. If you set the aging timer to a high value, this may cause reachability issues in stations within the network before the timer expires.

The Catalyst screen capture in Example 3-1 shows a bridge table example. This Catalyst knows about nine devices (see bolded line) on nine interfaces. Each Catalyst learns about each device on one and only one interface.

Example 3-1 *Catalyst 5000 Bridging Table*

```
Console> (enable) show cam dynamic
VLAN  Dest MAC/Route Des  Destination Ports or VCs
----  ------------------  -------------------------------------------------
2     00-90-ab-16-60-20   3/4
1     00-90-ab-16-b0-20   3/10
2     00-90-ab-16-4c-20   3/2
1     00-60-97-8f-4f-86   3/23
1     00-10-07-3b-5b-00   3/17
1     00-90-ab-16-50-20   3/91
3     00-90-ab-16-54-20   3/1
1     00-90-92-bf-74-00   3/18
1     00-90-ab-15-d0-10   3/3
Total Matching CAM Entries Displayed = 9
Console> (enable)
```

The bridge tables discussed so far contain two columns: the MAC address and the relative port location. These are seen in columns two and three in Example 3-1, respectively. But this table has an additional column. The first column indicates the VLAN to which the MAC address belongs. A MAC address belongs to only one VLAN at a time. Chapter 5, "VLANs," describes VLANs and why this is so.

Switching Modes

Chapter 2 discusses the differences between a bridge and a switch. Cisco identifies the Catalyst as a LAN switch; a switch is a more complex bridge. The switch can be configured to behave as multiple bridges by defining internal virtual bridges (i.e., VLANs). Each virtual bridge defines a new broadcast domain because no internal connection exists between them. Broadcasts for one virtual bridge are not seen by any other. Only routers (either external or internal) should connect broadcast domains together. Using a bridge to interconnect broadcast domains merges the domains and creates one giant domain. This defeats the reason for having individual broadcast domains in the first place.

Switches make forwarding decisions the same as a transparent bridge. But vendors have different switching modes available to determine *when* to switch a frame. Three modes in particular dominate the industry: store-and-forward, cut-through, and fragment-free. Figure 3-3 illustrates the trigger point for the three methods.

Figure 3-3 *Switching Mode Trigger Points*

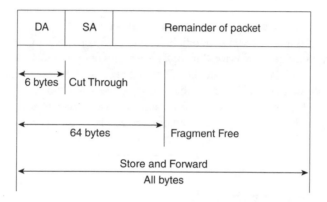

Each has advantages and trade offs, discussed in the sections that follow. As a result of the different trigger points, the effective differences between the modes are in error handling and latency. Table 3-3 compares the approaches and shows which members of the Catalyst family use the available modes. The table summarizes how each mode handles frames containing errors, and the associated latency characteristics.

Table 3-3 *Switching Mode Comparison*

Switching Mode	Errored Frame Handling	Latency	CAT Member*
Store-and-forward	Drop[*]	Variable	5500, 5000, 3920, 3900, 3000, 2900, 1900, 2820, 2600, 6000
Cut-through	Forwards	Low-fixed	3920, 3900, 3000, 2600
Fragment-free	Drops if error detected in first 64 octets	Moderate fixed	3000, 2820, 1900

*.   Note that when a model supports more than one switching mode, adaptive cut-through may be available. Check model specifics to confirm.

One of the objectives of switching is to provide more bandwidth to the user. Each port on a switch defines a new collision domain that offers full media bandwidth. If only one station attaches to an interface, that station has full dedicated bandwidth and does not need to share it with any other device. All the switching modes defined in the sections that follow support the dedicated bandwidth aspect of switching.

TIP   To determine the best mode for your network, consider the latency requirements for your applications and your network reliability. Do your network components or cabling infrastructure generate errors? If so, fix your network problems and use store-and-forward. Can your applications tolerate the additional latency of store-and-forward switching? If not, use cut-through switching. Note that you must use store-and-forward with the Cat 5000 and 6000 family of switches. This is acceptable because latency is rarely an issue, especially with high-speed links and processors and modern windowing protocols. Finally, if the source and destination segments are different media types, you must use store-and-forward mode.

Store-and-Forward Switching

The store-and-forward switching mode receives the entire frame before beginning the switching process. When it receives the complete frame, the switch examines it for the source and destination addresses and any errors it may contain, and then it possibly applies any special filters created by the network administrator to modify the default forwarding behavior. If the switch observes any errors in the frame, it is discarded, preventing errored frames from consuming bandwidth on the destination segment. If your network experiences a high rate of frame alignment or FCS errors, the store-and-forward switching mode may be best. The absolute best solution is to fix the cause of the errors. Using store-and-forward in this case is simply a bandage. It should not be the fix.

If your source and destination segments use different media, then you must use this mode. Different media often have issues when transferring data. The section "Source-Route Translation Bridging" discusses some of these issues. Store-and-forward mode is necessary to resolve this problem in a bridged environment.

Because the switch must receive the entire frame before it can start to forward, transfer latency varies based on frame size. In a 10BaseT network, for example, the minimum frame, 64 octets, takes 51.2 microseconds to receive. At the other extreme, a 1518 octet frame requires at least 1.2 milliseconds. Latency for 100BaseX (Fast Ethernet) networks is one-tenth the 10BaseT numbers.

Cut-Through Switching

Cut-through mode enables a switch to start the forwarding process as soon as it receives the destination address. This reduces latency to the time necessary to receive the six octet destination address: 4.8 microseconds. But cut-through cannot check for errored frames before it forwards the frame. Errored frames pass through the switch, consequently wasting bandwidth; the receiving device discards errored frames.

As network and internal processor speeds increase, the latency issues become less relevant. In high speed environments, the time to receive and process a frame reduces significantly, minimizing advantages of cut-through mode. Store-and-forward, therefore, is an attractive choice for most networks.

Some switches support both cut-through and store-and-forward mode. Such switches usually contain a third mode called *adaptive cut-through.* These multimodal switches use cut-through as the default switching mode and selectively activate store-and-forward. The switches monitor the frame as it passes through looking for errors. Although the switch cannot stop an errored frame, it counts how many it sees. If the switch observes that too many frames contain errors, the switch automatically activates the store-and-forward mode. This is often known as adaptive cut-through. It has the advantage of providing low latency while the network operates well, while providing automatic protection for the outbound segment if the inbound segment experiences problems.

Fragment-Free Switching

Another alternative offers some of the advantages of cut-through and store-and-forward switching. *Fragment-free switching* behaves like cut-through in that it does not wait for an entire frame before forwarding. Rather, fragment-free forwards a frame after it receives the first 64 octets of the frame (this is longer than the six bytes for cut-through and therefore has higher latency). Fragment-free switching protects the destination segment from fragments, an artifact of half-duplex Ethernet collisions. In a correctly designed Ethernet system, devices detect a collision before the source finishes its transmission of the 64-octet frame (this is driven by the slotTime described in Chapter 1). When a collision occurs, a fragment (a frame less than 64 octets long) is created. This is a useless Ethernet frame, and in the store-and-forward mode, it is discarded by the switch. In contrast, a cut-through switch forwards the fragment if at least a destination address exists. Because collisions must occur during the first 64 octets, and because most frame errors will show up in these octets, the fragment-free mode can detect most bad frames and discard them rather than forward them. Fragment-free has a higher latency than cut-through, however, because it must wait for an additional 58 octets before forwarding the frame. As described in the section on cut-through switching, the advantages of fragment-free switching are minimal given the higher network speeds and faster switch processors.

Token Ring Bridging

When IBM introduced Token Ring, they described an alternative bridging technique called *source-route bridging*. Although transparent bridging, as discussed in the previous section, works in a Token Ring environment, IBM networks have unique situations in which transparent bridging creates some obstacles. An example is shown in a later section, "Source-Route Transparent Bridging." Source-route bridging, on the other hand, overcomes these limitations.

Many networks have a combination of transparent and source-route bridged devices. The industry developed source-route transparent bridging for hybrid networks, allowing them to coexist. However, the source-route devices cannot inherently communicate with the transparent devices. Source-route translation bridging, yet another bridging method, offers some hope of mixed media communication. The sections that follow present all three Token Ring bridging methods (source-route, source-route transparent, and source-route translational). The switching aspects of Token Ring networks are described later in the section "Token Ring Switching."

Source-Route Bridging

In a Token Ring environment, rings interconnect with bridges. Each ring and bridge has a numeric identifier. The network administrator assigns the values and must follow several rules. Typically, each ring is uniquely identified within the bridged network with a value between 1 and 4095. (It is possible to have duplicate ring numbers, as long as the rings do not attach to the same bridge.) Valid bridge identifiers include 1 through 15 and must be unique to the local and target rings. A ring cannot have two bridges with the same bridge number. Source devices use ring and bridge numbers to specify the path that the frame will travel through the bridged network. Figure 3-4 illustrates a source-route bridging (SRB) network with several attached workstations.

Figure 3-4 *A Source-Route Bridged Network*

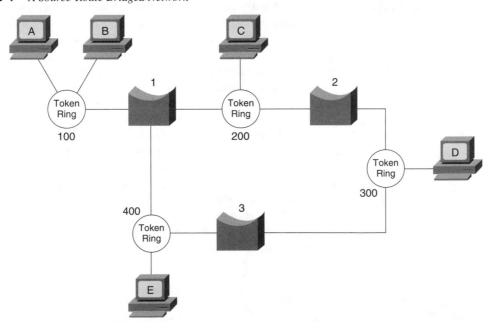

When Station A wants to communicate with Station B, Station A first sends a test frame to determine whether the destination is on the same ring as the source. If Station B responds to the test frame, the source knows that they are both on the same ring. The two stations communicate without involving any Token Ring bridges.

If, however, the source receives no response to the test frame, the source attempts to reach the destination on other rings. But the frame must now traverse a bridge. In order to pass through a bridge, the frame includes a *routing information field (RIF)*. One bit in the frame header signals bridges that a RIF is present and needs to be examined by the bridge. This bit, called the *routing information indicator (RII)*, is set to "zero" when the source and destination are on the same ring; otherwise, it is set to "one."

Most importantly, the RIF tells the bridge how to send the frame toward the destination. When the source first attempts to contact the destination, the RIF is empty because the source does not know any path to the destination. To complete the RIF, the source sends an *all routes explorer (ARE)* frame (it is also possible to use something called a Spanning Tree Explorer [STE]). The ARE passes through all bridges and all rings. As it passes through a bridge, the bridge inserts the local ring and bridge number into the RIF. If in Figure 3-5, Station A sends an ARE to find the best path to reach Station D, Station D will receive two AREs. The RIFs look like the following:

```
Ring100 - Bridge1 - Ring200 - Bridge2 - Ring300
Ring100 - Bridge1 - Ring400 - Bridge3 - Ring300
```

Each ring in the network, except for ring 100, see two AREs. For example, the stations on ring 200 receive two AREs that look like the following:

```
Ring100-Bridge1-Ring200
Ring100-Bridge1-Ring400-Bridge3-Ring300-Bridge2-Ring200
```

The AREs on ring 200 are useless for this session and unnecessarily consume bandwidth. As the Token Ring network gets more complex with many rings interconnected in a mesh design, the quantity of AREs in the network increases dramatically.

NOTE   A Catalyst feature, *all routes explorer reduction*, ensures that AREs don't overwhelm the network. It conserves bandwidth by reducing the number of explorer frames in the network.

Station D returns every ARE it receives to the source. The source uses the responses to determine the best path to the destination. What is the best path? The SRB standard does not specify which response to use, but it does provide some recommendations. The source could do any of the following:

- Use the first response it receives
- Use the path with the fewest hops
- Use the path with the largest MTU
- Use a combination of criteria
- Most Token Ring implementations use the first option.

Now that Station A knows how to reach Station D, Station A transmits each frame as a *specifically routed frame* where the RIF specifies the ring/bridge hops to the destination. When a bridge receives the frame, the bridge examines the RIF to determine if it has any responsibility to forward the frame. If more than one bridge attaches to ring 100, only one of them forwards the specifically routed frame. The other bridge(s) discard it. Station D uses the information in the RIF when it transmits back to Station A. Station D creates a frame with the RIF completed in reverse. The source and destination use the same path in both directions.

Note that transparent bridging differs from SRB in significant ways. First, in SRB, the source device determines what path the frame must follow to reach the destination. In transparent bridging, the bridge determines the path. Secondly, the information used to determine the path differs. SRB uses bridge/ring identifiers, and transparent bridging uses destination MAC addresses.

Source-Route Transparent Bridging

Although many Token Ring networks start out as homogenous systems, transparently bridged Ethernet works its way into many of these networks. As a result, network administrators face hybrid systems and support source-route bridged devices *and* transparently bridged devices. Unfortunately, the source-route bridged devices cannot communicate with the transparently bridged Ethernet devices. Non-source-routed devices do not understand RIFs, SREs, or any other such frames. To further confuse the issue, some Token Ring protocols run in transparent mode, a typically Ethernet process.

NOTE   Source-route translational bridging (SR/TLB), described in the next section, can overcome some of the limitations of source-route transparent bridging (SRT). The best solution, though, is to use a router to interconnect routed protocols residing on mixed media.

Source-route transparent bridging (SRT) supports both source-route and transparent bridging for Token Ring devices. The SRT bridge uses the RII bit to determine the correct bridging mode. If the bridge sees a frame with the RII set to "zero," the SRT bridge treats the frame using transparent bridging methods. It looks at the destination MAC address and determines whether to forward, flood, or filter the frame. If the frame contains a RIF (the RII bit set to "one"), the bridge initiates source-route bridging and uses the RIF to forward the frame. Table 3-4 compares how SRT and SRB bridges react to RII values

Table 3-4   *SRT and SRB Responses to RII*

RII Value	SRB	SRT
zero	Drop frame	Transparently bridge frame
one	Source-route frame	Source-route frame

This behavior causes problems in some IBM environments. Whenever an IBM Token Ring attached device wants to connect to another, it first issues a test frame to see whether the destination resides on the same ring as the source. If the source receives no response, it sends an SRB explorer frame.

The SRT deficiency occurs with the test frame. The source intends for the test frame to remain local to its ring and sets the RII to "zero." An RII set to "zero," however, signals the SRT bridge to transparently bridge the frame. The bridge floods the frame to all rings. After the test frame reaches the destination, the source and destination workstations communicate using transparent bridging methods as if they both reside on the same ring. Although this is functional, transparent bridging does not take advantage of parallel paths like source-route bridging can. Administrators often create parallel Token Ring backbones to distribute traffic and not overburden any single link. But transparent bridging selects a single path and does not use another link unless the primary link fails. (This is an aspect of the Spanning-Tree Protocol described in Chapter 6, "Understanding Spanning Tree," and Chapter 7, "Advanced Spanning Tree.") Therefore, all the traffic passes through the same links, increasing the load on one while another remains unused. This defeats the intent of the parallel Token Rings.

Another IBM operational aspect makes SRT unsuitable. To achieve high levels of service availability, some administrators install redundant devices, such as a 3745 controller, as illustrated in Figure 3-5.

Figure 3-5   *Redundant Token Ring Controllers*

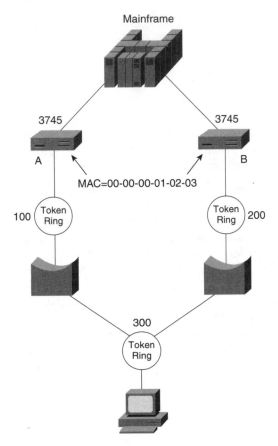

The redundant controllers use the same MAC address (00-00-00-01-02-03) to simplify workstation configuration; otherwise, multiple entries need to be entered. If the primary unit fails, the workstation needs to resolve the logical address to the new MAC address of the backup unit. By having duplicate MAC addresses, fully automatic recovery is available without needing to resolve a new address.

Duplicate MAC addresses within a transparently bridged network confuses bridging tables, however. A bridge table can have only one entry for a MAC address; a station cannot appear on two interfaces. Otherwise, if a device sends a frame to the MAC address for Controller A in Figure 3-5, how can the transparent bridge know whether to send the frame to Controller A or Controller B? Both have the same MAC address, but only one can exist in the bridging table. Therefore, the intended resiliency feature will not work in the source-route transparent bridge mode. When using the resiliency feature, configure the Token Ring Concentrator Relay Function (TrCRF) for source-route bridging. The TrCRF defines ports to a common ring. The TrCRF is discussed later in the chapter in the "Token Ring Switching" section.

Source-Route Translational Bridging

Unfortunately, not all networks are homogenous. They may contain a mixture of Ethernet and Token Ring access methods. How would you attach a Token Ring network to an Ethernet such as the one shown in Figure 3-6?

Figure 3-6   *Bridging Mixed Media Access Networks*

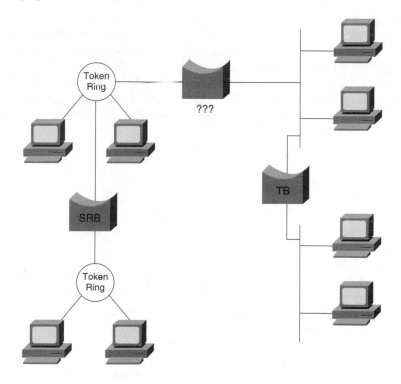

Several obstacles prevent devices on the two networks from communicating with each other. Some of the obstacles include the following:

- MAC address format
- MAC address representation in the protocol field
- LLC and Ethernet framing
- Routing information field translation
- MTU size mismatch

Translational bridging helps to resolve these issues, allowing the devices to communicate. But no standard exists for translational bridging, leaving a number of implementation details to the vendor. The following sections discuss in more detail each listed limitation. The sections provide a technical and a practical explanation of why transparent bridging might not be the best option.

MAC Address Format

When devices transmit frames, the bit sequence varies depending on the access method. An Ethernet frame has a format of **DA|SA|Type|Data**. But when the frame enters the media, which bit goes first? In Ethernet, the least significant bit of each octet does. Consider, for example, a hexadecimal value of 0x6A. In binary, this looks like: 0110 1010 with the most significant bit (MSB) on the left and the least significant bit (LSB) on the right. Ethernet transmits the LSB first. This is called the canonical address format. Token Ring and FDDI use a non-canonical format, transmitting the MSB first and the LSB last. The binary stream looks like 0101 0110 and has a hex value of 0x56. A translational bridge sequences the bits appropriately for the receiving network type so that the devices will see the correct MAC address. A canonical source MAC address of 0C-00-01-38-73-0B sent onto a Token Ring segment must have the address transmitted in non-canonical format as 30-00-80-1C-CE-D0. If the bridge does not perform address translation, the Token Ring device will respond to the wrong MAC address.

Embedded Address Format

Similarly, MAC address translation may need to occur at Layer 3. Some protocols embed the MAC address in the Layer 3 protocol header. IPX for example, uses a logical IPX address format comprising a network number and MAC address. In TCP/IP, the address resolution protocol (ARP) includes the source and destination MAC address in the frame as part of the IP protocol header. Other protocols that embed MAC addresses in the Layer 3 header include DECnet Phase IV, AppleTalk, Banyan VINES, and XNS. Many of these protocols respond to the MAC address contained in the Layer 3 header, not the data link layer. A translational bridge must therefore be intelligent and protocol-aware to know when to modify the Layer 3 information to correctly represent the MAC address. This is, of course, an activity normally relegated to a router, which operates at Layer 3. If a new protocol that needs translational bridging is added to the network, the bridge must be updated to know about the translation tasks. Translational bridging must keep abreast of industry protocols to allow inter-communication between the differently bridged devices.

LLC and Ethernet Frame Differences

Ethernet-formatted frames use a **DA|SA|Protocol_Type** format that, when bridged onto an IEEE 802 formatted network, presents the problem of what to do with the **Protocol_Type** value. IEEE 802 headers do not have a provision for the Protocol_Type value. The SNAP encapsulation approach was devised to carry the Protocol_Type value across IEEE 802-based networks. Figure 3-7 illustrates a translation from Ethernet to Token Ring SNAP.

Figure 3-7   *Frame Translation from Ethernet to Token Ring SNAP*

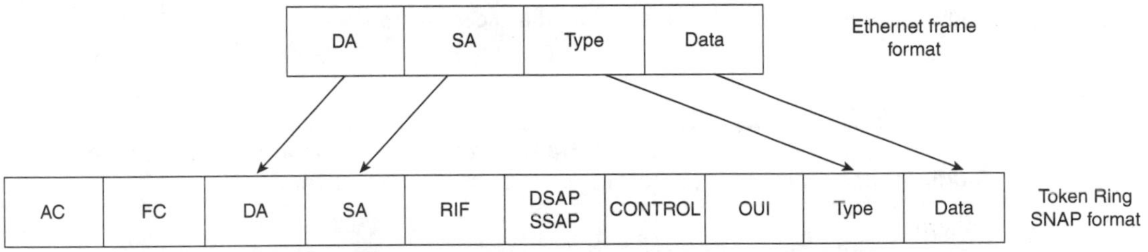

The frame fields illustrated in Figure 3-7 are as follows:

AC (access control)

FC (frame control)

DA (destination MAC address)

SA (source MAC address)

RIF (routing information field)

DSAP (destination service access point)

SSAP (source service access point)

Control (LLC control)

OUI (Organizational Unique Identifier—vendor ID)

Type (protocol type value)

RIF Interpretation

When connecting source-route devices to transparent devices, another issue involves the routing information field. The RIF is absent from transparent devices but is vital to the Token Ring bridging process. How then does a source-route bridged device specify a path to a transparently bridged device?

A translational bridge assigns a ring number to the transparent segment. To an SRB device, it appears that the destination device resides on a source-routed segment. To the transparent device, the SRB device appears to attach to a transparent segment. The translational bridge keeps a source-routing table to reach the Token Ring MAC address. When a transparent device transmits a frame to the Token Ring device, the bridge looks at the destination MAC address, finds a source-route entry for that address, and creates a frame with a completed RIF.

MTU Size

Ethernet, Token Ring, and FDDI support different frame sizes. Table 3-5 lists the minimum and maximum frame sizes for these media access methods.

Table 3-5   *Frame Size Comparison*

Media Access Method	Minimum Frame Size (Octets)	Maximum Frame Size (Octets)
Ethernet	64	1518
Token Ring (4 Mbps)	21	4511
Token Ring (16 Mbps)	21	17839
FDDI	28	4500

A frame from one network type cannot violate the frame size constraints of the destination network. If an FDDI device transmits to an Ethernet device, it must not create a frame over 1518 octets or under 64 octets. Otherwise, the bridge must drop the frame. Translational bridges attempt to adjust the frame size to accommodate the maximum transmission unit (MTU) mismatch. Specifically, a translational bridge may fragment an IP frame if the incoming frame exceeds the MTU of the outbound segment. Routers normally perform fragmentation because it is a Layer 3 process. Translational bridges that perform fragmentation actually perform a part of the router's responsibilities.

Note, however, that fragmentation is an IP process. Other protocols do not have fragmentation, so the source must create frames appropriately sized for the segment with the smallest MTU. In order for these protocols to work correctly, they exercise MTU discovery, which allows the stations to determine the largest allowed frame for the path(s) between the source and destination devices. This option exists in IP, too, and is preferred over fragmentation.

Catalyst and Translational Bridging

Catalyst Token Ring modules do not provide translational bridging. An external Cisco router or the Route Switch Module (RSM) operating in a bridging mode, however, does support translational bridging. The most reliable interconnection method between different access types, however, is routing. Because routers are protocol-aware, they reliably translate all necessary elements of the frame when converting from Token Ring to other network types.

Token Ring Switching

Token Ring switching offers many of the advantages found in switched Ethernet networks. Most notably, it offers more bandwidth by reducing the size of the Token Ring domain. In the extreme case, the smallest Token Ring domain is a dedicated workstation on a switch port. Catalyst Token Ring switching creates two virtual entities: the Token Ring Concentrator Relay Function (TrCRF) and the Token Ring Bridge Relay Function (TrBRF). Together, these functions form a switched Token Ring network with smaller token domains.

Source-route switching described in the later section "Source-Route Switching" provides a service within the TrCRF for transferring frames between ports within a ring, or to the TrBRF to transfer to another TrCRF.

Another Catalyst Token Ring feature protects you from misconfiguring the system with a duplicate ring on another Catalyst. This is an erroneous configuration, which, if actually performed, could prevent your Token Ring network from operating correctly. DRiP is described in the later section "Duplicate Ring Protocol (DRiP)."

Token Ring Concentrator Relay Function (TrCRF)

In Token Ring networks, multistation access units (MAUs) interconnect workstations to form a physical star topology. The MAU, a type of concentrator, maintains ring functionality and passes tokens and frames among all stations attached to the ring. All the stations attached to the MAU share the same token and bandwidth.

In the Catalyst, the network administrator assigns ports to a virtual concentrator called a Token Ring Concentrator Relay Function (TrCRF). All the ports assigned to a TrCRF belong to the same ring number. However, the workstations attached to each port experience full media bandwidth and have no perception that other stations share the ring.

The TrCRF defines the port to ring number association. The Catalyst in Figure 3-8 defines four TrCRFs to interconnect fourteen ports. (A port is a member of one and only one TrCRF.)

Figure 3-8 *Defining TrCRFs to Interconnect Ports*

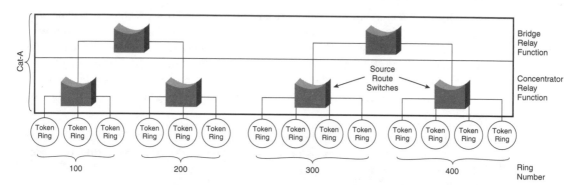

In general, a TrCRF can reside in only one Catalyst and cannot span outside of a Catalyst. This is called an *undistributed TrCRF*. An exception to this, the default TrCRF, spans Catalysts and is referred to as a *distributed TrCRF*. (A backup TrCRF may also span Catalysts.) The default TrCRF enables all Token Ring ports to belong to a common TrCRF without any administrator intervention. Users can attach to any Token Ring port and communicate with any other station in the distributed TrCRF network. The default TrCRF behaves like a giant ring extending across all Catalysts and provides the "plug and play" capability of the Catalyst in Token Ring networks.

When configuring a TrCRF, you must define the ring and VLAN numbers, and you must associate it with an existing parent TrBRF (TrBRFs are discussed in the next section). The parent TrBRF is assigned a VLAN number and is the identifier used to associate the TrCRF to the TrBRF. In addition, you may define whether the TrCRF will operate in the SRB or SRT mode. If left unspecified, the TrCRF will operate in SRB mode.

Token Ring Bridge Relay Function (TrBRF)

The Token Ring Bridge Relay Function (TrBRF) acts like a multiport bridge and interconnects rings. The TrBRF defines the TrCRF-to-bridge association. A TrCRF belongs to only one parent TrBRF, but multiple TrCRFs may attach to a parent bridge. Figure 3-8, for example, shows more than one TrCRF attached to a TrBRF. The TrCRFs interconnect through the TrBRF the same as rings do through the source-route bridges and source-route transparent bridges previously described. Unlike the TrCRF, the TrBRF can span between Catalysts, as shown in Figure 3-9. This allows TrCRFs on various Catalysts to belong to the same bridge

Figure 3-9   *TrBRF Extending Across Catalysts*

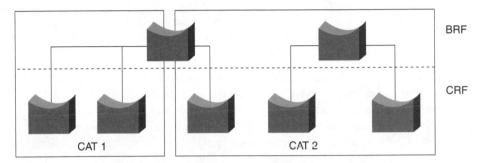

Enabling a TrBRF requires a bridge and VLAN number. The TrBRF's VLAN number is paired with the TrCRF VLAN number to create the parent-to-child relationship. Because a TrCRF must associate with a parent TrBRF, the default TrCRF belongs to a default TrBRF. When enabling Token Ring switching with a non-default TrCRF and TrBRF, you must first configure the TrBRF, then the TrCRF, and finally, group ports to TrCRFs. Referring to Figure 3-9, you would do the following:

1   Configure the TrBRF at the top of the drawing. To do this, you define the bridge number and the VLAN number as in the following:

    ```
    Console> (enable) set vlan 100 type trbrf bridge
    ```

2   Work down the figure to the TrCRF(s). Create the TrCRF, specifying the VLAN number, the ring number, the bridge type, and parent TrBRF. Here is an example:

    ```
    Console> (enable) set vlan 110 type trcrf parent 100 ring 10
    ```

3   After creating the TrCRF, associate ports to the correct TrCRF.

Source-Route Switching

Source-route switching describes the mechanism of bridging Token Ring traffic. The modes are determined based on the location of the source and destination devices relative to the bridging function. The source-route switch (SRS) decides whether to transparently bridge a frame within a TrCRF or to source-route bridge to another TrCRF. When a station on a switch port transmits to another station residing on a different port but belonging to the same TrCRF, the SRS forwards the frame based on the destination MAC address. The SRS learns source MAC addresses and makes forwarding decisions the same as a transparent bridge. However, if the source and destination are on different rings, the source creates a frame with a RIF. The SRS examines the RIF and passes the frame to the bridge relay function for forwarding.

Although this sounds like a source-route bridge, a significant difference distinguishes an SRS from an SRB. When a station transmits an ARE, an SRB modifies the RIF to indicate ring/bridge numbers. An SRS never modifies a RIF; it simply examines it. When a source sends an all-routes explorer, for example, it sets the RII bit to "one," indicating the presence of a RIF. Examination of the initial explorer frame, however, reveals that the RIF is empty. The SRS notices that the RII bit value is "one" and forwards the explorer to the TrBRF unmodified. The SRS simply says, "This is a source-routed frame; I better send it to the TrBRF and let the bridge worry about it." In contrast, an SRB or TrBRF modifies the explorer RIF by inserting ring and bridge numbers.

In Chapter 2, a broadcast domain was defined and equated to a VLAN; a broadcast domain describes the extent to which broadcast frames are forwarded or flooded throughout the network. The domain boundaries terminate at a router interface and include an interconnected set of virtual bridges. But Token Ring complexities present ambiguities when defining a VLAN. In a source-route bridged environment, Token Ring actually creates two kinds of broadcasts: the intra-ring and the inter-ring broadcast.

A device generates an intra-ring broadcast whenever it produces a broadcast frame without a RIF, and the explorer bit is set to "zero." A station may do this whenever it wants to determine whether the destination is on the same ring as the source. The SRS function floods this frame type to all ports within the TrCRF. The frame does not cross the TrBRF.

In contrast, an inter-ring broadcast frame sets the explorer bit to "one," enabling the frame to cross ring boundaries. The TrBRF floods the inter-ring frame to all attached rings; all rings receive a copy of the frame. Figure 3-10 illustrates Token Ring VLAN boundaries.

Figure 3-10 *Token Ring VLANs Illustrated*

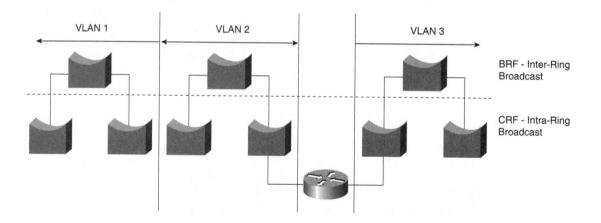

A network may see both the intra- and inter-ring broadcasts. Which one actually describes a VLAN? A VLAN in the Token Ring network includes the TrCRF and the TrBRF. A VLAN exists whenever Token Ring networks must interconnect through a router.

Duplicate Ring Protocol (DRiP)

In a Token Ring environment, each ring has a unique ring number identifying it for source-route bridging. Similarly, in a switched Token Ring, except for the default and backup TrCRFs mentioned earlier, each TrCRF has a unique ring number. If an administrator accidentally misconfigures another TrCRF with the same ring number, shown in Figure 3-11, the Token Ring switching process gets confused.

Figure 3-11 *Do not attempt this. Duplicate ring numbers are not allowed on multiple switches.*

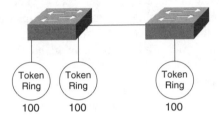

To mitigate the effects of duplicate ring numbers in a switched network, Cisco developed a proprietary protocol to detect them and react accordingly. The Duplicate Ring Protocol (DRiP) sends advertisements with the multicast address 01-00-0C-CC-CC-CC to its neighbors, announcing VLAN information for the source device only. By default, DRiP announcements occur every 30 seconds or whenever a significant configuration change occurs in the network. DRiP announcements only traverse ISL links and are constrained to VLAN1, the default VLAN. The receiving Catalyst then compares the information with its local configuration. If a user attempts to create a Token Ring VLAN that already exists on another Catalyst, the local unit denies the configuration.

Ethernet or Token Ring?

Since IBM introduced Token Ring to the industry, both Token Ring and Ethernet were recognized as candidates for corporate LAN infrastructures. The great debate among LAN specialists focused upon the question, "Which is better—Token Ring or Ethernet?" The answer to that question most often depended on the user application. Early Token Ring limitations offered connection speeds at only 4 Mbps, while Ethernet supported 10 Mbps. It was perceived, therefore, that Ethernet was better because it offered more bandwidth. Later, 16 Mbps Token Ring technology made Token Ring more attractive, but by no means ultimately superior. Some users felt that Ethernet's lack of guaranteed access made it unsuitable for environments such as manufacturing. If an equipment operator needed to control heavy equipment and send start/stop commands over a network, for example, the network administrator wanted to ensure that the command actually would make it to the device. Dangerous conditions could arise if the network lost a control command due to a collision. Because Ethernet offers no such promises in a collision environment, the manufacturing industry tended to select Token Ring. Token Ring promises a user the token at a predictable rate, thereby allowing access to the network to send critical commands. Ethernet could make no such claim; therefore, it was frequently dismissed as a viable networking alternative on the manufacturing floor.

Another factor that caused users to select Token Ring was their mainframe computer type. If the user had IBM equipment, they tended to use Token Ring because much of the IBM equipment had Token Ring LAN interfaces. Therefore, IBM shops were practically forced to use Token Ring to easily attach equipment to their networks.

In an office environment where no guarantees of predictability were necessary, Ethernet found popularity. Ethernet cabling schemes were simpler than Token Ring, and minicomputer manufacturers included Ethernet interfaces in their workstations. As users became more comfortable with Ethernet, network administrators selected it more frequently.

With the introduction of LAN switching technologies, Ethernet now finds application in the manufacturing environment where it previously could not. Switching reduces the size of a collision domain and provides a higher throughput potential that makes it possible to use in manufacturing. Switched Ethernet with ports dedicated to single devices performs equally as well or better than switched Token Ring networks in a similar configuration.

Migrating Token Ring to Ethernet

Many Token Ring users contemplate a migration from Token Ring to Ethernet. In some cases, the motivation is the available bandwidth of Fast Ethernet. Sometimes the motivation is to simplify cabling. But moving an infrastructure from Token Ring to Ethernet involves several considerations. For example, the media cabling type might differ. Many Token Ring systems utilize Category 3 cable (shielded twisted-pair), whereas Ethernet typically uses Category 5 cable (unshielded twisted-pair). Other elements to consider include changing workstations' adapters along with their drivers, performance requirements for existing protocols, and application demands.

A migration plan usually involves phases rather than a comprehensive one-time changeover. Cost, labor availability, and risk drive a migration plan to spread over time. But what should change first? Clients? Servers? Departments? If the cabling infrastructure needs to be upgraded to support the new Ethernet system, the migration may possibly involve geographical issues. This means that the network will change one room or one floor at a time.

If the primary concern is to minimize risk, the migration plan might be a hierarchical approach. Start by moving the backbone to a Fast Ethernet, and bridge or route between the backbone and the distribution segments. Then as the technology proves itself for the applications, move selected devices, such as servers, to the Ethernet system.

Whatever approach you take, be sure to plan it. Migrate—don't mutate—the network.

Summary

Bridging alternatives exist for Ethernet and Token Ring media types. Traditionally, Ethernet uses transparent bridging with the following operations: learning (adding a source address/interface to a bridge table), forwarding out a single interface (known unicast traffic), flooding out all interfaces (unknown unicast, multicast and broadcast), filtering (unicast traffic where the source and destination are on the same interface side), and aging (removing an entry from the bridge table.)

Token Ring usually implements source-route bridging in which the source specifies the path for the frame to the destination. This means the source identifies a sequence of ring/bridge hops. SRT (source-route transparent bridging), another Token Ring bridge method, does both source-route bridging and transparent bridging. Source-route bridging is employed if the frame includes a routing information field. Otherwise, transparent bridging is used.

When connecting transparently bridged segments (Ethernet) to source-routed segments (Token Ring), use routing or translational bridging. If you must use bridging, translational bridging resolves a number of issues in the way that frames are constructed for the different access methods. However, translational bridges must be aware of the protocols to be translated. The best solution, though, is to use routing to interconnect mixed media networks. Chapter 11, "Layer 3 Switching," discusses using routers in a switched environment.

Token Ring switching creates two functions to segment Token Rings: the concentrator relay function and the bridge relay function. In the Catalyst, the Token Ring Concentrator Relay Function (TrCRF) defines which ports belong to a ring. A TrCRF may operate either in SRB or SRT mode. A TrCRF cannot span across Catalysts. The Token Ring Bridge Relay Function (TrBRF) provides Token Ring bridging between TrCRFs. A TrBRF can span across Catalysts to allow ports on different units to communicate through a common bridge.

Source-route switching determines whether a frame may be forwarded within the TrCRF or whether the frame needs to be sent to the TrBRF. The SRS looks for the RII to make this decision. If the RII indicates the presence of a routing information field, it forwards the frame to the TrBRF. Otherwise, the SRS keeps the frame within the TrCRF and uses transparent bridging.

Review Questions

1 If a RIF is present in a source-routed frame, does a source-route switch ever examine the MAC address of a frame?

2 To how many VLANs can a TrBRF belong?

3 The transparent-bridge learning process adds entries to the bridging table based on the source address. Source addresses are never multicast addresses. Yet when examining the Catalyst bridge table, it is possible to see multicast. Why?

4 Two Cisco routers attach to a Catalyst. On one router you type **show cdp neighbor.** You expect to see the other router listed because CDP announces on a multicast address 01-00-0C-CC-CC-CC, which is flooded by bridges. But you see only the Catalyst as a neighbor. Suspecting that the other router isn't generating cdp announcements, you enter **show cdp neighbor** on the Catalyst. You see both routers listed verifying that both routers are generating announcements. Why didn't you see the second router from the first router? (Hint: neither router can see the other.)

This chapter covers the following key topics:

- **Catalyst 5000/6000 CLI Syntax Conventions**—Provides the standard Cisco representation for interpreting commands administered on Catalyst switches.

- **Catalyst 5000 Configuration Methods**—Provides information on how to operate under the Console, Telnet, and TFTP configuration modes for Catalyst configuration.

- **Using the Catalyst 5000/6000 Command-Line Interface**—Describes command-line recall, editing, and help for the Catalyst 5000 series.

- **Passwords**—Provides documentation on how to set, change, and recover passwords for the Catalyst 5000/6000 series of switches.

- **Configuration File Management**—Discusses how to store and restore configuration files on flash and TFTP servers for Supervisor I, II, and III modules.

- **Image File Management**—Describes how to transfer Supervisor I, II, and III module software images.

- **Redundant Supervisor Modules**—Discusses how to implement redundant Supervisor modules to ensure system operation in the event of a module failover.

- **Configuring Other Catalysts**—Provides a quick overview of the configuration methods for the 1900/2800 and the 3000 series of Catalyst switches.

CHAPTER 4

Configuring the Catalyst

Users familiar with Cisco routers exercise a command line interface (CLI) embedded in the IOS. The CLI characteristics are seen across nearly all of the router product line. However, most Catalysts CLIs differ from those found on Cisco routers. In fact, the Catalyst family has several CLIs based upon the model origins. The Catalyst 4000/5000/6000 series differs from the 3000 series, the 1900,2800 and the 8500 series. This chapter compares differences between the router CLI and the Catalyst 4000/5000/6000 family. It also describes the command line interface including aspects like command line recall, command editing, uploading and downloading code images and configuration files. An overview of the menu driven configuration for the other Catalysts is addressed in the last section, *Configuring Other Catalysts*. Examples of configuring the Catalyst 8500 series are included in Chapter 11, "Layer 3 Switching." This chapter deals primarily, however, with the *"XDI"* interface used by the Catalyst 4000/5000/6000 family.

NOTE   Cisco folklore has it that XDI is the name of a UNIX-like kernel purchased for use in equipment that evolved into the Catalyst 4000, 5000, and 6000 products of today. The XDI CLI is often referred to as "CatOS."

The Catalyst product family evolution does not have the same roots as the Cisco router products. Cisco's history begins with the development of routers to interconnect networks. As the router family increased, a number of differences between the early models and the later became evident. Particularly with the release of 9.1x, the command line interface vastly differed for the IOS. But the IOS essentially retained the same look and feel after that point across all of the router family. Users of the Catalyst on the other hand may encounter multiple CLIs dependent upon the model used. This occurs not because Cisco changed its mind on how to present the CLI, but because some of the products were acquired technologies with a previously installed user base. For example, some of the Catalysts such as the 1900 and 2800 came from Grand Junction and have their own configuration methods. Some come from Kalpana, such as the Catalyst 3000, and use a different menu structure. Some were developed by Cisco. For example, the 8500 and the 2900XL, and use IOS type configurations. The Catalyst 5000 family originated with Crescendo. When Cisco acquired Crescendo, a significant user base already familiar with the XDI/CatOS configuration modes existed. The Catalyst 5000 and 6000 series use a CLI which differs from all of the others.

This chapter provides an overview for configuring the Catalyst 4000/5000/6000 series products. The CLI syntax and conventions are covered, along with command recall and editing methods. Methods for storing and retrieving configuration files images are also explained. Finally, configuring and managing redundant supervisor modules in a Catalyst 5500/6000/6500 are discussed.

Catalyst 5000/6000 CLI Syntax Conventions

All well-documented equipment uses a standard representation for interpreting commands. The Catalyst is no exception. Cisco documents how to interpret the printed commands of its documentation. Table 4-1 summarizes the command syntax conventions used in the Catalyst documentation and in this book.

Table 4-1   *Catalyst Syntax Conventions*

Command Presentation	Interpretation
Boldface	Commands and keywords that are entered literally as shown are in boldface.
Italic	Arguments for which you supply values are in italics.
[ ]	Elements in square brackets are optional.
{x | y | z}	Alternative required keywords are grouped in braces and separated by vertical bars.
[x | y | z]	Optional alternative keywords are grouped in brackets and separated by vertical bars.
String	A nonquoted set of characters. Do not use quotation marks around the string or the string will include the quotation marks.

Catalyst 5000 Configuration Methods

When you attempt to log in to the Catalyst, the Catalyst presents you with a password prompt. If you enter the correct password, you enter the Catalyst's *NORMAL mode*. Normal mode equates to a router's *User EXEC* mode allowing you to view most Catalyst parameters, but not authorizing any configuration changes. To make changes, you must enter the Catalyst's *PRIVILEGED mode*. The privileged mode functionally equates to the router's *PRIVILEGED EXEC mode*. In the privileged mode, you can view configuration files and make configuration changes. You enter the Catalyst's privileged mode with the **enable** command. The Catalyst then prompts for a password.

You can access the Catalyst CLI through one of three methods: through the console interface, Telnet, or Trivial File Transfer Protocol (TFTP). The following sections detail each access method.

Like a router, commands are additive—adding configuration statements to an existing file does not completely overwrite the existing configuration. Suppose you have an existing configuration that assigns ports 2/1-10 to VLAN 5. If you add a configuration that assigns ports 2/1-5 to VLAN 5, but you do nothing to ports 2/6-10, 2/6-10 remain in VLAN 5. The absence of these ports in the new VLAN assignment does not remove them from VLAN 5. If, however, the additional configuration includes a line that assigns ports 2/6-10 to VLAN 20, they move VLAN membership.

A foolproof way of ensuring that a new configuration completely overwrites an existing file is to enter **clear config all** (see Example 4-1). If you clear the configuration from Telnet or TFTP, you do not see this output. You only see this when directly attached to the console. This CLI command returns the Catalyst Supervisor module to its default configuration where all ports belong to VLAN 1, there is no VTP domain (explained in Chapter 12, "VLAN Trunking Protocol"), and all Spanning Tree parameters back to default values. Note also that entering this command clears the console's IP address too. You can clear the configuration with any of the access methods, but if you do so while you access the Catalyst through Telnet, you disconnect from the Catalyst because the Catalyst no longer has an IP address either.

Example 4-1   **clear config all** *Output*

```
Console> (enable) clear config
Usage: clear config all
       clear config <mod_num>
       clear config rmon
Console> (enable) clear config all
This command will clear all configuration in NVRAM.
This command will cause ifIndex to be reassigned on the next system startup.
Do you want to continue (y/n) [n]? y
.
......
.........................
......
.....


System configuration cleared.
Use 'session' command to clear ATM or Router specific configurations.
Console> (enable)
```

From the Supervisor console, or via Telnet, you can clear the Catalyst configuration with the **clear config all** command. **clear config all** in Example 4-1 resets the Supervisor module to its defaults. Note that this command does not clear the files for the ATM LANE module, nor for the RSM (or MSM in a Catalyst 6000). This only affects the modules directly configured from the Supervisor module. To clear the configurations on the ATM or router modules, you need to access the modules with the **session** *module_number* command. This command performs the equivalent of an internal Telnet to the module so that you can make configuration changes. The ATM and router modules use IOS commands to change, save, and clear configurations.

TIP

Configuring the Catalyst through the console and through Telnet allows you to enter commands in real time, but only one at a time. Unlike Cisco routers, the Catalyst immediately stores commands in nonvolatile random-access memory (NVRAM) and does not require you to perform a **copy run start** like a router. Any command you type in a Catalyst is immediately remembered, even through a power cycle. This presents a challenge when reversing a series of commands. On a router, you can reverse a series of commands with reload, as long as you didn't write the running configuration into NVRAM.

Before making serious changes to a Catalyst, copy the configuration to an electronic notepad. On the Catalyst, use the command **set length 0** to terminate the *more* function, enable screen capture on your device, and enter **show config** to capture the current configuration. Then if you do not like the changes you made and cannot easily reverse them, **clear config all** and replay the captured configuration file to locally restore the starting configuration.

Console Configuration

The Catalyst 5000 series Supervisor module has one physical console connection. For a Supervisor I or a Supervisor II, the connection is an EIA-232 25-pin connection. For a Supervisor III module, the connection is an RJ-45 connector. Make sure that you know which kind of Supervisor module you are working with to ensure that you can attach to the console.

The console has an interesting feature in that it can operate in one of two modes: either as a console or slip interface. When used as a console, you can attach a terminal or terminal emulation device such as a PC with appropriate software to the interface. This provides direct access to the CLI regardless of the configuration. You use this access method when you have no IP addresses configured in the Catalyst; without an IP address, you cannot Telnet to the Catalyst over the network. You also use this method whenever you need to do password recovery. (Password recovery is discussed in a later section.) And, you will probably elect to access the Catalyst with this method whenever you are local to the Catalyst with an available terminal.

You can enable the console port as a SLIP interface. (SLIP [serial line interface protocol] is the precursor to PPP.) When used in the slip mode, you can Telnet directly to the console port. In a likely setup, you attach a modem to the console port enabling you to Telnet directly to the Catalyst without having to traverse the network. This can be useful when troubleshooting the Catalyst from a remote location when you cannot access it over the network. When used as a slip interface, the interface designator is sl0 [SL0]. You can use the interface as a direct console attachment or a slip interface, but not both. It can only operate as one or the other. By default, it operates as a console interface. To configure the console as a slip interface, you need to assign an IP address to sl0 using the **set interface** command.

Lastly, you can access the CLI through Telnet over the network. The Catalyst has an *internal logical* interface, **sc0,** that you can assign an IP address to. This address becomes the source address when generating traffic in the Catalyst, or the destination address when you attempt to reach the Catalyst. Assigning an address to this logical interface causes the

Catalyst to act like an IP end station on the network. You can use the address to perform Telnet, TFTP, BOOTP, RARP, ICMP, trace, and a host of other end station functions.

By default, the sc0 has no IP address and belongs to VLAN 1. If you want to change any of these parameters, use the **set interface** command. You can modify sc0's IP address and VLAN assignment in one statement. For example, **set int sc0 10 144.254.100.1 255.255.255.0** assigns sc0 to VLAN 10 and configures an IP address of 144.254.100.1 with a "Class C" IP mask.

Telnet Configuration

Before you can Telnet to a Catalyst, you need to assign an IP address to the sc0 interface on the Supervisor module. The previous section, "Console Configuration," demonstrated how to do this. You can Telnet to a Catalyst as long as your Telnet device can reach the VLAN and IP network that the sc0 interface belongs to. Telnetting to the Catalyst allows you to perform any command as if you were directly attached to the Catalyst console. You do, however, need to know the normal mode and privileged EXEC passwords to gain access.

It was also mentioned earlier that if you enter **clear config all** from a remote location, you effectively cut yourself off from communicating with the Catalyst through the network. Changing the IP address or VLAN assignment on sc0 can do the same thing. Therefore, be sure to thoroughly review the results of changing the Catalyst IP address or VLAN assignment remotely.

A Catalyst security feature allows you to specify an access list of authorized stations that can access the Catalyst through Telnet or Simple Network Management Protocol (SNMP). You can specify up to 10 entries through the **set ip permit** command. To enable the access list, you need to specify the set of authorized stations and then turn on the IP permit filter.

To specify the list of allowed stations, use the command syntax **set ip permit** *ip_address* [*mask*]. The optional mask allows you to specify wildcards. For example, if you type **set ip permit 144.254.100.0 255.255.255.0**, you authorize all stations in subnet 144.254.100.0 to access the console interface. If you enter the command **set ip permit 144.254.100.10** with no mask, the implied mask 255.255.255.255 is used, which specifies a specific host.

You can specify up to 10 entries this way. To activate the permit list, use the command **set ip permit enable**.

Activating the list does not affect any other transit or locally originated IP processes such as trace route and ICMP Echo Requests/Replies. The IP permit list only controls inbound Telnet and SNMP traffic addressed to the Catalyst. If the source IP address does not fall within the permitted range, the Catalyst refuses the connection.

TIP   If you apply a permit list from a remote Telnet connection, ensure that you include yourself in the permit list. Otherwise, you disconnect yourself from the Catalyst you are configuring.

You can also secure the Catalyst using Terminal Access Controller Access Control System Plus (TACACS+) authentication. TACACS+ enables a communication protocol between your Catalyst and a TACACS+ server. The server authenticates a user based upon the username and password for each individual you want to access the Catalyst console. Normally, the Catalyst authenticates using local parameters, the exec and enable passwords. If the user accessing the Catalyst knows these passwords, the user is authenticated to enter the corresponding mode.

TACACS+ allows you to demand not just a password, but also a username. The user attempting to log in must have a valid username/password combination to gain access.

If a user attempts to log in to the Catalyst when TACACS+ is enabled, the Catalyst sends a request to the TACACS+ server for authentication information. The server replies and the user is either authenticated or rejected.

To enable TACACS+, you need to have a functional and accessible TACACS+ server in your network. The specifics of configuring TACACS+ is beyond the scope of this book. See the Catalyst documentation for configuration details.

TIP   If you configure TACACS+ on a Catalyst and the TACACS+ server becomes unavailable for some reason, the locally configured normal and privileged passwords can be used as a "backdoor" (be sure to set these passwords to something other than the default of no password).

TFTP Configuration

The Catalyst has a TFTP client allowing you to retrieve and send configuration files from/to a TFTP server. The actual syntax to do TFTP configuration file transfers depends upon the version of Supervisor module installed in the Catalyst.

If you plan for the Catalyst to obtain the new configuration over the network after a **clear config all**, you either need to restore a valid IP address and default gateway setting or you need to have the configuration file on an accessible TFTP server. Details for using TFTP are described in the section, "Catalyst Configuration File Management."

Table 4-2 compares various access methods for configuring the Catalyst.

Table 4-2   *Comparing the Usage of Catalyst Access Methods*

Access Method	Attachment	When to Use
Console	Direct Supervisor module attachment	Use when network attachments not available, such as Telnet, TFTP, or SNMP. Also used for local access, initial configuration, and password recovery.
Sc0	Network	Use for Telnet, TFTP, or SNMP configurations to the built-in logical interface. Accessible through network connections.
Sl0	Supervisor module attachment	Use this for remote access to the Supervisor module when network access not available.
TFTP	Network	Use this to download a configuration to the Catalysts sc0 or sl0 interface.
SNMP	Network	Used to make configuration changes from a network management station.

Using the Catalyst 5000/6000 Command-Line Interface

Because the Catalyst has a different pedigree than the Cisco routers, the CLI differs between the two. For example, changes in a Cisco router are not permanent until you copy the running configuration to NVRAM. The Catalyst, on the other hand, immediately and automatically copies your commands to NVRAM. Individuals who suffer from an inability to remember to save configuration files on a router enjoy this feature. However, automatic configuration saves makes *restoring* a configuration more challenging, as discussed earlier.

The Catalyst does not have a special configuration mode like the routers. Rather, changes can be made directly from the privileged mode. Many users enjoy this feature because it allows them to make changes (**set**, **clear**) and view results (**show**) from the same command level. This eliminates the effort of bouncing between configuration mode and privileged mode to make changes and observe the results.

TIP   You might occasionally see Cisco refer to the Catalyst 5000/6000 interface as an XDI interface. This is Cisco's internal identification of the interface. Another name is "CatOS."

Command-line recall and editing vastly differed prior to Catalyst code version 4.4. With system codes prior to 4.4, command-line recall and editing consists of using UNIX shell-like commands. To recall a previous command, you need to specify how many commands back in the history file you want. Or, you can recall a command through pattern matching. To edit a command line, you need to use UNIX-like commands that specify a pattern and what to substitute in the pattern's place. Doing command-line editing in this manner is not self intuitive for many users, unless the user is a UNIX guru.

With Catalyst Supervisor engine software release 4.4, Cisco introduced IOS-type command-line recall and editing where up and down arrows on your terminal keypad scroll you through the Catalyst's command history buffer. If you are familiar with command-line recall and editing with a Cisco router, you will be comfortable with the Catalyst CLI. If however, you still have code levels prior to 4.4, regrettably, you must continue to use the UNIX structure.

The manner in which the Catalyst displays help differs from the router displays. The router uses a parameter-by-parameter method of displaying help, whereas the Catalyst displays a complete command syntax.

The following sections describe command-line recall, editing, and help for the Catalyst 5000 series with the XDI/CatOS style interface.

Command-Line Recall

When you enter a command in the Catalyst, it retains the command in a buffer called the *history buffer*. The history buffer can store up to 20 commands for you to recall and edit. Various devices have methods of recalling commands. The Catalyst uses abbreviated key sequences to recall commands. These sequences resemble what a UNIX c-shell user might use. UNIX users often live with awkward methods of recalling and editing commands. Therefore, their comfort level with the legacy Catalyst editing system is probably fairly high, but might be low for the rest of us.

In UNIX, you often perform commands with a *bang* included in the command line. A bang is nothing more than an exclamation point (!) on a keyboard, but "exclamation" is too difficult to say when dictating commands. Therefore, bang is used in its place. Table 4-3 summarizes the key sequence for recalling previous commands in the history buffer.

Table 4-3 *Command Recall from Catalyst History Buffer*

Command Sequence	Effect
!!	Repeats the previous command.
!-n	Repeats the command n places before the previous.
!n	Repeats command n in the buffer.
!aaa	Repeats the command that starts with the matching string aaa.
!?aaa	Repeats the command that contains the string aaa anywhere in the command.

Sometimes you not only want to recall a command, but also edit it. Table 4-4 shows the sequences to recall and edit previous commands.

Table 4-4   *Catalyst Command Recall with Substitution*

Command Sequence	Effect
^aaa^bbb	Recall previous command and substitute bbb for aaa.
!!aaa	Recall previous command and append aaa.
!n aaa	Recall command n and append aaa.
!aaa bbb	Recall command that starts with aaa and append bbb.
!?aaa bbb	Recall the command that contains aaa and append bbb.

Suppose, for example, that you enter a command **set vlan 3 2/1-10,4/12-216/1,5/7**.

This command string assigns a set of ports to VLAN 3. However, you realize after entering the command that you really mean for them to be in VLAN 4 rather VLAN 3. You could retype the whole command a second time and move the ports to VLAN 4, or you could simply type **^3^4**. This forces the Catalyst not only to use the previous command, but to change the number 3 to a number 4, which in this case, corrects the VLAN assignment.

One frustration when mentally recalling commands can be that you have a hard time remembering what command you entered, seven lines previously. This can become particularly challenging because the Catalyst history buffer can store up to 20 commands. Use the **history** command to see your history buffer. Example 4-2 shows output from a **history** command. Notice that the commands are numbered allowing you to reference a specific entry for command recall. For example, the output recalls command 2 from the history buffer. This caused the Catalyst to recall the **history** command. Note also that new commands add to the bottom of the list. Newer commands have higher numbers.

Example 4-2   *Catalyst History Buffer Example*

```
Console> history
       1 help
       2 history
Console> !2
history
       1 help
       2 history
       3 history
Console>
```

Using Help

In a Cisco router, you access help by entering **?** on a command line. The router then prompts you with all possible choices for the next parameter. If you type in the next parameter and type **?** again, the router displays the next set of command-line choices. In fact, the router displays help on a parameter-by-parameter basis. Additionally, when the router displays help options, it also ends by displaying the portion of the command that you entered so far. This enables you to continue to append commands to the line without needing to reenter the previous portion of the command.

The Catalyst help system functions differently from the router, though. You access help in the same manner as you do in a router, but the results differ. For example, where a router prompts you for the next parameter, the Catalyst displays the entire usage options for the command, if your command string is unique so that the Catalyst knows what command you want. Example 4-3 shows the help result for a partial command string. However, the string does not uniquely identify what parameter should be modified, so it lists all **set system** commands.

Example 4-3 *Catalyst Help Example*

```
Console> (enable) set system ?
Set system commands:
----------------------------------------------------------------
set system baud          Set system console port baud rate
set system contact       Set system contact
set system help          Show this message
set system location      Set system location
set system modem         Set system modem control (enable/disable)
set system name          Set system name
```

On the other hand, if you have enough of the command on the line that the Catalyst recognizes what command you intend to implement, it displays the options for that command. This time, in Example 4-4, the string identifies a specific command and the Catalyst displays help appropriate for that command. The user wants to modify the console interface in some way, but is unsure of the syntax to enter the command.

Example 4-4 *Another Catalyst Help Example*

```
Console> (enable) set interface ?
Usage: set interface <sc0¦sl0> <up¦down>
       set interface sc0 [vlan] [ip_addr [netmask [broadcast]]]
       set interface sl0 <slip_addr> <dest_addr>
Console> (enable)
```

Notice that when the console displays help, it returns the command line with a blank line. The command string you entered so far is not displayed for you as it is on a router. You can now elect to use command recall. Suppose you want to disable the logical interface, sc0. So you *want* to enter the command **set int sc0 down**. Being a clever network administrator, you elect to use command recall and complete the command. What happens if you type **!! sc0 down** ?

You see the command usage screen again, without the console changing state to down (see Example 4-5). This happens because the command recall executes the previous statement that was **set int ?** with the help question mark and your appended parameters. When you add the additional parameters, the Catalyst interprets the string as **set int ? sc0 down**, sees the question mark, and displays help.

Example 4-5 *Command Recall after Help*

```
CAT1> (enable) set int ?
Usage: set interface <sc0|sl0> <up|down>
set interface sc0 [vlan] [ip_addr [netmask [broadcast]]]
set interface sl0 <slip_addr> <dest_addr>
CAT1> (enable) !! sc0 down
set int ? sc0 down
Usage: set interface <sc0|sl0> <up|down>
        set interface sc0 [vlan] [ip_addr [netmask [broadcast]]]
        set interface sl0 <slip_addr> <dest_addr>
CAT1> (enable)
```

If you have system code 4.4 or later, you can use the up/down arrow to perform command recall after help, but the recall includes the question mark. The advantage here, though, over the **!!** recall is that you can edit out the question mark on the recalled command line using router editing commands. Therefore, you can perform command recall, remove the question mark, and enter the rest of the command. The Catalyst then correctly interprets the command, assuming that you subsequently enter correct and meaningful parameters.

A Catalyst invokes help when you enter a question mark on the command line. It also provides help if you enter a partial command terminated with **<ENTER>**. For example, the command in Example 4-4 displays the same screen if the user enters **set interface <ENTER>**. The Catalyst uniquely recognizes **set int**, but also observes that the command is not complete enough to execute. Therefore, the Catalyst displays the command usage screen. If you intend to modify the sc0 VLAN membership to VLAN 5 and change the IP address in the same line, you can enter the command **set int sc0 5 144.254.100.1 255.255.255.0**. Suppose that as you enter the command you enter the VLAN number, but forget the rest of the command line. You might be tempted to hit **<ENTER>** to get a command usage screen. But you do not see the usage screen. Instead, the Catalyst sees the current command line and says, "There is enough on this line to execute, so I will." You just successfully changed the sc0 VLAN membership without changing the IP address. If you do this through a Telnet session in a production network, you probably just completely removed Telnet access to the Catalyst. It is now time to walk, drive, or fly to the Catalyst to restore connectivity. (Or call someone who can do it for you and confess your mistake!)

TIP

In many cases, you can get usage help with a partial command and **<ENTER>**. However, it is best to use the question mark to ensure that you do not prematurely execute a command that might prove to be catastrophic to your network and career.

Supervisor Module Configuration

Modifying and viewing Catalyst 5000/6000 configuration files consists of using **set, clear,** and **show** commands. Because the Catalyst does not use a separate configuration mode to make changes, you can make changes and view system configurations all from the same prompt level. You must make all changes from the privilege mode, which requires an **enable** password.

Important show Statements

To view configurations, use the **show** command. Example 4-6 annotates a simple Supervisor module configuration file displayed through the **show config** command. Some configuration lines are editorially deleted because they are redundant and needlessly consume printed space. The remaining portion of the file enables you to see the general organization of the configuration file.

Example 4-6 *Annotated Supervisor Configuration File*

```
Console> (enable) show config
...
.........
.........
........
........
..
begin
set password $1$FMFQ$HfZR5DUszVHIRhrz4h6V70
set enablepass $1$FMFQ$HfZR5DUszVHIRhrz4h6V70
set prompt Console>
set length 24 default
set logout 20
set banner motd ^C^C
!
#system
set system baud  9600
set system modem disable
set system name
set system location
set system contact
!
#snmp
set snmp community read-only      public
set snmp community read-write     private
set snmp community read-write-all secret
!Other SNMP commands deleted
#IP
!This sets up the console or slip interfaces.
set interface sc0 1 144.254.100.97 255.255.255.0 144.254.100.255
!
```

Example 4-6 *Annotated Supervisor Configuration File (Continued)*

```
set interface sl0 0.0.0.0 0.0.0.0
set arp agingtime 1200
set ip redirect    enable
set ip unreachable    enable
set ip fragmentation enable
set ip alias default        0.0.0.0
!
#Command alias
!
#vmps
set vmps server retry 3
set vmps server reconfirminterval 60
set vmps tftpserver 0.0.0.0 vmps-config-database.1
set vmps state disable
!
#dns
set ip dns disable
!
#tacacs+
!This section configures the TACACS+ authentication parameters
!
#bridge
!This section defines FDDI module behavior
!
#vtp
!This section characterizes the virtual trunk protocol and vlan parameters
!
#spantree
#uplinkfast groups
set spantree uplinkfast disable
#vlan 1
set spantree enable     1
set spantree fwddelay 15    1
set spantree hello    2    1
set spantree maxage    20    1
set spantree priority 32768 1
!Other VLAN Spanning Tree information deleted. This section describes Spanning
!Tree for each VLAN.
!
#cgmp
!This group of commands controls the Catalyst multicast behavior
!
#syslog
set logging console enable
set logging server disable
!Other logging commands deleted. This characterizes what events are logged.
!
#ntp
!This sets up network time protocol
!
#set boot command
```

continues

Example 4-6 *Annotated Supervisor Configuration File (Continued)*

```
set boot config-register 0x102
set boot system flash bootflash:cat5000-sup3.3-1-1.bin
!Any special boot instructions are placed here.
!
#permit list
!The access list is found here
set ip permit disable
!
#drip
!This is Token Ring stuff to take care of duplicate ring numbers.
!
!On a per module basis, the Catalyst displays any module specific
!configurations.
#module 1 : 2-port 10/100BaseTX Supervisor
set module name    1
set vlan 1    1/1-2
set port channel 1/1-2 off
set port channel 1/1-2 auto
set port enable    1/1-2
set port level    1/1-2   normal
set port speed    1/1-2   auto
set port trap    1/1-2   disable
set port name    1/1-2
set port security  1/1-2   disable
set port broadcast 1/1-2   100%
set port membership 1/1-2   static
set cdp enable    1/1-2
set cdp interval 1/1-2 60
set trunk 1/1   auto 1-1005
set trunk 1/2   auto 1-1005
set spantree portfast    1/1-2 disable
set spantree portcost    1/1   100
set spantree portcost    1/2   100
set spantree portpri    1/1-2 32
set spantree portvlanpri 1/1   0
set spantree portvlanpri 1/2   0
set spantree portvlancost 1/1   cost 99
set spantree portvlancost 1/2   cost 99
!
#module 2 empty
!
#module 3 : 24-port 10BaseT Ethernet
set module name    3
set module enable  3
set vlan 1    3/1-24
set port enable    3/1-24
set port level    3/1-24   normal
set port duplex    3/1-24   half
set port trap    3/1-24   disable
set port name    3/1-24
```

Example 4-6   *Annotated Supervisor Configuration File (Continued)*

```
set port security   3/1-24  disable
set port broadcast  3/1-24  0
set port membership 3/1-24  static
set cdp enable    3/1-24
set cdp interval 3/1-24 60
set spantree portfast    3/1-24 disable
set spantree portcost    3/1-24 100
set spantree portpri     3/1-24 32
!
#module 5 : 1-port Route Switch
!Note that the only things in this configuration are Spanning Tree and bridge
!related. There are no routing configs here.
set module name    5
set port level      5/1  normal
set port trap       5/1  disable
set port name       5/1
set cdp enable    5/1
set cdp interval 5/1 60
set trunk 5/1  on 1-1005
set spantree portcost    5/1 5
set spantree portpri     5/1 32
set spantree portvlanpri 5/1  0
set spantree portvlancost 5/1   cost 4
!
#switch port analyzer
!If you set up the ability to monitor switched traffic, the
!the configs will show up here
set span disable
!
#cam
!set bridge table aging to five minutes
set cam agingtime 1,1003,1005 300
end
Console> (enable)
```

Note in Example 4-6 that the file collates in logical sections. First, the Catalyst writes any globally applicable configuration items such as passwords, SNMP parameters, system variables, and so forth. Then, it displays configurations for each Catalyst module installed. Note that the module configuration files refer to Spanning Tree and VLAN assignments. Further, it does not display any details about other functions within the module. For example, an RSM is installed in module 5 of this Catalyst. Although this is a router module, it attaches to a virtual bridge port internally. The Catalyst displays the bridge attachment parameters, but not the Route Switch Module (RSM) or ATM LANE configuration lines. To see the these module specific configurations, you need to access them with the **session** *module_number* and view its own configuration file.

Other **show** commands display item specific details. For example, to look at the current console configuration, you can use the **show interface** (**sh int**) command as demonstrated in Example 4-7.

Example 4-7 **show interface** *Display*

```
Console> (enable) show interface
sl0: flags=51<UP,POINTOPOINT,RUNNING>
        slip 0.0.0.0 dest 128.73.35.160
sc0: flags=63<UP,BROADCAST,RUNNING>
        vlan 1 inet 144.254.100.97 netmask 255.255.255.0 broadcast 144.254.100.255
Console> (enable)
```

Another useful **show** command displays the modules loaded in your Catalyst (see Example 4-8).

Example 4-8 **show module** *Output*

```
Console> (enable) show module
Mod Module-Name        Ports Module-Type           Model       Serial-Num Status
--- ------------------ ----- --------------------- ----------  ---------- -------
1                      2     10/100BaseTX Supervis WS-X5530    008700085  ok
3                      24    10BaseT Ethernet      WS-X5013    008678074  ok
4                      2     MM OC-3 Dual-Phy ATM  WS-X5158    008444947  ok
5                      1     Route Switch          WS-X5302    007600273  ok
13                           ASP

Mod MAC-Address(es)                          Hw     Fw      Sw
--- ---------------------------------------- ------ ------- ----------------
1   00-90-92-bf-70-00 thru 00-90-92-bf-73-ff 1.5    3.1(2)  3.1(1)
3   00-10-7b-4e-8d-d0 thru 00-10-7b-4e-8d-e7 1.1    2.3(1)  3.1(1)
4   00-10-7b-42-b0-59                        2.1    1.3     3.2(6)
5   00-e0-1e-91-da-e0 thru 00-e0-1e-91-da-e1 5.0    20.7    11.2(12a.P1)P1
Mod Sub-Type Sub-Model Sub-Serial Sub-Hw
--- -------- --------- ---------- ------
1   EARL 1+  WS-F5520  0008700721 1.1
1   uplink   WS-U5531  0007617579 1.1
Console> (enable)
```

The output in Example 4-8 displays details about the model number and description of the modules in each slot. The second block of the output tells you what MAC addresses are associated with each module. Notice that the Supervisor module reserves 1024 MAC addresses. Many of these addresses support Spanning Tree operations, but other processes are involved too. Module 3, the 24-port Ethernet module, reserves 24 MAC addresses, one for each port. These also support Spanning Tree in that they are the values used for the port ID in the Spanning Tree convergence algorithm. The third block of the display offers details regarding the Supervisor module.

Other key **show** statements are demonstrated throughout the rest of the book.

Modifying Catalyst Configurations

To modify a Catalyst parameter, you use either the **set** or **clear** commands. The **set** command changes a parameter to a value that you specify, whereas the **clear** command returns some parameters to their default setting.

To change system parameters, you use the **set system** command as demonstrated in Example 4-9.

Example 4-9   **set system** *Example*

```
Console> (enable) set system ?
Set system commands:
----------------         -----------------------------------------------
set system baud          Set system console port baud rate
set system contact       Set system contact
set system help          Show this message
set system location      Set system location
set system modem         Set system modem control (enable/disable)
set system name          Set system name
Console> (enable) set sys location whoneedsmarketing
System location set.
Console> (enable) show system
PS1-Status PS2-Status Fan-Status Temp-Alarm Sys-Status Uptime d,h:m:s Logout
---------- ---------- ---------- ---------- ---------- -------------- --------

ok         faulty     ok         off        faulty     0,00:31:09     20 min

PS1-Type   PS2-Type   Modem   Baud   Traffic Peak Peak-Time
---------- ---------- ------- ----- ------- ---- ------------------------
WS-C5508   WS-C5508   disable 9600   0%       0% Thu Aug 13 1998, 16:18:10

System Name            System Location         System Contact
---------------------- ----------------------- -----------------------
                       whoneedsmarketing
Console> (enable)
```

Clearly, there are several system variables that you can modify. Example 4-9 modifies the system location object.

Some commands provide a warning if your action might cause connectivity problems for you or the users. For example, in Example 4-10, the user intends to change the IP address of the console interface. If the user is making the change remotely—that is, the user is logged in to the Catalyst through a Telnet session—the user loses connectivity and needs to re-establish the Telnet session.

Example 4-10   **set interface** *Example*

```
Console> (enable) set interface sc0 1 144.254.100.97 255.255.255.0
This command may disconnect your Telnet session.
Do you want to continue (y/n) [n]? y
Interface sc0 vlan set, IP address and netmask set.
Console> (enable)
```

Use a **clear** command to restore a parameter to a default value. Suppose you have a VLAN 4 configured on the Catalyst and want to remove it. You use the command **clear vlan 4**. This eliminates references to VLAN 4 in the Catalyst. However, some things associated with VLAN 4 are not eliminated. For example, if you have ports assigned to VLAN 4 and you **clear vlan 4**, the ports assigned to VLAN 4 move into a disabled state. They do not move to VLAN 1. You need to manually reassign the ports to VLAN 1. The **clear config** command demonstrated in Example 4-1 returns the whole Catalyst to its default out-of-the-box configuration. The Catalyst warns you about potential connectivity issues with this command before executing it.

Catalyst Password Protection

When you first receive a Catalyst from Cisco, it has no password set. In other words, the password is **<ENTER>** to enter both the EXEC and privilege modes. Your first task as a conscientious network administrator should be to change the passwords to the unit. This helps to prevent unauthorized children in adult form from modifying the Catalyst and disrupting your network. Example 4-11 shows a Catalyst session where the user changes the EXEC and enable passwords. The user starts by changing the enable password for privilege mode with the command **set enablepass**. The Catalyst immediately prompts for the old password. If you are doing this to a Catalyst with a fresh configuration file, you should respond with **<ENTER>**. Otherwise, you need to know the existing enable password. If you do not know the existing enable password, see the following section, "Catalyst Password Recovery," for details on what to do next.

Example 4-11 *Modifying a Catalyst's Passwords*

```
Console> (enable) set enablepass
Enter old password: cntgetin
Sorry password incorrect.
Console> (enable) set enablepass
Enter old password: cantgetin
Enter new password: stillcantgetin
Retype new password: stillcantgetin
Password changed.
Console> (enable) set password
Enter old password: guessthis
Enter new password: guessthis2
Retype new password: guessthis2
Password changed.
Console> (enable)
```

Note that *italicized* text is not displayed in real output.

In Example 4-11, the user types in the wrong enable password, so the Catalyst shows an error message and stops the modification process. The user tries again, but this time enters a correct existing enable password. The Catalyst then asks the user to enter the new enable password, twice, to confirm the entry.

The user then changes the normal mode password with the **set password** command. As with the enable password, the user has to know the existing password before the Catalyst allows any changes to the password. Upon entering the correct password, the Catalyst asks for the new password and a confirmation.

Catalyst Password Recovery

If at any time you forget the normal mode or enable passwords, you need to start a password recovery process. Password recovery on the Catalyst 5000/6000 series differs from the methods used on a Cisco router or on other Catalyst models.

You must be at the Catalyst console to perform password recovery. Password recovery requires a power cycle of the system by toggling the power switch. After you power cycle the Catalyst, the Catalyst goes through its initialization routines and eventually prompts you for a password to enter the *normal* mode. At this point, you have 30 seconds to perform password recovery.

The trick in Catalyst password recovery lies in its behavior during the first 30 seconds after booting: when the Catalyst first boots, it ignores the passwords in the configuration file. It uses the default password **<ENTER>** during this time. So, when the Catalyst prompts you for an existing password at any time, simply type **<ENTER>** and the Catalyst accepts your response. Immediately enter **set password** or **set enablepass** to change the appropriate password(s).

TIP

When the Catalyst asks during the password recovery process what to use for the new password, simply respond with **<ENTER>** too. Otherwise, trying to type in new passwords sometimes leads to a need to reboot again, particularly if you are a poor typist. By initially setting the password to the default value, you minimize your probability of entering a bad value. After setting the enable and EXEC passwords to the default, you can at your leisure go back and change the values without the pressure of completing the process during the 30 seconds provided for password recovery.

TIP

As with many security situations, it is imperative that you consider physical security of your boxes. As demonstrated in the password recovery process, an attacker simply needs the ability to reboot the Catalyst and access to the console to get into the privilege mode. When in the privilege mode, the attacker can make any changes that he desires. Keep your Catalyst closets secured and minimize access to consoles.

<table>
<tr><td>TIP</td><td>A security configuration issue of which you should be aware: change the SNMP community strings from their default values. Example 4-6 shows the output from a Catalyst configuration file where the SNMP community strings are still at their default value. A system attacker might use SNMP to change your system. He starts with these common default values. Make them difficult to guess, but remember that they are transmitted over the network in clear text and are, therefore, snoopable.</td></tr>
</table>

Catalyst Configuration File Management

For complete system recovery, make sure that you have a copy of each Catalyst's configuration file stored somewhere other than on the Catalyst itself. If anything happens to the Catalyst Supervisor module, you might not be able to recover the configuration file. It is a crime to have to rebuild the entire configuration file from scratch during a system outage when it is easy to create a backup on a network accessible machine.

Through TFTP, you can store your configuration file on a TFTP server and recover it later when needed. The syntax varies depending upon the version of Supervisor module you have. Catalyst 5000 Supervisor III modules and Catalyst 6000s use a syntax more like a Cisco router than do the Catalyst 5000 Supervisor I or II modules.

<table>
<tr><td>TIP</td><td>TFTP servers are inherently weak, security wise. It is strongly recommended that you do not keep your configuration files in a TFTP directory space until you actually need to retrieve the file. System attackers who compromise your TFTP server can modify the configuration files without your knowledge to provide a security opening the next time a device downloads the configuration file from the server. Move your configuration files to secure directory spaces and copy them back to the TFTP directory space when you are ready to use them.

Although this adds another step to your recovery process, the security benefits frequently outweigh the procedural disadvantages.</td></tr>
</table>

Supervisor I and Supervisor II Module Configuration

To save a configuration file from either a Catalyst 5000 Supervisor I or Supervisor II module, use the **write net** command. Example 4-12 shows a session writing a configuration file to a TFTP server. The server's IP address and the filename are clearly seen in the output. Note that the filename is the name that you want to call the file on the server. This is not the name of the file in the Catalyst. There is only one configuration file residing in the Catalyst, so specifying a source file here is redundant.

Example 4-12 *Uploading a Configuration File to a TFTP Server*

```
Console> (enable) write ?
Usage: write network
       write terminal
       write <host> <file>
Console> (enable) write net
IP address or name of remote host? 144.254.100.50
Name of configuration file? cat
Upload configuration to cat on 144.254.100.50 (y/n) [n]? y
.....
.........
.........
........
........
..
Finished network upload. (6193 bytes)
Console> (enable)
```

Retrieving a file from the server uses the command **configure network**. When retrieving a file, you need to specify the source filename on the TFTP server (see Example 4-13).

Example 4-13 *Retrieving a Configuration File*

```
Console> (enable) configure ?
Usage: configure <host> <file>
Console> (enable) configure network
IP address or name of remote host? 144.254.100.50
Name of configuration file? cat
Configure using cat from 144.254.100.50 (y/n) [n]? y
/
Finished network download. (6193 bytes)
[Truncated output would show the configuration lines]
```

Note that in the command usage output, the configure network option is not displayed. However, it is a valid option to use.

Supervisor III Module Configuration

Transferring Supervisor III and Catalyst 6000 configuration files via TFTP to another device looks more like a router command. The command **copy config** {**flash** | *file-id* | **tftp**} copies the configuration file to one of three locations. You can store the configuration file in the bootflash memory, a flash card in a flash slot (with an appropriate Supervisor III module), or to a TFTP server. When copying configuration files from or to the Catalyst, you need to specify the source filename. Because of the flash architecture on the Supervisor III, you might have several configuration files local. However, only one can be active. Therefore, you need to specify which of the local files you are trying to copy.

Recovering a configuration file works in reverse. If you intend to retrieve the file from a TFTP server, use the command **copy tftp** {**flash** | *file-id* | **config**}. When retrieving, you can write the configuration file to your bootflash, a flash card, or to the running configuration. If you intend to write the configuration file to your running configuration, use the command form **copy tftp config**. Example 4-14 shows a session recovering the configuration filename *cat* to a flash device.

Example 4-14 *Recovering Configuration Files from a TFTP Server*

```
Console> (enable) copy tftp flash
IP address or name of remote host []? 144.254.100.50
Name of file to copy from []? cat
Flash device [slot0]? <ret>
Name of file to copy to [cat]? <ret>
```

If you store your configuration file in your flash, you can recover it with the command **copy flash** {**tftp** | *file-id* | **config**}. Again, any of three destinations are possible.

If the file is on any other flash device, use the command **copy** *file-id* {**tftp** | **flash** | *file-id* | **config**}.

Catalyst Image File Management

As with routers, Catalysts need software to function. The software loads into the flash memory of the Supervisor module and is referred to as the Supervisor Engine Software. The software provides the Catalyst CLI, Spanning Tree functions, VLAN configurations, VTP, and many other processes associated with the Supervisor.

The Catalyst 5000 Supervisor I and Supervisor II modules differ in how they transfer software images compared to the Supervisor III module. Therefore, they are treated separately in this section. As with the configuration files, the Supervisor III module behaves more like a Cisco router than do the Supervisor I and II modules.

The following sections assume that you have a single Supervisor module in your Catalyst. If you have redundant Supervisor modules, refer to the section, "Redundant Supervisor Modules," for more details.

Downloading image files to your Catalyst's flash memory causes the Catalyst to need a reboot for the new image to take effect. So be aware that any code changes temporarily take users off line if you elect to make the new image effective immediately. This might cause your beeper to beep or phone to ring.

Supervisor I and II Image File Management

To transfer Supervisor image files, use the commands **download** *host file* and **upload** *host file*. Example 4-15 shows a download from a TFTP server. Note that at the end of the transfer, the Catalyst prompts that you need to reset the image for it to take effect.

Example 4-15 *Supervisor Image Download from a TFTP Server*

```
Console> (enable) download 172.20.52.3 cat5000-sup.4-2-1.bin
Download image cat5000-sup.4-2-1.bin from 172.20.52.3 to module 1 FLASH (y/n)
 [n]? y
/
Finished network single module download. (2748504 bytes)
FLASH on Catalyst:

Type            Address             Location
Intel 28F016    20000000            NMP (P3) 8MB SIM

Erasing flash sector...done.
Programming flash sector...done.
Erasing flash sector...done.
Programming flash sector...done.
Erasing flash sector...done.
Programming flash sector...done.
The system needs to be reset to run the new image.
Console> (enable) reset system
This command will reset the system.
Do you want to continue (y/n) [n]? y
Console> (enable) 07/21/1998,10:52:36:SYS-5:System reset from Console
```

Supervisor III Image File Management

The same commands used to maneuver the configuration files on a Supervisor III module (and on Catalyst 6000s) apply to moving the image files. Use the **copy flash tftp** to upload a file or use **copy tftp flash** to download a file. You have the option of directing the copy operation towards the flash memory, a flash slot device, or a TFTP server.

Serial Port Download

One final method exists for importing an image file to the Supervisor module—through the console port. The Catalyst supports kermit transfers through the console. Kermit is a protocol for transferring files and is usually built into many terminal emulation software packages. If you have an image file on a UNIX host or PC connected to the Catalyst's console port, you can enable kermit on the Catalyst to receive the image file. Use **download serial** to receive the file through the console port. Be aware though, that this might take some time to transfer because you are transferring the code, a fairly large size, at the EIA-232 line rates. This is intended for emergency use only where a TFTP server is not available, nor are flash devices.

If you have the console port configured as a slip interface rather than a console, you can use TFTP to transfer the image through the port.

Redundant Supervisor Modules

One of the motivations for the introduction of the Catalyst 5500 series products was the customer need for system redundancy. The legacy Catalyst 5000 series contains one Supervisor module, which, if it fails, disables the entire unit. The Catalyst 5500/6000 family, on the other hand, enables you to put two Supervisor modules into the chassis at the same time. On power up, one of the modules becomes the active Supervisor engine, and the other becomes the standby Supervisor engine. The active Supervisor engine module takes care of all Catalyst operational details and provides the CLI for the administrator. The active module, therefore, takes care of the Spanning-Tree Protocol, SNMP, CLI, Telnet, VLAN assignments, VTP, CDP, and other aspects. If at any time the active engine fails, the Catalyst resets and the standby engine assumes the responsibility of the active Supervisor engine.

When a Supervisor module is in standby mode, its console interface is not active. All configuration changes must be made through the active Supervisor engine. And depending upon what version of Supervisor engine code is running, you might not be able to use the uplink ports on the standby unit either. If you are running an engine software version earlier than 4.1, you cannot use the uplinks on the standby unit. However, when the standby unit becomes the active module, the uplink ports are activated. If you have 4.1 or 4.2, the standby ports are active at all times, even if the module is in standby mode. If you have version 4.3 or later, the standby ports are inactive by default when in standby mode, but can be administratively enabled.

TIP   When using redundant uplink ports on a standby Supervisor, be sure that you do not configure more than 20 VLANs in current versions of the software. Doing so can potentially create Spanning Tree loops, increase convergence time, and decrease network stability.

There are a few things that must be true for the failover to function correctly:

1   The Catalyst 5000 Supervisor module must be a Supervisor Engine II or later. The legacy Supervisor module that is associated with the Catalyst 5000 series does not support the redundant features. In fact, the Supervisor I module does not even work in a 5500 chassis. All Catalyst 6000 Supervisors support redundancy.

2   The active and the standby Supervisor engines must be the same model. For Catalyst 5500s, they must both be Supervisor II or both be Supervisor III. You cannot mix a Supervisor II and a Supervisor III in the same unit. The reason for this will become clear shortly.

3   If you use two Catalyst 5000 Supervisor III modules, the feature cards on the two cards must be the same. If you have the NetFlow Feature Card (NFFC) card on one, they must both have NFFC capability.

4 Configuration files must match between the two modules.

5 The software images must be the same for both.

The first three items you must administratively ensure. You must select the appropriate hardware to support the redundancy feature. The Catalyst cannot do this for you.

However, the Catalyst can greatly help you regarding the last two items. The system code automatically synchronizes software between the two Supervisor modules to ensure that they are running the same files. This helps to ensure that, in the event of a failover, the failover condition can support all configured features that were running when the first unit was the active unit. Most network engineers can deal with a failover situation and replace a failed module. But when the network operational mode changes as a result of the failover ("oh no, everything now is in VLAN 1!"), they become very unhappy. So do users.

Synchronizing Configuration Between Redundant Supervisor Modules

Whenever you make a configuration change, you must make it in the active Supervisor module, because the console on the standby unit is disabled. If you make a change on the active Supervisor, how do you ensure that the configuration on the standby unit gets updated too? You don't need to, the Catalyst does it for you.

Configuration changes on the active unit are automatically updated to the standby unit. This happens internally to the Catalyst. If you swap standby modules, the active Supervisor automatically ensures that the standby gets a copy of the current configuration. It updates the configuration file in the standby unit.

TIP   Remember that any redundant Supervisor module you insert into the Catalyst acquires the configuration of the operating active Supervisor module. Do not insert a module with an "updated" configuration file and expect it to modify the active unit. You lose your updated file.

Synchronizing Image Files Between Redundant Supervisor Modules

Not only must the Supervisor modules be the same and running the same configuration file, but they must also have the same software image. As with the configuration file, the active Supervisor module ensures that the standby unit has the same software image. If they differ, the active Supervisor module loads the running image to the standby Supervisor and resets the standby module. The active unit checks the following to determine if the software images need to be synchronized:

1 The active unit checks to see if the boot images have the same time stamp. If they differ, the active Supervisor module updates the standby Supervisor module.

2 If you change the BOOT environment variable, the active Supervisor module copies the new target boot image to the standby, if necessary, and modifies the environment variable on the standby so that they start with the same image.

3 If you upgrade the boot image on the active unit, the active Supervisor module updates the standby.

Notice that images and configurations flow from the active to the standby units, never the other direction. You cannot update the image on the standby module first and then synchronize the active module with the standby. The standby always synchronizes to the active.

When using Catalyst 5000 Supervisor Engine III modules and all Catalyst 6000 modules, additional elements are compared between the active and standby engines. Specifically, the active module compares not just the *boot* image, but also the *run-time* image. The *run-time* image is the image used by the ROM monitor to boot the Supervisor module. If the run-time image successfully loads, and there is a boot image, and a BOOT environment variable pointing to the boot image, the Catalyst also loads the boot image, which is your desired operational image.

The Supervisor ensures that the run-time images are the same on the two modules. As with the boot image, if they differ, the active unit synchronizes the two by downloading a new run-time image. Therefore, the active Supervisor module performs the following to determine if there is a need to synchronize:

1 The active unit checks the timestamp on the run-time image. If they differ, it initiates the synchronization process.

2 If you overwrite the run-time image on the active unit, the active module synchronizes the standby unit.

Configuring Other Catalysts

As mentioned in the opening sections of this chapter, the other Catalysts (non-5000/6000 family) use other configuration methods. The three remaining types come from Grand Junction for the Catalyst 1900/2800 products, Kalpana for the Catalyst 3000 family, and Cisco IOS for the 2900XL and 8500. This section provides a quick overview of the configuration methods for the 1900/2800 and the 3000 because they use methods entirely different from the IOS methods of the 2900XL and 8500, and the CLI mode of the Catalyst 5000/6000. This section does not enter into any detail, but only serves to highlight the configuration interfaces.

After you understand how various aspects of the Catalyst 5000/6000 family operates, such as bridging, Inter-Switch Link (ISL), VLAN Trunking Protocol (VTP), and so forth, you basically understand what to configure on the other Catalysts. The difference is in what features are supported and how to effect configuration changes.

Catalyst 1900/2800 Configuration

The 1900/2800 products use a hierarchical menu structure to make changes. Example 4-16 shows one of the higher level menus from which you can make changes. To select a lower menu, type the letter of the menu item. To return to a higher menu, type **X**.

Example 4-16 *Catalyst 1900 Main Menu Display*

```
Catalyst 1900 - Main Menu

[C] Console Settings
[S] System
[N] Network Management
[P] Port Configuration
[A] Port Addressing
[D] Port Statistics Detail
[M] Monitoring
[V] Virtual LAN
[R] Multicast Registration
[F] Firmware
[I] RS-232 Interface
[U] Usage Summaries
[H] Help

[X] Exit Management Console
```

Catalyst 3000 Configuration

Like the 1900/2800, the Catalyst 3000 series also uses a hierarchical menu structure. It differs, however, from the 1900/2800 in how you maneuver through the menus. In the Catalyst 3000, you use the arrow keys from your terminal to highlight an item, and then you press **<ENTER>**. Example 4-17 illustrates the Catalyst 3000 series menu.

Example 4-17 *Catalyst 3000 Menu Example*

```
                        Configuration

            SwitchProbe...

    Switch/Stack Information…              EtherChannel...

    VLAN/VTP Configuration...              MAC Filter & Port Security...

    IP Configuration…                      Learn and Lock…

    SNMP Configuration…                    Address Aging...

    Spanning Tree…                         Port Switching Mode...

    Port Configuration…                    Broadcast Suppression…
```

continues

Example 4-17 *Catalyst 3000 Menu Example (Continued)*

```
    CDP Configuration…                      Password...

    CGMP Configuration…                     Console Configuration...

    Module Information…                     ATM Configuration…

    100VG Port Information…                 Router Configuration…

    RMON Configuration


                                      Display the Main Menu
            Use cursor keys to choose item. Press <RETURN> to confirm choice.
                     Press <CTRL><P> to return to Main Menu.
```

Review Questions

1 What happens if you replace the active Supervisor module?

2 If your redundant Supervisor engines are running software version 4.1, the uplink ports on the standby engine are disabled until it becomes the active Supervisor. What strategies might you need to employ to ensure that failover works for the uplinks?

3 Table 4-4 shows how to recall and edit a command from the history buffer. How would you recall and edit the following command so that you move the ports from VLAN 3 to VLAN 4?

    set vlan 3 2/1-10,3/12-21,6/1,5,7

4 What happens if you configure the Supervisor console port as sl0, and then you directly attach a PC with a terminal emulator through the PC serial port?

5 The Catalyst 5500 supports LS 1010 ATM modules in the last 5 slots of the chassis. Slot 13 of the 5500 is reserved for the LS1010 ATM Switch Processor (ASP). Can you use the **session** command to configure the ASP?

6 The command-line interface has a default line length of 24 lines. How can you confirm this?

This chapter covers the following key topics:

- **What is a VLAN?**—Provides a practical and technical definition of virtual LANs.

- **VLAN Types**—Describes how Layer 2, 3, and 4 switching operate under a VLAN.

- **802.1Q: VLAN Interoperability**—Describes the IEEE 802.1Q committee's effort to develop a vendor-independent method to create virtual bridged local area networks via shared VLANS (SVLs).

- **Justifying the Need for VLANs**—Describes how network security, broadcast distribution, bandwidth utilization, network latency from routers, and complex access lists justify the need for configuring VLANs. This section also details the improper motivation for setting up a VLAN.

- **Catalyst VLAN Configuration**—Describes how to plan for, create, and view VLAN configurations.

- **Moving Users in VLANs**—Describes how VLANs simplify moving a user from one location to another.

- **Protocol Filtering**—Describes how to control flooding of unneeded protocols.

CHAPTER 5

VLANs

When the industry started to articulate virtual LANs (VLANs) in the trade journals and the workforce, a lot of confusion arose. What exactly did they mean by *VLAN*? Authors had different interpretations of the new network terminology that were not always consistent with each other, much less in agreement. Vendors took varied approaches to creating VLANs which further muddled the understanding. This chapter presents definitions for VLANs as used in the Catalyst world and explains how to configure VLANs. It also discusses reasons to use and not use VLANs and attempts to clarify misinformation about them.

What Is a VLAN?

With many definitions for VLAN floating around, what exactly is it? The answer to this question can be treated in two ways because there is a technical answer and a practical answer. Technically, as set forth by IEEE, VLANs define broadcast domains in a Layer 2 network. As demonstrated in Chapter 2, "Segmenting LANs," a broadcast domain is the extent that a broadcast frame propagates through a network.

Legacy networks use router interfaces to define broadcast domain boundaries. The inherent behavior of routers prevents broadcasts from propagating through the routed interface. Hence routers automatically create broadcast domains. Layer 2 switches, on the other hand, create broadcast domains based upon the configuration of the switch. When you define the broadcast domain in the switch, you tell the switch how far it can propagate the broadcast. If the switch receives a broadcast on a port, what other ports are allowed to receive it? Should it flood the broadcast to all ports or to only some ports?

Unlike legacy network drawings, you cannot look at a switched network diagram and know where broadcast domains terminate. Figure 5-1 illustrates a legacy network where you can clearly determine the termination points for broadcast domains. They exist at each router interface. Two routers define three domains in this network. The bridge in the network extends Broadcast Domain 2, but does not create a new broadcast domain.

Figure 5-1 *Broadcast Domains in a Legacy Network*

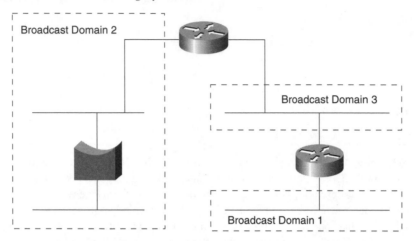

In the switched network of Figure 5-2, you cannot determine the broadcast domains by simple examination. The stations might belong to the same or multiple broadcast domains. You must examine configuration files in a VLAN environment to determine where broadcast domains terminate. Without access to configuration files, you can determine the broadcast domain extent with network analysis equipment, but it is a tedious process. How to do this is left as a review question at the end of this chapter.

Figure 5-2   *Broadcast Domains in a Switched Network*

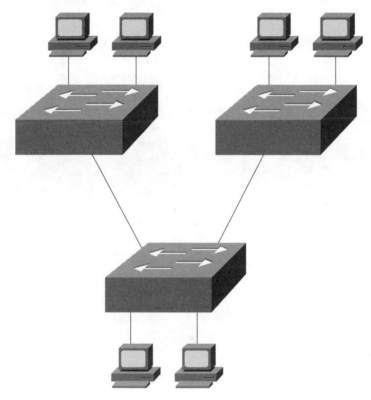

Even though you cannot easily see the broadcast domains in a switched network does not mean that they do not exist. They exist where you define and enable them. Chapter 2 presented a discussion on switches and compared them to bridges. A switch is a multi-port bridge that allows you to create multiple broadcast domains. Each broadcast domain is like a distinct virtual bridge within the switch. You can define one or many virtual bridges within the switch. Each virtual bridge you create in the switch defines a new broadcast domain (VLAN). Traffic from one VLAN cannot pass directly to another VLAN (between broadcast domains) within the switch. Layer 3 internetworking devices must interconnect the VLANs. You should not interconnect the VLANs with a bridge. Using a bridge merges the two VLANs into one giant VLAN. Rather, you must use routers or Layer 3 switches to interconnect the VLANs. Each of the four switches belong to two VLANs. A total of three broadcast domains are distributed across the switches. Figure 5-3 shows a logical representation of a switched network.

Figure 5-3 *A Switched Network with Virtual Bridges*

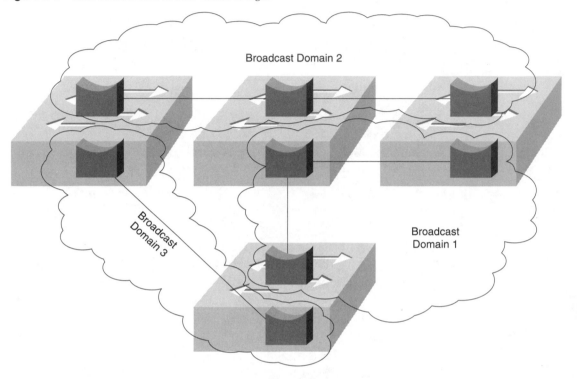

Rather than representing VLANs by designating the membership of each port, each switch has an internal representation for each virtual bridge. This is not a common way of illustrating a VLAN network, but serves to exaggerate the internal configuration of a LAN switch where each bridge within the switch corresponds to a single VLAN.

VLAN Types

The IEEE defines VLANs as a group of devices participating in the same Layer 2 domain. All devices that can communicate with each other without needing to communicate through a router (only use hubs/repeaters and bridges, real or virtual) share the broadcast domain. The Layer 2 internetworking devices move frames through the broadcast domain by examining the destination MAC address. Then, by comparing the destination address to a table, the device can determine how to forward the frame towards the destination.

Some devices use other header information to determine how to move the frame. For example, Layer 3 switches examine the destination and source IP address and forward frames between broadcast domains when needed. Traditionally, routers perform Layer 3 switching. Frames enter the router, the router chooses the best path to get to the destination, and the router then forwards the frame to the next router hop as shown in Figure 5-4. The routing protocol that you activate in the router determines the *best* path. A best path might be the fewest hops. Or, it might be the set of highest bandwidth segments. Or, it might be a combination of metrics. In Figure 5-4, only one choice exists to get from Station A to Station B.

Figure 5-4   *Traditional Frame Flow in a Routed Network*

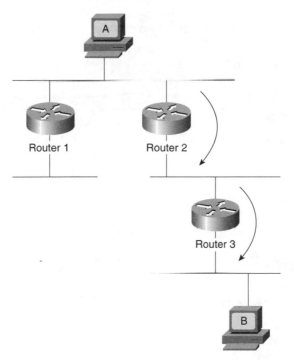

When the frame enters Router 2, the router not only determines the next hop to move the frame toward the destination, but it also performs a new Layer 2 encapsulation with a new destination/source MAC address pair, performs some Layer 3 activities such as decrementing the TTL value in an IP header, and calculates a new frame check sequence (FCS) value. Router 3 performs a similar set of actions before sending the frame to Station B. This is often called *packet-by-packet switching*.

The same process still occurs if you replace the shared wire segments in Figure 5-4 with a Layer 2 switched network. Figure 5-5 illustrates a similar network using Layer 2 switches and Layer 3 routers to interconnect the broadcast domains (VLANs). To get from Station A to B in the switched network, the frame must pass through three routers. Further, the frame must transit the link between Cat-C and Cat-D twice. Although this might be an exaggeration for such a small network, this can frequently happen in larger scale networks. In an extreme case, the frame can travel through the Layer 2 switched network multiple times as it passes from router to router on its way to the destination.

Figure 5-5 *Traditional Frame Flow in a Switched Network*

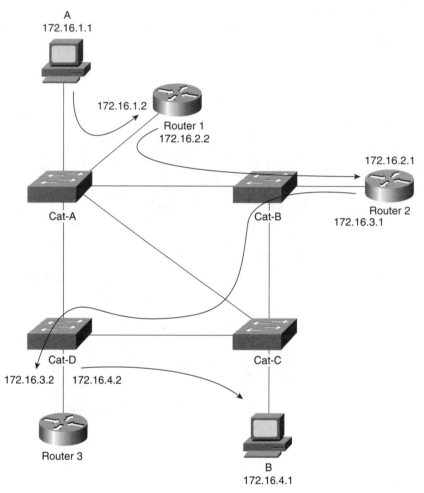

Layer 3 switching, on the other hand, circumvents the multiple entries and exits of the frame through routers. By adding a Netflow Feature Card and enabling Multilayer Switching (MLS) in a Catalyst 5000 supervisor module, a Catalyst 5000/5500 can rewrite a frame header like a router does. This gives the *appearance* of the frame passing through a router, yet it eliminates the need for a frame to actually pass in and out of a router interface. The Catalyst learns what to do with the frame header by watching a locally attached router. MLS is discussed in more detail in Chapter 11, "Layer 3 Switching." MLS creates a shortcut around each router as shown in Figure 5-6. When multiple routers are in the system, multiple MLS shortcuts exist between the source and destination devices. These shortcuts do not violate any Layer 3 routing rules because the NFFC does not perform any rewrites until the frames initially pass through a router. Further, when it does create the shortcut, the NFFC rewrites the frame header just as the router does.

Figure 5-6   *NetFlow Shortcuts Between Routed VLANs*

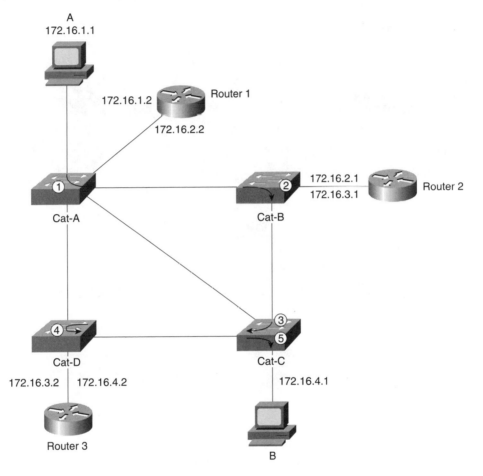

Another type of Layer 3 switching, Multiprotocol over ATM (MPOA), even eliminates the need to repeatedly pass a frame through the switched cloud. Functionally, MPOA in ATM equates to MLS in a frame network in that they both bypass routers. The routers in Figure 5-7 attach directly to an ATM cloud. Normally, when Station A wants to communicate with Station B, frames must pass in and out of the routers just as they do in the basic routed example of Figure 5-4. In Figure 5-7, the frames normally pass through the ATM cloud four times to reach Station B. However, MPOA creates a shortcut between two devices residing in different broadcast domains as shown in Figure 5-7. See Chapter 10, "Trunking with Multiprotocol Over ATM," for more details.

Figure 5-7 *MPOA Shortcut to Bypass Many Routers in an ATM Network*

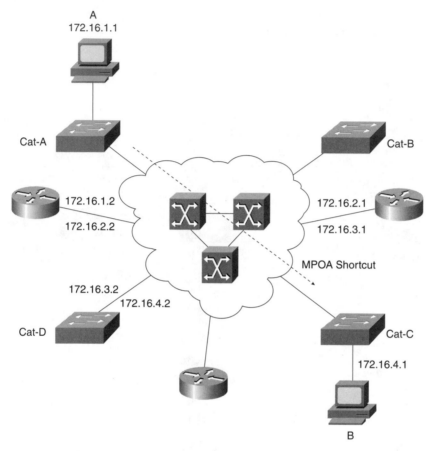

Other VLAN types use combinations of Layer 2, Layer 3, or even Layer 4 to create shortcuts in a system. Layer 4 switching creates shortcuts based upon the Layer 3 addresses and upon the Layer 4 port values. This is sometimes called *application switching* and provides a higher level of granularity for switching. Chapter 11 provides a more thorough discussion on this subject in the context of MLS.

Table 5-1 summarizes the various switch types found in the industry.

Table 5-1   *Layered Switching Comparison*

Switch Type	Switch Criteria
Layer 2	Destination MAC address
Layer 3	Source and destination MAC addresses and source and destination IP addresses
Layer 4	Layer 3 criteria plus Layer 4 source and destination port values

802.1Q: VLANs and Vendor Interoperability

Because vendors took individual approaches to create VLANs, network administrators were impaired whenever multiple vendor solutions were introduced into their system. A multi-vendor VLAN must be carefully handled to deal with interoperability shortcomings. Recognizing this deficiency in the industry, IEEE commissioned the 802.1Q committee to develop a vendor-independent method to create interoperable virtual bridged local area networks.

IEEE 802.1Q describes concepts called the *shared VLAN* (SVL) and *independent VLAN* (IVL). These define how bridges store MAC addresses in their bridging tables. SVL constrains a MAC address to only one VLAN. SVL-based devices build a giant bridge table, but allow a MAC address to appear only once in the table, regardless of how many VLANs exist. For many networks, this is fine. However, this can be an undesirable constraint when devices or protocols reuse MAC addresses in different broadcast domains. For example, SUN workstations reuse a MAC address whenever two NICs are installed in the workstation. Yet each NIC attaches to a different broadcast domain and has different logical addresses. Clearly, this violates the rules of SVL networks, but not legacy networks. DecNet IV has a similar characteristic, in that MAC addresses can be reused in different broadcast domains. This too, fails in an SVL network.

Yet a third situation where SVL devices cannot work is when a router interconnects VLANs by routing some protocols and bridging others. For example, in Figure 5-8, Stations A and B support multiple protocols: TCP/IP and NetBEUI. A router in the system interconnects VLAN1 (Switch-A Ports 1 and 2) and VLAN2 (Switch-A Ports 3 and 4). The router performs routing for TCP/IP traffic and bridging for NetBEUI. (Bridging is necessary because NetBEUI is a non-routable protocol.)

Figure 5-8 *An SVL Capable Switch and a Router that Routes and Bridges*

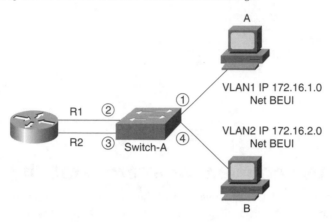

When Station A transmits an IP frame to Station B, Station A transmits a frame with the router's R1 MAC address as the destination and Station A's address as the source. The router routes the frame to Station B using the router's R2 MAC address for the source and Station B's MAC address for the destination. When Station B responds to Station A, the switch learns about Station B on Port 4 Switch-A's bridge table looks like that shown in Table 5-2, Event 1. The table shows the four ports on Switch-A (1, 2, 3, and 4) and the learned MAC addresses on each of the ports. Ports 1 and 2 belong to VLAN 1, and Ports 3 and 4 belong to VLAN 2. The MAC addresses are represented as A and B for the two workstations and R1 and R2 for the two router interfaces. Switch-A knows about Station A's MAC address on Port 1 and the router interfaces R1 and R2 MAC addresses on Ports 2 and 3, respectively. When Station A transmits a NetBEUI frame, the switch relearns Station A's MAC address on Port 1. When a router routes a frame, it replaces the source MAC address with its own MAC address. But, when the router bridges the frame out interface R2, the router does not replace the MAC address header and passes the original source MAC address through. Therefore, Switch-A now sees a frame from Station A on Port A.3. This causes the switch to believe that Station A moved. The bridge table now looks like Event 2 in Table 5-2. When Station B attempts to respond to Station A, the switch forwards the frame to router interface R2. But when the router sends the frame out interface R1, the switch does not forward the frame to Port 1. Rather, the switch filters the frame because the switch believes that Station A is on Port 3, a different VLAN.

Table 5-2 *Bridging Table*

VLAN	1		2	
Port	1	2	3	4
Event 1	A	R1	R2	B
Event 2		R1	R2,A	B

One final deficiency with 802.1Q concerns Spanning Tree. With 802.1Q, there is currently only one instance of Spanning Tree. This forces all VLANs to the same Spanning Tree topology which might not be optimal for all VLANs. The Catalyst, for example, uses multiple instances of Spanning Tree: one for each VLAN. This allows you to optimize the topology for each VLAN. Part II of this book, "Spanning Tree" provides details on the multiple instances of Spanning Tree.

The Catalyst does not use SVL tables. Rather, it uses Independent VLAN learning (IVL) which allows the same MAC address to appear in different broadcast domains. An IVL-capable device maintains independent bridge tables for each VLAN, allowing devices to reuse a MAC address in different VLANs. All of the Catalyst bridging examples in this book illustrate IVL methods.

Justifying the Need for VLANs

The previous section described the technical definition of a VLAN. This section describes practical answers. In a legacy network, administrators assign users to networks based on geography. The administrator attaches the user's workstation to the nearest network cable. If the user belongs to the engineering department and sits next to someone from the accounting department, they both belong to the same network because they attach to the same cable. This creates some interesting network issues. Discussing these issues highlights reasons for using VLANs. VLANs help to resolve many of the problems associated with legacy network designs. The sections that follow examine the five issues that warrant implementation of a VLAN.

Problem 1: Network Security

The first issue is the shared media nature of legacy networks. Whenever a station transmits in a *shared* network such as a legacy half-duplex 10BaseT system, all stations attached to the segment receive a copy of the frame, even if they are not the intended recipient. This does not prevent the network from functioning, but software packages to monitor network traffic are readily available and run on a number of workstation platforms. Anyone with such a package can capture passwords, sensitive e-mail (or embarrassing e-mail) and any other traffic on the network.

If the users on the network belong to the same department, this might not be disastrous, but when users from mixed departments share a segment, undesirable information captures can occur. If someone from human resources or accounting sends sensitive data such as salaries, stock options, or health records on the shared network, anyone with a network monitoring package can decode the information.

Neither of these scenarios are constrained to a single segment. These problems can occur in multisegment environments interconnected with routers. In Figure 5-9, accounting resides on two isolated segments. For users on one segment to transmit to users on the other segment, the frames must cross the engineering network. When they cross the engineering segment, they can be intercepted and misused.

Figure 5-9   *Security Problems in a Legacy Network*

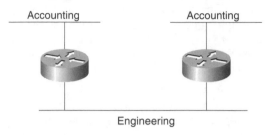

One way to eliminate the problem is to move all accounting users onto the same segment. This is not always possible because there might be space limitations preventing all accountants from sharing a common part of the building. Another reason might be due to geography. Users on one segment might be a considerable distance from users on the other segment. To move the users to a common location might mean moving the employee's household from one city to another.

A second method is to replace accounting with marketing. Who really wants to look at marketing data anyway, except for a good laugh? But accounting cannot distribute pay checks, and marketing tries to get our money. Clearly this is not a good solution.

A third approach is through the use of VLANs. VLANs enable you to place all process-related users in the same broadcast domain and isolate them from users in other broadcast domains. You can assign all accounting users to the same VLAN regardless of their physical location in the facility. You no longer have to place them in a network based upon their location. You can assign users to a VLAN based upon their function. Keep all of the accounting users on one VLAN, the marketing users on another VLAN, and engineering in yet a third.

By creating VLANs with switched network devices, you create another level of protection. Switches bridge traffic within a VLAN. When a station transmits, the frame goes to the intended destination. As long as it is a known unicast frame, the switch does not distribute the frame to all users in the VLAN (see Figure 5-10).

Figure 5-10   *A Known Unicast Frame in a Switched Network*

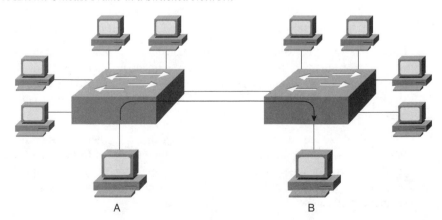

Station A in Figure 5-10 transmitted a frame to Station B attached to another Catalyst. Although the frame crosses through a Catalyst, only the destination receives a copy of the frame. The switch filters the frame from the other stations, whether they belong to a different VLAN or the same VLAN. This switch feature limits the opportunity for someone to promiscuously obtain traffic, thereby increasing the effectiveness of network security. What kind of traffic can be captured? Any traffic flooded within the VLAN is susceptible to capture. Flooded traffic includes broadcast, multicast, and unknown unicast. Note that a Catalyst feature Cisco Group Management Protocol (CGMP), if enabled, can restrict multicast flooding. This is discussed in Chapter 13, "Multicast and Broadcast Services."

Problem 2: Broadcast Distribution

Unfortunately, many, if not all, protocols create broadcasts. Some protocols create more than others. I happen to be particularly fond of Macintosh computers. Network administrators, however, despise AppleTalk due to the amount of broadcast traffic it generates. Every ten seconds, AppleTalk routers send routing updates that are broadcast frames in the network. Broadcasts go to all devices in the broadcast domain and must be processed by the receiving devices.

Other protocols share in the guilt. NetBEUI creates many broadcast frames, even when stations perform few network activities. TCP/IP stations create broadcasts for routing updates, ARP, and other processes. IPX generates broadcasts for SAP and GNS frames.

To add to the mix, many multimedia applications create broadcast and multicast frames that get distributed within a broadcast domain.

Why are broadcasts bad? Broadcasts are necessary to support protocol operations and are, therefore, overhead frames in the network. Broadcast frames rarely transport user data. (The exception might be for multimedia applications.) Because they carry no user data, they consume bandwidth in the network, reducing the effective available bandwidth for productive transfers.

Broadcasts also affect the performance of workstations. Any broadcast received by a workstation interrupts the CPU preventing it from working on user applications. As the number of broadcasts per second increases at the interface, effective CPU utilization diminishes. The actual level of degradation depends upon the applications running in the workstation, the type of network interface card and drivers, the operating system, and the workstation platform.

TIP	If broadcasts are a problem in your network, you might mitigate the effect by creating smaller broadcast domains. This was described in Chapter 2. In VLANs, this means creating additional VLANs and attaching fewer devices to each. The effectiveness of this action depends upon the source of the broadcast. If your broadcasts come from a localized server, you might simply need to isolate the server in another domain. If your broadcasts come from stations, creating multiple domains might help to reduce the number of broadcasts in each domain.

Problem 3: Bandwidth Utilization

When users attach to the same shared segment, they share the bandwidth of the segment. The more users that attach to the shared cable means less average bandwidth for each user. If the sharing becomes too great, user applications start to suffer. You start to suffer too, because users harass you for more bandwidth. VLANs, which are usually created with LAN switch equipment, can offer more bandwidth to users than is inherent in a shared network.

Each port in a Catalyst behaves like a port on a legacy bridge. Bridges filter traffic that does not need to go to segments other than the source. If a frame needs to cross the bridge, the bridge forwards the frame to the correct interface and to no others. If the bridge (switch) does not know where the destination resides, it floods the frame to all ports in the broadcast domain (VLAN).

NOTE   Although each port of a Catalyst behaves like a port on a bridge, there is an exception. The Catalyst family has group switch modules where ports on the module behave like a shared hub. When devices attach to ports on this module, they share bandwidth like a legacy network. Use this module when you have high density requirements, and where the devices have low bandwidth requirements, yet need connectivity to a VLAN.

In most normal situations, then, a station only sees traffic destined specifically for it. The switch filters most other background traffic in the network. This allows the workstation to have full dedicated bandwidth for sending and/or receiving frames interesting traffic.Unlike a shared hub system where only one station can transmit at a time, the switched network in Figure 5-11 allows many concurrent transmissions within a broadcast domain without directly affecting other stations inside or outside of the broadcast domain. Station pairs A/B, C/D, and E/F can all communicate with each other without affecting the other station pairs.

Figure 5-11 *Concurrent Transmissions in a Catalyst*

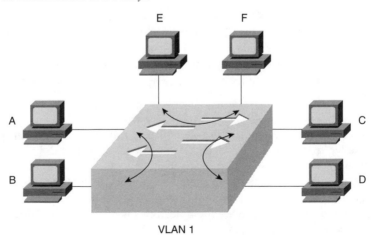

VLAN 1

Problem 4: Network Latency from Routers

In the legacy network of Figure 5-9, accounting users on the two segments had to cross the engineering segment to transfer any data. The frames had to pass through two routers. Older software-based routers tend to be comparatively slower than other internetworking products such as a Layer 2 bridge or switch. As a frame passes through a router, the router introduces latency—the amount of time necessary to transport a frame from the ingress port to the egress port. Every router that the frame transits increases the end-to-end latency. Further, every congested segment that a frame must cross increases latency. By moving all of the accounting users into one VLAN, the need to cross through multiple routers and segments is eliminated. This reduces latency in a network that might improve performance for your users, especially if they use a send-acknowledge protocol. Send-acknowledge protocols do not send more data until an acknowledgement is received about the previous data. Network latency dramatically reduces the effective throughput for send-acknowledge protocols. If you can eliminate the need for user traffic to pass through a router by placing users in the same VLAN, you can eliminate cumulative router latency. If frames must pass through routers, enabling Layer 3 switching reduces router transit latencies, too.

VLANs help to reduce latency by reducing segment congestion. This can be a dramatic improvement if the workstations' connections originally attached to congested shared segments and the workstations' new connections all have dedicated switch ports.

Problem 5: Complex Access Lists

Cisco routers allow administrators to introduce policies controlling the flow of traffic in the network. Access lists control traffic flow and provide varied degrees of policy granularity. Through the implementation of access lists, you can prevent a specific user from communicating with another user or network, or you can prevent an entire network from accessing a user or network. You might exercise these capabilities for security reasons, or you might elect to prevent traffic from flowing through a segment to protect local bandwidth.

In any case, the management of access lists is cumbersome. You must develop the access list according to a set of rules designed by Cisco for the access list to correctly filter traffic.

In the network example of Figure 5-9, filters in the routers attached to the engineering segment can include access lists allowing the accounting traffic to pass through the engineering segment, but to never talk to any engineering devices. That does not prevent engineers from monitoring the traffic, but does prevent direct communication between the engineering and accounting devices. Accounting never sees the engineering traffic, but engineering sees all of the accounting transit traffic. (Accounting yells, "That hardly seems fair!")

VLANs can help by allowing you to keep all accounting users in one VLAN. Then their traffic does not need to pass through a router to get to peers of the VLAN. This can simplify your access list design because you can treat networks as groups with similar or equal access requirements.

Wrong Motives for Using VLANs

One common motivation for using VLANs tends to get network administrators excited about VLANs. Unfortunately, reality quickly meets enthusiasm revealing errors in motivation. The advent of VLANs led many to believe that life as a network administrator would simplify. They thought that VLANs would eliminate the need for routers, everyone could be placed in one giant flat network, and they could go home at 5:00 PM each evening like everyone else in their office. Wrong. VLANs do not eliminate Layer 3 issues. They might allow you to more easily perform some Layer 3 tasks such as developing simpler access lists. But Layer 3 routing still exists.

If anything, VLANs make networks more complex due to the introduction of the Spanning-Tree Protocol in the system and the dispersed nature of broadcast domains. Spanning Tree (discussed in Chapters 6 and 7) adds additional background traffic to your network by flooding "hello packets" (BPDUs) throughout the system every two seconds. Although hello messages do not consume significant bandwidth on segments, it does make use of a network analyzer more challenging. You might need to filter out the hello messages to find the interesting traffic that you are trying to troubleshoot. A more significant Spanning Tree element making VLANs complex is the selection of a Root Bridge. Spanning Tree participants elect a Root Bridge around which the rest of the network revolves. Depending upon the location of the Root Bridge in the network, traffic flow might not always pass through the most desirable links. Traffic might flow through less desirable links with lower bandwidth or might require more hops to reach the destination. The network administrator might need to tweak Spanning Tree default values to select a more appropriate Root Bridge. The default selection of a root bridge is not arbitrary, but is based upon the MAC address of the bridge. The bridge with the lowest MAC address becomes the Root Bridge. This means the Root Bridge selection is repeatable every time the system powers up, as long as no other bridges are introduced to the system with a lower MAC address, or other default values are changed. See Chapters 6 and 7 for more detailed information.

This discussion does not imply that you should not use VLANs. Rather, it raises the point that you need to consider not just *why*, but also *how* you plan to deploy VLANs. All networks are candidates for VLANs and switches. Your network might have one VLAN with switches, but it is still a VLAN. However, you should consider limiting the size or extent of the VLAN. As mentioned, a single VLAN extending throughout the entire network usually defies practicality and scalability. Smaller VLAN islands interconnected with Layer 3 devices typically deploy much more easily in a large scale, while allowing you to take advantage of Layer 2 VLANs within a workgroup area.

Moving Users in VLANs

VLANs reduce the problems associated with moving a user in a legacy network from one location to another. As you move a user in a legacy network, you need to consider many factors. In a VLAN, however, a number of the factors disappear. Consider the following example in Figure 5-12.

Figure 5-12 *Moving a User in a Legacy Network*

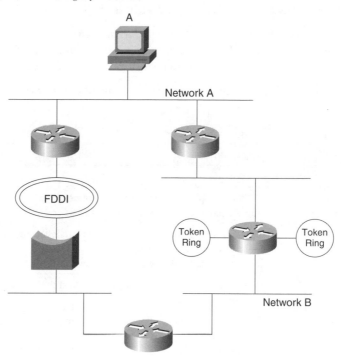

Figure 5-12 shows Station A attached to Network A in a legacy network. The user's highly educated, capable, and rational manager decides that the user needs to move to another location. As the network administrator, you inquire about the motivation for the move and learn that, "It's none of your business," which is shorthand for, "I don't have anything better to do than to reassign employee locations." Being a diligent network administrator, you quickly recognize an important task, so you set about to plan the move.

OSI Logistics for Moving Network Users

During the early 1990s, a movement was afoot to eliminate routers from the networks and create one large, flat-bridged network. These were known as end-to-end VLANs. The motivations for this type of design are considered in this section. However, as a preamble, it is important to note that experience with the end-to-end VLANs demonstrated that they do not scale well in networks and forced users to reinstate routers in the network. One of the scaling issues was with Spanning Tree. Today's design recommendations incorporate VLANs in local areas and use Layer 3 routing/switching between smaller areas. Part V of this book, "Real-World Campus Design and Implementation," discusses in more detail various approaches to VLAN deployments. Even though the end-to-end designs did not prove to be feasible, the motivations still apply in smaller areas. That is why this section covers the initial benefits of end-to-end VLANs.

What issues do you need to consider to support the move? Many issues ranging from Layer 1 through Layer 7 of the OSI model. Ignore Layers 8 (financial), 9 (political), and 10 (religious) for now because these are not officially in the OSI definition.

Table 5-3 summarizes a number of issues that should concern you.

Table 5-3   *Logistics Issues in a Legacy Network*

Issue	Explanation
Layer 1	
Distance to network hub	The new employee location might not be close to an existing network. You might need to extend the network or even create a new one.
Media type	The user already has an adapter card installed in the workstation. Is the media compatible with the equipment at the new location? Is the new location using Category 5 cable? Fiber optic? Coax? Other?
Port availability	Are there any ports or attachment points at the new location suitable for the user?
Link speed	Can the hub or segment at the new location offer the bandwidth that the user needs?
Layer 2	
Access method	Is the network at the new location of the same type as at the original location? Is the network new/old Ethernet, Fast Ethernet, Token Ring, FDDI, or other?
NIC compatibility	Is the existing NIC compatible with the new network hardware? If you have to change the NIC, are the new drivers compatible with the upper layers?
Layer 3	
Logical address	You might need to assign a new protocol address to the user at the new location.
Default gateway	The user's workstation might need to be reconfigured to point to a different gateway.
Firewalls/access lists	By moving the user, you might need to modify router access lists and firewall configurations to allow the user to reach the resources that support his functions.
Higher Layers	
Available bandwidth to resources	Layer 1 issues listed link speed. This is for the local link. But the user's resources might be located on another segment forcing the traffic to cross other segments. Do the transit segments have enough bandwidth to support the user's applications?

You must deal with all of these issues when you move users in a legacy network environment. Layer 1 and Layer 2 issues can create some undesirable situations like forcing you to change a user from Ethernet to Token Ring because the new location uses that access method. This should cause you to worry about compatibility with the user's upper layer protocols. If you need to attach to a different network type, you need to change the workstation's NIC and associated drivers. You might think that the drivers are compatible with the upper layers, but you might discover at 5:00 PM on a Friday evening that they are not.

Maybe you need to use fiber optics to reach from the new location to a hub because the distance is too long. Or, you might use fiber because the cable runs through an electrically noisy environment.

Possibly, new switches or hubs need to be installed to support the relocated user because all of the other interfaces might be occupied. If you install a new repeater/hub, make sure that you do not exceed the collision domain extent. If you install a new switch, you need to configure the correct VLAN setting and any other appropriate parameters.

Although all layers create headaches at one time or another for network administrators, Layer 3 creates irksome migraines. Layer 3 issues are even more complex, because they frequently involve changes in equipment configuration files. When you move the user, he might attach to an entirely different logical network than where he was originally. This creates a large set of potential actions on your part. For example, because the user now attaches to a different network, you need to modify his host address. Some of this pain is lessened through the use of Dynamic Host Configuration Protocol (DHCP) to automatically acquire an IP address. This works even when moving a user from one VLAN to another.

Even more annoying, you might need to modify any policy-based devices to allow the new address to reach the same services as prior to the move. For example, you might need to modify access lists in routers to enable the station's frames to transit the network to reach a file server. Remember that routers evaluate access lists from the top of the list to the bottom and stop whenever a match occurs. This means that you need to be sure to place the new entry in the correct location in the access list so that it is correctly evaluated. If any firewalls exist between the station and its resources, you need to ensure that the firewall's settings permit access to all desired resources.

Yet another item you must consider involves a combination of higher and lower layers. What bandwidth does the user's applications require? Can the network provide the same bandwidth for the paths that the frames must now transit? If not, you might have some serious network redesign in front of you.

Deploying VLANs to Eliminate Broadcast Domain Issues

Now consider a similar network designed with Catalysts rather than a legacy design. By using Catalysts as in Figure 5-13, you can deploy VLANs to distribute and constrain broadcast domains. When deploying VLANs, some items in Table 5-3 become irrelevant when moving a user from one location to another in the network.

Figure 5-13 *A Switched Version of the Legacy Network of Figure 5-12*

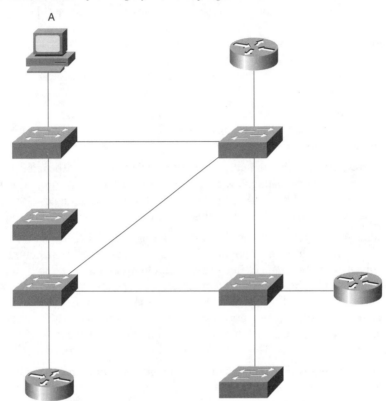

VLANs do not eliminate Layer 1 or Layer 2 issues. You still need to worry about port availability, media and access types, and the distance from the station to the switch.

You still need to worry about higher layer issues such as bandwidth to resources. The switched network cannot implicitly guarantee bandwidth. It does, however, offer you flexible alternatives to install more bandwidth between switches without redesigning a whole network infrastructure. For example, you can install more links between Catalysts, or you can move to higher speed links. (Inter-Catalyst connection options are reviewed in Chapter 8, "Trunking Technologies and Applications.") Upgrading to a higher speed link does not force you to install a new access method. You can upgrade from a 10 Mbps to a Fast Ethernet or Gigabit Ethernet solution fairly easily and transparently to users. Obviously, similar solutions are available in routers too, but you might not be able to obtain the port density that you want to service many stations.

VLANs do not directly help mitigate lower layer or higher layer difficulties in a legacy LAN. Other than for the possibility of user stations experiencing more bandwidth with switched VLAN equipment, why use VLANs? Here is the good news: in a VLAN environment, Layer 3 issues no longer need to be a concern as they were in legacy network designs. When moving the user in Figure 5-13, you can configure the switch port at the new location to belong to the same VLAN as at the old location. This allows the user to remain in the same broadcast domain. Because the user belongs to the same broadcast domain, the routers and firewalls view the user as belonging to the same network even though a new physical location is involved. This eliminates the need to perform any Layer 3 tasks such as changing host addresses for the new location and leaves access list and firewall configurations intact.

The VLAN approach just described is sometimes called *end-to-end VLANs*, or *VLAN everywhere* or the *distributed VLAN* design method. It has the clear advantage of allowing you to keep a user in the same broadcast domain regardless of the physical location. As good as it seems to take this approach, it does have disadvantages. (Alas, nothing is ever as good as it seems.) Issues arise whenever the network grows in extent. As you add more Catalysts to the system, you add more bridges which increases the Spanning Tree topology complexity. This was mentioned in the previous section.

Deploying Layer 3 Distribution for Network Access Management and Load Distribution

In contrast, another approach to deploying VLANs potentially simplifies Spanning Tree issues. Some network designers use a Layer 3 approach in the system for distribution and backbone layers and use Layer 2 devices for access layers. Figure 5-14 shows such a network concept. In this system, the network design uses Layer 2 switches to the desktop and Layer 3 switches, such as the Catalyst 8500 and Catalyst 6000 series, for the distribution and backbone segments.

Figure 5-14 *Layer 3 Design in a Switched Network*

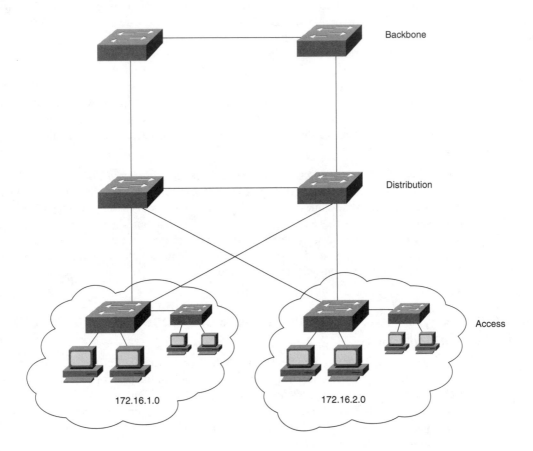

Part V of this book describes VLAN design philosophies. One approach, the Layer 3 distribution design, minimizes the Spanning Tree extent and topology because the Spanning Tree is constrained to the pockets of access devices. Access pockets can be placed on floors as in Figure 5-15. Each floor has its own access network. Users on the floor share the access network regardless of their community of interest. Engineering and accounting might share the VLAN. If necessary, the access network can be divided into a couple of VLANs to provide additional isolation between users or departments. Further, it enables load balancing, which is not easily obtainable in a Layer 2 design. These advantages lead many network engineers to avoid the end-to-end VLAN approach in favor of the Layer 3 design approach.

Figure 5-15   *Layer 3 Design Approach Applied to a Facility*

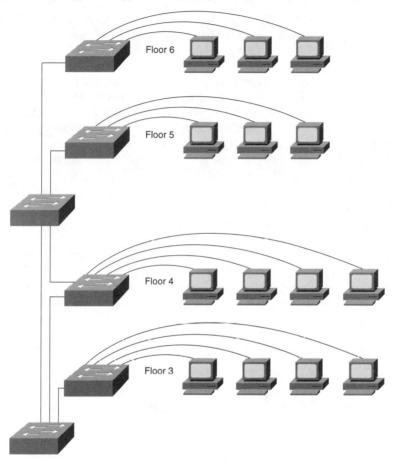

Historically, network approaches swayed from Layer 2 to Layer 3 back to Layer 2 and now back to Layer 3. The earliest networks were by default Layer 2. At some point in history, someone realized that they didn't scale very well, and they wanted to connect Layer 2 segments together. So routers were invented. Soon, the whole world deployed routers. But because routers were slow, designers started to look at high-performance bridges to interconnect the networks on a large scale. This was the advent of the Layer 2 switching products during the late 1980s to early 1990s. Until recently, Layer 2 switching plans dominated new network designs. Then came the realization that large scale Layer 2 networks created other problems, and router speeds have increased dramatically since the early 1990s. Engineers reexamined Layer 3 approaches for the backbone and distribution networks and now tend to consider Layer 3 designs a more desirable approach. It can, however, restore the disadvantages of Layer 3 complexities in a legacy network if poorly implemented.

Catalyst VLAN Configuration

Some VLAN components assign stations to VLANs based upon MAC addresses. The Catalyst, on the other hand, associates *ports* to a VLAN. Any device attached to the port belongs to the VLAN describing the switch interface. Even if a shared hub attaches to the port, all stations on the hub belong to the same VLAN. This is called a *port-centric* approach to VLANs. To configure VLANs in a Catalyst, you must first plan the VLAN membership and then assign ports to the correct VLAN. Planning VLAN membership involves knowing what Layer 3 networks should belong to the VLAN, what inter-VLAN connectivity you require, and where the VLAN will be distributed. Are you going to use end-to-end VLANs or use a Layer 3 approach to deploy your networks? After you proceed through the planning stages, you are ready to create the VLANs.

Planning VLANs

Before you enable new VLANs, make sure that you know what you really want to do and how your actions can affect other VLANs or stations already present in your system. The planning at this stage can primarily focus around Layer 3 issues. What networks need to be supported in the VLAN? Is there more than one protocol that you want in the VLAN? Because each VLAN corresponds to a broadcast domain, you can support multiple protocols in the VLAN. However, you should only have one network for each protocol in the VLAN.

A multiswitch system like that shown in Figure 5-16 can have several VLANs.

Figure 5-16   *A Typical VLAN Network Address Deployment*

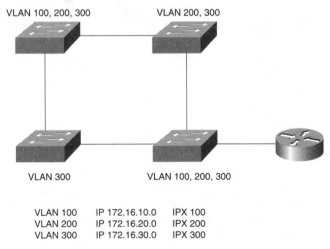

VLAN 100, 200, 300   VLAN 200, 300

VLAN 300   VLAN 100, 200, 300

VLAN 100	IP 172.16.10.0	IPX 100
VLAN 200	IP 172.16.20.0	IPX 200
VLAN 300	IP 172.16.30.0	IPX 300

Each VLAN in Figure 5-16 supports multiple protocols. For the networks to communicate with each other, they must pass through a router. The *router on a stick* in Figure 5-16 interconnects several networks together. Example 5-1 shows a configuration file for this router.

Example 5-1 *Router on a Stick Configuration File*

```
interface fastethernet 2/0.1
 ip address 172.16.10.1 255.255.255.0
 ipx network 100
 encapsulation isl 100
interface fastethernet 2/0.2
 ip address 172.16.20.1 255.255.255.0
 ipx network 200
 encapsulation isl 200
interface fastethernet 2/0.3
 ip address 172.16.30.1 255.255.255.0
 encapsulation isl 300
```

Example 5-1 sets up a trunk between a device and the router. Trunks and Inter-Switch Link (ISL) encapsulation are discussed in more detail in Chapter 8. Trunks allow traffic from more than one VLAN to communicate over one physical link. The **encapsulation isl** command in Example 5-1 instructs the router to use ISL trunking to communicate with the broadcast domain for each subinterface. Note that the router configuration uses subinterfaces. Normally, in a router, you assign a single address per protocol on an interface. However, when you want to use a single physical interface in a way that, to the routing protocols, appears as multiple interfaces, you can use subinterfaces—for example, when creating a trunk between a Catalyst and a router, as in Example 5-1. The router needs to identify a separate broadcast domain for each VLAN on the trunk.

Cisco routers use a concept of subinterfaces to spoof the router into thinking that a physical interface is actually more than one physical interface. Each subinterface identifies a new broadcast domain on the physical interface and can belong to its own IP network, even though they all actually belong to the same major interface. The router configured in Example 5-1 uses three subinterfaces making the router think that the one physical interface (the major interface) **interface fastethernet 2/0** is actually three physical interfaces, and therefore, three broadcast domains. Each belongs to a different IP subnet. You can recognize a subinterface on a Cisco router because the major interface designator has a **.x** after it. For example, subinterface 3 is identified in Example 5-1 as **int fastethernet 2/0.3** where **.3** designates the specific subinterface for the major interface.

The subinterface concept arises again when configuring LANE and MPOA on routers and on the Catalyst ATM modules.

In Example 5-1, which network is isolated from the others? IPX network 300 is isolated because the router does not have this network defined on any of its interfaces.

At times, a physical network configuration can confuse you. A common question we hear in class or consulting situations is, "Can I do this with a VLAN?" Frequently, an answer can be devised by representing the VLANs in a logical configuration. Figure 5-16 shows a physical network; Figure 5-17 shows the same network, but redrawn to show the logical connectivity.

The drawing replaces each VLAN with a wire representation labeled with the networks assigned to the VLAN. This more conventional representation helps when trying to design and deploy a VLAN, because it places networks and components into their logical relationship.

Figure 5-17 *A Logical Representation of Figure 5-16*

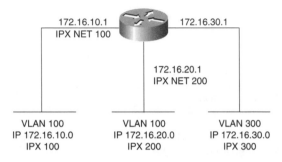

The network could be redrawn as in Figure 5-19 where clearly there are two isolated broadcast domains. As long as you do not attempt to interconnect them with a router, this configuration is completely valid. Why can they not be connected with a router? Because this forces a router to have two interfaces that belong to the same IP subnetwork. The router does not let you do this.

Figure 5-18 shows another network configuration where two VLANs carry the same IP network. Nothing prevents this configuration and it is valid. It is not, however, recommended for most networks. This configuration represents the same subnet on two logical wires.

Figure 5-18 *Overlapping IP Networks*

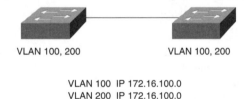

The network could be redrawn as in Figure 5-19 where clearly there are two isolated broadcast domains. As long as you do not attempt to interconnect them with a router, this configuration is completely valid. Why can they not be connected with a router? Because this forces a router to have two interfaces that belong to the same IP subnetwork. The router does not let you do this.

Figure 5-19 *Logical Representation of Figure 5-18*

```
       VLAN 100            VLAN 200
      172.16.10.0         172.16.10.0
```

The logical connectivity drawing loses information regarding physical interconnectivity which is important for bandwidth planning. For example, Figure 5-19 might lead you to believe that all devices in VLAN 100 have full bandwidth available between all components.

You might also believe the same regarding VLAN 200. However, the physical representation of Figure 5-18 makes it clear that the two VLANs share a link between the switches. This must be a shared bandwidth link which is not obvious from the logical representation.

TIP   Use the logical representation to plan and troubleshoot Layer 3 issues and use the physical drawings to determine Layer 2-related issues.

Creating VLANs

Creating a VLAN involves the following steps:

Step 1   Assign the Catalyst to a VTP domain

Step 2   Create the VLAN

Step 3   Associate ports to a VLAN

To facilitate creation, deletion, and management of VLANs in Catalysts, Cisco developed a protocol called VLAN Trunking Protocol (VTP). Chapter 12, "VLAN Trunking Protocol," covers VTP in more detail. However, a brief introduction is necessary here. You can divide a large Catalyst network into VTP management domains to ease some configuration and management tasks. Management domains are loosely analogous to autonomous systems in a routed network where a group of devices share some common attributes. Catalysts share VLAN information with each other within a VTP domain. A Catalyst must belong to a VTP domain before you can create a VLAN. You cannot create a VLAN on any Catalyst. The Catalyst must be configured in either the *server* or *transparent* mode to *create* the VLAN. By default, the Catalyst operates in the server mode. These modes and the command details to set them are described in Chapter 12.

You can configure a Catalyst's VTP domain membership with the **set vtp domain** *name* command. Each domain is uniquely identified by a text string. Note that the name is case sensitive. Therefore, a domain name of *Cisco* is not the same as *cisco*. Other rules about VTP domains that you need to consider are also detailed in Chapter 12.

Whenever you create or delete a VLAN, VTP transmits the VLAN status to the other Catalysts in the VTP domain. If the receiving Catalyst in the VTP domain is configured as a server or client, it uses this information to automatically modify its VLAN list. This saves you the task of repeating the command to create the same VLAN in all participating Catalysts within the domain. Create the VLAN in one Catalyst, and all Catalysts in the domain automatically learn about the new VLAN. The exception to the rule occurs if the receiving Catalyst is in transparent mode. In this case, the receiving Catalyst ignores the VTP. Transparent Catalysts only use locally configured information.

After the Catalyst belongs to a named VTP domain, you can create a VLAN. Use the **set vlan** command to create a VLAN in a Catalyst.

Example 5-2 shows three attempts to create VLAN 2. Note that in the second attempt the Catalyst fails to create the VLAN as indicated in the bolded line of the output. It fails because the Catalyst was not assigned to a VTP management domain. Only after the Catalyst is assigned to a VTP domain is Catalyst able to create the VLAN. What is the domain name that the Catalyst belongs to? The Catalyst belongs to the VTP domain *wally.*

Example 5-2 set vlan *Screen Example*

```
Console> (enable) set vlan 2 willitwork
Usage: set vlan <vlan_num> [name <name>] [type <type>] [state <state>]
                           [said <said>] [mtu <mtu>] [ring <ring_number>]
                           [bridge <bridge_number>] [parent <vlan_num>]
                           [mode <bridge_mode>] [stp <stp_type>]
                           [translation <vlan_num>] [backupcrf <off¦on>]
                           [aremaxhop <hopcount>] [stemaxhop <hopcount>]
        (name = 1..32 characters, state = (active, suspend)
         type = (ethernet, fddi, fddinet, trcrf, trbrf)
         said = 1..4294967294, mtu = 576..18190, ring_number = 0x1..0xfff
         bridge_number = 0x1..0xf, parent = 2..1005, mode = (srt, srb)
         stp = (ieee, ibm, auto), translation = 1..1005
         hopcount = 1..13)
Console> (enable) set vlan 2 name willitwork
Cannot add/modify VLANs on a VTP server without a domain name.
Console> (enable)
Console> (enable) set vtp domain wally
VTP domain wally modified
Console> (enable) set vlan 2 willitwork
Vlan 2 configuration successful
Console> (enable)
```

Note that the usage information indicates that the minimum input necessary to create a VLAN is the VLAN number. Optionally, you can specify a VLAN name, type, and other parameters. Many of the other parameters configure the Catalyst for Token Ring or FDDI VLANs. If you do not specify a VLAN name, the Catalyst assigns the name **VLAN#.** If you do not specify a VLAN type, the Catalyst assumes that you are configuring an Ethernet VLAN. Assigning a name does not change the performance of the Catalyst or VLAN. If used well, it enables you to document the VLAN by reminding yourself what the VLAN is for. Use meaningful names to document the VLAN. This helps you with troubleshooting and configuration tasks.

After you create a VLAN, you can assign ports to the VLAN. Assigning ports to a VLAN uses the same command as for creating the VLAN. Example 5-3 shows an attempt to assign a block of ports to VLAN 2. Unfortunately, the command is entered incorrectly the first time. What is wrong with the command? The **set vlan** command fails in the first case because the range specifies a non-existent interface on the Supervisor module. 1/8 indicates the eighth port on the Supervisor.

Example 5-3 *Assigning Ports to a VLAN*

```
Console> (enable) set vlan 2 2/1-1/8
Usage: set vlan <vlan_num> <mod/ports...>
       (An example of mod/ports is 1/1,2/1-12,3/1-2,4/1-12)
Console> (enable) set vlan 2 2/1-2/8
VLAN 2 modified.
VLAN 1 modified.
VLAN  Mod/Ports
----  ---------------------
2     2/1-8

Console> (enable)
```

After the port designation is corrected, the Catalyst successfully reassigns the block of ports to VLAN 2. When designating ports, remember that you can assign a block by using hyphens and commas. Do not insert any spaces, though, between the ports on the line. This causes the Catalyst to parse the command leaving you with only some of the ports assigned into the VLAN.

NOTE   In many instances where administrators install Catalysts, legacy hubs already exist. You might have network areas where stations do not need the dedicated bandwidth of a switch port and can easily share bandwidth with other devices. To provide more bandwidth, you can elect to not attach as many devices as were originally attached, and then attach the hub to a Catalyst interface. Be sure to remember, though, that all of the devices on that hub belong to the same Layer 2 VLAN because they all ultimately attach to the same Catalyst port.

Deleting VLANs

You can remove VLANs from the management domain using the **clear vlan** *vlan_number* command. For example, if you want to remove VLAN 5 from your VTP management domain, you can type the command **clear vlan 5** on a Catalyst configured as a VTP server. You cannot delete VLANs from a VTP client Catalyst. If the Catalyst is configured in transparent mode, you can delete the VLAN. However, the VLAN is removed only from the one Catalyst and is not deleted throughout the management domain. All VLAN creations and deletions are only locally significant on a transparent Catalyst.

When you attempt to delete the VLAN, the Catalyst warns you that all ports belonging to the VLAN in the management domain will move into a disabled state. If you have 50 devices as members of the VLAN when you delete it, all 50 stations become isolated because their local Catalyst port becomes disabled. If you recreate the VLAN, the ports become active again because the Catalyst remembers what VLAN you want the port to belong to. If the VLAN exists, the ports become active. If the VLAN does not exist, the ports become inactive. This could be catastrophic if you accidentally eliminate a VLAN that still has active users on it.

Also, realize that if you have a VTP management domain where you have most of your Catalysts configured as VTP servers and clients with a few Catalysts configured in transparent mode, you can inadvertently cause another situation when you delete a VLAN in the transparent device when the VLAN exists throughout the management domain. For example, suppose you have three Catalysts in a row with Cat-A configured in server mode, Cat-B configured in transparent mode, and Cat-C configured in client or server mode. Each Catalyst has a member of VLAN 10, so you create the VLAN on Cat-B, and you create it on Cat-A (Cat-C acquires the VLAN information from Cat-A as a result of VTP). From a Spanning Tree point of view, you have one Spanning Tree domain, and therefore, one Spanning Tree Root Bridge. But suppose that you decide you no longer need VLAN 10 on Cat-B, because there are no longer members of the VLAN. So, you delete the VLAN with the **clear vlan 10** command. From a VLAN point of view, this is perfectly acceptable. However, from a Spanning Tree point of view, you now created two Spanning Tree domains. Because Cat-B no longer participates in the VLAN, it no longer contributes to the Spanning Tree for that VLAN. Therefore, Cat-A and Cat-C each become a Root Bridge for VLAN 10 in each of their Spanning Tree domains.

Although Spanning Tree reconverges as a result of the apparent topology change, users in VLAN 10 cannot communicate with each other until the Spanning Tree topology finally places ports into the forwarding state.

TIP   When deleting VLANs from a management domain, whether it is on a Catalyst configured in server or transparent mode, be sure that you consider how you can affect the network. You have the possibility of isolating a lot of users and of disrupting Spanning Tree in a network.

Viewing VLAN Configurations

Of course, you want to examine your VLAN configurations at one time or another. Example 5-4 shows a Catalyst output for the **show vlan** command.

Example 5-4 show vlan *Command and Output*

```
Console> (enable) show vlan
VLAN Name                              Status   Mod/Ports, Vlans
---- -------------------------------- -------- ----------------------------
1    default                          active   1/1-2
                                               2/9-24

2    willitwork                       active   2/1-8
1002 fddi-default                     active
1003 token-ring-default               active
1004 fddinet-default                  active
1005 trnet-default                    active


VLAN Type  SAID    MTU   Parent RingNo BrdgNo Stp  BrdgMode Trans1 Trans2
---- ----- ------- ----- ------ ------ ------ ---- -------- ------ ------
1    enet  100001  1500  -      -      -      -    -        0      0
2    enet  100002  1500  -      -      -      -    -        0      0
1002 fddi  101002  1500  -      0x0    -      -    -        0      0
1003 trcrf 101003  1500  0      0x0    -      -    -        0      0
1004 fdnet 101004  1500  -      -      0x0    ieee -        0      0
1005 trbrf 101005  1500  -      -      0x0    ibm  -        0      0


VLAN AREHops STEHops Backup CRF
---- ------- ------- ----------
1003 7       7       off
Console> (enable)
```

VLAN 2, created in the previous section, is highlighted in the output of Example 5-4. The **show vlan** output is divided into three portions. The first portion shows the VLAN number, name, status, and ports assigned to the VLAN. This provides a quick evaluation of the condition of a VLAN within the Catalyst. The second portion displays the VLAN type and other parameters relevant to the VLAN—for example, the MTU size. The other columns display information for Token Ring and FDDI VLANs. The third portion of the output displays further information for source-routed VLANs.

Note that there are several VLANs present in the output. All of the entries in the display, except for VLAN 2, show default VLANs which are always present in the Catalyst. These default VLANs cannot be removed from the Catalyst. When you first power a new Catalyst, all Ethernet interfaces belong to VLAN 1. Also, the Supervisor module **sc0** or **sl0** interface belongs to this VLAN by default. If you interconnect several Catalysts, each populated with Ethernet modules and with only default configurations, all of the Catalyst interfaces belong to the same VLAN. You have one giant broadcast domain.

VMPS and Dynamic VLANs: Advanced Administration

Normally, when you configure a VLAN, you must perform three steps:

Step 1   Ensure that the Catalyst belongs to a VTP domain

Step 2   Create a VLAN

Step 3   Assign ports to the VLAN

The first two steps globally affect Catalysts. When you create a VLAN, VTP announces the addition or deletion of the VLAN throughout the VTP domain. Assigning ports to a VLAN, however, is a local event. VTP does not announce what ports belong to which VLAN. You must log in to the Catalyst where you want to assign ports. After you assign the port to a VLAN, any device attached to the port belongs to the assigned VLAN. (The exception to this is the port security feature that allows one and only one MAC address on the port to belong to the VLAN.) When you attach a station to a port on the Catalyst, you need to ensure that the port belongs to the correct VLAN. Unfortunately, you might not always have access to the CLI to make a change. Or, you might have users who frequently relocate within their facilities environment. But you do not want them to bother you every time they relocate a station, especially when it happens after midnight or during a weekend.

Cisco built a feature into the Catalyst to facilitate dynamic port configurations. The dynamic VLAN feature automatically configures a port to a VLAN based upon the MAC address of the device attached to the port as shown in the following sequence:

Step 1   When you attach a device to the port and the device transmits a frame, the Catalyst learns the source MAC address.

Step 2   The Catalyst then interrogates a VLAN membership policy server (VMPS). The VMPS server has a database of MAC addresses and the authorized VLAN for each MAC address.

Step 3   The VMPS responds to the client Catalyst with the authorized VLAN.

Step 4   The VMPS client Catalyst configures the port to the correct VLAN based upon the information received from the VMPS.

The bulk of your work as the network administrator is to initially build the database. After you build the database, you (or your users) do not have to statically configure a Catalyst every time that a device moves from one port to another.

This feature also provides a level of security because the user's MAC address for the device must be in a database before the Catalyst assigns the port to a VLAN. If the MAC address is not in the database, the Catalyst can refuse the connection or assign the user to a default VLAN.

Three components enable a dynamic VLAN environment. First, you must have a TFTP server. The VMPS database resides as a text file on the TFTP server. The second component, the VMPS server, reads the database from the TFTP server and locally remembers all of the data. Dynamic VLAN clients interrogate the VMPS whenever a device attaches to a port on the Catalyst. You can configure up to two backup VMPS servers. The third component, the VMPS client, communicates with the VMPS server using UDP transport and a socket value of 1589. This is a well known protocol value registered with the Internet Assigned Numbers Authority (IANA) as VQP (VMPS Query Protocol).

Figure 5-20 illustrates the relationship between the components. Cat-A serves as the primary VMPS server, with two other Catalysts also enabled as backup VMPS servers. The section on configuring the VMPS client details how to identify primary and backup VMPS servers. The VMPS server (Cat-A) accesses the TFTP server when you initially enable the VMPS server, or whenever you manually force the VMPS to download a new configuration table. The VMPS server must have an IP address and it might need a default route to the TFTP server for the VMPS server to initialize. The VMPS server needs a default route if the VMPS and TFTP servers reside on different subnets/VLANs.

Cat-B and Cat-C are each configured as VMPS clients and get port-to-VLAN authorizations from the VMPS server. Therefore, they need to be able to communicate with the VMPS server.

Figure 5-20 *Dynamic VLAN Architecture*

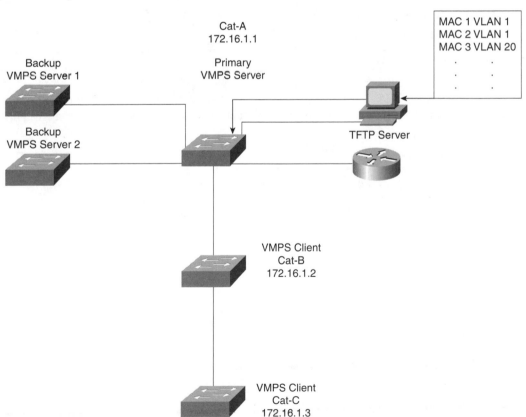

The following list outlines the steps for configuring dynamic VLANs:

Step 1   Build the VLAN database and load into a TFTP server.

Step 2   Configure the VMPS server IP address.

Step 3   On the VMPS server, enter the IP address of the TFTP server.

Step 4   Enable the VMPS server.

Step 5   Configure VMPS clients with an IP address.

Step 6   On the VMPS clients, configure the IP address of the VMPS server.

Step 7   Identify dynamic ports on clients.

The sections that follow provide more detail on this seven-step sequence for configuring dynamic VLANs.

Building the VMPS Database for TFTP Download

The bulk of your configuration activity resides in building the VMPS database, a simple text file. The VMPS server downloads the text file database and uses it to determine whether devices are authorized to join a VLAN. Example 5-5 shows a representative database. The database divides into three portions. The first part modifies global parameters for the VMPS system. The second part defines the MAC address and the authorized VLAN for the address. The third part defines other policies to restrict VLANs to specific ports or groups of ports.

Example 5-5   *VLAN Database Example*

```
!PART 1:   GLOBAL SETTINGS
!vmps domain <domain-name>
! The VMPS domain must be defined.
!vmps mode { open ¦ secure }
! The default mode is open.
!vmps fallback <vlan-name>
!vmps no-domain-req { allow ¦ deny }
!
! The default value is allow.
! The VMPS domain name MUST MATCH the VTP domain name.
vmps domain testvtp
vmps mode open
vmps fallback default
vmps no-domain-req deny
!
!
!PART 2:   MAC ADDRESS DATABASE
!MAC Addresses
!
vmps-mac-addrs
```

continues

Example 5-5   *VLAN Database Example (Continued)*

```
!
! address <addr> vlan-name <vlan_name>
!
address 0060.0893.dbc1 vlan-name Engineering
address 0060.08aa.5279 vlan-name --NONE--
address 0060.08b6.49fb vlan-name Engineering
!
!PART 3:  OTHER POLICIES
!Port Groups
!
!vmps-port-group <group-name>
! device <device-id> { port <port-name> | all-ports }
vmps-port-group restrictengineering
device 172.16.1.2 port 3/1
device 172.16.1.2 port 3/2
device 172.16.1.3 port 4/1
device 172.16.1.3 port 4/3
device 172.16.1.3 port 4/5
!
!
!
!VLAN groups
! USE THIS TO ASSOCIATE A GROUP OF VLANs TOGETHER. THE DATABASE TREATS
! ALL OF THE VLANs AS A SINGLE GROUP.
!
!vmps-vlan-group <group-name>
! vlan-name <vlan-name>
!
!
!
!VLAN port Policies
!
!vmps-port-policies {vlan-name <vlan_name> | vlan-group <group-name> }
! { port-group <group-name> | device <device-id> port <port-name> }
vmps-port-policies vlan-name port-group restrictengineering
!
```

VMPS Database Global Settings

In the global configuration portion of the database (Part 1 in Example 5-5), you configure the VMPS domain name, the security mode, the fallback VLAN, and the policy regarding VMPS and VTP domain name mismatches.

The VMPS domain name must match the VTP domain name for the VMPS server to respond to a VMPS client. You can force the VMPS server to accept requests from VMPS clients with a domain name mismatch by setting the parameter **vmps no-domain-req allow** in the database.

The database entry **vmps mode { open | secure }** defines what action to take if the VMPS server does not have an entry for a MAC address. The **open** mode means that, if there is no entry for the MAC address, assign the port to the fallback VLAN. If you do not define a fallback, the port remains unassigned. If you set the mode to **secure**, the VMPS server instructs the VMPS client to shut down the interface instead of leaving it unassigned. An unassigned port can continue to try to assign a port through repeated requests. A shutdown port stays that way until you enable it.

The fallback VLAN is like a miscellaneous VLAN. If the database does not have an entry for the MAC address, the VMPS server assigns the device to the fallback VLAN, if one is configured.

VMPS Database VLAN Authorizations

The heart of the database is found here in the middle portion (Part 2 of Example 5-5). This defines the MAC address-to-VLAN association. Each device that you want to dynamically assign needs to have an entry in the database indicating its MAC address and the authorized VLAN. If the host attaches to a dynamic port, the Catalyst refers to the database for the VLAN assignment. Note that the VLAN assignment is by name, not by VLAN number. Also note a reserved VLAN name, **--NONE--**. This VLAN explicitly denies a MAC address from any dynamic VLAN port. Use this to ensure that certain devices never work when attached to a dynamic port. You can achieve a similar result by setting the security mode to enabled and not defining a fallback VLAN. But that affects all devices not in the database, not just a specific MAC address.

You can elect to enable these services for security reasons. For example, you might have specific devices that you never want to gain access through dynamic ports, in which case you can use the mapping to **NONE** option. This prevents the device from even joining the fallback VLAN. On the other hand, you might not want any station that is not in the database to dynamically join any VLAN. In this case, you should enable the security mode. This saves you from having to explicitly identify every excluded device.

VMPS Database Group Policies

Through the third part of the VMPS database (Part 3 in Example 5-5), you can restrict VLANS to specific ports on the VMPS client. Suppose, for example, that you want to ensure that hosts in the engineering VLAN only get authorized when they attach to Ports 3/1 and 3/2 on Cat-B, and Ports 4/1,3,5 on Cat-C in Figure 5-20. If the host attaches to any other dynamic port, do not authorize the port configuration, even if the MAC address is in the database. You can configure this in the database as shown in the third part of Example 5-5. Note that the database depends upon the IP address to specify the VMPS client and the policies regarding it.

Configuring the VMPS Server

You should complete the TFTP file configuration before you enable the VMPS server. You can have up to three VMPS servers, the active and two backups. When you enable the server, it attempts to download the database from the TFTP server. If it fails to download the database, the Catalyst does not enable the VMPS server function.

Two commands configure the VMPS server—**set vmps tftpserver** *ip_addr* [*filename*] and **set vmps state enable**. The first command points the VMPS server to the TFTP server and optionally specifies the database filename. If you do not specify a filename, the VMPS tries the filename *vmps-config-database.1*. Use the command **set vmps tftpserver** *ip_addr* [*filename*] to inform the VMPS server of the TFTP server's IP address and the VMPS database filename to request.

After you configure the TFTP server information, you can enable the VMPS server with the command **set vmps state enable**. At this point, the VMPS server attempts to download the VMPS database from the TFTP server.

If at some point after you enable the server you modify the VMPS database on the TFTP server, you can force the VMPS server to acquire the new database with the command **download vmps**.

You can check the status of the VMPS server with the command **show vmps**. This command reports all of the current configuration information for the server, as shown in Example 5-6.

Example 5-6 *show vmps Output*

```
Console> show vmps
VMPS Server Status:
--------------------
Management Domain:     Accounting
State:                 enbabled
Operational Status:    active
TFTP Server:           144.254.10.33
TFTP File:             myvmpsdatabase.db
Fallback VLAN:         miscbucket
Secure Mode:           open
VMPS No Domain Req:    allow

VMPS Client Status:
--------------------
VMPS VQP Version:      1
Reconfirm Interval:    20 min
Server Retry Count:    3
VMPS domain server:    172.16.1.1

No dynamic ports configured.
Console>
```

The **show vmps** command works for both the VMPS server and client. The top half of the display shows the server configuration information, and the bottom half displays client values. If you have trouble getting the VMPS server operational, use this command to view a summary of the parameters. In particular, check that the VMPS domain name matches the VTP domain name. State is either **enabled** or **disabled**. You should see **enabled** if you entered the **set vmps state enable** command. Check the operational status. This displays either **active**, **inactive**, or **downloading**. The **downloading** status implies that the VMPS server is retrieving the VMPS database from the TFTP server. The **inactive** status means that the VMPS server tried to get the database, but failed and became inactive. Finally, check the database filename and ensure that the Catalyst can reach the server, that the file exists, and that it is a VMPS file.

Cisco has two optional tools for the VMPS database—the User Registration Tool (URT) and the User Tracker for Cisco Works for Switched Internetworks (CWSI). The tools help with the creation of the database and allow you to place the VMPS server in a non-Catalyst device. The sections that follow provide additional information on these two tools.

URT

Cisco's User Registration Tool (URT) allows you to have a VLAN membership database built based upon a user's Windows/NT login information rather than based upon a MAC address. You can only use URT with Windows 95/98 and Windows NT 4 clients running Microsoft Networking (NetBios or Client for Microsoft Networks) running over TCP/IP using the Dynamic Host Control Protocol (DHCP). URT does not support other operating systems or network layer protocols. You must manually load a URT client package on the NT 4 clients/servers so it can interact with the URT server. However, Windows 95/98 clients automatically install the URT client service from their NT domain controller.

URT sets up an NT 4 database and behaves like a VMPS server. You still need to enable Catalysts as VMPS clients pointing to the NT server with the URT database.

Managing the URT server requires CWSI 2.1 as it interacts with the CWSI 2.1 ANI server to define workstation relationships to VLANs.

User Tracker for CWSI

User Tracker simplifies the task of building the TFTP server database. With Cisco Works for Switched Internetworks (CWSI), you can use the User Tracker function to build the database. User Tracker keeps track of individual stations in your network. Through a series of screens, you can use the information gleaned by User Tracker to automatically add entries to the VMPS database on your TFTP server. This eliminates the need for you to manually type entries in the database eliminating typographical errorrorrorrs in the database.

Configuring the VMPS Client

The VMPS client configuration includes steps to inform the client of the IP address of the VMPS server and to set ports to dynamic mode. By default, ports are in static mode which means that you must manually configure the VLAN membership. Setting the port to dynamic means that the Catalyst automatically configures the port VLAN membership based upon the response of the VMPS server.

Use the command **set vmps server** *ip_addr* [**primary**] to inform the client about the VMPS server IP address. You can specify up to three VMPS servers in the configuration file. One server functions as the primary server, the other two as backups.

To configure ports as dynamic, use the command **set port membership** *mod_num/ port_num* **dynamic**. You cannot make a trunk port a dynamic port. You must first turn off trunking before you set port membership to dynamic. Nor can you set a secure port to dynamic. If you have port security enabled, you must disable it before you set it to dynamic. After you enter the **set port membership** command, the Catalyst attempts to communicate with the VMPS server using VQP when the attached device initially transmits. If the client successfully communicates with the server, the server responds in one of four ways:

- Assigns the port to an authorized VLAN
- Assigns the port to a fallback VLAN
- Denies access
- Disables the port

If the VMPS server finds an entry for the MAC address in the VMPS database, the server responds with the authorized VLAN for that device. The VMPS client enables the port and configures the port to the correct VLAN. If the VMPS server does not find the MAC address in the database, it assigns the device to the fallback VLAN if you set one up in the database. If you do not have a fallback specified, the VMPS server responds with instructions to deny access or shut down the interface, depending upon the VMPS security setting. Deny access differs from shutdown in that deny allows devices to try again (the behavior if the security option is disabled), whereas shutdown literally shuts down the port and prevents any further attempts to dynamically assign the port (the default behavior if the security option is enabled).

You can have multiple hosts on the dynamic port; however, all hosts must be authorized for the same VLAN, and you cannot have more than 50 hosts on the port.

Note that a Catalyst does not initiate a VQP to the server until the device attached to the port transmits. When the local Catalyst sees the source MAC address, it can generate a request to the VMPS server. If you use the **show port** command, you can determine what VLAN a port is assigned to. Dynamic ports have a VLAN nomenclature of **dyn-** as shown in Example 5-7.

Example 5-7 *Displaying Dynamic Ports*

```
Console> show port
Port    Name    Status    Vlan    Level    Duplex    Speed    Type
1/1             connect   dyn-3   normal   full      100      100 BASE-TX
1/2             connect   trunk   normal   half      100      100 BASE-TX
2/1             connect   trunk   normal   full      155      OC3 MMF ATM
3/1             connect   dyn-    normal   half      10       10 BASE-T
3/2             connect   dyn-5   normal   half      10       10 BASE-T
3/3             connect   dyn-5   normal   half      10       10 BASE-T
Console> (enable)
```

Note the entry for Port 1/1. It has a dynamic VLAN assignment. But the highlighted Port 3/1 is a dynamic port without a VLAN assignment. The Catalyst does not forward any frames from the host attached to this port. When you first attach a host to the port, the Catalyst does not know the source MAC address and automatically configures the port in this mode.

After the host transmits and the VMPS client receives a valid response from the VMPS server, the VMPS client Catalyst enables the interface in the correct VLAN. If the client sits idle for awhile causing the bridge aging timer to expire for the entry, the Catalyst returns the port to an unassigned state. The VMPS client issues a new query to the VMPS server when the host transmits again.

Confirm the VMPS client configuration with the **show vmps** command as was shown in Example 5-6. The bottom half of this output shows the client settings. The *reconfirm interval* defines how often the client interrogates the VMPS server to see if a policy changed for locally attached hosts. In Example 5-6, the interval is for every 20 minutes. The *Server Retry Count,* in this case three, specifies how many times the VMPS client should try to reach the VMPS server. If it fails to receive a response from the server after three attempts, the client attempts to reach one of the backup servers. Finally, the output shows how the IP address of the VMPS server the client is attempting to use, 172.16.1.1.

Protocol Filtering

A switch forwards traffic within a broadcast domain based upon the destination MAC address. The switch filters, forwards, or floods the frame depending upon whether or not the switch knows about the destination in its address table. The switch normally does not look at any Layer 3 information (or Layer 2 protocol type) to decide how to treat the frame. (MLS and MPOA are exceptions). Refer to Figure 5-21 for another example of the Catalyst blocking traffic based upon the protocol.

Figure 5-21   *Protocol Filtering*

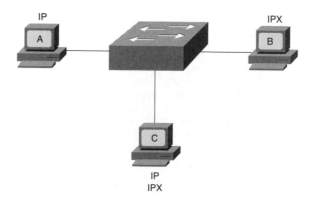

If Station A in Figure 5-21 sends a frame to Station B, the switch forwards the frame, even if Station B does not share the same Layer 3 protocol as Station A. This is an unusual situation. Suppose, however, that the VLAN contains stations with a mix of protocols in use. Some stations use IP, some use IPX, and others might even have a mix of protocols. If a switch needs to flood an IP frame, it floods it out all ports in the VLAN, even if the attached station does not support the frame's protocol. This is the nature of a broadcast domain.

A Catalyst 5000 equipped with a NetFlow Feature Card and a Supervisor III engine, as well as many other Catalysts, can override this behavior with *protocol filtering*. Protocol filtering works on Ethernet, Fast Ethernet, or Gigabit Ethernet non-trunking interfaces. Protocol filtering prevents the Catalyst from flooding frames from a protocol if there are no stations on the destination port that use that protocol. For example, if you have a VLAN with a mix of IP and IPX protocols, any flooded traffic appears on all ports in the VLAN. Protocol filtering prevents the Catalyst from flooding traffic from a protocol if the destination port does not use that protocol. The Catalyst listens for active protocols on an interface. Only when it sees an active protocol does it flood traffic from that protocol. In Figure 5-21, there is a mix of protocols in the VLAN. Some of the stations in the network support only one protocol, either IP or IPX. Some of the stations support both. The Catalyst learns that Station A uses IP, Station B uses IPX, and Station C uses both by examining the Layer 2 protocol type value. When Station A creates an IP broadcast, Station B does not see the frame, only Station C. Likewise, if Station B creates a frame for the switch to flood, the frame does not appear on Station A's interface because this is an IP-only interface.

The Catalyst enables and disables protocols in groups. They are the following:

- IP
- IPX
- AppleTalk, DECnet, and Vines
- All others

Review Questions

This section includes a variety of questions on the topic of campus design implementation. By completing these, you can test your mastery of the material included in this chapter as well as help prepare yourself for the CCIE written test.

1 Early in this chapter, it was mentioned that you can determine the extent of a broadcast domain in a switched network without configuration files. How do you do it?

2 Two Catalysts interconnect stations as shown in Figure 5-22. Station A cannot communicate with Station B. Why not? Example 5-8 provides additional information for the system.

Figure 5-22 *Figure for Review Question 2*

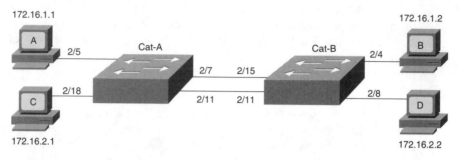

Example 5-8 *Cat-A and Cat-B Configurations*

```
Cat-A > (enable) show vlan
VLAN Name                             Status    Mod/Ports, Vlans
---- -------------------------------- --------- ----------------------------
1    default                          active    1/1-2
                                                2/1-8
2    vlan2                            active    2/9-24
1002 fddi-default                     active
1003 token-ring-default               active
1004 fddinet-default                  active
1005 trnet-default                    active


Cat-B> (enable) show vlan
VLAN Name                             Status    Mod/Ports, Vlans
---- -------------------------------- --------- ----------------------------
1    default                          active    1/1-2
                                                2/9-24
2    vlan2                            active    2/1-8
1002 fddi-default                     active
1003 token-ring-default               active
1004 fddinet-default                  active
1005 trnet-default                    active
```

3   Again referring to Figure 5-22 and Example 5-8, can Station C communicate with Station D?

4   Are there any Spanning Tree issues in Figure 5-22?

5   Draw a logical representation of Figure 5-22 of the way the network actually exists as opposed to what was probably intended.

6   Is there ever a time when you would bridge between VLANs?

7   List the three components of dynamic VLANs using VMPS.

Spanning Tree

The authors would like to thank Radia Perlman for graciously contributing her time to review the material in this chapter.

This chapter covers the following key topics:

- **What Is Spanning Tree and Why Use Spanning Tree**—Briefly explains the purpose of the Spanning-Tree Protocol (STP). Explains why some form of loop-prevention protocol is required to prevent broadcast storms and bridge table corruption.

- **Four-Step STP Decision Sequence**—Describes the process that the Spanning-Tree Protocol uses for all evaluations and calculations.

- **Initial STP Convergence**—A detailed examination of the three steps that STP uses to initially converge on a loop-free active topology.

- **STP States**—Explains the five STP states and how the algorithm progresses through each state.

- **STP Timers**—Discusses the three configurable timers utilized by the Spanning-Tree Protocol.

- **The show spantree Command**—Provides a detailed explanation of the fields contained in this powerful command. Several useful tips are discussed.

- **BPDUs**—Provides a detailed discussion of the frames used by bridges and switches to convey STP information. Decodes of actual BPDUs are explained.

- **Topology Change Process**—Explains how the Topology Change process allows the network to reconverge more quickly after changes in the physical network.

- **Setting the Root Bridge**—Explains how to manually place Root Bridges in your network for improved stability and performance.

- **Per VLAN Spanning Tree**—Explains how Cisco supports one instance of the Spanning-Tree Protocol per VLAN. This features allows for extremely flexible designs and is detailed in Chapter 7, "Advanced Spanning Tree."

CHAPTER 6

Understanding Spanning Tree

Most network administrators and designers underestimate the importance of the Spanning-Tree Protocol (STP). As routers became popular in the early 1990s, STP faded into the background as a "less important protocol that just worked." However, with the recent rise of switching technology, Spanning Tree has once again become an important factor that can have a tremendous impact on your network's performance.

In fact, STP often accounts for more than 50 percent of the configuration, troubleshooting, and maintenance headaches in real-world campus networks (especially if they are poorly designed). When I first encountered switching technology, I had the typical "I'm a Layer 3 pro, how hard could this STP stuff be?" mentality. However, I soon learned that STP is a complex protocol that is generally very poorly understood. I found it difficult to locate good Spanning Tree information, especially information about *modern* implementations of STP. The goal of this chapter (and Chapter 7) is to make your STP journey smooth sailing.

This chapter covers the mechanics of the Spanning-Tree Protocol as it performs its basic loop-prevention duties. To build a baseline knowledge of STP, the chapter begins by answering the questions "What is Spanning Tree?" and "Why do I need Spanning Tree?" From there, the chapter walks through the Spanning Tree algorithm in detail. In short, this chapter sets the stage for Chapter 7, "Advanced Spanning Tree," where complex topics such as load balancing and minimizing convergence time are presented in detail.

This chapter uses the terms bridge, switch, and Layer 2 switch interchangeably. Although some argue that there are differences between these types of devices, these differences are irrelevant when discussing Spanning Tree. This is particularly true when discussing the STP standards that were written prior to the development of hardware-based switches. For example, you will learn about the Root Bridge concept (don't worry about what it means yet). Although the term Root Switch is becoming more common, I find it awkward when first learning how the Spanning-Tree Protocol functions. However, the term switch is used when discussing particular network designs and deployments because it is rare to deploy a traditional, software-based bridge today.

CAUTION Please note that the examples used in this chapter (and Chapter 7) are designed to illustrate the operation of the Spanning-Tree Protocol, *not necessarily good design practices*. Design issues are addressed in Chapter 11, "Layer 3 Switching," Chapter 14, "Campus Design Models," Chapter 15, "Campus Design Implementation," and Chapter 17, "Case Studies: Implementing Switches."

What Is Spanning Tree and Why Use Spanning Tree?

In its most basic sense, the Spanning-Tree Protocol (STP) is a loop-prevention protocol. It is a technology that allows bridges to communicate with each other to discover physical loops in the network. The protocol then specifies an algorithm that bridges can use to create a *loop-free logical* topology. In other words, STP creates a tree structure of loop-free leaves and branches that spans the entire Layer 2 network. The actual mechanics of how the bridges communicate and how the STP algorithm works is the subject of the rest of the chapter.

Loops occur in networks for a variety of reasons. The most common reason you find loops in networks is the result of a deliberate attempt to provide redundancy—in case one link or switch fails, another link or switch can take over. However, loops can also occur by mistake (of course, that would never happen to you). Figure 6-1 shows a typical switch network and how loops can be intentionally used to provide redundancy.

Figure 6-1 *Networks Often Include Bridging Loops to Provide Redundancy*

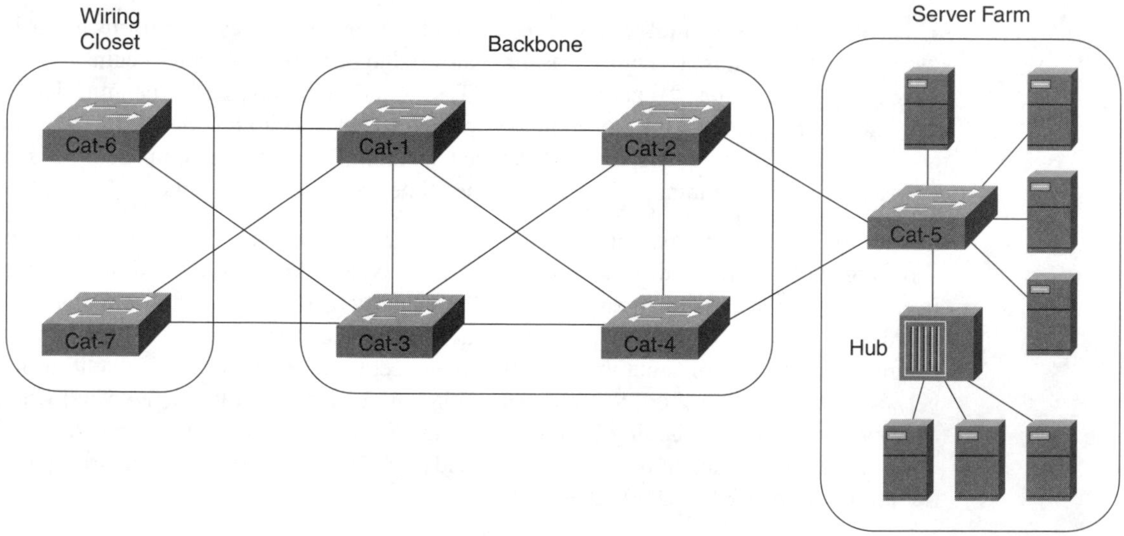

The catch is that loops are potentially disastrous in a bridged network for two primary reasons: broadcast loops and bridge table corruption.

Broadcast Loops

Broadcasts and Layer 2 loops can be a dangerous combination. Consider Figure 6-2.

Figure 6-2 *Without STP, Broadcasts Create Feedback Loops*

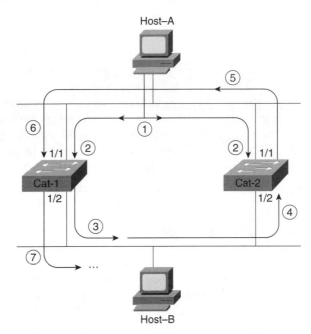

Assume that neither switch is running STP. Host-A begins by sending out a frame to the broadcast MAC address (FF-FF-FF-FF-FF-FF) in Step 1. Because Ethernet is a bus medium, this frame travels to both Cat-1 and Cat-2 (Step 2).

When the frame arrives at Cat-1:Port-1/1, Cat-1 will follow the standard bridging algorithm discussed in Chapter 3, "Bridging Technologies," and flood the frame out Port 1/2 (Step 3). Again, this frame will travel to all nodes on the lower Ethernet segment, including Cat-2:Port1/2 (Step 4). Cat-2 will flood the broadcast frame out Port 1/1 (Step 5) and, once again, the frame will show up at Cat-1:Port-1/1 (Step 6). Cat-1, being a good little switch, will follow orders and send the frame out Port 1/2 for the second time (Step 7). By now I think you can see the pattern—there is a pretty good loop going on here.

Additionally, notice that Figure 6-2 quietly ignored the broadcast that arrived at Cat-2:Port-1/1 back in Step 2. This frame would have also been flooded onto the bottom Ethernet segment and created a loop in the reverse direction. In other words, don't forget that this "feedback" loop would occur in both directions.

Notice an important conclusion that can be drawn from Figure 6-2—bridging loops are much more dangerous than routing loops. To understand this, refer back to the discussion of Ethernet frame formats in Chapter 1, "Desktop Technologies." For example, Figure 6-3 illustrates the layout of a DIX V2 Ethernet frame.

Figure 6-3   *DIX Version 2 Ethernet Frame Format*

Notice that the DIX V2 Ethernet frame only contains two MAC addresses, a Type field, and a CRC (plus the next layer as Data). By way of contrast, an IP header contains a time to live (TTL) field that gets set by the original host and is then decremented at every router. By discarding packets that reach TTL=0, this allows routers to prevent "run-away" datagrams. Unlike IP, Ethernet (or, for that matter, any other common data link implementation) doesn't have a TTL field. Therefore, after a frame starts to loop in the network above, it continues forever until one of the following happens:

- Someone shuts off one of the bridges or breaks a link.

- The sun novas.

As if that is not frightening enough, networks that are more complex than the one illustrated in Figure 6-2 (such as Figure 6-1) can actually cause the feedback loop to grow at an exponential rate! As each frame is flooded out multiple switch ports, the total number of frames multiplies quickly. I have witnessed a single ARP filling two OC-12 ATM links for 45 minutes (for non-ATM wizards, each OC-12 sends 622 Mbps in each direction; this is a total of 2.4 Gbps of traffic)! For those who have a hard time recognizing the obvious, this is bad.

As a final note, consider the impact of this broadcast storm on the poor users of Host-A and Host-B in Figure 6-2. Not only can these users not play Doom (a popular game on campus networks) with each other, they can't do anything (other than go home for the day)! Recall in Chapter 2, "Segmenting LANs," that broadcasts must be processed by the CPU in all devices on the segment. In this case, both PCs lock up trying to process the broadcast storm that has been created. Even the mouse cursor freezes on most PCs that connect to this network. If you disconnect one of the hosts from the LAN, it generally returns to normal operation. However, as soon as you reconnect it to the LAN, the broadcasts again consume 100 percent of the CPU. If you have never witnessed this, some night when only your worst enemy is still using the network, feel free to create a physical loop in some VLAN (VLAN 2, for example) and then type **set spantree 2 disable** into your Catalyst 4000s, 5000s, and 6000s to test this theory. Of course, don't do this if your worst enemy is your boss!

Bridge Table Corruption

Many switch/bridge administrators are aware of the basic problem of broadcast storms as discussed in the previous section. However, fewer people are aware of the fact that even unicast frames can circulate forever in a network that contains loops. Figure 6-4 illustrates this point.

Figure 6-4 *Without STP, Even Unicast Frames Can Loop and Corrupt Bridging Tables*

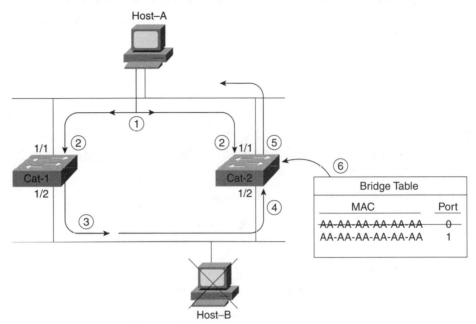

For example, suppose that Host-A, possessing a prior ARP entry for Host-B, wants to send a unicast Ping packet to Host-B. However, Host-B has been temporarily removed from the network, and the corresponding bridge-table entries in the switches have been flushed for Host-B. Assume that both switches are not running STP. As with the previous example, the frame travels to Port 1/1 on both switches (Step 2), but the text only considers things from Cat-1's point of view. Because Host-C is down, Cat-1 does not have an entry for the MAC address CC-CC-CC-CC-CC-CC in its bridging table, and it floods the frame (Step 3). In Step 4, Cat-2 receives the frame on Port 1/2. Two things (both bad) happen at this point:

1 Cat-2 floods the frame because it has never learned MAC address CC-CC-CC-CC-CC-CC (Step 5). This creates a feedback loop and brings down the network.

2 Cat-2 notices that it just received a frame on Port 1/2 with a source MAC of AA-AA-AA-AA-AA-AA. It changes its bridging entry for Host-A's MAC address to the wrong port!

As frames loop in the reverse direction (recall that the feedback loop exists in both directions), you actually see Host-A's MAC address flipping between Port 1/1 and Port 1/2.

In short, not only does this permanently saturate the network with the unicast ping packet, but it corrupts the bridging tables. Remember that it's not just broadcasts that can ruin your network.

Two Key Spanning-Tree Protocol Concepts

Spanning Tree calculations make extensive use of two key concepts when creating a loop-free logical topology:

- Bridge ID (BID)
- Path Cost

Bridge IDs

A Bridge ID (BID) is a single, 8-byte field that is composed of two subfields as illustrated in Figure 6-5.

Figure 6-5   *The Bridge ID (BID) Is Composed of Bridge Priority and a MAC Address*

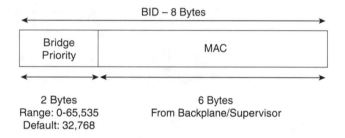

The low-order subfield consists of a 6-byte MAC address assigned to the switch. The Catalyst 5000 and 6000 use one of the MAC addresses from the pool of 1024 addresses assigned to every supervisor or backplane. This is a hard-coded number that is not designed to be changed by the user. The MAC address in the BID is expressed in the usual hexadecimal (base 16) format.

NOTE   Some Catalysts pull the MAC addresses from the supervisor module (for example, the Catalyst 5000), whereas others pull the addresses from the backplane (such as the Catalyst 5500 and 6000).

The high-order BID subfield is referred to as the *Bridge Priority*. Do not confuse *Bridge Priority* with the various versions of *Port Priority* that are discussed in Chapter 7, "Advanced Spanning Tree." The Bridge Priority field is a 2-byte (16-bit) value. The C programmers in the crowd might recall that an unsigned 16-bit integer can have 2^{16} possible values that range from 0–65,535. The default Bridge Priority is the mid-point value, 32,768. Bridge Priorities are typically expressed in a decimal (base 10) format.

NOTE	This book only covers the IEEE version of the Spanning-Tree Protocol. Although the basic mechanics of both are identical, there are some differences between IEEE STP and DEC STP (the original implementation of the Spanning-Tree Protocol). For example, DEC STP uses an 8-bit Bridge Priority. Layer 2 Catalysts (such as the 4000s, 5000s, and 6000s) only support IEEE STP. Cisco routers support both varieties. A third variety, the VLAN-Bridge Spanning Tree, is being introduced in 12.0 IOS code for the routers. This version can be useful in environments that mix routing and bridging and is discussed in Chapter 11.

Path Cost

Bridges use the concept of cost to evaluate how close they are to other bridges. 802.1D originally defined cost as 1000 Mbps divided by the bandwidth of the link in Mbps. For example, a 10BaseT link has a cost of 100 (1000/10), Fast Ethernet and FDDI use a cost of 10 (1000/100). This scheme has served the world well since Radia Perlman first began working on the protocol in 1983. However, with the rise of Gigabit Ethernet and OC-48 ATM (2.4 Gbps), a problem has come up because the cost is stored as an integer value that cannot carry fractional costs. For example, OC-48 ATM results in 1000 Mbps/2400 Mbps=.41667, an invalid cost value. One option is to use a cost of 1 for all links equal to or greater than 1 Gbps; however, this prevents STP from accurately choosing "the best path" in Gigabit networks.

As a solution to this dilemma, the IEEE has decided to modify cost to use a non-linear scale. Table 6-1 lists the new cost values.

Table 6-1   *STP Cost Values for Network Bridges*

Bandwidth	STP Cost
4 Mbps	250
10 Mbps	100
16 Mbps	62
45 Mbps	39
100 Mbps	19
155 Mbps	14
622 Mbps	6
1 Gbps	4
10 Gbps	2

The values in Table 6-1 were carefully chosen so that the old and new schemes interoperate for the link speeds in common use today.

The key point to remember concerning STP cost values is that *lower costs are better.* Also keep in mind that Versions 1.X through 2.4 of the Catalyst 5000 NMP use the old, linear values, whereas version 3.1 and later use the newer values. All Catalyst 4000s and 6000s utilize the new values.

Four-Step STP Decision Sequence

When creating a loop-free logical topology, Spanning Tree always uses the same four-step decision sequence:

Step 1   Lowest Root BID

Step 2   Lowest Path Cost to Root Bridge

Step 3   Lowest Sender BID

Step 4   Lowest Port ID

Bridges pass Spanning Tree information between themselves using special frames known as bridge protocol data units (BPDUs). A bridge uses this four-step decision sequence to save a copy of the best BPDU seen on every port. When making this evaluation, it considers all of the BPDUs received on the port *as well as the BPDU that would be sent on that port.* As every BPDU arrives, it is checked against this four-step sequence to see if it is more attractive (that is, lower in value) than the existing BPDU saved for that port. If the new BPDU (or the locally generated BPDU) is more attractive, the old value is replaced.

TIP   Bridges send configuration BPDUs until a more attractive BPDU is received.

In addition, this "saving the best BPDU" process also controls the sending of BPDUs. When a bridge first becomes active, all of its ports are sending BPDUs every 2 seconds (when using the default timer values). However, if a port hears a BPDU from another bridge that is more attractive than the BPDU it has been sending, the local port *stops sending BPDUs*. If the more attractive BPDU stops arriving from a neighbor for a period of time (20 seconds by default), the local port can once again resume the sending of BPDUs.

NOTE   There are actually two types of BPDUs: Configuration BPDUs and Topology Change Notification (TCN) BPDUs. The first half of this chapter only discusses Configuration BPDUs. The second half discusses TCNs and the differences between the two.

Three Steps of Initial STP Convergence

This section considers the algorithm that the Spanning-Tree Protocol uses to initially converge on a loop-free logical topology. Although there are many facets to the Spanning-Tree Protocol, the initial convergence can be broken down into three simple steps:

Step 1   Elect one Root Bridge

Step 2   Elect Root Ports

Step 3   Elect Designated Ports

When the network first starts, all of the bridges are announcing a chaotic mix of BPDU information. However, the bridges immediately begin applying the four-step decision sequence discussed in the previous section. This allows the bridges to hone in on the set of BPDUs that form a single tree spanning the entire network. A single Root Bridge is elected to act as the "center of the universe" for this network (Step 1). All of the remaining bridges calculate a set of Root Ports (Step 2) and Designated Ports (Step 3) to build a loop-free topology. You can think of the resulting topology as a wheel—the Root Bridge is the hub with loop-free active paths (spokes) radiating outward. In a steady-state network, BPDUs flow from the Root Bridge outward along these loop-free spokes to every segment in the network.

After the network has converged on a loop-free active topology utilizing this three-step process, additional changes are handled using the Topology Change process. This subject is covered later in the "Topology Change Process" section.

For the discussion that follows in the rest of the chapter, refer to Figure 6-6 as the model layout of a three switches/bridges network.

Figure 6-6   *Model Network Layout for Discussion of Basic STP Operations*

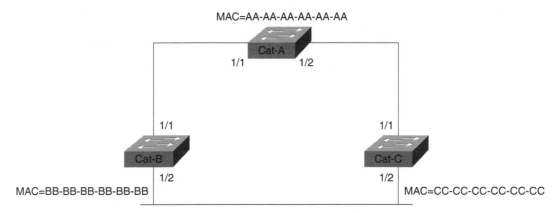

This network consists of three bridges connected in a looped configuration. Each bridge has been assigned a fictitious MAC address that corresponds to the device's name (for example, Cat-A uses MAC address AA-AA-AA-AA-AA-AA).

Step One: Elect One Root Bridge

The switches first need to elect a single Root Bridge by looking for the bridge with the *lowest Bridge ID (BID)*. Remember, in "STP economics", *the lowest BID wins!* This process of selecting the bridge with the lowest BID often goes by the exciting title of a Root War.

TIP	Many texts use the term highest priority when discussing the results of the Root War. However, notice that the bridge with the highest priority actually has the lowest value. To avoid confusion, this text always refers to the values.

As discussed in the "Bridge ID" section earlier, a BID is an 8-byte identifier that is composed of two subfields: the Bridge Priority and a MAC address from the supervisor or backplane. Referring back to Figure 6-6, you can see that Cat-A has a default BID of 32,768.AA-AA-AA-AA-AA-AA. Note the mixing of a decimal Bridge Priority with a hexadecimal MAC address. Although this might look a little strange, this convention enables you to view each section of the BID in its most common format.

TIP	Remember, the lowest BID wins.

Continuing with the example, Cat-B assumes a default BID of 32,768.BB-BB-BB-BB-BB-BB, and Cat-C uses 32,768.CC-CC-CC-CC-CC-CC. Because all three bridges are using the default Bridge Priority of 32,768, the lowest MAC address (AA-AA-AA-AA-AA-AA) serves as the tie-breaker, and Cat-A becomes the Root Bridge. Figure 6-7 illustrates this process.

Figure 6-7 *The Network Must Select a Single Root Bridge*

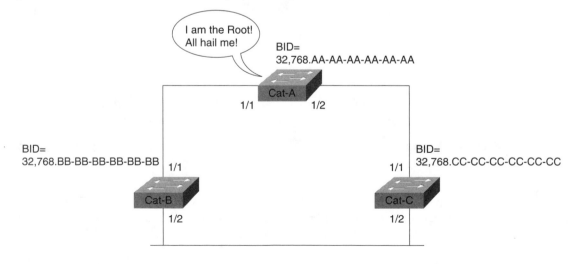

Okay, but how did the bridges learn that Cat-A had the lowest BID? This is accomplished through the exchange of BPDUs. As discussed earlier, BPDUs are special packets that bridges use to exchange topology and Spanning Tree information with each other. By default, BPDUs are sent out every two seconds. BPDUs are bridge-to-bridge traffic; they do not carry any end-user traffic (such as Doom or, if you are boring, e-mail traffic). Figure 6-8 illustrates the basic layout of a BPDU. (BPDU formats are covered in detail in the "Two Types of BPDUs" section.)

Figure 6-8   *Basic BPDU Layout*

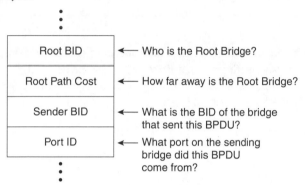

For the purposes of the Root War, the discussion is only concerned with the Root BID and Sender BID fields (again, the real names come later). When a bridge generates a BPDU every 2 seconds, it places *who it thinks is the Root Bridge* at that instant in time in the Root BID field. The bridge always places its own BID in the Sender BID field.

TIP   Remember that the Root BID is the bridge ID of the current Root Bridge, while the Sender BID is the bridge ID of the local bridge or switch.

It turns out that a bridge is a lot like a human in that it starts out assuming that the world revolves around itself. In other words, when a bridge first boots, it always places its BID in both the Root BID and the Sender BID fields. Suppose that Cat-B boots first and starts sending out BPDUs announcing itself as the Root Bridge every 2 seconds. A few minutes later, Cat-C boots and boldly announces itself as the Root Bridge. When Cat-C's BPDU arrives at Cat-B, Cat-B discards the BPDU because it has a lower BID saved on its ports (its *own* BID). As soon as Cat-B transmits a BPDU, Cat-C learns that it is not quite as important as it initially assumed. At this point, Cat-C starts sending BPDUs that list Cat-B as the *Root BID* and Cat-C as the *Sender BID*. The network is now in agreement that Cat-B is the Root Bridge.

Five minutes later Cat-A boots. As you saw with Cat-B earlier, Cat-A initially assumes that it is the Root Bridge and starts advertising this fact in BPDUs. As soon as these BPDUs arrive at Cat-B and Cat-C, these switches abdicate the Root Bridge position to Cat-A. All three switches are now sending out BPDUs that announce Cat-A as the Root Bridge and themselves as the Sender BID.

Step Two: Elect Root Ports

After the bloodshed of the Root War is behind them, the switches move on to selecting Root Ports. A bridge's Root Port is the port that is closest to the Root Bridge. *Every non-Root Bridge must select one Root Port.*

TIP   Every non-Root Bridge will select one Root Port.

As discussed earlier, bridges use the concept of cost to judge closeness. Specifically, bridges track something called *Root Path Cost*, the cumulative cost of all links to the Root Bridge. Figure 6-9 illustrates how this value is calculated across multiple bridges and the resulting Root Port election process.

Figure 6-9   *Every Non-Root Bridge Must Select One Root Port*

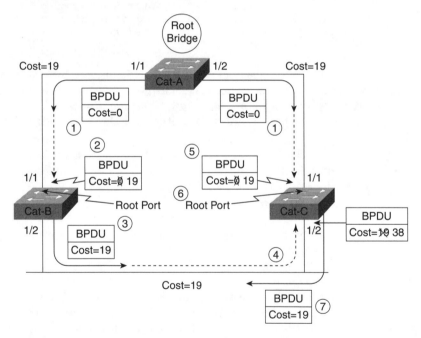

When Cat-A (the Root Bridge) sends out BPDUs, they contain a Root Path Cost of 0 (Step 1). When Cat-B receives these BPDUs, it adds the Path Cost of Port 1/1 to the Root Path Cost contained in the received BPDU. Assume the network is running Catalyst 5000 switch code greater than version 2.4 and that all three links in Figure 6-9 are Fast Ethernet. Cat-B receives a Root Path Cost of 0 and adds in Port 1/1's cost of 19 (Step 2). Cat-B then uses the value of 19 internally and sends BPDUs with a Root Path Cost of 19 out Port 1/2 (Step 3).

When Cat-C receives these BPDUs from Cat-B (Step 4), it increases the Root Path Cost to 38 (19+19). However, Cat-C is also receiving BPDUs from the Root Bridge on Port 1/1. These enter Cat-C:Port-1/1 with a cost of 0, and Cat-C increases the cost to 19 internally (Step 5). Cat-C has a decision to make: it must select a single Root Port, the port that is closest to the Root Bridge. Cat-C sees a Root Path Cost of 19 on Port 1/1 and 38 on Port 1/2—Cat-C:Port-1/1 becomes the Root Port (Step 6). Cat-C then begins advertising this Root Path Cost of 19 to downstream switches (Step 7).

Although not detailed in Figure 6-9, Cat-B goes through a similar set of calculations: Cat-B:Port-1/1 can reach the Root Bridge at a cost of 19, whereas Cat-B:Port-1/2 calculates a cost of 38…Port-1/1 becomes the Root Port for Cat-B. Notice that costs are incremented as BPDUs are *received* on a port.

TIP   Remember that STP costs are incremented as BPDUs are *received* on a port, not as they are sent out a port.

For example, BPDUs arrive on Cat-B:Port-1/1 with a cost of 0 and get increased to 19 "inside" Cat-B. This point is discussed in more detail in the section "Mastering the **show spantree** Command."

TIP   Remember the difference between Path Cost and Root Path Cost.

Path Cost is a value assigned to each port. It is added to BPDUs received on that port to calculate the Root Path Cost.

Root Path Cost is defined as the cumulative cost to the Root Bridge. In a BPDU, this is the value transmitted in the cost field. In a bridge, this value is calculated by adding the receiving port's Path Cost to the value contained in the BPDU.

Step Three: Elect Designated Ports

The loop prevention part of STP becomes obvious during the third step of initial STP convergence: electing Designated Ports. *Each **segment** in a bridged network has one Designated Port*. This port functions as the single bridge port that both sends and receives traffic to and from that segment and the Root Bridge. The idea is that if only one port handles traffic for each link, all of the loops have been broken! The bridge containing the Designated Port for a given segment is referred to as the *Designated Bridge* for that segment.

As with the Root Port selection, the Designated Ports are chosen based on cumulative Root Path Cost to the Root Bridge (see Figure 6-10).

Figure 6-10 *Every Segment Elects One Designated Port Based on the Lowest Cost*

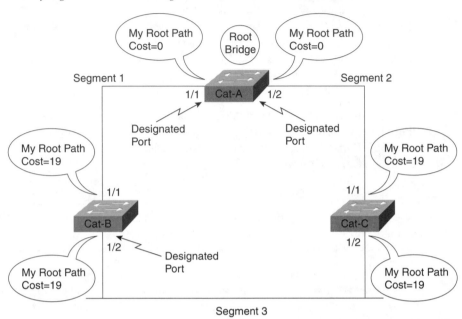

To locate the Designated Ports, take a look at each segment in turn. First look at Segment 1, the link between Cat-A and Cat-B. There are 2 bridge ports on the segment: Cat-A:Port-1/1 and Cat-B:Port-1/1. Cat-A:Port-1/1 has a Root Path Cost of 0 (after all, it *is* the Root Bridge), whereas Cat-B:Port-1/1 has a Root Path Cost of 19 (the value 0 received in BPDUs from Cat-A plus the Path Cost of 19 assigned to Cat-B:Port1/1). Because Cat-A:Port-1/1 has the lower Root Path Cost, it becomes the Designated Port for this link.

For Segment 2 (Cat-A to Cat-C link), a similar election takes place. Cat-A:Port-1/2 has a Root Path Cost of 0, whereas Cat-C:Port-1/1 has a Root Path Cost of 19. Cat-A:Port-1/2 has the lower cost and becomes the Designated Port. Notice that *every active port on the Root Bridge becomes a Designated Port*. The only exception to this rule is a Layer 1 physical loop to the Root Bridge (for example, you connected two ports on the Root Bridge to the same hub or you connected the two ports together with a crossover cable).

Now look at Segment 3 (Cat-B to Cat-C): both Cat-B:Port-1/2 and Cat-C:Port-1/2 have a Root Path Cost of 19. There is a tie! When faced with a tie (or any other determination), STP always uses the four-step decision sequence discussed earlier in the section "Four-Step STP Decision Sequence." Recall that the four steps are as follows:

Step 1   Lowest Root BID

Step 2   Lowest Path Cost to Root Bridge

Step 3   Lowest Sender BID

Step 4   Lowest Port ID

In the example shown in Figure 6-10, all three bridges are in agreement that Cat-A is the Root Bridge, causing Root Path Cost to be evaluated next. However, as pointed out in the previous paragraph, both Cat-B and Cat-C have a cost of 19. This causes BID, the third decision criteria, to be the deciding factor. Because Cat-B's BID (32,768.BB-BB-BB-BB-BB-BB) is lower than Cat-C's BID (32,768.CC-CC-CC-CC-CC-CC), Cat-B:Port-1/2 becomes the Designated Port for Segment 3. Cat-C:Port-1/2 therefore becomes a *non-Designated Port*.

Initial STP Convergence Review

Before continuing, this section recaps the points already discussed. Recall that switches go through three steps for their initial convergence:

Step 1   Elect one Root Bridge

Step 2   Elect one Root Port per non-Root Bridge

Step 3   Elect one Designated Port per segment

First, the bridged network elects a single Root Bridge. Second, every non-Root Bridge elects a single Root Port, the port that is the closest to the Root Bridge. Third, the bridges elect a single Designated Port for every segment.

For example, in a network that contains 15 switches and 146 segments (remember every switch port is a unique segment), the number of STP components that exist corresponds to the values documented in Table 6-2.

Table 6-2   *STP Components in a 15 Switch and 146 Segment Network*

STP Component	Number
Root Bridge	1
Root Port	14
Designated Ports	146

Also, all STP decisions are based on a predetermined sequence as follows:

Step 1   Lowest Root BID

Step 2   Lowest Path Cost to Root Bridge

Step 3   Lowest Sender BID

Step 4   Lowest Port ID

Every BPDU received on a port is compared against the other BPDUs received (as well as the BPDU that is sent on that port). Only the best BPDU (or superior BPDU) is saved. Notice in all cases that "best" is determined by the *lowest* value (for example, the lowest BID becomes the Root Bridge, and the lowest cost is used to elect the Root and Designated Ports). A port stops transmitting BPDUs if it hears a better BPDU that it would transmit itself.

Five STP States

After the bridges have classified their ports as Root, Designated, or non-Designated, creating a loop-free topology is straightforward: *Root and Designated Ports forward traffic*, whereas *non-Designated Ports block traffic*. Although Forwarding and Blocking are the only two states commonly seen in a stable network, Table 6-3 illustrates that there are actually five STP states.

Table 6-3   *STP States*

State	Purpose
Forwarding	Sending/receiving user data
Learning	Building bridging table
Listening	Building "active" topology
Blocking	Receives BPDUs only
Disabled	Administratively down

You can view this list as a hierarchy in that bridge ports start at the bottom (Disabled or Blocking) and work their way up to Forwarding. The *Disabled* state allows network administrators to manually shut down a port. It is not part of the normal, dynamic port processing. After initialization, ports start in the *Blocking* state where they listen for BPDUs.

A variety of events (such as a bridge thinking it is the Root Bridge immediately after booting or an absence of BPDUs for certain period of time) can cause the bridge to transition into the *Listening* state. At this point, no user data is being passed—the port is sending and receiving BPDUs in an effort to determine the active topology. It is during the Listening state that the three initial convergence steps discussed in the previous section take place. Ports that lose the Designated Port election become non-Designated Ports and drop back to the Blocking state.

Ports that remain Designated or Root Ports after 15 seconds (the default timer value) progress into the *Learning* state. This is another 15-second period where the bridge is still not passing user data frames. Instead, the bridge is quietly building its bridging table as discussed in Chapter 3. As the bridge receives frames, it places the source MAC address and port into the bridging table. The Learning state reduces the amount of flooding required when data forwarding begins.

NOTE   In addition to storing source MAC address and port information, Catalysts learn
information such as the source VLAN.

If a port is still a Designated or Root Port at the end of the Learning state period, the port
transitions into the *Forwarding* state. At this stage, it finally starts sending and receiving
user data frames. Figure 6-11 illustrates the port states and possible transitions.

Figure 6-11 *Possible Port States and Transitions*

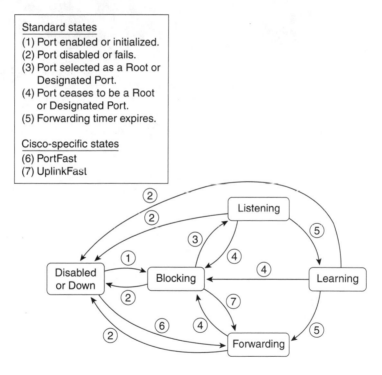

Figure 6-12 shows the sample network with the port classifications and states listed. Notice
that all ports are forwarding except Cat-C:Port-1/2.

Figure 6-12   *Sample Network with Port States Identified*

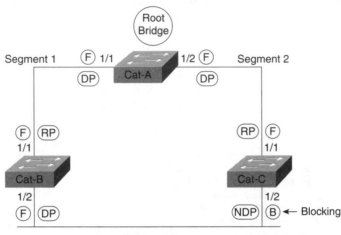

Table 6-4 documents the symbols used throughout the book to represent Spanning Tree states.

Table 6-4   *STP State and Port Symbols*

State/Port	Symbol
Blocking	B
Forwarding	F
Designated Port	DP
Root Port	RP
Non-Designated Port	NDP

Three STP Timers

The previous section mentioned that a bridge spends 15 seconds in each of the Listening and Learning states by default. In all, the Spanning-Tree Protocol is controlled by the three timers documented in Table 6-5.

Table 6-5   *STP Timers*

Timer	Primary Purpose	Default
Hello Time	Time between sending of Configuration BPDUs by the Root Bridge	2 Secs
Forward Delay	Duration of Listening and Learning states	15 Secs
Max Age	Time BPDU stored	20 Secs

The *Hello Time* controls the time interval between the sending of Configuration BPDUs. 802.1D specifies a default value of two seconds. Note that this value really only controls Configuration BPDUs as they are generated at the Root Bridge—other bridges propagate BPDUs from the Root Bridge as they are received. In other words, if BPDUs stop arriving for 2–20 seconds because of a network disturbance, non-Root Bridges stop sending periodic BPDUs during this time. (If the outage lasts more than 20 seconds, the default Max Age time, the bridge invalidates the saved BPDUs and begins looking for a new Root Port.) However, as discussed in the "Topology Change Notification BPDUs" section later, *all* bridges use their locally configured Hello Time value as a *TCN retransmit timer.*

Forward Delay is the time that the bridge spends in the Listening and Learning states. This is a single value that controls both states. The default value of 15 seconds was originally derived assuming a maximum network size of seven bridge hops, a maximum of three lost BPDUs, and a Hello Time interval of two seconds (see the section "Tuning Forward Delay" in Chapter 7 for more detail on how Forward Delay is calculated). As discussed in the "Topology Change Notification BPDUs" section, the Forward Delay timer also controls the bridge table age-out period after a change in the active topology.

Max Age is the time that a bridge stores a BPDU before discarding it. Recall from the earlier discussions that each port saves a copy of the best BPDU it has seen. As long as the bridge receives a continuous stream of BPDUs every 2 seconds, the receiving bridge maintains a continuous copy of the BPDU's values. However, if the device sending this best BPDU fails, some mechanism must exist to allow other bridges to take over.

For example, assume that the Segment 3 link in Figure 6-12 uses a hub and Cat-B:Port-1/2's transceiver falls out. Cat-C has no immediate notification of the failure because it's still receiving Ethernet link from the hub. The only thing Cat-C notices is that BPDUs stop arriving. Twenty seconds (Max Age) after the failure, Cat-C:Port-1/2 ages out the stale BPDU information that lists Cat-B as having the best Designated Port for Segment 3. This causes Cat-C:Port-1/2 to transition into the Listening state in an effort to become the Designated Port. Because Cat-C:Port-1/2 now offers the most attractive access from the Root Bridge to this link, it eventually transitions all the way into Forwarding mode. In practice, it takes 50 seconds (20 Max Age + 15 Listening + 15 Learning) for Cat-C to take over after the failure of Port 1/2 on Cat-B.

In some situations, bridges can detect topology changes on directly connected links and immediately transition into the Listening state without waiting Max Age seconds. For example, consider Figure 6-13.

Figure 6-13 *Failure of a Link Directly Connected to the Root Port of Cat-C*

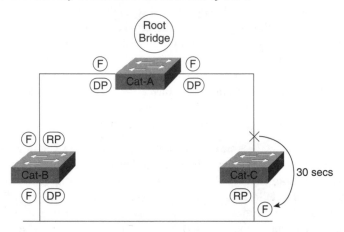

In this case, Cat-C:Port-1/1 failed. Because the failure results in a loss of link on the Root Port, there is no need to wait 20 seconds for the old information to age out. Instead, Cat-C:Port-1/2 immediately goes into Learning mode in an attempt to become the new Root Port. This has the effect of reducing the STP convergence time from 50 seconds to 30 seconds (15 Listening + 15 Learning).

TIP   The default STP convergence time is 30 to 50 seconds. The section "Fast STP Convergence" in Chapter 7 discusses ways to improve this.

There are two key points to remember about using the STP timers. First, *don't change the default timer values without some careful consideration.* This is discussed in more detail in Chapter 7. Second, assuming that you are brave enough to attempt timer tuning, *you should only modify the STP timers from the Root Bridge.* As you will see in the "Two Types of BPDUs" section, the BPDUs contain three fields where the timer values can be passed from the Root Bridge to all other bridges in the network. Consider the alternative: if every bridge was locally configured, some bridges could work their way up to the Forwarding state before other bridges ever leave the Listening state. This chaotic approach could obviously destabilize the entire network. By providing timer fields in the BPDUs, the single bridge acting as the Root Bridge can dictate the timing parameters for the entire bridged network.

TIP   You can only modify the timer values from the Root Bridge. Modifying the values on other bridges has no effect. However, don't forget to update any "backup" Root Bridges.

Mastering the show spantree **Command**

The most important Catalyst command for working with STP is the **show spantree** command. Although this command offers several useful parameters, this section only explains the basic syntax (see Chapter 7 for the full syntax). A sample of the **show spantree** output from Cat-B in the sample network from Figure 6-6 would contain the information shown in Example 6-1.

Example 6-1 *show spantree Output from Cat-B in the Network Shown in Figure 6-6*

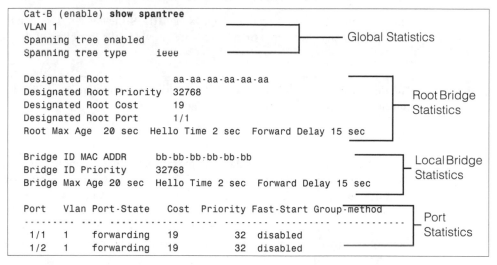

This **show spantree** output in Example 6-1 can be broken down into four sections as follows:

1 Global statistics for the current switch/bridge (lines 2–4)

2 Root Bridge statistics (lines 5–9)

3 Local bridge statistics (lines 10–12)

4 Port statistics (lines 13–16)

The global statistics appear at the top of the screen. The first line of this section (**VLAN 1**) indicates that the output only contains information for VLAN 1. The second line indicates that STP is enabled on this Catalyst for this VLAN. The final line of this section shows that the IEEE version of STP is being utilized (this cannot be changed on most Catalyst switches). Additional details about these values are discussed in the "All of This Per VLAN!" section at the end of the chapter.

The first two lines of the Root Bridge statistics display the BID of the current Root Bridge. The BID subfields are displayed separately—**Designated Root** shows the MAC address contained in the low-order six bytes, whereas **Designated Root Priority** holds the high-order two bytes. The cumulative Root Path Cost to the Root Bridge is displayed in the

Designated Root Cost field. The fourth line of this section (**Designated Root Port**) shows the current Root Port of the local device. The last line of the Root Bridge statistics section shows the timer values currently set on the Root Bridge. As the previous section discussed, these values are used throughout the entire network (at least for VLAN 1) to provide consistency. The term designated is used here to signify that these values pertain to the bridge that this device currently believes is the Root Bridge. However, because of topology changes and propagation delays during network convergence, this information might not reflect the characteristics of the true Root Bridge.

The local bridge statistics section displays the BID of the current bridge in the first two lines. The locally configured timer values are shown in the third line of this section.

TIP   The timer values shown in the local bridge statistics section are not utilized unless the current bridge becomes the Root Bridge at some point.

The port statistics section is displayed at the bottom of the screen. Depending on the number of ports present in the Catalyst, this display can continue for many screens using the **more** prompt. This information displays the Path Cost value associated with each port. This value is the cost that is added to the **Root Path Cost** field contained in BPDUs *received* on this port. In other words, Cat-B receives BPDUs on Port 1/1 with a cost of 0 because they are sent by the Root Bridge. Port 1/1's cost of 19 is added to this zero-cost value to yield a Designated Root Cost of 19. In the outbound direction, Cat-B sends BPDUs downstream with a cost of 19—Port 1/2's Path Cost of 19 is *not* added to transmitted BPDUs.

TIP   The cost values displayed in the port statistics section **show spantree** are added to BPDUs that are *received* (not sent) on that port.

The information displayed by **show spantree** can be critical to learning how Spanning Tree is working in your network. For example, it can be extremely useful when you need to locate the Root Bridge. Consider the network shown in Figure 6-14.

Figure 6-14 *Using **show spantree** to Locate the Root Bridge*

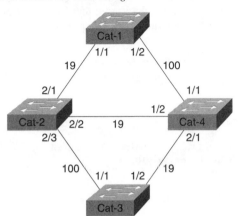

Example 6-2 shows the output of **show spantree** on Cat-1 for VLAN 1.

Example 6-2 *Locating the Root Bridge with **show spantree** on Cat-1 for VLAN 1*

```
Cat-1 (enable) show spantree
VLAN 1
Spanning tree enabled
Spanning tree type      ieee

Designated Root            00-e0-f9-16-28-00
Designated Root Priority   100
Designated Root Cost       57
Designated Root Port       1/1
Root Max Age  10 sec  Hello Time 1 sec  Forward Delay 10 sec

Bridge ID MAC ADDR     00-e0-f9-af-5d-00
Bridge ID Priority     32768
Bridge Max Age 20 sec  Hello Time 2 sec  Forward Delay 15 sec

Port   Vlan Port-State   Cost  Priority Fast-Start Group-method
-------- ---- ------------- ----- -------- ---------- -----------
 1/1   1    forwarding    19       32 disabled
 1/2   1    blocking     100       32 disabled
```

Although this information indicates that the Root Bridge has a BID of 100.00-E0-F9-16-28-00, locating the specific MAC address 00-E0-F9-16-28-00 in a large network can be difficult. One approach is to maintain a list of all MAC addresses assigned to all Catalyst—a tedious and error-prone activity. A more effective approach is to simply use the output of **show spantree** to "walk" the network until you locate the Root Bridge. By looking at the Designated Root Port field, you can easily determine that the Root Bridge is located somewhere out Port 1/1. By consulting our topology diagram (or using the **show cdp neighbor** command), you can determine that Cat-2 is the next-hop switch on Port 1/1. Then, Telnet to Cat-2 and issue the **show spantree** command as in Example 6-3.

Example 6-3 *Locating the Root Bridge with **show spantree** on Cat-2 for VLAN*

```
Cat-2 (enable) show spantree
VLAN 1
Spanning tree enabled
Spanning tree type      ieee

Designated Root             00-e0-f9-16-28-00
Designated Root Priority  100
Designated Root Cost        38
Designated Root Port        2/2
Root Max Age  10 sec  Hello Time 1 sec  Forward Delay 10 sec

Bridge ID MAC ADDR        00-e0-f9-1d-32-00
Bridge ID Priority        32768
Bridge Max Age 20 sec  Hello Time 2 sec  Forward Delay 15 sec

Port   Vlan Port-State   Cost  Priority Fast-Start Group-method
---------- ---- ------------- ----- -------- ---------- -----------
 2/1   1    forwarding     19        32 disabled
 2/2   1    forwarding     19        32 disabled
 2/3   1    blocking      100        32 disabled
```

Cat-2's Root Port is Port 2/2. After determining Port 2/2's neighboring bridge (Cat-4), Telnet to Cat-4 and issue the **show spantree** command as in Example 6-4.

Example 6-4 *Locating the Root Bridge with **show spantree** on Cat-4 for VLAN 1*

```
Cat-4 (enable) show spantree
VLAN 1
Spanning tree enabled
Spanning tree type      ieee

Designated Root             00-e0-f9-16-28-00
Designated Root Priority  100
Designated Root Cost        19
Designated Root Port        2/1
Root Max Age  10 sec  Hello Time 1 sec  Forward Delay 10 sec

Bridge ID MAC ADDR        00-e0-f9-52-ba-00
Bridge ID Priority        32768
Bridge Max Age 20 sec  Hello Time 2 sec  Forward Delay 15 sec

Port   Vlan Port-State   Cost  Priority Fast-Start Group-method
---------- ---- ------------- ----- -------- ---------- -----------
 1/1   1    forwarding     19        32 disabled
 1/2   1    forwarding    100        32 disabled
 2/1   1    forwarding     19        32 disabled
```

Because Cat-4's Root Port is 2/1, you will next look at Cat-3 (see Example 6-5).

Example 6-5 *Locating the Root Bridge with **show spantree** on Cat-3 for VLAN 1*

```
Cat-3 (enable) show spantree
VLAN 1
Spanning tree enabled
Spanning tree type      ieee

Designated Root               00-e0-f9-16-28-00
Designated Root Priority  100
Designated Root Cost        0
Designated Root Port        1/0
Root Max Age  10 sec  Hello Time 1 sec  Forward Delay 10 sec

Bridge ID MAC ADDR        00-e0-f9-16-28-00
Bridge ID Priority        100
Root Max Age  10 sec  Hello Time 1 sec  Forward Delay 10 sec

Port   Vlan Port-State   Cost  Priority Fast-Start Group-method
-------- ---- ------------- ----- -------- ---------- -----------
 1/1   1    forwarding    100      32  disabled
 1/2   1    forwarding     19      32  disabled
```

Several fields highlight the fact that Cat-3 is the Root Bridge:

- The Root Port is Port 1/0. Note that Catalyst 4000s, 5000s, and 6000s do not have a physical port labeled 1/0. Instead, the NPM software uses a reference to the logical console port, SC0, as a "logical Root Port."
- The local BID matches the Root Bridge BID.
- The Root Path Cost is zero.
- The timer values match.
- All ports are in the Forwarding state.

The search is over—you have found the Root Bridge located at Cat-3.

Two Types of BPDUs

To this point, the chapter has referred to all BPDUs as a single type. Actually, there are two types of BPDUs:

- Configuration BPDUs
- Topology Change Notification (TCN) BPDUs

Configuration BPDUs are originated by the Root Bridge and flow outward along the active paths that radiate away from the Root Bridge. *Topology Change Notification BPDUs* flow upstream (toward the Root Bridge) to alert the Root Bridge that the active topology has changed. The following sections discuss both of these BPDUs in detail.

Configuration BPDUs

All of the BPDUs discussed so far (and the vast majority of BPDUs on a healthy network) are Configuration BPDUs. Figure 6-15 illustrates a BPDU's protocol format.

Figure 6-15 *Configuration BPDU Decode*

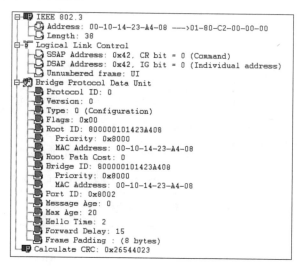

```
IEEE 802.3
   Address: 00-10-14-23-A4-08 --->01-80-C2-00-00-00
   Length: 38
Logical Link Control
   SSAP Address: 0x42, CR bit = 0 (Command)
   DSAP Address: 0x42, IG bit = 0 (Individual address)
   Unnumbered frame: UI
Bridge Protocol Data Unit
   Protocol ID: 0
   Version: 0
   Type: 0 (Configuration)
   Flags: 0x00
   Root ID: 800000101423A408
      Priority: 0x8000
      MAC Address: 00-10-14-23-A4-08
   Root Path Cost: 0
   Bridge ID: 800000101423A408
      Priority: 0x8000
      MAC Address: 00-10-14-23-A4-08
   Port ID: 0x8002
   Message Age: 0
   Max Age: 20
   Hello Time: 2
   Forward Delay: 15
   Frame Padding : (8 bytes)
Calculate CRC: 0x26544023
```

NOTE

For simplicity, the chapter has so far ignored the fact that there are two types of BPDUs and simply has used the term BPDU. However, recognize that all of these cases were referring to Configuration BPDUs. The second type of BPDU, the Topology Change BPDU, is discussed in the next section.

The decode in Figure 6-15 was captured and displayed by the NetXRay software from Network Associates (formerly Network General). Although considerably newer versions are available for sale, the version shown in Figure 6-15 is useful because it provides a very easy-to-read representation and decode of the Spanning-Tree Protocol. At the top of the screen you can observe the Ethernet 802.3 header. The source address is the MAC address of the individual port sending the BPDU. Every port on a Catalyst uses a unique Source MAC Address value for BPDUs sent out that port. Note the difference between this MAC address and the MAC address used to create the BID. The source MAC address is different on every Catalyst port. The BID is a global, box-wide value (within a single VLAN) that is formed from a MAC address located on the supervisor card or backplane. The source MAC is used to build the frame that carries the BPDU, whereas the BID's MAC is contained within the actual Configuration BPDU.

The Destination MAC Address uses the well-known STP multicast address of 01-80-C2-00-00-00. The Length field contains the length of the 802.2 LLC (Logical Link Control) header, BPDU, and pad that follows. Note that the CRC shown at the bottom of the screen is also part of the 802.3 encapsulation (specifically, the 802.3 trailer).

Below the 802.3 header lies the 802.2 LLC header. This 3-byte header consists of three fields that essentially identify the payload (in this case, a BPDU). The IEEE has reserved the DSAP (destination service access point) and SSAP (source service access point) value 0x42 hex to signify STP. This value has the unique advantage of being the same regardless of bit ordering (0x42 equals 0100 0010 in binary), avoiding confusion in environments that use translational bridging. Don't worry about the next byte, the control byte. It turns out that every non-SNA protocol you can name (including STP) always uses the value 0x03 to represent an Unnumbered Information (UI) frame.

The lower two-thirds of the output contains the actual BPDU. Configuration BPDUs consist of the following 12 fields (although many displays break the two BIDs out into separate subfields as shown in Figure 6-15):

- **Protocol ID**—Always 0. Future enhancements to the protocol might cause the **Protocol ID** values to increase.

- **Version**—Always 0. Future enhancements to the protocol might cause the **Version** value to increase.

- **Type**—Determines which of the two BPDU formats this frame contains (Configuration BPDU or TCN BPDU). See the next section, "Topology Change Notification BPDUs," for more detail.

- **Flags**—Used to handle changes in the active topology and is covered in the next section on Topology Change Notifications.

- **Root BID (Root ID in Figure 6-15)**—Contains the Bridge ID of the Root Bridge. After convergence, all Configuration BPDUs in the bridged network should contain the same value for this field (for a single VLAN). NetXRay breaks out the two BID subfields: Bridge Priority and bridge MAC address. See the "Step One: Elect One Root Bridge" section for more detail.

- **Root Path Cost**—The cumulative cost of all links leading to the Root Bridge. See the earlier "Path Cost" section for more detail.

- **Sender BID (Bridge ID in Figure 6-15)**—The BID of the bridge that created the current BPDU. This field is the same for all BPDUs sent by a single switch (for a single VLAN), but it differs between switches. See the "Step Three: Elect Designated Ports" section for more detail.

- **Port ID**—Contains a unique value for every port. Port 1/1 contains the value 0x8001, whereas Port 1/2 contains 0x8002 (although the numbers are grouped into blocks based on slot numbers and are not consecutive). See the "Load Balancing" section of Chapter 7 for more detail.

- **Message Age**—Records the time since the Root Bridge originally generated the information that the current BPDU is derived from. If a bridge looses connectivity to the Root Bridge (and hence, stops receiving BPDU refreshes), it needs to increment this counter in any BPDUs it sends to signify that the data is old. Encoded in 256[th]s of a second.

- **Max Age**—Maximum time that a BPDU is saved. Also influences the bridge table aging timer during the Topology Change Notification process (discussed later). See the "Three STP Timers" section for more detail. Encoded in 256[th]s of a second.

- **Hello Time**—Time between periodic Configuration BPDUs. The Root Bridge sends a Configuration BPDU on every active port every **Hello Time** seconds. This causes the other bridges to propagate BPDUs throughout the bridged network. See the "Three STP Timers" section for more detail. Encoded in 256[th]s of a second.

- **Forward Delay**—The time spent in the Listening and Learning states. Also influences timers during the Topology Change Notification process (discussed later). See the "Three STP Timers" section for more detail. Encoded in 256[th]s of a second.

Table 6-6 summarizes the Configuration BPDU fields.

Table 6-6 *Configuration BPDU Fields*

Field	Octets	Use
Protocol ID	2	Always 0
Version	1	Always 0
Type	1	Type of current BPDU 0 = Configuration BPDU
Flags	1	LSB = Topology Change (TC) flag MSB = Topology Change Acknowledgment (TCA) flag
Root BID	8	Bridge ID of current Root Bridge
Root Path Cost	4	Cumulative cost to Root Bridge
Sender BID	8	Bridge ID of current bridge
Port ID	2	Unique ID for port that sent this BPDU
Message Age	2	Time since Root Bridge-created BPDU used to derive current BPDU
Max Age	2	Period to save BPDU information
Hello Time	2	Period between BPDUs
Forward Delay	2	Time spent in Listening and Learning states

Topology Change Notification BPDUs

Although the majority of BPDUs on a healthy network should be Configuration BPDUs, all bridged networks see at least a few of the second type of BPDU, the Topology Change Notification (TCN) BPDU. TCN BPDUs, as their name suggests, play a key role in handling changes in the active topology. Figure 6-16 illustrates a decode of a TCN BPDU.

Figure 6-16 *Topology Change Notification BPDU Decode*

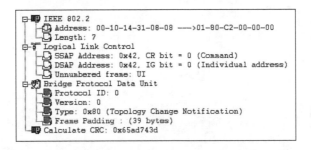

```
┌─■┏ IEEE 802.2
│   ┌─┚ Address: 00-10-14-31-08-08 ---->01-80-C2-00-00-00
│   └─┚ Length: 7
├─┚┚ Logical Link Control
│   ├─┚ SSAP Address: 0x42, CR bit = 0 (Command)
│   ├─┚ DSAP Address: 0x42, IG bit = 0 (Individual address)
│   └─┚ Unnumbered frame: UI
├─┚┚ Bridge Protocol Data Unit
│   ├─■ Protocol ID: 0
│   ├─■ Version: 0
│   ├─■ Type: 0x80 (Topology Change Notification)
│   └─■ Frame Padding : (39 bytes)
└─■┏ Calculate CRC: 0x65ad743d
```

The TCN BPDU is much simpler than the Configuration BPDU illustrated in Figure 6-15 and consists of only three fields. TCN BPDUs are identical to the first three fields of a Configuration BPDU with the exception of a single bit in the **Type** field. After all, at least one bit is needed to say "this is a TCN BPDU, not a Configuration BPDU." Therefore, the **Type** field can contain one of two values:

- **0x00** (Binary: 0000 0000) Configuration BPDU
- **0x80** (Binary: 1000 0000) Topology Change Notification (TCN) BPDU

That's it. TCN BPDUs don't carry any additional information.

Topology Change Process

If TCN BPDUs are so simple, how then do they play such an important role? Before answering that question directly, consider a subtle side effect of topology changes. The discussion that follows refers to the scenario illustrated in Figure 6-17.

Figure 6-17 *TCN BPDUs are Required to Update Bridge Tables More Quickly*

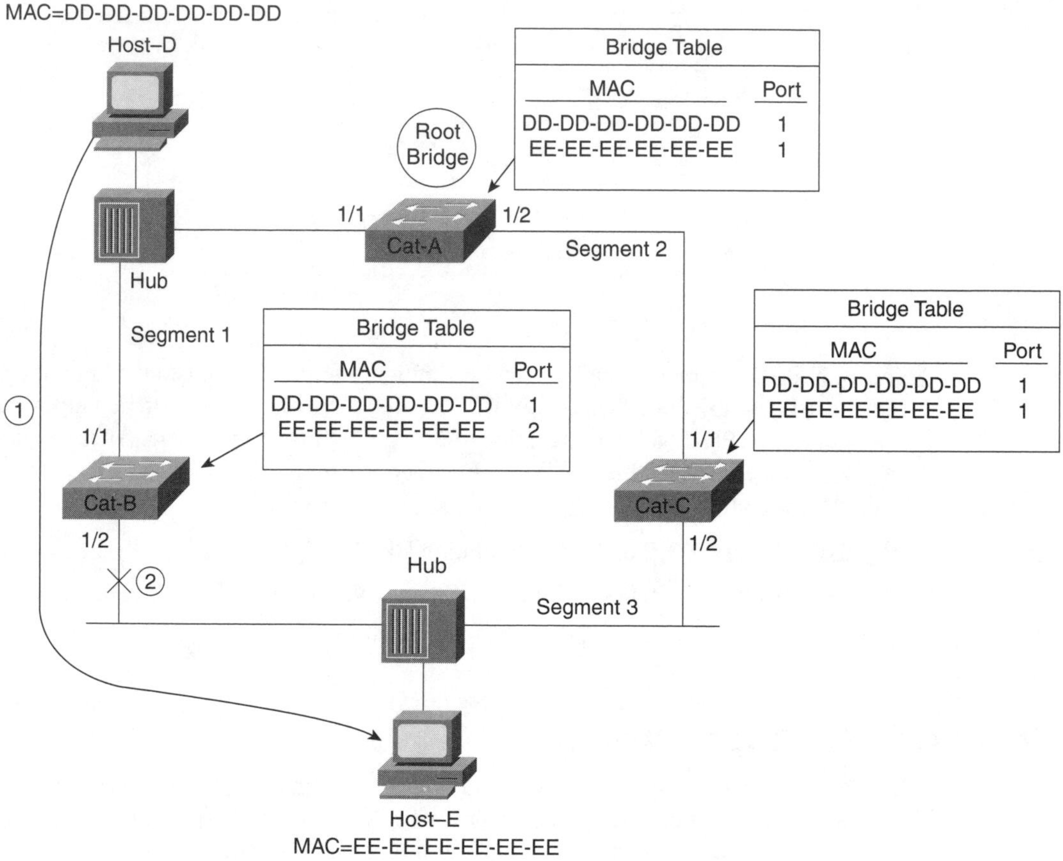

Suppose that Host-D is playing Doom with Host-E. As discussed earlier in Figure 6-12, the traffic from Host-D flows directly through Cat-B to reach Host-E (Step 1). Assume that the Ethernet transceiver on Cat-B:Port-1/2 falls out (Step 2). As discussed earlier, Cat-C: Port 1/2 takes over as the Designated Port in 50 seconds. However, without TCN BPDUs, the game continues to be interrupted for another 250 seconds (4 minutes, 10 seconds). Why is this the case? Prior to the failure, the bridging table entries for MAC address EE-EE-EE-EE-EE-EE on all three switches appeared as documented in Table 6-7.

Table 6-7   *Bridge Table Values Before Topology Change*

Bridge Table	Port Associated with EE-EE-EE-EE-EE-EE
Cat-A	Port 1/1
Cat-B	Port 1/2
Cat-C	Port 1/1

In other words, all frames destined for Host-E before the failure had to travel counterclockwise around the network because Cat-C:Port-1/2 was Blocking. When Cat-B:Port 1/2 fails, Cat-C:Port-1/2 takes over as the Designated Port. This allows traffic to start flowing in a clockwise direction and reach Host-E. *However, the bridging tables in all three switches still point in the wrong direction.* In other words, it appears to the network as if Host-E has moved and the bridging tables still require updating. One option is to wait for the natural timeout of entries in the bridging table. However, because the default address timeout is 300 seconds, this unfortunately results in the 5-minute outage calculated previously.

TCN BPDUs are a fairly simple way to improve this convergence time (and allow us to continue playing Doom sooner). TCN BPDUs work closely with Configuration BPDUs as follows:

1 A bridge originates a TCN BPDU in two conditions:

   • It transitions a port into the Forwarding state and it has at least one Designated Port.

   • It transitions a port from either the Forwarding or Learning states to the Blocking state.

   These situations construe a change in the active topology and require notification be sent to the Root Bridge. Assuming that the current bridge is not the Root Bridge, the current bridge begins this notification process by sending TCN BPDU out its *Root Port*. It continues sending the TCN BPDU every Hello Time interval seconds until the TCN message is acknowledged (note: this is the locally configured Hello Time, not the Hello Time distributed by the Root Bridge in Configuration BPDUs).

2 The upstream bridge receives the TCN BPDU. Although several bridges might hear the TCN BPDU (because they are directly connected to the Root Port's segment), only the Designated Port accepts and processes the TCN BPDU.

3 The upstream bridge sets the Topology Change Acknowledgment flag in the next Configuration BPDU that it sends downstream (out the Designated Port). This acknowledges the TCN BPDU received in the previous step and causes the originating bridge to cease generating TCN BPDUs.

4 The upstream bridge propagates the TCN BPDU out its Root Port (the TCN BPDU is now one hop closer to the Root Bridge).

5 Steps 2 through 4 continue until the Root Bridge receives the TCN BPDU.

6 The Root Bridge then sets the Topology Change Acknowledgment flag (to acknowledge the TCN BPDU sent by the previous bridge) *and* the Topology change flag in the next *Configuration BPDU* that it sends out.

7 The Root Bridge continues to set the Topology Change flag in all Configuration BPDUs that it sends out for a total of Forward Delay + Max Age seconds (default = 35 seconds). This flag instructs all bridges to shorten their bridge table aging process from the default value of 300 seconds to the current Forward Delay value (default=15 seconds).

Figure 6-18 summarizes the use of these bits during the seven-step TCN procedure (the steps numbers are circled):

Figure 6-18 *Sequence of Flows in Topology Change Processes*

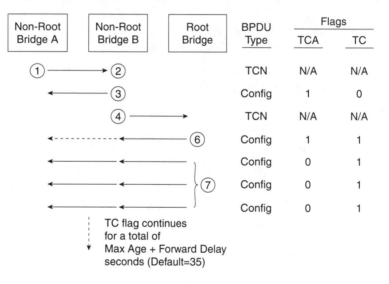

Applying these steps to the topology in Figure 6-17 (for simplicity, the steps are not shown in Figure 6-17), Cat-B and Cat-C send TCN BPDUs out their Port 1/1 (Step 1). Because the upstream bridge is also the Root Bridge, Steps 2 and 5 occur simultaneously (and allow Steps 3 and 4 to be skipped). In the next Configuration BPDU that it sends, the Root Bridge sets the TCN ACK flag to acknowledge receipt of the TCN from both downstream Catalysts. Cat-A also sets the Topology Change flag for 35 seconds (assume the default Forwarding Delay and Max Age) to cause the bridging tables to update more quickly (Step 6 and 7). All three switches receive the Topology Change flag and age out their bridging tables in 15 seconds.

Notice that shortening the aging time to 15 seconds does not flush the entire table, it just accelerates the aging process. Devices that continue to "speak" during the 15-second age-out period never leave the bridging table. However, if Host-D tries to send a frame to Host-E in 20 seconds (assume that Host-E has been silent), it is flooded to all segments by the switches because the EE-EE-EE-EE-EE-EE MAC address is no longer in any of the bridging tables. As soon as this frame reaches Host-E and Host-E responds, the switches learn the new bridge table values that are appropriate for the new topology.

Table 6-8 shows the bridge table entries for MAC address EE-EE-EE-EE-EE-EE on all three bridges after the new topology has converged and traffic has resumed.

Table 6-8 *Bridge Table Value after Topology Change*

Bridge Table	Port Associated with EE-EE-EE-EE-EE-EE
Cat-A	Port 1/2
Cat-B	Port 1/1
Cat-C	Port 1/2

At this point, connectivity between Host-D and Host-E is reestablished and our Doom Deathmatch can resume. Notice that the TCN BPDU reduced the failover time from 5 minutes to 50 seconds.

As previously mentioned in the "Configuration BPDUs" section, both **Flag** fields are stored in the same octet of a Configuration BPDU. This octet is laid out as illustrated in Figure 6-19.

Figure 6-19 *Layout of Configuration BPDU Flag Fields*

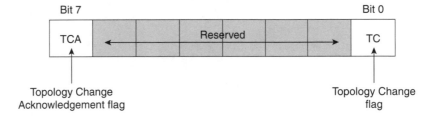

As discussed in the previous section, the TCA flag is set by the upstream bridge to tell the downstream bridge to stop sending TCN BPDUs. The TC flag is set by the Root Bridge to shorten the bridge table age-out period from 300 seconds to Forward Delay seconds.

Using Spanning Tree in Real-World Networks

Look at Figure 6-20 for a more complex topology, and see how all this STP detail adds up in the real world.

Figure 6-20 *A Complex Network with All Links Shown*

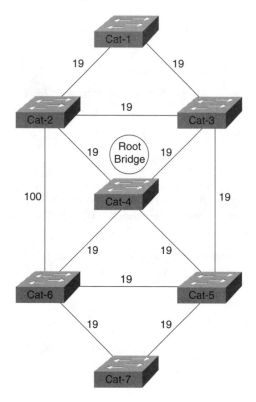

Figure 6-20 illustrates a network of seven switches connected in a highly redundant (that is, looped) configuration. Link costs are indicated—all are Fast Ethernet (cost of 19) except for the vertical link on the far left that is 10BaseT (cost of 100).

Assuming that Cat-4 wins the Root War, Figure 6-21 shows the active topology that results.

Figure 6-21 *Complex Network with Central Root Bridge and Active Topology*

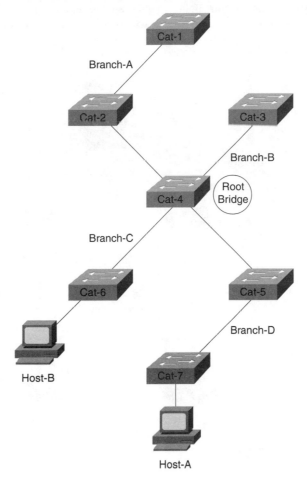

The setup in Figure 6-21 clearly illustrates the basic objective of the Spanning-Tree Protocol: make one bridge the center of the universe and then have all other bridges locate the shortest path to that location ("all roads lead to Rome"). This results in an active topology consisting of spoke-like branches that radiate out from the Root Bridge.

Notice that the Root Bridge is acting as the central switching station for all traffic between the four branches and must be capable of carrying this increased load. For example, Cat-7 and Cat-5 on Branch-D must send all traffic through the Root Bridge (Cat-4) to reach any of the other switches. In other words, don't use your slowest bridge in place of Cat-4!

Figure 6-21 also illustrates the importance of a centrally located Root Bridge. Consider the traffic between Host-A on Cat-7 and Host-B on Cat-6. When these two users want to fire up a game of Doom, the traffic must cross four bridges despite the fact that Cat-7 and Cat-6 are directly connected. Although this might seem inefficient at first, it could be much worse! For example, suppose Cat-1 happened to win the Root War as illustrated in Figure 6-22.

Figure 6-22   *Complex Network with Inefficient Root Bridge and Active Topology*

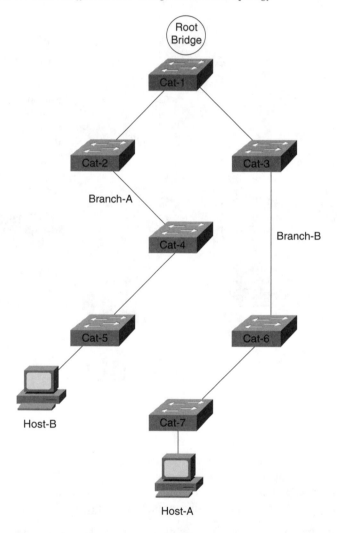

In this scenario, the network has converged into two branches with all traffic flowing through the Root Bridge. However, notice how suboptimal the flows are—Doom traffic between Host-A and Host-B must now flow through all seven bridges!

In the event that I haven't convinced you to avoid a randomly chosen Root Bridge, let me point out that the deck is stacked against you. Assume that Cat-1 is a vintage Cisco MGS or AGS router doing software bridging (Layer 2 forwarding capacity equals about 10,000 packets per second) and the remaining six devices are Catalyst 5500 or 6000 switches (Layer 2 forwarding capacity equals millions of packets per second). Without even thinking, I can guarantee you that the MGS becomes the Root Bridge every time by default!

How can I be so sure? Well, what determines who wins the Root War? The lowest BID. And as you saw earlier, BIDs are composed of two subfields: Bridge Priority and a MAC address. Because all bridges default to a Bridge Priority of 32,768, the lowest MAC address becomes the Root Bridge by default. Catalysts use MAC addresses that begin with OUIs like 00-10-FF and 00-E0-F9 (for example, MAC address 00-10-FF-9F-85-00). All Cisco MGSs use Cisco's traditional OUI of 00-00-0C (for example, MAC address 00-00-0C-58-AF-C1). 00-00-0C is about as low an OUI as you can have—there are only twelve numbers mathematically lower. Therefore, your MGS always has a lower MAC address than any Catalyst you could buy, and it always wins the Root War by default in a Cisco network (and almost any other network on the planet).

In other words, by ignoring Root Bridge placement, you can lower the throughput on your network by a factor of 1,000! Obviously, manually controlling your Root Bridge is critical to good Layer 2 performance.

Deterministic Root Bridge Placement

Based on the previous discussion, you should now agree that deterministically setting your Root Bridge is a must. In fact, you should *always set more than one Root Bridge*—one to act as the primary and another to act as a backup in the event the primary fails. If your bridged network is really large, you might want to even set a tertiary Root Bridge in case both the primary and the secondary fail.

This section considers how to deterministically place Root Bridges in your network. For considerations and recommendations on *where* you should place these devices, please consult Chapter 7.

There are two techniques available for setting Root Bridges:

- The **set spantree priority** command
- The **set spantree root** command

Manual Root Bridge Placement: set spantree priority

To force a particular bridge to win the Root War, you need to ensure that its BID is lower than all other bridges. One option might be to tweak the MAC address, but that could get ugly (trust me on this). A much simpler option is to modify the Bridge Priority. Because the high-order 16 bits of the BID consist of the Bridge Priority, lowering this number by even one (from 32,768 to 32,767) allows a bridge to *always* win the Root War against other bridges that are using the default value.

Bridge Priority is controlled through the **set spantree priority** command. The syntax for this command is:

```
set spantree priority priority [vlan]
```

Although the *vlan* parameter is optional, I suggest that you get in the habit of always typing it (otherwise, someday you will accidentally modify VLAN 1 when you intended to modify some other VLAN). The text revisits the *vlan* parameter in more detail later. For now, just assume VLAN 1 in all cases.

TIP Almost all of the Spanning Tree **set** and **show** commands support an optional *vlan* parameter. If you omit this parameter, VLAN 1 is implied. Get in the habit of always explicitly entering this parameter, even if you are only interested in VLAN 1. That way you don't accidentally modify or view the wrong VLAN.

Suppose that you want to force Cat-4 to win the Root War. You could Telnet to the switch and enter:

```
set spantree priority 100 1
```

This lowers the priority to 100 for VLAN 1, causing Cat-4 to always win against other switches with the default of 32,768 (including the MGS with its lower MAC address).

But what happens if Cat-4 fails? Do you really want to fail back to the MGS? Probably not. Make Cat-2 the secondary Root Bridge by entering the following on Cat-2:

```
set spantree priority 200 1
```

As long at Cat-4 is active, Cat-2 never wins the Root War. However, as soon as Cat-4 dies, Cat-2 always takes over.

TIP Notice that I used 100 for the primary Root Bridge and 200 for the secondary. I have found this numbering convention to work well in the real world and recommend that you adopt it. It is easy to understand and, more importantly, easy to remember. For example, if you ever look at a **show** command and see that your current Root Bridge has a Bridge Priority of 200, you instantly know that something has gone wrong with the primary Root Bridge. This scheme also comes in handy when the subject of load balancing is discussed later.

Using a Macro: set spantree root

Starting in version 3.X of the Catalyst 5000 NMP code, Cisco introduced a powerful new macro to automatically program Bridge Priorities and other values. The full syntax of this macro is as follows:

```
set spantree root [secondary] [vlan_list] [dia network_diameter] [hello hello_time]
```

To make a particular Catalyst the Root Bridge for VLAN 1, simply Telnet to that device and enter the following:

```
set spantree root 1
```

This causes the Catalyst to look at the Bridge Priority of the existing Root Bridge. If this value is higher than 8,192, the **set spantree root** macro programs the local Bridge Priority to 8,192. If the existing Root Bridge is less than 8,192, the macro sets the local bridge priority to one less than the value used by the existing Root Bridge. For example, if the existing Root Bridge is using a Bridge Priority of 100, **set spantree root** sets the local Bridge Priority to 99.

NOTE

The current documentation claims that **set spantree root** sets the value to 100 less than the current value if 8,192 is not low enough to win the Root War. However, I have always observed it to reduce the value only by 1.

To make another Catalyst function as a backup Root Bridge, Telnet to that device and enter the following:

```
set spantree root 1 secondary
```

This lowers the current Catalyst's Bridge Priority to 16,384. Because this value is higher than the value used by the primary, but lower than the default of 32,867, it is a simple but effect way to provide deterministic Root Bridge failover.

The **dia** and **hello** parameters can be used to automatically adjust the STP timer values according to the recommendations spelled out in the 802.1D specification. Tuning STP timers is discussed in detail in the "Fast STP Convergence" section of Chapter 7.

This might seem like a subtle point, but **set spantree root** is not a normal command—it is a macro that programs other commands. In other words, **set spantree root** never appears in a **show config** listing. However, the *results* of entering **set spantree root** *do* appear in the configuration. For example, suppose that you run the macro with **set spantree root 1**. Assuming that the existing Root Bridge is using a Bridge Priority higher than 8192, the macro automatically issues a **set spantree priority 1 8191** command. After the **set spantree priority** command is written to NVRAM, there is no evidence that the macro was ever used.

However, just because **set spantree root** is a macro, don't let that fool you into thinking that it is "unnecessary fluff." On the contrary, using the **set spantree root** macro has several benefits over manually using the commands yourself:

- It can be easier to use.
- It doesn't require you to remember lots of syntax.

- If you must resort to timer tuning, **set spantree root** is safer than manually setting the timers because it calculates the values recommended in the 802.1D spec. See the "Fast Convergence" section of Chapter 7 for more detail on timer tuning.

All of This Per VLAN!

As if the Spanning-Tree Protocol isn't exciting enough all by itself, it turns out that everything already discussed in the chapter actually occurs once per VLAN! In other words, *Cisco uses one instance of STP per VLAN*. This feature is generally referred to as PVST: per VLAN Spanning Tree.

In other words, every VLAN can have a different Root Bridge and active topology. For example, VLAN 2 could look like part A of Figure 6-23, whereas VLAN 3 could look like part B.

Figure 6-23 *PVST Allows You to Create Different Active Topologies for Each VLAN*

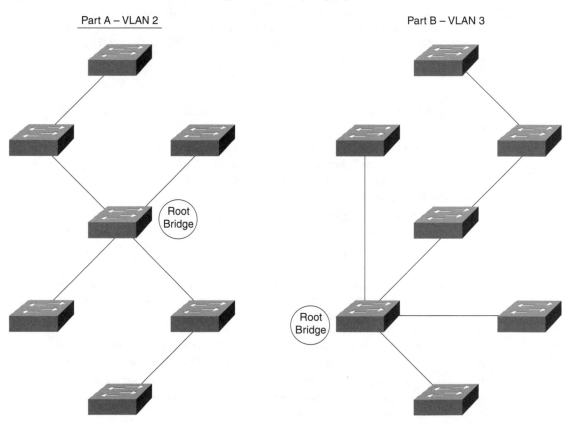

Part A – VLAN 2   Part B – VLAN 3

In fact, this is why there is a *vlan* parameter on the **set spantree** command that you saw in the previous section. Every VLAN could have a different set of active paths. Every VLAN could have different timer values. You get the idea.

The fact that Cisco uses one instance of STP per VLAN has two important implications:

- It can allow you to tap into many wonderful features such as load balancing and per-VLAN flows.
- It can make your life miserable (if you don't know what you are doing).

The goal here is to show you how to maximize the first point and avoid the second.

On the whole, having multiple instances of Spanning Tree gives you a phenomenal tool for controlling your network. Be aware that many vendors only use one instance of STP for all VLANs. Not only does this reduce your control, but it can lead to broken networks. For example, suppose that the single instance of Spanning Tree in VLAN 1 determines the active topology for all VLANs. However, what if you remove VLAN 5 from a link used by VLAN 1—if that link is selected as part of the active topology for all VLANs, VLAN 5 becomes partitioned. The VLAN 5 users are probably pretty upset about now.

Chapter 7 explores how to take advantage of the multiple instances of STP to accomplish advanced tasks such as STP load balancing.

Exercises

This section includes a variety of questions and hands-on lab exercises. By completing these, you can test your mastery of the material included in this chapter as well as help prepare yourself for the CCIE written and lab tests. You can find the answers to the Review Questions and the Hands-On Lab Exercises in Appendix A, "Answers to End of Chapter Exercises."

Review Questions

1 Summarize the three-step process that STP uses to initially converge on an active topology.

2 How many of the following items does the network shown in Figure 6-24 contain: Root Bridges, Root Ports, Designated Ports? Assume all devices are operational.

Figure 6-24 *Sample Network of Four Switches and 400 Users*

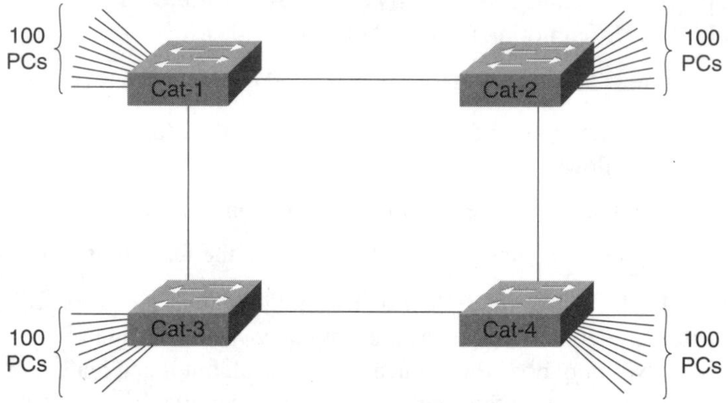

3 When running the Spanning-Tree Protocol, every bridge port saves a copy of the best information it has heard. How do bridges decide what constitutes the best information?

4 Why are Topology Change Notification BPDUs important? Describe the TCN process.

5 How are Root Path Cost values calculated?

6 Assume that you install a new bridge and it contains the lowest BID in the network. Further assume that this devices is running experimental Beta code that contains a severe memory leak and, as a result, reboots every 10 minutes. What effect does this have on the network?

7 When using the **show spantree** command, why might the timer values shown on the line that begins with Root Max Age differ from the values shown on the Bridge Max Age line?

8 Label the port types (RP=Root Port, DP=Designated Port, NDP=non-Designated Port) and the STP states (F=Forwarding, B=Blocking) in Figure 6-25. The Bridge IDs are labeled. All links are Fast Ethernet.

Figure 6-25 *Sample Network*

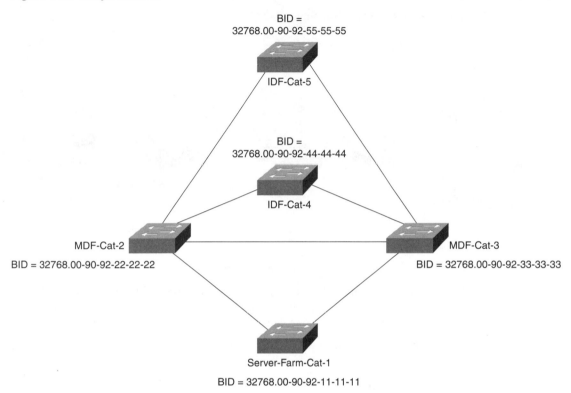

9 What happens to the network in Figure 6-26 if Cat-4 fails?

Figure 6-26 *Cat-4 Connects Two Groups of Switches*

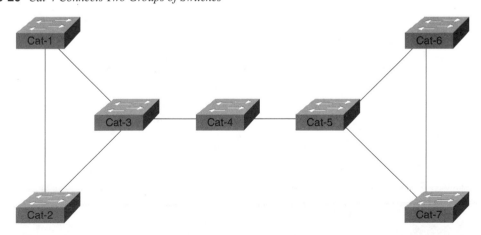

Hands-On Lab

Build a network that resembles Figure 6-27.

Figure 6-27 *Hands-On Lab Diagram*

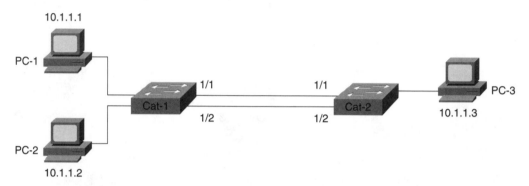

Using only VLAN 1, complete the following steps:

1 Start a continuous ping (tip: under Microsoft Windows, use the **ping -t** *ip_address* command) between PC-1 and PC-3. Break the link connecting PC-3 to Cat-2. After reconnecting the link, how long does it take for the pings to resume?

2 Start a continuous ping between PC-1 and PC-2. As in Step 1, break the link between PC-3 and Cat-2. Does this affect the traffic between PC-1 and PC-2?

3 Use the **show spantree** command on Cat-1 and Cat-2. What bridge is acting as the Root Bridge? Make a note of the state of all ports.

4 Why is the 1/2 port on the non-Root Bridge Blocking? How did the Catalyst know to block this port?

5 Start a continuous ping between PC-1 and PC-3. Break the 1/1 link connecting Cat-1 and Cat-2. How long before the traffic starts using the 1/2 link?

6 Reconnect the 1/1 link from Step 2. What happens? Why?

7 With the continuous ping from Step 3 still running, break the 1/2 link connecting Cat-1 and Cat-2. What effect does this have?

The authors would like to thank Radia Perlman for graciously contributing her time to review the material in this chapter.

This chapter covers the following key topics:

- **Typical Campus Design: A Baseline Network**—Introduces a baseline network for use throughout most of the chapter.

- **STP Behavior in the Baseline Network: A Spanning Tree Review**—Reviews the concepts introduced in Chapter 6, "Understanding Spanning Tree," while also introducing some advanced STP theory.

- **Spanning Tree Load Balancing**—Master this potentially confusing and poorly documented feature that can double available bandwidth for free. Four Spanning Tree load balancing techniques are discussed in detail.

- **Fast STP Convergence**—Seven techniques that can be used to improve on the default STP failover behavior of 30–50 seconds.

- **Useful STP Display Commands**—Several commands that can be extremely useful for understanding and troubleshooting STP's behavior in your network.

- **Per-VLAN Spanning Tree Plus (PVST+)**—An important feature introduced by Cisco, PVST+ allows interoperability between traditional per-VLAN Spanning Tree (PVST) Catalysts and devices that support 802.1Q.

- **Disabling STP**—Explains how to disable Spanning Tree on Catalyst devices. Also considers reasons why this might be done and why it shouldn't be done.

- **Tips and Tricks: Mastering STP**—A condensed listing of Spanning Tree advice to help you avoid STP problems in your network.

Advanced Spanning Tree

Chapter 6, "Understanding Spanning Tree," constructed a solid foundation of Spanning Tree knowledge. This chapter builds on that base by looking at a variety of advanced issues related to the Spanning-Tree Protocol (STP). After a quick review of some key points from Chapter 6, the discussion examines the important issue of load balancing. The techniques discussed in this section might allow you to double your available bandwidth in a redundant configuration without buying any new equipment! The chapter then discusses methods for improving Spanning Tree convergence and failover times. After a detailed look at some important show commands and new features, the chapter concludes with a section called "Tips and Tricks: Mastering STP." This information is designed to be a compendium of useful Spanning Tree information and best practices.

If you skipped Chapter 6, "Understanding Spanning Tree," consider that some of the techniques discussed in this chapter are not intuitively obvious. For example, a good understanding of STP basics is required to comprehend Spanning Tree load balancing. At the very least, I recommend that you do the exercises located at the end of Chapter 6. If these seem straightforward, by all means, continue. However, if they seem strange and mysterious, you might want to go back and read Chapter 6.

CAUTION   As with Chapter 6, the examples in this chapter are designed to illustrate the intricacies of the Spanning-Tree Protocol, *not good design practices.* For more information on Spanning Tree and campus design principles, please refer to Chapter 11, "Layer 3 Switching," Chapter 14, "Campus Design Models," Chapter 15, "Campus Design Implementation," and Chapter 17, "Case Studies: Implementing Switches."

Typical Campus Design: A Baseline Network

Chapter 14, "Campus Design Models," takes a detailed look at overall campus design principals. Although there are many options available when laying out a campus network, most are some variation of the network illustrated in Figure 7-1.

Figure 7-1 *Typical Design for a Single Building in a Switched Campus Network*

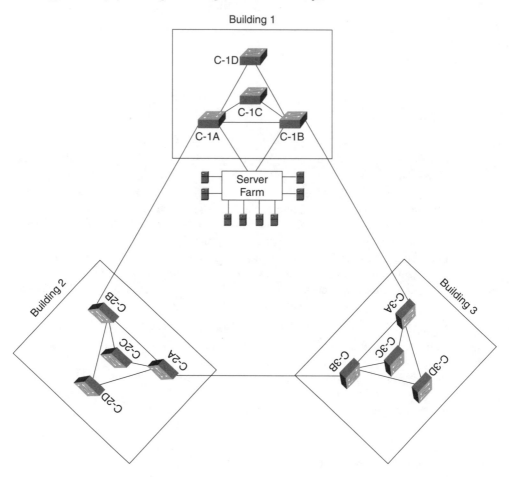

Figure 7-1 shows a network that might be contained within several buildings of a large campus environment. The PCs and workstations directly connect on one of the Intermediate Distribution Frame (IDF) switches located on every floor. These IDF switches also link to Main Distribution Frame (MDF) switches that are often located in the building's basement or ground floor. Because the MDF is carrying traffic for the entire building, it is usually provisioned with a pair of redundant switches for increased bandwidth and reliability. The MDF switches then connect to the rest of the campus backbone where a server farm is generally located.

By looking at this network from the point of view of a single IDF wiring closet, much of the complexity can be eliminated as shown in Figure 7-2.

Figure 7-2   *Typical Campus Network Simplified to Show a Single IDF*

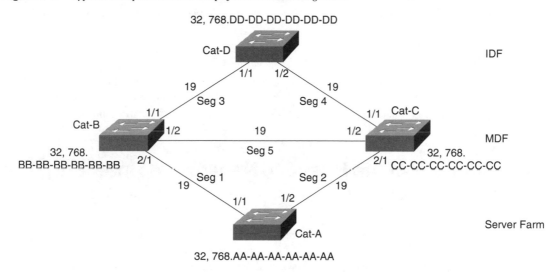

By reducing the clutter of multiple IDFs and MDFs, Figure 7-2 allows for a much clearer picture of what is happening at the Spanning Tree level and focuses on the fact that most campus designs utilize triangle-shaped STP patterns. (These patterns and their impact on campus design are discussed in detail during Chapters 14, 15, and 17.) Furthermore, because modern traffic patterns tend to be highly centralized, it eliminates the negligible level of IDF-to-IDF traffic present in most networks.

NOTE   Chapter 14 discusses the differences between two common campus design modules: the campus-wide VLANs model and the multilayer model. In campus-wide VLANs, the network consists of many large and overlapping triangle- and diamond-shaped patterns that can be simplified in the manner shown in Figure 7-2. Because these triangles and diamonds overlap and interconnect, it often leads to significant scaling problems. The multilayer model avoids these issues by using Layer 3 switching (routing) to break the network into many small triangles of Layer 2 connectivity. Because these triangles are isolated by the Layer 3 switching component, the network is invariably more scalable.

A detailed discussion of the differences between these two models is beyond the scope of this chapter. Obviously, consult Chapter 14 for more information. However, it is worth noting that this chapter often uses examples from the campus-wide VLANs model because they present more Spanning Tree challenges and opportunities. Nevertheless, you should generally consider using Layer 3 switching for reasons of scalability.

Cat-D in Figure 7-2 is an IDF switch that connects to a pair of MDF switches, Cat-B and Cat-C. The MDF switches connect through the campus backbone to a server farm switch, Cat-A.

TIP	Utilize this technique of simplifying the network when trying to understand STP in your network. When doing this, be sure to include paths where unusually heavy traffic loads are common. Having a modular design where a consistent layout is used throughout the network can make this much easier (see Chapters 14 and 15 for more information).

STP Behavior in the Baseline Network: A Spanning Tree Review

This section analyzes Spanning Tree's default behavior in a network such as that in Figure 7-2. Not only does this serve as a useful review of the material in Chapter 6, it provides a baseline network that can be used throughout the remainder of this chapter. In doing so, the text makes no attempt to be an exhaustive tutorial—it is only capturing the critical and easily missed aspects of the protocol (see Chapter 6 for a more complete discussion of Spanning Tree basics).

General BPDU Processing

Recall from Chapter 6 that bridges share information using Bridge Protocol Data Units (BPDUs). There are two types of BPDUs:

- **Configuration BPDUs**—Account for the majority of BPDU traffic and allow bridges to carry out STP elections
- **Topology Change Notification (TCN) BPDUs**—Assist in STP failover situations

When people use the term BPDU without indicating a specific type, they are almost always referring to a Configuration BPDU.

Determining the Best Configuration BPDU

Every bridge port running the Spanning-Tree Protocol saves a copy of the best Configuration BPDU it has seen. In doing this, the port not only considers every BPDU it receives from other bridges, but it also evaluates the BPDU that it would send out that port.

To determine the best Configuration BPDU, STP uses a four-step decision sequence as follows:

Step 1 The bridges look for the lowest Root Bridge Identifier (BID), an eight-byte field composed of a Bridge Priority and a Media Access Control (MAC) address. This allows the entire bridged network to elect a single Root Bridge.

Step 2   The bridges consider Root Path Cost, the cumulative cost of the path to the Root Bridge. Every non-Root Bridge uses this to locate a single, least-cost path to the Root Bridge.

Step 3   If the cost values are equal, the bridges consider the BID of the sending device.

Step 4   Port ID (a unique index value for every port in a bridge or switch) is evaluated if all three of the previous criteria tie.

TIP   A shortened, easy-to-remember outline of the four-step STP decision sequence to determine the best Configuration BPDU is as follows:

Step 1   Lowest Root BID

Step 2   Lowest Root Path Cost

Step 3   Lowest Sending BID

Step 4   Lowest Port ID

As long as a port sees its own Configuration BPDU as the most attractive, it continues sending Configuration BPDUs. A port begins this process of sending Configuration BPDUs in what is called the *Listening* state. Although BPDU processing is occurring during the Listening state, no user traffic is being passed. After waiting for a period of time defined by the Forward Delay parameter (default=15 seconds), the port moves into the *Learning* state. At this point, the port starts adding source MAC addresses to the bridging table, but all incoming data frames are still dropped. After another period equal to the Forward Delay, the port finally moves into the *Forwarding* state and begins passing end-user data traffic. However, if at any point during this process the port hears a more attractive BPDU, it immediately transitions into the *Blocking* state and stops sending Configuration BPDUs.

Converging on an Active Topology

Configuration BPDUs allow bridges to complete a three-step process to initially converge on an active topology:

Step 1   Elect a *single Root Bridge* for the entire Spanning Tree domain.

Step 2   Elect *one Root Port* for *every non-Root Bridge*.

Step 3   Elect *one Designated Port* for *every segment*.

First, the bridges elect a single Root Bridge by looking for the device with the lowest Bridge ID (BID). By default, all bridges use a Bridge Priority of 32,768, causing the lowest MAC address to win this Root War. In the case of Figure 7-2, Cat-A becomes the Root Bridge.

Second, every non-Root Bridge elects a single Root Port, its port that is closest to the Root Bridge. Cat-B has to choose between three ports: Port 1/1 with a Root Path Cost of 57, Port 1/2 with a cost of 38, or Port 2/1 with a cost of 19. Obviously, Port 2/1 is the most attractive and becomes the Root Port. Similarly, Cat-C chooses Port 2/1. However, Cat-D calculates a Root Path Cost of 38 on both ports—a tie. This causes Cat-D to evaluate the third decision criterion—the *Sending BID*. Because Cat-B has a lower Sending BID than Cat-C, Cat-D:Port-1/1 becomes the Root Port.

Finally, a Designated Port is elected for every LAN segment (the device containing the Designated Port is referred to as the *Designated Bridge*). By functioning as the only port that both sends and receives traffic to/from that segment and the Root Bridge, Designated Ports are the mechanism that actually implement a loop-free topology. It is best to analyze Designated Port elections on a per-segment basis. In Figure 7-2, there are five segments. Segment 1 is touched by two bridge ports—Cat-A:Port-1/1 at a cost of zero and Cat-B:Port-2/1 at a cost of 19. Because the directly-connected Root Bridge has a cost of zero, Cat-A:Port-1/1 obviously becomes the Designated Port. A similar process elects Cat-A:Port-1/2 as the Designated Port for Segment 2. Segment 3 also has two bridge ports: Cat-B:Port-1/1 at a cost of 19 and Cat-D:Port-1/1 at a cost of 38. Because it has the lower cost, Cat-B:Port-1/1 becomes the Designated Port. Using the same logic, Cat-C:Port-1/1 becomes the Designated Port for Segment 4. In the case of Segment 5, there are once again two options (Cat-B:Port-1/2 and Cat-C:Port-1/2), however both are a cost of 19 away from the Root Bridge. By applying the third decision criterion, both bridges determine that Cat-B:Port-1/2 should become the Designated Port because it has the lower Sending BID.

Figure 7-3 shows the resulting active topology and port states.

Figure 7-3   *Active Topology and Port States in the Baseline Network*

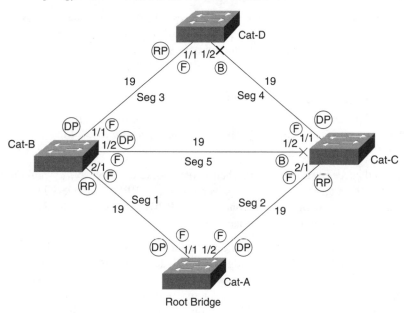

Two ports remain in the Blocking state: Cat-C:Port-1/2 and Cat-D:Port-1/2. These ports are often referred to as *non-Designated Ports*. They provide a loop-free path from every segment to every other segment. The Designated Ports are used to send traffic away from the Root Bridge, whereas Root Ports are used to send traffic toward the Root Bridge.

NOTE   From a technical perspective, it is possible to debate the correct ordering of Steps 2 and 3 in what I have called the 3-Step Spanning Tree Convergence Process. Because 802.1D (the Spanning Tree standards document) specifically excludes Designated Ports from the Root Port election process, the implication is that Designated Ports must be determined first. However, 802.1D also lists the Root Port selection process before the Designated Port selection process in its detailed pseudo-code listing of the complete STP algorithm. This text avoids such nerdy debates. The fact of the matter is that both occur constantly and at approximately the same time. Therefore, from the perspective of learning how the protocol operates, the order is irrelevant.

In addition to determining the path and direction of data forwarding, Root and Designated Ports also play a key role in the sending of BPDUs. In short, Designated Ports send Configuration BPDUs, whereas Root Ports send TCN BPDUs. The following sections explore the two types of BPDUs in detail.

Configuration BPDU Processing

Configuration BPDUs are sent in three cases. The discussion that follows breaks these into two categories, normal processing and exception processing. (This terminology is non-standard, but useful for understanding how STP works.)

Normal Configuration BPDU Processing

Normal processing occurs every Hello Time seconds on all ports of the Root Bridge (unless there is a physical layer loop). This results in the *origination* of Configuration BPDUs at the Root Bridge.

Normal processing also occurs when a non-Root Bridge receives a Configuration BPDU on its Root Port and sends an updated version of this BPDU out every Designated Port. This results in the *propagation* of Configuration BPDUs away from the Root Bridge and throughout the entire Layer 2 network.

These two conditions account for the normal flow of Configuration BPDUs that constantly stream away from the Root Bridge during steady state processing. The Root Bridge originates Configuration BPDUs on its Designated Ports every two seconds (the default value of Hello Time). Note that every active port on the Root Bridge should be a Designated Port unless there is a physical layer loop to multiple ports on this bridge. As these Configuration BPDUs arrive at the Root Ports of downstream bridges, these bridges then propagate Configuration BPDUs on their Designated Ports. Figure 7-4 illustrates how this process propagates Configuration BPDUs away from the Root Bridge.

Figure 7-4   *Normal Sending of Configuration BPDUs*

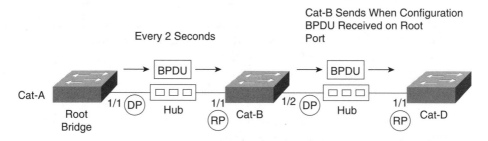

Figure 7-4 shows Cat-A, the Root Bridge, originating Configuration BPDUs every two seconds. As these arrive on Cat-B:Port-1/1 (the Root Port for Cat-B), Configuration BPDUs are sent out Cat-B's Designated Ports, in this case Port 1/2.

Several observations can be made about the normal processing of Configuration BPDUs:

- Configuration BPDUs flow away from the Root Bridge.
- Root Ports receive Configuration BPDUs.

- Root Ports do not send Configuration BPDUs.

- Blocking ports do not send Configuration BPDUs.

- If the Root Bridge fails, Configuration BPDUs stop flowing throughout the network. This absence of Configuration BPDUs continues until another bridge's Max Age timer expires and starts taking over as the new Root Bridge.

- If the path to the Root Bridge fails (but the Root Bridge is still active), Configuration BPDUs stop flowing downstream of the failure. If an alternate path to the Root Bridge is available, this absence of Configuration BPDUs continues until another path is taken out of the Blocking state. If an alternate path to the Root Bridge is not available, the bridged network has been partitioned and a new Root Bridge is elected for the isolated segment of the network.

Therefore, under the normal behavior, a non-Root Bridge only sends Configuration BPDUs when a Root Bridge-originated BPDU arrives on its Root Port.

Exception Configuration BPDU Processing

Exception Configuration BPDU processing, by contrast to normal processing, occurs when a Designated Port hears an inferior BPDU from some other device and sends a Configuration BPDU in response. The Spanning Tree algorithm includes this exception processing to squelch less attractive information as quickly as possible and speed convergence. For example, consider Figure 7-5 where the Root Bridge failed (Step 1 in the figure) just before Cat-C was connected to the Ethernet hub (Step 2 in the figure).

Figure 7-5 *The Root Bridge Failed Just Before Cat-C Was Connected*

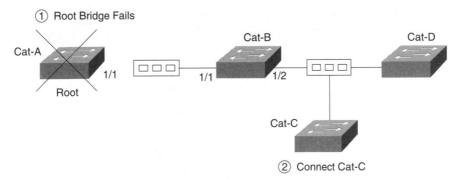

Figure 7-6 illustrates the conversation that ensues between Cat-C and Cat-B.

Figure 7-6   *Exception Processing of Configuration BPDUs*

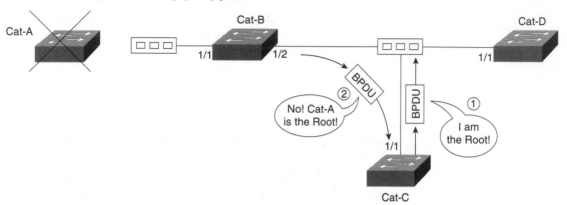

As discussed in Chapter 6, Cat-C initially assumes it is the Root Bridge and immediately starts sending BPDUs to announce itself as such. Because the Root Bridge is currently down, Cat-B:Port-1/2 has stopped sending Configuration BPDUs as a part of the normal processing. However, because Cat-B:Port-1/2 is the Designated Port for this segment, it immediately responds with a Configuration BPDU announcing Cat-A as the Root Bridge. By doing so, Cat-B prevents Cat-C from accidentally trying to become the Root Bridge or creating loops in the active topology.

The sequence illustrated in Figure 7-6 raises the following points about Configuration BPDU exception processing:

- Designated Ports can respond to inferior Configuration BPDUs at any time.

- As long as Cat-B saves a copy of Cat-A's information, Cat-B continues to refute any inferior Configuration BPDUs.

- Cat-A's information ages out on Cat-B in Max Age seconds (default=20 seconds). In the case of Figure 7-5, Cat-B begins announcing itself as the Root Bridge at that time.

- By immediately refuting less attractive information, the network converges more quickly. Consider what might happen if Cat-B only used the normal conditions to send a Configuration BPDU—Cat-C would have 20 seconds to incorrectly assume that it was functioning as the Root Bridge and might inadvertently open up a bridging loop. Even if this did not result in the formation of a bridging loop, it could lead to unnecessary Root and Designated Port elections that could interrupt traffic and destabilize the network.

- Because Cat-D:Port-1/1 is not the Designated Port for this segment, it does not send a Configuration BPDU to refute Cat-C.

TIP   Configuration BPDUs are sent in three cases:

- When the Hello Timer expires (every two seconds by default), the Root Bridge originates a Configuration BPDU on every port (assuming no self-looped ports). This is a part of the normal Configuration BPDU processing.

- When non-Root Bridges receive a Configuration BPDU on their Root Port, they send (propagate) updated Configuration BPDUs on all of their Designated Ports (normal processing).

- When a Designated Port hears an inferior Configuration BPDU from another switch, it sends a Configuration BPDU of its own to suppress the less attractive information.

TCN BPDU Processing

Whereas Configuration BPDUs are the general workhorse of the STP algorithm, TCN BPDUs perform a very specific role by assisting in network recovery after changes in the active topology. When a non-Root Bridge detects a change in the active topology, a TCN BPDU is propagated upstream through the network until the Root Bridge is reached. The Root Bridge then tells every bridge in the network to shorten their bridge table aging periods from 300 seconds to the interval specified by Forward Delay. In other words, TCN BPDUs are used to tell the Root Bridge that the topology has changed so that Configuration BPDUs can be used to tell every other bridge of the event.

TCN BPDUs are sent in three cases. It is useful to group these into two categories, change detection and propagation:

- **Change detection**—Occurs in the event that a bridge port is put into the Forwarding state and the bridge has at least one Designated Port. Change detection also occurs when a port in the Forwarding or Learning states transitions to the Blocking state.

- **Propagation**—Occurs in the event that a non-Root Bridge receives a TCN (from a downstream bridge) on a Designated Port.

The first two conditions categorized under change detection constitute a change in the active topology that needs to be reflected in bridging tables throughout the network. The last condition is used to propagate TCN BPDUs up through the branches of the Spanning Tree until they reach the Root Bridge.

TIP

TCN BPDUs are sent in three cases:

- When a port is put in the Forwarding state and the bridge has at least one Designated Port (this is a part of change detection).

- When a port is transitioned from the Forwarding or Learning states back to the Blocking state (change detection).

- When a TCN BPDU is received on Designated Port, it is forwarded out the bridge's Root Port (propagation).

Several observations can be made about TCN BPDUs:

- TCN BPDUs are only sent out Root Ports.

- TCN BPDUs are the only BPDUs sent out Root Ports (Configuration BPDUs are only sent out Designated Ports, not Root Ports).

- TCN BPDUs are received by Designated Ports.

- TCN BPDUs flow upstream toward the Root Bridge.

- TCN BPDUs use a reliable mechanism to reach the Root Bridge. When a bridge sends a TCN BPDU, it continues repeating the BPDU every Hello Time seconds until the upstream bridge acknowledges receipt with a Topology Change Acknowledgement flag in a Configuration BPDU. TCN BPDUs are not periodic in the same sense as Configuration BPDUs. Other than the retransmission of already generated TCN BPDUs discussed in the previous bullet and used as a reliability mechanism, *completely new* TCN BPDUs are not sent until the next topology change occurs (this could be hours, days, or weeks later).

- TCN BPDUs are acknowledged even if the normal Configuration BPDU processing discussed earlier has stopped (because the flow of Configuration BPDUs from the Root Bridge has stopped flowing).

TIP

The TCN process is discussed in considerably more detail in Chapter 6 (see the section "Topology Change Notification BPDUs").

STP Timers

The Spanning-Tree Protocol provides three user-configurable timers: Hello Time, Forward Delay, and Max Age. To avoid situations where each bridge is using a different set of timer values, all bridges adopt the values specified by the Root Bridge. The current Root Bridge places its timer values in the last three fields of every Configuration BPDU it sends. Other bridges do not alter these values as the BPDUs propagate throughout the network. Therefore, timer values can only be adjusted on Root Bridges.

TIP	Avoid the frustration of trying to modify timer values from non-Root Bridges—they can only be changed from the Root Bridge. However, do not forget to modify the timer values on any backup Root Bridges so that you can keep a consistent set of timers even after a primary Root Bridge failure.

The *Hello Time timer* is used to control the sending of BPDUs. Its main duty is to control how often the Root Bridge originates Configuration BPDUs; however, it also controls how often TCN BPDUs are sent. By repeating TCN BPDUs every Hello Time seconds until a Topology Change Acknowledgement (TCA) flag is received from the upstream bridge, TCN BPDUs are propagated using a reliable mechanism. 802.1D, the Spanning Tree standard document, specifies an allowable range 1–10 seconds for Hello Time. The syntax for changing the Hello Time is as follows (see the section "Lowering Hello Time to One Second" for more information):

```
set spantree hello interval [vlan]
```

The *Forward Delay timer* primarily controls the length of time a port spends in the Listening and Learning states. It is also used in other situations related to the topology change process. First, when the Root Bridge receives a TCN BPDU, it sets the Topology Change (TC) flag for Forward Delay+Max Age seconds. Second, this action causes all bridges in the network to shorten their bridge table aging periods from 300 seconds to Forward Delay seconds. Valid Forward Delay values range from 4–30 seconds with the default being 15 seconds. To change the Forward Delay, use the following command (see the section "Tuning Forward Delay" for more information):

```
set spantree fwddelay delay [vlan]
```

The *Max Age timer* controls the maximum length of time that a bridge port saves Configuration BPDU information. This allows the network to revert to a less attractive topology when the more attractive topology fails. As discussed in the previous paragraph, Max Age also plays a role in controlling how long the TC flag remains set after the Root Bridge receives a TCN BPDU. Valid Max Age values are 6 to 40 seconds with the default being 20 seconds. The command for changing the Max Age time is shown in the following (see the section "Tuning Max Age" for more information):

```
set spantree maxage agingtime [vlan]
```

Configuration BPDUs also pass a fourth time-related value, the Message Age field (don't confuse this with Max Age). The Message Age field is not a periodic timer value—it contains the length of time since a BPDU's information was first originated at the Root Bridge. When Configuration BPDUs are originated by the Root Bridge, the Message Age field contains the value zero. As other bridges propagate these BPDUs through the network, the Message Age field is incremented by one at every bridge hop. Although 802.1D allows for more precise timer control, in practice, bridges simply add one to the existing value, resulting in something akin to a reverse TTL. If connectivity to the Root Bridge fails and all normal Configuration BPDU processing stops, this field can be used to track the age of any information that is sent during this outage as a part of Configuration BPDU exception processing discussed earlier.

The Spanning-Tree Protocol also uses a separate Hold Time value to prevent excessive BPDU traffic. The Hold Time determines the minimum time between the sending of any two back-to-back Configuration BPDUs on a given port. It prevents a cascade effect of where BPDUs spawn more and more other BPDUs. This parameter is fixed at a non-configurable value of one second.

How Far Does Spanning Tree Reach?

It is important to note the impact of placing routers (or Layer 3 switches) in a campus network. Figure 7-7 illustrates an example.

Figure 7-7   *A Network Consisting of Two Bridge Domains*

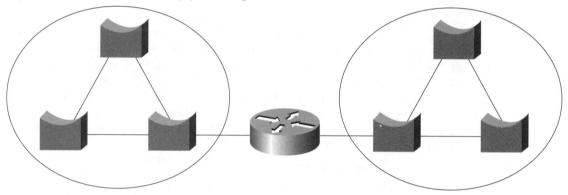

Each half in this network has a completely independent Spanning Tree. For example, each half elects a single Root Bridge. When a topology change occurs on the left side of the network, it has no effect on the right side of the network (at least from a Spanning Tree perspective). As Chapter 14, "Campus Design Models," discusses, you should strive to use Layer 3 routers and Layer 2 switches together to maximize the benefit that this sort of separation can have on the stability and scalability of your network.

On the other hand, routers do not always break a network into separate Spanning Trees. For example, there could be a backdoor connection that allows the bridged traffic to bypass the router as illustrated in Figure 7-8.

Figure 7-8   *Although This Network Contains a Router, It Represents a Single Bridge Domain*

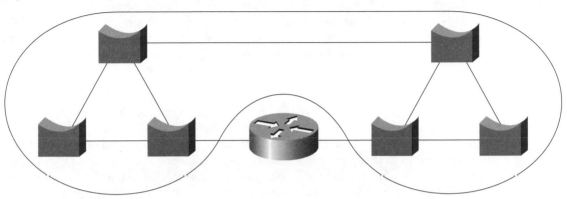

In this case, there is a single, contiguous, Layer 2 domain that is used to bypass the router. The network only elects a single Root Bridge, and topology changes can create network-wide disturbances.

TIP   By default, Route Switch Modules (RSMs) (and other router-on-a-stick implementations) do *not* partition the network as shown in Figure 7-7. This can *significantly* limit the scalability and stability of the network. See Chapter 11, "Layer 3 Switching," Chapter 14, "Campus Design Models," and Chapter 15, "Campus Design Implementation," for more information.

As Chapter 6 explained, Cisco uses a separate instance of Spanning Tree for each VLAN (per-VLAN Spanning Tree—PVST). This provides two main benefits: control and isolation.

Spanning Tree control is critical to network design. It allows each VLAN to have a completely independent STP configuration. For example, each VLAN can have the Root Bridge located in a different place. Cost and Priority values can be tuned on a per-VLAN basis. Per-VLAN control allows the network designer total flexibility when it comes to optimizing data flows within each VLAN. It also makes possible Spanning Tree load balancing, the subject of the next section.

Spanning Tree isolation is critical to the troubleshooting and day-to-day management of your network. It prevents Spanning Tree topology changes in one VLAN from disturbing other VLANs. If a single VLAN loses its Root Bridge, connectivity should not be interrupted in other VLANs.

Although Spanning Tree processing is isolated between VLANs, don't forget that a loop in a single VLAN can saturate your trunk links and starve out resources in other VLANs. This can quickly lead to a death spiral that brings down the entire network. See Chapter 15 for more detail and specific recommendations for solving this nasty problem.

However, there are several technologies that negate the control and isolation benefits of PVST. First, standards-based 802.1Q specifies a single instance of Spanning Tree for all VLANs. Therefore, if you are using vanilla 802.1Q devices, you lose all of the advantages offered by PVST. To address this limitation, Cisco developed a feature called PVST+ that is discussed later in this chapter. Second, bridging between VLANs defeats the advantages of PVST by merging the multiple instances of Spanning Tree into a single tree.

NOTE   Although the initial version of 802.1Q only specified a single instance of the Spanning-Tree Protocol, future enhancements will likely add support for multiple instances. At presstime, this issue was being explored in the IEEE 802.1s committee.

To avoid the confusion introduced by these issues and exceptions, it is often useful to employ the term *Spanning Tree domain*. Each Spanning Tree domain contains its own set of STP calculations, parameters, and BPDUs. Each Spanning Tree domain elects a single Root Bridge and converges on one active topology. Topology changes in one domain do not effect other domains (other than the obvious case of shared equipment failures). The term Spanning Tree domain provides a consistent nomenclature that can be used to describe STP's behavior regardless of whether the network is using any particular technology.

Spanning Tree Load Balancing

The previous section discussed the concepts of PVST and how it allows Spanning Tree isolation and control. One of the most important benefits of this isolation and control is load balancing, the capability to utilize multiple active paths.

There is both good and bad news associated with load balancing. The good news is that it can be used to effectively double your network's throughput. The bad news is that it can triple the complexity to your network! Although I might be exaggerating a bit, the added complexity can be especially burdensome in a poorly designed network (see Chapters 14 and 15 for more information). This section takes a detailed look at the techniques that are available for implementing this advanced feature. By examining the theory behind each feature, you will be well equipped to maximize your available bandwidth with minimal added complexity.

It is important to realize that the term load balancing is a bit of a euphemism. In reality, Spanning Tree load balancing almost never achieves an even distribution of traffic across the available links. However, by allowing the use of more than one path, it can have a significant impact on your network's overall performance. Although some people prefer to use terms such as load distribution or load sharing, this text uses the more common term of load balancing.

There are four primary techniques for implementing Spanning Tree load balancing on Catalyst gear. Table 7-1 lists all four along with the primary command used to implement each.

Table 7-1   *Techniques for Spanning Tree Load Balancing*

Technique	Command
Root Bridge Placement	set spantree priority
Port Priority	set spantree portvlanpri
Bridge Priority	set spantree priority
Port Cost	set spantree portvlancost

Each of these is discussed in the separate sections that follow. Note that the discussion only addresses load balancing techniques based on the Spanning-Tree Protocol. For a discussion of non-STP load balancing techniques, see Chapter 11 and Chapter 15.

General Principles of Spanning Tree Load Balancing

Spanning Tree load balancing requires that two characteristics be built into the network:

- Multiple paths that form loops
- Multiple VLANs

If the network doesn't contain loops, there cannot be multiple paths over which the load can be distributed. By way of illustration, if two switches only have one Fast Ethernet link between them, it is fairly difficult to do any load balancing. This concept is obviously tightly coupled with the desire to have redundancy in campus networks. For example, most networks employ at least two links to every IDF wiring closet to meet reliability and availability requirements even if the bandwidth requirements are low. However, after the redundant paths are available, the question becomes, "How do you make use of them?" In fact, load balancing is all about having the best of both worlds—redundancy *and* speed.

However, if loops exist in the network, isn't Spanning Tree designed to remove them from the active topology? In other words, how can you use multiple paths if Spanning Tree prunes the network back to a single set of paths that reach from every location to every other location? Well, with only one Spanning Tree domain, you can't. On the other hand, VLANs make it possible to create multiple Spanning Tree domains over a single physical infrastructure. By intentionally designing different active topologies into each VLAN, you can utilize multiple redundant paths. Within a single VLAN, the traffic is loop free and only utilizes a single path to reach each destination. But two VLANs can use both redundant links that you have installed to a wiring closet switch.

For example, consider Figure 7-9, a variation of the simplified campus network used in Figure 7-2.

Figure 7-9   *A Simplified Campus Network*

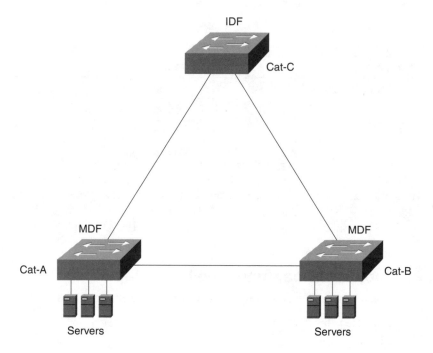

In this version of the simplified campus network, the campus backbone has been eliminated so that the entire network is contained within a single building. Instead of locating the server farm in a separate building, the servers have been moved to the MDF closets. Redundant links have been provided to the IDF switches (only one IDF is shown). Assume that the wiring closet switch only supports 20 users that rarely generate more than 100 Mbps of traffic. From a bandwidth perspective, a single riser link could easily handle the load. However, from a redundancy perspective, this creates a single point of failure that most organizations are not willing to accept. Given the assumption that corporate policy dictates multiple links to every wiring closet, wouldn't it be nice to have all the links available for carrying traffic? After all, after both links have been installed, Spanning Tree load balancing can potentially double the available bandwidth for free! Having three paths to every closet is indicative of two things: You work for a really paranoid organization and you can possibly *triple* your bandwidth for free!

Even when redundant links are available, don't overlook the second STP requirement for Spanning Tree load balancing—multiple VLANs. Many organizations prefer to place a single VLAN on each switch to ease VLAN administration. However, this is in conflict with the goal of maximizing bandwidth through load balancing. Just remember—one VLAN=one active path. This is not meant to suggest that it's wrong to place a single VLAN on a switch, just that it prevents you from implementing Spanning Tree load balancing.

TIP   If you only place a single VLAN on a switch, you cannot implement Spanning Tree load balancing. Either add VLANs or consider other load balancing techniques such as EtherChannel or MHSRP. See Chapter 11 and Chapter 15 for more information.

Root Bridge Placement Load Balancing

Fortunately, one of the most effective load balancing techniques is also the simplest. By carefully placing the Root Bridge for each VLAN in different locations, data can be forced to follow multiple paths. Each VLAN looks for the shortest path to its Root Bridge.

For example, Figure 7-10 adds load balancing to the network in Figure 7-9.

Figure 7-10 *Load Balancing through Root Bridge Placement*

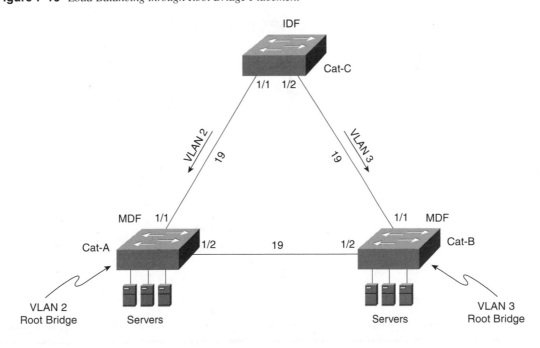

This network contains two VLANs. Cat-A is the Root Bridge for VLAN 2, and Cat-B is the Root Bridge for VLAN 3. From Cat-C's perspective, the available bandwidth to the servers has been doubled. First, examine VLAN 2. Cat-C has two possible paths to the Root Bridge: Cat-C:Port-1/1 can reach the Root Bridge with a cost of 19, whereas Cat-C:Port-1/2 can get there at a cost of 38. Obviously, Port 1/1 is chosen as Cat-C's Root Port for VLAN 2. VLAN 3 also has two paths to the Root Bridge, but this time the costs are reversed: 38 through Port 1/1 and 19 through Port 1/2. Therefore, VLAN 3's traffic uses Cat-C:Port-1/2. Both links are active and carrying traffic. However, if either link fails, Spanning Tree places all bandwidth on the remaining link to maintain connectivity throughout the network.

Root Bridge Placement in Hierarchical Networks

The advantage of Root Bridge placement load balancing is that it can provide a simple yet effective increase in the network's aggregate bandwidth. This is especially true with networks that utilize Layer 3 switching in designs such as the multilayer model discussed in Chapters 14 and 15. In this case, the Root Bridges should simply be co-located (or located near) the routers serving as the default gateways. For example, Figure 7-11 uses this approach to load balancing traffic for VLANs 2 and 3.

Figure 7-11 *Co-locating Root Bridges with Default Gateways*

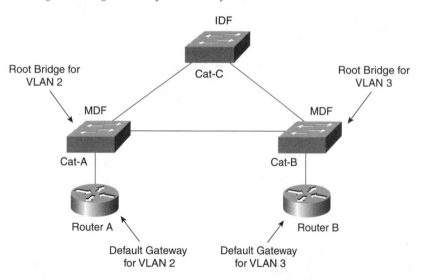

Not only has the load been distributed between the two routers (Router A is handling VLAN 2, whereas Router B is handling VLAN 3), the Layer 2 load has also been spread across both IDF uplinks. By placing the Root Bridge for VLAN 2 on Cat-A, the Spanning-Tree

Protocol automatically creates the best Layer 2 path to the default gateway, the first-hop destination of most traffic in modern campus networks. The same has been done with Cat-B and VLAN 3.

More information on this technique (including how to use HSRP for redundancy) is discussed in Chapter 11.

Root Bridge Placement in Flat Networks

Although Root Bridge placement is appropriate for most well-designed campus networks such as that shown in Figure 7-11, the disadvantage is that many topologies do not support this approach. This is especially true of non-hierarchical, flat-earth networks. In some of these networks, traffic patterns are not clearly enough defined (or understood) for this technique to be effective. In other cases, the traffic between the VLANs is too similar.

As Chapter 15 discusses, the general rule of thumb in non-hierarchical networks is that you should try to place your Root Bridges in the path of your high-volume traffic flows. In the case of flat-earth networks, this usually translates into locating the Root Bridges as close to your servers as possible. Because end-station-to-server farm traffic accounts for over 90 percent of the load on most modern networks, this approach causes Spanning Tree to look for the shortest paths where your load is heaviest. If you place the Root Bridge at the other end of the network from your server farm, the high-volume traffic might be forced to take a very inefficient path.

Therefore, the Root Bridge placement load balancing technique is most effective in flat-earth networks where there is a clearly defined server location for every VLAN. Simply place the Root Bridge on the server farm switches and Spanning Tree naturally looks for the most efficient path. Figure 7-12 illustrates such a network.

Figure 7-12 *Root Bridge Placement Load Balancing Requires Well-Defined Traffic Patterns*

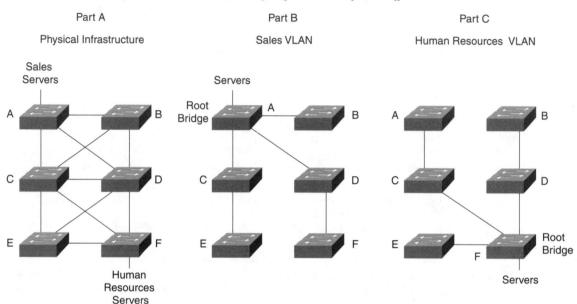

Part A of Figure 7-12 illustrates the physical topology and the location of servers. The Sales department has its servers attached to Cat-A, whereas the Human Resources department has connected their servers to Cat-F. Part B of Figure 7-12 shows the active topology for the Sales VLAN. By placing the Root Bridge at the servers, the Spanning Tree topology automatically mirrors the traffic flow. Part C of Figure 7-12 shows the active topology for the Human Resources VLAN. Again, the paths are optimal for traffic destined to the servers in that VLAN. Consider what happens if the Root Bridges for both VLANs are placed on Cat-F. This forces a large percentage of the Sales VLAN's traffic to take an inefficient path through Cat-F.

A potential problem with using this technique is that the traffic between the VLANs might be too similar. For example, what if a single server farm handles the entire network? You are left with two unappealing options. First, you could optimize the traffic flow by placing all of the Root Bridges at the server farm, but this eliminates all load balancing. Second, you could optimize for load balancing by distributing the Root Bridges, but this creates unnecessary bridge hops for traffic that is trying to reach the servers.

Implementing Root Bridge Placement

To implement Root Bridge placement load balancing, use the **set spantree priority** command discussed in the "Manual Root Bridge Placement: **set spantree priority**" section of Chapter 6. For instance, load balancing could be achieved in Figure 7-12 with the following commands:

```
Cat-A (enable) set spantree priority 100 2
Cat-F (enable) set spantree priority 100 3
```

The first command lowers the Bridge Priority on Cat-A to 100 for VLAN 2 (the Sales VLAN) so that it wins the Root Bridge election. In a similar fashion, the second command configures Cat-F to be the Root Bridge for VLAN 3 (the Human Resources VLAN).

Port/VLAN Priority Load Balancing

Another topology where Root Bridge placement load balancing does not work is with back-to-back switches or bridges. For example, consider Figure 7-13.

Figure 7-13 *Back-to-Back Switches Cannot Use Root Bridge Placement Load Balancing*

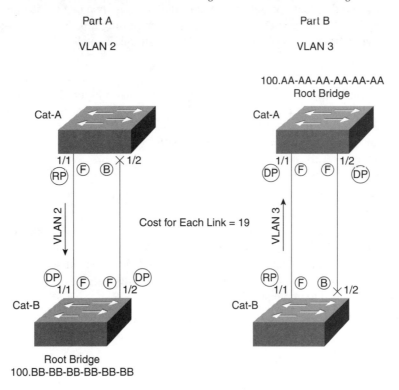

First, examine VLAN 2 as shown in Part A. Cat-A needs to pick a single Root Port to reach Cat-B, the Root Bridge for VLAN 2. As soon as Cat-A recognizes Cat-B as the Root Bridge, Cat-A begins evaluating Root Path Cost. Because both Cat-A:Port-1/1 and Cat-A:Port-1/2 have a cost of 19 to the Root Bridge, there is a tie. In an effort to break the tie, Cat-A considers the Sending BID that it is receiving over both links. However, both ports are connected to the same bridge, causing Cat-A to receive the same Sending BID (100.BB-BB-BB-BB-BB-BB) on both links. This results in another tie. Finally, Cat-A evaluates the Port ID values received in Configuration BPDUs on both ports. Cat-A:Port-1/1 is receiving a Port ID of 0x8001, and Cat-A:Port-1/2 is receiving a Port ID of 0x8002. Cat-A chooses the lower value for a Root Port, causing it to send all traffic out Port 1/1 while Blocking on Port 1/2.

With VLAN 3 in Part B of Figure 7-13, the roles are reversed but the outcome is the same—all traffic is passing over the left link. In this case, it is Cat-B that must elect a Root Port to reach the Root Bridge, Cat-A. Cat-B calculates identical values for Root Path Cost and Sending BID as discussed in the previous paragraph. To resolve the resulting tie, Cat-B evaluates the received Port ID values, chooses Port 1/1 as the Root Port, and places Port 1/2 in the Blocking state.

Although the Root Port selection and traffic flow is happening in the opposing direction, both switches have selected Port 1/1 as the Forwarding link. The result—the left link is carrying 100 percent of the traffic, and the right link is totally idle.

NOTE   Note that it is possible to implement load balancing in Figure 7-13 by crossing the cables such that Cat-B:Port-1/1 connects to Cat-A:Port-1/2 and Cat-B:Port-1/2 connects to Cat-A:Port-1/1. However, this approach is not very scalable and can be difficult to implement in large networks. Exercise 1 at the end of this chapter explores this load balancing technique.

Although the network in Figure 7-13 fails to implement load balancing, it does raise two interesting points. First, notice that it is the *non-Root Bridge* that must implement load balancing. Recall that all ports on the Root Bridge become Designated Ports and enter the Forwarding state. Therefore, it is the non-Root Bridge that must select a single Root Port and place the other port in a Blocking state. It is precisely this decision process that must be influenced to implement load balancing.

Second, it is the *received values* that are being used here. Cat-A is *not* evaluating its own BID and Port ID; it is looking at the values contained in the BPDUs being received from Cat-B.

NOTE   There is one case where the local Port ID is used. As shown in Figure 7-14, imagine two ports on Cat-B connecting to a hub that also connects to Cat-A, the Root Bridge. In this case, the received Port ID is the same on both ports of Cat-B. To resolve the tie, Cat-B needs to evaluate its own local Port ID values (the lower Port ID becomes the Root Port). This topology is obviously fairly rare in modern networks and not useful for load balancing purposes.

Figure 7-14 *Using the Local Port ID Value As a Tie-Breaker*

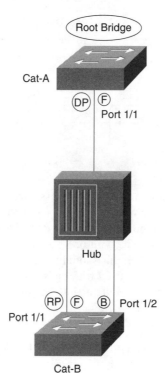

How can the load balancing be fixed in Figure 7-13? Given that Port ID is being used as decision criterion to determine which path to use, one strategy is to focus on influencing these Port ID values. On Catalysts using the XDI/CatOS interface (such as the Catalyst 4000s, 5000s, and 6000s), this can be done by applying the **set spantree portvlanpri** command. The full syntax for this command is

```
set spantree portvlanpri mod_num/port_num priority [vlans]
```

where *mod_num* is the slot number that a line card is using and *port_num* is the port on an individual line card.

As with the other **set spantree** and **show spantree** commands already discussed, the *vlans* parameter is optional. However, I suggest that you always code it so that you don't accidentally modify VLAN 1 (the default) one day.

The *priority* parameter can have the values ranging from 0 to 63, with 32 being the default. The *priority* parameter adjusts the Port ID field contained in every Configuration BPDU. Although the Port ID field is 16 bits in length, **set spantree portvlanpri** just modifies the high-order 6 bits of this field. In other words, Port ID consists of the two subfields shown in Figure 7-15.

Figure 7-15 *Port ID Is a 16-Bit Field Consisting of Two Subfields*

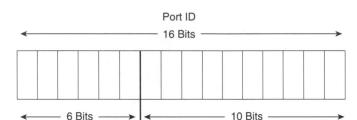

Port Number is a unique value statically assigned to every port: 1 for Port 1/1, 2 for Port 1/2, and so on (because number ranges are assigned to each slot, not all of the numbers are consecutive). Being 10 bits in length, the Port Number subfield can uniquely identify 2^{10}, or 1,024, different ports. The high-order 6 bits of the Port ID field hold the Port Priority subfield. As a 6-bit number, this subfield can mathematically hold $2^6=64$ values (0 to 63, the same values that can be used with the **set spantree portvlanpri** command). Because the Port Priority subfield is contained in the high-order bits of Port ID, lowering this value by even one (to 31 from the default of 32) causes that port to be preferred.

The overly observant folks in the crowd might notice that Cisco routers use a different range of Port Priority values than do Catalyst switches. Whereas Catalysts accept Port Priority values between 0 and 63, the routers accept any value between 0 and 255. This difference comes from the fact that the routers are actually using the values specified in the 802.1D standard. Unfortunately, the 802.1D scheme only uses 8 bits for the Port Number field, limiting devices to 256 ports (2^8). Although this is more than adequate for traditional routers, it is a significant issue for high-density switches such as the Catalyst 5500. By shifting the subfield boundary two bits, the Catalysts can accommodate the 1,024 ports calculated in the previous paragraph (2^{10}). Best of all, this difference is totally harmless— as long as every port has a unique Port ID, the Spanning-Tree Protocol is perfectly happy. In fact, as combined Layer 2/Layer 3 devices continue to grow in popularity and port densities continue to increase, this sort of modification to the 802.1D specification should become more common.

NOTE Starting in 12.0 IOS, the routers started using a subfield boundary that allows the Port Number subfield to be between 9 and 10 bits in length. This was done to support high-density bridging routers such as the 8540. The new scheme still allows Port Priority to be specified as an 8-bit value (0–255) and then the value is divided by either two (9-bit Port Number) or four (10-bit Port Number) to scale the value to the appropriate size.

How does all this bit-twiddling cause traffic to flow across multiple paths? Figure 7-16 redraws the VLANs originally presented in Figure 7-13 to locate the Root Bridge for both VLANs on Cat-B.

Figure 7-16 *Back-to-Back Switches: The Root Bridge for Both VLANs Is on Cat-B*

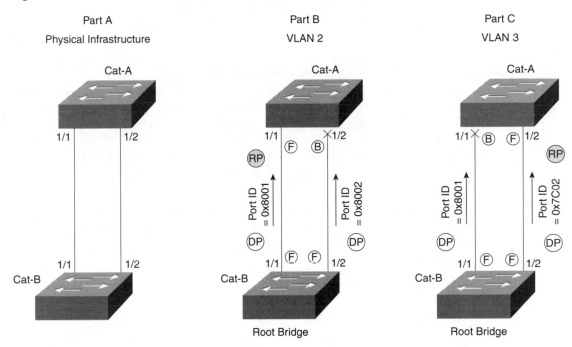

As was the case with Part A of Figure 7-13, the default Configuration BPDUs received on Port 1/1 of Cat-A contains a Port ID of 0x8001, but Port 1/2 receives the value 0x8002. Because 0x8001 is lower, Port 1/1 becames the Root Port for all VLANs by default. However, if you lower VLAN 3's Port Priority to 31 on Cat-B:Port-1/2, it lowers the Port ID that Cat-A:Port-1/2 receives for VLAN 3 to 0x7C01. Because 0x7C01 is less than 0x8001, Cat-A now elects Port 1/2 as the Root Port for VLAN 3 and sends traffic over this link. The syntax to implement this change is as follows:

```
Cat-B (enable) set spantree portvlanpri 1/2 31 3
```

Voilá, you have load balancing—VLAN 2 is using the left link and VLAN 3 is using the right link.

TIP	Note that the **portvlanpri** value must be less than the value specified by **portpri**.

By default, Cat-A is already sending traffic over the 1/1 link, so it is not necessary to add any commands to influence this behavior. However, it is probably a good idea to explicitly put in the command so that you can document your intentions and avoid surprises later:

```
Cat-B (enable) set spantree portvlanpri 1/1 31 2
```

This command lowers Cat-B's Port Priority on Port 1/1 to 31 for VLAN 2 and reinforces Cat-A's default behavior of sending traffic over this link for VLAN 2.

Precautions for Using Port/VLAN Priority Load Balancing

Notice that you must adjust the Port Priority on Cat-B to influence the load balancing on Cat-A. Adjusting the Port Priority on Cat-A has no effect as long as Cat-B is the Root Bridge. Recall that the Root Bridge is forwarding on all of its ports and therefore not making any load balancing decisions. This scheme of adjusting one switch's Port Priorities to influence another switch's load balancing is very counterintuitive. Just remember, to use port/VLAN priority load balancing, *you must adjust the upstream bridge* (the one closer to the Root Bridge, or, in this case, the Root Bridge itself).

Confusion can really set in when you take a look at the output of **show spantree** when using this form of load balancing. For example, Example 7-1 lists the output for VLAN 3 on Cat-A.

Example 7-1   **show spantree** *Output for VLAN 3 on Cat-A*

```
Cat-A (enable) show spantree 3
VLAN 3
Spanning tree enabled
Spanning tree type          ieee

Designated Root             00-e0-f9-16-28-00
Designated Root Priority    100
Designated Root Cost        19
Designated Root Port        1/2
Root Max Age   20 sec    Hello Time 2  sec   Forward Delay 15 sec

Bridge ID MAC ADDR          00-e0-f9-52-ba-00
Bridge ID Priority          32768
Bridge Max Age 20 sec    Hello Time 2  sec   Forward Delay 15 sec

Port      Vlan  Port-State      Cost   Priority  Fast-Start  Group-method
--------- ----  -------------   -----  --------  ----------  ------------
 1/1       1    blocking          19        32   disabled
 1/2       1    forwarding        19        32   disabled
```

As you might expect on a device performing load balancing, one port is forwarding and one is blocking (see the last two lines from Example 7-1). You can also observe that the load balancing is having the desired effect because Port 1/2 is the forwarding port. However, notice how the Port Priority is still set at 32. At first this might appear to be a bug. On the contrary, the Port Priority field of **show spantree** only shows the *outbound* Port Priority. To see the values Cat-A is *receiving*, you must look at Cat-B's outbound values as shown in Example 7-2.

Example 7-2 **show spantree** *Output for VLAN 3 on Cat-B*

```
Cat-B (enable) show spantree 3
VLAN 3
Spanning tree enabled
Spanning tree type          ieee

Designated Root             00-e0-f9-16-28-00
Designated Root Priority    100
Designated Root Cost        0
Designated Root Port        1/0
Root Max Age   20 sec    Hello Time 2  sec    Forward Delay 15 sec

Bridge ID MAC ADDR          00-e0-f9-16-28-00
Bridge ID Priority          100
Bridge Max Age 20 sec    Hello Time 2  sec    Forward Delay 15 sec

Port     Vlan  Port-State     Cost   Priority  Fast-Start  Group-method
-------- ----  -------------  -----  --------  ----------  ------------
 1/1      1    forwarding      19       32      disabled
 1/2      1    forwarding      19       31      disabled
```

There it is—Port 1/2's Priority has been set to 31. If you think about the theory behind using **set spantree portvlanpri**, this makes perfect sense. However, it's very easy to look for the value on Cat-A, the device actually doing the load balancing.

TIP   The received Port ID can be viewed on Cat-A with the **show spantree statistics** command. This feature is discussed in the "Useful STP Display Commands" section toward the end the chapter.

Keeping all of this straight is especially fun when you are trying to track down some network outage and the pressure is on! In fact, it is this counterintuitive nature of port/VLAN priority that makes it such a hassle to use.

As if the confusing nature of port/VLAN priority wasn't bad enough, **set spantree portvlanpri** can *only* be used in back-to-back situations. Recall that Port ID is evaluated last in the STP decision sequence. Therefore, for it to have any effect on STP's path sections, both Root Path Cost and Sending BID must be identical. Although identical Root Path Costs are fairly common, identical Sending BIDs only occur in one topology: back-to-back bridges. For example, look back at Figure 7-3. Cat-D never receives the same Sending BID on both links because they are connected to completely different switches, Cat-B and Cat-C. Modifying port/VLAN priority in this case has no effect on load balancing.

TIP   Don't use **set spantree portvlanpri** in the typical model where each IDF switch is connected to redundant MDF switches; it does not work.

Although port/VLAN priority is useful in back-to-back configurations, I recommend that you never use it for that purpose. Why? Because Cisco's EtherChannel technology provides much better performance. Not only does it offer faster failover response, but it often results in better load balancing. EtherChannel is discussed in Chapter 8, "Trunking between Catalysts."

TIP   Don't use **set spantree portvlanpri** with back-to-back configurations. Instead, use Fast or Gigabit EtherChannel.

Unfortunately, many documents simply present **set spantree portvlanpri** as *the* way to do load balancing in a switched network. By failing to mention its limitations and proper use (for example, that it should be coded on the upstream bridge), many users are led on a frustrating journey and never get load balancing to work.

Given all the downsides, why would anyone use port/VLAN priority load balancing? In general, Root Bridge placement and port/VLAN cost provide a much more intuitive, flexible, and easy-to-understand options. However, there are two cases where **set spantree portvlanpri** might be useful. First, if you are running pre-3.1 NMP code, the port/VLAN cost feature is not available. Second, you might be using back-to-back switches in a configuration where Etherchannel is not an option—for example, if you are using non-EtherChannel capable line cards in your Catalyst or the device at the other end of the link is from another vendor (God forbid!).

NOTE   The version numbers given in this chapter are for Catalyst 5000 NMP images. Currently, this is the same numbering scheme that the Catalyst 4000s and 6000s use. Other Cisco products might use different numbering schemes.

Finally, don't confuse **set spantree portvlanpri** with the **set spantree portpri** command. The **set spantree portpri** command allows you to modify the high-order 6 bits of the Port ID field; however, it modifies these bits for *all* VLANs on a particular port. This obviously does not support the sort of per-VLAN load balancing being discussed in this section. On the other hand, **set spantree portvlanpri** allows Port Priority to be adjusted on a per-port *and* per-VLAN basis.

NOTE   To save NVRAM storage space, **set spantree portvlanpri** only allows you to set a total of
two priority values for each port. One is the actual value specified on the **set spantree
portvlanpri** command line. The other is controlled through the **set spantree portpri**
command. This behavior can appear very strange to uninformed users. See the section
"Load Balancing with Port/VLAN Cost" for more detail (port/VLAN cost also suffers from
the same confusing limitation). However, this limitation rarely poses a problem in real-
world networks (in general, it is only required for back-to-back switches linked by more
than two links, a situation much better handled by EtherChannel).

Potential Issues in Real-World Networks

Before discussing the remaining two load balancing techniques, this section examines
issues that arise when trying to load balance in more complex campus networks. In doing
so, it demonstrates the potential ineffectiveness of Root Bridge placement and **set spantree
portvlanpri** load balancing as covered in previous sections.

Although Root Bridge placement and **set spantree portvlanpri** can be effective tools in
certain topologies, what if your network consists of two buildings that form a campus as
illustrated in Figure 7-17?

Figure 7-17 *A Campus Network where Root Bridge Placement and Port Priority Load Balancing Are Not Effective*

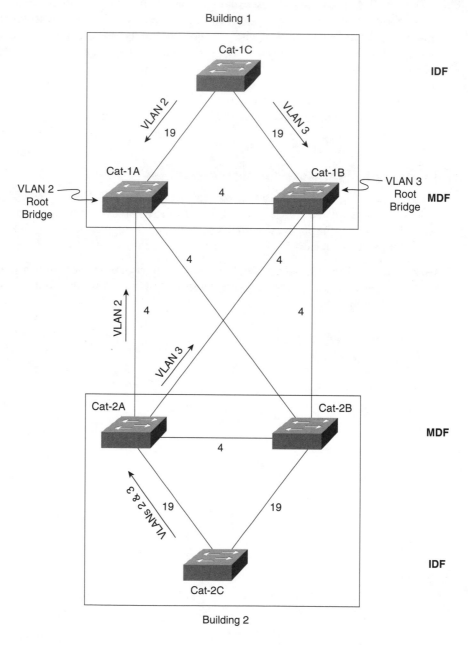

Figure 7-17 is a simplified diagram of a typical (but not necessarily recommended) campus design. In this design, VLANs 2 and 3 span all switches in both buildings. Each building consists of a pair of redundant MDF (Main Distribution Frame) switches in the main wiring closet. Both MDF switches connect to the IDF (Intermediate Distribution Frame) switches sitting on every floor (only one IDF switch in each building is shown to simplify the diagram). Link costs are also indicated (the IDF links are Fast Ethernet and MDF links are Gigabit Ethernet).

To implement load balancing, you cannot use the Port Priority load balancing technique because the switches are not back-to-back. How about using Root Bridge placement? To load balance in Building 1, you could place the Root Bridge for VLAN 2 on Cat-1A while placing the Root Bridge for VLAN 3 on Cat-1B. This causes VLAN 2's traffic to use the left riser link and VLAN 3's traffic to use the riser on the right. So far so good.

But what does this do to the traffic in Building 2? The IDF switch in Building 2 (Cat-2C) has several paths that it can use to reach the Root Bridge for VLAN 2 (Cat-1A). Which of these paths does it use? Well, refer back to the four-step STP decision criteria covered earlier. The first criterion evaluated is always the Root Bridge. Because everyone is in agreement that Cat-1A is the Root Bridge for VLAN 2, Cat-2C proceeds to the second criterion—Root Path Cost. One possibility is to follow the path Cat-2C to Cat-2B to Cat-2A to Cat-1A at a Root Path Cost of 27 (19+4+4). A better option is Cat-2C to Cat-2B to Cat-1A at a cost of 23 (19+4). However, path Cat-2C to Cat-2A to Cat-1A also has a Root Path Cost of 23 (19+4).

Because there are two paths tied for the lowest cost, Cat-2A proceeds to the third decision factor—Sending BID. Assume that both Cat-2A and Cat-2B are using the default Bridge Priority (32,768). Also assume that Cat-2A has a MAC address of AA-AA-AA-AA-AA-AA and Cat-2B has a MAC address of BB-BB-BB-BB-BB-BB. Because Cat-2A has the lower BID (32,768.AA-AA-AA-AA-AA-AA), all traffic for VLAN 2 uses the path Cat-2C to Cat-2A to Cat-1B.

OK, how about VLAN 3? Because all switches are in agreement that Cat-1B is the Root Bridge of VLAN 3, Root Path Cost is considered next. One option is to follow the path Cat-2C to Cat-2A to Cat-1A to Cat-1B at a cost of 27 (19+4+4). A better option is Cat-2C to Cat-2A to Cat-1B at a cost of 23 (19+4). However, again, there is an equal cost path along Cat-2C to Cat-2B to Cat-1B (cost =19+4=23). Cat-2C then evaluates the BIDs of Cat-2A and Cat-2B, choosing Cat-2A. VLAN 3 traffic therefore follows the path Cat-2C to Cat-2A to Cat-1B. This does provide load balancing across the campus core, but now both VLANs are using the same IDF riser cable. In other words, the load balancing in Building 1 destroyed the load balancing in Building 2.

Clearly, a new technique is required. Assuming that you want to maintain both VLANs across both buildings (I am using this assumption because it is a common design technique; however, in general, I recommend against it—see Chapter 14 for more details), there are two options:

- Bridge Priority
- Port/VLAN cost

Of these, port/VLAN cost is almost always the better option. However, because **set spantree portvlancost** was not available until 3.1 Catalyst images, the Bridge Priority technique is discussed first.

Bridge Priority Load Balancing

How can Bridge Priority be used to accomplish load balancing in the two-building campus illustrated in Figure 7-17? As discussed in the previous section, the IDF switch (Cat-2C) found multiple equal cost paths to the Root Bridge. This caused the third decision criterion, Bridge ID, to be evaluated. Because Cat-2A and Cat-2B were using the default Bridge ID values, Cat-2A had the lower BID for *all* VLANs (32,768.AA-AA-AA-AA-AA-AA versus 32,768.BB-BB-BB-BB-BB-BB). This is precisely what ruined the load balancing in Building 2.

Given this scenario, try lowering the BID on Cat-2B, but just for VLAN 3. For example, you could enter the following command on Cat-2B:

```
Cat-2B (enable) set spantree priority 1000 3
```

For consistency, you should also enter the following command on Cat-2A (although this command merely reinforces the default behavior, it helps document your intentions):

```
Cat-2A (enable) set spantree priority 1000 2
```

Figure 7-18 illustrates the resulting topology and traffic flows.

Figure 7-18 *Load Balancing Using Bridge Priority*

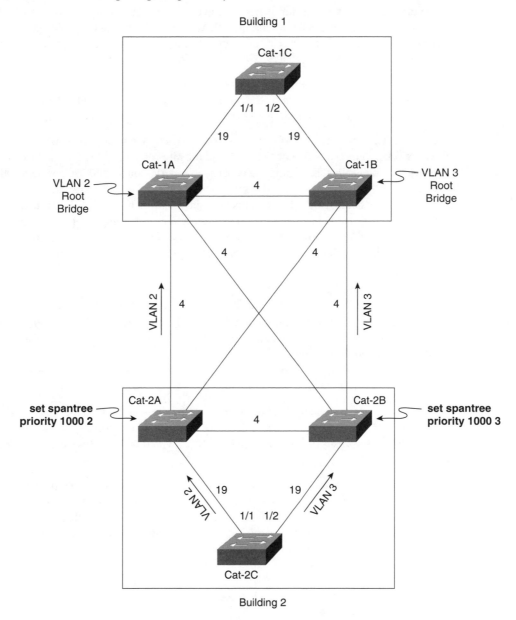

Note that these commands are adjusting Bridge Priority, not Port Priority. **set spantree portvlanpri**, the previous technique, was used to adjust Port Priority (the high-order 6 bits of the Port ID field) on a per-port and per-VLAN basis. On the contrary, Bridge Priority is a parameter that is global across all ports on a given switch, but it can be individually set for *each VLAN* on that switch.

"Wait a minute!" you exclaim. "Isn't this the same value I used to set the Root Bridge?" Yes, it is! The Bridge Priority must be low enough to influence the load balancing of traffic flows, but if it is too low, the bridge wins the Root War and disturbs the entire topology.

Picking the right balance of Port Priorities can be a tricky job in large, complex, and overly flat networks. In fact, it is one of the most significant problems associated with Bridge Priority load balancing. To maintain a consistent pattern, you should use a scheme such as 100, 200, 300,... to position your Root Bridges and 1000, 2000, 3000,... to influence load balancing. This numbering scheme helps you make your network self-documenting while also keeping the load balancing adjustments safely out of the range of the Root Bridge adjustments. This approach assumes that you don't have more than eight backup Root Bridges (if that's not the case, you probably have bigger problems than worrying about load balancing!).

TIP

Use a Bridge Priority numbering scheme that clearly delineates Root Bridge placement from load balancing. For example, use multiples of 100 for your Root Bridges and multiples of 1000 for load balancing.

An additional caveat of using Bridge Priorities to implement load balancing is that it can scale poorly. As your network grows, it is very difficult to keep track of which device has had its Bridge Priority adjusted for each VLAN for which reason (Root Bridge or load balancing).

Furthermore, the technique shares much of the confusion of **set spantree portvlanpri**. Namely, you must modify MDF switches to implement load balancing on IDF switches. Because it is the *received* BPDUs that are being evaluated on Cat-2C, changing the BID on Cat-2C has no effect. In short, you must modify the upstream switch when load balancing with either Bridge Priorities or port/VLAN priority.

To make matters even worse, this load balancing scheme creates an awkward situation where one technique is used in Building 1 (Root Bridge placement) and another technique is used in Building 2 (Bridge Priority). It is much more straightforward to use a simple technique that is flexible enough to implement load balancing in both buildings.

Why, then, does anyone choose to use Bridge Priorities to implement load balancing? For one simple reason—prior to 3.1 Catalyst 5000 code it was your only choice in certain topologies. However, don't get discouraged—starting in 3.1, Cisco offered a feature called port/VLAN cost load balancing that addresses these downsides.

Load Balancing with Port/VLAN Cost

Although Root Bridge placement is attractive because of its simplicity, port/VLAN cost load balancing can be very useful because of its flexibility. By virtue of this versatility, Port/VLAN cost can be an intuitive and effective load balancing scheme for almost every topology.

The port/VLAN priority and Bridge Priority load balancing sections looked at techniques for influencing STP when the costs were equal. The strategy behind port/VLAN cost is based on a very simple and sensible observation: if Root Path Cost is the second STP decision criterion, why are the third and fourth decision criteria being used to implement load balancing? In other words, why not just modify the cost directly?

Catalysts have always supported the **set spantree portcost** command. However, this command is not useful as a primary technique for load balancing because it changes the cost for *every* VLAN on a given port. It wasn't until 3.1 Catalyst 5000 code (all Catalyst 4000s and 6000s support it) that Cisco added **set spantree portvlancost**, a command that allows you to tune cost on both a per-port *and* per-VLAN basis.

NOTE   Somewhat ironically, the Catalyst 3000s (3000, 3100, and 3200) supported per-port and per-VLAN cost configuration well before the feature was moved into the high-end products such as the Catalyst 5000.

Increasing Path Cost for Load Balancing

Figure 7-19 illustrates how **set spantree portvlancost** can be used to implement STP load balancing. For simplicity, this example uses Cat-1A as the Root Bridge for all VLANs.

Figure 7-19 *Load Balancing Using the* ***set spantree portvlancost*** *Command*

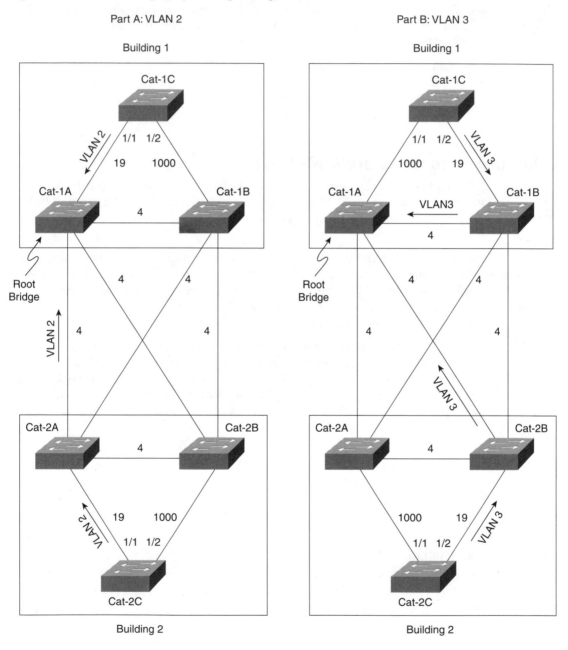

First, consider load balancing in Building 1. Cat-1C, the IDF switch in Building 1, has two potential paths to the Root Bridge. It can go directly to Cat-1A over the 1/1 link at a cost of 19, or it can use the 1/2 link to go through Cat-1B at a cost of 23 (19+4). The 1/1 link is fine for VLAN 2, but load balancing requires that VLAN 3 use the 1/2 link. This can be accomplished by increasing the Root Path Cost on the 1/1 link to anything greater than 23 for VLANs that should take the 1/2 link. For example, enter the command from Example 7-3 on Cat-1C to increase the Root Path Cost for VLAN 3 on Port 1/1 to 1000.

Example 7-3 *Increasing the Cost for VLAN 3 on Cat-1C:Port-1/1*

```
Cat-1C (enable) set spantree portvlancost 1/1 cost 1000 3
Port 1/1 VLANs 1-2,4-1005 have path cost 19.
Port 1/1 VLANs 3 have path cost 1000.
```

Although a comparable entry is not required for VLAN 2 on the 1/2 link, it is generally a good idea to add it for consistency as illustrated in Example 7-4.

Example 7-4 *Increasing the Cost for VLAN 2 on Cat-1C:Port-1/2*

```
Cat-1C (enable) set spantree portvlancost 1/2 cost 1000 2
Port 1/2 VLANs 1,3-1005 have path cost 19.
Port 1/2 VLANs 2 have path cost 1000.
```

The previous two commands increase the Root Path Cost on the undesirable link high enough to force traffic across the other IDF-to-MDF link. For example, the command in Example 7-3 discourages VLAN 3's traffic from using the 1/1 link, causing it to use the 1/2 link. However, if either riser link fails, all of the traffic rolls over to the remaining connection.

As mentioned earlier, it is important to understand the difference between *Root Path Cost* and *Path Cost*. This point is especially true when working with port/VLAN cost load balancing. Root Path Cost is the *cumulative* Spanning Tree cost from a bridge or switch to the Root Bridge. Path Cost is the *amount that is added to Root Path Cost* as BPDUs are *received* on a port. Notice that **set spantree portvlancost** is manipulating *Path Cost, not Root Path Cost*. It might help if you remember the command as **set spantree portvlan*path*cost** (just don't try typing that in!).

Decreasing Path Cost for Load Balancing

An alternate approach is to decrease the cost on the desirable link. In fact, this is actually the manner in which the **set spantree portvlancost** command syntax was designed to support. Here is the full syntax of the **set spantree portvlancost** command:

```
set spantree portvlancost mod_num/port_num [cost cost_value] [preferred_vlans]
```

Notice that the **set spantree portvlancost** command allows you to omit several of the parameters as a shortcut. If you omit the **cost** parameter, it lowers the cost by one from its current value. If you omit the *preferred_vlans* parameter, it uses the VLAN list from the last time the command was used. In other words, the command in Example 7-5 is designed to make Port 1/2 the preferred path for VLAN 3.

Example 7-5 *Selecting Cat-1C:Port-1/2 As the Preferred Path for VLAN 3 Using the Automatically Calculated Value*

```
Cat-1C> (enable) set spantree portvlancost 1/2 3
Port 1/2 VLANs 1-2,4-1005 have path cost 19.
Port 1/2 VLANs 3 have path cost 18.
```

TIP   Unlike most Spanning Tree commands on Catalysts that substitute the default value of 1 when the vlan parameter is omitted, **set spantreee portvlancost** uses the same VLAN (or VLANs) as the previous use of this command. To avoid surprises, it is safer to always specify both the **cost** and the *preferred_vlans* parameters.

However, lowering the cost to 18 on Port 1/2 for VLAN 3 does not work in situations such as Cat-1C in Figure 7-19. In this case, Cat-1C sees two paths to the Root Bridge. As explained earlier, the Root Path Cost values before tuning are 19 on the 1/1 link and 23 (19+4) on the 1/2 link. Lowering the 1/2 Path Cost by one results in a Root Path Cost for Port 1/2 of 22, not enough to win the Root Port election.

One solution is to manually specify a **cost** parameter that is low enough to do the trick as in Example 7-6.

Example 7-6 *Selecting Cat-1C:Port-1/2 As the Preferred Path for VLAN 3 By Manually Specifying a Lower Cost on Port 1/2*

```
Console> (enable) set spantree portvlancost 1/2 cost 14 3
Port 1/2 VLANs 1-2,4-1005 have path cost 19.
Port 1/2 VLANs 3 have path cost 14.
```

This lowers the *cumulative* Root Path Cost on Port 1/2 to 18 (14+4) and causes it to win out against the cost of 19 on Port 1/1.

However, this approach might not be stable in the long run. What if the link between Cat-1A and Cat-1B is replaced with Fast Ethernet or Fast EtherChannel? Or what if an additional switch is added in the middle of this link? In fact, if anything is done to increase the cost between Cat-1A and Cat-1B, this load balancing scheme fails. Therefore, as a general rule of thumb, it is better to increase the cost of undesirable paths than decrease the cost of desirable paths.

TIP   Increasing the cost of undesirable paths is more flexible and scalable than decreasing the cost of desirable paths.

Advantages of Port/VLAN Cost Load Balancing

Getting back to the example in Figure 7-19, now consider the load balancing for Building 2. First, force STP to use the Cat-2C:Port-1/2 link for VLAN 3 by entering the commands in Example 7-7 and 7-8 on Cat-2C.

Example 7-7   *Selecting Cat-2C:Port-1/2 As the Preferred Path for VLAN 3 By Manually Specifying a Higher Cost on Port 1/1*

```
Cat-2C (enable) set spantree portvlancost 1/1 cost 1000 3
Port 1/1 VLANs 1-2,4-1005 have path cost 19.
Port 1/1 VLANs 3 have path cost 1000.
```

Then, force VLAN 2 over the 1/1 link, as shown in Example 7-8.

Example 7-8   *Selecting Cat-2C:Port-1/1 As the Preferred Path for VLAN 2*

```
Cat-2C (enable) set spantree portvlancost 1/2 cost 1000 2
Port 1/2 VLANs 1,3-1005 have path cost 19.
Port 1/2 VLANs 2 have path cost 1000.
```

See how much easier **set spantree portvlancost** is to use than the port/VLAN priority and Bridge Priority load balancing? First, it is much easier to visualize the impact that the commands are having on the network. Second, both IDF switches use similar and consistent commands. Third, and best of all, the commands are entered on the very switch where the load balancing is occurring—the IDF switch. If you have an IDF switch with multiple uplinks, just Telnet to that device and use **set spantree portvlancost** to spread the load over all available links. With port/VLAN cost, there is no need to make strange modifications to upstream switches.

The results of using **set spantree portvlancost** are also much easier to read in **show spantree**. For example, the output in Example 7-9 would appear for VLAN 2 on Cat-2C, the IDF switch in Building 2.

Example 7-9 *show spantree Output for VLAN 2 After Using Port/VLAN Cost Load Balancing*

```
Cat-2C (enable) show spantree 2
VLAN 2
Spanning tree enabled
Spanning tree type              ieee

Designated Root                 00-e0-f9-16-28-00
Designated Root Priority        100
Designated Root Cost            23
Designated Root Port            1/1
Root Max Age    20 sec      Hello Time 2  sec    Forward Delay 15 sec

Bridge ID MAC ADDR              00-e0-f9-F2-44-00
Bridge ID Priority              32768
Bridge Max Age 20 sec       Hello Time 2  sec    Forward Delay 15 sec

Port       Vlan  Port-State      Cost    Priority  Fast-Start  Group-method
---------  ----  --------------  -----   --------  ----------  ------------
  1/1       1    forwarding       19        32     disabled
  1/2       1    blocking        1000       32     disabled
```

The increased cost on the 1/2 link is plainly shown along with the fact that Port 1/1 is in the Forwarding state. Also notice that Port 1/1 is acting as the Root Port.

The output in Example 7-10 shows the Spanning Tree information for VLAN 3 on the same switch.

Example 7-10 show spantree *Output for VLAN 3 After Using Port/VLAN Cost Load Balancing*

```
Cat-2C (enable) show spantree 3
VLAN 3
Spanning tree enabled
Spanning tree type              ieee

Designated Root                 00-e0-f9-16-28-00
Designated Root Priority        100
Designated Root Cost            23
Designated Root Port            1/2
Root Max Age    20 sec      Hello Time 2  sec    Forward Delay 15 sec

Bridge ID MAC ADDR              00-e0-f9-F2-44-00
Bridge ID Priority              32768
Bridge Max Age 20 sec       Hello Time 2  sec    Forward Delay 15 sec

Port       Vlan  Port-State      Cost    Priority  Fast-Start  Group-method
---------  ----  --------------  -----   --------  ----------  ------------
  1/1       1    blocking        1000       32     disabled
  1/2       1    forwarding       19        32     disabled
```

In the case of Example 7-10, the 1/1 port is Blocking, whereas the 1/2 port is Forwarding. The Root Port has also shifted to 1/2 with a Root Path Cost of 23 (19 for the riser link plus 4 to cross the Gigabit Ethernet link between Cat-2B and Cat-1A).

TIP   Carefully observe the difference between Root Path Cost and Path Cost. Root Path Cost is the cumulative cost to the Root Bridge. Path Cost is the amount that each port contributes to Root Path Cost.

Because it is both flexible and easy to understand, port/VLAN cost is one of the most useful STP load balancing tools (along with Root Bridge placement). The only requirement is that you run 3.1 or higher code on the switches where you want to implement the load balancing (generally your IDF switches). Note that you do not need to run 3.1+ code everywhere, it is only necessary on the actual devices where **set spantree portvlancost** load balancing is configured (modifying the **set spantree portvlancost** on some devices does not create any interoperability problems with your other switches).

Precautions for Using Port/VLAN Cost Load Balancing

However, there is one potentially confusing matter that you should keep in mind when using **set spantree portvlancost**: each port is only allowed two Port Cost values (very similar to how each port is only allowed two port/VLAN priority values). The first value is the default cost for the port. This value is derived from the bandwidth chart presented in Table 6-1 of Chapter 6 and can be modified with the **set spantree portcost** command (it modifies cost for *every* VLAN on a port). The second value is the one configured with **set spantree portvlancost**. However, only a single **set spantree portvlancost** value can exist on a given port. If you configure multiple **set spantree portvlancost** values on a single port, all of the VLANs ever configured with **set spantree portvlancost** adopt the most recent value.

TIP   As with port/VLAN priority, the per-VLAN value must be less than the per-port value. In other words, the **set spantree portvlancost** value must be less than the **set spantree portcost** value.

For example, the command in Example 7-11 increases the cost to 1000 for VLANs 2 and 3 on Port 1/1.

Example 7-11 *Increasing Port/VLAN Cost on Port 1/1 for VLANs 2 and 3*

```
Cat-A> (enable) set spantree portvlancost 1/1 cost 1000 2-3
Port 1/1 VLANs 1,4-1005 have path cost 19.
Port 1/1 VLANs 2-3 have path cost 1000.
```

Next, try increasing the Path Cost for VLAN 5 to 2000 as in Example 7-12.

Example 7-12 *Trying to Specify a Different Port/VLAN Cost Value*

```
Console> (enable) set spantree portvlancost 1/1 cost 2000 5
Port 1/1 VLANs 1,4,6-1005 have path cost 19.
Port 1/1 VLANs 2-3,5 have path cost 2000.
```

Notice how it also changes the Path Cost for VLANs 2 and 3. A quick look at the output of **show spantree** in Example 7-13 confirms the change.

Example 7-13 *Only the Most Recently Specified Port/VLAN Cost Value Is Used*

```
Console> (enable) show spantree 1/1
Port      Vlan  Port-State    Cost   Priority  Fast-Start  Group-Method
--------- ----  ------------- -----  --------  ----------  ------------
  1/1      1    forwarding      19      31      disabled
  1/1      2    forwarding    2000      31      disabled
  1/1      3    forwarding    2000      31      disabled
  1/1      4    forwarding      19      31      disabled
  1/1      5    forwarding    2000      31      disabled
  1/1      6    forwarding      19      31      disabled
  1/1      7    forwarding      19      31      disabled
  1/1      8    forwarding      19      31      disabled
  1/1      9    forwarding      19      31      disabled
  1/1     10    forwarding      19      31      disabled
```

Poof! The cost of 1000 is gone. As mentioned in the "Port/VLAN Priority Load Balancing" section that covered the **set spantree portvlanpri** command (which also exhibits the behavior seen in Example 7-13), this sleight of hand is a subtle side effect caused by a technique the Catalysts use to save NVRAM storage. Internally, Catalysts store three different values related to cost per port:

- A global cost for that port
- A single **set spantree portvlancost** value
- A list of VLANs using the **set spantree portvlancost** value

Therefore, separate cost values cannot be stored for every VLAN. However, the good news is that, apart from its strange appearances, this is not a significant drawback in most situations. Networks with lots of redundancy and multiple links might find it a limitation, but most never notice it at all.

Spanning Tree Load Balancing Summary

In review, there are four techniques available for Spanning Tree load balancing on Catalyst equipment:

- **Root Bridge Placement**—Traffic flows can be influenced by carefully locating Root Bridges throughout your network. This option is extremely viable and useful for organizations utilizing the multilayer design model discussed in Chapter 14. However, for networks employing less hierarchical designs, it can be hopeless.

- **Port/VLAN Priority**—**set spantree portvlanpri** can be used to load balance between back-to-back switches. This technique allows network administrators to modify Port ID values on upstream switches to influence forwarding and blocking decisions on neighboring downstream switches. For a variety of reasons, the option is rarely useful.

- **Bridge Priority**—Bridge Priorities can be used. In general, this technique is only useful in older software images (pre-3.1) where **set spantree portvlancost** is not available. As with **set spantree portvlanpri**, it requires that load balancing parameters be entered on the switch that is upstream of the switch actually performing the load balancing.

- **Port/VLAN Cost**—**set spantree portvlancost** can be utilized. This technique is the most flexible option available for STP load balancing. In flat networks, it is also the simplest to implement. The only requirement is that you use 3.1 or later code on your devices. It allows the command to be entered and observed on the actual switch where the load balancing is being performed.

In short, Spanning Tree load balancing almost always boils down to one of two options. First, when using the MLS form of Layer 3 switching to build networks according to the multilayer design model (see Chapters 11 and 14), the Root Bridge Placement form of load balancing is generally most appropriate. Second, port/VLAN cost load balancing should be used in almost all other situations.

Fast STP Convergence

When discussing the five STP states, Chapter 6 mentioned that Spanning Tree starts ports in a Blocking state. Over a period of 30 to 50 seconds, ports work their way through the Listening and Learning states to finally reach the Forwarding state where user data is actually passed. Spanning Tree was intentionally designed with this conservative logic. Consider the alternative: if STP immediately brought ports into the Forwarding state, loops could form and prevent STP from ever getting any BPDUs through! Instead, STP keeps all ports from forwarding anything but BPDUs for at least 30 seconds by default. This is designed to give the bridges in almost all networks plenty of time to learn the physical topology and then create a loop-free logical topology.

However, the downside to this conservative behavior is slow convergence time. In a world that has grown accustomed to sub-ten-second-failover protocols such as Open Shortest Path First (OSPF), Enhanced IGRP (EIGRP), and Hot Standby Routing Protocol (HSRP), Spanning Tree's default behavior can be intolerably sluggish. In response to this need for speed, there are a variety of techniques available on Catalyst switches to improve on Spanning Tree's default performance. Some of these techniques merely implement features originally designed into the 802.1D protocol. Others take advantage of new and patented features researched and implemented by Cisco. These capabilities can play an important role in building large and stable switched backbones.

In total, Catalysts offer seven techniques to improve Spanning Tree's convergence time:

- Tuning Max Age
- Tuning Forward Delay
- Lowering Hello Time
- PortFast
- UplinkFast
- BackboneFast
- Disabling PAgP on EtherChannel-capable ports

Tuning Max Age

Recall that Spanning Tree centers around a process of each port saving a copy of the best BPDU it has heard. However, there must be some process to age out this stored information, otherwise, the network would never repair itself after the failure of a bridge or link. The Max Age timer controls the length of this age out period.

The Root Bridge generates Configuration BPDUs on all of its ports every 2 seconds (the default Hello Time interval). This triggers a cascade of Configuration BPDUs that, under normal conditions, should reach every segment in the network. As long as a non-Designated Port continues to receive Configuration BPDUs from the segment's Designated Port, the port's saved information never ages out. In other words, this continual refresh of more attractive BPDU information keeps the non-Designated Port in a Blocking state.

However, if an upstream bridge or link fails, the flow of Configuration BPDUs is interrupted. After Max Age seconds, the port starts sending its own Configuration BPDUs as it transitions into the Listening state. As long as no more attractive BPDUs are heard from other devices, the port eventually transitions through the Learning state and ends up in the Forwarding state. At this point, the port has restored connectivity to the local segment.

In practice, Max Age is used to detect *indirect* failures. For example, the directly connected failure illustrated in Figure 7-20 does not require Cat-C to use the Max Age timer.

Figure 7-20 *Direct Failures Take Approximately 30 Seconds to Reconverge*

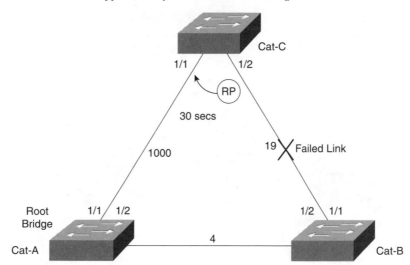

In this network, Cat-A is the Root Bridge, and Cat-C (an IDF switch) has selected Port 1/2 as its Root Port because it has a lower Root Path Cost (23 versus 1000). Assume that the cable connecting Cat-C and Cat-B fails. This produces an immediate physical layer loss of link on Cat-C:Port-1/2 and causes that port to be placed in the not-connected state. Port 1/2 is then immediately excluded from STP processing and causes Cat-C to start searching for a new Root Port. 30 seconds later (twice the Forward Delay), Port 1/1 enters the Forwarding state and connectivity resumes.

TIP   Max Age is used to detect and recover from *indirect* failures.

On the other hand, Figure 7-21 depicts an indirect failure.

Figure 7-21 *Indirect Failures Take Approximately 50 Seconds to Reconverge*

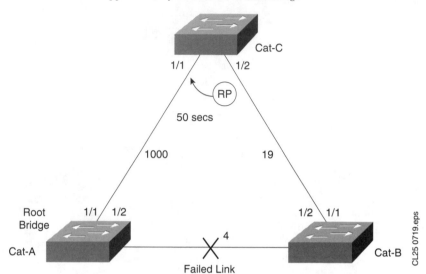

In this case, the link between Cat-A and Cat-B fails. Cat-C:Port-1/2 receives no direct notification that anything has changed. All Cat-C notices is that Configuration BPDUs stop arriving on Port 1/2. After waiting for the number of seconds specified by the Max Age timer, Cat-C:Port-1/1 starts to take over as the Root Port. This reconvergence takes considerably longer: 50 seconds as opposed to 30 seconds.

The default Max Age value of 20 seconds is designed to take two factors into account:

- End-to-End BPDU Propagation Delay
- Message Age Overestimate

Calculating End-to-End BPDU Propagation Delay for Max Age

End-to-End BPDU Propagation Delay is the amount of time that it takes for a BPDU to travel from one edge of the network to the other edge of the network. The 802.1D specification assumes that up to three BPDUs can get lost along the way, the maximum distance between any two nodes in the network is seven bridge hops, and each bridge can take up to one second to propagate a BPDU after receiving it. Also, the default Hello Time interval of two seconds is assumed. Table 7-2 documents these assumptions.

Table 7-2 *Assumptions Used to Calculate the Default Max Age*

Parameter	Value	Tunable	Description
lost_msgs	3	N	Lost Messages: Number of BPDUs that can be lost as a message moves from one end of the bridged network to the other. Reasons for the potential loss of BPDUs include issues such as congestion, CRC errors, physical layer issues, and software deficiencies (that is, bugs).
dia	7 hops	Y	Diameter: The maximum number of bridge hops between any two end-station nodes in the network.
bpdu_delay	1 sec	N	BPDU Transmission Delay: The maximum time a single bridge takes to propagate a BPDU after receiving it on another port.
hello_t	2 secs	Y	Hello Time: The time between Configuration BPDUs that are originated on the Root Bridge.

These values can be used to calculate the End-to-End BPDU Propagation Delay using the following formula:

end-to-end_bpdu_propagation_delay
$= ((lost\_msgs + 1) \times hello\_t) + (bpdu\_delay \times (dia - 1))$
$= ((3 + 1) \times 2) + (1 \times (7 - 1))$
$= 8 + 6 = 14$ seconds

Calculating Message Age Overestimate for Max Age

The other component of Max Age is something referred to as *Message Age Overestimate*. This is the amount of time that the Message Age field carried in BPDUs can be overstated. Recall from the earlier section "STP Timers" that Message Age is the amount of time that has passed since the Root Bridge first originated the information the current BPDU is based on.

Although the 802.1D specification forbids a bridge from underestimating the Message Age field, it can become overstated because many bridges have limited timer resolution and just add a second at every hop. As a result, each bridge hop generally increases the amount of this overstatement, causing downstream bridges to potentially expire the Max Age counter too soon. 802.1D assumes that each bridge can contribute one second of Message Age Overstatement. Therefore, the total Message Age Overestimate can be calculated as follows:

message_age_overestimate
$= (dia - 1) \times overestimate\_per\_bridge$
$= (7 - 1) \times 1$
$= 6$ seconds

Note that this process of simply incrementing the Message Age field in each bridge causes bridges farther from the Root Bridge to age out their Max Age counters first. Therefore, this effect is more pronounced in flat-earth networks that consist of many Layer 2 switches connected without any intervening routers or Layer 3 switches. This is another advantage to creating hierarchy with Layer 3 switching as prescribed by the multilayer model in Chapter 14.

Calculating and Using Max Age

Max Age is simply the sum of these two previously calculated values:

Max Age = end-to-end_bpdu_propagation_delay + message_age_overestimate
= 14 + 6 = 20 seconds

Of the values assumed in this calculation, two are something you can consider tunable:

- Diameter
- Hello Time

If your bridged network diameter is considerably smaller than seven hops or your Hello Time has been set to one second, you might want to recalculate a new Max Age value. The result can then be entered at your Root Bridges using the following command:

```
set spantree maxage agingtime [vlan]
```

TIP When using Layer 3 switching to limit the size of your Spanning Tree domains, the Max Age timer can be safely tuned. The extent of tuning that is possible is based on the style of Layer 3 switching in use and the overall campus network design. See Chapter 15 for specific details and recommendations.

You can only modify the timer values on Root Bridges. Don't forget to also change the values on any backup Root Bridges.

If you do lower the Hello Time interval, carefully consider the impact that it has on your CPU. STP can easily be the single most intensive CPU process running on a modern bridge (which does all of the frame forwarding in hardware). Cutting the Hello Time interval in half doubles the load that STP places on your CPU. See the sections "Lowering Hello Time to One Second" and "Tips and Tricks: Mastering STP" later in this chapter for more guidance.

TIP	Decreasing Hello Time to one second doubles the STP load placed on your CPU. Use the formula presented at the end of the chapter to be certain that this does not overload your CPU. However, in networks that contain a limited numbers of VLANs, lowering Hello Time to one second can be an excellent way to improve convergence times. See the section "Lowering Hello Time to One Second" for more information.

Precautions for Tuning Max Age

If you assume a lower network diameter, be careful to look for unexpected bridge hops that can crop up during failure conditions. Also, diameter is defined as the largest number of bridge hops between any two end-station nodes in your network. It is not just the number of hops between your primary Root Bridge and the farthest leaf node.

TIP	Be careful when calculating bridge diameter—unexpected hops can creep in when other links or devices fail.

Some of the 802.1D values might appear overly conservative. For instance, most users would argue that their networks would never drop three BPDUs while transferring information a mere seven bridge hops. Likewise, the assumption that each bridge takes one second to propagate a BPDU seems strange in a world of high-horsepower switching. Although it might be tempting to recalculate the formula with more "real-world" values, I strongly recommend against this. Keep in mind that these values were chosen to provide adequate margin in networks experiencing failure conditions, not just networks happily humming along while everything is operating at peak efficiency. When a failure does occur, your bandwidth and CPU capacity can be depleted as the network tries to recover. Be sure to leave some reserves to handle these situations.

TIP	Only modify the diameter and Hello Time variables in the Max Age calculation. Modifying the other values can surprise you some day (when you least expect it!).

Although any form of STP timer tuning can be dangerous, reducing Max Age can be less risky than other forms. If you set Max Age too low, a brief interruption in the flow of Configuration BPDUs in the network can cause Blocking ports to age out their BPDU information. When this happens, this rogue bridge starts sending Configuration BPDUs in an attempt to move into the Forwarding state. If there is a functioning Designated Port available for that segment, it refutes the BPDU with a Configuration BPDU of its own (this is the exception processing discussed earlier in the "Configuration BPDU Processing" section). However, if the Designated Port has failed, no device will refute the BPDU, and the rogue bridge might form a bridging loop before it hears from any neighboring bridges.

TIP	Modifying Max Age is less dangerous than changing the other timer values. Unfortunately, it only improves convergence in the case of an indirect failure.

Tuning Forward Delay

Forward Delay can add an agonizing amount of delay to the recovery time experienced in your network. Unlike Max Age, where direct failures cause that stage to be bypassed, *all failures must wait through the Forward Delay stage twice* (Listening and then Learning).

Given this sluggishness, it can be very tempting to try improving STP's performance by lowering the Forward Delay timer. However, unless this is done with considerable planning and care, it can have a devastating impact on your network. This section explores the thought process behind Forward Delay's default value and explores reasonable guidelines for tuning this parameter.

Forward Delay is used to control the migration of a port from the Blocking state to the Forwarding state. If this was an instantaneous transition, a loop could easily form and the network would collapse under the resulting load. Instead, bridges wait for twice the Forward Delay to allow BPDUs to propagate across the network and all traffic on the old topology to die. In addition, it must allow time for the same overestimate error in Message Age seen in the previous section.

To accommodate these three items, the default Forward Delay value recommended in the 802.1D specification accounts for the following four components that affect STP reconvergence:

- End-to-End BPDU Propagation Delay
- Message Age Overestimate
- Maximum Transmission Halt Delay
- Maximum Frame Lifetime

You might recognize the first two factors affecting convergence as being the same two used to calculate Max Age. These values represent the same two factors here: the time that it takes for BPDUs to move across the network and nodes expiring information too early because of an overstatement in the Message Age field. Conversely, the combination of the last two items allows time for information to age out of the old topology before the new topology takes effect.

The Forward Delay calculation uses the values shown in Table 7-3.

Table 7-3   *Assumptions Used to Calculate the Default Forward Delay*

Parameter	Value	Tunable	Description
lost_msgs	3	N	Lost Messages: Number of BPDUs that could get lost as a message moves from one end of the bridged network to the other.
dia	7 hops	Y	Diameter: The maximum number of bridge hops between any two nodes in the network.
bpdu_delay	1 sec	N	BPDU Transmission Delay: The maximum time a single bridge takes to propagate a BPDU after receiving it on another port.
hello_t	2 secs	Y	Hello Time: The time between Configuration BPDUs that are originated on the Root Bridge.
tx_halt_delay	1 sec	N	Transmit Halt Delay: The time it takes for a bridge to stop sending traffic on a port after it enters the Blocking state.
transit_delay	1 sec	N	Bridge Transit Delay: The time it takes for a bridge to propagate a data frame.
med_access_delay	.5 sec	N	Maximum Medium Access Delay: The time it takes for a device to gain access to the wire to initially transmit a frame.

Calculating End-to-End BPDU Propagation Delay and Message Age Overestimate for Forward Delay

These components are used to calculate Forward Delay as follows:

$$\text{end-to-end\_bpdu\_propagation\_delay}$$
$$= ((lost\_msgs + 1) \times hello\_t) + (bpdu\_delay \times (dia - 1))$$
$$= ((3 + 1) \times 2) + (1 \times (7 - 1))$$
$$= 8 + 6 = 14 \text{ seconds}$$
$$\text{message\_age\_overestimate}$$
$$= (dia - 1) \times overestimate\_per\_bridge$$
$$= (7 - 1) \times 1$$
$$= 6 \text{ seconds}$$

These two calculations are the same two used to derive Max Age. With Forward Delay, just as in Max Age, they account for the time it takes to propagate BPDUs across the network and for the error present in the Message Age field of Configuration BPDUs.

Calculating Maximum Transmission Halt Delay

Maximum Transmission Halt Delay is designed to account for the lag that can occur before a bridge puts a port into the Blocking state. In other words, the Spanning-Tree Protocol might determine that a port should be placed in the Blocking state. However, it might take the bridge or switch some time to follow through on this decision. As Table 7-3 indicates, 802.1D allows one second for this event.

Calculating Maximum Frame Lifetime

In addition to the delay that it takes for a bridge to "close the door" by blocking the port, the algorithm needs to account for frames that have already "gone out the door" and are running around the network looking for their final destination. This is done with the Maximum Frame Lifetime. Maximum Frame Lifetime can be calculated with the following formula:

max_frame_lifetime
$= (dia \times transit\_delay) + med\_access\_delay$
$= (7 \times 1) + .5 = 8$ seconds (rounded)

The *dia* × *transit_delay* part allows time for frames to die out, whereas the *med_access_delay* accounts for the time that it takes for a frame to initially gain access to the wire.

Calculating and Using Forward Delay

The entire pre-forwarding period can be calculated by combining these four parts:

pre-forwarding_period
= end-to-end_bpdu_propagation_delay + message_age_overestimate + tx_halt_delay
   + max_frame_lifetime
$= 14 + 6 + 1 + 8 = 29$ seconds

Because the pre-forwarding period is divided into two halves, this number can be divided by two to calculate Forward Delay:

forward_delay
$= 29 / 2 = 15$ seconds (rounded)

As with Max Age, you can substitute the appropriate values for your network to potentially calculate a smaller Forward Delay value (only modify diameter and Hello Time). This value can then be set on Root Bridges using the following command:

```
set spantree fwddelay delay [vlan]
```

TIP   You can only modify the timer values on Root Bridges. Don't forget to also change the values on any backup Root Bridges so as to be consistent during primary Root Bridge failure. As with other Spanning Tree commands, it is best to get into the habit of always specifying the VLAN parameter.

Precautions for Tuning Forward Delay

You should be very careful when adjusting Forward Delay. If you are too aggressive, you can disable the entire network for extended periods of time. Recall that one of the goals of Forward Delay is to let the entire network learn the active topology before any of the ports start passing traffic. If ports are brought into the Forwarding state without giving ample time for information to propagate, loops can be the result. The other goal of Forwarding Delay is to let frames in the old topology die out. If this does not occur, some frames might be delivered in duplicate, something the 802.1D specification prohibits. Although this can corrupt certain applications, it is generally far less dangerous than the bridging loops created by the first issue (bridge loops can take down *every* application and device on the network).

Note that if a bridging loop forms in even a small area, it can quickly spread throughout the entire network. As the loop grows in size, the number of ports replicating the data grows. As the volume of data grows, output buffers and available link bandwidth begin to exhaust—it's become harder to send BPDUs that might fix the problem. Then bridge CPUs become overburdened with broadcast and multicast traffic—making it harder to generate BPDUs to fix the loop. The resulting downward spiral can quickly lead to a network-wide meltdown.

TIP   Be very careful and conservative when you adjust Forward Delay. If you set Forward Delay too low, it can create network-wide outages.

Lowering Hello Time to One Second

The previous two sections mention the impact that a lower Hello Time can have on the network. By causing the Root Bridge to generate Configuration BPDUs twice as often, information, in general, propagates twice as quickly through the network.

However, *notice that merely lowering Hello Time from the default of two seconds to one second does not improve convergence times.* It causes the network to learn information more quickly, but only by reducing Max Age or Forward Delay does this actually lead to a faster convergence time.

TIP	Unlike Forward Delay and Max Age, lowering the Hello Time value does not improve convergence. On the contrary, you lower the Hello Time to make it possible for you to also lower the Forward Delay and/or Max Age timers. In general, it is simplest to use the **set spantree root** macro discussed in Chapter 6 (it automatically makes all necessary adjustments based on the suggested formulas in 802.1D).

The Hello Time can be adjusted with the **set spantree hello** command. For instance, the following command lowers the Hello Time for VLAN 3 to one second:

```
set spantree hello 1 3
```

If you do lower the Hello Time value, carefully consider the CPU overload warning mentioned in the "Tuning Max Age" section. For more information, see the formula presented in the "Tips and Tricks: Mastering STP" section.

PortFast

PortFast is a feature that is primarily designed to optimize switch ports that are connected to end-station devices. By using PortFast, these devices can be granted instant access to the Layer 2 network.

Think for a moment about what happens when you boot your PC every morning. You flip the big red switch, the monitor flickers, it beeps and buzzes. Somewhere during that process your network interface card (NIC) asserts Ethernet link, causing a Catalyst port to jump from *not connected* to the STP Learning state. Thirty seconds later, the Catalyst puts your port into Forwarding mode, and you are able to play Doom to your heart's content.

Normally, this sequence never even gets noticed because it takes your PC at least 30 seconds to boot. However, there are two cases where this might not be true.

First, some NICs do not enable link until the MAC-layer software driver is actually loaded. Because most operating systems try to use the network almost immediately after loading the driver, this can create an obvious problem. Several years ago, this problem was fairly common with certain Novell ODI NIC drivers. With more modern NICs, this problem is fairly common with PC Card (PCMCIA) NICs used in laptop computers.

Second, there is a race—a race between Microsoft and Intel. Intel keeps making the CPUs faster and Microsoft keeps making the operating systems slower…and so far Intel is winning. In other words, PCs are booting faster than ever. In fact, some modern machines are done booting (or at least far enough along in the process) and need to use the network before STP's 30-second countdown has finished. Dynamic Host Control Protocol (DHCP) and NT Domain Controller authentication are two common activities that occur late in the initialization process.

In both cases, STP's default settings can create a problem. How do you know if you have this problem? Probably the easiest is to plug both the PC *and* the Catalyst port into a hub. This provides a constant link to the Catalyst and keeps the port in Forwarding mode regardless of whether the PC is booted or not. Another classic symptom is if your PC always has problems when you first cold boot it in the morning, but it never has problems when you warm boot it during the day or try to manually complete login or DHCP sequences after booting.

This problem motivates some network administrators to disable STP altogether. This certainly fixes any STP booting problems, but it can easily create other problems. If you employ this strategy, it requires that you eliminate all physical loops (a bad idea from a resiliency standpoint) and carefully avoid all physical layer loops (something that can be difficult to do in the real world). Also, keep in mind that you can't disable STP for a single port. **set spantree disable** [*vlan*] is a per-VLAN global command that disables STP for every port that participates in the specified VLAN (and, as you would expect, VLAN 1 is the default if you do not specify the VLAN parameter). Moreover, some of the Layer 3 switching technologies, such as the Catalyst 5000 Supervisor Module III NetFlow Feature Card (NFFC), require that Spanning Tree be disabled on the *entire box* (all VLANs)!

In short, rather than disabling STP, you should consider using Cisco's PortFast feature. This feature gives you the best of both worlds—immediate end-station access and the safety net of STP.

PortFast works by making a fairly simple change in the STP process. Rather than starting out at the bottom of the Blocking-to-Listening-to-Learning-to-Forwarding hierarchy of states as with normal STP, PortFast starts at the top. As soon as your switch sees the link, the port is placed in the Forwarding state (Catalyst 3000s actually spend one second in both Listening and Learning, but who's counting?). If STP later detects that you have a loop, it does all of the Root and Designated Port calculations discussed earlier. If a loop is detected, the port is put in the Blocking state.

This magic only occurs when the port first initializes. If the port is forced into the Blocking state for some reason and later needs to return to the Forwarding state, the usual Listening and Learning processing is done.

Precautions for Using PortFast

You will probably run into people who recommend that you only enable PortFast if it is absolutely necessary. The stern warning that Catalysts issue when you enable this feature backs up this opinion:

```
Warning: Spantree port fast start should only be enabled on ports connected
to a single host. Connecting hubs, concentrators, switches, bridges, etc. to
a fast start port can cause temporary Spanning Tree loops. Use with caution.
```

However, to the contrary, PortFast can actually improve the stability of large networks! Recall the discussion of TCN BPDUs. TCN BPDUs are sent every time a bridge detects a change in the active topology to shorten the bridge table age-out time to the Forward Delay interval. Do you really want to potentially flush large sections of your bridging tables every time a user boots? Probably not.

TIP	Use PortFast on your end-station ports. Not only does it avoid problems when these devices boot, it reduces the amount of Topology Change Notifications in your network.

Despite all of PortFast's benefits, you should not carelessly enable it on every port. Only enable it on ports that connect to workstations. Because servers rarely reboot (you hope), don't enable it here.

TIP	One exception to the rule of not using PortFast on server ports involves the use of fault-tolerant NICs. If you are using one of these NICs that toggles link-state during failover (most don't), you should enable PortFast on these server ports.

Finally, you cannot use PortFast on trunk ports. Although Catalysts allow the command to be entered on trunk links, it is ignored. In short, PortFast is like any other power tool: it is extremely useful, but only if used correctly.

TIP	Do not enable PortFast on looped ports.

Using PortFast

Enabling PortFast is simple. Simply use the **set spantree portfast** command:

```
set spantree portfast mod_num/port_num {enable | disable}
```

For example, to enable PortFast on every port of a 24-port module in slot 3, issue the following command:

```
set spantree portfast 3/1-24 enable
```

You can later disable PortFast with the following command:

```
set spantree portfast 3/1-24 disable
```

If you want to check to see where you have PortFast enabled, you can use the **show spantree** command as in Example 7-14.

Example 7-14 *Showing Where PortFast Is Enabled*

```
Cat-A (enable) show spantree 1
VLAN 1
Spanning tree enabled
Spanning tree type          ieee

Designated Root             00-90-92-16-28-00
Designated Root Priority    100
Designated Root Cost        19
Designated Root Port        1/1
Root Max Age   20 sec    Hello Time 2  sec   Forward Delay 15 sec

Bridge ID MAC ADDR          00-90-92-bf-70-00
Bridge ID Priority          32768
Bridge Max Age 20 sec    Hello Time 2  sec   Forward Delay 15 sec

Port    Vlan  Port-State      Cost   Priority  Fast-Start  Group-method
......... ....  .............   .....  ........  .........   ...........
 1/1     1    forwarding        19       32     disabled
 1/2     1    blocking        1000       32     disabled
 3/1     1    forwarding       100       32     enabled
 3/2     1    forwarding       100       32     enabled
 3/3     1    forwarding       100       32     enabled
```

Look under the Fast-Start column. Notice how the end-station ports on module three have PortFast enabled, whereas the uplink ports on the Supervisor do not.

TIP	In many cases, you might experience a 17–20 second delay even after you have enabled PortFast. This is almost always caused by a side effect of the Port Aggregation Protocol (PAgP) used to handle EtherChannel negotiations. As discussed in the "Disabling Port Aggregation Protocol" section later in this chapter, PAgP hides port initialization changes for approximately 17–18 seconds. In other words, although PortFast might enable the link as soon as it is aware that the port has transitioned, PAgP delays this notification. In a future software release, Cisco is considering disabling PAgP on ports where PortFast is enabled, a change that would avoid this problem.

UplinkFast

UplinkFast is an exciting feature that Cisco rolled out in the 3.1 NMP release. This exclusive feature (it is patented) allows wiring closet switches to converge in two to three seconds!

The syntax for UplinkFast is even simpler than PortFast:

```
set spantree uplinkfast {enable | disable} [rate station_update_rate]
```

You should only enable UplinkFast on IDF-like wiring closet switches in correctly designed networks. UplinkFast is designed to only operate on switches that are leaves (end nodes) in your Spanning Tree. If you enable it in the core of you network, it generally leads to unexpected traffic flows.

For example, consider Figure 7-22, the typical campus introduced earlier.

Figure 7-22 *A Typical Campus Network Using UplinkFast*

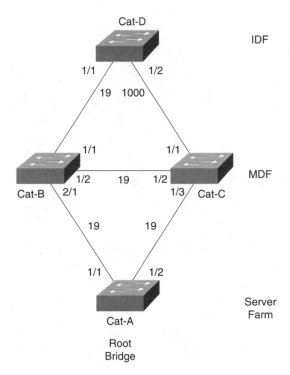

Cat-D is an IDF switch that is connected to two MDF switches (Cat-B and Cat-C). Although **set spantree uplinkfast** is a global command that applies to all VLANs, this section only analyzes a single VLAN: VLAN 2. Cat-A, the server farm switch, is the Root Bridge for VLAN 2. Cat-D has two uplink ports that are potential Root Port candidates. Utilizing the load balancing techniques discussed earlier, the cost on Port 1/2 has been increased to 1000 to force VLAN 2's traffic across the 1/1 link. Notice that Port 1/1 becomes the Root Port. UplinkFast is then enabled on Cat-D with the following command:

```
Cat-D> (enable) set spantree uplinkfast enable
```

This causes Cat-D to notice that Port 1/2 is Blocking and therefore constitutes a redundant connection to the Root Bridge. By making a note of this backup uplink port, Cat-D can set itself up for a quick rollover in the event that Port 1/1 fails. The list of potential uplink ports can be viewed with the **show spantree uplinkfast** command as in Example 7-15.

Example 7-15 *Showing Forwarding and Backup Ports with UplinkFast*

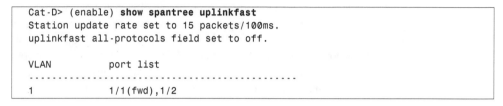

```
Cat-D> (enable) show spantree uplinkfast
Station update rate set to 15 packets/100ms.
uplinkfast all-protocols field set to off.

VLAN            port list
-----------------------------------------------
1               1/1(fwd),1/2
```

Port 1/1 is shown as the primary port (it is in the Forwarding state) and Port 1/2 is the backup. If three uplink ports exist, all three appear in the output.

It is important to recognize that UplinkFast is a Root Port optimization. It allows wiring closet switches to quickly bring up another Root Port in the event that the primary port fails.

TIP   UplinkFast is a Root Port optimization.

Therefore, it is futile to enable UplinkFast on a Root Bridge—because Root Bridges contain no physical Root Ports there is nothing for UplinkFast to optimize. In other words, only implement this feature on leaf-node switches sitting at the ends of the branches of your Spanning Tree. These leaf-node switches should not be used as a transit switches to reach the Root Bridge. So, as a general rule, only enable UplinkFast on your IDF wiring closet switches.

TIP   Do not enable UplinkFast on every switch in your network! Only enable UplinkFast on leaf-node Catalysts such as your IDF switches.

To enforce the requirement of leaf-node status, Cisco modifies several STP parameters when UplinkFast is enabled. Take a look at the output of the **set spantree uplinkfast** command in Example 7-16.

Example 7-16 **set spantree uplinkfast** *Command Output*

```
Cat-D> (enable) set spantree uplinkfast enable
VLANs 1-1005 bridge priority set to 49152.
The port cost and portvlancost of all ports set to above 3000.
Station update rate set to 15 packets/100ms.
uplinkfast all-protocols field set to off.
uplinkfast enabled for bridge.
```

First, the Bridge Priority is modified to an unusually high value of 49,152. This causes the current switch to effectively take itself out of the election to become the Root Bridge. Second, it adds 3000 to the cost of all links. This is done to discourage other switches from using the current switch as a transit switch to the Root Bridge. Notice that neither of these actions limits STP failover in your network. The Bridge Priority modification only discourages other switches from electing this switch as the Root Bridge. If the other switches fail, this switch happily becomes the Root Bridge. Also, the increase to Path Cost only discourages other switches from using the current switch as a transit path to the Root Bridge. However, if no alternate paths are available, the current switch gleefully transfers traffic to and from the Root Bridge.

Notice the third line in the output in Example 7-16 (in bold). This is evidence of a subtle trick that is the crux of what UplinkFast is all about. It should probably be fairly obvious by now that a failure on Cat-D:Port-1/1 forces Cat-D to take all MAC addresses associated with Port 1/1 in the Bridging Table and points them to Port 1/2. However, a more subtle process must take place to convert the bridging tables in other switches. Why is this extra step necessary? Figure 7-23 shows the network with the left-hand link broken.

Figure 7-23 *UplinkFast Behavior When the Primary Uplink Is Lost*

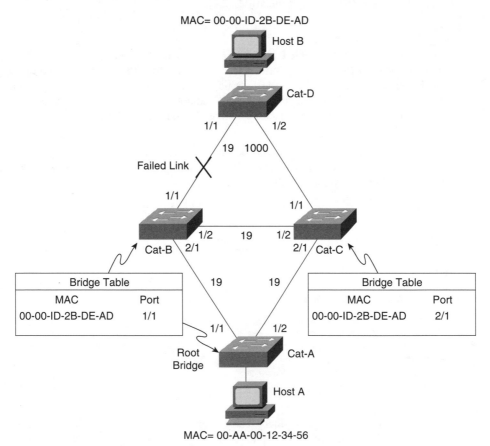

Cat-D changes MAC address 00-AA-00-12-34-56 (Host-A) to Port 1/2 so that it has a correct view of the network. However, notice that Cat-A, Cat-B, and Cat-C are still trying to send traffic for 00-00-1D-2B-DE-AD (Host-B) to the broken link! This is where the real ingenuity of UplinkFast comes in: Cat-D sends out a dummy multicast frame for the addresses in its local Bridging Table. One frame is sent for each MAC address that is not associated with one of the uplink ports. These packets are sent to a multicast 01-00-0C-CD-CD-CD destination address to ensure that they are flooded throughout the bridged network. Recall from Chapter 3 that multicast addresses are flooded as with broadcast frames. However, note that Cisco does not use the traditional multicast address of 01-00-0C-CC-CC-CC. Because this multicast address is reserved for single hop protocols such as Cisco Discovery Protocol (CDP), VLAN Trunk Protocol (VTP), Dynamic ISL (DISL), and Dynamic Trunk Protocol (DTP), Cisco devices have been programmed to not flood the 01-00-0C-CC-CC-CC. To avoid this behavior, a new multicast address needed to be introduced.

Each frame contains the source address of a different entry in the local Bridging Table. As these packets are flooded through the network, all of the switches and bridges make a note of the new interface the frame arrived on and, if necessary, adjust their bridging tables. By default, the Catalyst sends 15 of these dummy frames every 100 milliseconds, but this rate can be adjusted with the [**rate** *station_update_rate*] parameter (the number represents how many dummy updates to send every 100 milliseconds).

However, adjusting the **rate** parameter usually does not improve failover performance. Notice that only MAC addresses *not* learned over the uplinks are flooded. Because UplinkFast only runs on leaf-node switches where the vast majority of the MAC addresses in the bridging table *are* associated with the uplink ports, usually only a few hundred addresses require flooding. The default rate floods 450 to 600 addresses in the 3–4 second UplinkFast convergence period. Therefore, it only makes sense to increase the rate if you have more than about 500 devices connected to your wiring closet switch.

UplinkFast is an extremely effective and useful feature. It provides much faster convergence than any of the timer tuning techniques discussed earlier and is much safer. As long as you only deploy it in leaf-node switches, it can be a wonderful way to maintain the safety of STP while dramatically improving failover times in most situations.

BackboneFast

BackboneFast is a complementary (and patented) technology to UplinkFast. Whereas UplinkFast is designed to quickly respond to failures on links directly connected to leaf-node switches, it does not help in the case of indirect failures in the core of the backbone. This is where BackboneFast comes in.

Don't expect BackboneFast to provide the two to three second rollover performance of UplinkFast. As a Max Age optimization, BackboneFast can reduce the indirect failover performance from 50 to 30 seconds (with default parameters; and from 14 to 8 seconds with the tunable values set their minimums). However, it never eliminates Forwarding Delay and provides no assistance in the case of a direct failure (recall from the "Tuning Max Age" section that direct failures do not use Max Age).

TIP	BackboneFast is a Max Age optimization. It allows the default convergence time for indirect failures to be reduced from 50 seconds to 30 seconds.

As discussed in the previous section, UplinkFast should only be enabled on a subset of all switches in your network (leaf-node, wiring closet switches). On the other hand, *BackboneFast should be enabled on every switch* in your network. This allows all of the switches to propagate information about link failures throughout the network.

TIP	BackboneFast should be enabled on every switch in your network.

When a device detects a failure on the link directly connected to its Root Port, the normal rules of STP dictate that it begin sending Configuration BPDUs in an attempt to become the Root Bridge. What other devices do with these Configuration BPDUs depends on where the Designated Ports are located. If a Designated Port hears these inferior BPDUs, it immediately refutes them with a Configuration BPDU as discussed in the "Configuration BPDU" section earlier. If a non-Designated Port receives the inferior BPDU, it is ignored. However, in either case, the 802.1D standard does not provide a mechanism that allows switches receiving inferior BPDUs to make any judgments about the state of the network.

How does BackboneFast magically eliminate Max Age from the STP convergence delay? By taking advantage of the following two mechanisms:

- The first allows switches to detect a possible indirect failure.
- The second allows them to verify the failure.

The BackboneFast detection mechanism is built around the concept that inferior BPDUs are a signal that another bridge *might* have lost its path to the Root Bridge. BackboneFast's verification mechanism employs a request and response protocol that queries other switches to determine if the path to the Root Bridge has actually been lost. If this is the case, the switch can expire its Max Age timer immediately, reducing the convergence time by 20 seconds.

To detect the possible failure of the Root Bridge path, BackboneFast checks the source of the inferior BPDU. If the BPDU is from the local segment's Designated Bridge, this is viewed as a signal of an indirect failure. If the inferior BPDU came from another switch, it is discarded and ignored.

The verification process is more complex than the detection process. First, BackboneFast considers if there are alternate paths to the Root Bridge. If the switch receiving an inferior BPDU has no ports in the Blocking state (ports looped to itself are excluded), it knows that it has no alternate paths to the Root Bridge. Because it just received an inferior BPDU from its Designated Bridge, the local switch can recognize that it has lost connectivity to the Root Bridge and immediately expire the Max Age timer.

If the switch does have blocked ports, it must utilize a second verification mechanism to determine if those alternate paths have lost connectivity to the Root Bridge. To do this, the Catalysts utilize a Root Link Query (RLQ) protocol. The RLQ protocol employs two types of packets—RLQ Requests and RLQ Responses.

RLQ Requests are sent to query upstream bridges if their connection to the Root Bridge is stable. RLQ Responses are used to reply to RLQ Requests. The switch that originates the RLQ Request sends RLQ frames out all non-Designated Ports except the port that received the inferior BPDU. A switch that receives an RLQ Request replies with an RLQ Response if it is the Root Bridge or it knows that it has lost its connection to the Root Bridge. If neither of these conditions is true, the switches propagate the RLQ Requests out their Root Ports until the stability of the Root Bridge is known and RLQ Responses can be sent. If the RLQ Response is received on an existing Root Port, the switch knows that its path to the Root Bridge is stable. On the other hand, if the RLQ Response is received on some port other than the current Root Port, it knows that it has lost its connection to the Root Bridge and can immediately expire the Max Age timer. A switch propagates BPDUs out all Designated Ports until the switch that originated the RLQ Request is reached.

To illustrate this process, consider the simplified campus network shown in Figure 7-24.

Figure 7-24 *BackboneFast Operation*

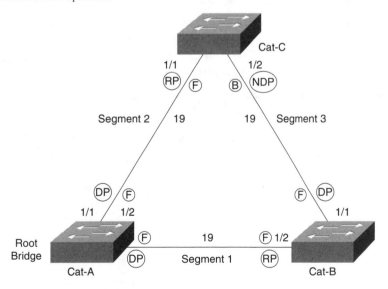

As discussed earlier, BackboneFast must be enabled on all three switches in this network. Assume that Cat-A is the Root Bridge. This results in Cat-B:Port-1/2 and Cat-C:Port-1/1 becoming Root Ports. Because Cat-B has the lower BID, it becomes the Designated Bridge for Segment 3, resulting in Cat-C:Port-1/2 remaining in the Blocking state.

Next, assume that Segment 1 fails. Cat-A and Cat-B, the switches directly connected to this segment, instantly know that the link is down. To repair the network, it is necessary that Cat-C:Port-1/2 enter the Forwarding state. However, because Segment 1 is not directly connected to Cat-C, Cat-C does not start sending any BPDUs on Segment 3 under the normal rules of STP until the Max Age timer has expired.

BackboneFast can be used to eliminate this 20-second delay with the following eight-step process (illustrated in Figure 7-25):

Step 1 Segment 1 breaks.

Step 2 Cat-B immediately withdraws Port 1/2 as its Root Port and begins sending Configuration BPDUs announcing itself as the new Root Bridge on Port 1/1. This is a part of the normal STP behavior (Steps 3–7 are specific to BackboneFast).

Step 3 Cat-C:Port-1/2 receives the first Configuration BPDU from Cat-B and recognizes it as an inferior BPDU.

Step 4 Cat-C then sends an RLQ Request out Port 1/1.

Step 5 Cat-A:Port-1/1 receives the RLQ Request. Because Cat-A is the Root Bridge, it replies with an RLQ Response listing itself as the Root Bridge.

Step 6 When Cat-C receives the RLQ Response on its existing Root Port, it knows that it still has a stable connection to the Root Bridge. Because Cat-B originated the RLQ Request, it does not need to forward the RLQ Response on to other switches.

Step 7 Because Cat-C has a stable connection to the Root Bridge, it can immediately expire the Max Age timer on Port-1/2.

Step 8 As soon as the Max Age timer expires in Step 7, the normal rules of STP require Port Cat-C:Port-1/2 to start sending Configuration BPDUs. Because these BPDUs list Cat-A as the Root Bridge, Cat-B quickly learns that it is not the Root Bridge and it has an alternate path to Cat-A.

Figure 7-25 *BackboneFast Steps to Eliminating the 20-Second Delay*

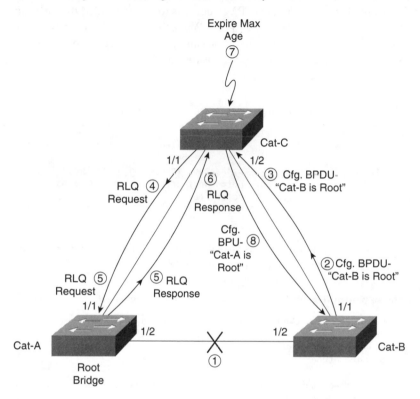

Although this allows Cat-B to learn about the alternate path to the Root Bridge within
several seconds, it still requires that Cat-C:Port-1/2 go through the normal Listening and
Learning states (adding 30 seconds of delay to the convergence with the default values and
8 seconds with the minimum value for Forward Delay).

TIP   BackboneFast requires 4.1 or later code on the Catalyst 5000. All Catalyst 4000s and 6000s
support BackboneFast.

Disabling Port Aggregation Protocol

In certain situations, the Port Aggregation Protocol (PAgP) can create "unexplainable STP
delays" after link initialization. By default, current implementations of EtherChannel-
capable ports reserve the first 15–20 seconds after link initialization for PAgP negotiations.
As is discussed in Chapter 8, "Trunking Technologies and Applications," PAgP is a protocol

that assists in correctly configuring bundles of Fast and Gigabit Ethernet links that act as one large EtherChannel pipe. PAgP defaults to a mode called the **auto** state where it looks for other EtherChannel-capable ports. While this process is occurring, STP is not aware that the link is even active. This condition can be observed with **show** commands. For example, **show port** displays a connected status for Port 1/1 immediately after it has been connected as a trunk link (see Example 7-17).

Example 7-17 show port *Output Immediately After Port 1/1 Is Connected*

```
Cat-D (enable) show port
Port  Name              Status     Vlan      Level  Duplex Speed Type
----- ----------------- ---------- --------- ------ ------ ----- ------------
 1/1                    connected  trunk     normal a-half a-100 10/100BaseTX
 1/2                    notconnect trunk     normal a-half a-100 10/100BaseTX
 3/1                    notconnect 1         normal half   10    10BaseT
 3/2                    notconnect 1         normal half   10    10BaseT
```

However, if **show spantree** is issued at the same time, it still displays the port as not-connected as demonstrated in Example 7-18.

Example 7-18 show spantree *Output Immediately After Port 1/1 is Connected*

```
Cat-D (enable) show spantree 1
VLAN 1
Spanning tree enabled
Spanning tree type          ieee

Designated Root             00-90-92-16-28-00
Designated Root Priority    100
Designated Root Cost        19
Designated Root Port        1/1
Root Max Age   20 sec    Hello Time 2  sec    Forward Delay 15 sec

Bridge ID MAC ADDR          00-90-92-bf-70-00

Bridge ID Priority          32768
Bridge Max Age 20 sec    Hello Time 2  sec    Forward Delay 15 sec

Port      Vlan  Port-State     Cost   Priority  Fast-Start  Group-method
--------- ----  -------------  -----  --------  ----------  ------------
 1/1       1    non-connected   19       32     disabled
 1/2       1    forwarding      19       32     disabled
 3/1       1    not-connected  100       32     disabled
 3/2       1    not-connected  100       32     disabled
```

After approximately 15–20 seconds, PAgP releases the port for use by the rest of the box. At this point, the port enters Listening, Learning, and then Forwarding. In short, because of PAgP, the port took 50 seconds instead of 30 seconds to become active.

Therefore, you should carefully consider the impact of PAgP in your campus implementations. First, it is advisable to use the **desirable** channeling state for links where an EtherChannel bundle *is desired*. Specifically, you should avoid using the **on** state because it hard-codes the links into a bundle and disables PAgP's capability to intelligently monitor the bundle. For example, all STP BPDUs are sent over a single link of the EtherChannel. If this one link fails, the entire bundle can be declared down if PAgP is not running in the **auto** or **desirable** states.

However, in cases where EtherChannel is not in use, disabling PAgP can improve Spanning Tree performance dramatically. In general, campus networks benefit from disabling PAgP in three situations:

- End-Station Ports
- Servers using fault-tolerant NICs that toggle link state during failover
- Testing

End-stations can benefit from disabling PAgP on their switching ports. This can be especially noticeable when used in conjunction with PortFast. Even with PortFast enabled, EtherChannel-capable ports still require almost 20 seconds for activation because PAgP hides the port activation from STP. By disabling PAgP with the **set port channel** *mod_num/port_num* **off** command, this 20-second delay can be almost eliminated, allowing PortFast to function as expected.

Fault-tolerant server NICs that toggle link state during failover can also benefit from a similar performance improvement (however, most fault-tolerant NICs do *not* toggle link). Otherwise, the PAgP delay needlessly interrupts server traffic for almost 20 seconds.

Finally, you should consider disabling PAgP on non-channel ports when performing STP performance. Otherwise, the 20-second PAgP delay can skew your results.

The good news is that this should not affect trunk link failover performance in production in most situations. For example, assume that Cat-D is using Port 1/1 and Port 1/2 as uplinks. If Port 1/1 fails, failover can start immediately because both links have been active for some time and are therefore past the initial PAgP lockout period. On the other hand, if Port 1/2 was acting as a cold standby and not connected when Port 1/1 failed, that is a different matter. In this case, you need to walk up and physically plug in Port 1/2 and PAgP *does* add to the STP failover time.

Useful STP Display Commands

Many Spanning Tree **show** commands have already been discussed. This section mentions some additional **show spantree** capabilities and introduces some extremely useful commands not discussed earlier.

General show spantree Guidelines

A quick look at the output of **show spantree ?** provides an overview of the options available for this powerful and useful command. Example 7-19 displays the output of **show spantree ?** from 4.5.1 Catalyst 5000 code.

Example 7-19 *Online Help Listing of* **show spantree** *Options*

```
Cat-D> (enable) show spantree ?
Usage: show spantree [vlan] [active]
       show spantree <mod_num/port_num>
       show spantree backbonefast
       show spantree blockedports [vlan]
       show spantree portstate <trcrf>
       show spantree portvlancost <mod_num/port_num>
       show spantree statistics <mod_num/port_num> [vlan]
       show spantree statistics <trcrf> <trbrf>
       show spantree summary
       show spantree uplinkfast
```

The primary options are displayed in the following syntax listing:

show spantree [*vlan* | *mod_num/port_num*] [**blockedports** | **active** | **statistics** | **summary**]

These options (and more) are described in the following sections.

Using show spantree *mod_num/port_num*

It is extremely useful to utilize the *mod_num/port_num* option when analyzing Spanning Tree behavior on trunk links. It only lists port-level information and does not show the global and local timer values displayed with the VLAN parameter. For example, the command output in Example 7-20 looks at Port 1/1 which is configured as a trunk link carrying several VLANs.

Example 7-20 *Output of* **show spantree** *mod_num/port_num*

```
Cat-A> (enable) show spantree 1/1
Port      Vlan  Port-State     Cost   Priority  Fast-Start  Group-Method
--------- ----  ------------   -----  --------  ----------  ------------
 1/1       1    listening        19      32      disabled
 1/1       2    listening        16      32      disabled
 1/1       3    listening        19      32      disabled
 1/1       4    listening        16      32      disabled
 1/1       5    listening        19      32      disabled
 1/1       6    listening        16      32      disabled
 1/1       7    listening        19      32      disabled
 1/1       8    listening        19      32      disabled
 1/1       9    listening        19      32      disabled
 1/1      10    listening        19      32      disabled
 1/1    1003    not-connected    19      32      disabled
 1/1    1005    not-connected    19       4      disabled
```

Using show spantree active

Another useful **show spantree** option is the **active** keyword. The **active** keyword filters out all of the not-connected ports. This feature can be especially useful during deployments where many ports are not yet connected to end stations or on Catalysts with very high port densities. Example 7-21 shows some sample **show spantree** output using the **active** keyword.

Example 7-21 *Output of* **show spantree active**

```
Cat-A> (enable) show spantree 1 active
VLAN 1
Spanning tree enabled
Spanning tree type          ieee

Designated Root             00-90-92-16-18-00
Designated Root Priority    32768
Designated Root Cost        19
Designated Root Port        1/1
Root Max Age   20 sec    Hello Time 2  sec    Forward Delay 15 sec

Bridge ID MAC ADDR          00-90-92-1B-CB-00
Bridge ID Priority          32768
Bridge Max Age 20 sec    Hello Time 2  sec    Forward Delay 15 sec

Port      Vlan  Port-State     Cost   Priority  Fast-Start  Group-Method
--------- ----  ------------   -----  --------  ----------  ------------
 1/1       1    forwarding       19      32      disabled
 1/2       1    blocking         19      32      disabled
 2/10      1    forwarding      100      32      disabled
 2/23      1    listening       100      32      disabled
```

Although optional, it is best to get into the habit of always specifying the *vlan* parameter. Otherwise, it is easy to waste crucial time looking at output for VLAN 1 (the default) when you thought you were looking at some other VLAN. The same is also true of **show spantree statistics** and **show spantree blockedports**.

Using show spantree summary

The **show spantree summary** command can be useful for getting an overview of the port states on an entire Catalyst device. As illustrated in the output in Example 7-22, port states are listed for every VLAN along with totals for the entire device listed at the bottom.

Example 7-22 *Output of show spantree summary*

```
Cat-D> (enable) show spantree summary
Summary of connected Spanning Tree ports by vlan

Uplinkfast disabled for bridge.

Vlan  Blocking Listening Learning Forwarding STP Active
----- -------- --------- -------- ---------- ----------
    1        1         0        0          2          3
    2        0         0        0          2          2
    3        0         0        0          2          2
    4        0         0        0          2          2
    5        0         0        0          2          2
    6        0         0        0          2          2
    7        0         0        0          2          2
    8        0         0        0          2          2
 1003        1         0        0          1          2
 1005        1         0        0          1          2

      Blocking Listening Learning Forwarding STP Active
----- -------- --------- -------- ---------- ----------
Total        3         0        0         20         23
```

Using show spantree blockedports

The **show spantree blockedports** command can be used to quickly list all of the blocked (and therefore looped) ports on a Catalyst. The VLAN, trunk, and EtherChannel information is listed for every port. A total is presented on the last line. Example 7-23 displays some sample output from the **show spantree blockedports** command.

Example 7-23 *Output of* **show spantree blockedports**

```
Console> (enable) show spantree blockedports
T = trunk
g = group
Ports       Vlans
-----       ----------
 1/2        1
 2/14       1
Number of blocked ports (segments) in the system : 2
```

Using Spanning Tree Logging

In some situations, it is more important to see real-time feedback of Spanning Tree events. This can be enabled with the **set logging** command, as shown in Example 7-24. For example, **set logging level spantree 7** displays STP state transitions. The logging feature was initially released in 2.2 NMP images. Early versions of this feature only show limited information such as when ports enter or leave the Forwarding and Blocking states. Later versions, such as 4.X, show all transitions (such as Listening and Learning mode). This command can also be used to send Spanning Tree transition information to a Syslog server for analysis later or to monitor STP on an ongoing basis.

Example 7-24 *Output of Spanning Tree Logging*

```
06/12/1999,19:33:45:SPANTREE-6: port 3/5 state in vlan 2 changed to blocking.
06/12/1999,19:33:45:SPANTREE-6: port 3/5 state in vlan 2 changed to Listening.
06/12/1999,19:33:51:SPANTREE-6: port 3/5 state in vlan 2 changed to Learning.
06/12/1999,19:33:58:SPANTREE-6: port 3/5 state in vlan 2 changed to forwarding.
```

Using show spantree statistics

If you have a yearning for detailed Spanning Tree information, the **show spantree statistics** command should keep you happy for a while. This command presents several screens full of information for a single VLAN on a single port. For instance, the output in Example 7-25 displays information for VLAN 1 on Port 1/1 of a Catalyst.

Example 7-25 *Output of* **show spantree** *statistics*

```
Cat-D> (enable) show spantree statistics 1/1 1
Port  1/1    VLAN 1


SpanningTree enabled for vlanNo = 1

              BPDU-related parameters
port Spanning Tree              enabled
state                           forwarding
port_id                         0x8001
port number                     0x1
path cost                       19
message age (port/VLAN)         0(20)
designated_root                 00-90-92-55-80-00
designated_cost                 0
designated_bridge               00-90-92-55-80-00
designated_port                 0x8001
top_change_ack                  FALSE
config_pending                  FALSE
port_inconsistency              none


              PORT based information & statistics
config bpdu's xmitted (port/VLAN)   1(393)
config bpdu's received (port/VLAN)  402(804)
tcn bpdu's xmitted (port/VLAN)      1(1)
tcn bpdu's received (port/VLAN)     0(0)
forward trans count                 1
scp failure count                   0


              Status of Port Timers
forward delay timer             INACTIVE
forward delay timer value       15
message age timer               ACTIVE
message age timer value         0
topology change timer           INACTIVE
topology change timer value     0
hold timer                      INACTIVE
hold timer value                1
delay root port timer           INACTIVE
delay root port timer value     0


              VLAN based information & statistics
spanningtree type               ieee
spanningtree multicast address  01-80-c2-00-00-00
bridge priority                 32768
bridge mac address              00-90-92-55-94-00
bridge hello time               2 sec
bridge forward delay            15 sec
topology change initiator:      1/1
last topology change occured:   Fri Dec 11 1998, 14:25:00
topology change                 FALSE
topology change time            35
topology change detected        FALSE
```

Example 7-25 *Output of* **show spantree** *statistics (Continued)*

```
topology change count              1
topology change last recvd. from   00-00-00-00-00-00

                    Other port-specific info
dynamic max age transitions        0
port bpdu ok count                 0
msg age expiry count               0
link loading                       1
bpdu in processing                 FALSE
num of similar bpdus to process    0
received_inferior_bpdu             FALSE
next state                         3
src mac count:                     0
total src mac count                0
curr_src_mac                       00-00-00-00-00-00
next_src_mac                       00-00-00-00-00-00
channel_src_mac                    00-00-00-00-00-00
channel src count                  0
channel ok count                   0
```

The output of **show spantree statistics** is broken into five sections. Several of the more useful fields are discussed here. The **message age (port/VLAN)** field under the **BPDU-related parameters** section displays two values. The first value (outside the parentheses) displays the age of the most recently received BPDU plus any time that has elapsed since it arrived. This can be useful to determine if the flow of Configuration BPDUs has stopped arriving from the Root Bridge. The second value (inside the parentheses) displays the Max Age for the VLAN, currently at the default of 20 seconds in the sample output. This is the *locally configured* value, not the value received from the Root Bridge (and actually in use).

The **PORT based information & statistics** presents some very useful BPDU counter statistics. The first two lines display the number of Configuration BPDUs transmitted and received. The next two lines display the same information for TCN BPDUs. Each line contains two values. The first value (outside the parentheses) displays the number of BPDUs transmitted or received on that port for the specified VLAN (if it is a trunk). The second value (inside the parentheses) shows the total number of BPDUs received for the entire VLAN (all ports).

If you are experiencing STP problems, this information can be used to verify that BPDUs are flowing. However, notice that both ends of a link generally do not increment both the transmit and the receive counters. During steady state processing, only the Designated Port increments the Configuration BPDU transmit counter, whereas the Root Port (or Ports) at the other end only increments the receive counter. The BPDU counters can be invaluable when troubleshooting situations where a link has failed in such a way that traffic cannot flow in both directions. Without this information, it can take days to narrow down the source of the instability.

TIP

Use the BPDU transmit and receive counters to troubleshoot link failure problems. Also, Cisco's UniDirectional Link Detection (UDLD) can be very useful.

The **VLAN based information & statistics** section contains helpful information on topology changes. **Last topology change occurred** shows the time and date that the last change took place. The **topology change count** field shows the total number of topology changes that have occurred since Spanning Tree initialized on this port. The **topology change last recvd. from** field shows the port MAC address (the MAC address used in the 802.3 header, *not* the MAC address used for the BID) of the last bridge or switch to send the current bridge a TCN BPDU. Use these fields to track instability caused by excessive Topology Change Notifications. However, notice that unless you are using PortFast on all of your end-station ports, every time a PC or workstation boots or shuts down it generates a TCN BPDU.

TIP

Use the topology change information in the **VLAN based information & statistics** section to track down TCN BPDU problems.

Per-VLAN Spanning Tree Plus

As discussed in Chapter 5, 802.1Q has defined standards-based technologies for handling VLANs. To reduce the complexity of this standard, the 802.1 committee specified only a single instance of Spanning Tree for all VLANs. Not only does this provide a considerably less flexible approach than the Per-VLAN Spanning Tree (PVST) adopted by Cisco, it creates an interoperability problem. To address both of these issues, Cisco introduced the Per-VLAN Spanning Tree Plus (PVST+) protocol in 4.1 code on the Catalyst 5000s (all 4000s and 6000s support PVST+). This feature allows the two schemes to interoperate in a seamless and transparent manner in almost all topologies and configurations.

There are both advantages and disadvantages to using a single Spanning Tree. On the upside, it allows switches to be simpler in design and place a lighter load on the CPU. On the downside, a single Spanning Tree precludes load balancing and can lead to incomplete connectivity in certain VLANs (the single STP VLAN might select a link that is not included in other VLANs). Given these tradeoffs, most network designers have concluded that the downsides of having one Spanning Tree outweigh the benefits.

NOTE

Although the initial release of 802.1Q only specified a single instance of the Spanning-Tree Protocol, the IEEE is working on multiple instances of STP in the 802.1s working group.

PVST+ Network Region Types

PVST+ allows for three types of regions in the network:

- A group of traditional (pre-4.1) Catalysts form a PVST region with each VLAN using a separate instance of the Spanning-Tree Protocol.

- Pure 802.1Q switches use a single instance of the Spanning-Tree Protocol, the Mono Spanning Tree (MST). A group of these switches forms an MST region.

- Catalysts running 4.1 and later code form a PVST+ region.

Given that pure 802.1Q switches only support 802.1Q-style trunks and PVST switches only support ISL trunks, these regions can only be connected in a limited set of combinations:

- PVST and PVST+ regions can connect over ISL trunk links.

- MST and PVST+ regions can connect over an 802.1Q trunk.

Notice that an MST and PVST region cannot be connected via a trunk link. Although it is possible to provide a non-trunk connection between the two regions by using an access (non-trunk) link, this is of limited usefulness in real-world networks. Figure 7-26 illustrates the three types of STP regions and potential linkages.

Figure 7-26 *Three Types of Regions Supported under PVST+*

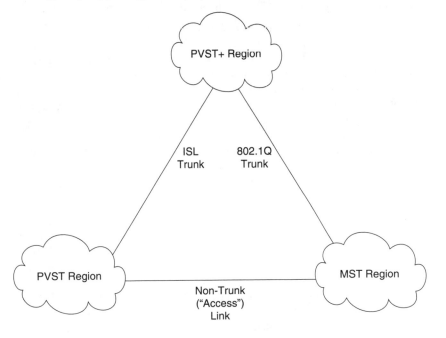

Because it provides interoperability between the other two types of regions, a PVST+ region is generally used in the backbone. It connects to MST regions via 802.1Q trunks and PVST regions via ISL links. However, more flexible configurations are allowed. For example, two PVST+ regions can connect via an MST backbone region.

PVST+ Mapping and Tunneling

PVST+ utilizes two techniques to provide transparent STP support across the three types of regions:

- Mapping
- Tunneling

Mapping is used between PVST and PVST+ regions. Each Spanning Tree in a PVST region maps to a separate Spanning Tree in PVST+ on a one-to-one basis. The same occurs in the reverse direction. This process is both simple and obvious.

On the other hand, when converting between MST and PVST+ regions, both mapping and tunneling must be used. The single Spanning Tree used in the MST region maps to a single Spanning Tree in the PVST+ region. This Spanning Tree is referred to as the *Common Spanning Tree (CST)* and uses VLAN 1. When going in the opposite direction, all Spanning Trees other than the CST belonging to VLAN 1 use tunneling. The BPDUs for these VLANs are flooded throughout the MST region and reach other PVST+ bridges on the far side.

How does Cisco implement the tunneling approach that allows these PVST+ BPDUs to be flooded? In the case of mapped VLANs, the BPDUs are sent to the well-known STP MAC address of 01-80-C2-00-00-00. All bridges conforming to the 802.1D specification do not flood these frames. Rather, the frames are forwarded to the CPU for STP processing. If necessary, the STP process generates *new* BPDUs to pass on to other devices. If the PVST+ BPDUs were sent into the MST region using this MAC address, they would only travel as far as the first bridge or switch. Because MST devices do not understand multiple instances of the Spanning-Tree Protocol, these BPDUs would be dropped. However, because PVST+ uses a different multicast MAC address, the MST devices would flood the BPDUs as if they were normal data. As these BPDUs reach other PVST+ switches on the far side of the MST region, they can be processed as if they were sent to the well-known MAC address.

To accomplish this flooding process, Cisco has utilized the destination MAC address 01-00-0C-CC-CC-CD. Notice that this address differs from the usual Cisco multicast address used by CDP, VTP, DISL, PAgP, and DTP: 01-00-0C-CC-CC-CC. Although these only differ by one bit, the difference is critical. Just as all 802.1D bridges absorb frames sent to 01-80-C2-00-00-00 for processing (in other words, they are *regenerated, not flooded*), all Cisco devices absorb 01-00-0C-CC-CC-CC for processing. If the usual Cisco Multicast were used, all existing Catalyst devices would not flood the PVST+ BPDUs, breaking the tunneling process. However, by using a new multicast address, older Cisco bridging devices flood the BPDUs as normal data. As mentioned in the previous paragraph, also notice that the CST BPDUs must be sent to the well-known MAC of 01-80-C2-00-00-00 (this is the MAC addresses specified for STP in the 802.1D specification) so that they can be processed normally by the devices in the MST region.

PVST+ and Spanning Tree Load Balancing

An interesting question arises when using PVST+: How do you implement STP load balancing? Fortunately, most of the techniques discussed earlier work the same under PVST+ as they were explained under the PVST rules used earlier. The most significant difference has to do with the mechanics of the tunneling process. Specifically, when MST switches flood the PVST+ BPDUs, they are only flooded out ports that are in the Forwarding state. Not only can this delay the initial propagation of PVST+ BPDU through the MST region, it can affect STP load balancing. For example, consider Figure 7-27, the simplified campus backbone used throughout this chapter.

Figure 7-27 *PVST+ Load Balancing*

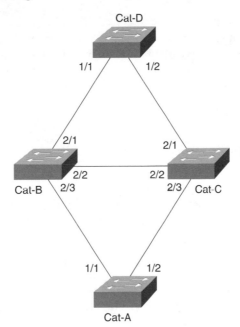

Five basic combinations of MST, PVST, and PVST+ switches can be used in this network:

- **All switches are PVST devices**—This is the case discussed in the "Spanning Tree Load Balancing" section earlier. All of the load balancing techniques covered in that section obviously work here.

- **All switches are PVST+ devices**—Load balancing can be implemented using exactly the same techniques as with PVST switches. The PVST+ and CST BPDUs are handled without any user configuration.

- **All switches are MST devices**—No STP load balancing is possible under the current version of 802.1Q.

- **An IDF switch is an MST device and remaining devices are PVST+ devices**— For PVST+ BPDUs and traffic to pass through both uplink ports on the IDF switch, both ports need to be in the STP Forwarding state. Beyond that, normal STP load balancing techniques can be utilized.

- **An MDF switch is an MST device and remaining devices are PVST+ devices**— For PVST+ BPDUs and traffic to pass through all ports of the MDF switch, all of the ports must be placed in the Forwarding state. After that has been accomplished, normal STP load balancing can be done.

In short, PVST+ allows all of the usual Spanning Tree load balancing techniques to be used with one exception—all inter-switch ports on MST devices should be in the Forwarding state.

NOTE   Load balancing might be possible if some MST ports are Blocking. However, the load balancing design requires careful analysis. In general, it is easiest to design the network to have all inter-switch MST ports in the Forwarding state (if possible).

Two problems arise when the MST ports are not forwarding:

- PVST+ BPDUs are only flooded out a subset of the ports, and therefore only learn a subset of the topology.

- Blocking MST ports destroy the capability to implement load balancing. Recall that when an MST switch puts a port in the Blocking state, it blocks that port for *all* VLANs. Because this forces all traffic to use a single path, load balancing is no longer possible.

TIP   The mapping and tunneling aspects of PVST+ require no user configuration or intervention. This allows plug-and-play interoperability. However, load balancing might require some extra STP tuning to force the MST ports into the Forwarding state.

It can be tricky to meet the requirement that all ports on the MST switches forward while also distributing the traffic across multiple paths. A couple of examples illustrate this point. First, consider the case of an MDF MST switch as shown in Figure 7-28. Cat-B has been replaced by Sw-B, a generic 802.1Q MST switch.

Figure 7-28 *MDF MST Switch Load Balancing*

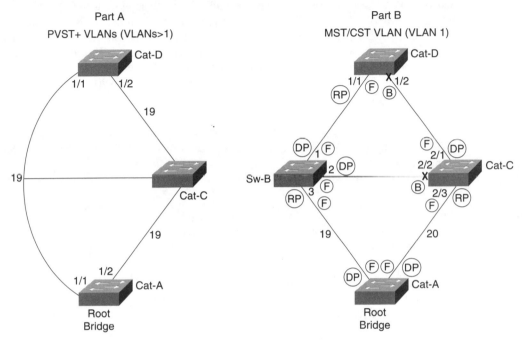

Part A in Figure 7-28 illustrates the tunneling process of PVST+ BPDUs through an MST switch (this is used for VLANs other than VLAN 1). Because the MST switch floods the PVST+ BPDUs out all inter-switch ports (assuming that the requirement of all ports Forwarding is met), it is as though the MST switch does not exist. An interesting consequence of this is that the left path appears to only have a cost of 19, whereas the right path has the usual cost of 38 (19+19). In other words, Cat-A, the Root Bridge, originates Configuration BPDUs with a cost of zero. These BPDUs arrive without any modification on Cat-D:Port-1/1 where the cost is increased to 19. On the right link, Cat-C receives the BPDUs and increases the Root Path Cost to 19. When Cat-D:Port-1/2 receives these, it increases the Root Path Cost to 38. This issue is easily overcome by increasing cost to some large value such as 1000 on the link you do not want the traffic to take (this is another example of a case where using the default **portvlancost** behavior of lowering the cost by one does not work as discussed in the earlier section "Decreasing Path Cost for Load Balancing"). For example, traffic for VLAN 3 could be forced to take the right link by increasing VLAN 3's Path Cost on Cat-D:Port-1/1 to 1000 (the cost of the right path would remain 38 and be more attractive).

Part B in Figure 7-28 illustrates the active topology seen in VLAN 1, the MST/CST VLAN. This is the VLAN where the STP parameters must be tuned to meet the requirement that all ports on the MST switch be Forwarding. One easy way to meet this requirement is to make Sw-B the Root Bridge for VLAN 1. In a simple topology such as that shown in Figure 7-28, this is probably the most effective approach. However, a more flexible technique is generally required for larger networks. Part B shows a solution that can be utilized in these cases (note that Cat-A is the Root Bridge). Sw-B:Port-1 and Sw-B:Port-3 are Forwarding by default (Sw-B:Port-1 becomes a Designated Port and Sw-B:Port-3 becomes the Root Port). Sw-B:Port-2, on the other hand, might or might not become a Designated Port (if Cat-C has a lower BID, Cat-C:Port-2/2 wins the election). To eliminate this chance and force Sw-B:Port-2 to win the Designated Port election, the Path Cost of Cat-C:Port-2/3 can be increased from 19 to 20 (or something even higher).

TIP	Load balancing generally requires all inter-switch ports on MST switches to be in the Forwarding state.

Figure 7-29 illustrates the case of an IDF MST switch. Cat-B has been put back into service and the generic 802.1Q switch has been relocated to the IDF wiring closet in place of Cat-D (it is called Sw-D).

Figure 7-29 *IDF MST Switch Load Balancing*

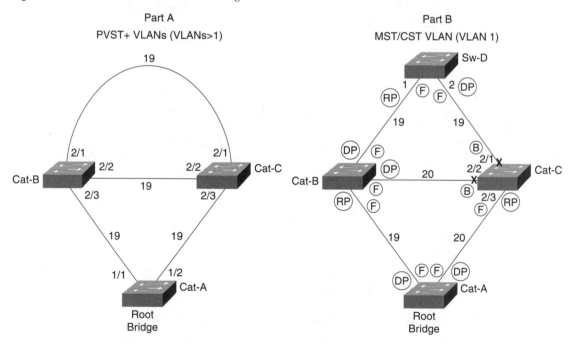

In this case, both uplink ports on Sw-D must be Forwarding. However, to ensure this behavior, one of Sw-D's ports must become a Root Port and the other must become a Designated Port. This can be accomplished by increasing the cost on Cat-C:Port-2/2 and Cat-C:Port-2/3

enough to force Cat-C:Port-2/1 into the Blocking state (because Sw-D:Port-2 has the most attractive port for the Cat-C to Sw-D segment). Now that the MST switch has all inter-switch ports in the Forwarding state, load balancing can be addressed. In this case, Cat-B should be configured to forward half of the VLANs (for example, the even VLANs) while Cat-C handles the other half (the odd VLANs). This can be done by increasing (or decreasing) the Path Cost on Ports 2/3 of Cat-B and Cat-C for alternating VLANs.

NOTE   Note that the Path Cost on Cat-C:Port-2/3 needs to be set between 20 and 37 for the topology to work as described in Figure 7-29. If it were set lower, Cat-C:Port-2/1 would have a lower Root Path Cost than Sw-D:Port-2, causing Sw-D:Port-2 to enter the Blocking state. On the other hand, if Cat-C:Port-2/3's Path Cost were set to higher than 37, Cat-C:Port-2/1 would become the Root Port for Cat-C, causing Cat-C:Port-2/3 to enter the Blocking state.

Disabling STP

It might be necessary to disable Spanning Tree in some situations. For example, some network administrators disable STP in frustration after not being able to resolve STP bugs and design issues. Other people disable STP because they have loop-free topologies. Some shops resort to disabling STP because they are not aware of the PortFast feature (not to mention its interaction with PAgP as discussed earlier).

If you do need to disable STP, Catalysts offer the **set spantree disable** command. On most Catalyst systems, STP can be disabled on a per-VLAN basis. For example, **set spantree disable 2** disables STP for VLAN 2. However, don't forget that this disables STP for all ports in the specified VLAN—Layer 2 Catalyst switches such as the 4000s, 5000s, and 6000s currently do not offer the capability to disable STP on a per-port basis. Example 7-26 shows the use of the **set spantree disable** command to disable STP for VLAN 1 on Cat-A.

Example 7-26 *Disabling STP for VLAN 1*

```
Cat-A> (enable) set spantree disable 1
Spantree 1 disabled.
```

If you are using certain Layer 3 switching technologies such as the NetFlow Feature Card, STP can only be disabled for an entire device (all VLANs).

TIP

STP cannot be disabled per port on Layer 2-oriented Catalyst equipment such as the 4000s, 5000s, and 6000s. When these Catalysts are not using a NFFC, you are allowed to disable STP per VLAN, but this applies to all ports in the VLAN on the specified device. Because devices such as the Catalyst 8500 use the full router IOS, you have complete control over where Spanning Tree runs (through the use of **bridge-group** statements).

Disabling STP on an entire device can be accomplished with the **set spantree disable all** command.

However, it is generally better to use features such as PortFast, UplinkFast, Layer 3 switching, and a scalable design than it is to completely disable Spanning Tree. When Spanning Tree is disabled, your network is vulnerable to misconfigurations and other mistakes that might create bridging loops.

TIP

Don't take disabling STP lightly. If loops are formed by mistake, the entire network can collapse. In general, it is preferable to utilize features such as UplinkFast than to entirely disable STP.

One of the more common places where Spanning Tree can be disabled is when using an ATM campus core. Because LANE naturally provides a loop-free environment, some ATM-oriented vendors leave Spanning Tree disabled by default. However, for this to work, you must be very careful to avoid loops in the Ethernet portion of your network. Besides preventing loops between end-user ports, you generally must directly connect every IDF switch to the ATM core (in other words, redundant Ethernet links cannot be used from the MDF closets to the IDF closets because they would form loops).

Finally, notice that when STP is disabled on Layer 2 Catalyst equipment such as the 4000s, 5000s, and 6000s, BPDUs are flooded through the box. In other words, as soon as Spanning Tree is disabled, the 01-80-C2-00-00-00 multicast address is again treated as a normal multicast frame (rather than being directed to the Supervisor where the frames are absorbed and possibly regenerated). The net effect of this is that Catalysts with Spanning Tree disabled are invisible to neighboring switches that are still running the protocol. To these switches, the Catalyst with STP disabled is indistinguishable from a Layer 1 hub (at least as far as STP goes).

Tips and Tricks: Mastering STP

This section summarizes some of the advice given in earlier sections while also introducing some other STP best practices.

Manually position Root Bridges. Leaving Root Bridge placement to chance can dramatically affect the stability and scalability of your network. For more information, see the sections "Using Spanning Tree in Real-World Networks" and "Deterministic Root Bridge Placement" in Chapter 6.

Always have at least one backup Root Bridge. If you design your network around a single Root Bridge, all of your carefully laid plans can unravel when the Root Bridge fails. All Layer 2 networks should have at least one backup Root Bridge. Large networks might require more than one.

Try to locate Root Bridges on devices near heavily used traffic destinations. For flat networks lacking sufficient Layer 3 hierarchy, this usually means placing the Root Bridges for all VLANs on a pair of redundant switches at the server farm entrance. For more hierarchical networks, collocate the Root Bridges with the routers acting as the default gateways for the end-user segments (see Chapters 11, 15, and 17 for more information).

Diagram your primary and backup topologies. Most network managers recognize the value in having network diagrams. However, most of these diagrams only show the Layer 3 topology. Furthermore, tools such as HP OpenView tend to be very Layer 3 centric (although this is starting to change). Unfortunately, these Layer 3 diagrams tell you nothing about your Layer 2 topology—it all appears as one big subnet. CiscoWorks for Switched Internetworks (CWSI) in CiscoWorks 2000 has a simplistic but effective STP mapping tool.

Network managers running a large switched infrastructure should consider placing the same care and effort into Layer 2 diagrams as they do with Layer 3 diagrams. When doing this, be sure to capture the primary and back up active Spanning Tree topologies. The diagram should indicate which ports are Forwarding and which ports are Blocking for each VLAN. Knowing this ahead of time can be a huge lifesaver when the network is down. It can be confusing enough just to figure out your STP topology on a calm day—trying to figure it out when the network is down is no fun at all!

TIP   Many CWSI/CiscoWorks 2000 users are not aware that it contains a Spanning Tree mapping tool. To use it, first pull up VLAN Director. Then select a VTP domain. Then pick a VLAN in that domain. This highlights the nodes and links that participate in the VLAN. It also brings up the VLAN section (it has a yellow light bulb next to it). Click the Spanning Tree checkbox and the Blocking ports, which are marked with a sometimes-hard-to-see X.

Update your design after adding to the network. After carefully implementing load balancing and Root Bridge failover strategies, be sure to evaluate the impact of network additions and modifications. By adding devices and paths, it is easy for innocent-looking changes to completely invalidate your original design. Also be sure to update your documentation and diagrams. This is especially true if you are using a flat-earth design (see the section "Campus-Wide VLANs Model" in Chapter 14).

Avoid timer tuning in flat designs. Unless you have a narrow Spanning Tree diameter and a very controlled topology, timer tuning can do more harm than good. It is usually safer and more scalable to employ techniques such as UplinkFast and BackboneFast.

Max Age tuning is less risky than Forward Delay tuning. Although overly-aggressive Max Age tuning can lead to excessive Root Bridge, Root Port, and Designated Port elections, it is less dangerous than overly-aggressive Forward Delay tuning. Because Forward Delay controls the time a device waits before placing ports in the Forwarding state, a very small value can allow devices to create bridging loops before accurate topology information has had time to propagate. See the sections "Tuning Max Age" and "Tuning Forward Delay" earlier in this chapter for more information.

If you do resort to timer tuning, consider using the **set spantree root** macro. This macro sets Spanning Tree parameters based on the recommended formulas at the end of the 802.1D spec. For more information, see the section "Using A Macro: set spantree root" in Chapter 6.

Use timer tuning in networks using the multilayer design model. Because this approach constrains the Layer 2 topology into lots of Layer 2 triangles, consider using STP timer tuning in networks using the multilayer design model. In general, it is recommended to use the **set spantree root** command and specify a diameter of 2–3 hops and a Hello Time of two seconds. See the section "Timer Tuning" in Chapter 15 for more detailed information.

Utilize Root Bridge placement load balancing in networks employing MLS and the multilayer design model. This chapter discussed the importance of using Layer 3 switching to limit the size of your Spanning Tree domains. Chapters 11, 14, 15, and 17 look at the use of various approaches to Layer 3 switching and make some specific recommendations on how to use this technology for maximum benefit. Chapter 14 details one of the most successful campus design architectures, the so-called multilayer model. When implemented in conjunction with Cisco's MLS/NFFC, the multilayer model seeks to reduce Spanning Tree domains to a series of many small Layer 2 triangles. Because these triangles have very predictable and deterministic traffic flows, they are very well suited to using the Root Bridge Placement form of STP load balancing. In general, the Root Bridges should be located near or collocated with the default gateway router for that VLAN.

Port/VLAN cost is the most flexible STP load balancing technique. Other than Root Bridge placement, which can be useful in networks with well-defined traffic patterns for each VLAN, port/VLAN cost load balancing is the preferable option. In general, it should be used in all situations other than the case mentioned in the previous tip. For details, see "Load Balancing with Port/VLAN Cost" earlier in this chapter.

Spanning Tree load balancing requires that multiple VLANs be assigned to IDF wiring closet switches. Although assigning a single VLAN to IDF switches can make administration easier, it prevents STP load balancing from being possible. In some cases, non-STP load balancing techniques such as MHSRP and EtherChannel might still be possible with a single IDF VLAN.

Use a separate management VLAN. Just like end-stations, Catalysts must process all broadcast packets in the VLAN where they are assigned. In the case of a Layer 2 Catalyst, this is the VLAN where SC0 is placed. If this VLAN contains a large amount of broadcast traffic, it can then overload the CPU and cause it to drop frames. If end-user traffic is dropped, no problem. However, if STP (or other management) frames are dropped, the network can quickly destabilize. Isolating the SC0 logical interfaces in their own VLAN protects them from end-user broadcasts and allows the CPU to focus only on important management traffic. In many cases, the factory default VLAN (VLAN 1 for Ethernet) works well as the management VLAN. Chapter 15 discusses management VLAN design issues and techniques.

Minimize Layer 2 loops in the management VLAN. Many networks contain lots of redundancy in the management VLAN. The thought is that it prevents failovers from isolating switch management capabilities. Unfortunately, this can also destabilize the network. In networks with lots of management VLAN loops, all it takes is a single switch to become overloaded or run into an STP bug. If this switch then opens up a bridging loop in the management VLAN, suddenly neighboring bridges see a flood of broadcast and multicast traffic. As this traffic inevitably overloads the neighboring switches, they can create additional bridging loops. This phenomenon can pass like a wave across the entire network with catastrophic results. Although it might only directly effect VLAN 1, by disabling the CPUs in all bridges and switches, it effectively shuts down the entire Layer 2 network. To avoid these problems, it is advisable to use Layer 3 routing, not Layer 2 bridging, to provide redundancy in the management VLAN. This point is discussed further in Chapter 15.

Use Layer 3 switching to reduce the size of Spanning Tree domains. Now that you are armed with a truck-load of STP knowledge, creating scalable and flexible STP designs should be a breeze! However, this knowledge should also lead you to the conclusion that excessively large Spanning Tree domains are a bad idea. Small STP domains provide the best mix of failover performance and reliability. See Chapters 11, 14, 15, and 17 for more information.

Try to design your network such that Spanning Tree domains consist of MDF-IDF-MDF triangles. This maximizes STP's value as a Layer 2 failover feature minimizes any scalability concerns.

Use PortFast on end-station ports to reduce Topology Change Notifications. Not only can PortFast eliminate problems associated with devices that boot and access the network quickly, it reduces the number of Topology Change Notifications in the network. See the "PortFast" section in the chapter for more information.

Use UplinkFast to improve IDF wiring closet failover time. UplinkFast is an extremely effective and clever STP optimization that reduces most wiring closet failover times to two or three seconds. See the "UplinkFast" section in this chapter for more information.

PVST+ load balancing requires all inter-switch ports on MST switches to be in the Forwarding state. PVST+ allows traditional PVST Catalysts to interoperate with 802.1Q switches that only use a single Spanning Tree (MST). Best of all, it does this without any additional configuration! However, it might require careful planning to maintain effective STP load balancing. See the "PVST+" section of this chapter for more information.

Always specify the VLAN parameter with Spanning Tree commands to avoid accidental changes to VLAN 1. Many of the Spanning Tree **set** and **show** commands allow you to omit the VLAN parameter. When doing so, you are implying VLAN 1. To avoid confusion and unintentional modifications to VLAN 1, it is best to get in the habit of always specifying this parameter.

The original implementations of Fast EtherChannel in 2.2 and 2.3 NMP images did not support STP over EtherChannel. Spanning Tree still viewed the link as two or four separate ports and would block all but one (obviously defeating the purpose of EtherChannel). The limitation was solved in 3.1 and later versions of code. Don't be misled by older or incorrect documentation that does not reflect this enhancement—using STP over EtherChannel is generally a good idea.

Utilize the "desirable" EtherChannel mode for maximum Spanning Tree stability. When using the on mode, it is possible for the entire channel to be declared down when only the single link carrying STP failed. See Chapter 8 for more information on EtherChannel technology.

Be certain that you do not overload your CPU with Spanning Tree calculations. Keep the total number of logical ports below the values specified in Table 7-4.

Table 7-4 *Maximum Logical Ports*

Cat 5000 Supervisor	Max Logical Ports
Supervisor I	400
Supervisor II	1500
Supervisor III	3500

Use the following formula to calculate the number of logical ports on your devices:

Logical Port = number VLANs on non-ATM trunks +
(2 × number VLANs on ATM trunks) + number non-trunk ports

In other words, you want to add up the total number of VLANs on every port in your box. ATM VLANs (these are called ELANs; see Chapter 9, "Trunking with LAN Emulation") are more heavily weighed by counting them twice.

For example, consider a Catalyst 5000 MDF switch with 100 Ethernet trunk ports, each of which carry 25 VLANs. Also assume that the MDF switch is 32 Ethernet-attached servers using non-trunk links. In this case, the total number of logical ports would be:

2,532 = (100 trunks × 25 VLANs) + 32 non-trunk ports

Although this is by no means the largest MDF switch possible with Catalyst equipment, notice that it requires a Supervisor III. If the trunks were ATM trunks, the total number of logical ports swell to 5,032—more than even a Catalyst 5000 Supervisor III can handle.

Finally, note that this calculation assumes a Hello Time of two seconds. If you have decreased your Hello Time to one second to speed convergence, double the value you calculate in the formula. For instance, the number of Ethernet logical ports in the previous example would be 5,032, and the number of ATM logical ports would swell to 10,064!

Exercises

This section includes a variety of questions and hands-on lab exercises. By completing these you can test your mastery of the material included in this chapter as well as help prepare yourself for the CCIE written and lab tests.

Review Questions

1 Label the port types (RP=Root Port, DP=Designated Port, NDP=non-Designated Port) and the STP states (F=Forwarding, B=Blocking) in Figure 7-30. The Bridge IDs are labeled. All links are Fast Ethernet. Assume that there is only a single VLAN and that the **portvlanpri** command has not been used.

Figure 7-30 *Two Back-to-Back Catalysts with Crossed Links*

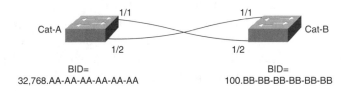

2 When do bridges generate Configuration BPDUs?

3 When do bridges generate Topology Change Notification BPDUs?

4 How many Spanning Tree domains are shown in Figure 7-31? Assume that all of the switches are using ISL trunks and PVST Spanning Tree.

Figure 7-31 *Multiple Spanning Tree Domains*

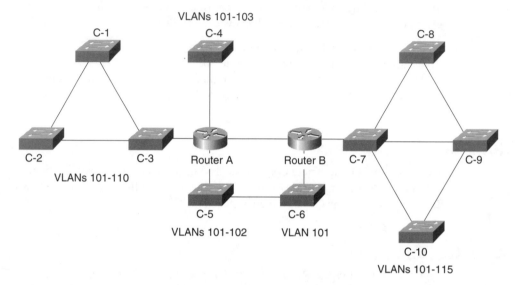

5 When is the Root Bridge placement form of STP load balancing most effective? What command(s) are used to implement this approach?

6 When is the Port Priority form of STP load balancing useful? What command(s) are used to implement this approach? What makes this technique so confusing?

7 When is the Bridge Priority form of STP load balancing useful? What command(s) are used to implement this approach? What makes this technique so confusing?

8 When is the **portvlancost** form of load balancing useful? What is the full syntax of the **portvlancost** command? What is the one confusing aspect of this technique?

9 What technology should be used in place of **portvlanpri**?

10 What are the components that the default value of Max Age is designed to account for? There is no need to specify the exact formula, just the major components captured in the formula.

11 What are the components that the default value of Forwarding Delay is designed to account for? There is no need to specify the exact formula, just the major components captured in the formula.

12 What are the main considerations when lowering the Hello Time from the default of two seconds to one second?

13 Where should PortFast be utilized? What does it change about the STP algorithm?

14 Where should UplinkFast be utilized? In addition to altering the local bridging table to reflect the new Root Port after a failover situation, what other issue must UplinkFast address?

15 Where should BackboneFast be utilized?

16 Where is PVST+ useful?

17 Can MST regions be connected to PVST regions?

18 Can you disable STP on a per-port basis?

19 Why is it important to use a separate management VLAN?

20 What happens if UplinkFast sends the fake multicast frames to the usual Cisco multicast address of 01-00-0C-CC-CC-CC?

Hands-On Lab

Complete an STP design for the network shown in Figure 7-32.

Figure 7-32 *A Three-Building Campus Design*

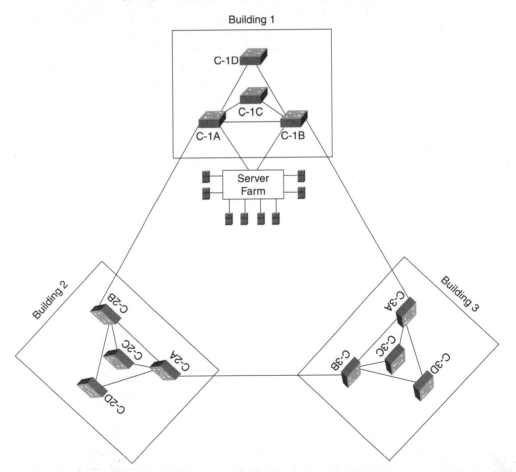

Figure 7-32 shows a three-building campus. Each building contains two MDF switches (A and B) and two IDF switches (C and D). The number of IDF switches in each building is expected to grow dramatically in the near future. The server farm has its own switch that connects to Cat-1A and Cat-1B. The network contains 20 VLANs. Assume that each server can be connected to a single VLAN (for example, the SAP server can be connected to the Finance VLAN). Assume that all links are Fast Ethernet except the ring of links between the MDF switches, which are Gigabit Ethernet.

Be sure to address the following items: STP timers, Root Bridges, Load Balancing, failover performance, and traffic flows. Diagram the primary and backup topologies for your design.

NOTE   This design utilizes what Chapters 14 and 15 refer to as the campus-wide VLANs design model. In general, this design is not recommended for large campus designs. However, it is used here because it makes extensive use of the Spanning-Tree Protocol. For more information on campus-wide VLANs and other design alternatives, please consult Chapters 11, 14, 15, and 17.

Trunking

This chapter covers the following key topics:

- **Why Trunks?**—Describes the advantages of trunks and compares various trunk connection methods for interconnecting Catalysts, routers, and servers.

- **Ethernet Trunks**—Details the trunk options over Fast Ethernet and Gigabit Ethernet. EtherChannel technologies are also discussed. Also describes ISL and 802.1Q encapsulation over trunks. Automatic methods of establishing trunks through DISL and DTP are also considered.

- **FDDI Trunks and 802.10 Encapsulation**—Provides an overview of trunking technology over FDDI in a Cisco environment and the associated encapsulation technology, 802.10.

- **ATM Trunks**—Offers an overview of LANE and MPOA for trunking over ATM. Both LANE and MPOA are detailed in subsequent chapters.

- **Trunk Options**—Provides guidelines for choosing an appropriate trunk technology by comparing the advantages and disadvantages of each.

CHAPTER 8

Trunking Technologies and Applications

Except for the simplest of network configurations, a network comprises multiple Catalysts. Although each Catalyst can stand autonomously, they usually interconnect through ATM, FDDI, or Ethernet technologies. Administrators often face the challenge of choosing the best method to interconnect geographically disbursed members of a VLAN. Some of the issues involved in the decision include the following: technology availability, resources, bandwidth, and resiliency.

This chapter reviews the advantages of trunks and discusses the various technologies available for Catalyst trunks. Specifically, the following sections describe trunks for Fast and Gigabit Ethernet, FDDI, and ATM. The sections also explain Inter-Switch Link (ISL), 802.1Q, Dynamic ISL (DISL), Dynamic Trunk Protocol (DTP), Token Ring ISL (TRISL), 802.10, LAN Emulation (LANE), and Multiprotocol over ATM (MPOA). Guidelines for choosing a method are included at the end of the chapter.

Why Trunks?

When all of the Catalysts in a network support one VLAN and need connectivity, you can establish links between the Catalysts to transport intra-VLAN traffic. One approach to interconnecting Catalysts uses links dedicated to individual VLANs. For example, the network in Figure 8-1 connects several Catalysts together. All of the Catalyst configurations include only one VLAN—all ports belong to the same VLAN. Catalysts A and B interconnect with two direct links for resiliency. If one link fails, Spanning Tree enables the second link.

Figure 8-1 *A Single VLAN Catalyst Design*

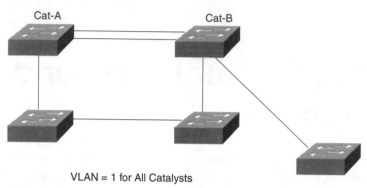

VLAN = 1 for All Catalysts

When you dedicate a link to a single VLAN, this is called an *access link*. Access links never carry traffic from more than one VLAN. You can build an entire switched network with access links. But as you add VLANs, dedicated links consume additional ports in your network when you extend the VLAN to other switches.

In Figure 8-1, multiple links interconnect the Catalysts, but each link belongs to only 1 VLAN. This is possible because there is only one VLAN in the network. What if there were more than one? To interconnect multiple VLANs, you need a link for each VLAN. The network in Figure 8-2 interconnects six Catalysts and contains three distributed VLANs. Notice that Cat-B has members of all three VLANs, whereas its neighbors only have members of two VLANs. Even though the neighbors do not have members of all VLANs, an access link for all three VLANs is necessary to support Cat-B. Without the VLAN 3 access links attached to Cat-B, VLAN 3 members attached to Cat-B are isolated from VLAN 3 members on other Catalysts.

Figure 8-2   *A Multi-VLAN Network Without Trunks*

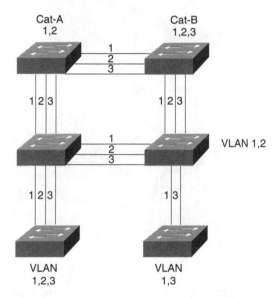

When deploying a network with access links, each link supplies dedicated bandwidth to the VLAN. The link could be a standard 10-Mbps link, a Fast Ethernet, or even a Gigabit Ethernet link. You can select the link speed appropriate for your VLAN requirements. Further, the link for each VLAN can differ. You can install a 10-Mbps link for VLAN 1 and a 100-Mbps link for VLAN 2.

Unfortunately, access links do not scale well as you increase the number of VLANs or switches in your network. For example, the network of Figure 8-1 uses 34 interfaces and 17 links to interconnect the VLANs. Imagine if there were 20 switches in the network with multiple VLANs. Not only does your system cost escalate, but your physical layer tasks as an administrator quickly become unbearable as the system expands.

Alternatively, you can enable a *trunk link* between Catalysts. Trunks allow you to distribute VLAN connectivity without needing to use as many interfaces and cables. This saves you cost and administrative headaches. A trunk multiplexes traffic from multiple VLANs over a single link. Figure 8-3 illustrates the network from Figure 8-2 deployed with trunks.

Figure 8-3 *The Figure 8-2 Network with Trunk Links*

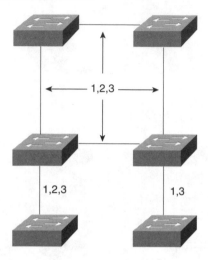

In this network, only 12 ports and six links are used. Although VLANs share the link bandwidth, you conserve capital resources in your network by sharing the links. The majority of this chapter focuses on connectivity between switches. As a practical introduction to trunks, the following section describes reasons to attach routers and file servers to switches with trunks.

Trunks, Servers, and Routers

Trunks are not limited to use between Catalysts. They can also connect routers and file servers to switches. You can do this to support multiple VLANs without using additional ports (see Figure 8-4).

Figure 8-4 *Connecting File Servers and Routers in a Multi-VLAN Network*

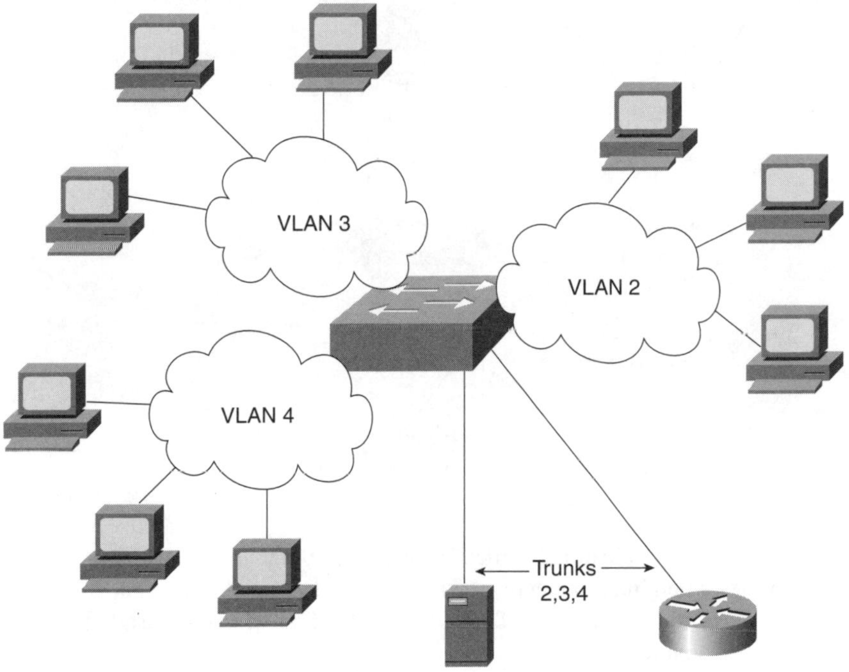

In Figure 8-4, workstations belong to VLANs 2, 3, and 4. Because these stations attach to different broadcast domains, they cannot communicate with each other except through a router. Trunks connect a file server and a router to the switched network. The trunk connection to the router enables inter-VLAN connectivity. Without trunks, you can use multiple interfaces on the router and attach each to a different port on the switch as in Figure 8-5. The difficulty you might experience, though, is in the number of VLANs that this configuration supports. If the connections are high-speed interfaces like Fast Ethernet, you might only install a couple of interfaces. If you use 10-Mbps interfaces, you might not have the bandwidth that you want to support the VLANs.

Figure 8-5 *A Brute Force Method of Attaching Routers and Servers to Multiple VLANs*

Likewise, you could attach a file server to more than one VLAN through multiple interface cards. As when interconnecting switches with dedicated links, this does not scale well and costs more than a trunk link. Therefore, the trunk connectivity used in Figure 8-4 is usually more reasonable.

When a router or file server attaches as a trunk to the switch, it must understand how to identify data from each of the VLANs. The router must, therefore, understand the multiplexing technique used on the link. In a Cisco environment, this can be either ISL or 802.1Q over Ethernet, 802.10 over FDDI, or LANE/MPOA over ATM. In a mixed vendor environment, you must trunk with 802.1Q or LANE/MPOA.

NOTE Some vendors such as Intel and others supply ISL-aware adapter cards for workstations allowing you to use Cisco's trunk protocols. This is beneficial if you want to attach a file server to the Catalyst using a trunk link rather than multiple access links.

Ethernet Trunks

Most trunk implementations use Ethernet. You can construct Ethernet trunks using Fast Ethernet or Gigabit Ethernet, depending upon your bandwidth needs. EtherChannel (defined in greater detail in the sections that follow) creates additional bandwidth options by combining multiple Fast Ethernet or Gigabit Ethernet links. The combined links behave as a single interface, load distribute frames across each segment in the EtherChannel, and provide link resiliency.

Simply inter-connecting Catalysts with Ethernet does not create trunks. By default, you create an access link when you establish an Ethernet interconnection. When the port belongs to a single VLAN, the connection is not a trunk in the true sense as this connection never carries traffic from more than one VLAN.

To make a trunk, you must not only create a link, but you must enable trunk processes. To trunk over Ethernet between Catalysts, Cisco developed a protocol to multiplex VLAN traffic. The multiplexing scheme encapsulates user data and identifies the source VLAN for each frame. The protocol, called Inter-Switch Link (ISL), enables multiple VLANs to share a virtual link such that the receiving Catalyst knows in what VLAN to constrain the packet.

TIP   Trunks allow you to more easily scale your network than access links. However, be aware that Layer 2 broadcast loops (normally eliminated with Spanning Tree) for a VLAN carried on a trunk degrades all VLANs on the trunk. Be sure to enable Spanning Tree for all VLANs when using trunks.

The following sections describe EtherChannel and ISL. The physical layer aspects of EtherChannel are covered first followed by a discussion of ISL encapsulation.

EtherChannel

EtherChannel provides you with incremental trunk speeds between Fast Ethernet and Gigabit Ethernet, or even at speeds greater than Gigabit Ethernet. Without EtherChannel, your connectivity options are limited to the specific line rates of the interface. If you want more than the speed offered by a Fast Ethernet port, you need to add a Gigabit Ethernet module and immediately jump to this higher-speed technology. You do not have any intermediate speed options. Alternatively, you can create multiple parallel trunk links, but Spanning Tree normally treats these as a loop and shuts down all but one link to eliminate the loop. You can modify Spanning Tree to keep links open for some VLANs and not others, but this requires significant configurations on your part.

EtherChannel, on the other hand, allows you to build incremental speed links without having to incorporate another technology. It provides you with some link speed scaling options by effectively merging or bundling the Fast Ethernet or Gigabit Ethernet links and making the Catalyst or router use the merged ports as a single port. This simplifies Spanning Tree while still providing resiliency. EtherChannel resiliency is described later. Further, if you want to get speeds greater than 1 Gbps, you can create Gigabit EtherChannels by merging Gigabit Ethernet ports into an EtherChannel. With a Catalyst 6000 family device, this lets you create bundles up to 8 Gbps (16 Gbps full duplex).

Unlike the multiple Spanning Tree option just described, EtherChannel treats the bundle of links as a single Spanning Tree port and does not create loops. This reduces much of your configuration requirements simplifying your job.

EtherChannel works as an access or trunk link. In either case, EtherChannel offers more bandwidth than any single segment in the EtherChannel. EtherChannel combines multiple Fast Ethernet or Gigabit Ethernet segments to offer more apparent bandwidth than any of the individual links. It also provides link resiliency. EtherChannel bundles segments in groups of two, four, or eight. Two links provide twice the aggregate bandwidth of a single link, and a bundle of four offers four times the aggregate bandwidth. For example, a bundle of two Fast Ethernet interfaces creates a 400-Mbps link (in full-duplex mode). This enables you to scale links at rates between Fast Ethernet and Gigabit Ethernet. Bundling Gigabit Ethernet interfaces exceeds the speed of a single Gigabit Ethernet interface. A bundle of four Gigabit Ethernet interfaces can offer up to 8 Gbps of bandwidth. Note that the actual line rate of each segment remains at its native speed. The clock rate does not change as a result of bundling segments. The two Fast Ethernet ports comprising the 400-Mbps EtherChannel each operate at 100 Mbps (in each direction). The combining of the two ports does not create a single 200-Mbps connection. This is a frequently misunderstood aspect of EtherChannel technology.

EtherChannel operates as either an access or trunk link. Regardless of the mode in which the link is configured, the basic EtherChannel operation remains the same. From a Spanning Tree point of view, an EtherChannel is treated as a single port rather than multiple ports. When Spanning Tree places an EtherChannel in either the Forward or Blocking state, it puts all of the segments in the EtherChannel in the same state.

Bundling Ports

When bundling ports for EtherChannel using *early* EtherChannel-capable line modules, you must follow a couple of rules:

- Bundle two or four ports.
- Use contiguous ports for a bundle.
- All ports must belong to the same VLAN. If the ports are used for trunks, all ports must be set as a trunk.
- If you set the ports to trunk, make sure that all ports pass the same VLANs.
- Ensure that all ports at both ends have the same speed and duplex settings.
- You cannot arbitrarily select ports to bundle. See the following descriptions for guidelines.

These rules are generally applicable to many EtherChannel capable modules, however, some exceptions exist with later Catalyst modules. For example, the Catalyst 6000 line cards do not constrain you to use even numbers of links. You can create bundles with three links if you so choose. Nor do the ports have to be contiguous, or even on the same line card, as is true with some Catalyst devices and line modules. The previously mentioned exceptions of the Catalyst 6000 EtherChannel rules come from newer chipsets on the line modules. These newer chips are not present on all hardware. Be sure to check your hardware features before attempting to create any of these other bundle types.

Early EtherChannel-capable modules incorporate a chip called the Ethernet Bundling Controller (EBC) which manages aggregated EtherChannel ports. For example, the EBC manages traffic distribution across each segment in the bundled link. The distribution mechanism is described later in this section.

When selecting ports to group for an EtherChannel, you must select ports that belong to the same EBC. On a 24-port EtherChannel capable module, there are three groups of eight ports. On a 12-port EtherChannel capable module, there are three groups of four ports.

Table 8-1 shows 24- and 12-port groupings.

Table 8-1   *24-Port and 12-Port Groupings for EtherChannel*

1	2	3	4	5	6	7	8	9	10	11	12	13	14	15	16	17	18	19	20	21	22	23	24
1	1	1	1	1	1	1	1	2	2	2	2	2	2	2	2	3	3	3	3	3	3	3	3
1	1	1	1	2	2	2	2	3	3	3	3												

Table 8-2   *Valid and Invalid 12-Port EtherChannel Examples (for Original Catalyst 5000 Implementations)*

Port		1	2	3	4	5	6	7	8	9	10	11	12
Example A	OK	1	1	2	2	3	3	4	4	5	5	6	6
Example B	OK	1	1			2	2			3	3		
Example C	OK	1	1	1	1	2	2						
Example D	NOK			1	1								
Example E	NOK	1	1	2	2	2	2						
Example F	NOK	1		1									
Example G	NOK		1	1									

For example, in a 12-port module, you can create up to two dual segment EtherChannels within each group as illustrated in Example A of Table 8-2. Or, you can create one dual segment EtherChannel within each group as in Example B of Table 8-2. Example C illustrates a four-segment and a two-segment EtherChannel.

You must avoid some EtherChannel configurations on early Catalyst 5000 equipment. Example D of Table 8-2 illustrates an invalid two-segment EtherChannel using Ports 3 and 4 of a group. The EBC must start its bundling with the first ports of a group. This does not mean that you have to use the first group. In contrast, a valid dual segment EtherChannel can use Ports 5 and 6 with no EtherChannel on the first group.

Example E illustrates another invalid configuration. In this example, two EtherChannels are formed. One is a dual-segment EtherChannel, the other is a four-segment EtherChannel. The dual-segment EtherChannel is valid. The four-segment EtherChannel, however, violates the rule that all ports must belong to the same group. This EtherChannel uses two ports from the first group and two ports from the second group.

Example F shows an invalid configuration where an EtherChannel is formed with discontiguous segments. You must use adjacent ports to form an EtherChannel.

Finally, Example G shows an invalid EtherChannel because it does not use the first ports on the module to start the EtherChannel. You cannot start the EtherChannel with middle ports on the line module.

All of the examples in Table 8-2 apply to the 24-port modules too. The only difference between a 12- and 24-port module is the number of EtherChannels that can be formed within a group. The 12-port module allows only two EtherChannels in a group, whereas the 24-port module supports up to four EtherChannels per group.

One significant reason for constraining bundles within an EBC stems from the load distribution that the EBC performs. The EBC distributes frames across the segments of an EtherChannel based upon the source and destination MAC addresses of the frame. This is accomplished through an **Exclusive OR (X-OR)** operation. **X-OR** differs from a normal **OR** operation. **OR** states that when at least one of two bits is set to a **1**, the result is a **1**. **X-OR** means that when two bits are compared, at least one bit, but only one bit can have a value of **1**. Otherwise, the result is a **0**. This is illustrated in Table 8-3.

Table 8-3   *Exclusive-OR Truth Table*

Bit-1	Bit-2	Result
0	0	0
0	1	1
1	0	1
1	1	0

The EBC uses **X-OR** to determine over what segment of an EtherChannel bundle to transmit a frame. If the EtherChannel is a two-segment bundle, the EBC performs an **X-OR** on the last bit of the source and destination MAC address to determine what link to use. If the **X-OR** generates a **0**, segment 1 is used. If the **X-OR** generates a **1**, segment 2 is used. Table 8-4 shows this operation.

Table 8-4   *Two-Segment Link Selection*

MAC	Binary of Last Octet	Segment Used
Example 1		
MAC Address 1	xxxxxxx0	
MAC Address 2	xxxxxxx0	
X-OR	xxxxxxx0	1
Example 2		
MAC Address 1	xxxxxxx0	
MAC Address 2	xxxxxxx1	
X-OR	xxxxxxx1	2
Example 3		
MAC Address 1	xxxxxxx1	
MAC Address 2	xxxxxxx1	
X-OR	xxxxxxx0	1

The middle column denotes a binary representation of the last octet of the MAC address. An **x** indicates that the value of that bit does not matter. For a two-segment link, only the last bit matters. Note that the first column only states Address 1 or Address 2. It does not specify which is the source or destination address. **X-OR** produces exactly the same result regardless of which is first. Therefore, Example 2 really indicates two situations: one where the source address ends with a **0** and the destination address ends in a **1**, and the inverse. Frames between devices use the same link in both directions.

A four-segment operation performs an **X-OR** on the last two bits of the source and destination MAC address. An **X-OR** of the last two bits yields four possible results. As with the two-segment example, the **X-OR** result specifies the segment that the frame travels. Table 8-5 illustrates the **X-OR** process for a four-segment EtherChannel.

NOTE   Newer Catalyst models such as the 6000 series have the ability to perform the load distribution on just the source address, the destination address, or both. Further, they have the ability to use the IP address or the MAC addresses for the X-OR operation.

Some other models such as the 2900 Series XL perform X-OR on either the source or the destination MAC address, but not on the address pair.

Table 8-5   *Four-Segment Link Selection*

MAC	Binary of last octet	Segment Used
Example 1		
MAC Address 1	xxxxxx00	
MAC Address 2	xxxxxx00	
X-OR	xxxxxx00	1
Example 2		
MAC Address 1	xxxxxx00	
MAC Address 2	xxxxxx01	
X-OR	xxxxxx01	2
Example 3		
MAC Address 1	xxxxxx00	
MAC Address 2	xxxxxx10	
X-OR	xxxxxx10	3
Example 4		
MAC Address 1	xxxxxx01	
MAC Address 2	xxxxxx10	
X-OR	xxxxxx11	4
Example 5		
MAC Address 1	xxxxxx11	
MAC Address 2	xxxxxx11	
X-OR	xxxxxx00	1

The results of Examples 1 and 5 force the Catalyst to use Segment 1 in both cases because the **X-OR** process yields a **0**.

The end result of the **X-OR** process forces a source/destination address pair to use the same link for each frame they transmit. What prevents a single segment from becoming overwhelmed with traffic? Statistics. Statistically, the MAC address assignments are fairly random in the network. A link does not likely experience a traffic loading imbalance due to source/destination MAC address values. Because the source and destination use the same MAC address for every frame between each other, the frames always use the same EtherChannel segment. It is possible, too, that a workstation *pair* can create a high volume of traffic creating a load imbalance due to their application. The **X-OR** process does not remedy this situation because it is not application aware.

TIP   Connecting RSMs together with a Catalyst EtherChannel might not experience load distribution. This occurs because the RSM MAC addresses remain the same for every transmission, forcing the **X-OR** to use the same segment in the bundle for each frame. However, you can force the RSM to use multiple user-assigned MAC addresses, one for each VLAN, with the **mac-address** command. This forces the switch to perform the X-OR on a per-VLAN basis and enable a level of load distribution.

Configuring EtherChannel and PAgP

To simplify the configuration of EtherChannel, Cisco created the Port Aggregation Protocol (PAgP). This protocol helps to automatically form an EtherChannel between two Catalysts. PAgP can have any of four states: **on**, **off**, **auto**, **desirable**. You specify which PAgP state the Catalyst should enable when you configure EtherChannel. Example 8-1 shows the syntax to create an EtherChannel and determine the PAgP mode.

Example 8-1   *EtherChannel Syntax Example*

```
Console> (enable) set port channel ?
Usage: set port channel port_list {on¦off¦auto¦desirable}
   (example of port_list: 2/1-4 or 2/1-2 or 2/5,2/6)
```

The **set port channel** command enables EtherChannel. It does not establish a trunk. With only this configuration statement, a single VLAN crosses the EtherChannel. To enable a trunk, you must also enter a **set trunk** command. The **set trunk** command is described in following sections.

The **on** and **off** options indicate that the Catalyst always (or never) bundles the ports as an EtherChannel. The **desirable** option tells the Catalyst to enable EtherChannel as long as the other end agrees to configure EtherChannel and as long as all EtherChannel rules are met. For example, all ports in the EtherChannel must belong to the same VLAN, or they must all be set to trunk. All ports must be set for the same duplex mode. If any of the parameters mismatch, PAgP refuses to enable EtherChannel. The **auto** option allows a Catalyst to enable EtherChannel if the other end is set as either **on** or **desirable**. Otherwise, the Catalyst isolates the segments as individual links.

Figure 8-6 shows two Catalysts connected with two Fast Ethernet segments. Assume that you desire to enable EtherChannel by bundling the two segments.

Figure 8-6   *A Catalyst 5000 and a Catalyst 5500 Connected with EtherChannel*

Examples 8-2 and 8-3 show sample configurations for both Cat-A and Cat-B.

Example 8-2 *A Two-Port EtherChannel Configuration for Cat-A*

```
Cat-A> (enable) set port channel 2/1-2 on
Port(s) 2/1-2 channel mode set to on.
```

Example 8-3 *A Two-Port EtherChannel Configuration for Cat-B*

```
Cat-B> (enable) set port channel 10/1-2 on
Port(s) 10/1-2 channel mode set to on.
```

TIP

Note that when you enable PAgP on a link where Spanning Tree is active, Spanning Tree takes about 18 more seconds to converge. This is true because PAgP takes about 18 seconds to negotiate a link. The link negotiation must be completed before Spanning Tree can start its convergence algorithm.

TIP

If you change an attribute on one of the EtherChannel segments, you must make the same change on all of the segments for the change to be effective. All ports must be configured identically.

EtherChannel and Routers

Enabling EtherChannel on a Cisco router requires you to define a virtual channel and then to associate specific interfaces to the channel. Up to four EtherChannels can be created in a router. The router views the EtherChannel as a single interface. Example 8-4 shows a configuration for a Cisco 7200 series router. You assign logical addresses to a bundle, not to individual segments in the EtherChannel. The router views the EtherChannel as a single interface.

Example 8-4 *7200 Series EtherChannel Configuration Session Example*

```
Router# config terminal
! This creates the virtual channel
Router(config)# interface port-channel 1
! Assign attributes to the channel just like to a real interface.
Router(config-if)# ip address 10.0.0.1 255.0.0.0
Router(config-if)# ip route-cache distributed
Router(config-if)# exit
!Configure the physical interfaces that comprise the channel
Router(config)# interface fasteth 0/0
Router(config-if)# no ip address
!This statement  assigns fasteth 0/0 to the EtherChannel
Router(config-if)# channel-group 1
%LINEPROTO-5-UPDOWN: Line protocol on Interface Port-Channel1,
changed to UP
Router(config-if)# exit
!You must have at least two interfaces to form an EtherChannel
Router(config-if)# interface fasteth 0/1
Router(config-if)# no ip address
Router(config-if)# channel-group 1
FastEthernet 0/1 added as member-2 to fechannel1
```

In the Catalyst, hardware forms an EtherChannel. In most of the routers, an EtherChannel is formed in software. Unlike the Catalyst, therefore, the router interfaces do not need to be contiguous. However, it might make it administratively easier for you if they are.

Load distribution in a router happens differently than for the Catalyst. Rather than distributing frames based upon the MAC addresses, the router performs an **X-OR** on the last two bits of the source and destination IP address. Theoretically, you should be able to maintain load balancing with this, but because IP addresses are locally administered (you assign them) you can unintentionally assign addresses with a scheme that might favor one link or another in the EtherChannel. If you have EtherChannel to a router, evaluate your IP address assignment policy to see if you are doing anything that might prevent load distribution. If you use protocols other than IP, all non-IP traffic uses a single link. Only the IP traffic experiences load distribution.

If you have a Layer 3 switch such as the Catalyst 8500 series switch/router, it can perform load balancing based upon the IP address and upon an IPX address. Because IPX incorporates the station's MAC address as part of the logical address, load distribution occurs just like it does for any other Catalyst, based upon the MAC address. As mentioned previously, this ensures a fairly high degree of randomness for load distribution, but cannot guarantee load balancing. A particular workstation/server pair can create a high bandwidth load. All of the frames for that pair always cross the same link—even if another link in the EtherChannel remains unused. Load distribution is not based upon bandwidth utilization.

EtherChannel Resiliency

What happens when an EtherChannel segment fails? When a Catalyst detects a segment failure, it informs the Encoded Address Recognition Logic (EARL) ASIC on the Supervisor module. The EARL is a special application-specific integrated circuit that learns MAC addresses. In essence, the EARL is the learning and address storage device creating the bridge tables discussed in Chapter 3. The EARL ages any addresses that it learned on that segment so it can relearn address pairs on a new segment in the bundle. On what segment does it relearn the source? In a two-segment EtherChannel, frames must cross the one remaining segment. In a four- or eight-segment bundle, traffic migrates to the neighboring segment.

When you restore the failed segment, you do not see the traffic return to the original segment. When the segment fails, the EARL relearns the addresses on a new link. Until addresses age out of the bridge table, the frames continue to cross the backup link. This requires that the stations not transmit for the duration of the bridge aging timer. You can manually clear the bridge table, but that forces the Catalyst to recalculate and relearn all the addresses associated with that segment.

EtherChannel Development

EtherChannel defines a bundling technique for standards-based segments such as Fast Ethernet and Gigabit Ethernet. It does not cause the links to operate at clock rates different than they were without bundling. This makes the segments non Fast Ethernet- or Gigabit Ethernet-compliant. EtherChannel enables devices to distribute a traffic load over more than one segment while providing a level of resiliency that does not involve Spanning Tree or other failover mechanisms. The IEEE is examining a standards-based approach to bundling in the 802.3ad committee.

ISL

When multiplexing frames from more than one VLAN over a Fast Ethernet or Fast EtherChannel, the transmitting Catalyst must identify the frame's VLAN membership. This allows the receiving Catalyst to constrain the frame to the same VLAN as the source, thereby maintaining VLAN integrity. Otherwise, the frame crosses VLAN boundaries and violates the intention of creating VLANs.

Cisco's proprietary Inter-Switch Link (ISL) encapsulation enables VLANs to share a common link between Catalysts while allowing the receiver to separate the frames into the correct VLANs.

When a Catalyst forwards or floods a frame out an ISL enabled trunk interface, the Catalyst encapsulates the original frame identifying the source VLAN. Generically, the encapsulation looks like Figure 8-7. When the frame leaves the trunk interface at the source Catalyst, the Catalyst prepends a 26-octet ISL header and appends a 4-octet CRC to the frame. This is called *double-tagging* or *two-level tagging encapsulation*.

Figure 8-7   *ISL Double-Tagging Encapsulation*

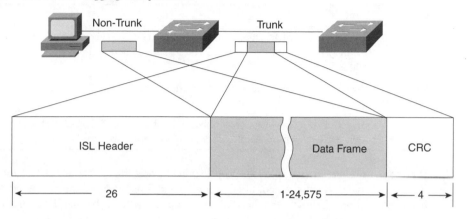

The ISL header looks like that described in Table 8-6.

Table 8-6   *ISL Encapsulation Description*

Octet	Description
DA	A 40-bit multicast address with a value of 0x01-00-0C-00-00 that indicates to the receiving Catalyst that the frame is an ISL encapsulated frame.
Type	A 4-bit value indicating the source frame type. Values include 0 0 0 0 (Ethernet), 0 0 0 1 (Token Ring), 0 0 1 0 (FDDI), and 0 0 1 1 (ATM).
User	A 4-bit value usually set to zero, but can be used for special situations when transporting Token Ring.
SA	The 802.3 MAC address of the transmitting Catalyst. This is a 48-bit value.
Length	The LEN field is a 16-bit value indicating the length of the user data and ISL header, but excludes the DA, Type, User, SA, and Length and ISL CRC bytes.
SNAP	A three-byte field with a fixed value of 0xAA-AA-03.
HSA	This three-byte value duplicates the high order bytes of the ISL SA field.
VLAN	A 15-bit value to reflect the numerical value of the source VLAN that the user frame belongs to. Note that only 10 bits are used.
BPDU	A single-bit value that, when set to 1, indicates that the receiving Catalyst should immediately examine the frame as an end station because the data contains either a Spanning Tree, ISL, VTP, or CDP message.
Index	The value indicates what port the frame exited from the source Catalyst.

continues

Table 8-6 *ISL Encapsulation Description (Continued)*

Octet	Description
Reserved	Token Ring and FDDI frames have special values that need to be transported over the ISL link. These values, such as AC and FC, are carried in this field. The value of this field is zero for Ethernet frames.
User Frame	The original user data frame is inserted here including the frame's FCS.
CRC	ISL calculates a 32-bit CRC for the header and user frame. This double-checks the integrity of the message as it crosses an ISL trunk. It does not replace the User Frame CRC.

ISL trunk links can carry traffic from LAN sources other than Ethernet. For example, Token Ring and FDDI segments can communicate across an ISL trunk. Figure 8-8 shows two Token Rings on different Catalysts that need to communicate with each other. Ethernet-based VLANs also exist in the network. The connection between the Catalysts is an Ethernet trunk.

Figure 8-8 *Using Token Ring ISL (TRISL) to Transport Token Ring Over an Ethernet Trunk*

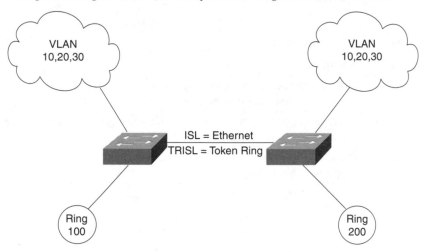

Unfortunately, Token Ring attributes differ significantly from Ethernet. Differences between Token Ring and Ethernet include the following:

- **Frame sizes**—Token Ring supports frames both smaller and extremely larger than Ethernet.

- **Routing Information Field**—Token Ring frames can include an RIF which is meaningless in an Ethernet system.

- **Explorer frames**—Token Ring stations can transmit an explorer frame to discover the relative location of a destination device. This frame type includes a bit indicating that the encapsulated frame is an explorer.

These differences make transporting Token Ring frames over an Ethernet segment challenging at the least.

To effectively transport Token Ring frames over an Ethernet link, the Catalyst must deal with each of these issues.

When Cisco developed ISL, it included a provision for Token Ring and FDDI over Ethernet. The ISL header includes a space for carrying Token Ring- and FDDI-specific header information. These are carried in the **Reserved** field of the ISL header.

When specifically dealing with Token Ring over ISL, the encapsulation is called Token Ring ISL (TRISL). TRISL adds seven octets to the standard ISL encapsulation to carry Token Ring information. The trunk passes both ISL- and TRISL-encapsulated frames.

Dynamic ISL (DISL)

Two Catalysts interconnected with a Fast Ethernet, Gigabit Ethernet, Fast EtherChannel, or Gigabit EtherChannel can operate in a non-trunk mode using access links. When so configured, the traffic from only one VLAN passes over the link. More often, however, you desire to transport traffic from more than one VLAN over the link. Multiplexing the data from the different VLANs over the link requires ISL as described in the previous section. Both ends must agree upon enabling ISL to successfully trunk over the Fast Ethernet or Fast EtherChannel link. If one end enables ISL and the other end disables ISL, the packet encapsulation mismatch prevents successful user data communication over the link. One end generates encapsulated frames and expects to see encapsulated frames, whereas the other end expects the inverse. Conversely, the non-trunking end transmits unencapsulated frames, whereas the receiving trunking end looks for encapsulation, but does not see it and rejects the frame.

In the earliest versions of Catalyst code, you had to manually enable ISL at both ends of the link. With release 2.1 of the Catalyst software, an automatic method of enabling ISL was introduced requiring you to only configure one end of a link. The Cisco proprietary Dynamic Inter-Switch Link (DISL) protocol enables a Catalyst to negotiate with the remote side of a point-to-point Fast Ethernet, Gigabit Ethernet, or EtherChannel to enable or disable ISL. DISL, a data link layer protocol, transmits ISL configuration information with a destination MAC multicast address of 01-00-0C-CC-CC-CC. Note that Cisco uses this multicast address for several proprietary protocols. Cisco uses a different SNAP value, though, to distinguish the packet's purpose. For example, CDP uses the multicast address and a SNAP value of 0x2000, whereas DISL uses the multicast with a SNAP value of 0x2004. When a Catalyst receives a frame with this destination address, it does not forward the frame out any interface. Rather, it processes the frame on the Supervisor module.

A Catalyst trunk (both Fast Ethernet and Gigabit Ethernet) interface can support one of five trunk modes: **off**, **on**, **desirable**, **auto**, or **nonegotiate**. When set to **off**, **on**, **auto**, or **desirable**, the Catalyst sends ISL configuration frames every 30 seconds to ensure that the other end synchronizes to the current configuration. The syntax to enable trunking is as follows:

```
set trunk mod_num/port_num [on | desirable | auto | nonegotiate]
```

Note that **off** is not listed because it disables trunking as described below.

When configured as **off**, the interface locally disables ISL and negotiates (informs) the remote end of the local state. If the remote end configuration allows dynamic trunk state changes (**auto** or **desirable**), it configures itself as a non-trunk. If the remote side cannot change state (such as when configured to **on**), the local unit still disables ISL. Additionally, if the local unit is configured as **off** and it receives a request from the remote Catalyst to enable ISL, the local Catalyst refuses the request. Setting the port to **off** forces the interface to remain **off**, regardless of the ISL state at the remote end. Use this mode whenever you don't want an interface to be a trunk, but want it to participate in ISL negotiations to inform the remote side of its local policy.

On the other hand, if the local interface configuration is **on**, the Catalyst locally enables ISL and negotiates (informs) the remote side of the local state. If the remote side configuration is **auto** or **desirable**, the link enables trunking and ISL encapsulation. If the remote end state is **off**, the link never negotiates to an enabled trunk mode. The local Catalyst enables trunking while the remote end remains disabled. This creates an encapsulation mismatch preventing successful data transfers. Use trunk mode **on** when the remote end supports DISL, and when you want the local end to remain in trunk mode regardless of the remote end's mode.

The **desirable** mode causes a Catalyst interface to inform the remote end of its *intent* to enable ISL, but does not actually enable ISL unless the remote end agrees to enable it. The remote end must be set in the **on**, **auto**, or **desirable** mode for the link to establish an ISL trunk. Do not use the **desirable** mode if the remote end does not support DISL.

NOTE   Not all Catalysts, such as the older Catalyst 3000 and the Catalyst 1900, support DISL. If you enable the Catalyst 5000 end as desirable and the other end does not support DISL, a trunk is never established. Only use the **desirable** mode when you are confident that the remote end supports DISL, and you want to simplify your configuration requirements.

Configuring a Catalyst in **auto** mode enables the Catalyst to receive a request to enable ISL trunking and to automatically enter that mode. The Catalyst configured in **auto** never initiates a request to create a trunk and never becomes a trunk unless the remote end is configured as **on** or **desirable**. The **auto** mode is the Catalyst default configuration. If when enabling a trunk you do not specify a mode, **auto** is assumed. A Catalyst never enables trunk mode when left to the default values at both ends. When one end is set as **auto**, you must set the other end to either **on** or **desirable** to activate a trunk.

The **nonegotiate** mode establishes a Catalyst configuration where the Catalyst enables trunking, but does not send any configuration requests to the remote device. This mode prevents the Catalyst from sending DISL frames to set up a trunk port. Use this mode when establishing a trunk between a Catalyst and a router to ensure that the router does not erroneously forward the DISL requests to another VLAN component. You should also use this whenever the remote end does not support DISL. Sending DISL announcements over the link is unproductive when the receiving device does not support it.

Table 8-7 shows the different combinations of trunk modes and the corresponding effect.

Table 8-7   *Results of Mixed DISL Modes*

Local Mode→ Remote Mode ↓	off	on	auto	desirable	nonegotiate
off	Local:off Remote:off	Local:on Remote:off	Local:off Remote:off	Local:off Remote:off	Local:on Remote:off
on	Local:off Remote:on	Local:on Remote:on	Local:on Remote:on	Local:on Remote:on	Local:on Remote:on
auto	Local:off Remote:off	Local:on Remote:on	Local:off Remote:off	Local:on Remote:on	Local:on Remote:off
desirable	Local:off Remote:off	Local:on Remote:on	Local:on Remote:on	Local:on Remote:on	Local:on Remote:on
nonegotiate	Local:off Remote:on	Local:on Remote:on	Local:off Remote:on	Local:on Remote:on	Local:on Remote:on

With all of these combinations, the physical layer might appear to be operational. If you do a **show port**, the display indicates connected. However, that does not necessarily mean that the trunk is operational. If both the remote and local sides of the link do not have the same indication (on or off), you cannot transmit any traffic due to encapsulation mismatches. Use the **show trunk** command to examine the trunk status. For example, in Table 8-7, the combination **on/auto** results in both sides trunking. The combination **auto/auto** results in both sides remaining configured as access links. Therefore, trunking is not enabled. Both of these are valid in that both ends agree to trunk or not to trunk. However, the combination **on/off** creates a situation where the two ends of the link disagree about the trunk condition. Both sides pass traffic, but neither side can decode the received traffic. This is because of the encapsulation mismatch that results from the disagreement. The end with trunking enabled looks for ISL encapsulated frames, but actually receives nonencapsulated frames. Likewise, the end that is configured as an access link looks for nonencapsulated Ethernet frames, but sees encapsulation headers that are not part of the Ethernet standard and interpret these as errored frames. Therefore, traffic does not successfully transfer across the link.

Do not get confused between DISL and PAgP. In the section on EtherChannel, PAgP was introduced. PAgP allows two Catalysts to negotiate how to form an EtherChannel between them. PAgP does not negotiate whether or not to enter trunk mode. This is the domain of DISL and Dynamic Trunk Protocol (DTP). DTP is a second generation of DISL and allows the Catalysts to negotiate whether or not to use 802.1Q encapsulation. This is discussed further in a later section in this chapter. On the other hand, note that DISL and DTP do not negotiate anything about EtherChannel. Rather, they negotiate whether to enable trunking.

TIP	It is best to hard code the trunk configuration on critical links between Catalysts such as in your core network, or to critical servers that are trunk attached.

TIP	If you configure the Catalyst trunk links for dynamic operations (**desirable**, **auto**), ensure that both ends of the link belong to the same VTP management domain. If they belong to different domains, Catalysts do not form the trunk link.

802.1Q/802.1p

In an effort to provide multivendor support for VLANs, the IEEE 802.1Q committee defined a method for multiplexing VLANs in local and metropolitan area networks. The multiplexing method, similar to ISL, offers an alternative trunk protocol in a Catalyst network. Like ISL, 802.1Q explicitly tags frames to identify the frame's VLAN membership. The tagging scheme differs from ISL in that ISL uses an external tag, and 802.1Q uses an internal tag.

The IEEE also worked on a standard called 802.1p. 802.1p allows users to specify priorities for their traffic. The priority value is inserted into the priority field of the 802.1Q header. If a LAN switch supports 802.1p, the switch might forward traffic flagged as higher priority before it forwards other traffic.

ISL's external tag scheme adds octets to the beginning and to the end of the original data frame. Because information is added to both ends of a frame, this is sometimes called *double-tagging*. (Refer back to Table 8-6 for ISL details.) 802.1Q is called an *internal tag scheme* because it adds octets inside of the original data frame. In contrast to double-tagging, this is sometimes called a *single-tag scheme*. Figure 8-9 shows an 802.1Q tagged frame.

Figure 8-9 *802.1Q/802.1p Frame Tagging Compared to ISL*

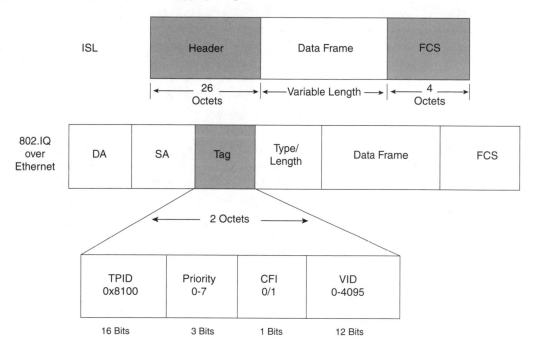

The following bullets describe each of the fields in the 802.1Q header illustrated in Figure 8-9:

- **TPID (Tag Protocol Identifier)**—This indicates to the receiver that an 802.1Q tag follows. The value for the TPID is a hexadecimal value of 0x8100.

- **Priority**—This is the 802.1p priority field. Eight priority levels are defined in 802.1p and are embedded in the 802.1Q header.

- **CFI (Canonical format indicator)**—This single bit indicates whether or not the MAC addresses in the MAC header are in canonical (0) or non-canonical (1) format.

- **VID (VLAN Identifier)**—This indicates the source VLAN membership for the frame. The 12-bit field allows for VLAN values between 0 and 4095. However, VLANs 0, 1, and 4095 are reserved.

An interesting situation arises from the 802.1Q tag scheme. If the tag is added to a maximum sized Ethernet frame, the frame size exceeds that specified by IEEE 802.3. To carry the tag in a maximum sized Ethernet frame requires 1522 octets, four more than the specification allows. The 802.3 committee created a workgroup, 802.3ac, to extend Ethernet's maximum frame size to 1522 octets.

If you have equipment that does not support the larger frame size, it might complain if it receives these oversized frames. These frames are sometimes called *baby giants*.

802.1Q, ISL, and Spanning Tree

When Cisco introduced switched LAN solutions, it recognized the possibility of a complex Catalyst topology. Consequently, Cisco supports multiple instances of Spanning Tree. You can create a different Spanning Tree topology for every VLAN in your network where each VLAN can have a different Catalyst for a Root Bridge. This allows you to optimize the bridged network topology for each VLAN. The selection of a Root Bridge for VLAN 10 might not be the best choice for VLAN 11, or any VLAN other than VLAN 10. Cisco's capability to support multiple instances of Spanning Tree in the Catalyst is called Per-VLAN Spanning Tree (PVST).

802.1Q, however, defines a single instance of Spanning Tree for all VLANs. All VLANs have the same Root Bridge in an 802.1Q network. This is called a *Mono Spanning Tree (MST)* topology. 802.1Q does not exclude the use of more than one instance of Spanning Tree, it just does not address the issues of how to support it.

A complication could arise in a hybrid ISL and 802.1Q environment. Without any special provisions, you need to restrict your Spanning Tree topology to a common topology for all VLANs. Cisco developed PVST+ which allows you to retain multiple Spanning Tree topologies, even in an 802.1Q mixed vendor environment. PVST+ tunnels PVST frames through the 802.1Q MST Spanning Tree network as multicast frames. Cisco uses the multicast address **01-00-0C-CC-CC-CD** for PVST+. Unlike 802.1Q, PVST+ enables you to reuse a MAC address in multiple VLANs. If you have devices that need to do this, you need to use ISL and PVST+. Chapter 7, "Advanced Spanning Tree," provides more details on PVST+.

Configuring 802.1Q

Configuration tasks to enable 802.1Q trunks include the following:

1 Specify the correct encapsulation mode (ISL or 802.1Q) for the trunk.

2 Enable the correct DTP trunking mode or manually ensure that both ends of the link support the same trunk mode.

3 Select the correct native VLAN-id on both ends of the 802.1Q trunk.

The following syntax enables an 802.1Q trunk on a Catalyst:

```
set trunk mod_num/port_num [on|desirable|auto|nonegotiate] dot1q
```

dot1q specifies the trunk encapsulation type. Specifically, it enables the trunk using 802.1Q encapsulation. This is an optional field for ISL trunks, but mandatory if you want dot1q. Of course, if you want an ISL trunk, you do not use **dot1q**, but rather **ISL**. If you do not specify the encapsulation type, the Catalyst uses the default value (ISL). Not all modules support both ISL and 802.1Q modes. Check current Cisco documentation to determine which modes your hardware supports. Further, not all versions of the Catalyst software support 802.1Q. Only since version 4.1(1) does the Catalyst 5000 family support dot1q encapsulation. Automatic negotiation of the encapsulation type between the two ends of the trunk was not available until version 4.2(1) of the Catalyst 5000 software. 4.2(1) introduced DTP, which is described in the following section. Prior to 4.2(1), you must manually configure the trunk mode.

Example 8-5 shows a sample output for configuring Port 1/1 for dot1q encapsulation. This works whether the interface is Fast Ethernet or Gigabit Ethernet.

Example 8-5   *Sample Catalyst Configuration for 802.1Q Trunk*

```
Console> (enable) set trunk 1/1 desirable dot1q
Port(s) 1/1 trunk mode set to desirable.
Port(s) 1/1 trunk type set to dot1q.
Console> (enable) 11/11/1998,23:03:17:DTP-5:Port 1/1 has become dot1q trunk
```

Enabling 802.1Q trunks on a router is similar to enabling ISL. Like ISL, you must include an **encapsulation** statement in the interface configuration. Example 8-6 shows a sample router configuration.

Example 8-6   *Sample Router Configuration for 802.1Q*

```
! Specify the interface to configure
interface fastether 2/0.1
   ip address 172.16.10.1 255.255.255.0
   ipx network 100
   encapsulation dot1q 200
```

The number at the end of the **encapsulation** statement specifies the VLAN number. The 802.1Q specification allows VLAN values between 0 and 4095 (with reserved VLAN values as discussed previously). However, a Catalyst supports VLAN values up to 1005. Generally, do not use values greater than 1005 when specifying the 802.1Q VLAN number to remain consistent with Catalyst VLAN numbers. Note that newer code releases allow you to map 802.1Q VLAN numbers into the valid ISL number range. This is useful in a hybrid 802.1Q/ISL environment by enabling you to use any valid 802.1Q value for 802.1Q trunks, while using valid ISL values on ISL trunks.

Dynamic Trunk Protocol (DTP)

802.1Q offers an alternative to Cisco's proprietary ISL encapsulation protocol. That means a Fast Ethernet/EtherChannel link now has even more possible combinations because a trunk can use ISL encapsulation or 802.1Q tags. Just like ISL, 802.1Q trunks can be set for **on**, **off**, **desirable**, or **auto**. Both ends of a link must, however, be either in ISL or in 802.1Q mode. With version 4.1, you need to manually configure the encapsulation mode at both ends to make them compatible. In release 4.2, Cisco introduced a new link negotiation protocol called Dynamic Trunk Protocol (DTP) which enhances DISL functionality. DTP negotiates the two ends of the link to a compatible mode, reducing the possibility of incompatibly when configuring a link. Note the highlighted DTP message in Example 8-7 indicating that the interface became a trunk. If you select an ISL trunk, DTP reports the action if you have software release 4.2 or later as shown in the output in Example 8-7. Note that PAgP also reports messages. Although PAgP sets up EtherChannel, it reports port status even for non-EtherChannel segments.

Example 8-7 *DTP Message When Establishing an ISL Trunk*

```
Port(s) 1/1 trunk mode set to on.
Console> (enable) 11/12/1998,17:56:39:DTP-5:Port 1/1 has become isl trunk
11/12/1998,17:56:40:PAGP-5:Port 1/1 left bridge port 1/1.
11/12/1998,17:56:40:PAGP-5:Port 1/1 joined bridge port 1/1
```

Restricting VLANs on a Trunk

You can elect to restrict what VLANs can cross a trunk. By default, the Catalyst is authorized to transport all VLANs over a trunk. You might want, instead, to allow only VLANs 5–10 over a trunk. You can specify the VLANs to transport as part of the **set trunk** command. Or, you can remove authorized VLANs from a trunk with the **clear trunk** command. Example 8-8 shows an example of clearing VLANs from a trunk and adding VLANs.

Example 8-8 *Modifying Authorized VLANs on a Trunk*

```
Console> (enable) clear trunk 1/1 10-20
Removing Vlan(s) 10-20 from allowed list.
Port 1/1 allowed vlans modified to 1-9,21-1005.
Console> (enable) set trunk 1/1 15
Adding vlans 15 to allowed list
```

At the end of Example 8-8, the complete list of allowed VLANs is 1-9, 15, 21-1005.

You can use these commands on any trunk, regardless of its tagging mode. Note that if you enter these commands on an EtherChannel trunk, the Catalyst modifies all ports in the bundle to ensure consistency. Ensure that you configure the remote link to carry the same set of VLANs.

FDDI Trunks and 802.10 Encapsulation

ISL trunk encapsulation is designed for trunking over a point-to-point connection between two Catalysts using Ethernet. Only two Catalysts connect to the link. This contrasts with connectivity over an FDDI system. FDDI operates as a shared network media (half duplex) and can have more than two participants on the network. A different encapsulation scheme, therefore, is used when trunking over an FDDI network. Cisco adapted an IEEE standard for secure bridging over an 802-based network and applied it to FDDI trunking between Catalysts. IEEE 802.10 devised the standard to facilitate the transport of multiple traffic sources over shared local and metropolitan networks and yet retain logical isolation between the source networks at the receiver.

You can create interconnections between Catalysts where all Catalyst FDDI interfaces belong to the same VLAN. Only one VLAN transports over the FDDI, however. You can do this if you have a simple VLAN design and have an existing FDDI segment that you need to continue to use. The legacy network components might not support 802.10, forcing you to configure your Catalysts so they can share the FDDI network. A more typical use, however, might allow for multiple VLANs to share the backbone, as in Figure 8-10.

Figure 8-10 *An FDDI Trunk Example with 802.10 Encapsulation*

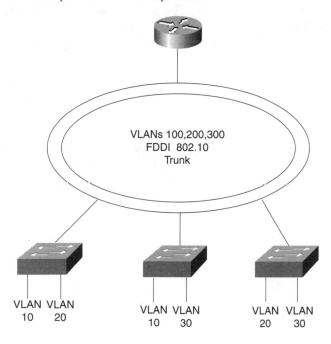

By enabling 802.10 encapsulation on the FDDI interfaces in the network, the FDDI backbone becomes a Catalyst trunk. The network in Figure 8-10 attaches many Catalysts allowing them to transport data from distributed VLANs over the FDDI trunk. Member stations of VLAN 10 on Cat-A can communicate with stations belonging to VLAN 10 on Cat-B. Likewise, members of VLAN 20 can communicate with each other regardless of their location in the network.

As with any multiple VLAN network, routers interconnect VLANs. The Cisco router in Figure 8-10 attached to the FDDI network understands 802.10 encapsulation and can therefore route traffic between VLANs.

The configuration in Example 8-9 demonstrates how to enable 801.10 encapsulation on a Cisco router so that VLAN 100 can communicate with VLAN 200.

Example 8-9 *Router Configuration for 802.10 Trunk*

```
int fddi 2/0.1
 ip address 172.16.1.1 255.255.255.0
 encapsulation sde 100
int fddi 2/0.2
 ip address 172.16.2.1 255.255.255.0
 encapsulation sde 200
```

The configuration applies to FDDI subinterfaces. Each VLAN must be configured on a subinterface and should support a single subnetwork. The **encapsulation sde 100** statement under subinterface 2/0.1 enables 802.10 encapsulation and associates VLAN 100 with the interface, whereas the statement **encapsulation sde 200** associates VLAN 200 with subinterface 2/0.2.

Figure 8-11 illustrates 802.10 encapsulation. The 802.10 header contains the MAC header, a Clear header, and a Protected header. The MAC header contains the usual 48-bit destination and source MAC addresses found in FDDI, Ethernet, and Token Ring networks. The Clear and Protected headers, however, are additions from the 802.10 standard. The Protected header duplicates the source MAC address to ensure that a station is not spoofing the real source. If the source address in the MAC and Protected headers differ, another station took over the session.

Figure 8-11 *802.10 Encapsulation*

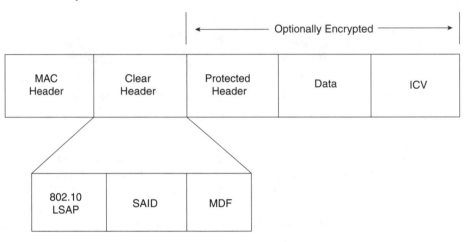

Figure 8-11 shows three fields in the Clear header portion. Only the **Security Association Identifier (SAID)** field is relevant to VLANs. Therefore, the other two fields (802.10 LSAP and MDF) are ignored in this discussion.

The **SAID** field as used by Cisco identifies the source VLAN. The four-byte **SAID** allows for many VLAN identifiers on the FDDI network. When you create an FDDI VLAN, you provide the VLAN number. By default, the Catalyst adds 100,000 to the VLAN number to create a **SAID** value. The receiving Catalyst subtracts 100,000 to recover the original FDDI VLAN value. Optionally, you can specify a **SAID** value. But this is not usually necessary. The Catalyst commands in Example 8-10 enable 802.10 encapsulation for VLANs 500 and 600 and modify the VLAN 600 **SAID** value to 1600.

Example 8-10 *802.10 VLAN Configuration*

```
Console> (enable) set vlan 500 type fddi
Vlan 500 configuration successful
Console> (enable) set vlan 600 type fddi said 1600
Vlan 600 configuration successful
```

After establishing the VLANs, the **show vlan** command displays the addition of the VLANs with the specified SAID value as in Example 8-11. Note that VLAN 500 has a SAID value of 100,500 because a SAID value was not specified and the Catalyst by default added 100,000 to the VLAN number.

Example 8-11 *show vlan Command Output*

```
Console> (enable) show vlan
VLAN Name                             Status    Mod/Ports, Vlans
---- -------------------------------- --------- ------------------------
1    default                          active    1/1-2
                                                2/1-24
100  VLAN0100                         active    110, 120
110  VLAN0110                         active
120  VLAN0120                         active
500  VLAN0500                         active
600  VLAN0600                         active
1002 fddi-default                     active
1003 trcrf-default                    active
1004 fddinet-default                  active
1005 trbrf-default                    active    1003


VLAN Type  SAID       MTU   Parent RingNo BrdgNo Stp  BrdgMode Trans1 Trans2
---- ----- ---------- ----- ------ ------ ------ ---- -------- ------ ------
1    enet  100001     1500  -      -      -      -    -        0      0
100  trbrf 100100     4472  -      -      0x5    ibm  -        0      0
110  trcrf 100110     4472  100    0x10   -      -    srb      0      0
120  trcrf 100120     4472  100    0x20   -      -    srb      0      0
500  fddi  100500     1500  -      0x0    -      -    -        0      0
600  fddi  1600       1500  -      0x0    -      -    -        0      0
1002 fddi  101002     1500  -      0x0    -      -    -        0      0
1003 trcrf 101003     4472  1005   0xccc  -      -    srb      0      0
1004 fdnet 101004     1500  -      -      0x0    ieee -        0      0
1005 trbrf 101005     4472  -      -      0xf    ibm  -        0      0


VLAN AREHops STEHops Backup CRF
---- ------- ------- ----------
110  7       7       off
120  7       7       off
1003 7       7       off
Console> (enable)
```

Although the FDDI VLANS were successfully created, all that was accomplished was the creation of yet another broadcast domain. The Catalysts treat the FDDI VLAN as distinct from any of the Ethernet VLANs unless you associate the broadcast domains as a single domain. Use the **set vlan** command to merge the FDDI and the Ethernet broadcast domains. Until you do this, the Catalyst cannot transport the Ethernet VLAN over the FDDI trunk. To make an Ethernet VLAN 10 and an FDDI VLAN 100 part of the same broadcast domain, you enter the following command:

```
Console> (enable) set vlan 10 translation 100
```

Conversely, the following command is equally effective, where you specify the FDDI VLAN first, and then translate it into the Ethernet VLAN:

```
Console> (enable) set vlan 100 translation 10
```

These are bidirectional commands. You do not need to enter both commands, only one or the other.

ATM Trunks

Asynchronous Transfer Mode (ATM) technology has the inherent capability to transport voice, video, and data over the same infrastructure. And because ATM does not have any collision domain distance constraints like LAN technologies, ATM deployments can reach from the desktop to around the globe. With these attributes, ATM offers users the opportunity to deploy an infrastructure suitable for consolidating what are traditionally independent networks. For example, some companies have a private voice infrastructure between corporate and remote offices. The business leases T1 or E1 services to interconnect private branch exchanges (PBXs) between the offices. The company can deploy or lease a separate network to transport data between the offices. And finally, to support video conferencing, an ISDN service can be installed. Each of these networks has its own equipment requirements, maintenance headaches, and in many cases recurring costs. By consolidating all of the services onto an ATM network, as in Figure 8-12, the infrastructure complexities significantly reduce. Even better, the recurring costs can diminish. Most importantly, this keeps your employer happy.

Figure 8-12 *Service Consolidation over an ATM Network*

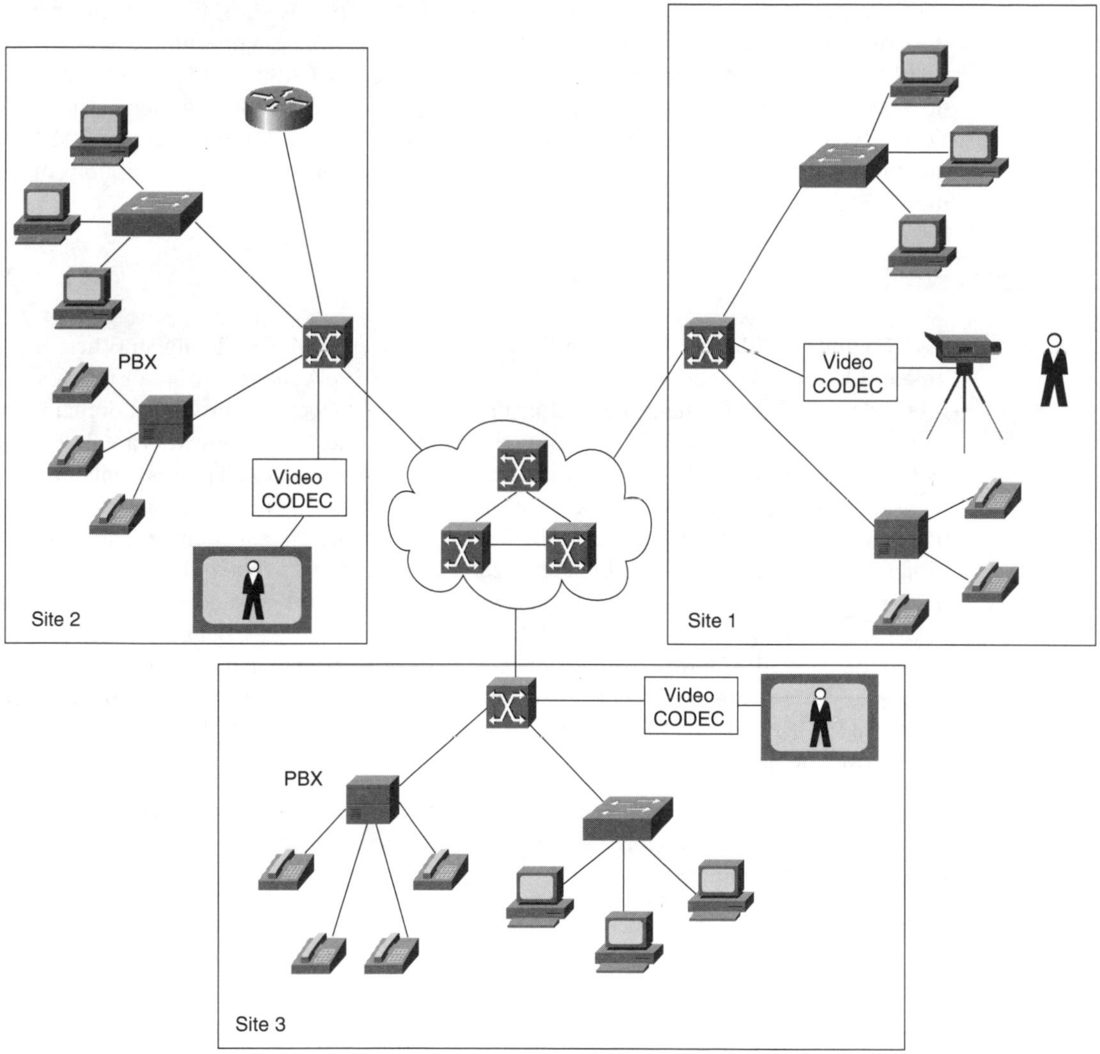

For those installations where ATM provides a backbone service (either at the campus or WAN levels), users can take advantage of the ATM infrastructure to trunk between Catalysts. By inserting a Catalyst LANE module, the Catalyst can send and receive data frames over the ATM network. The Catalyst bridges the LAN traffic onto the ATM network to transport the frames (segmented into ATM cells by the LANE module) through the ATM system and received by another ATM-attached Catalyst or router.

Catalysts support two modes of transporting data over the ATM network: LANE and MPOA. Each of these are covered in detail in other chapters. LANE is discussed in Chapter 9, "Trunking with LAN Emulation," and Chapter 10, "Trunking with Multiprotocol over ATM," covers MPOA operations. The ATM Forum defined LANE and MPOA for data networks. If you plan to use ATM trunking, you are strongly encouraged to visit the ATM Forum Web site (`www.atmforum.com`) and obtain, for free, copies of the LANE and MPOA documents. The following sections on LANE and MPOA provide brief descriptions of these options for trunking over ATM.

LANE

LANE emulates Ethernet and Token Ring networks over ATM. Emulating an Ethernet or Token Ring over ATM defines an Emulated LAN (ELAN). A member of the ELAN is referred to as a LANE Client (LEC). Each ELAN is an independent broadcast domain. An LEC can belong to only one ELAN. Both Ethernet and Token Ring networks are described as broadcast networks; if a station generates a broadcast message, all components in the network receive a copy of the frame. ATM networks, on the other hand, create direct point-to-point connections between users. This creates a problem when a client transmits a broadcast frame. How does the broadcast get distributed to all users in the broadcast domain? ATM does not inherently do this. A client could create a connection to all members of the ELAN and individually forward the broadcast to each client, but this is impractical due to the quantity of virtual connections that need to be established even in a small- to moderately-sized network. Besides, each client does not necessarily know about all other clients in the network. LANE provides a solution by defining a special server responsible for distributing broadcasts within an ELAN.

In Figure 8-13, three Catalysts and a router interconnect over an ATM network. On the LAN side, each Catalyst supports three VLANs. On the ATM side, each Catalyst has three clients to be a member of three ELANs.

Figure 8-13 *Catalysts in a LANE Environment Attached to Three ELANs*

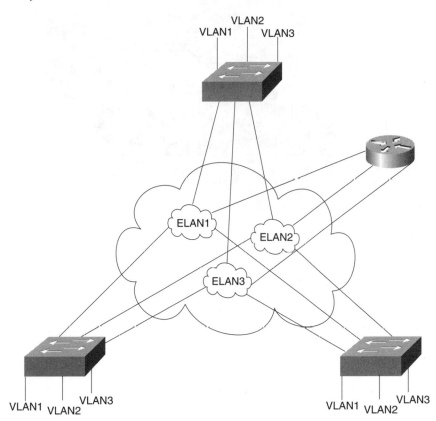

Within the Catalyst configurations, each VLAN maps to one ELAN. This merges the broadcast domains so that the distributed VLANs can intercommunicate over the ATM network. Figure 8-14 shows a logical depiction of the VLAN to ELAN mapping that occurs inside a Catalyst.

Figure 8-14 *A Catalyst with Three LECs Configured to Attach to Three ELANs*

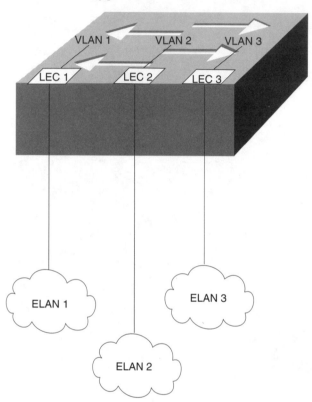

You need the router shown in Figure 8-13 if workstations in one VLAN desire to communicate with workstations in another VLAN. The router can reside on the LAN side of the Catalysts, but this example illustrates the router on the ATM side. When a station in VLAN 1 attempts to communicate with a station in VLAN 2, the Catalyst bridges the frame out LEC 1 to the router. The router, which also has three clients, routes the frame out the LEC which is a member of ELAN 2 to the destination Catalyst. The destination Catalyst receives the frame on LEC 2 and bridges the frame to the correct VLAN port.

MPOA

In most networks, several routers interconnect subnetworks. Only in the smallest networks is a router a member of all subnetworks. In larger networks, therefore, a frame can cross multiple routers to get to the intended destination. When this happens in an ATM network, the same information travels through the ATM cloud as many times as there are inter-router hops. In Figure 8-15, a station in VLAN 1 attached to Cat-A desires to communicate with a station in

VLAN 4 on Cat-B. Normally, the frame exits Cat-A toward Router 1, the default gateway. Router 1 forwards the frame to Router 2, which forwards the frame to Router 3. Router 3 transfers the frame to the destination Cat-B. This is the *default path* and requires four transfers across the ATM network, a very inefficient use of bandwidth. This is particularly frustrating because the ATM network can build a virtual circuit directly between Cat-A and Cat-B. IP rules, however, insist that devices belonging to different subnetworks interconnect through routers.

Figure 8-15 *Catalysts in an MPOA Environment*

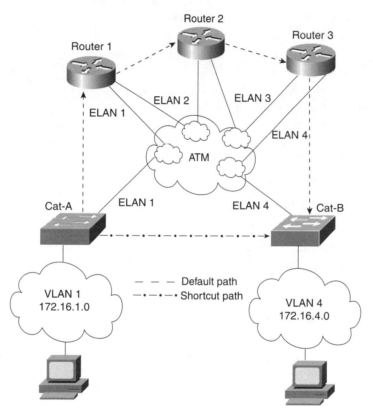

MPOA enables devices to circumvent the default path and establish a direct connection between the devices, even though they belong to different subnets. This shortcut path, illustrated in Figure 8-15, eliminates the multiple transits of the default path conserving ATM bandwidth and reducing the overall transit delay.

MPOA does not replace LANE, but supplements it. In fact, MPOA requires LANE as one of its components. Intra-broadcast domain (transfers within an ELAN) communications use LANE. MPOA kicks in only when devices on different ELANs try to communicate with each other. Even so, MPOA might not always get involved. One reason is that MPOA is protocol dependent. A vendor must provide MPOA capabilities for a protocol. Currently, IP is the dominant protocol supported. Another reason MPOA might not create a shortcut is that it might not be worth it. For MPOA to request a shortcut, the MPOA client must detect enough traffic between two hosts to merit any shortcut efforts. This is determined by an administratively configurable threshold of packets per second between two specific devices. If the client detects a packets per second rate between an IP source and an IP destination greater than the configured threshold, the client attempts to create a shortcut to the IP destination. But if the packets per second rate never exceeds the threshold, frames continue to travel through the default path.

Trunk Options

Three trunk methods and their encapsulation methods were described in the previous sections. Fast Ethernet and Gigabit Ethernet use ISL or 802.1Q encapsulation. FDDI trunks encapsulate with a Cisco proprietary adaptation of 802.10. With ATM, you can use LANE encapsulation. Optionally, you can augment LANE operations with MPOA. Which option should you use?

Criteria you need to consider include the following:

- Existing infrastructure
- Your technology comfort level
- Infrastructure resiliency needs
- Bandwidth requirements

Existing Infrastructure

Your trunk choice might be limited to whatever technology you currently deploy in your network. If your Catalyst interfaces are Ethernet and Fast Ethernet, and your cabling is oriented around that, you probably elect to use some form of Ethernet for your trunk lines. The question becomes one, then, of how much bandwidth do you need to support your users.

If your backbone infrastructure currently runs FDDI, you might not be able to do much with other trunk technologies without deploying some additional cabling. You might need to shift the FDDI network as a distribution network and use another technology for the core backbone. Figure 8-16 shows the FDDI network below the core network.

Figure 8-16 *Integrating an Existing FDDI Into Your Network*

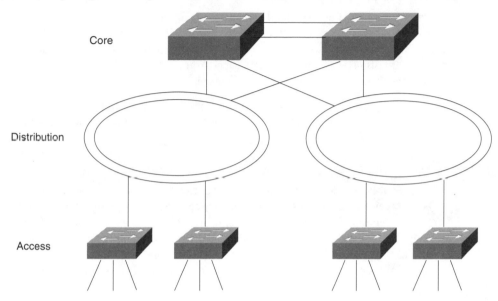

The FDDI segments are dual-homed to core-level Catalysts providing fault tolerance in the event that a primary Catalyst fails. The connection type between the core Catalysts is again determined by the bandwidth requirements. Remember that the FDDI segment is shared. The bandwidth is divided between all of the attached components and operates in half-duplex mode. Today, FDDI is probably your last choice for a backbone technology.

ATM proves to be a good choice if you are interested in network consolidation as described in the ATM trunk section, or if you need to trunk over distances not easily supported by Ethernet or FDDI technologies.

Your Technology Comfort Level

Another consideration might be your personal experience with the network technologies. Although you might not want to admit to your employer that you are uncomfortable with a particular technology because you do not have experience with or knowledge of it, the reason is still valid. Obviously, you prefer to select a technology based solely on technology merits. But, you are the one who needs to fix the network at 2:30 AM when the network fails. Stick with what you know unless there is an absolutely compelling technical reason to do otherwise.

Infrastructure Resiliency Needs

By definition, a lot of users depend upon trunk availability. A trunk carries traffic from more than one VLAN and can, in fact, carry traffic from all VLANs. If a trunk fails between critical points in the network, services become unreachable, causing your pager and/or phone to go off. This is not a desirable event. You might, therefore, need to consider how each of the trunk methods operate in the presence of failures.

The good news is that each of the trunk technologies have resiliency capabilities. The difference between them, however, is deployment requirements and failover times.

FDDI Resiliency

FDDI probably has the quickest failover rate because its resiliency operates at Layer 1, the physical layer. FDDI operates in a dual counter-rotating ring topology. Each ring runs in the opposite direction of the other ring. If a cable breaks between Cat-A and Cat-B as in Figure 8-17, both Catalysts see the loss of optical signal and enter into a *wrapped* state. Data continues to flow between all components in the network in spite of the cable outage. The cutover time is extremely fast because failure detection and recovery occur at Layer 1.

Figure 8-17 *FDDI Resiliency*

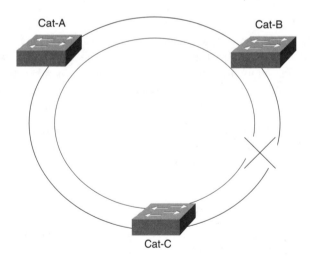

ATM Resiliency

ATM also provides physical layer recovery. However, the failover time is longer than for FDDI. In an ATM network, a cable or interface failure can occur at the Catalyst or between ATM switches. If the failure occurs between ATM switches, the Catalyst requests the ATM network to re-establish a connection to the destination client(s). The ATM network attempts to find an alternate path to complete the connection request. This happens automatically.

Figure 8-18 shows a Catalyst attached to two ATM switches for redundancy. One link, the preferred link, is the active connection. The second link serves as a backup and is inactive. Traffic only passes over the active link.

Figure 8-18 *Catalyst ATM Resiliency*

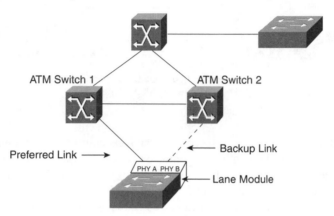

A failure can occur at the Catalyst. To account for this, the Catalyst LANE module provides two physical interfaces, PHY A and PHY B. In Figure 8-18, a Catalyst attaches to two ATM switches. PHY A attaches to ATM Switch 1 and PHY B attaches to ATM Switch 2. The Catalyst activates only one of the interfaces at a time. The other simply provides a backup path. If the active link fails, the Catalyst activates the backup port. The Catalyst must rejoin the ELAN and then reattach to the other client(s) in the network. Although ATM connections can establish quickly, the additional complexity increases the failover time as compared to FDDI links. The actual failover time varies depending upon the tasks that the ATM switches are performing when the Catalyst requests a connection to the ELAN or to another client.

Other types of failures can also occur in a LANE environment. For example, various server functions must be enabled for LANE to function. The LANE version 1 standard provides for only one of the servers in each ELAN. If these servers fail, it disables the ELAN. Cisco has a protocol called Simple Server Redundancy Protocol (SSRP) that enables backup servers so that the LANE can remain functional in the event of a server failure. This is discussed in more detail in Chapter 9, "Trunking with LAN Emulation."

Ethernet Resiliency

Ethernet options (both Fast Ethernet and Gigabit Ethernet) rely upon Spanning Tree for resiliency. Spanning Tree, discussed in Chapter 6, "Understanding Spanning Tree," operates at Layer 2, the data link layer. Components detect failures when they fail to receive BPDUs from the Root Bridge. Spanning Tree recovery can take as much as 50 seconds depending upon at what values you set the timers.

EtherChannel, both Fast and Gigabit, provide local resiliency. Figure 8-19 shows two Catalysts interconnected with an EtherChannel.

Figure 8-19 *EtherChannel Resiliency*

Normal 800 Mbps Bandwidth
Single Failure 600 Mbps Bandwidth

An EtherChannel has more than one link actively carrying data. If one of the links in Figure 8-19 fails, the remaining link(s) continue to carry the load, although with a reduced aggregate bandwidth. This happens without triggering any Spanning Tree events. Therefore, Spanning Tree times do not get involved. Failover for EtherChannel occurs quickly, because it uses Layer 1 failure detection and recovery. If you implement redundant EtherChannels, Spanning Tree activation times must be anticipated.

Resiliency: Failover Mechanisms

One final thought on resiliency. Many network engineers pride themselves in their forethought regarding failover mechanisms. They implement redundant interfaces, taking into account bandwidth planning in failover configurations. They even plan redundant power supplies. And yet they fail to recognize two particular failure modes: power source failures and cable plant routing. Although the redundant supplies can take care of internal equipment supply failures, to be fully protected, the redundant supplies should be attached to alternate sources on different circuit breakers in the facility. If both supplies attach to the same source and that source fails, the whole unit becomes dysfunctional. Place them on redundant sources!

An even more egregious error concerns cable paths. Although you can deploy redundant cable segments, make sure the segments take diverse paths! For example, if you deploy EtherChannel between Catalysts and the cable bundle is cut, the EtherChannel cannot carry data. The electrons fall on the floor. To provide full resiliency, use cable segments from different bundles, through different cable trays and patch panels, through different risers and conduits. Otherwise, if they are all in the same bundle, you are likely to lose the whole connection. Bundles get cut, not individual wires.

Bandwidth Requirements

Right or wrong, network engineers most often use bandwidth capabilities for selecting a trunk technology. Catalyst offers a spectrum of options ranging from half-duplex FDDI through full-duplex Gigabit EtherChannel. Figure 8-20 illustrates a number of Fast Ethernet and Fast EtherChannel options with increasing bandwidth.

Figure 8-20 *Bandwidth Options for Ethernet-Based Trunks*

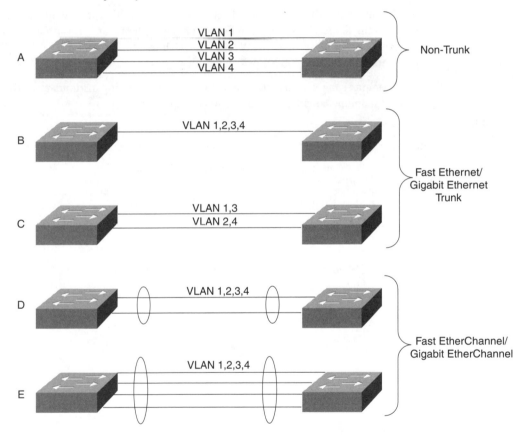

Part A of Figure 8-20 shows an interconnection where each link is dedicated to a VLAN. No trunk encapsulation is used and frames are transported in their native format. Only one link per VLAN between the Catalysts can be active at any time. Spanning Tree disables any additional links. Therefore, bandwidth options are only 10/100/1000 Mbps.

By enabling ISL trunking, you can share the link bandwidth with multiple VLANs. A single Fast Ethernet or Gigabit Ethernet link as in Part B of Figure 8-20 offers 100 or 1000 Mbps bandwidth with no resiliency. Running multiple trunks in parallel provides additional bandwidth and resiliency. However, VLAN traffic from any single VLAN can only use one path while the other path serves as a backup. For example, in Part C of Figure 8-20, two links run between the Catalysts. One link carries the traffic for VLANs 1 and 3, and the other link carries the traffic for VLANs 2 and 4. Each serves as a Spanning Tree backup for the other. This provides more bandwidth than in Part B of Figure 8-20 by having fewer VLANs contend for the bandwidth while providing another level of resiliency. However, each VLAN can still have no more than 100 or 1000 Mbps of bandwidth, depending upon whether the link is Fast Ethernet or a Gigabit Ethernet.

On the other hand, the VLANs in Parts D and E of Figure 8-20 share the aggregate bandwidth of the links. These links use Fast or Gigabit EtherChannel. With a two-port EtherChannel, the VLANs share a 400/4000 Mbps bandwidth. (Each link is full duplex.) A four-port version has 800/8000 Mbps bandwidth.

Table 8-8 compares the various interconnection modes providing a summary of the bandwidth capabilities, resiliency modes, and encapsulation types.

Table 8-8 *A Comparison of Different Trunk Modes*

Trunk Mode	Bandwidth (Mbps)	Resiliency	Encapsulation	Comments
Per VLAN link	Dedicated per VLAN 10/100/1000	Spanning Tree	None	VLANs traffic dedicated per link.
Ethernet	Shared 100/1000	Spanning Tree	ISL/802.1Q	Bandwidth reflects half duplex. Full duplex doubles bandwidth.
EtherChannel	Shared 200/400/2000/8000	Layer 1	ISL/802.1Q	Spanning Tree might activate in some cases.
FDDI	Shared 100	Layer 1 wrap	802.10	
ATM	Shared 155/622	Layer 1 Diverse path	LANE/MPOA	Resiliency against network and local failures.

Review Questions

This section includes a variety of questions on the topic of campus design implementation. By completing these, you can test your mastery of the material included in this chapter as well as help prepare yourself for the CCIE written test.

1 What happens in a traffic loading situation for EtherChannel when two servers pass files between each other?

2 If you have access to equipment, attempt to configure a two-segment EtherChannel where one end is set to transport only VLANs 1–10 and the other end of the segment is set to transport all VLANs. What gets established?

3 In Figure 8-13, the configuration shows an 802.1Q encapsulation for VLAN 200 on a router. How would you add VLAN 300 to the trunk?

4 Configure a Catalyst trunk to transport VLAN 200 and VLAN 300 with 802.1Q. Repeat the exercise with ISL.

This chapter covers the following key topics:

- **A Brief ATM Tutorial**—For engineers accustomed to working in frame-based technologies such as Ethernet, ATM can seem strange and mysterious. However, as this section discusses, it is based on many of the same fundamental concepts as technologies that are probably more familiar.

- **LANE: Theory of Operation**—Introduces the theory used by LAN Emulation (LANE) to simulate Ethernet and Token Ring networks over an ATM infrastructure. Explores the conceptual approach used by LANE and its four main components. This is followed by a detailed description of the LANE initialization sequence and the required overhead connections.

- **Configuration Concepts**—Discusses several concepts used to configure LANE on Cisco equipment.

- **Configuration Syntax**—Introduces a five-step process that can be used to configure LANE on Cisco routers and Catalyst equipment.

- **A Complete LANE Network**—Pulls together the material discussed in previous sections by examining a complete end-to-end LANE configuration in a sample campus network.

- **Testing the Configuration**—Explains several useful and important commands used to troubleshoot and maintain LANE networks on Cisco equipment.

- **Advanced Issues and Features**—Discusses a variety of advanced LANE topics such as LANE design, Simple Server Redundancy Protocol (SSRP), PVC-based connectivity, and traffic shaping.

CHAPTER 9

Trunking with LAN Emulation

Asynchronous Transfer Mode (ATM) has received considerable press and attention since the early 1990s. As one of the original four founders of the ATM Forum (ATMF, or The Forum), Cisco has played a significant role in ATM's development. The ATM Forum has produced a large number of standards aimed at improving the acceptance and interoperability of ATM. By 1996, several key standards were complete and available in commercial products, finally allowing network administrators to build viable networks using ATM. Today, ATM is an extremely feature-rich and high performance technology. Of the several approaches devised by the ATM Forum, LAN Emulation (LANE) has become the most popular for campus data networking.

Before getting started, two cautions are in order. First, ATM is a very complex subject—don't be surprised if it takes a little while to feel comfortable with this new and complex technology. Most users find it very difficult to "ramp up" on ATM. For example, it uses a lot of geeky concepts and acronyms (you will come to learn that ATM really stands for Acronym Training Method). Second, it is impossible to cover everything there is to know about ATM in this chapter. There are obviously many books devoted entirely to the subject. Our purpose is more specific: learn as much as possible about using ATM in the real world to build LANE campus backbones (while also setting the stage for Chapter 10, which covers Multiprotocol over ATM—MPOA).

However, do not despair. Believe it or not, ATM and LANE are subjects that you actually can decipher and understand. By focusing specifically on LANE, this chapter glosses over some of the murkier issues of ATM theory. By discussing it from a real-world perspective, the text avoids the labyrinth of ATM's theoretical questions and issues. By stressing the important *concepts*, this chapter promises to make you an effective LANE designer, planner, implementer, and troubleshooter.

A Brief ATM Tutorial

This section looks at some basic ATM concepts and terminology before diving into the deep waters of LANE. The principal concepts covered here include the following:

- Understanding ATM Cells (Five Questions about Cells That You Were Always Afraid to Ask)
- ATM is Connection Oriented
- ATM Addressing
- ATM Devices
- ATM Overhead Protocols
- When to Use ATM

Understanding ATM Cells: Five Questions about Cells (That You Were Always Afraid to Ask)

The single most important characteristic of ATM is that it uses cells. Whereas other technologies transport large and variable-length units of data, ATM is completely based around small, fixed-length units of data called cells.

Why Cells?

Most readers are probably aware that ATM uses fixed-length packages of data called *cells*. But what's the big deal about cells? Because it takes quite a lot of work for network devices hardware to cellify all of their data, what is the payoff to justify all of this extra work and complexity? Fortunately, cells do have many advantages, including the following:

- High throughput
- Advanced statistical multiplexing
- Low latency
- Facilitate multiservice traffic (voice, video, and data)

Each of these advantages of ATM cells is addressed in the sections that follow.

High Throughput

High throughput has always been one of the most compelling benefits of ATM. At the time ATM was conceived, routers were slow devices that required software-based processing to handle the complex variable-length and variable-format multiprotocol (IP, IPX, and so forth) traffic. The variable data lengths resulted in inefficient processing and many complex buffering schemes (to illustrate this point, just issue a **show buffers** command on a Cisco router). The variable data formats required every Layer 3 protocol to utilize a different set of logic and routing procedures. Run this on a general-purpose CPU and the result is a low-throughput device.

The ATM cell was designed to address both of these issues. Because cells are fixed in length, buffering becomes a trivial exercise of simply carving up buffer memory into fixed-length cubbyholes. Because cells have a fixed-format, 5-byte header, switch processing is drastically simplified. The result: it becomes much easier to build very high-speed, hardware-based switching mechanisms.

Advanced Statistical Multiplexing

Large phone and data carriers funded the majority of early ATM research. One of the key factors that motivated carriers to explore ATM was their desire to improve utilization and statistical multiplexing in their networks. At the time, it was very common (and still is) to link sites using channelized T1 circuits (or E1 circuits outside the United States). Figure 9-1 illustrates a typical use of this approach.

Figure 9-1   *A Typical Channelized Network*

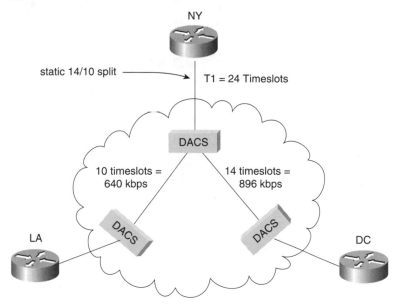

Figure 9-1 illustrates a small corporate network with three sites: headquarters is located in New York City with two remote sites in Washington, DC and Los Angeles. The NY site has a single T1 to the carrier's nearest Central Office (CO). This T1 has been channelized into two sections: one channel to DC and another to LA.

T1 technology uses something called time-division multiplexing (TDM) to allow up to 24 voice conversations to be carried across a single 4-wire circuit. Each of these 24 conversations is assigned a timeslot that allows it to send 8 bits of information at a time (typically, these 8 bits are pulse code modulation [PCM] digital representations of human voice conversations). Repeat this pattern 8000 times per second and you have the illusion that all 24 conversations are using the wire at the same time. Also note that this results in each timeslot receiving 64,000 bits/second (bps) of bandwidth (8 bits/timeslot×8,000 timeslots per second).

However, the data network in Figure 9-1 does not call for 24 low-bandwidth connections— the desire is for two higher-bandwidth connections. The solution is to group the timeslots into two bundles. For example, a 14-timeslot bundle can be used to carry data to the remote site in DC, whereas the remaining 10 timeslots are used for data traveling to the remote site in LA. Because each timeslot represents 64 Kbps of bandwidth, DC is allocated 896 Kbps and LA receives 640 Kbps. This represents a form of static multiplexing. It allows two connections to share a single link, but it prevents a dynamic reconfiguration of the 896/640 bandwidth split. In other words, if no traffic is being transferred between NY and LA, the NY-to-DC circuit is still limited to 896 Kbps. The 640 Kbps of bandwidth allocated to the other link is wasted.

Figure 9-2 shows an equivalent design utilizing ATM.

Figure 9-2   *An ATM-Based Network Using Virtual Circuits*

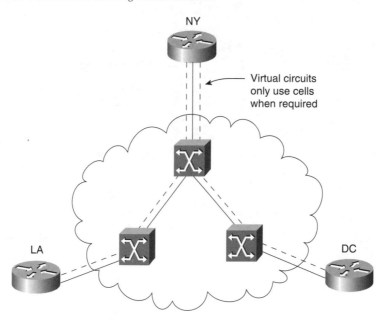

In Figure 9-2, the NY office still has a T1 to the local CO. However, this T1 line is unchannelized—it acts as a single pipe to the ATM switch sitting in the CO. The advantage of this approach is that cells are only sent when there is a need to deliver data (other than some overhead cells). In other words, if no traffic is being exchanged between the NY and LA sites, 100 percent of the bandwidth can be used to send traffic between NY and DC. Seconds later, 100 percent of the bandwidth might be available between NY and LA. Notice that, although the T1 still delivers a constant flow of 1,544,000 bps, this fixed amount of bandwidth is better utilized because there are no hard-coded multiplexing patterns that inevitably lead to unused bandwidth. The result is a significant improvement over the static multiplexing configured in Figure 9-1. In fact, many studies have shown that cell multiplexing can double the overall bandwidth utilization in a large network.

Low Latency

Latency is a measurement of the time that it takes to deliver information from the source to the destination. Latency comes from two primary sources:

- Propagation delay
- Switching delay

Propagation delay is based on the amount of time that it takes for a signal to travel over a given type of media. In most types of copper and fiber optic media, signals travel at approximately two-thirds the speed of light (in other words, about 200,000 meters per second). Because this delay is ultimately controlled by the speed of light, propagation delay cannot be eliminated or minimized (unless, of course, the two devices are moved closer together).

Switching delay results from the time it takes for data to move through some internetworking device. Two factors come into play here:

- **The length of the frame**—If very large frames are in use, it takes a longer period of time for the last bit of a frame to arrive after the first bit arrives.
- **The switching mechanics of the device**—Software-based routers can add several hundred microseconds of delay during the routing process, whereas hardware-based devices can make switching and routing decisions in only several microseconds.

Cells are an attempt to address both of these issues simultaneously. Because cells are small, the difference between the arrival time of the first and last bit is minimized. Because cells are of a fixed size and format, they readily allow for hardware-based optimizations.

Facilitates Multiservice Traffic

One of the most touted benefits of ATM is its capability to simultaneously support voice, video, and data traffic over the same switching infrastructure. Cells play a large part in making this possible by allowing all types of traffic to be put in a single, ubiquitous container.

Part of this multiservice benefit is derived from points already discussed. For example, one of the biggest challenges facing voice over IP is the large end-to-end latency present in most existing IP networks. The low latency of cell switching allows ATM to easily accommodate existing voice applications. In addition, the advanced multiplexing of cells allows ATM to instantly make bandwidth available to data applications when video and voice traffic is reduced (either through compression or tearing down unused circuits). Furthermore, the small size of cells prevents data logjams that can result in many other architectures when small packets clump up behind large packets (much like small cars clumping up behind trucks on the highway).

Why 53 Bytes?

As discussed in the previous section, every cell is a fixed-length container of information. After considerable debate, the networking community settled on a 53-byte cell. This 53-byte unit is composed of two parts: a 5-byte header and a 48-byte payload. However, given that networking engineers have a long history of using even powers of two, 53 bytes seems like a very strange number. As it turns out, 53 bytes was the result of an international compromise. In the late 1980s, the European carriers wanted to use ATM for voice traffic. Given the tight latency constraints required by voice, the Europeans argued that a 32-byte cell payload would be most useful. U.S. carriers, interested in using ATM for data traffic, were more interested in the efficiency that would be possible with a larger, 64-byte payload. The two groups compromised on the mid-point value, resulting in the 48-byte payload still used today. The groups then debated the merits of various header sizes. Although several sizes were proposed, the 5-byte header was ultimately chosen.

How Does an IP Packet Fit Inside a Cell?

To answer this question, this section examines the three-step process that ATM uses to transfer information:

Step 1   Slice & Dice

Step 2   Build Header

Step 3   Ship Cells

Each of these steps equates to a layer in the ATM stack shown in Figure 9-3.

Figure 9-3   *Three-Layer ATM Stack*

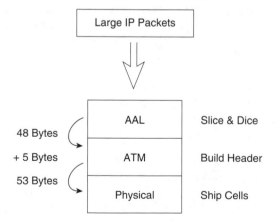

First, ATM must obviously chop up large IP packets before transmission. The technical term for this function is the *ATM Adaptation Layer* (AAL); however, I use the more intuitive term Slice & Dice Layer. The purpose of the Slice & Dice Layer is to act like a virtual Cuisinart® that chops up large data into small, fixed size pieces. This is frequently referred to as SAR, a term that stands for Segmentation And Reassembly, and accurately portrays this Slice & Dice function (it is also one of the two main functions performed by the AAL). Just as Cuisinarts are available with a variety of different blades, the AAL blade can Slice & Dice in a variety of ways. In fact, this is exactly how ATM accommodates voice, video, and data traffic over a common infrastructure. In other words, the ATM Adaptation Layer adapts all types of traffic into common ATM cells. However, regardless of which Slice & Dice blade is in use, the AAL is guaranteed to pass a fixed-length, 48-byte payload down to the next layer, the ATM layer.

The middle layer in the ATM stack, the ATM layer, receives the 48-byte slices created by the AAL. Note the potential for confusion here: all three layers form the *ATM stack,* but the middle layer represents the *ATM layer* of the ATM stack. This layer builds the 5-byte ATM cell header, the heart of the entire ATM process. The primary function of this header is to identify the remote ATM device that should receive each cell. After this layer has completed its work, the cell is guaranteed to be 53 bytes in length.

NOTE   Technically, there is a small exception to the statement that the ATM Layer always passes 53-byte cells to the physical layer. In some cases, the physical layer is used to calculate the cell header's CRC, requiring only 52-byte transfers. In practice, this minor detail can be ignored.

At this point, the cells are ready to leave the device in a physical layer protocol. This physical layer acts like a shipping department for cells. The vast majority of campus ATM networks use Synchronous Optical Network (SONET) as a physical layer transport. SONET was developed as a high-speed alternative to the T1s and E1s discussed earlier in this chapter.

NOTE   SONET is very similar to T1s in that it is a framed, physical layer transport mechanism that repeats 8,000 times per second and is used for multiplexing across trunk links. On the other hand, they are very different in that SONET operates at much higher bit rates than T1s while also maintaining much tighter timing (synchronization) parameters. SONET was devised to provide efficient multiplexing of T1, T3, E1, and E3 traffic.

Think of a SONET frame as a large, 810-byte moving van that leaves the shipping dock every $1/8000^{th}$ of a second (810 bytes is the smallest/slowest version of SONET; higher speeds use an even larger frame!). The ATM Layer is free to pack as many cells as it can fit into each of these 810-byte moving vans. On a slow day, many of the moving vans might be almost empty. However, on a busy day, most of the vans are full or nearly full.

One of the most significant advantages of ATM is that it doesn't require any particular type of physical layer. That is, it is media independent. Originally, ATM was designed to run only over SONET. However, the ATM Forum wisely recognized that this would severely limit ATM's potential for growth and acceptance, and developed standards for many different types and speeds of physical layers. In fact, the Physical Layer Working Group of the ATM Forum has been its most prolific group. Currently, ATM runs over just about any media this side of barbed wire.

Why Is It *Asynchronous* Transfer Mode?

The term Asynchronous Transfer Mode has created significant confusion. Many ask, "What's asynchronous about it? Is this a throwback to using start and stop bits like my modem?"

ATM is asynchronous in the sense that *cells* are generated asynchronously on an as-needed basis. If two ATM devices have a three-second quiet period during an extended file transfer, ATM does not need to send any cells during this three-second interval. This unused bandwidth is instantly available to any other devices sharing that link. In other words, it is the asynchronous nature of ATM that delivers the advanced statistical multiplexing capabilities discussed earlier.

This confusion is further complicated by the common use of SONET as a physical layer for ATM. Because *Synchronous* Optical Network is obviously synchronous, how can ATM be asynchronous if SONET is in use? To answer this question, apply the logic of the previous paragraph: ATM is only referring to the generation of cells as being asynchronous. How cells get shipped from point A to point B is a different matter. In the case of SONET, the shipment from point A to point B is most definitely synchronous in that SONET moving vans (frames) leave the shipping dock (the ATM device) at exactly 1/8000th of a second intervals. However, *filling* these moving vans is done on an as-needed or asynchronous basis. Again, this is exactly what gives ATM its amazing statistical multiplexing capabilities. All of the empty space in the moving van is instantly available to other devices and users in the network.

What Is the Difference Between ATM and SONET?

As discussed in the previous sections, ATM and SONET are closely related technologies. In fact, they were originally conceived to always be used together in a global architecture called BISDN (Broadband Integrated Digital Services Network). However, they have been developed (and often implemented) as two different technologies. ATM is a *cloud* technology that deals with the high-speed generation and transportation of fixed-size units of information called cells. SONET, on the other hand, is a *point-to-point* technology that deals with the high-speed transportation of anything, including ATM cells.

In other words, referring back to the three-layer model, ATM makes the cells and SONET ships the cells.

TIP	ATM and SONET are two different concepts. ATM deals with cells and SONET is simply one of the many physical layers available for moving ATM cells from point to point.

ATM Is Connection Oriented

ATM is always connection oriented. Before any data can be exchanged, the network must negotiate a connection between two endpoints. ATM supports two types of connections:

- Permanent virtual circuits (PVCs)
- Switched virtual circuits (SVCs)

PVCs act like virtual leased lines in that the circuits are always active. PVCs are manually built based on human intervention (either via a command-line interface [CLI] or some action at a management console).

SVCs are "dialup" ATM connections. Think of them as ATM phone calls. When two devices require connectivity via a SVC, one device *signals* the ATM network to build this temporary circuit. When the connection is no longer required, one of the devices can destroy the SVC via signaling.

ATM always requires that one of these two types of circuits be built. At the cell layer, it is not possible for ATM to provide a connectionless environment like Ethernet. However, it is entirely possible for this connection-oriented cell layer to emulate a connectionless environment by providing a connectionless service at some higher layer. The most common example of such a connectionless service is LANE, the very subject of this chapter.

ATM supports two configurations for virtual circuits (VCs):

Step 1 Point-to-point Virtual Circuits

Step 2 Point-to-multipoint Virtual Circuits

Figure 9-4 illustrates both types of circuits.

Figure 9-4   *Point-to-Point and Point-to-Multipoint Vcs*

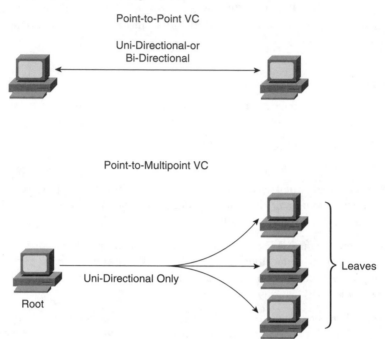

Point-to-point virtual circuits behave exactly as the name suggests: one device can be located at each end of the circuit. This type of virtual circuit is also very common in technologies such as Frame Relay. These circuits support bi-directional communication—that is, both end points are free to transmit cells.

Point-to-multipoint virtual circuits allow a single root node to send cells to multiple leaf nodes. Point-to-multipoint circuits are very efficient for this sort of one-to-many communication because it allows the root to generate a given message only once. It then becomes the duty of the ATM switches to pass a copy of the cells that comprise this message to all leaf nodes. Because of their unidirectional nature, point-to-multipoint circuits only allow the root to transmit. If the leaf nodes need to transmit, they need to build their own virtual circuits.

TIP   Do not confuse the root of a point-to-multipoint ATM VC with the Spanning Tree Root Bridge and Root Port concepts discussed in Chapter 6, "Understanding Spanning Tree." They are completely unrelated concepts.

ATM Addressing

As with all other cloud topologies, ATM needs some method to identify the intended destination for each unit of information (cell) that gets sent. Unlike most other topologies, ATM actually uses two types of addresses to accomplish this task: Virtual Path Indicator/ Virtual Channel Indicator (VPI/VCI) addresses and Network Services Access Point (NSAP) addresses, both of which are discussed in greater detail in the sections that follow.

VPI/VCI Addresses

VPI/VCI, the first type of address used by ATM, is placed in the 5-byte header of every cell. This address actually consists of two parts: the Virtual Path Indicator (VPI) and the Virtual Channel Indicator (VCI). They are typically written with a slash separating the VPI and the VCI values—for example, 0/100. The distinction between VPI and VCI is not important to a discussion of LANE. Just remember that together these two values are used by an ATM edge device (such as a router) to indicate to ATM switches which virtual circuit a cell should follow. For example, Figure 9-5 adds VPI/VCI detail to the network illustrated in Figure 9-2 earlier.

Figure 9-5   *VPI/VCI Usage in an ATM Network*

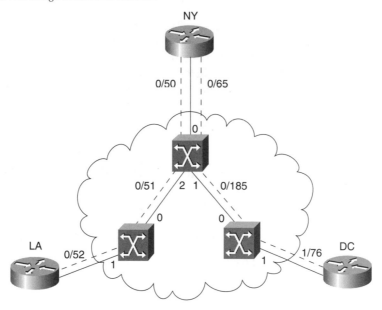

The NY router uses a single physical link connected to Port 0 on the NY ATM switch carrying both virtual circuits. How, then, does the ATM switch know where to send each cell? It simply makes decisions based on VPI/VCI values placed in ATM cell headers by the router. If the NY router (the ATM edge device) places the VPI/VCI value 0/50 in the cell header, the ATM switch uses a preprogrammed table indicating that the cell should be forwarded out Port 2, sending it to LA. Also, note that this table needs to instruct the switch to convert the VPI/VCI value to 0/51 as the cells leave the Port 1 interface (only the VCI is changed). The ATM switch in LA has a similar table indicating that the cell should be switched out Port 1 with a VPI/VCI value of 0/52. However, if the NY router originates a cell with the VPI/VCI value 0/65, the NY ATM switch forwards the cell to DC. The ATM switching table in the NY ATM switch would contain the entries listed in Table 9-1.

Table 9-1   *Switching Table in NY ATM Switch*

Input			Output		
Port	VPI	VCI	Port	VPI	VCI
0	0	50	2	0	51
0	0	65	1	0	185
1	0	185	0	0	65
2	0	51	0	0	50

Notice the previous paragraph mentions that the ATM switch had been preprogrammed with this switching table. How this preprogramming happens depends on whether the virtual circuit is a PVC or an SVC. In the case of a PVC, the switching table is programmed through human intervention (for example, through a command-line interface). However, with SVCs, the table is built dynamically at the time the call is established.

NSAPs

The previous section mentioned that SVCs build the ATM switching tables dynamically. This requires a two-step process:

Step 1   The ATM switch must select a VPI/VCI value for the SVC.

Step 2   The ATM switch must determine where the destination of the call is located.

Step 1 is a simple matter of having the ATM switch look in the table to find a value currently not in use *on that port* (in other words, the same VPI/VCI can be in use on every port of the same switch; it just cannot be used twice on the same port).

To understand Step 2, consider the following example. If the NY router places an SVC call to DC, how does the New York ATM switch know that DC is reachable out Port 1, not Port 2? The details of this process involve a complex protocol called Private Network-Network Interface (PNNI) that is briefly discussed later in this chapter. For now, just remember that the NY switch utilizes an NSAP address to determine the intended destination. NSAP addresses function very much like regular telephone numbers. Just as every telephone on the edge of a phone network gets a unique phone number, every device on an ATM network gets a unique NSAP address. Just as you must dial a phone number to call your friend named Joe, an ATM router must signal an NSAP address to call a router named DC. Just as you can look at a phone number to determine the city and state in which the phone is located, an NSAP tells you where the router is located.

However, there is one important difference between traditional phone numbers and NSAP addresses: the length. NSAPs are fixed at 20 bytes in length. When written in their standard hexadecimal format, these addresses are 40 characters long! Try typing in a long list of NSAP addresses and you quickly learn why an ATM friend of mine refers to NSAPs as Nasty SAPs! You also learn two other lessons: the value of cut-and-paste and that even people who understand ATM can have friends (there's hope after all!).

NSAP addresses consist of three sections:

* A 13-byte *prefix*. This is a value that uniquely identifies every *ATM switch* in the network. Logically, it functions very much like the area code and exchange of a U.S. phone number (for example, the 703-242 of 703-242-1111 identifies a telephone switch in Vienna, Virginia). Cisco's campus ATM switches are preconfigured with 47.0091.8100.0000, followed by a unique MAC address that gets assigned to every switch. For example, a switch that contains the MAC address 0010.2962.E801 uses a prefix of 47.0091.8100.0000.0010.2962.E801. No other ATM switch in your network can use this prefix.

* A 6-byte *End System Identifier (ESI)*. This value identifies every *device* connected to an ATM switch. A MAC address is typically used (but not required) for this value. Logically, it functions very much like the last four digits of a U.S. phone number (for example, the 1111 of 703-242-1111 identifies a particular phone attached to the Vienna, Virginia telephone switch).

* A 1-byte *selector byte*. This value identifies a particular software process running in an ATM-attached device. It functions very much like an extension number associated with a telephone number (for example, 222 in 703-242-1111 x222). Cisco devices typically use a subinterface number for the selector byte.

Figure 9-6 illustrates the ATM NSAP format.

Figure 9-6 *ATM NSAP Format*

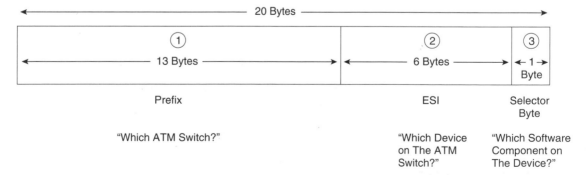

An actual NSAP appears as follows:

> 47.0091.8100.0000.0060.8372.56A1 . 0000.0c33.BFC1 . A1

Extra spaces have been inserted to clearly delineate the three sections. The pattern of dots above is optional. If you are a particularly adept typist, feel free to completely omit the dots. However, most people find a pattern such as the one above to be a very useful typing aid.

Using NSAP and VPI/VCI Addresses Together

In short, the purpose of the two types of ATM addresses can be summarized as follows:

- NSAP addresses are used to *build* SVCs.
- VPI/VCIs are used after the circuit (SVC or PVC) has already been built to *deliver cells across the circuit*.

TIP ATM NSAP addresses are only used to build an SVC. After the SVC is built, only VPI/VCI addresses are used.

Figure 9-7 illustrates the relationship between NSAP and VPI/VCI addresses. The NSAPs represent the endpoints whereas VPI/VCIs are used to address cells as they cross each link.

Figure 9-7 *Using NSAP Addresses to Build VPI/VCI Values for SVCs*

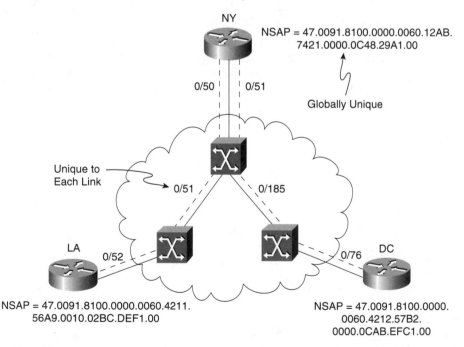

Table 9-2 documents the characteristics of NSAP and VPI/VCI addresses for easy comparison.

Table 9-2 *NSAP Versus VPI/VCI Address Characteristics*

NSAP Addresses	VPI/VCI Addresses
40 hex characters (20 bytes) in length	24 to 28 bits in length (depending on what type of link the cell is traversing)
Globally significant (that is, globally unique)	Locally significant (that is, only need to be unique to a single link)
Physically reside in the signaling messages used to build SVCs	Physically reside in the 5-byte header of *every* ATM cell
Not used for PVCs	Used for PVCs *and* SVCs

ATM Device Types

ATM devices can be divided into one of two broad categories, each of which is covered in greater detail in the sections that follow:

- ATM edge devices
- ATM switches

ATM Edge Devices

ATM edge devices include equipment such as workstations, servers, PCs, routers, and switches with ATM interface cards (for example, a Catalyst 5000 containing a LANE module). These devices act as the termination points for ATM PVCs and SVCs. In the case of routers and switches, edge devices must also convert from frame-based media such as Ethernet to ATM cells.

ATM Switches

ATM switches only handle ATM cells. Cisco's campus switches include the LightStream LS1010 and 8500 MSR platforms (Cisco also sells several carrier-class switches developed as a result of their Stratacom acquisition). ATM switches are the devices that contain the ATM switching tables referenced earlier. They also contain advanced software features (such as PNNI) to allow calls to be established and high-speed switching fabrics to shuttle cells between ports. Except for certain overhead circuits, ATM switches generally do not act as the termination point of PVCs and SVCs. Rather, they act as the intermediary junction points that exist for the circuits connected between ATM edge devices.

Figure 9-8 illustrates the difference between edge devices and ATM switches.

Figure 9-8 *Catalyst ATM Edge Devices Convert Frames to Cells, Whereas ATM Switches Handle Only Cells*

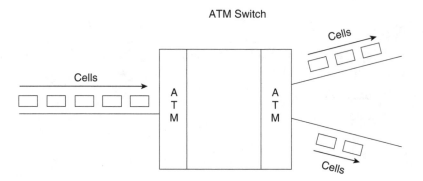

TIP   Remember the difference between ATM edge devices and ATM switches. ATM edge devices sit at the edge of the network, but ATM switches actually *are* the ATM network.

Products such as the Catalyst 5500 and 8500 actually support multiple functions in the same chassis. The 5500 supports LS1010 ATM switching in its bottom five slots while simultaneously accommodating one to seven LANE modules in the remaining slots. However, it is often easiest to think of these as two separate boxes that happen to share the same chassis and power supplies. The bottom five slots (slots 9–13) accommodate ATM switch modules while slots 2–12 accommodate ATM edge device modules (note that slots 9–12 can support either service).

TIP   Cisco sells several other devices that integrate ATM and frame technologies in a single platform in a variety of different ways. These include the Catalyst 5500 Fabric Integration Module (FIM), the Catalyst 8500 MSR, and the ATM Router Module (ARM). See Cisco's Product Catalog for more information on these devices.

ATM Overhead Protocols

Although ATM theory can be extremely complex, the good news is that it can be amazingly easily to implement in most networks. This plug-and-play nature is due in large part to two automation protocols: Integrated Local Management Interface (ILMI) and Private Network-Network Interface (PNNI).

ILMI

Integrated Local Management Interface (ILMI) is a protocol created by the ATM Forum to handle various automation responsibilities. Initially called the Interim Local Management Interface, ILMI utilizes SNMP to allow ATM devices to "automagically" learn the configuration of neighboring ATM devices. The most common use of ILMI is a process generally referred to as address registration. Recall that NSAP addresses consist of three parts: the switch's prefix and the edge device's ESI and selector byte. How do the two devices learn about each other's addresses? This is where ILMI comes in. Address registration allows the edge device to learn the prefix from the switch and the switch to learn the ESI from the edge device (because the selector byte is locally significant, the switch doesn't need to acquire this value).

PNNI

Private Network-Network Interface (PNNI) is a protocol that allows switches to dynamically establish SVCs between edge devices. However, edge devices do not participate in PNNI—it is a switch-to-switch protocol (as the Network-Network Interface portion of the name suggests). Network-Network Interface (NNI) protocols consist of two primary functions:

- Signaling
- Routing

Signaling allows devices to issue requests that create and destroy ATM SVCs (because PVCs are manually created, they do not require signaling for setup and tear down).

Routing is the process that ATM switches use to locate the destination the NSAP addresses specified in signaling requests. Note that this is very different from IP-based routing. IP routing is a connectionless process that is performed for each and every IP datagram (although various caching and optimization techniques do exist). *ATM routing is only performed at the time of call setup.* After the call has been established, all of the traffic associated with that SVC utilizes the VPI/VCI cell-switching table. Note that this distinction allows ATM to simultaneously fulfill the conflicting goals of flexibility and performance. The unwieldy NSAP addresses provide flexible call setup schemes, and the low-overhead VPI/VCI values provide high-throughput and low-latency cell switching.

TIP	Do not confuse ATM routing and IP routing. ATM routing is only performed during call setup when an ATM SVC is being built. On the other hand, IP routing is a process that is performed on each and every IP packet.

When to Use ATM

Although ATM has enjoyed considerable success within the marketplace, the debate continues: which is better—ATM or competing technologies such as Gigabit Ethernet in the campus and Packet Over SONET in the WAN? Well, like most other issues in the internetworking field, the answer is "it depends."

Specifically, ATM has distinct advantages in the following areas:

- Full support for timing-critical applications
- Full support for Quality of Service (QoS)
- Communication over long geographic distances
- Theoretically capable of almost unlimited throughput

Die-hard geeks often refer to timing-critical applications as *isochronous applications.* Isochronous is a fancy term used to describe applications such as voice and video that have very tight timing requirements. Stated differently, the *chronous* (greek word for timing) must be *isos* (Greek word for equal). Traditional techniques used to encode voice and video such as PCM for voice and H.320 for video are generally isochronous and can benefit greatly from ATM's *circuit emulation* capabilities. If your voice and video traffic is isochronous *and* you want to use a single network infrastructure for voice, video, and data, ATM is about your only choice other than bandwidth-inefficient TDM circuits. However, note that there is a growing movement away from isochronous traffic. For example, voice over IP and H.323 video are non-isochronous mechanisms that can run over frame-based media such as Ethernet.

At the time of writing, ATM is the only data technology in common use that reliably supports Quality of Service (QoS). This allows bandwidth and switch processing to be reserved and guaranteed for critical applications like voice and video. Although Ethernet, IP, and other data communication technologies are beginning to offer QoS, these efforts are still in their infancy. Many ATM users argue that Ethernet and IP-based forms of QoS are be better termed Class of Service (CoS) because the reservation and isolation mechanisms are not as strong as can be found in ATM (ATM was built from the ground up to support QoS).

For many network designers, one of the most compelling advantages of ATM is freedom from distance constraints. Even without repeaters, ATM supports much longer distances than any form of Ethernet. With repeaters (or additional switches), ATM can cover any distance. For example, with ATM it is very simple and cost-effective to purchase dark fiber between two sites that are up to 40 kilometers apart (much longer distances are possible) and connect the fiber to OC-12 long-reach ports on LS1010 ATM switches (no repeaters are required). By using repeaters and additional switches, ATM can easily accommodate networks of global scale. However, on the other hand, a number of vendors have introduced forms of Gigabit Ethernet ports capable of reaching 100 kilometers without a repeater such as Cisco's ZX GBIC. Although this does not allow transcontinental Ethernet connections, it can accommodate many campus requirements.

ATM has historically been considered one of the fastest (if not *the* fastest) networking technologies available. However, this point has recently become the subject of considerable debate. The introduction of hardware-based, Gigabit-speed routers (a.k.a. Layer 3 switches) has nullified the view that routers are slow, causing many to argue that modern routers can be just as fast as ATM switches. On the other hand, ATM proponents argue that ATM's low-overhead switching mechanisms will always allow for higher bandwidth than Layer 3 switches can support. Only time will tell.

In short, the decision to use ATM is no longer a clear-cut choice. Each organization must carefully evaluate its current requirements and plans for future growth. For additional guidelines on when to use ATM and when not to use ATM, see Chapter 15, "Campus Design Implementation."

LANE: Theory of Operation

Now that the chapter has built a common foundation of ATM knowledge, the following sections dive into the specifics of LAN Emulation. Before beginning, let me reiterate that the goal is not to clobber you with every subtle nuance of LANE (although it will probably feel like that in ten pages). For example, the LANE specifications contain many optional features—rather than trying to highlight every option, the material focuses on the real-world applications and common practices of LANE.

VLAN Versus ELAN

Many documents treat the terms Virtual LAN (VLAN) and Emulated LAN (ELAN) as synonyms; however, although related, they are arguably different concepts. As discussed in Chapter 5, "VLANs," the term VLAN is used to describe a broadcast domain, in other words, an IP subnet. In a similar fashion, ELANs also act as broadcast domains, and each ELAN has a unique IP subnet address. However, an ELAN is also a specific type of a VLAN: a LAN emulated over ATM. Whereas VLANs can exist over any medium, ELANs only exist in an ATM environment. Whereas all ELANs are VLANs, not all VLANs are ELANs.

The LANE Fake Out: Simulating LANs

As it creates emulated LANs, LANE functions as a sophisticated fake out. Specifically, it fools higher-layer protocols into believing that the network infrastructure consists of Ethernet or Token Ring links when, in fact, the network is composed of an ATM cloud. In this chapter, we focus exclusively on Ethernet-style LANE.

To fool higher-layer protocols into believing that Ethernet is in use, LANE must simulate two important aspects of Ethernet not found in normal ATM networks:

- **MAC addresses**—As discussed in Chapter 1, "Desktop Technologies," Ethernet devices use 6-byte MAC addresses. However, as discussed earlier in this chapter, ATM uses NSAP addresses to create new ATM SVC connections. Some means to convert between these two addressing schemes must exist.

- **Broadcasting**—Given the connection-oriented nature of ATM discussed earlier, broadcasting and multicasting become non-trivial exercises in an ATM environment. However, because higher-layer protocols have always made extensive use of Ethernet's broadcast capabilities, some broadcast mechanism must be devised.

NOTE   Recall that LANE is a technique for *bridging* traffic over an ATM network. As a bridging technology, LANE therefore uses the Spanning-Tree Protocol discussed in Chapters 6 and 7. Note that this also implies a lower limit on failover performance: features such as SSRP, discussed later, might fail over in 10–15 seconds, however, Spanning Tree prevents traffic from flowing for approximately 30 seconds by default.

Because of this delay, some ATM vendors disable Spanning Tree by default. Because of the risks associated with doing this (loops can easily be formed in the Ethernet portion of the network), Cisco *enables Spanning Tree over LANE by default.*

Let's Go to The LANE Bar

This section uses the analogy of a play or skit called "The LANE Bar." Not only does this provide an opportunity for some comic relief in the middle of a long and technically challenging chapter, it provides a strong parallel and memory aid for how LANE functions.

The director of this play is none other than the ATM Forum, world-renowned producers of such Broadway hits as "UNI 3.1," "PNNI," and "Circuit Emulation Service." The play is about deception and deceit—about a group of thugs who fake out a bunch of innocent Ethernet hosts one night. The director has chosen to include four characters.

The Four Characters (Components) of LANE

LANE uses four characters (components) to create the fake out discussed in the previous section. Most vendors implement these components in software that runs on edge devices (although hardware-assisted, hardware-based, and switch-based components are possible). In total, LANE uses one client character and three server characters. The characters (described in the ensuing sections) are as follows:

- LAN Emulation Clients (LECs)
- LAN Emulation Configuration Server (LECS)
- LAN Emulation Server (LES)
- Broadcast and Unknown Server (BUS)

Starring Role: LEC

LAN Emulation Clients (LECs, note the lowercase "s") are edge devices where the fake out actually occurs. In the case of Catalyst LECs, the Catalyst LANE module runs software that fools Ethernet-attached hosts into believing that the ATM backbone is actually Ethernet. LECs are often referred to as Clients and have a starring role in the play. There are two types of LECs: Normal LECs and Proxy LECs.

Normal LECs are everyday devices that happen to contain an ATM interface. For example, take a Windows NT server and place an ATM NIC in one of its expansion slots. Configure it to run LEC software, and the PC can now communicate directly to other devices over the ATM backbone.

Proxy LECs (PLECs) are a slightly different animal. Proxy LECs also directly connect to the ATM backbone and run some sort of LEC software, however, they usually generate very little traffic by themselves. For example, take a Catalyst 5000 that contains a LANE uplink module. Left alone, the Catalyst 5000 generates minute amounts of overhead traffic such as Spanning-Tree Protocol, VLAN Trunking Protocol (VTP), and so forth. The vast majority of traffic that the Catalyst needs to send is on behalf of the Ethernet-attached devices connected to 10/100 Ethernet ports (some B-grade supporting actors sitting just off-stage). However, these Ethernet-attached PCs, workstations, and servers cannot become LECs— after all, they aren't connected to the ATM cloud! It is the Catalyst LANE module that acts as a proxy or agent on behalf of these devices.

LANE Clients serve as the front lines of the fake out; however, left to their own capabilities, LECs would be hopeless. To complete the fake out, our stars (LECs) require the services of three supporting actors (server components). In fact, these three servers allow a Client to join an Emulated LAN.

Supporting Actor: LECS

To begin this joining process, Clients require two things: security and hospitality.

These two functions are provided by a character (component) referred to as the LAN Emulation Configuration Server, or LECS (note the uppercase "S"). This character has been cast as a large, burly fellow with a huge neck, bald head, and a large tattoo on his left arm. He is affectionately referred to as The Bouncer. This character stands at the front door of the nightclub to provide security ("Hey, I need to see your ID!") and hospitality ("The bartender is located over there.") to thirsty Clients.

TIP   The acronyms used by LANE can lead to considerable confusion. This is especially true when using the terms LECs (more than one LANE Client) and LECS (a single LANE Configuration Server). You might want to always pronounce LEC as "Client" and LECS as "Config Server" to avoid this confusion.

Supporting Actor: LES

No barroom would be complete without a Bartender. This important character runs the show in each bar (ELAN). The other characters typically refer to the Bartender by his nickname, LES. Because the directors see this as a high-class bar, they have asked LES to carefully keep track of every Client sitting in the bar (joined the ELAN). To not fail at this task, LES keeps of a list of every Client's name (MAC address) on a clipboard. In addition, LES makes a note of the table number (NSAP address) where every Client is sitting. Therefore, Client actors can ask questions like, "Where's Billy Bob (MAC address 0000.0C12.3456) sitting?" LES can then easily give an answer: "He's at table 219 (NSAP address 47.0091.8100.0000.0060.8372.56A1.0000.0c33.BFC1.A1)!"

Supporting Actor: BUS

The owner of the bar has noticed that the situation sometimes gets a little out of hand in the bar. Get a room full of Clients together and you never know what will happen! One of the problems, especially on Friday nights, is that Clients tend to jump on the tables and start dancing around to attract attention from all other Clients in the bar. Because this has proven to be hard on both the tables and the Clients, our director has requested a special supporting actor called the Broadcast and Unknown Server, or BUS for short. This sly character has earned the title of The Barroom Gossip—you tell him one thing and he's guaranteed to tell everyone else in the bar!

The Setting

Our play is set in the exciting community of Geektown. In building the set, the director has spared no expense. On stage, the workers have carefully built an entire nightclub. This is a single, large brick building (ATM cloud) that contains two separate barrooms (ELANs). On the right, we have The Funky Bit-Pipe, a popular local discotheque. On the left, The Dusty Switch, an always-crowded country-western bar.

Plot Synopsis

Act I is where the main drama occurs and consists of five scenes:

- **Scene 1**—*Configuration Direct*—Client Contacts the Bouncer (LECS): The play begins with a lone Client standing outside the barroom. The Client is clad in a pair of shiny new cowboy boots, a wide-brimmed Stetson hat, and a Garth Brooks look-alike shirt. Before the Client can enter the bar and quench his thirst, he must locate the Bouncer (LECS) standing at the front door to the nightclub. The Bouncer performs a quick security check and, noticing the Client's cowboy attire, points the Client in the direction of the Bartender (LES) for the Dusty Switch barroom (ELAN).

- **Scene 2**—*Control Direct*—Client Contacts the Bartender (LES): As soon as the Client enters the bar, it must approach the Bartender. Then, the Bartender makes a note of the Client's name (MAC address) and table number (NSAP address). Notice that this solves the first requirement of the LANE fake out by providing MAC address to NSAP address mapping.

- **Scene 3**—*Control Distribute* —Bartender (LES) Contacts the Client: As every Client enters the barroom, the Bartender adds it as a leaf node to a special fan-out point-to-multipoint VC. After the new Client contacts the Bartender, the Bartender must add this Client as well. This fan-out circuit allows the Bartender to easily send a single frame that gets distributed to all Clients in the ELAN by the ATM switches. "Happy Hour!" and "Last Call!" are commonly heard messages.

- **Scene 4**—*Multicast Send*—Client Contacts the Gossip (BUS): The Client then acquires the location of the Gossip (BUS) from the Bartender (LES). Next, the Client uses this address to build a connection to the Gossip, allowing the Client to easily send broadcasts and multicasts to everyone in the bar. Notice that this solves the second requirement of the fake out: the capability to send broadcast and multicast frames.

- **Scene 5**—*Multicast Forward*—The Gossip (BUS) Contacts the Client: Just as the Bartender has special fan-out point-to-multipoint circuits that can be used to efficiently reach every Client in the barroom, The Gossip maintains a similar circuit. This allows the Gossip to quickly distribute all of the information he collects.

After the five scenes of Act I are complete, the Client has joined the ELAN, Act II. Notice that Acts I and II only consider the action in the Dusty Switch ELAN. While the cowboys are having fun in their ELAN, another group of Clients is dancing the night away in the discotheque ELAN. Although both barrooms share the services of the Bouncer, each bar requires its own Bartender and Gossip.

Five-Step LANE Initialization Sequence

As introduced in the previous section, the four LANE characters have to do some fancy footwork before they are allowed to communicate via LANE. This section discusses in detail each of the five scenes used to describe the complete process. Now that you are awake (and hopefully have a smile on your face), the text begins to transition away from The LANE Bar analogy (for example, Scenes 1–5 are now referred to as Steps 1–5). However, because it has proven to be a useful memory aid, the text continues to refer to the analogy with parenthetical comments.

Step 1: Configuration Direct—Client Contacts the LECS

As the first step in the joining process, the Client must locate the LECS (Bouncer). Clients can use four techniques to locate the Configuration Server:

- A manually configured NSAP address
- ILMI
- Well-known NSAP (47.0079…)
- Well-known VPI/VCI (0/17)

In reality, locating the Bouncer consists of building an ATM virtual circuit to the LECS. The first three options in the preceding list all make use of SVCs, and the last option utilizes a PVC.

The manually configured NSAP address option for LECS discovery uses the **lane config-atm-address** command to hard-code the NSAP address of the LECS on every Client. Although this approach does provide for technical simplicity, it can lead to administrative headaches.

The ILMI approach uses the capabilities of ILMI to automate the distribution of the LECS' NSAP. This still requires the NSAP to be manually configured on *every ATM switch*, but because most networks have far fewer ATM switches than Clients, this can result in significantly less configuration effort. Cisco recommends this approach because it is both simple and effective (it also works well with the Simple Server Redundancy Protocol [SSRP] discussed later in this chapter).

The well-known NSAP technique is similar to dialing the police in the United States: regardless of where you are, just dial 911 and the phone system connects you to the nearest police station. In the case of LANE, dialing the well-known NSAP connects you to the nearest LECS. Although the full address is 47.00790000000000000000000000.00A03E000001.00 (00A03E is the Organizational Unique Identifier [OUI] assigned by the ATM Forum), any time you see an address that begins with 47.0079 you can be fairly confident that this is an attempt to contact the LECS via the well-known NSAP. You might also run into another version of this address that begins with a C5 in place of a 47 (this uses an ATM feature called anycasting).

NOTE   Anycast addresses are special ATM NSAPs that allow multiple devices to advertise a single service. As clients request connections to these addresses, ATM switches automatically connect them to the nearest available device providing that service. Not only can this optimize traffic flows, it can provide an automatic form of redundancy (if the nearby server goes away, the client simply is sent to a more distant device when it tries to reconnect).

Under the well-known VPI/VCI approach, Clients always use 0/17 to communicate with the LECS. Because this method doesn't lend itself well to failure recovery, the well-known VPI/VCI technique is rarely used (it's also not included in the second version of the LANE specification).

Assuming that the LEC has acquired the Configuration Server's NSAP via ILMI, the Client then places an ATM phone call (SVC) to the LECS. This SVC is referred to as the *Configuration Direct* (it is a direct connection to the Configuration Server). After the Configuration Direct has been established, the Client tells the Configuration Server its NSAP address and the desired ELAN (barroom). The LECS then lives up to its title of the Bouncer by providing the Client with the following:

- **Security**—Optionally checks the Client's NSAP address as a security measure
- **Hospitality**—Tells the Client how to reach the bartender (LES) of the desired barroom (ELAN)

Also, if the Client doesn't request a specific ELAN, the Bouncer can optionally provide a default ELAN.

Figure 9-9 illustrates the Configuration Direct VC.

Figure 9-9 *Step 1: The Client Contacts the Configuration Server to Get the NSAP of the LES*

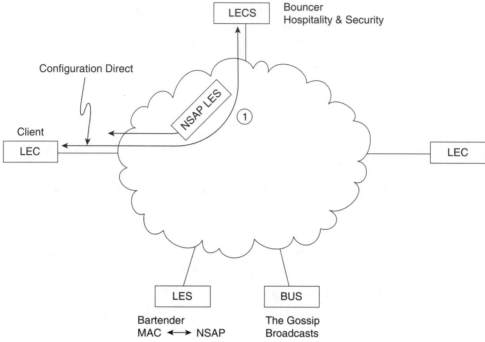

Assuming that the Client meets the security requirements and the requested ELAN exists, the LECS provide the *NSAP of the LES* to the Client. At this point, the Configuration Direct can optionally be torn down to conserve virtual circuits on the ATM switch (Cisco devices take advantage of this option).

Step 2: Control Direct—Client Contacts the LES

After the Client has acquired the LES's NSAP address, it requests an SVC to this location. This SVC is known as a *Control Direct*, the direct connection to the device that controls the ELAN, the LES. The Client sends his MAC address (Name) and NSAP address (barroom table he is sitting at) to the LES (bartender). The LES then makes a note of these entries in its database. Figure 9-10 shows the Control Direct VC.

Figure 9-10 *Step 2: The Client Contacts the LES and Registers Its MAC and NSAP Addresses*

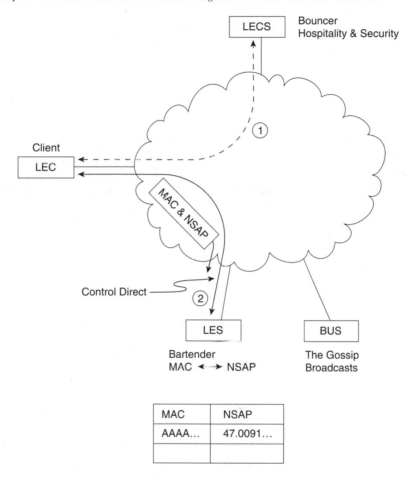

Step 3: Control Distribute—LES Contacts the Client

Using the NSAP address registered over the Control Direct, the LES needs to call back the Client. However, this is not a normal, point-to-point phone call. Prior to this Client's attempt to join, the LES already owned a point-to-multipoint VC to every Client in the ELAN. In other words, every existing Client is a leaf node and the LES is the root node of this unidirectional circuit. The LES then issues an ADD_PARTY message to add the new Client as a leaf node. Figure 9-11 illustrates the resulting Control Distribute VC.

Figure 9-11 *Step 3: The LES Adds the Client to the Already Existing Control Distribute Point-to-Multipoint Circuit*

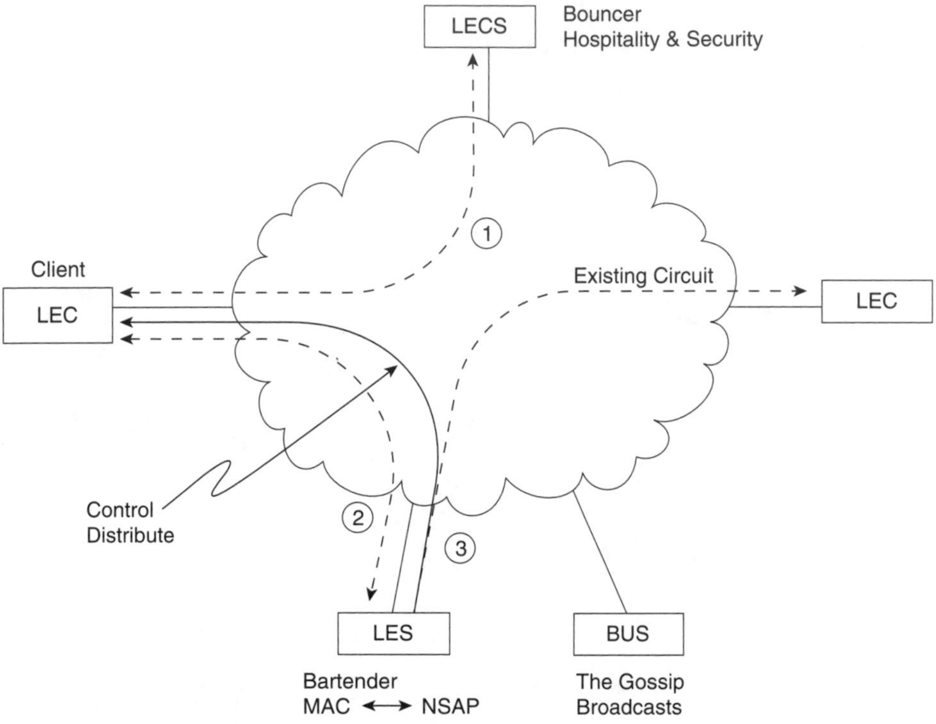

Step 4: Multicast Send—The Client Contacts the BUS

As might be expected, the Client ultimately uses the Control Direct VC established in Step 3 to map MAC addresses into NSAP addresses. The name of the message used to perform this mapping process is an LE_ARP message. An LE_ARP_REQUEST allows a Client to locate the NSAP address associated with another Client's MAC address. LE_ARP_REPLIES are used by the LES to answer LE_ARP_REQUESTS.

Notice that the Client is still in the process of joining and LE_ARPs cannot be used to contact other Clients until the join process is complete. However, the Client LE_ARPs to locate the BUS (the Gossip). The Client issues an LE_ARP_REQUEST for the MAC address FFFF.FFFF.FFFF to resolve the NSAP of the BUS. In other words, the Client LE_ARPs for the broadcast MAC address to locate the device that handles broadcast traffic: the BUS. After the Client LE_ARPs for FFFF.FFFF.FFFF, the LES responds with the NSAP address of the BUS. The Client uses this information to build a *Multicast Send* VC to the BUS as shown in Figure 9-12.

Figure 9-12 *Step 4: The Client Builds the Multicast Send to the BUS*

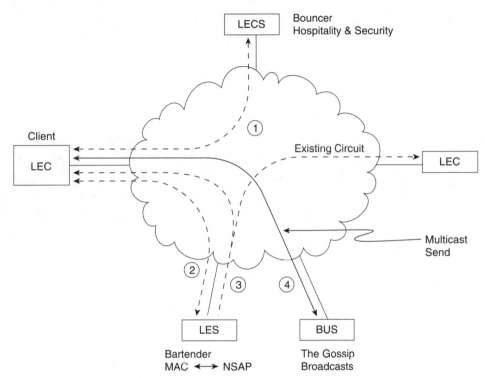

Step 5: Multicast Forward—The BUS Contacts the Client

As with the LES, the BUS maintains a point-to-multipoint connection to every Client in the ELAN. After the BUS learns of the new Client via the Multicast Send, it calls back the Client by issuing an ADD_PARTY message for that device. This VC is referred to as the *Multicast Forward*.

This point-to-multipoint VC provides a fairly efficient method for Clients to issue broadcast and multicast traffic to each other. After Clients forward traffic to the BUS, it sends the traffic out the Multicast Forward to all devices in the ELAN. Figure 9-13 illustrates the Multicast Forward.

Figure 9-13 *Step 5: The BUS Adds the Client to the Multicast Forward*

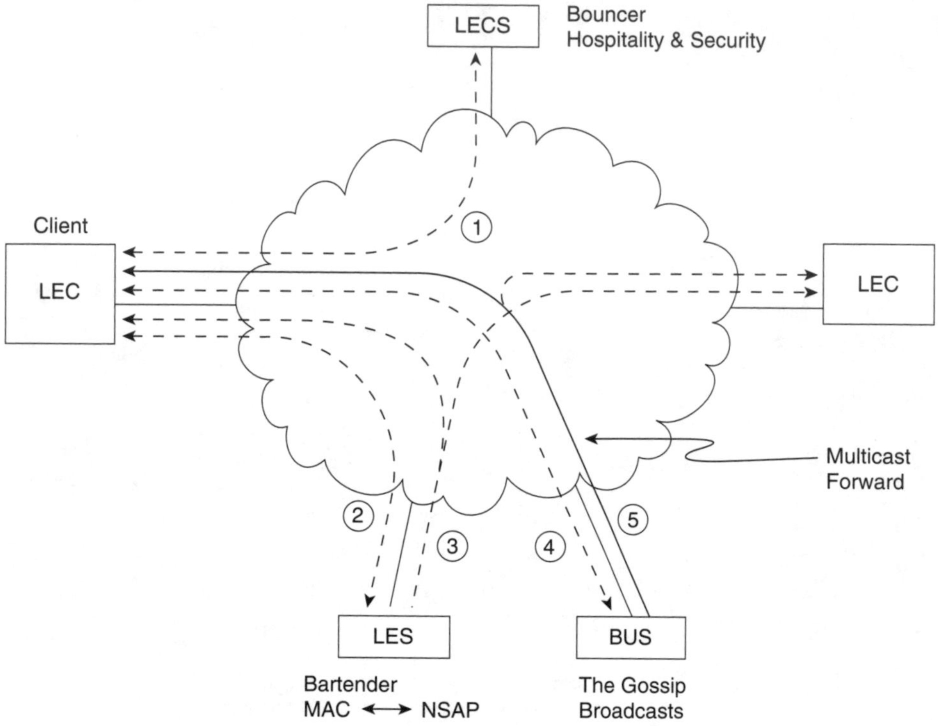

The Client Has Joined!

After the five overhead connections have been built, the Client has officially *joined* the ELAN. At this point, the Client is free to issue LE_ARP_REQUESTs for other Clients in the ELAN. The resulting connections, *Data Direct VCs*, are the primary communication path between LANE Clients. Figure 9-14 illustrates a Data Direct circuit.

Figure 9-14 *Data Direct VCs are created by Clients after they have joined the ELAN*

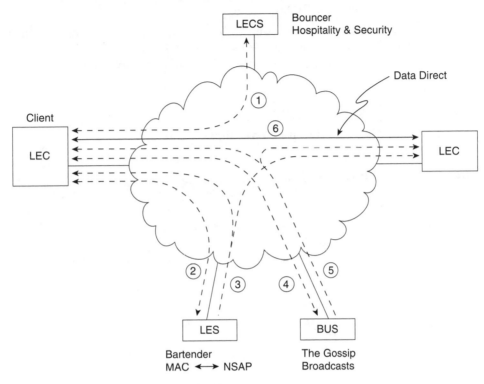

Using The LANE Bar as a Memory Aid

Because LANE obviously contains many unusual and complex mechanisms, use the LANE Bar analogy to keep your bearings. Many elements of the analogy were specifically chosen to mirror how LANE works in reality. In particular:

- Just as one physical building can be used to house two barrooms, one physical ATM cloud can house multiple ELANs.

- Just as a Bouncer provides security and hospitality, the LECS can check Client NSAP addresses for security and point the Clients toward the LES.

- Just as both barrooms were served by a single Bouncer, a single LECS serves an entire network.

- Just as each barroom required its own Bartender and Gossip, each ELAN requires a LES and BUS.

- Just as a Bartender runs a barroom, an LES runs an ELAN.

- Just as Gossips tell everyone everything they hear, BUSs are used to spray information to all Clients in an ELAN.

- Just as Clients are not allowed to come through the bar's back door when they are thrown out (they must dust themselves off and go back to see the Bouncer first), LANE Clients must rejoin an ELAN by visiting the LECS first.

Ethernet LANE Frame Format

Ethernet LANE traffic that passes over the Data Direct uses the frame format illustrated in Figure 9-15.

Figure 9-15 *Ethernet Data Frame Format for LANE*

Ethernet

Dest. MAC	Src. MAC	Type/ Length	Payload	CRC

Bytes: 6   6   2   46 – 1500   4

Max = 1518 Bytes

Version 1.0 (& Version 2.0 Without Multiplexing):

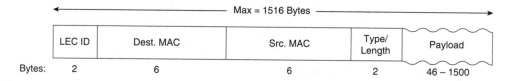

LEC ID	Dest. MAC	Src. MAC	Type/ Length	Payload

Bytes: 2   6   6   2   46 – 1500

Max = 1516 Bytes

Version 2.0 (With Multiplexing):

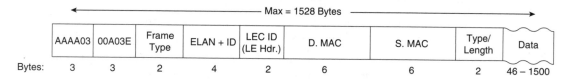

AAAA03	00A03E	Frame Type	ELAN + ID	LEC ID (LE Hdr.)	D. MAC	S. MAC	Type/ Length	Data

Bytes: 3   3   2   4   2   6   6   2   46 – 1500

Max = 1528 Bytes

If you compare the LANE Version 1.0 format to the traditional Ethernet frame you will notice two changes:

- **The addition of the 2-byte LEC ID field**—As LECs contact the LES, they are assigned a unique, 2-byte LECID identifier. In practice, the first LEC that joins is 1, the second is 2, and so on.

- **The removal of the 4-byte CRC**—Because ATM has its own CRC mechanism, the ATM Forum removed the Ethernet CRC.

Notice that this changes the Ethernet MTU for LANE. As discussed in Chapter 1, the traditional Ethernet MTU is 1,518 bytes: 14 bytes of header, 1500 bytes of payload, and 4 bytes of CRC. Because Ethernet LANE removes the 4-byte CRC but adds a 2-byte LEC ID, the resulting MTU is 1516. However, notice that *the payload portion is still 1500 bytes* to ensure interoperability with all Ethernet devices.

LANE version 2.0 adds an optional 12-byte header to the front of the format used in version 1.0. The 12 bytes of this header are composed of the following four fields:

- **802.2 Logical Link Control (LLC) header**—The value AAAA03 signifies that the next five bytes are a SNAP header.

- **SNAP Organizationally Unique Identifier (OUI)**—Used to specify the organization that created this protocol format. In this case, the OUI assigned to the ATM Forum, 00A03E, is used.

- **SNAP Frame Type**—Used to specify the specific frame type. This field allows each of the organizations specified in the previous field to create up to 65,535 different protocols. In the LANE of LANE V2, the value 000C is used.

- **LANE V2 ELAN ID**—A unique identifier for every ELAN.

This allows the second version of LANE to multiplex traffic from multiple ELANs over a single Data Direct VC (the ELAN-ID is used to differentiate the traffic).

Building a Data Direct VC

This section details the sequence of events that allow two Clients to establish a Data Direct VC. The example uses the network illustrated in Figure 9-16.

Figure 9-16 *Two Ethernet Hosts Connected via Proxy Clients*

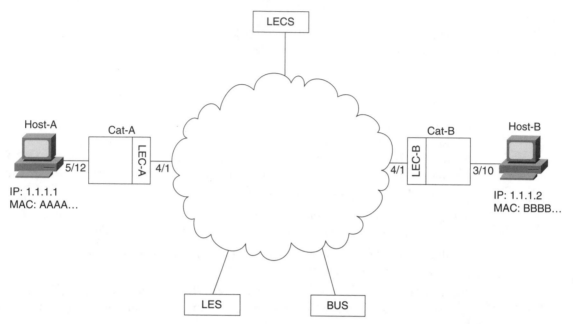

In the example, Host-A issues an IP **ping** to Host-B. Both devices are Ethernet-attached PCs connected to Catalysts that contain LANE uplink cards in slot 4. Host-A is using IP address 1.1.1.1 and MAC address AAAA.AAAA.AAAA. Host-B has IP address 1.1.1.2 and MAC address BBBB.BBBB.BBBB. Notice that this example focuses only on the building of a Data Direct—both Clients (Catalyst LANE cards) are assumed to have already joined the ELAN (using the five-step process discussed earlier). All caches and LANE tables are assumed to be at a state just after initialization. The following sequence outlines the steps that allow two Clients to establish a Data Direct VC.

Step 1   The user of Host-A enters **ping 1.1.1.2** at a command prompt.

Step 2   Host-A issues an IP ARP for the IP address 1.1.1.2. Figure 9-17 illustrates this ARP packet.

Figure 9-17 *IP ARP Request*

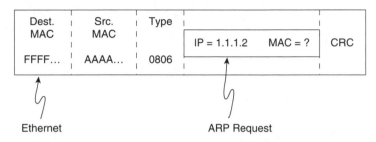

The ARP payload contains the destination IP address in question, 1.1.1.2, but contains all zeros for the associated MAC address. This ARP packet is then encapsulated in an Ethernet frame. As discussed in Chapter 2, "Segmenting LANs," the Ethernet encapsulation has a destination MAC address of FFFF.FFFF.FFFF and a source address of AAAA.AAAA.AAAA, the originating node.

Step 3   The LEC-A Catalyst receives the IP ARP frame on Port 5/12 and floods the frame out all ports in the same VLAN (there are no loops here, so Spanning Tree is ignored). Because LEC-A has been assigned to the same VLAN as Host-A, this Client needs to forward the frame across the LANE cloud. Because the destination address is FFFF.FFFF.FFFF, the Client forwards the frame to the BUS via the Multicast Send. Also notice that LEC-A adds an entry into its bridging table associating MAC address AAAA.AAAA.AAAA with Port 5/12.

Step 4   The BUS floods the packet to all Clients, including LEC-B, via the Multicast Forward. Notice that LEC-A also receives this frame, but is able to discard the frame because it recognizes its own LECID in the first two bytes.

Step 5   Because the LEC-B is operating as a transparent bridge, it also notices the broadcast destination address of the IP ARP and floods the packet to all ports in that VLAN, including Host-B's Port of 3/10. It also makes a new entry in its bridging table to reflect the fact that it just received a source MAC address of AAAA.AAAA.AAAA on Port 4/1.

Figure 9-18 illustrates the first five steps of the Data Direct Process.

Figure 9-18 *The first five steps of the Data Direct VC Creation Process*

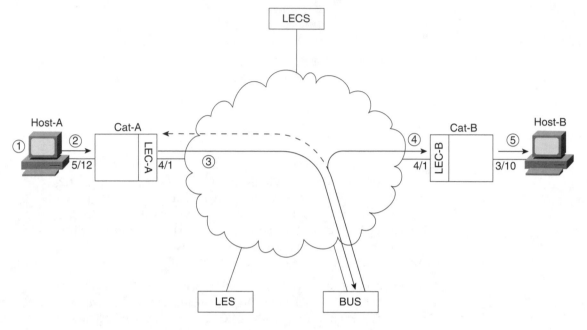

Step 6   Host-B receives the IP ARP request. Recognizing its IP address in the ARP packet, it builds an IP ARP reply packet. Figure 9-19 illustrates the reply.

Figure 9-19 *IP ARP Reply*

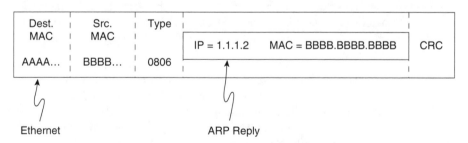

In this case, the ARP message contains the MAC address in question. Also notice that ARP unicasts the reply back to the source node; it is not sent to all nodes via the broadcast address.

Step 7   The LEC-B Catalyst receives the IP ARP reply. Having just added a bridging table entry for AAAA.AAAA.AAAA in Step 5, the frame is forwarded to the LANE module in slot 4.

Step 8   The LEC-B software running on the LANE module must then send the IP ARP reply over the ATM backbone. At this point, two separate threads of activities take over. The first thread, an LE_ARP process, is detailed in Step 8; the second thread, forwarding the IP ARP, is explained in Step 9.

    (a) LEC-B must resolve MAC address AAAA.AAAA.AAAA into an NSAP address. To do this, LEC-B sends an LE_ARP_REQUEST to the LES. Notice the important differences between this LE_ARP and the earlier IP ARP. With the IP ARP, the destination IP address was known but the MAC address was not known. In the case of the LE_ARP, the MAC address is now known (via the IP ARP) and the NSAP address is unknown. In other words, the LE_ARP is only possible after the IP ARP has already resolved the MAC address.

    (b) The LES consults its local MAC-address-to-NSAP-address mapping table. Although this table contains a mapping entry for LEC-A, *it does not contain a mapping entry for Host-A*. It is important to realize that LEC-A and Host-A are using different MAC addresses. Just because LEC-A is acting as a Proxy Client for Host-A doesn't mean that it has assumed Host-A's MAC address. When LEC-A joined the ELAN, it could have optionally registered all known addresses for its Ethernet-attached hosts. However, because transparent bridges rarely know all MAC addresses (after all, they are learning bridges), most vendors opt to only register the MAC address specifically assigned to the Proxy LEC.

        If it still seems unclear why the LES wouldn't learn about MAC address AAAA.AAAA.AAAA at the time LEC-A joined the ELAN, consider the following: What if Host-A wasn't even running at the time LEC-A joined? In this case, the MAC address isn't even active, so it is impossible for LEC-A to register MAC address AAAA.AAAA.AAAA.

    (c) Because the LES doesn't have a mapping for the requested MAC address, it forwards the LE_ARP message on to all Proxy Clients via the Control Distribute VC.

Figure 9-20 diagrams Steps 6 through 8c.

Figure 9-20 *Steps 6–8c in the Data Direct VC Creation Process*

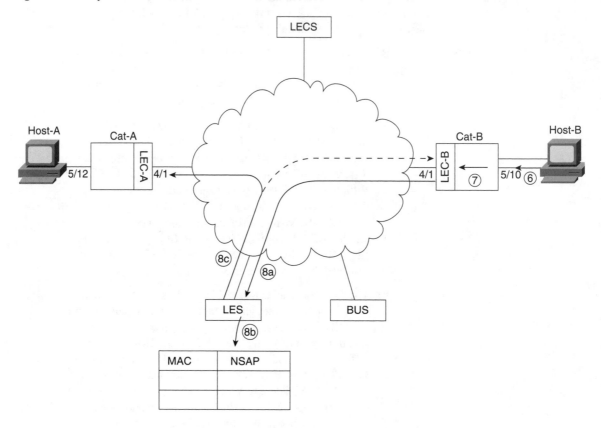

(d) All Clients, including LEC-A, receive the LE_ARP_REQUEST. LEC-A answers with an LE_ARP_REPLY using the bridging table entry added in Step 3.

(e) The LES receives the LE_ARP_REPLY from LEC-A and forwards it to LEC-B.

(f) LEC-B builds a Data Direct VC to LEC-A.

Figure 9-21 illustrates Steps 8d through 8f.

Figure 9-21   *Steps 8d–8f in the Data Direct VC Creation Process*

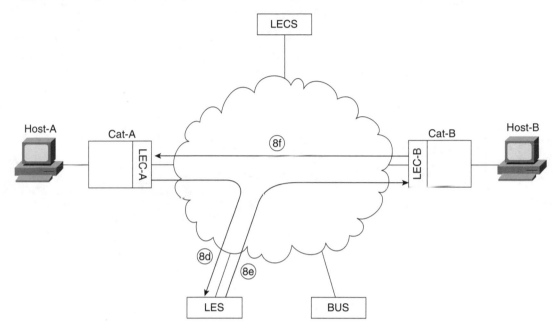

Step 9   As mentioned in Step 8, LEC-B performed two tasks in parallel. Steps 8a through 8f detailed the LE_ARP resolution process. However, while this sequence of events was taking place, LEC-B also forwarded the IP ARP frame via the BUS. Steps 9a through 9f detail this process of forwarding the IP ARP.

   (a)   LEC-B sends the IP ARP frame over its Multicast Send to the BUS.

   (b)   The BUS forwards this frame to all Clients via the Multicast Forward.

   (c)   All Clients, including LEC-A, receive the IP ARP packet. LEC-B recognizes its LECID and drops the frame. LEC-A uses the bridging table entry added in Step 3 to forward the IP ARP out Port 5/12 to Host-A. LEC-A also adds a bridging table entry associating Port 4/1 with MAC address BBBB.BBBB.BBBB.

Figure 9-22 illustrates Steps 9a through 9c.

Figure 9-22 *Steps 9a–9c in the Data Direct VC Creation Process*

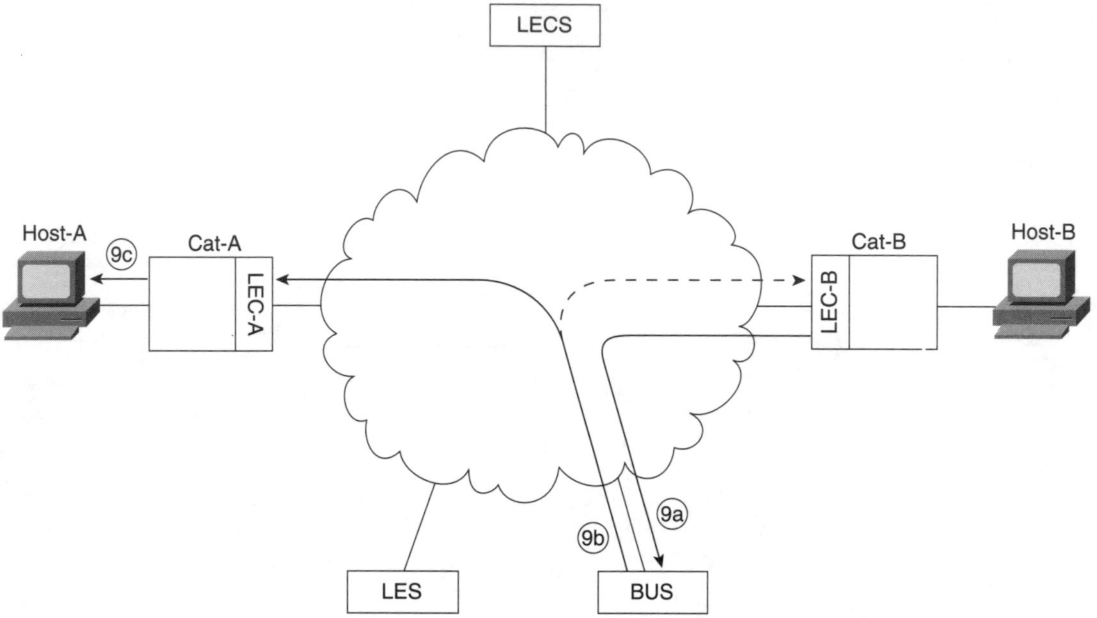

(d) Having received the IP ARP reply, Host-A caches the IP ARP data, and sends the IP **ping** packet that has been waiting since Step 2. The destination MAC address is BBBB.BBBB.BBBB (a unicast frame).

(e) The LEC-A Catalyst receives the ping packet on Port 5/12 and uses the bridging table entry added in Step 9c to forward the frame out Port 4/1.

(f) LEC-A then performs the same two parallel tasks discussed in the text preceding Step 8: it issues an LE_ARP_REQUEST over the Control Direct to build a Data Direct, and it floods the ping packet via the BUS. Although the intervening steps are not shown, LEC-A ultimately receives an LE_ARP_REPLY.

(g) LEC-A uses the information contained in the LE_ARP_REPLY to build a Data Direct VC to LEC-B.

Figure 9-23 illustrates the remaining portions of Step 9.

Figure 9-23 *Steps 9d–9g in the Data Direct VC Creation Process*

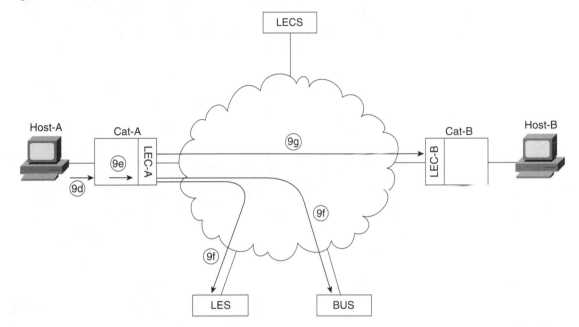

Step 10 At this point, both LECs have attempted to build a Data Direct VC. Which Data Direct VC is built first can be different in every case and depends on the timing of Steps 8 and 9. Assume that LEC-B completes its Data Direct VC first and the timing is such that LEC-A also builds a Data Direct VC. In this case, both LECs begin using the Data Direct VC built by the LEC with the lower NSAP address. Assume that LEC-A has the lower NSAP. This causes all traffic to flow over the Data Direct VC created by LEC-A (LEC-B's Data Direct VC times out after five minutes by default on Cisco equipment).

Step 11 Before the Clients can begin communicating, they must take an extra step to ensure the in-order delivery of information. Notice that both LEC-B (Step 9b) *and* LEC-A (Step 9f) have sent information via the BUS. If the Clients were to start sending information via the Data Direct VC as soon as it became available, this could lead to out-of-order information. For example, the Data Direct frame (the second frame sent) could arrive before the frame sent via the BUS (the first frame sent). To prevent this, the Clients can optionally use a *Flush* protocol. Steps 11a–11e follow the Flush protocol from LEC-A's perspective:

    (a) LEC-A sends an LE_FLUSH_REQUEST message over the Multicast Send.

    (b) The BUS forwards the LE_FLUSH_REQUEST to LEC-B.

(c) LEC-B answers the Flush with a LE_FLUSH_RESPONSE over the Control Direct.

(d) The LES forwards the LE_FLUSH_RESPONSE over the *Control Direct to LEC-A*.

(e) Having now flushed all data out of its connection to the BUS, LEC-A can safely begin using the Data Direct VC. The remaining ping packets use this Data Direct VC.

Figure 9-24 diagrams the Data Direct VC completion and Flush processes.

Figure 9-24 *Steps 10 and 11a–11e in the Data Direct VC Creation Process*

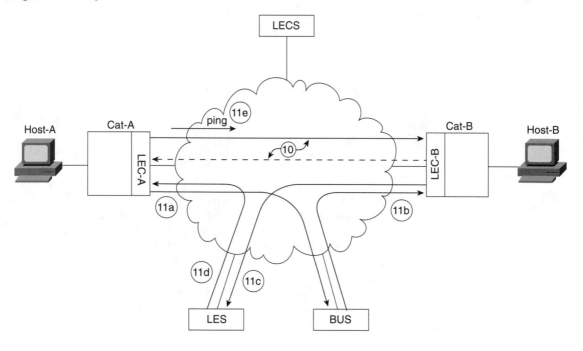

Notice that after the process forks in Step 8, the order of the events becomes indeterminate. In some cases, LEC-A is the first to build a Data Direct VC; in other cases, LEC-B is the first.

Configuration Concepts

There are several important concepts used in configuring LANE on Cisco devices, including the following:

- Mapping VLAN numbers to ELAN names
- Addressing
- Subinterfaces

Mapping VLAN Numbers to ELAN Names

Whereas the Catalyst refers to broadcast domains with VLAN numbers, LANE always uses textual ELAN names. The LEC is used to map the VLAN number into an ELAN name (as is discussed in the "Configuration Syntax" section later, this mapping is established via the command that creates the Client). ELAN names can be up to 32 characters in length. Be very careful when configuring ELAN names because they are case sensitive.

Subinterfaces

As explained in Chapter 8, "Trunking Technologies and Applications," Cisco uses the subinterface concept to create logical partitions on a single physical interface. In this case, each partition is used for a separate ELAN as shown in Figure 9-25.

Figure 9-25 *Each Subinterface Is Used for a Separate ELAN*

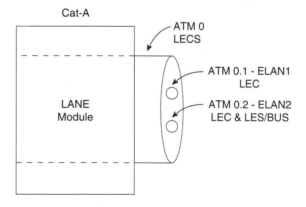

In Figure 9-25, subinterface ATM 0.1 is used for ELAN1, and ATM 0.2 is used for ELAN2. Cat-A is a client on both ELANs and therefore requires a LEC on both subinterfaces. Because Cat-A is also acting as the LES and BUS for ELAN2 (but not ELAN1), these services are only configured on subinterface ATM 0.2. However, notice that the LECS is configured on the major interface, ATM 0. This placement mirrors the roles that each component plays:

- Because the LECS doesn't belong to any particular ELAN, it is placed on the major interface. As a global concept, the LECS should be placed on the global interface.
- LECs, LESs, and BUSs that do belong to specific ELANs are placed on subinterfaces.

In short, subinterfaces allow the interface configuration to match the LANE configuration.

TIP	Although most LANE components are configured on a subinterface, the LECS is always configured on the major interface of Cisco equipment.

Addressing

LANE's reliance on SVCs requires careful planning of NSAP addresses (recall that SCVs are built by placing an ATM phone call to an NSAP address). Although Cisco allows you to manually configure NSAP addresses, an automatic NSAP addressing scheme is provided to allow almost plug-and-play operation.

Recall from Figure 9-6 that NSAP addresses have three sections:

- A 13-byte prefix from the ATM switch (LS1010)
- A 6-byte ESI from the edge device (Catalyst LANE module)
- A 1-byte selector byte from the edge device (Catalyst LANE module)

The LANE components automatically acquire the prefix from the ATM switch. However, what does the Catalyst provide for the ESI and selector byte values? Cisco has created a simple scheme based on MAC addresses to fulfill this need. Every ATM interface sold by Cisco has a block of at least eight MAC addresses on it (some interfaces have more). This allows each LANE component to automatically adopt a unique NSAP address using the pattern shown in Table 9-3.

Table 9-3 *Automatic ESI and Selector Byte Values*

LANE Component	ESI	Selector Byte
LEC	MAC Address	.**
LES	MAC Address + 1	.**
BUS	MAC Address + 2	.**
LECS	MAC Address + 3	.00

** Represents the subinterface where a LANE component is created

For example, assume that an ATM switch is using a prefix of
47.0091.8100.0000.0060.1234.5678 and the first MAC address on a LANE blade is
0000.0CAB.5910. If you build all four components on this device and use subinterface
ATM 0.29, Table 9-4 shows the resulting NSAP addresses.

Table 9-4   *Sample NSAP addresses*

LANE Component	NSAP
LEC	47.0091.8100.0000.0060.1234.5678.0000.0CAB.5910.1D
LES	47.0091.8100.0000.0060.1234.5678.0000.0CAB.5911.1D
BUS	47.0091.8100.0000.0060.1234.5678.0000.0CAB.5912.1D
LECS	47.0091.8100.0000.0060.1234.5678.0000.0CAB.5913.00

As discussed earlier, notice that the LECS always appears on the major interface and uses
.00 as a selector byte. Also note that although subinterfaces are expressed in decimal to the
IOS (interface ATM 0.29), the selector byte is expressed in hexadecimal (0x1D).

TIP	Although subinterface numbers are expressed in decimal in the IOS configuration, they are expressed in hex when used for the ATM NSAP's selector byte.

In practice, Cisco makes it extremely easy to determine the NSAP addresses for a specific
Catalyst LANE module—just use the **show lane default** command. For example, the
Catalyst output in Example 9-1 is connected to an ATM switch with the prefix
47.0091.8100.0000.0010.2962.E801.

Example 9-1   *Determining NSAP Addresses for a Catalyst LANE Module*

```
ATM#show lane default
interface ATM0:
LANE Client:      47.00918100000000102962E801.00102962E430.**
LANE Server:      47.00918100000000102962E801.00102962E431.**
LANE Bus:         47.00918100000000102962E801.00102962E432.**
LANE Config Server: 47.00918100000000102962E801.00102962E433.00
note: ** is the subinterface number byte in hex
```

The selector byte is shown as .** for the LEC, LES, and BUS because the subinterface
numbers are not revealed by this command.

Configuration Syntax

The good news is that, although the theory of LANE is very complex and cumbersome, Cisco has made the configuration very simple. In fact, LANE uses the same configuration syntax across almost the entire product line. In other words, learn how to configure LANE on a Catalyst and you already know how to configure it on a Cisco router or ATM switch.

To configure a Catalyst LANE module, you must first use the **session** command to open a LANE command prompt. For example, if you currently have a Telnet session into the Catalyst 5000 Supervisor and you want to configure a LANE blade in slot 4, you issue the command in Example 9-2.

Example 9-2 *Opening a LANE Command Prompt*

```
MyCat> (enable) session 4
Trying ATM-4...
Connected to ATM-4.
Escape character is '^]'.

ATM>
```

This suddenly catapults you to the IOS-style command prompt on the LANE module! That's right, the LANE module runs the traditional IOS software (although it's obviously a separate binary image that must be downloaded from CCO). Almost all of the router's command-line interface (CLI) features you know and love are available:

- BASH-style command-line recall (using the arrow keys)
- **config term** to alter the configuration
- **debug** commands
- **copy run start** or **write mem** to save the configuration

Don't forget the last bullet: unlike the Catalyst Supervisor, you must remember to save the configuration. Forget to do this and you are guaranteed to have a miserable day (or night) after the next power outage!

TIP   Don't forget to use the **copy run start** command to save your LANE configuration!

It is easiest to think of the LANE module as an independent device that connects to the Catalyst backplane. In other words, it has its own DRAM and CPU for use while operational. When the Catalyst is powered down, the LANE module uses its own NVRAM to store the configuration and flash to store the operating system.

The Catalyst LANE module can be configured in five simple steps, each of which are detailed in the sections that follow:

Step 1   Build overhead connections

Step 2   Build the LES and BUS

Step 3   Build the LECS

Step 4   Build the LECs

Step 5   Add LECS' NSAP to ATM Switch

Step 1: Build Overhead Connections

LANE makes extensive use of the ATM overhead protocols mentioned earlier in the chapter. Specifically, the LEC must be configured to use signaling and ILMI. Signaling allows the LEC to build the many SVCs required by LANE, whereas ILMI provides address registration and allows the ATM switch to provide the LECS' (Bouncer's) NSAP address. Both of these overhead protocols are enabled by creating two ATM PVCs. The basic syntax for the ATM PVC commands is (there are other options available, but they are not relevant to LANE) as follows:

```
atm pvc VCD VPI VCI encapsulation
```

The *VCD* parameter is used to specify a locally significant Virtual Circuit Descriptor. The IOS uses a unique VCD to track every ATM connection. In the case of PVCs, you must manually specify a unique value. In the case of SVCs, the Catalyst automatically chooses a unique value.

The *VPI* and *VCI* parameters are used to specify the Virtual Path Indicator and Virtual Channel Indicator, respectively. Recall that these are the two addressing fields in the 5-byte ATM cell header.

The two PVCs listed in Example 9-3 must exist on every LEC.

Example 9-3   *Mandatory PVCs for LECs*

```
ATM(Config)# int atm 0
ATM(Config-if)# atm pvc 1 0 5 qsaal
ATM(Config-if)# atm pvc 2 0 16 ilmi
```

The first PVC provides signaling (QSAAL stands for Q.Signaling ATM Adaptation Layer), whereas the second PVC obviously provides ILMI. You are free to use any VCD values you want; however, they must be unique, and the values 1 and 2 are most common.

Be careful not to enter commands in Example 9-4.

Example 9-4 *Eliminating a PVC by Mistake*

```
ATM(Config)# int atm 0
ATM(Config-if)# atm pvc 1 0 5 qsaal
ATM(Config-if)# atm pvc 1 0 16 ilmi
```

This common mistake results in only one PVC (ILMI) because the VCD numbers are the same.

The best news of all is that *Step 1 is not required for Catalyst LANE modules!* All Catalyst LANE images since 3.X automatically contain the two overhead PVCs. On the other hand, if you are configuring LANE on a Cisco router, don't forget to enter these two commands.

TIP   The ATM PVC statements for signaling and ILMI are not required for Catalyst LANE module configuration. However, they *are* required for LANE configurations on Cisco routers.

Step 2: Build the LES and BUS (Bartender and Gossip)

The first LANE-specific components to be configured are the LES and BUS (you can create the LANE components in any order you want, however, I recommend the order presented here). To allow the components to function more efficiently, Cisco requires the LES and BUS to be co-located on the same device. Therefore, a single command is used to enable both devices:

```
lane server-bus ethernet ELAN_Name
```

For example, the configuration in Example 9-5 creates a LES and BUS for the ELAN named ELAN1.

Example 9-5 *Creating the LES and BUS for an ELAN*

```
ATM(Config)# int atm 0.1 multipoint
ATM(Config-subif)# lane server-bus ethernet ELAN1
```

CAUTION   Enter ELAN names carefully—they are case sensitive.

After completing the configuration in Example 9-5, you should be able to view the status of the LES with the **show lane server** command as demonstrated in Example 9-6.

Example 9-6   *Viewing the LES Status*

```
ATM#show lane server
LE Server ATM0.1  ELAN name: ELAN1  Admin: up  State: operational
type: ethernet         Max Frame Size: 1516
ATM address: 47.00918100000000102962E801.00102962E431.01
LECS used: 47.0079000000000000000000.00A03E000001.00 NOT yet connected
```

Finally, be sure to make note of the LES' address on the second to last line (the **ATM address:** field), it is used in Step 3.

Unless you are using SSRP server redundancy (discussed later), be sure to only configure one LES/BUS for each ELAN.

Step 3: Build the LECS (Bouncer)

Every LANE network requires a single LECS (although redundant LECSs are possible using SSRP). The LECS is configured using a two-step process:

Step 1   You must build the LECS database.

Step 2   You must enable the LECS on the major interface.

Building the LECS Database

The LECS database is a table that lists all of the available ELANs and their corresponding LES NSAP addresses. It can also list optional information such as NSAP addresses for security verification and ELAN IDs. To create a basic LECS database, use the **lane database** command to enter the database configuration mode of the IOS CLI. The following is the syntax for the **lane database** command:

    lane database *database-name*

At this point, you can now enter one line per ELAN. Each line lists the name of the ELAN and the NSAP of the LES for that ELAN using the following syntax (some advanced options have been omitted for simplicity):

    name *elan-name* **server-atm-addres** *atm-addr*

NOTE   Multiple lines are possible if you are using a feature known as SSRP. This option is discussed later.

For example, the commands in Example 9-7 build a database for two ELANs.

Example 9-7 *Building a Database for Two ELANS*

```
ATM(Config)# lane database My_LECS_Db
ATM(lane-config-database)# name ELAN1 server-atm-address
   47.009181000000000102962E801.00102962E431.01
ATM(lane-config-database)# name ELAN2 server-atm-address
   47.009181000000000102962E801.00101F266431.02
```

A common mistake is to configure the NSAP of the *LECS* in the database (instead of the *LES'* NSAP). The LECS doesn't need to have its own address added to the database (it already knows that), it needs to know the NSAP of the *LES*. Just remember, the LECS (Bouncer) needs to tell Clients how to reach the LES (Bartender).

TIP   Be certain that you specify the name of the LES, not the LECS, in the LECS database.

Be aware that the capability to edit the LECS database on the ATM device itself is a very useful Cisco-specific feature. Several other leading competitors require you to build the file on a TFTP server using cryptic syntax and then TFTP the file to the ATM device, an awkward process at best.

Enabling the LECS

After you have built the LECS, you can enable the LECS. As discussed earlier, the LECS must run on a major interface because it is a global component that serves the entire network and does not belong to any particular ELAN.

You must enter the two required commands in Example 9-8 to start the LECS.

Example 9-8 *Required Commands for Starting the LECS*

```
ATM(Config)# int atm 0
ATM(Config-if)# lane config database My_LECS_Db
ATM(Config-if)# lane config auto-config-atm-address
```

The **lane config database** command binds the database built in the previous step to the specified major interface. The complete syntax for this command is as follows:

```
lane config database database-name
```

The **lane config auto-config-atm-address** command tells the IOS to use the automatic addressing scheme (MAC Address + 3 . 00) discussed earlier. The following is the complete syntax for this command:

```
lane config auto-config-atm-address
```

Step 4: Build the LECs (Clients)

The fourth step adds LANE Clients to the appropriate subinterfaces. If a single Catalyst LANE module needs to participate in ten ELANs, it requires ten Clients. To create a single client, issue the command in Example 9-9.

Example 9-9 *Creating an LEC*

```
ATM(Config)# int atm 0.1 multipoint
ATM(Config-subif)# lane client ethernet 1 ELAN1
```

The **1** ties VLAN 1 to ELAN1, merging the two into a single broadcast domain.

The following is the complete syntax for the **lane client** command:

```
lane client [ethernet | tokenring] vlan-num [elan-name]
```

TIP   It is necessary to specify a VLAN number to ELAN name mapping when creating a LEC on a Catalyst LANE module. This is not required when configuring LANE on a Cisco router (by default, they route, not bridge, between the LEC and other interfaces).

Step 5: Add the LECS' NSAP to ATM Switch

Recall that Cisco devices prefer to have LECs learn the NSAP of the LECS via ILMI. This requires that ATM switches be configured with the LECS' NSAP address. To do this, enter the following command on the LS1010 (the LS1010 also uses an IOS-style interface):

```
Switch(Config)# atm lecs-address-default 47.0091.8100.0000.0010.2962.
e801.0010.2962.e433.00
```

This is a global command that applies to all ports on the switch. You can obtain the LECS' address by issuing the **show lane config** command or the **show lane default** command on the device functioning as the Configuration Server. This command must be configured on all ATM switches (there is not an automated protocol to disseminate the LECS' NSAP between ATM switches). The full syntax of the **atm lecs-address-default** command is as follows:

```
atm lecs-address-default lecs-address [sequence-#]
```

The *sequence-#* parameter is used by the SSRP feature discussed later in the chapter.

A Complete LANE Network

Figure 9-26 pulls together many of the concepts and commands discussed earlier in previous sections. This section also shows the configuration for an ATM-attached router.

Figure 9-26 *A Complete LANE Network*

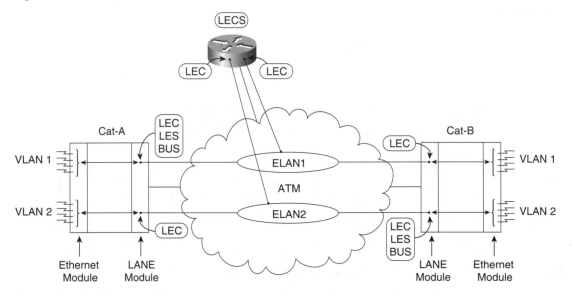

The network consists of two Catalysts that contain Ethernet and LANE modules. Each Catalyst has been configured with two VLANs that use ATM as a trunk media. VLAN 1 is transparently bridged to ELAN1, creating a single broadcast domain. VLAN 2 uses ELAN2. Both Catalysts have two LANE Clients, one for each ELAN. Cat-A is acting as the LES/BUS for ELAN1, and Cat-B is serving as the LES/BUS for ELAN2. Example 9-10 shows the configuration code for Cat-A.

Example 9-10 *Cat-A Configuration for the LANE Network in Figure 9-26*

```
int atm 0
 atm pvc 1 0 5 qsaal
 atm pvc 2 0 16 ilmi
 !
int atm 0.1 multipoint
 lane server-bus ethernet ELAN1
 lane client ethernet 1 ELAN1
 !
int atm 0.2 multipoint
 lane client ethernet 2 ELAN2
```

Example 9-11 shows the configuration code for Cat-B.

Example 9-11 *Cat-B Configuration for the LANE Network in Figure 9-26*

```
int atm 0
 atm pvc 1 0 5 qsaal
 atm pvc 2 0 16 ilmi
 !
int atm 0.1 multipoint
 lane client ethernet 1 ELAN1
 !
int atm 0.2 multipoint
 lane server-bus ethernet ELAN2
 lane client ethernet 2 ELAN2
```

An ATM-attached router on a stick has also been configured to provide routing services between the VLANs/ELANs. To function in this capacity, the router must be configured with the two overhead PVCs on the major interface and two subinterfaces containing LANE Clients and IP addresses. The router is also acting as the LECS for the network. Example 9-12 shows the configuration code for the router.

Example 9-12 *Router Configuration for the LANE Network in Figure 9-26*

```
lane database my_database
 name ELAN1 server-atm-address 47.0091.8100.0000.0010.2962.E801.0010.2962.E431.01
 name ELAN2 server-atm-address 47.0091.8100.0000.0010.2962.E801.0010.1F26.6431.02
 !
int atm 1/0
 atm pvc 1 0 5 qsaal
 atm pvc 2 0 16 ilmi
 lane config database my_database
 lane config auto-config-atm-address
 !
int atm 1/0.1 multipoint
 ip address 10.0.1.1 255.255.255.0
 lane client ethernet 1 ELAN1
 !
int atm 1/0.2 multipoint
 ip address 10.0.2.1 255.255.255.0
 lane client ethernet 2 ELAN2
```

Testing the LANE Configuration

At this point, you should have a working LANE configuration. Use the **show lane client** command to troubleshoot your configuration—it is a deceptively powerful and useful command. Notice that, for two reasons, I recommend using **show lane client** before you even try a ping. First, the LANE module does not have a **ping** command (requiring that you use the **exit** command to return to the Supervisor). Second, **show lane client** provides much more useful information.

Example 9-13 demonstrates the **show lane client** display from a working configuration.

Example 9-13 *show lane client Command Output*

```
ATM#show lane client
LE Client ATM0.1  ELAN name: ELAN1  Admin: up  State: operational
Client ID: 3                 LEC up for 8 seconds
Join Attempt: 1
HW Address: 0010.2962.e430   Type: ethernet          Max Frame Size: 1516
        VLANID: 1
ATM Address: 47.009181000000000102962E801.00102962E430.01

 VCD  rxFrames  txFrames  Type       ATM Address
   0        0         0  configure  47.009181000000000102962E801.00102962E433.00
  22        1         3  direct     47.009181000000000102962E801.00102962E431.01
  23        7         0  distribute 47.009181000000000102962E801.00102962E431.01
  25        0         1  send       47.009181000000000102962E801.00102962E432.01
  26        6         0  forward    47.009181000000000102962E801.00102962E432.01
```

The breakdown for the output in Example 9-13 is as follows:

- The first line (after the **show lane client** command, of course) shows the subinterface, the ELAN name, whether the LEC is administratively up, and whether the LEC is in an operational state.

- The second line shows the LEC-ID assigned by the LES to this LEC and how long the LEC has been active.

- The third line displays how many attempts it took the LEC to join (in some cases, this information might appear at the end of the second line).

- The fourth line shows the MAC address being used by the Client (it should tie to the first line in **show lane default**), whether the LEC is an Ethernet or Token Ring Client, and the MTU being used.

- The VLAN mapped to the ELAN specified in the first line generally wraps on the display to be shown on the fifth line.

- The sixth line shows the NSAP address being used by the LEC (if you have used the auto-NSAP addresses, it should include the MAC address on line four as the ESI).

- The remaining output shows the five overhead connections created during the joining process. Notice that they are shown in the order they are created. Remember to use this great reference tool when you forget the joining order! Each line shows the VCD currently in use for that connection, the number of frames transmitted and received on that connection, the name of the connection (abbreviated), and the NSAP of the device at the other end of the connection. Notice that the Configuration Direct VC to the Configuration Server has a VCD of 0. This reflects the fact that Cisco closes this control connection as soon as the LECS has provided the NSAP of the LES. As Data Direct VCs are built, they appear as additional lines after the five overhead VCs.

TIP   Use the **show lane client** command to remember the order of the LANE joining process.

There are several items in Example 9-13 showing that the LEC has successfully joined the ELAN:

- The State is **operational**.
- The LEC has been up for eight seconds.
- All five overhead VCs have valid NSAPs listed.

Example 9-14 shows a common failure condition.

Example 9-14 *LEC Failure*

```
ATM#show lane client
LE Client ATM0.1  ELAN name: ELAN1  Admin: up  State: initialState
Client ID: unassigned          Next join attempt in 9 seconds
Join Attempt: 7
Last Fail Reason: Config VC being released
HW Address: 0010.2962.e430  Type: ethernet           Max Frame Size: 1516
        VLANID: 1
ATM Address: 47.00918100000000102962E801.00102962E430.01

 VCD  rxFrames  txFrames  Type        ATM Address
  0       0        0  configure  47.00790000000000000000000.00A03E000001.00
  0       0        0  direct     00.000000000000000000000000.000000000000.00
  0       0        0  distribute 00.000000000000000000000000.000000000000.00
  0       0        0  send       00.000000000000000000000000.000000000000.00
  0       0        0  forward    00.000000000000000000000000.000000000000.00
```

Several sections of the output in Example 9-14 point to the failure, including:

- The State is **initialState**.

- The LEC attempts to join again in nine seconds.

- A Last Fail Reason is provided.

- Only the first VC (the Configuration Direct) lists a non-zero NSAP.

Because the first line represents the Configuration Direct to the LECS, the information in this display is strong evidence of a problem very early in the joining process. Also look carefully at the NSAP for the Configuration Direct—it is the well-known NSAP. Because Cisco uses the well-known NSAP as a last gasp effort to contact the LECS if all other measures have failed, it is often a sign that the join process failed. In fact, this display is almost always the result of three specific errors:

- **The ATM switch provided the wrong NSAP (or no NSAP) for the LECS**—When the LEC contacted the device specified by this NSAP and tried to begin the joining process, it was rudely told the equivalent of "Join an ELAN?? I don't know what you are talking about!" Look at the **atm lecs-address-default** command on the LS1010 to verify and fix this problem.

- **The LEC was given the correct NSAP address LECS, but the LECS is down**—In this case, the Client contacted the correct devices, but it was still rebuffed because the LECS couldn't yet handle LE_CONFIGURE_REQUESTS (the message sent between Clients and LECSs). Look at the configuration of the LECS to verify and fix this problem. The **show lane config** command is often useful for this purpose.

- **The LEC requested an ELAN that doesn't exist**—To verify this condition, issue a **terminal monitor** command on the LANE module to display error messages. If you see "CFG_REQ failed, no configuration (LECS returned 20)" messages, use the **show**

lane client command to check the ELAN name. Make certain that this ELAN name is identical to one of the ELANs displayed in **show lane database** on the LECS. Carefully check for incorrect case—ELAN names are case sensitive.

The output in Example 9-15 shows the results of an LEC that made it past contacting the LECS but has run into problems contacting the LES.

Example 9-15 *LEC Can't Contact LES*

```
ATM#show lane client
LE Client ATM0.1  ELAN name: ELAN1  Admin: up  State: initialState
Client ID: unassigned          Next join attempt in 10 seconds
Join Attempt: 8
Last Fail Reason: Control Direct VC being released
HW Address: 0010.2962.e430   Type: ethernet              Max Frame Size: 1516
      VLANID: 1
ATM Address: 47.00918100000000102962E801.00102962E430.01

 VCD  rxFrames  txFrames  Type      ATM Address
   0        0         0   configure 47.00918100000000102962E801.00102962E433.00
   0        0         0   direct    47.00918100000000102962E801.00102962E431.01
   0        0         0   distribute 00.00000000000000000000000.000000000000.00
   0        0         0   send      00.00000000000000000000000.000000000000.00
   0        0         0   forward   00.00000000000000000000000.000000000000.00
```

The output in Example 9-15 shows most of the same symptoms as the output in Example 9-14; however, the first two overhead connections have NSAPs listed. For two reasons, this pair of overhead connections proves that the LEC successfully reached the LECS. First, the Configuration Direct (first overhead circuit) lists the correct NSAP for the LECS. Second, the LEC could not have attempted a call to the LES (second overhead circuit) without having received an NSAP from the LECS. In this case, the LEC called the LES (Control Direct, second VC), but the LES didn't call the LEC back (Control Distribute, third VC). This diagnosis is further supported by the Last Fail Reason indicating "Control Direct VC being released." In almost all cases, one of two problems is the cause:

- **The LEC received the incorrect NSAP address for the LES from the LECS**—The LEC again "jumped off in the weeds" and called the wrong device only to receive an "I don't know what you're talking about!" response. Use the **show lane database** command on the LECS to verify LES' NSAP addresses for the appropriate ELAN. If necessary, correct the LECS database.

- **The LEC was given the right NSAP address for the LES, but the LES is down**— The LEC called the correct device, but the device was not a functioning LES. Verify the problem with the **show lane server** command on the LES (make certain that the LES is operational). If necessary, adjust the LES configuration parameters.

It is very uncommon to have a problem with only the Multicast Send and Multicast Forward VCs on Cisco equipment. Such behavior suggests a problem with the BUS: either the LES provided the wrong NSAP for the BUS or the BUS was not active. Because Cisco requires that the LES and BUS be co-located, the BUS should always be reachable if the LES is reachable. However, if you are using a third-party device for the LES and BUS, it is possible to run into this problem.

If you are still not able to successfully join the ELAN, consult the more detailed information given in Chapter 16, "Troubleshooting." Chapter 16 explores additional troubleshooting techniques.

Advanced LANE Issues and Features

This section explores several advanced issues that might be relevant in large LANE networks, including the following:

- Where to run LANE services
- Using hard-coded addresses
- SSRP
- Dual-PHY
- Using the well-known NSAP for LECS discovery
- PVCs and traffic shaping

Where to Run LANE Services

One of the first questions facing most implementers of LANE is "Where should I locate my three server components (LECS, LES, and BUS)?"

Because the LECS function is a very low-CPU function, you have a fair amount of latitude in terms of where you place the LECS. The main criterion is to pick a device with high availability. Some network designers argue that the best location is an ATM switch because it provides a centrally-located database. However, other designers argue that during a partial network outage, the ATM switch has its hands full just trying to build new SVCs. To further burden it with handling LECS duties hampers network resiliency. I generally try to locate the LECS in a Catalyst LANE module. However, a platform such as a 7500 router can also be a good choice.

The LES function requires more CPU effort than the LECS function, but it is generally not a burdensome amount. On the other hand, the BUS *does* require a tremendous amount of effort—it must be able to handle all broadcasts and all multicasts on the network while also supporting unicast traffic until the Flush process can occur. Because Cisco requires the LES to be co-located with the BUS, the BUS becomes the component that must be carefully positioned. In practice, the Catalyst 5000 currently provides the best BUS performance of the Cisco product line (as well as having top performance within the industry). Table 9-5 shows the BUS performance for various Cisco ATM devices expressed in kilopackets (thousands of packets) per second. When released, the Catalyst 6000 OC-12 ATM module is expected to have performance comparable to that of the Catalyst 5000 OC-12 module.

Table 9-5   *BUS Performance by Hardware Platform (in Kilopackets per Second)*

Platform	KPPS
Catalyst 5000 OC-12 LANE Module	500+
Catalyst 5000 OC-3 LANE Module	125
ATM PA (in 7500 and 7200)	70
Catalyst 3000	50
4700 NMP-1A	41
LS1010	30
7000 AIP	27

NOTE   Although Catalyst LANE modules provide the highest throughput in Cisco's products line, routers with very powerful CPUs (such as the 7500 RSP4) can provide faster recovery during network failover (the additional CPU capacity allows them to build VCs more quickly). In general, this is less important than the throughput numbers presented in Table 9-5.

Using Hard-Coded Addresses

Although the automatic NSAP scheme based on MAC addresses and subinterface numbers does allow for very easy configuration of LANE across Cisco devices, it can lead to maintenance problems. Because the MAC addresses used for the NSAP scheme are tied to the chassis or Supervisor module, swapping cards can create a need for minor reconfigurations. Chassis that support redundant Supervisors such as the 55XX family derive their MAC address from chips located on the backplane. Each slot is assigned a block of addresses, causing problems if either the chassis is changed or the LANE module is moved to a different slot. Chassis that only support a single Supervisor engine (such as the Catalyst 5000) pull their MAC addresses from the Supervisor module itself. Again, each slot is assigned a block of addresses. However, in this case, problems do not result from a change in the chassis (after all, the backplane in these platforms is passive) but from a change in Supervisor modules or if the LANE module is moved to another slot.

Note that reconfiguration is only required if the device acting as the LECS or the LES is changed. If the LECS changes, you need to modify the NSAP address configured on every ATM switch (but, assuming ILMI or well-known LECS NSAPs are in use, this does *not* require a change on the LECs). If the LES changes, you need to modify the LES' NSAP listed in the LECS database.

SSRP

The LANE 1.0 spec released in January 1995 did not provide for a server-to-server protocol (known as the LNNI [LANE Network-Network Interface] protocol). Because this limitation prohibited multiple servers from communicating and synchronizing information with each other, the ATM Forum had a simple solution: allow only a single instance of each type of server. The entire network was then dependent on a single LECS, and each ELAN was dependent on a single LES and BUS. Because this obviously creates multiple single points of failure, most ATM vendors have created their own redundancy protocols. Cisco's protocol is known as the Simple Server Redundancy Protocol (SSRP).

SSRP allows for an unlimited number of standby LECS and LES/BUS servers, although one standby of each type is most common. It allows the standby servers to take over if the primary fails, but it does not allow multiple active servers. One of the primary benefits of SSRP is that it is interoperable with most third-party LECs.

An additional benefit of SSRP is that it is easy and intuitive to configure. To provide for multiple LECSs, you simply need to configure multiple **atm lecs-address-default** commands on every ATM switch. To provide for multiple LES/BUSs for every ELAN, just add multiple **name *ELAN_NAME* server-atm-address *NSAP*** commands to the LECS database. For example, the commands in Example 9-16 configure two LECSs on a LS1010 ATM switch.

Example 9-16   *Configuring Two LECSs on a LS1010 ATM Switch*

```
Switch(Config)# atm lecs-address-default 47.0091.8100.0000.0010.2962.
 e801.0010.2962.e433.00
Switch(Config)# atm lecs-address-default 47.0091.8100.0000.0010.29BC.
 5604.0010.2972.7713.00
```

If the first LECS is available, the LS1010 always provides this address to LECs via ILMI. However, if the first LECS becomes unavailable, the ATM switch just returns the second LECS' NSAP to the LEC. Other than an address change, the LEC doesn't even know the first LECS failed.

CAUTION   You must be certain to enter redundant LECS addresses in the same order on all ATM switches.

The commands in Example 9-17 configure redundant LES/BUS servers for ELAN1 and ELAN2.

Example 9-17 *Configuring Redundant LES/BUS Servers for Multiple ELANs*

```
ATM(Config)# lane database My_LECS_Db
ATM(lane-config-database)# name ELAN1 server-atm-address
 47.00918100000000102962E801.00102962E431.01
ATM(lane-config-database)# name ELAN1 server-atm-address
 47.009181000000001029BC5604.001029727711.01
ATM(lane-config-database)# name ELAN2 server-atm-address
 47.00918100000000102962E801.00101F266431.02
ATM(lane-config-database)# name ELAN2 server-atm-address
 47.009181000000001029BC5604.00101F727711.02
```

If the first LES listed is available, the LECS returns this address to the LEC in the LE_CONFIGURE_REPLY. If the first LES fails, the LECS returns the second LES' NSAP when the LEC tries to rejoin. Again, the LEC isn't aware of the change (other than it was given a different address).

CAUTION   Make certain that all of the LECS database are identical.

The LECS redundancy mechanism is implemented by control connections between the LECSs. The LECS uses ILMI to acquire the complete list of LECSs servers from the ATM switch (just as an LEC does). Each LECS then builds an SVC to every LECS listed below itself on the list. The one LECS with no inbound connections is the primary LECS. However, if the primary fails, its connection to the second LECS closes, causing the second LECS to no longer have any inbound connections. For example, imagine three LECS devices A, B, and C. A is listed first on the LS1010 and C is listed last. After all three switches acquire the complete list of LECSs via ILMI, the A device opens a connection to B and C, and B opens a connection to C. Because B has one inbound connection and C has two inbound connections, both of these devices are backup LECSs. Because it has no inbound connections, A becomes the primary LECS. However, if A fails, the connection to B fails causing B to become the primary. If B fails, its connection to C drops and C becomes the primary.

The LES/BUS redundancy mechanism also utilizes ILMI. Upon startup, all LES/BUSs use ILMI to locate the primary LECS. Every LES/BUS then builds a connection to this single LECS. The Configuration Server then evaluates all of the inbound connections to determine which connection is from the LES/BUS listed first in the LECS database. That LES/BUS' NSAP is then provided in LE_CONFIGURE_REPLY messages to LANE Clients.

Dual-PHY

Cisco offers Dual-PHY on all of the high-end Catalyst LANE Modules (such as the Catalyst 5000 and 6000). Although these cards still have only a single set of ATM and AAL logic, it provides dual physical layer paths for redundant connections. This allows the LANE card to connect to two different ATM switches (in case one link or switch fails), but only one link can be active at a time. You can configure which link is preferred with the **atm preferred phy** command.

Although this feature is of great value in large networks, it does introduce a subtle configuration change. Notice the configuration in Figure 9-27.

Figure 9-27 *Dual-PHY Connection to Two ATM Switches*

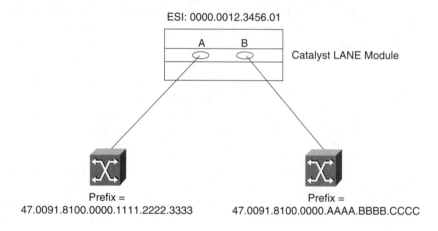

If A is the preferred port, the resulting NSAP is the following:

47.0091.8100.0000.1111.2222.3333.0000.0C12.3456.01

However, if the left-hand switch fails, the NSAP changes when the B port becomes active:

47.0091.8100.0000.AAAA.BBBB.CCCC.0000.0C12.3456.01

Although this change does not affect LANE Clients, it has a significant influence on LECS and LES/BUS configurations that use SSRP. In practice, this means that the LS1010 must list four LECS addresses to provide a single redundant LECS device. In addition, the LECS database must list four LES addresses to provide a single redundant LES/BUS.

TIP　　Using SSRP with Dual-PHY connections generally requires careful planning of the order of SSRP entries.

For example, Figure 9-28 illustrates two LES/BUSs linked to two LS1010s through dual-PHY connections.

Figure 9-28   *Redundant LES/BUSs Connected via Dual-PHY to Two ATM Switches*

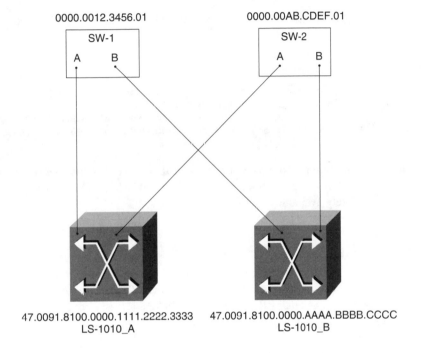

The LECS database should contain four **name** *ELAN_NAME* **server-atm-address** *NSAP* commands for each ELAN. Look at Example 9-18.

Example 9-18   *Inefficient LECS Configuration for SSRP*

```
name ELAN1 server-atm-address 47.0091.8100.0000.1111.2222.3333.0000.0C12.3456.01
name ELAN1 server-atm-address 47.0091.8100.0000.AAAA.BBBB.CCCC.0000.0C12.3456.01
name ELAN1 server-atm-address 47.0091.8100.0000.1111.2222.3333.0000.0CAB.CDEF.01
name ELAN1 server-atm-address 47.0091.8100.0000.AAAA.BBBB.CCCC.0000.0CAB.CDEF.01
```

Although this provides LES/BUS redundancy, it introduces another complication. Assume that both Catalysts are using PHY-A as the preferred link and LS-1010-A fails. The LECs instantly try to rejoin ELAN1 and be directed by the LECS to the second LES listed in the database, Port B on the SW-1. However, because this port has not completed its ILMI address registration process (when LS-1010-A failed, PHY-A went down with it and it typically takes about 10–15 seconds to bring up ILMI on another port), the call fails and the LECs try the third LES listed, Port A on SW-2. The call succeeds and all the LECs rejoin the ELAN. However, a few seconds later Port B on SW-1 completes the ILMI addresses registration process and becomes active. Now that the second LES in the database is active, Port A on SW-2 reverts to backup mode, causing all of the LECs to again be thrown out of the ELAN. When the LECs try again to rejoin, the LECS sends them to Port B on SW-1.

This unnecessary backtracking can be avoided by carefully coding the order of the LECS database as in Example 9-19.

Example 9-19 *Coding the LECS Database Order*

```
name ELAN1 server-atm-address 47.0091.8100.0000.1111.2222.3333.0000.0C12.3456.01
name ELAN1 server-atm-address 47.0091.8100.0000.1111.2222.3333.0000.0CAB.CDEF.01
name ELAN1 server-atm-address 47.0091.8100.0000.AAAA.BBBB.CCCC.0000.0C12.3456.01
name ELAN1 server-atm-address 47.0091.8100.0000.AAAA.BBBB.CCCC.0000.0CAB.CDEF.01
```

The configuration in Example 9-19 offers faster failover because the second device listed completes address registration before Port A on SW-1 fails. This allows the second LES to be immediately available without backtracking.

Using the Well-Known NSAP for LECS Discovery

Earlier in the chapter, the text mentioned that Cisco recommends using ILMI to pass the NSAP address of the LECS to the LECs. However, Cisco also supports using hard-coded NSAP addresses and using the well-known NSAP address. Because the well-known NSAP address is used in many networks (for example, it is the default method used on Fore Systems equipment), this section briefly looks at the configuration syntax and issues involved in using the well-known NSAP.

To configure use of the well-known NSAP, merely modify the command used to enable the LECS—use the **lane config fixed-config-atm-address** command as opposed to the **lane config auto-config-atm-address** command. The causes the LECS to register the 47.0079000000000000000000000.00A03E000001.00 so that it can be made reachable via PNNI.

Example 9-20 illustrates a complete configuration that uses the well-known LECS NSAP and places all four LANE components for two ELANs on a single device.

Example 9-20 *Using the Well-Known LECS NSAP*

```
lane database WKN
  name ELAN1 server-atm-address 47.00918100000000102962E801.00102962E431.01
  name ELAN2 server-atm-address 47.00918100000000102962E801.00102962E431.02
!
interface ATM0
 atm preferred phy A
 atm pvc 1 0 5 qsaal
 atm pvc 2 0 16 ilmi
 lane config fixed-config-atm-address
 lane config database WKN
!
interface ATM0.1 multipoint
 lane server-bus ethernet ELAN1
 lane client ethernet 1 ELAN1
!
interface ATM0.2 multipoint
 lane server-bus ethernet ELAN2
 lane client ethernet 2 ELAN2
```

One of the advantages of using the well-known NSAP is that it does not require any configuration at all on the LS1010 ATM switch. Because the LECs automatically try the well-known NSAP if the hard-coded NSAP and ILMI options fail, the LEC reaches the LECS with minimal configuration.

Although the well-known NSAP is potentially easier to configure in small networks, Cisco recommends the ILMI approach because it provides better support for SSRP server redundancy. There is a problem if multiple LECS servers try to use the well-known NSAP for LECS discovery: both servers try to register the same 47.0079… address! With ILMI and SSRP, every device registers a unique NSAP address, avoiding any PNNI routing confusion.

If you run into a situation where you need to run SSRP and also support the well-known NSAP (this can be the case if you are using third-party LECs that do not support the ILMI LECS discovery method), there is a solution. First, configure all of the LECS devices with the **lane config fixed-config-atm-address** command. Next, be sure to also configure every LECS for ILMI support with the **lane config auto-config-atm-address** command. This allows SSRP to function properly and elects only a single primary LECS. Because the backup LECS servers do not register the well-known NSAP, only the primary originates the 47.0079… route into PNNI. You now have the resiliency of SSRP combined with the simplicity and widespread support of the well-known NSAP!

PVCs and Traffic Shaping

The Catalyst LANE module allows connections to one or more Catalysts using PVCs. When implementing this, the LECS, LES, and BUS server functions are not utilized. You simply build a PVC and then bind a VLAN to that circuit as in Example 9-21.

Example 9-21   *Catalyst ATM PVC Configuration*

```
int atm 0
atm pvc 3 0 50 aal5snap
atm bind pvc vlan 3 1
```

This creates a PVC using VPI 0 and VCI 50 and then binds it to VLAN 1. PVCs can be useful in small networks, especially when connecting two Catalyst LANE blades back-to-back without using an ATM switch. Another advanced feature offered by the Catalyst is PVC-based traffic shaping. This allows you to set a peak bandwidth level on a particular circuit. It can be very useful for controlling bandwidth across expensive wide-area links. This feature requires you to load a special image into flash on the LANE module and does not work with SVCs. For example, Example 9-22 adds traffic shaping to the configuration in Example 9-21.

Example 9-22   *Traffic Shaping and ATM PVCs*

```
int atm 0
atm pvc 3 0 50 aal5snap 11000
atm bind pvc vlan 3 1
```

The final parameter on the **atm pvc** command limits the traffic to a peak rate of 11 Mbps.

Exercises

This section includes a variety of questions and hands-on lab exercises. By completing these you can test your mastery of the material included in this chapter as well as help prepare yourself for the CCIE written and lab tests.

Review Questions

1 What are the three layers of the ATM stack? What does each do?

2 What is the difference between ATM and SONET?

3 What is the difference between a Catalyst with two LANE modules and a two-port ATM switch?

4 What is the difference between a VPI, a VCI, and an NSAP? When is each used?

5 Assume you attached an ATM network analyzer to an ATM cloud consisting of one LS1010 ATM switch and two Catalysts with LANE modules. What types of cells could you capture to observe VPI and VCI values? What type of cells could you capture to observe NSAP addresses?

6 What are the three sections of an NSAP address? What does each part represent?

7 How do Catalysts automatically generate ESI and selector byte values for use with LANE?

8 What is the five-step initialization process used by LANE Clients to join an ELAN?

9 What are the names of the six types of circuits used by LANE? What type of traffic does each carry?

10 What is the difference between an IP ARP and an LE_ARP?

11 In a network that needs to trunk two VLANs between two Catalysts, how many LECs are required? How many LECSs? How many LESs? How many BUSs?

12 If the network in Question 12 grows to ten Catalysts and ten VLANs, how many LECs, LECSs, LESs and BUSs are required? Assume that every Catalyst has ports assigned to every VLAN.

13 Trace the data path in Figure 9-26 from an Ethernet-attached node in VLAN 1 on Cat-A to an Ethernet-attached node in VLAN 2 on Cat-B. Why is this inefficient?

Hands-On Lab

Build a network that resembles Figure 9-29.

Figure 9-29 *Hands-On Lab Diagram*

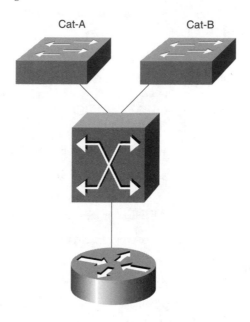

Table 9-6 shows the LANE components that should be configured on each device.

Table 9-6 *LANE Components to Be Configured*

Device	VLAN1/ELAN1	VLAN2/ELAN2	VLAN3/ELAN3
LEC-A	LEC, LES/BUS	LEC	LEC
LEC-B	LEC	LEC, LES/BUS	LEC
Router	LEC	LEC	LEC, LES/BUS
LS1010	LEC	LEC	LEC

The LS1010 is the LECS.

Configure IP addresses on the SC0 interfaces of both Catalysts, the router subinterfaces, and the LS1010 subinterfaces (use interface atm 2/0/0 or 13/0/0 for the LS1010). Configure HSRP between the ATM router and an RSM located in LEC-A. Table 9-7 provides IP addresses that can be used.

Table 9-7   *IP Addresses for Hands-On Lab*

Device	VLAN1/ELAN1	VLAN2/ELAN2	VLAN3/ELAN3
LEC-A SC0	10.1.1.1		
LEC-A RSM	10.1.1.252	10.1.2.252	10.1.3.252
LEC-B SC0	10.1.1.2		
Router	10.1.1.253	10.1.2.253	10.1.3.253
LS1010	10.1.1.110	10.1.2.110	10.1.3.110
HSRP Address	10.1.1.254	10.1.2.254	10.1.3.254

When you are done building the network, perform the following tasks:

- Test connectivity to all devices.

- Turn on **debug lane client all** and ping another device on the network (you might need to clear the Data Direct if it already exists). Log the results.

- With **debug lane client all** still running, issue **shut** and **no shut** commands on the atm major interface. Log the results.

- Examine the output of the **show lane client**, **show lane config**, **show lane server**, **show lane bus**, and **show lane database** commands.

- Add SSRP to allow server redundancy.

- If you have multiple ATM switches, add dual-PHY support (don't forget to update your SSRP configurations).

This chapter covers the following key topics:

Why Two ATM Modes?—Describes the relationship between LANE and MPOA, and discusses the choices of when to use one as opposed to the other.

MPOA Components and Model—Provides an overview of MPOA including the various components defined and utilized by MPOA, their relationship with each other, and how they interact to support MPOA. Various traffic flows for management and user data are also described.

MPOA Configuration—Details the commands to enable MPOA on an MPOA-capable Catalyst LANE module and on a Cisco MPOA-capable router. This details the configuration for both the Multiprotocol Server (MPS) and the Multiprotocol Client (MPC).

Sample MPOA Configuration—This section puts it all together, and shows a sample network and the supporting MPOA configurations.

Troubleshooting an MPOA Network—Offers guidelines for getting MPOA functional. It provides steps for ensuring that the MPOA components are operational, and provides insight for using MPOA debug.

CHAPTER 10

Trunking with Multiprotocol Over ATM

Catalysts rarely stand alone. More often than not, they interconnect with other Catalysts. Chapter 8, "Trunking Technologies and Applications," discussed various methods for interconnecting Catalysts. Methods range from multiple links with each dedicated to a single VLAN, to a variety of trunk technologies. Fast Ethernet, Gigabit Ethernet, FDDI, and ATM technologies are all suitable for trunking Catalysts. Within ATM, you can use LAN Emulation (LANE) or Multiprotocol over ATM (MPOA) data transfer modes to trunk Catalysts. Chapter 9, "Trunking with LAN Emulation," described that option. This chapter focuses on (MPOA) in a Catalyst environment, specifically, when to use MPOA, its components, and configuring and troubleshooting MPOA.

Why Two ATM Modes?

Two modes exist for geographic scalability and efficiency. LANE emulates a local-area network and creates many virtual circuits to support each LAN Emulation Client (LEC) in each Emulated LAN (ELAN). Each LEC maintains four virtual circuits to retain ELAN membership. Two are point-to-point connections (one to the LAN Emulation Server [LES] and one to the broadcast and unknown server [BUS]), and two are point-to-multipoint connections (one from the LES and one from the BUS). The LEC connects as a leaf for the point-to-multipoint connection, with the LES and BUS as roots. An ELAN with 100 LECs then has 200 point-to-point connections, and 200 leaf node connections just for the control virtual circuits to maintain VLAN membership.

This scenario does not even count the data direct connections required for data transfers between LECs. Clearly, many more connections can be present in the ELAN to support peer-to-peer communications.

If LECs for an ELAN are geographically dispersed in a campus or enterprise network, the connections can consume a lot of virtual circuits in many ATM switches. And, if the user leases ATM services, they can be billed for each circuit established in the system. From a technical point of view, there are no limitations on the LEC distribution. But practically, LECs within an ELAN should reside in geographically limited areas to reduce the number of virtual circuit resources consumed in the ATM switches throughout the network.

Further, consider what happens when a LEC in one ELAN needs to communicate with a LEC in another ELAN. The traffic must pass through a router because each ELAN defines a unique broadcast domain. ELANs interconnect through routers, just like VLANs.

Frames traveling from a source LEC in one ELAN to a destination LEC in a second ELAN must traverse routers, as discussed in Chapter 9. If a frame passes through multiple routers to get from the source LEC to the destination LEC, multiple data direct circuits must be established so routers can pass the frame from one ELAN to another. A source LEC must establish a data direct circuit to its default gateway, another data direct must be established from that router to the next router, and so on to the final router. The last router must establish a data direct to the destination LEC. Consider the network in Figure 10-1. When an Ethernet frame from VLAN 1 (destined for VLAN 2) hits the switch, the switch LEC segments the frame into cells and passes it to the default router LEC (Router 1). The default router LEC reassembles the cells into a frame, and routes it to the LEC on the next ELAN. This LEC segments the data and forwards the frame (cells) to the next hop router LEC (Router 2) over ATM. When the cells hit Router 2's ATM interface, Router 2 reassembles the cells, routes the frame, and then segments the frame before it can pass the frame to Router 3. Router 3 reassembles the cells, routes the frame, segments the frame into cells, and forwards them to the destination Catalyst. This Catalyst reassembles the cells into a frame and passes the frame onto the destination Ethernet segment.

Each hop through a router introduces additional latency and consumes routing resources within each router. Some of the latency stems from the segmentation/reassembly process. Another latency factor includes the route processing time to determine the next hop. This element can be less significant in routers that do hardware routing (as opposed to legacy software-based routers).

Figure 10-1 *A Multi-ELAN Network Data Flow*

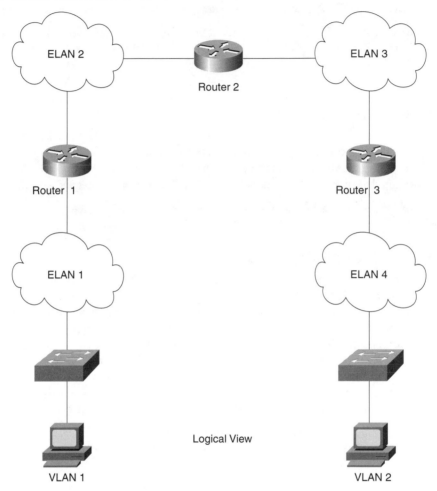

The hop-by-hop approach was necessary when networks interconnected with shared media systems such as Ethernet. Physical connections force frames to pass through a router whenever a device in one network wants to connect to a device in another network. LANE maintains this model. It honors the rule that devices in different networks must interconnect through a router. MPOA, however, creates a virtual circuit directly between two devices residing in different ELANs.

MPOA, in fact, bypasses intermediate routers but gives the appearance that traffic from a device in one ELAN passes through routers to reach the destination device in another ELAN.

To get from one VLAN to another over ATM can require communication across several ELANs. The following sections compare how traffic flows within an ELAN as opposed to when it needs to cross more than one ELAN.

Intra-Subnet Communications

When Catalysts need to communicate with each other within the same ELAN, the Catalysts use LANE. Intra-subnet (or intra-ELAN) communications occur whenever devices in the same broadcast domain trunk to each other. The Catalyst LANE module was exclusively designed to support LANE operations with high performance to handle flows at LAN rates.

Details for intra-subnet communications are described in Chapter 9.

Inter-Subnet Communications

As discussed earlier, occasions arise where hosts in different VLANs need to communicate with each other over ATM. VLANs have similarities to ELANs on the ATM network. VLANs describe broadcast domains in a LAN environment, whereas ELANs describe broadcast domains in an ATM environment. Whenever hosts in one VLAN need to communicate with hosts in another VLAN, the traffic must be routed between them. If the inter-VLAN routing occurs on Ethernet, Multilayer Switching (MLS) is an appropriate choice to bypass routers. If the routing occurs in the ATM network, MPOA is a candidate to bypass routers. MLS and MPOA both have the same objective: to bypass routers. One does it in the LAN world (VLANs), the other does it in the ATM world (ELANs).

This chapter details the inter-VLAN/inter-ELAN communications performed with MPOA. Without MPOA, the traffic follows the hop-by-hop path described earlier in the chapter.

MPOA Components and Model

Various components comprise an MPOA system. The following sections describe each of the significant components. Figure 10-2 illustrates the components and their positional relationship. Note that there are ingress and egress devices, inbound and outbound flows, and configuration, control, and data flows.

Figure 10-2 *MPOA Model*

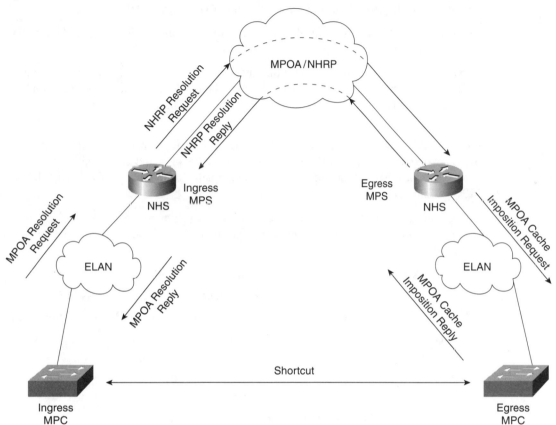

Note also the presence of LANE components. MPOA depends upon LANE for intra-ELAN communications. Communication between a Multiprotocol Client (MPC) and a Multiprotocol Server (MPS) occurs over an ELAN. Communication between adjacent Next Hop Servers (NHSs), another MPOA component discussed later in the section on Next Hop Resolution Protocol (NHRP), also occurs over ELANs. Finally, MPSs also communicate over ELANs. Additionally, if frames are sent between MPCs before a shortcut is established, the frames transit ELANs. The objective of MPOA is to ultimately circumvent this situation by transmitting frames over a shortcut between MPCs. However, the shortcut is not immediately established. It is the responsibility of the ingress MPC to generate a shortcut request with the egress MPC as the target. The ingress MPC request asks for the egress MPC's ATM address from the ingress MPS. The ingress MPS receives the shortcut request from the ingress MPC and resolves the request into a Next Hop Resolution Protocol (NHRP) request. NHSs forward the request to the final NHS, which resides in the egress

MPS. The egress MPS resolves the request, informs the egress MPC to expect traffic from the ingress MPC, and returns the resolution reply to the ingress MPC.

In this process, three kinds of information flows exist: configuration, inbound/outbound, and control.

MPOA components acquire configuration information from the LECS. LANE version 2 defines this configuration flow. Both the MPC and the MPS can obtain configuration parameters from the LECS. Alternatively, they can get configurations from internal statements.

Inbound and outbound flows occur between the MPCs and the MPSs. The inbound flow occurs between the ingress MPC and MPS, whereas the outbound flow occurs between the egress MPC and MPS. Inbound and outbound are defined from the perspective of the MPOA cloud.

MPOA defines a set of control flows used to establish and maintain shortcut information. Control flows occur over ELANs between adjacent devices. Control flows as defined by MPOA include:

- **MPOA Resolution Request**—Sent from the ingress MPC to the ingress MPS.
- **MPOA Resolution Reply**—Sent from the ingress MPS to the ingress MPC.
- **MPOA Cache Imposition Request**—Sent from the egress MPS to the egress MPC.
- **MPOA Cache Imposition Reply**—Sent from the egress MPC to the egress MPS.
- **MPOA Egress Cache Purge Request**—Sent from the egress MPC to the egress MPS.
- **MPOA Egress Cache Purge Reply**—Sent from the egress MPS to the egress MPC.
- **MPOA Keep-Alive**—Sent from an MPS to an MPC.
- **MPOA Trigger**—Sent from an MPS to an MPC. If an MPS detects a flow from an MPC, the MPS issues a request to the MPC to issue an MPOA resolution request.
- **NHRP Purge Request**—Sent from the egress MPC to the ingress MPC.
- **NHRP Purge Reply**—Sent from the ingress MPC to the egress MPC.

Another approach to describe the control flows categorizes the flows by the components that exercise the flow. Flows between an MPC and an MPS manage the MPC cache. These include the MPOA resolution request/reply and the MPOA cache imposition request/reply. The MPC/MPS control flows communicate over the common ELAN.

Control flows between MPCs include the MPOA egress cache purge request and reply. This control flow occurs over the shortcut, which normally carries only user data. It is used to eliminate cache errors in the ingress MPC. When the egress MPC detects errors, it sends the purge request to the ingress MPC, forcing the ingress MPC to reestablish its cache information.

Control flows also exist between MPSs. However, these are defined by the internetwork layer routing protocols and NHRP. MPOA does not define any new control flows between MPSs.

The control flow list does not define the actual sequence of the messages. Figure 10-3 shows two MPCs and MPSs interconnected in an ATM network.

Figure 10-3 *Control Flow Sequence in an MPOA System*

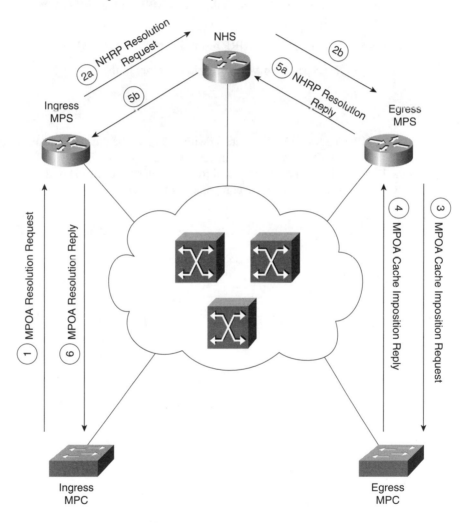

The message sequence occurs as follows:

1 The ingress MPC sends an MPOA resolution request to the ingress MPS.

2 The ingress MPS translates the request into an NHRP request that gets forwarded toward the egress MPS.

3 The egress MPS issues an MPOA cache imposition request to the egress MPC.

4 The egress MPC responds back to the egress MPS with an MPOA cache imposition reply.

5 The egress MPS returns an NHRP resolution to the ingress MPS.

6 The ingress MPS sends an MPOA resolution reply to the ingress MPC.

MPS

The Multiprotocol Server (MPS) interacts with NHRP on behalf of the Multiprotocol Client (MPC). An MPS always resides in a router and includes a full NHS. The MPS works with the local NHS and consults the local routing tables to resolve shortcut requests from an MPC. Figure 10-4 illustrates the components of an MPS.

Figure 10-4 *MPS Anatomy*

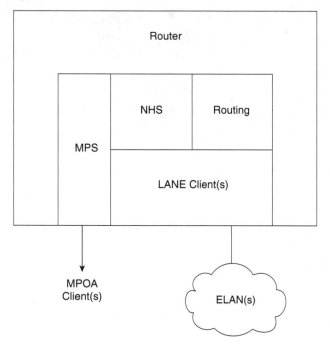

The MPS has a set of interfaces attached to the ATM cloud and at least one interface for internal services. The external connections pointing to the ATM cloud consist of LANE client(s) and an MPS interface. The LANE clients support the MPOA device discovery protocol described later, and the actual flow of data before the shortcuts are established. The MPS also uses the LEC to forward resolution requests to the next NHS in the system. The service interface interacts with internal processes such as the router processes and the NHS to facilitate MPOA resolution requests and replies.

When an MPC detects an inter-ELAN flow, the ingress MPC issues a shortcut request to the MPS asking if there is a better way to the target MPC. The ingress MPS translates the MPC's request into an NHRP request, which is forwarded to the egress MPS. The egress MPS resolves the request and performs a couple of other activities. These activities include cache imposition to the egress MPC and resolution reply back toward the ingress MPC.

MPC

In most cases, an MPC detects an inter-ELAN flow and subsequently initiates an MPOA resolution request. The MPC detects inter-ELAN flows by watching the internetwork layer destination address. When the destination and source network addresses differ, the MPC identifies a candidate flow. The MPC continues to transmit using hop-by-hop Layer 3 routing. But, it counts the number of frames transmitted to the target. If the frame count exceeds a threshold configured by the network administrator (or default values), the MPC triggers an MPOA resolution request to an appropriate MPS. The threshold is defined by two parameters: the number of frames sent and the time interval.

When the ingress MPC receives a resolution reply from the ingress MPS, the MPC can then establish a shortcut to the target MPC. Additional frames between the ingress and egress MPCs flow through the shortcut bypassing the routers in the default path.

MPOA identifies two types of MPC devices: a host device and an edge device. They differ in how they originate data in the MPOA system. The sections that follow discuss these two types of MPOA devices in greater detail.

MPOA Host Devices

Host devices originate traffic to traverse the MPOA network. A typical example of an MPC host device includes a workstation with an ATM network interface card (NIC), and MPOA drivers. An MPOA Host, then, includes at least one MPC, at least one LEC, and an internetworking layer protocol stack. An MPOA host generates traffic on its own behalf. Figure 10-5 shows an MPOA Host logical representation.

Figure 10-5 *MPOA Host Device Anatomy*

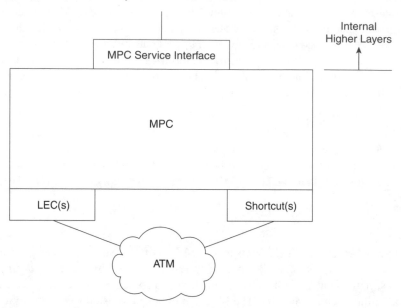

Like the MPS, the MPC host device has internal and external interfaces. The external interfaces include the LEC and the MPC. The MPC communicates to the LES through the LEC to detect MPOA neighbors. Also, traffic transmissions that are initiated before a shortcut is established will pass through the LEC.

The MPC interface, on the other hand, is used for shortcuts. When the MPC detects a flow, it issues a resolution request through its MPC interface. The MPC receives the resolution reply through the MPC interface too. After the MPC establishes a shortcut, the MPC interface becomes the origination point of the data circuit to the other MPC.

When you enable MPOA, all outbound traffic is forced through the MPC, whether or not a shortcut exists. The MPC internal service interface accepts the host's outbound traffic and passes it through the MPC. This enables the MPC to watch for flows so that shortcuts can be established as needed.

MPOA Edge Devices

Edge devices inject traffic into an MPOA system on behalf of non ATM-capable devices. As such, edge devices integrate at least one MPC, at least one LEC, and a bridge port. Bridges, LAN switches, and routers represent typical edge devices. Figure 10-6 illustrates an MPOA edge device logical representation.

Figure 10-6 *MPOA Edge Device Anatomy*

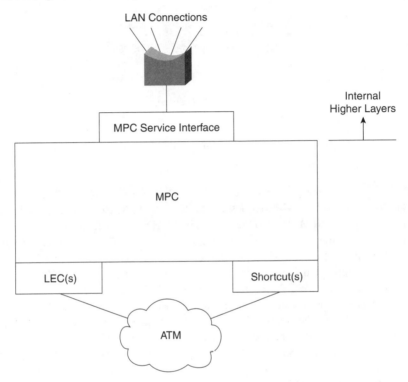

The MPC edge device is nearly identical to the MPC host device, except that its service interface connects to bridging processes. This happens because the edge device is facilitating connectivity of non-ATM capable devices onto the ATM network. These non-ATM capable devices are connected into the MPOA environment through bridged interfaces in the MPC edge device.

MPOA Operational Summary

Refer to Figure 10-7 for the following summary of data flows in MPOA.

Figure 10-7 *MPOA Data Flow Summary*

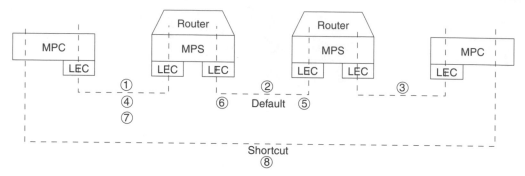

(1)Before the ingress MPC requests a shortcut, the MPC forwards frames through the LEC interface to the ATM cloud to the MPS. The MPS receives the flow on its LEC interface, performs routing and (2) forwards the frame to the next MPS. This continues until the frame reaches the egress MPS where the frame is forwarded (3) over the ELAN to the egress MPC. Until the ingress MPC establishes a shortcut, all frames pass through LECs at each device. When the ingress MPC detects a flow that exceeds the configured threshold levels (# of frames/ time), the MPC issues an MPOA resolution request (4) through the MPC control interface to the ingress MPS. The ingress MPS forwards the request (5) to the next NHS which may or may not reside in an MPS. The resolution request continues to be forwarded until it reaches the device that serves as the egress MPS. Note that the resolution request propagates through LANE clients. Resolution replies propagate back to the ingress MPS (6) through LANE clients. The ingress MPS forwards the reply (7) to the ingress MPC through the MPOA control circuit. Then the ingress MPC establishes a shortcut (8) to the egress MPC. The shortcut is established to the MPC interface, not the LEC interface. Subsequent data frames stop transiting the LEC interfaces and pass through the MPC interface directly to the egress LEC.

In summary, intra-ELAN sessions flow through LANE clients, whereas inter-ELAN flows pass through the MPC interfaces.

LANE V2

In July of 1997, the ATM Forum released LANE version 2, which introduces enhancements over version 1. MPOA depends upon some of the enhancements to support MPOA operations. For example, one of the enhancements was the addition of the elan-id. MPOA uses the elan-id to identify what broadcast domains (ELANs) MPOA devices belong to. This is expected behavior in MPOA. In a non-MPOA environment, LECs use the elan-id value to filter traffic from other ELANs. If a LEC in one ELAN somehow obtains the NSAP of a LEC in another ELAN, the LEC can issue a connection request. However, because they are in different ELANs, the receiving ELAN can (and should) reject the connection request. Why? Because they are in different ELANs, they also belong to different subnetworks. A direct connection between them, then, is illegal outside of the scope of MPOA. Another LANEv2 enhancement supports neighbor discovery. When a LEC registers with the LES, it reports the MPOA device type associated with it. For example, if the LEC is associated with an MPC, the LEC informs the LES that the LEC serves an MPC. LECs associated with MPSs also report to the LES. The MPOA devices can then interrogate the LES to discover any other MPOA devices on the ELAN.

NHRP

Frequently, networks are described as having logically independent IP subnets (LISs). In legacy LANs, devices on each segment normally belong to a different IP subnet and interconnect with devices in other subnets through routers. The physical construction of the networks force traffic through the routers. In an ATM environment, a hard physical delineation doesn't exist. Connections exist whenever one ATM device requests the ATM network to create a logical circuit between the two devices. In a LAN environment, devices in the same subnet usually are located within a close proximity of each other. But in the ATM network, the devices can be located on opposite sides of the globe and still belong to the same LIS. In Figure 10-8, several LISs exist in an ATM network. But the illustration provides no hint as to the geographical proximity of devices in the system.

Figure 10-8 *LISs in a Nonbroadcast Multi-Access (NBMA) Environment*

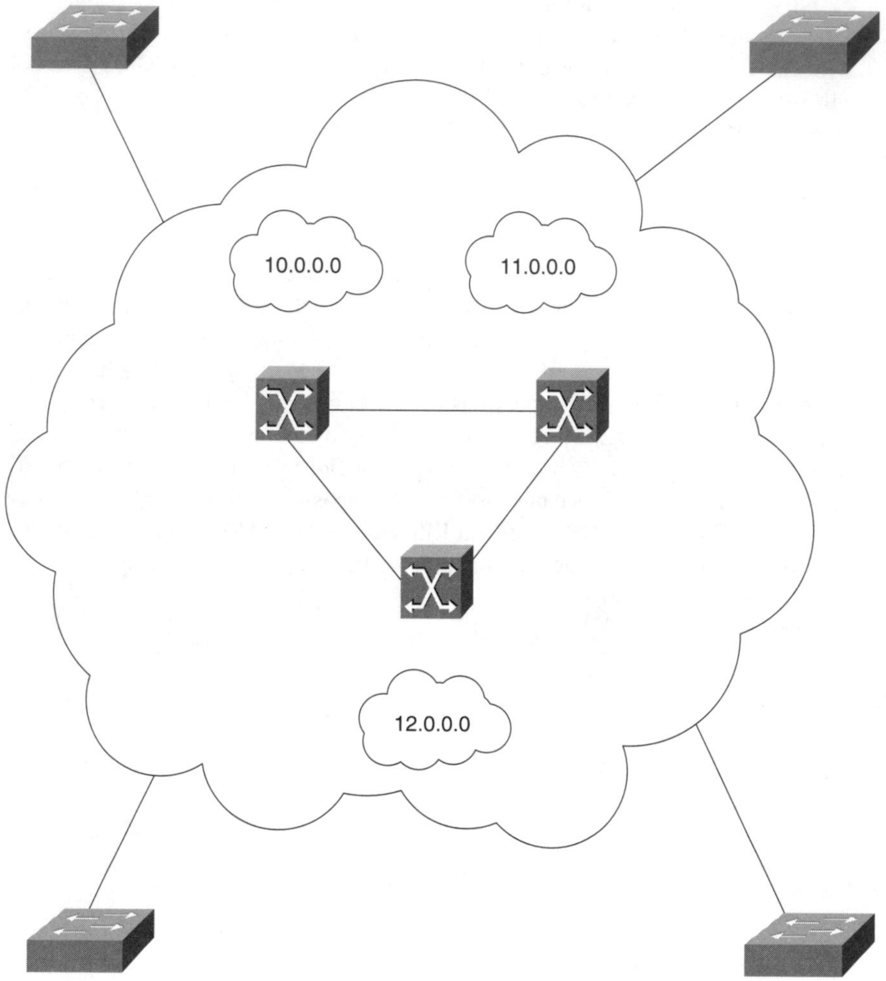

NHRP describes the attributes of each LIS in an NBMA network. Quoting RFC 2332 (NHRP):

- All members of an LIS have the same IP network/subnet number and address mask.
- All members of an LIS are directly connected to the same NBMA subnetwork.
- All hosts and routers outside of the LIS are accessed via a router.
- All members of an LIS access each other directly (without routers).

Whenever an IP station in a LIS desires to talk to another IP station in the same LIS, the source station issues an ARP request to the destination station. If the source desires to communicate with a destination in another LIS, the source must ARP for a router that is a member of at least two LISs. A router must belong to the LIS of the source device and the next hop LIS. In other words, traffic in a LIS flows hop by hop just as it does for legacy networks interconnected with Layer 3 routers. Routers must, therefore, interconnect multiple LISs to provide a Layer 3 path between networks.

NHRP identifies another method of modeling stations in an NBMA network. Logical Address Groups (LAGs) differ from LISs in that LISs forward traffic in a hop-by-hop manner. Traffic must always be forwarded to another device in the same LIS. LAGs, on the other hand, associate devices based on Quality of Service (QoS) or traffic characteristics. LAGs do not group stations according to their logical addresses. Therefore, in a LAG model, two devices in the same NBMA network can talk directly with each other, even if they belong to different LISs. MPOA shortcuts interconnect devices belonging to different LISs, creating a LAG.

NHRP works directly with routing protocols to resolve a shortcut between workstations in different LISs. The primary NHRP component to do this is the Next Hop Server (NHS) which interacts with the router to determine next hop information. Each MPS has an NHS collocated with it. The MPS translates a resolution request to an NHS request. The NHS interrogates the router for next hop information. If the destination is local, the NHS finishes its job and reports the egress information to the ingress MPS. If the destination is not local, the NHS forwards the request to the next NHS toward the destination. The NHS determines the next NHS based upon the local routing tables. It answers the question, "What is the next hop towards the destination?" The request is forwarded from NHS to NHS until it reaches the final NHS, whereupon the egress information is returned to the ingress MPS.

MPOA Configuration

Surprisingly, in spite of all of the background complexity of MPOA, configuring the MPS and MPC is quite simple. You must first have LANE configured, though. Without proper LANE configurations, MPOA never works.

NOTE   Before attempting to configure MPOA on your Catalyst LANE module, ensure that you have an MPOA-capable module. The legacy LANE modules do not support MPOA. The MPOA-capable modules include hardware enhancements to support the MPC functions.

Generally, the LANE module must be a model number WS-X5161, WS-X5162 for OC-12, or WS-X5167 and WS-X5168 for OC-3c support.

Although you can configure the MPOA components in any sequence, the following sequence helps to ensure that the initialization processes acquire all necessary values to enable the components.

Step 1   Configure LECS database with elan-id

Step 2   Enable LECS

Step 3   Configure MPS

Step 4   Configure MPC

Step 5   Enable LANE server and bus

Step 6   Enable LANE clients

A configuration sequence other than that listed does not prevent MPOA from functioning, but you might need to restart the LANE components so that MPOA can correctly operate. Specifically, you should ensure that the LEC can acquire the elan-id from the LECs before you enable the LEC. The elan-id is used by the MPOA components to identify broadcast domain membership. This is useful when establishing shortcuts.

Cisco implementations of LANE and MPOA use a default NSAP address scheme. Chapter 9 describes the NSAP format in detail. Remember, however, that the NSAP is comprised of three parts:

- The 13-byte prefix
- The 6-byte end-station identifier (esi)
- The 1-byte selector (sel)

The **show lane default** command enables you to see what the NSAP address for each LANE component will be if you enable that service within that device. Cisco's implementation of MPOA also uses a default addressing scheme that can be observed with the **show mpoa default** command. Example 10-1 shows the output from these two commands.

Example 10-1 *LANE and MPOA Component Addresses*

```
router#show lane default
interface ATM1/0:
LANE Client:          47.009181000000009092BF7401.0090AB165008.**
LANE Server:          47.009181000000009092BF7401.0090AB165009.**
LANE Bus:             47.009181000000009092BF7401.0090AB16500A.**
LANE Config Server: 47.009181000000009092BF7401.0090AB16500B.00
note: ** is the subinterface number byte in hex

router#show mpoa default
interface ATM1/0:
MPOA Server: 47.009181000000009092BF7401.0090AB16500C.**
MPOA Client: 47.009181000000009092BF7401.0090AB16500D.**
note: ** is the MPS/MPC instance number in hex
```

Note that the *esi* portion highlighted in *italics* of the MPS and MPC NSAP continue to increment beyond the esi portion of the LECS NSAP address. The selector byte, however, does not correlate to a subinterface as happens with the LANE components. Rather, the selector byte indicates which MPS or MPC sources the traffic. A host, edge device, or router can have more than one MPC or MPS enabled. The selector byte identifies the intended device.

Configuring the LECS Database with elan-id

In addition to the LECS configuration statements necessary to enable LANE, another database statement must be present to enable the MPOA servers and clients to identify their membership in a broadcast domain. Each broadcast domain (ELAN) in the ATM domain must be uniquely identified with a numerical ELAN identifier value. The *elan-id* value is a 4-octet value. Every LEC in an ELAN must have the same elan-id. Every ELAN serviced by the LECS must have a unique elan-id. Because the MPC and MPS must associate with a LEC, the MPC and MPS have an elan-id by association. They have the elan-id of the LEC.

The syntax to identify the ELAN is as follows:

```
name elan_name elan-id id
```

Example 10-2 shows how to configure the LECS database for MPOA.

Example 10-2 *LECS Database Configured for MPOA*

```
lane database usethis
  name elan1 server-atm-address 47.009181000000009092BF7401.0090AB165009.01
! The elan-id number identifies the broadcast domain
  name elan1 elan-id 101
name elan2 server-atm-address 47.009181000000009092BF7401.0090AB165009.02
! Each ELAN must have a unique elan-id
  name elan2 elan-id 102
```

Every ELAN with MPC components must have an elan-id assigned to it. In Example 10-2, two ELANs are defined, elan1 and elan2, each with a unique elan-id of 101 and 102, respectively. The actual value used does not matter, so long as the value is unique to the ATM domain.

Rather than letting the LECs obtain the elan-id value from the LECS, you can manually configure the elan-id value in each of the LECs in your network. But this can become administratively burdensome and is not, therefore, a widely used approach. By having the elan-id configured in the LECS database, you simplify your configuration requirements by placing the value in one location rather than many.

Whenever a LANE client connects to the LECS as part of the initialization process, the LEC acquires the elan-id. This value is then used by the MPS and the MPC during their initialization processes, and during the shortcut establishment.

Confirm that the LEC acquired the elan-id with the **show lane client** command. The bold highlight in Example 10-3 indicates that the Cat-A LEC belongs to the ELAN with an elan-id value of 101. This value came from the ELAN configuration statement in the LECS database.

Example 10-3 *show lane client with ELAN-ID Acquired from LECS*

```
Cat-A#show lane client
LE Client ATM0.1  ELAN name: elan1  Admin: up  State: operational
Client ID: 2                LEC up for 13 minutes 42 seconds
ELAN ID: 101
Join Attempt: 1
HW Address: 0090.ab16.b008  Type: ethernet        Max Frame Size: 1516
ATM Address: 47.009181000000009092BF7401.0090AB16B008.01

  VCD  rxFrames  txFrames  Type      ATM Address
    0         0         0  configure 47.009181000000009092BF7401.0090AB16500B.00
    3         1         7  direct    47.009181000000009092BF7401.0090AB165009.01
    4        10         0  distribute 47.009181000000009092BF7401.0090AB165009.01
    6         0        38  send      47.009181000000009092BF7401.0090AB16500A.01
    7        76         0  forward   47.009181000000009092BF7401.0090AB16500A.01
```

If you enable the LANE components before you put the necessary MPOA statements in the
LECS database, the LANE components do not acquire the elan-id value. In this case, you need
to restart the LEC so it reinitializes and obtains the elan-id. Without the elan-id, the MPS and
MPC cannot establish neighbor relationships. Nor can the egress MPS issue a cache imposition
request, as the elan-id is one of the parameters passed in the request as defined by MPOA.

Configuring the MPS

Configuring the MPS requires three categories of configuration:

- Global configurations to set MPS parameters
- Major interface configurations to enable the server
- Subinterface configurations to associate LECs with the MPS

To create a functional MPOA system, you must have an MPS at the ingress and egress
points in the network to resolve MPC to MPC values.

MPSs must be created on routers to interact with NHSs and routing tables. In the Catalyst
product line, you can enable an MPS on a route-switch module (RSM) if the RSM has a
versatile Interface Processor 2 (VIP2) containing an ATM port adapter. You cannot enable
an MPS on the LANE module.

MPS Global Configuration

You have the option to modify MPS default configuration parameters. For example, you can
modify the MPS's control NSAP address to a value other than the one used by default Cisco
methods.

MPOA defines several timers and default values for those timers. You can modify the
defaults if you so choose. Table 10-1 shows the names and descriptions for each of the MPS
configurable timers.

Table 10-1 *MPS Configurable Timers*

Timer Name	Timer Description
Keepalive-time	How often the MPS issues a keepalive frame to the MPC. The default value is 10 seconds. Values can range from 1 second to 300 seconds.
Keepalive-lifetime	How long the MPC should consider a keepalive valid. This should be at least three times the keepalive-time value. The default value is 35 seconds. Values can range from 3 seconds to 1000 seconds.
Holding-time	How long an MPC should retain an MPOA resolution reply. The default is 20 minutes (1200 seconds). Values can range from 1 minute to 120 minutes.

The MPS issues keepalive messages to the neighbor MPCs at a frequency defined by the keepalive-time value. This maintains the neighbor relationship between the MPC and the MPS.

Example 10-4 shows a sample global configuration for the MPS. The global configuration requires you to name the MPS. The name is only locally significant, so you can name it whatever you want. If you enable more than one MPS in the unit, they need to be uniquely named within the device.

Example 10-4 *MPS Global Configuration Example*

```
router(config)#mpoa server ?
  config  configure it now

router(config)#mpoa server config ?
  name  name to be given to the MPS
router(mpoa-server-config)#! This is a global config statement
router(config)#mpoa server config name mps
router(mpoa-server-config)#?
MPOA server configuration mode subcommands:
  atm-address        specify the control atm address of the MPS
  default            Set a command to its defaults
  exit               exit the MPOA Server config mode
  holding-time       specify the cache entry holding time of the MPS
  keepalive-lifetime specify the keepalive lifetime of the MPS
  keepalive-time     specify the keepalive time of the MPS
  network-id         specify the network id of the MPS
  no                 Negate a command or set its defaults

router(mpoa-server-config)# ! Insert optional MPS configurations here
```

The *network-id* parameter allows you to prevent shortcuts between LECs on ELANs served by one MPS and LECs on ELANs served by another MPS. By default, all MPSs belong to network-id 1. If you have two MPSs, one with a network-id of 1 and the other with a network-id of 2, LECs associated with network-id 1 cannot develop a shortcut to LECs associated with network-id 2.

TIP   Even if you elect to retain the default values, you must still enter the global configuration statement **mpoa server config name MPS_server_name**.

MPS Major Interface Configuration

Enabling the MPS requires one statement on the ATM major interface. Note that, although multiple MPSs can be enabled in a router, even on the same major interface, an MPS can be associated with only one hardware interface. If you have two ATM modules, you need to enable at least two uniquely named MPSs. Example 10-5 shows the configuration required on the ATM major interface. The single statement enables the MPS.

Example 10-5 *MPS Major Interface Configuration Example*

```
int a1/0
!Enables MPS component
 mpoa server name MPS_Server_name
```

MPS Subinterface Configuration

The MPS must have an LEC associated with it so the MPS can communicate with other MPOA devices in the ELAN. Although more than one MPS can be associated with an interface, you can bind an LEC to only one MPS. Example 10-6 shows how to associate an MPS with an LEC. Note that only one statement is required to do this. If you enter the **lane client mpoa** command before you actually enable the LEC, you receive an alert informing you of this. This is all right and can be ignored, as long as you remember to enable an LEC. Without the LEC, the MPS is operating, but incapable of supporting MPOA operations. This results from its inability to communicate with any other MPOA devices in the ELAN.

Example 10-6 *MPS Subinterface Configuration Example*

```
int a1/0.x
!Associates MPS with LEC
 lane client mpoa server name MPS_Server_name
!Create LEC
 lane client ethernet elan_name
```

Examining the MPOA Server

If you correctly configure the MPS, you should see output as shown in Example 10-7.

Example 10-7 *Output from* **show mpoa** *server Command*

```
router#show mpoa server
MPS Name: mps, MPS id: 0, Interface: ATM1/0, State: up
network-id: 1, Keepalive: 10 secs, Holding time: 1200 secs
Keepalive lifetime: 35 secs, Giveup time: 40 secs
MPS actual operating address: 47.009181000000009092BF7401.0090AB16500C.00
Lane clients bound to MPS mps: ATM1/0.1 ATM1/0.2
Discovered neighbours:
MPC 47.009181000000009092BF7401.0090AB16A80D.00 vcds: 75(R,A)
MPC 47.009181000000009092BF7401.0090AB16B00D.00 vcds: 77(R,A)
```

In Example 10-7, the MPS sees two MPC neighbors. The output displays the virtual circuits used to communicate with each of the MPCs. These circuits should not experience idle timeouts and should, therefore, remain open. The default idle timeout for Cisco equipment is 5 minutes. If the device sees no traffic on the circuit for the idle timeout value, it releases the circuit. However, by default, the MPS issues keepalives to MPCs every 10 seconds. You can modify this value, but generally you should leave the timers at the default values.

If any of the neighbors are MPSs, the display would also present their NSAP address along with the MPC addresses.

Configuring the MPC

Like the configuration tasks for the MPS, configuration of the MPC requires three categories of configuration:

- Global configurations to define MPC parameters
- Major interface configurations to enable the server
- Subinterface configurations to associate LECs with the MPC

MPC Global Configuration

From the LANE module global configuration prompt, you can specify MPC parameters to modify the default behavior. Specifically, you can change the MPCs NSAP address from the Cisco default value displayed in the **show mpoa default** command. You can also modify the threshold that causes the MPC to issue an MPOA resolution request to the MPS. The MPOA document specifies a default threshold of 10 frames in 1 second. If the MPC observes a flow with more than 10 frames per second between devices in two different ELANs, it issues the resolution request. You can modify the frame count and the integration period. Example 10-8 shows a sample global configuration for an MPC in a Catalyst LANE module, along with some results from the Help menu. Multiple MPCs can be enabled in your Catalyst, but each must be uniquely named and individually configured.

Example 10-8 *MPC Global Configuration Example*

```
! This is a global config statement
Cat-A(config)#mpoa client config name MPC_client_name
! Insert optional MPC configurations here
Cat-A(mpoa-client-config)#?
MPOA client configuration mode subcommands:
  atm-address             specify the control atm address of the MPC
  default                 Set a command to its defaults
  exit                    exit the MPOA Client config mode
  no                      Negate a command or set its defaults
  shortcut-frame-count    specify the shortcut-setup frame count of the MPC
  shortcut-frame-time     specify the shortcut-setup frame time of the MPC
```

TIP   Even if you elect to retain the default values of 10 frames per second, you must still enter the global configuration statement **mpoa client config name *MPC_client_name***.

MPC Major Interface Configuration

As with the MPS configuration, the MPC is not enabled until you enter the **mpoa client** command on the major interface. Example 10-9 shows a major interface configuration to enable the client. Notice its similarity to the command to enable an MPS as in Example 10-5.

Example 10-9 *MPC Major Interface Configuration Example*

```
int a1/0
!Creates MPC function
 mpoa client name MPC_client_name
```

MPC Subinterface Configuration

Each VLAN for which you want MPOA capability must have an MPC associated with an LEC on the appropriate subinterfaces. Example 10-10 demonstrates how to build the LEC to MPC association. A three-way relationship exists in the configuration. In Example 10-10, the first **lane client** command enables the LEC/VLAN to participate in MPOA. The LEC associates with a VLAN 12 in the second **lane client** command. *VLAN 12* and *ELAN_name* correlate to the same broadcast domain.

Example 10-10 *MPC Subinterface Configuration Example*

```
int a0.x
!Associates MPC with LEC
 lane client mpoa client name MPC_client_name
!Create LEC
 lane client ethernet 12 elan_name
```

Remember that you can bind the LEC to only one MPC. If you bind the MPC to the LEC before you enable the LEC, you receive a warning indicating that no LEC is configured. You can ignore this warning as long as you remember to eventually enable a LEC. When you complete the **lane client mpoa** command, you can create the LEC on the subinterface. If you create the LEC first, you can enable the MPC afterwards. In either case, make sure that the LEC acquires the elan-id.

Examining the MPOA Client

If you configure MPOA correctly, you should see output for your client as shown in Example 10-11. This output displays the MPC situation before any shortcuts are established. You can identify shortcuts when there are entries under the **Remote Devices known** section of the MPC output display.

Example 10-11 *MPOA Client Show Output*

```
Cat-A#show mpoa client
MPC Name: mpc2, Interface: ATM0, State: Up
MPC actual operating address: 47.009181000000009092BF7401.0090AB16A80D.00
Shortcut-Setup Count: 10, Shortcut-Setup Time: 1
Lane clients bound to MPC mpc2: ATM1/0.2
Discovered MPS neighbours                  kp-alv    vcd      rxPkts      txPkts
47.009181000000009092BF7401.0090AB16500C.00    31        9        76           2
Remote Devices known                                 vcd      rxPkts      txPkts
```

Suppose that you send an extended **ping** to an egress MPC with 20 **ping**s in the sequence. When the ingress MPC sends enough frames to cross the shortcut threshold, it issues the shortcut request to its neighbor MPS. Assuming that the MPS resolved the shortcut, the ingress MPC can establish the shortcut and start using it rather than the default path.

But during the extended **ping** operation, the egress MPC sends an echo reply for each echo request issued from the ingress MPC. If the shortcut threshold is set for the same or less than for the ingress MPC, the echo replies cause the egress MPC to issue a shortcut request too. Ultimately, both the ingress and egress MPCs develop shortcuts between each other as illustrated by Example 10-12.

Example 10-12 *show mpoa client Display after Shortcut*

```
Cat-A#show mpoa client

MPC Name: mpc, Interface: ATM0, State: Up
MPC actual operating address: 47.000601171000008100530606.0090AB16500D.00
Shortcut-Setup Count: 10, Shortcut-Setup Time: 1
Lane clients bound to MPC mpc: ATM0.20
Discovered MPS neighbours                  kp-alv    vcd      rxPkts      txPkts
47.000601171000008100530606.0090AB16B00C.00    28       35       125          4
Remote Devices known                                 vcd      rxPkts      txPkts
47.000601171000008100530606.0090AB16A80D.00             49        7           8
                                                       47        0           0
```

The MPCs use only one of the shortcuts, though. The shortcut established by the MPC with lowest NSAP address is used by both clients. The ingress MPC of Example 10-12 has the lowest MAC address and should be the one used by the two MPCs. Issuing the **show atm vc 49** command confirms that the local device originated from virtual circuit (VC) 49 (see Example 10-13).

Example 10-13 *Confirm Call Origination*

```
Cat-A#show atm vc 49
ATM0: VCD: 49, VPI: 0, VCI: 80, etype:0x0, AAL5 - LLC/SNAP, Flags: 0x50
PeakRate: 0, Average Rate: 0, Burst Cells: 0, VCmode: 0x0
OAM DISABLED, InARP DISABLED
InPkts: 7, OutPkts: 8, InBytes: 724, OutBytes: 766
InPRoc: 7, OutPRoc: 8, Broadcasts: 0
InFast: 0, OutFast: 0, InAS: 0, OutAS: 0
OAM F5 cells sent: 0, OAM cells received: 0
Status: ACTIVE  , TTL: 4
interface =  ATM0, call locally initiated, call reference = 118
vcnum = 49, vpi = 0, vci = 80, state = Active(U10)
 , point-to-point call
Retry count: Current = 0
timer currently inactive, timer value = 00:00:00
Remote Atm Nsap address: 47.00060117100008100530606.0090AB16A80D.00
```

VC 47 eventually times out and disappears. Until a device tears down the circuit, both circuits remain in place, but only one is used. Note that the traffic counters for VC 47 show zero frames sent or received. Whether or not this happens is a function of your traffic flows. Not all application/protocol flows create a one for one reply-response and will therefore only create one VC.

Sample MPOA Configuration

This section presents a sample network to summarize the configuration for MPCs and MPSs. Figure 10-9 Sample MPOA Network illustrates the network where two MPCs interconnect through one MPS.

Figure 10-9 *Sample MPOA Network*

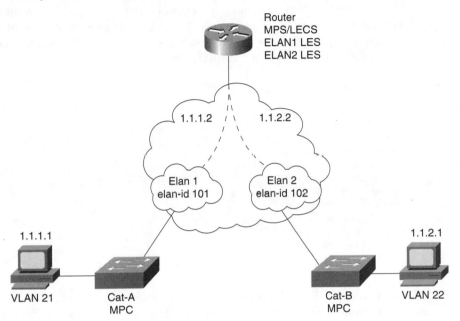

The MPCs reside inside of Catalysts equipped with MPOA-capable LANE modules. The MPS resides in a 7204 router. Each MPC has one LEC enabled. The MPS has two LECs enabled, one for each of the two ELANs. The LECS and LESs reside in the 7204 router, although it could just as easily have been configured in either of the Catalysts.

Example 10-14 shows the relevant configuration statements for Cat-A.

Example 10-14 *Cat-A MPOA Configuration*

```
!
mpoa client config name mpc1
!interface ATM0
 no ip address
 atm pvc 5 0 5 qsaal
 atm pvc 16 0 16 ilmi
 mpoa client name mpc1
!
interface ATM0.1 multipoint
 lane client mpoa client name mpc1
 lane client ethernet 21 elan1
```

Similarly, Cat-B's configuration reflects Cat-A's. Note that no IP address is configured on the Catalysts because the LANE module does not let you assign one. This results from the LANE module behaving like a bridge port. Example 10-15 shows Cat-B's configuration. The MPC names differ in the two configurations (Cat-A and Cat-B), but they could be the same because the names are only locally significant.

Example 10-15 *Cat-B MPOA Client Configuration*

```
!
mpoa client config name mpc2
!
interface ATM0
 no ip address
 atm pvc 5 0 5 qsaal
 atm pvc 16 0 16 ilmi
 mpoa client name mpc2
!
interface ATM0.2 multipoint
 lane client mpoa client name mpc2
 lane client ethernet 22 elan2
```

The MPS configuration of Example 10-16 resides in a router and has an IP address associated with each subinterface. Not shown in this abbreviated output, but vitally important in the configuration, is a routing protocol configuration. You must have routing enabled for the MPS/NHS to function correctly.

Example 10-16 *Router MPOA Server Configuration*

```
lane database usethis
  name elan1 server-atm-address 47.009181000000009092BF7401.0090AB165009.01
  name elan1 elan-id 101
  name elan2 server-atm-address 47.009181000000009092BF7401.0090AB165009.02
  name elan2 elan-id 102
!
mpoa server config name mps
!
interface ATM1/0
 no ip address
 atm pvc 5 0 5 qsaal
 atm pvc 16 0 16 ilmi
 lane config auto-config-atm-address
 lane config database usethis
 mpoa server name mps
!
interface ATM1/0.1 multipoint
 ip address 1.1.1.2 255.255.255.0
 lane server-bus ethernet elan1
 lane client mpoa server name mps
 lane client ethernet elan1
!
interface ATM1/0.2 multipoint
 ip address 1.1.2.2 255.255.255.0
 lane server-bus ethernet elan2
 lane client mpoa server name mps
 lane client ethernet elan2
```

Troubleshooting an MPOA Network

Troubleshooting an MPOA network is not conceptually difficult. Generically, the first step is to characterize the problem. The most likely symptom is an inability to create a shortcut. Assuming all media is intact between the source and the destination (not always a good assumption), troubleshooting consists of the following:

1 Ensuring that all ELANs are functional between the source and destination.

2 Determining that all MPCs and MPSs are operational.

3 Determining that MPCs and MPSs discovered each other.

4 Determining if the threshold is crossed at the MPC to initiate an MPOA resolution request.

5 Ensuring that NHSs or MPSs exist along the default path at each hop to participate in resolution activities.

The following sections expand upon each of the troubleshooting activities listed in the preceding.

Ensuring the ELANs Are Functional between the Source and the Destination

If you configure the ELANs correctly, you should be able to **ping** each of the interfaces for each MPS and NHS along the default path between the source and destination client. If not, you either configured the ELAN incorrectly, you have a Layer 3 issue such as a bad IP address, or you have some routing protocol issues.

Examine your intra-ELAN connectivity first. See if you can **ping** the neighbor device(s) within the ELAN. If you can, **ping** the next device in the next ELAN, either from your current device or from the next hop component within your ELAN. Do this along each ELAN to ensure that each ELAN is completely functional.

Also ensure that each LEC bound to an MPOA device acquired an elan-id as demonstrated in the Catalyst output of Example 10-3.

Determining That All MPCs and MPSs Are Functional

Check the configuration results of the MPC and MPS with the **show mpoa client** and **show mpoa server** commands. Each command should provide you with basic information such as name of the device, the interface where it is enabled, and the current state (up or down).

Determining That MPCs and MPSs Discovered Each Other

Each MPOA device attempts to discover its MPOA neighbors through the ELAN's LES. MPOA has a neighbor discovery protocol enabling MPCs to discover MPSs, and for MPSs to discover other MPSs. Output from the **show mpoa client** and **show mpoa server** commands verify if the device knows any neighbors. The MPS and MPC discover each other by registering their device type values with the LES of their local ELAN. They then send an inquiry to the LES to discover the neighbor devices.

Determining If the Threshold Is Crossed at the MPC to Initiate an MPOA Resolution Request

MPOA defines a default value of 10 frames over 1 second as a threshold for an MPC to trigger a resolution request. If the traffic type never exceeds the configured threshold, the MPC never attempts to establish a shortcut to the egress MPC. You can get an indication if the client even issued a resolution request with the **show mpoa client cache** command. Example 10-17 shows client statistics for an MPC, and shows that it issued and received an MPOA resolution request and reply.

Example 10-17 *An MPOA Client Statistics Screen*

```
Cat-A#sh mp cl statistics
MPC Name: mpc2, Interface: ATM1/0, State: Up
MPC actual operating address: 47.009181000000009092BF7401.0090AB16A80D.00
Shortcut-Setup Count: 10, Shortcut-Setup Time: 1
                                  Transmitted         Received
  MPOA Resolution Requests             1                 0
  MPOA Resolution Replies              0                 1
  MPOA Cache Imposition Requests       0                 1
  MPOA Cache Imposition Replies        1                 0
  MPOA Cache Purge Requests            0                 0
  MPOA Cache Purge Replies             0                 0
  MPOA Trigger Request                 0                 0
  NHRP Purge Requests                  0                 0

Invalid MPOA Data Packets Received: 0

Cat-A#
```

If the resolution request counter does not increment, the MPC does not see interesting traffic to trigger a request to an MPS. If the resolution request counter increments, but the resolution reply counter does not match the request counter, the MPC did not receive a reply to its request. When this happens, ensure that the MPSs are operational. Also check that a default path actually exists to the egress MPC. If the default path does not exist, the MPS cannot resolve a shortcut.

Another method of examining the MPC behavior uses **debug**. The **debug mpoa client** command provides an opportunity to track how the MPC monitors a potential flow and to determine if the MPC actually triggers an MPOA resolution request. Example 10-18 shows an abbreviated **debug** output from an MPC.

Example 10-18 *Sample **debug mpoa client** Command Output*

```
Cat-A#debug mp cl ?
  all                Enable all MPOA Client debugging
  data               Debugs MPOA Client Data Processing
  egress             Debugs MPOA Client Egress Activity
  general            Debugs MPOA Client General/Common Activity
  ingress            Debugs MPOA Client Ingress Activity
  keep-alives        Debugs keep-alives received from MPOA servers
  platform-specific  Hardware platform specific debug
Cat-A#debug mp cl all


. . . . . .

MPOA CLIENT: mpc_trigger_from_lane: mac 0090.ab16.5008 on out ATM0.20
MPOA CLIENT: Is MAC 0090.ab16.5008 interesting on i/f: ATM0.20
MPOA CLIENT MPC: MAC 0090.ab16.5008 interesting
MPOA CLIENT: lower levels detected 1 packets to 0090.ab16.5008 (3.0.0.1)
MPOA CLIENT MPC: mpc_ingress_cache_state_machine called for icache 3.0.0.1:
    current state: INIT, event MPC_ELIGIBLE_PACKET_RECEIVED
MPOA CLIENT: mpc_count_and_trigger: cache state INIT
MPOA CLIENT: mpc_trigger_from_lane: mac 0090.ab16.5008 on out ATM0.20
MPOA CLIENT: Is MAC 0090.ab16.5008 interesting on i/f: ATM0.20
MPOA CLIENT MPC: MAC 0090.ab16.5008 interesting
MPOA CLIENT: lower levels detected 1 packets to 0090.ab16.5008 (3.0.0.1)
MPOA CLIENT MPC: mpc_ingress_cache_state_machine called for icache 3.0.0.1:
    current state: INIT, event MPC_FLOW_DETECTED
MPOA CLIENT MPC: MPOA Resolution process started for 3.0.0.1
MPOA CLIENT MPC: Sending MPOA Resol. req(ReqId=2) for 3.0.0.1
MPOA CLIENT: mpc_count_and_trigger: cache state TRIG
```

The first two highlighted portions of the output illustrate where the MPC recognized what is called interesting traffic. Interesting traffic targets a host in another ELAN. Therefore, the source and destination Layer 3 addresses differ. But the destination MAC address targets a neighbor ingress MPS. Why does it see a MAC address for the MPS? The MPC sees a MAC address for the MPS because this is the first router in the default path. The MPC puts the first hop router's MAC address in the data link header. The two highlighted statements are for frames 9 and 10 within the configured one-second period (the first eight frames were removed for simplicity). There is no indication of the frame count, so you might need to sort through the **debug** output to see if at least ten frames were seen. Because there are ten frames per second, the MPC triggers a resolution request to the ingress MPS. This is shown in the third highlighted area of Example 10-18.

Eventually, the MPC should receive a resolution reply from the MPS as shown in Example 10-19.

Example 10-19 *MPOA Resolution Reply from* **debug**

```
MPOA CLIENT: received a MPOA_RESOLUTION_REPLY packet of size 127 bytes on ATM1/0
  vcd 832
dumping nhrp packet:
fixed part:
    op_type 135 (MPOA_RESOLUTION_REPLY), shtl 20, sstl 0

mandatory part:
    src_proto_len 4, dst_proto_len 4, flags 0, request_id 2
    src_nbma_addr: 47.00918100000100020030099.0090AB16540D.00
    src_prot_addr: 0.0.0.0
    dst_prot_addr: 3.0.0.1
cie 0:
    code 0, prefix_length 0, mtu 1500, holding_time 1200
    cli_addr_tl 20, cli_saddr_tl 0, cli_proto_len 0, preference 0
    cli_nbma_addr: 47.00918100000100020030099.0090AB164C0D.00
tlv 0:
    type 4097, length 4
    data: 15 05 00 01
tlv 1:
    type 4096, length 23 compulsory
    data: 00 00 00 01 00 00 00 67 0E 00 90 AB 16 4C 08 00 90 AB 16 B0 08 08 00

MPOA CLIENT MPC: Resol Reply- IP addr 3.0.0.1, mpxp addr=47.00918100000100020003
0099.0090AB164C0D.00, TAG=352649217
MPOA CLIENT MPC: mpc_ingress_cache_state_machine called for icache 3.0.0.1:
    current state: TRIG, event MPC_VALID_RESOL_REPLY_RECVD
```

The middle portion of the **debug** output displays various items from the MPOA resolution reply messages. For example, **cie** refers to a *client information element* as specified by MPOA. **code 0** means that the operation was successful. Reference the MPOA documents for decode specifics. The important parts of the **debug** for the immediate purposes of troubleshooting are highlighted.

Ensuring That the MPS and NHS Components ARE Functional

Check along the default path and ensure that all MPOA server related devices found each other and can communicate over LANE. Without functional pieces, MPOA cannot resolve a shortcut.

Other Causes of MPOA Failures

One other event can prevent a shortcut from getting established. When the ingress MPC issues the resolution request, the request gets forwarded to the egress MPS. The egress MPS issues a cache imposition request to the egress MPC. If the egress MPC cannot accept a cache imposition, it rejects the imposition request forcing the ingress MPC to continue to use the default paths.

The egress MPC can reject the imposition whenever its local resources prevent it from doing so. For example, the egress MPC might not have enough memory resources to hold another cache entry. It might be that the egress MPC already has too many virtual circuits established and cannot support another circuit. Any of these can cause the egress MPC to reject the imposition preventing a shortcut from getting established.

If you use the MPC **debug**, you should see a line like that shown at the end of Example 10-19 to confirm that the cache imposition worked successfully.

Review Questions

This section includes a variety of questions on the topic of this chapter—MPOA. By completing these, you can test your mastery of the material included in this chapter as well as help prepare yourself for the CCIE written and lab tests.

1 A network administrator observes that the MPC cannot develop a shortcut. An ATM analyzer attached to the network shows that the MPC never issues a shortcut request, even though the 10 frames per second threshold is crossed. Why doesn't the MPC issue a shortcut request? The **show mpoa client** command displays as shown in Example 10-20.

Example 10-20 *Client Output for Review Question 1*

```
Cat-C#sh mpoa client
MPC Name: mpc2, Interface: ATM1/0, State: Up
MPC actual operating address: 47.009181000000009092BF7401.0090AB16A80D.00
Shortcut-Setup Count: 10, Shortcut-Setup Time: 1
Lane clients bound to MPC mpc2:
```

2 When might the ingress and egress MPS reside in the same router?

3 What creates the association of an MPC with a VLAN?

4 Example 10-6 has the following configuration statement in it: **lane client ethernet elan_name**. Where is the VLAN reference?

5 If a frame must pass through three routers to get from an ingress LEC to an egress LEC, do all three routers need to be configured as an MPS?

6 Can you configure both an MPC and an MPS in a router?

Advanced Features

This chapter covers the following key topics:

- **Layer 3 Switching Terminology**—Examines the confusing subject of Layer 3 switching terminology and jargon.

- **The Importance of Routing**—Discusses how routing, and therefore Layer 3 switching, is the key to building large-scale networks that are stable and easy to manage.

- **Router-on-a-Stick**—This section explores the use of traditional router platforms for inter-VLAN routing. As the earliest form of Layer 3 switching, this approach can use either multiple interfaces or a single interface configured for a trunking protocol such as ISL or 802.1Q.

- **The RSM**—Cisco's route-switch module was a natural evolution of the router-on-a-stick approach by bringing the routing function into the Catalyst 5000 chassis. This section discusses issues such as RSM configuration and the advantages of their use.

- **Routing Switches**—Explores the use of the NetFlow Feature Cards (NFFCs) to provide high-performance, ASIC-based Layer 3 switching. After a detailed examination of the theory behind MLS, this section also considers configuration and the appropriate use of MLS technology.

- **Switching Routers**—Discusses an alternate approach to Layer 3 switching represented by devices such as the Catalyst 8500. Resembling traditional router platforms from a design and configuration standpoint, the technology and configuration behind this approach is explained.

- **Routing Switches versus Switching Routers**—Although both styles of Layer 3 switching offer high-performance routing, they are very different from a design and implementation standpoint. This section takes a detailed look at these differences.

- **Catalyst 6000 Layer 3 Switching**—Examines how the Catalyst 6000 both evolves and blends the various Layer 3 switching technologies introduced before it.

- **HSRP**—This section discusses the use of Cisco's Hot Standby Router Protocol for both resiliency and performance.

- **Integration between Routing and Bridging**—Looks at several technologies that are available for blending Layer 2 and Layer 3 technologies.

CHAPTER 11

Layer 3 Switching

Layer 3 switching is one of the most important but over-hyped technologies of recent memory. On one hand, vendors have created a labyrinth of names, architectures, and options that have done little but confuse people. On the other hand, Layer 3 switching (routing) is one of the most important ingredients in a successful campus design. While providing the bandwidth necessary to build modern campus backbones, it also provides the scalability necessary for growth and ease of maintenance.

The goal of this chapter is to clear up any confusion created by competing marchitectures (marketing architectures). By digging into the details behind Cisco's approach to Layer 3 switching, myth and fact can be separated. The chapter takes a chronological look at inter-VLAN (VLAN) routing. It begins with a brief discussion of switching terminology and the importance of routing. It then dives into the first technique commonly used to connect virtual LANs (VLANs) in a switched environment: the router-on-a-stick design. The chapter then looks at more integrated approaches such as the Catalyst Route Switch Module (RSM), followed by a discussion of two hardware-based approaches to Layer 3 switching. The chapter concludes with coverage of Cisco's Hot Standby Router Protocol (HSRP) and bridging between VLANs.

Layer 3 Switching Terminology

Several factors have created significant confusion surrounding the subject of Layer 3 switching. Some of this bewilderment arises from the recent merging of several technologies. In the past, switches and routers have been separate and distinct devices. The term *switch* was reserved for hardware-based platforms that generally functioned at Layer 2. For example, ATM switches perform hardware-based forwarding of fixed-length cells, whereas Ethernet switches use MAC addresses to make forwarding decisions. Conversely, the term *router* has been used to refer to a device that runs routing protocols to discover the Layer 3 topology and makes forwarding decisions based on hierarchical Layer 3 addresses. Because of the complexity of these tasks, routers have traditionally been software-based devices. Routers have also performed a wide variety of "high touch" and value added features such as tunneling, data-link switching (DLSw), protocol translation, access lists, and Dynamic Host Configuration Protocol (DHCP) relay.

Layer 3 switching is a term that encompasses a wide variety of techniques that seek to merge the benefits of these previously separate technologies. The goal is to capture the speed of switching and the scalability of routing. In general, Layer 3 switching techniques can be grouped into two categories:

- Routing switches
- Switching routers

As a broad category, routing switches uses hardware to create shortcut paths through the middle of the network, bypassing the traditional software-based router. Some routing switch devices have been referred to as *router accelerators*. Routing switches do not run routing protocols such as Open Shortest Path First (OSPF) or Enhanced Interior Gateway Routing Protocol (EIGRP). Instead, they utilize various techniques to discover, create, or cache shortcut information. For example, Multiprotocol over ATM was discussed in Chapter 10, "Trunking with Multiprotocol over ATM." This is a standards-based technique that allows ATM-attached devices to build a virtual circuit that avoids routers for sustained flows of information. Although Cisco obviously supports MPOA, it has developed another shortcut technique that does not require an ATM backbone. This feature is called Multilayer Switching (MLS), although many people (and Cisco documents) still refer to it by an earlier name, NetFlow LAN Switching (NFLS). MLS is discussed in detail during this chapter.

WARNING   Do not confuse MLS with other shortcut Layer 3 switching techniques that are not standards-compliant (many of these use the term cut-through switching). Many of these other techniques quickly switch the packets through the network *without* making the necessary modifications to the packet (such as decrementing the TTL field and rewriting the source and destination MAC addresses). MLS makes all of same modifications as a normal router and is therefore completely standards-compliant.

Unlike routing switches, switching routers *do* run routing protocols such as OSPF. These operations are typically run on a general-purpose CPU as with a traditional router platform. However, unlike traditional routers that utilize general-purpose CPUs for both control-plane *and* data-plane functions, Layer 3 switches use high-speed application specific integrated circuits (ASICs) in the data plane. By removing CPUs from the data-forwarding path, wire-speed performance can be obtained. This results in a much faster version of the traditional router. Switching routers such as the Catalyst 8500 are discussed in more detail later in this chapter.

Although the terms routing switch and switching router seem arbitrarily close, the terms are actually very descriptive of the sometimes subtle difference between these types of devices. For example, in the case of routing switch, switch is the noun and routing is the adjective (you didn't know you were in for a grammar lesson in this chapter, did you?). In other words, it is primarily a switch (a Layer 2 device) that has been enhanced or taught some routing (Layer 3) capabilities. In the case of a switching router, it is primarily a router (Layer 3 device) that uses switching technology (high-speed ASICs) for speed and performance (as well as also supporting Layer 2 bridging functions).

TIP	Routing switches are Layer 2-oriented devices that have been enhanced to provide Layer 3 (and 4) functionality. On the other hand, switching routers are primarily Layer 3 devices that can also do Layer 2 processing (like any Cisco router).

Of the variety of other switching devices and terminology released by vendors, Layer 4 and Layer 7 switching have received considerable attention. In general, these approaches refer to the capability of a switch to act on Layer 4 (transport layer) information contained in packets. For example, Transmission Control Protocol (TCP) and User Datagram Protocol (UDP) port numbers can be used to make decisions affecting issues such as security and Quality of Service (QoS). However, rather than being viewed as a third type of campus switching devices, these should be seen as a logical extension and enhancement to the two types of switches already discussed. In fact, both routing switches and switching routers can perform these upper-layer functions.

The Importance of Routing

Although Chapter 14, "Campus Design Models," discusses the advantages of routing from a design perspective, it is also useful to consider the importance of routing when discussing Layer 3 switching—after all, Layer 3 switching is routing. This section is designed to serve only as a brief reminder of routing's benefits in a large network (campus or WAN). For a more thorough discussion of this subject, please see the section "Advantages of Routing" in Chapter 14.

Probably the most important benefit of routing is its proven history of facilitating large networks. Although the Internet serves as the obvious example here, this point is true of any type of network, such as a large campus backbone. Because routers prevent broadcast propagation and use more intelligent forwarding algorithms than bridges, routers provide much more efficient use of bandwidth. This simultaneously results in flexible and optimal path selection. For example, it is very easy to implement load balancing across multiple paths in most networks when using routing. On the other hand, as Chapter 7, "Advanced Spanning Tree," discussed, Layer 2 load balancing can be very difficult to design, implement, and maintain. The data forwarding benefits of routers are especially important when multicast traffic is in use. As multicast traffic becomes increasingly common in campus networks, routers play an increasingly important role.

Routers provide additional benefits that reach beyond the area of data forwarding. Because Layer 3 addresses are hierarchical, routers can be used to implement summarized designs. By reducing routing protocol overhead, increasing table lookup performance, and improving network stability, this can further facilitate networks of almost unlimited size. Most routers provide extensive access list capabilities that can be used to provide important policy controls. Finally, routers can also provide important features such as DHCP relay, proxy Address Resolution Protocol (ARP), and Get Nearest Server (GNS) functions in IPX networks.

TIP	You should build routing (Layer 3 switching) into all but the smallest campus networks. See Chapters 14, "Campus Design Models," and 15, "Campus Design Implementation," for more information.

Router-on-a-Stick

Early VLAN designs relied on routers connected to VLAN-capable switches in the manner shown in Figure 11-1.

Figure 11-1 *Router-on-a-Stick Design*

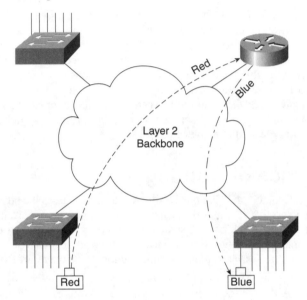

In this approach, traditional routers are connected via one or more links to a switched network. Figure 11-1 shows a single link, the stick, connecting the router to the rest of the campus network. Inter-VLAN traffic must cross the Layer 2 backbone to reach the router where it can move between VLANs. It then travels back to the desired end station using normal Layer 2 forwarding. This "out to the router and back" flow is characteristic of all router-on-a stick designs.

Figure 11-1 portrays the router connection in a general sense. When discussing specific options for linking a router to a switched network, two alternatives are available:

- One-link-per-VLAN
- Trunk-connected router

One-Link-per-VLAN

One of the earliest techniques for connecting a switched network to a router was the use of one-link-per-VLAN as shown in Figure 11-2.

Figure 11-2 *One-Link-per-VLAN*

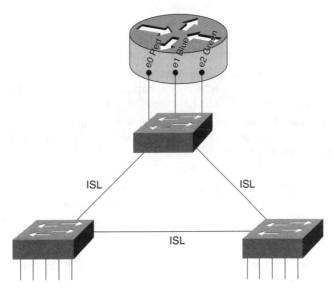

In this case, the switched network carries three VLANs: Red, Blue, and Green. Inter-Switch Link (ISL) trunks are used to connect the three switches together, allowing a single link to carry all three VLANs. However, connections to the router use a separate link for every VLAN. Figure 11-2 illustrates the use of 10 Mbps router ports; however, Fast Ethernet, Gigabit Ethernet, or even other media such as Asynchronous Transfer Mode (ATM) or Fiber Distributed Data Interface (FDDI) can be used.

There are several advantages to using the one-link-per-VLAN approach:

- It allows existing equipment to be redeployed in a switched infrastructure, consequently saving money.

- It is simple to understand and implement. Network administrators do not have to learn any new concepts or configuration commands to roll out the one-link-per-VLAN approach.

- Because it relies of multiple interfaces, it can provide high performance.

Furthermore, notice that every router interface is unaware of the VLAN infrastructure (they are access ports). This allows the router to utilize normal processing to move packets between VLANs. In other words, there is no additional processing or overhead.

Although there are advantages to the one-link-per-VLAN design, it suffers from several critical flaws:

- It can require more interfaces than is practical. In effect, this limits the one-link-per-VLAN approach to networks carrying less than 10 VLANs. Trying to use this model with networks that carry 15 or more VLANs is generally not feasible because of port-density and cost limitations.

- Although it can initially save money because it allows the reuse of existing equipment, it can become very expensive as the number of VLANs grows over time. Keep in mind that every VLAN requires an additional port on both the router and the switch.

- It can become difficult to maintain the network over time. Although the one-link-per-VLAN design can be simple to initially configure, it can become very cumbersome as the number of VLANs (and therefore cables) grows.

In short, the downside of the one-link-per-VLAN approach can be summarized as a lack of scalability. Therefore, you should only consider this to be a viable option in networks that contain a small number of VLANs.

TIP   The one-link-per-VLAN model can be appropriate in networks with a limited number of VLANs.

Example 11-1 presents a possible configuration for the router in Figure 11-2.

Example 11-1 *One-Link-Per-VLAN Router Configuration*

```
interface Ethernet0
 ip address 10.1.1.1 255.255.255.0
 !
interface Ethernet1
 ip address 10.1.2.1 255.255.255.0
 ipx network 2
 !
interface Ethernet2
 ip address 10.1.3.1 255.255.255.0
 appletalk cable-range 300-310 304.101
 appletalk zone ZonedOut
 ipx network 3
```

The configuration in Example 11-1 provides inter-VLAN routing services for three VLANs:

- VLAN 1 is connected to the Ethernet0 interface and is only using the IP protocol.
- VLAN 2 is linked the Ethernet1 interface and uses the IP and IPX protocols.
- VLAN 3 is linked to the Ethernet2 interface and supports three network layer protocols: IP, IPX, and AppleTalk.

Notice that the router is unaware of VLANs directly—it sees the network as three normal segments.

Trunk-Connected Routers

As technologies such as ISL became more common, network designers began to use trunk links to connect routers to a campus backbone. Figure 11-3 illustrates an example of this approach.

Figure 11-3 *Trunk-Connected Router*

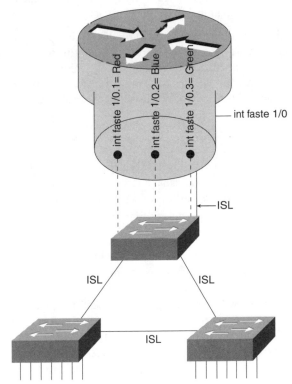

Although any trunking technology such as ISL, 802.1Q, 802.10, LAN Emulation (LANE), or MPOA can be used, Ethernet-based approaches are most common (ISL and 802.1Q). Figure 11-3 uses ISL running over Fast Ethernet. The solid lines refer to the single *physical* link running between the top Catalyst and the router. The dashed lines refer to the multiple *logical* links running over this physical link.

The primary advantage of using a trunk link is a reduction in router and switch ports. Not only can this save money, it can reduce configuration complexity. Consequently, the trunk-connected router approach can scale to a much larger number of VLANs than the one-link-per-VLAN design.

However, there are disadvantages to the trunk-connected router configuration, including the following:

- Inadequate bandwidth for each VLAN
- Additional overhead on the router
- Older versions of the IOS only support a limited set of features on ISL interfaces

With regard to inadequate bandwidth for each VLAN, consider, for example, the use of a Fast Ethernet link where all VLANs must share 100 Mbps of bandwidth. A single VLAN could easily consume the entire capacity of the router or the link (especially if there is a broadcast storm or Spanning Tree problem).

With regard to the additional overhead on the router caused by using a trunk-connected router, not only must the router perform normal routing and data forwarding duties, it must handle the additional encapsulation used by the trunking protocol. Take ISL running on a 7500 router as an example. Cisco's software-based routers have a number of different switching modes, a term that Cisco uses to generically refer to the process of data forwarding in a router.

NOTE   Don't confuse the term *switching* here with how it normally gets used throughout this book. These software-based routers use the term switching to refer to the process of forwarding frames through the box, regardless of whether the frames are routed or bridged.

Every Cisco router supports multiple forwarding techniques. Although a full discussion of these is not appropriate for a campus-oriented book, it is easiest to think of them as gears in an automobile transmission. For example, just as every car has a first gear, every Cisco router (including low-end routers such as the 2500) supports something called Process Switching. Process Switching relies on the CPU to perform brute-force routing on each and every packet. Just as first gear is useful in all situations (uphill, flat roads, rain, snow, dry, and so on), Process Switching can route all packets and protocols. However, just as first gear is the slowest in a car, Process Switching is slowest forwarding technique for a router.

Every Cisco router also has a second gear—this is referred to as Fast Switching. By taking advantage of software-based caching techniques, it provides faster data forwarding. However, just as second gear is not useful in all situations (going up a steep hill, starting away from a traffic signal, and so on), Fast Switching cannot handle all types of traffic (for example, many types of SNA traffic).

Finally, just as high-end automobiles offer fancy six-speed transmissions, high-end Cisco routers offer a variety of other switching modes. These switching modes go by names such as Autonomous Switching, Silicon Switching, Optimum Switching, and Distributed Switching. Think of these as gears three, four, five, and six (respectively) in a Ferrari's transmission—they can allow you to move very quickly, but can be useful only in ideal conditions and very limited situations (that is, dry pavement, a long country road, and no police!).

Getting back to the example of an ISL interface on a 7500 router, 7500 routers normally use techniques such as Optimum Switching and Distributed Switching to achieve data forwarding rates from 300,000 to over 1,000,000 packets per second (pps).

NOTE	Several performance figures are included in this chapter to allow you to develop a general sense of the throughput you can expect from the various Layer 3 switching options. Any sort of throughput numbers are obviously highly dependent on many factors such as configuration options, software version, and hardware revision. You should not treat them as an absolute indication of performance (in other words, "your mileage may vary").

However, when running ISL, that interface becomes limited to second gear Fast Switching. Because of this restriction, ISL routing is limited to approximately 50,000 to 100,000 pps on a 7500 (and considerably less on many other platforms).

Some of this limitation is due to the overhead of processing the additional 30-byte ISL encapsulation. With older interfaces such as the Fast Ethernet Interface Processor (FEIP), this can be especially noticeable because the second CRC (cyclic redundancy check) contained in the ISL trailer must be performed in software. In the case of newer interfaces such as the PA-FE (Fast Ethernet port adapter for 7200 and VIP interfaces) or the FEIP2, hardware assistance has been provided for tasks such as the ISL CRC. However, even in the case of the PA-FE and the FEIP2, the Fast Switching limitation remains.

TIP	The RSM Versatile Interface Processor (VIP) (the card into which you put port adapters) is *not* the same as a 7500 VIP. It is port adapters themselves that are the same in both platforms.

Note that switching routers such as the Catalyst 8500s use ASICs to handle ISL and 802.1Q encapsulations, effectively removing the overhead penalty of trunk links. However, devices such as the 8500 are rarely deployed in router-on-a-stick configurations. See the section on 8500-style switching routers later in this chapter.

Software-based routers containing Fast Ethernet interfaces, such as the 7500, 7200, 4000, and 3600, are limited to Fast Switching speeds for ISL operations. ASIC-based routers such as the Catalyst 8500 do not have this limitation and can perform ISL routing at wire speed.

The third disadvantage of the trunk-connected router design is that older versions of the IOS only support a limited set of features on ISL interfaces. Although most limitations were removed in 11.3 and some later 11.2 images, networks using older images need to carefully plan the inter-VLAN routing in their network. Some of the more significant limitations prior to 11.3 include the following:

- Support for only IP and IPX. All other protocols (including AppleTalk and DECnet) must be bridged. Inter-VLAN bridging is almost always a bad idea and is discussed later in the section "Integration between Routing and Bridging."

- IPX only supports the **novell_ether** encapsulation (Novell refers to this as Ethernet_802.3).

- HSRP is not supported. This can make it very difficult or impossible to provide default gateway redundancy.

- Secondary IP addresses are not supported.

ISL interfaces prior to 11.3 (and some later versions of 11.2) only support a limited set of protocols and features. 11.3+ code addresses all four of the issues mentioned in the preceding list.

As discussed in Chapter 9, "Trunking with LAN Emulation," subinterfaces allow Cisco routers to create multiple logical partitions on a single physical interface. Just as subinterfaces allow each ELAN on a single ATM interface to belong to its own logical grouping, subinterfaces on Fast Ethernet (or other media) interfaces allow a logical partition for each VLAN. If the physical interface is Fast Ethernet1/0 (this is also called the major interface), subinterfaces can use designations such as Fast Ethernet1/0.1, Fast Ethernet1/0.2, and Fast Ethernet1/0.3. For example, the configuration in Example 11-2 configures a Fast Ethernet port to perform ISL routing for three VLANs.

Example 11-2   *ISL Router-on-a-Stick Configuration*

```
interface FastEthernet1/0
no ip address
!
interface FastEthernet1/0.1
 encapsulation isl 1
 ip address 10.1.1.1 255.255.255.0
!
interface FastEthernet1/0.2
 encapsulation isl 2
 ip address 10.1.2.1 255.255.255.0
 ipx network 2
!
interface FastEthernet1/0.3
 encapsulation isl 3
 ip address 10.1.3.1 255.255.255.0
 appletalk cable-range 300-310 304.101
 appletalk zone ZonedOut
 ipx network 3
```

The major interface contains no configuration statements (the **no ip address** command appears by default). One subinterface is created per VLAN. Each subinterface must receive the **encapsulation isl** *vlan* command to specify the VLAN to associate with that subinterface. (This must be done before the IP and AppleTalk parameters are configured, otherwise the router generates an error message.) Commands specific to each VLAN are also placed on the subinterface. For example, the first subinterface (Fast Ethernet1/0.1) is configured to handle VLAN 1. Because only an IP address is specified on this subinterface, the router does not perform services for other protocols that might be present in VLAN 1. On the other hand, subinterface 1/0.3 is used to handle traffic for IP, IPX, and AppleTalk.

Notice that this router must be running 11.3+ code to support the AppleTalk protocol. Also notice that this configuration is functionally identical to the example presented in the "One-Link-per-VLAN" section.

TIP	Although the router allows the subinterface numbers and VLAN numbers to differ, using the same numbers provides easier maintenance. For example, configure VLAN 2 on subinterface X.2 (where X equals the major interface designation).

When to Use the Router-On-A-Stick Design

In general, the router-on-a-stick approach to inter-VLAN routing is most appropriate when other options are not available. This is not to say that the router-on-a-stick design is a poor choice, it is only a reflection that other options tend to provide higher throughput and functionality. Also, because the router-on-a-stick technique functions as if the router were sitting on the edge of the network (at least as far as the Layer 2 network is concerned), it tends to be less tightly integrated with the rest of the campus network. Newer approaches, such as MLS and the 8500s, seek to place routing in the *middle* of the network where it can have a greater influence on the overall scalability and stability of the network. However, before looking into MLS and 8500 technology, the next section looks at Cisco's first attempt to provide a more integrated approach to inter-VLAN routing—the Catalyst 5000 Catalyst Route Switch Module (RSM).

The RSM

In the case of the router-on-a-stick design, traffic flows to the router within the source VLAN where it is routed into the destination VLAN. This created an out and back flow to the router. Technically, the Catalyst 5000 RSM uses a very similar flow, but with one important difference: the stick becomes the Catalyst 5000 backplane (the high-speed switching path used inside the Catalyst chassis). This difference provides two key benefits:

- Speed
- Integration

Because the RSM directly connects to the Catalyst 5000 backplane, it allows the router to be much more tightly integrated into the Catalyst switching mechanics. Not only can this ease configuration tasks, it can provide intelligent communication between the Layer 2 and Layer 3 portions of the network (several examples are discussed later in the chapter). Also, because it provides a faster link than a single Fast Ethernet ISL interface, the performance can be greater. In general, the RSM provides 125,000–175,000 pps for IP and approximately 100,000 pps for other protocols.

TIP	If necessary, more than one RSM can be used in a single Catalyst chassis for additional throughput.

RSM Configuration

One of the appealing benefits of the RSM is its familiarity. From a hardware perspective, it is almost identical to an RSP2 (the second version of the Route Switch Processor) from a Cisco 7500. It has the same CPU and contains the same console and auxiliary ports for out-of-band configuration. It has its own flash, dynamic random-access memory (DRAM), and nonvolatile random-access memory (NVRAM). And, because it runs the full IOS, RSM is configured almost exactly like any Cisco router.

TIP   Although the IOS is identical from a configuration standpoint, do not try to use a 7500 router image on an RSM—the RSM uses its own image sets. Under Cisco's current naming convention, RSM images begin with the characters **c5rsm**.

The most obvious modification is a set of dual direct memory access (DMA) connections to the Catalyst 5000 backplane. (The backplane connection remains 1.2 Gbps even in 3.6 Gbps devices such as the Catalyst 5500.) The status of these two connections is indicated by the Channel 0 and Channel 1 LEDs on the front panel. Each channel provides 200 Mbps of throughput for a total of 400 Mbps.

Because the RSM runs the full IOS and contains its own image and memory, it shares some of the same configuration aspects as the LANE module discussed in Chapter 9. To configure the RSM, you need to enter the **session** *slot* command. For example, to configure an RSM located in slot 3, you enter **session 3**. This instantly transports you from the Catalyst world of **set** and **show** commands to the router world of **config t**. The full range of IOS help and command-line editing features are available. The RSM also requires you to save your configuration changes to NVRAM using the **copy run start** command.

TIP   Don't forget to save your RSM configurations with **copy run start** or **write mem**. Unlike the Catalyst Supervisor, the RSM does not automatically save configuration changes.

Although the **session** command is the most common way to configure an RSM, the console and auxiliary ports can be useful in certain situations. Many organizations use the auxiliary port to connect a modem to the Catalyst. This is especially useful for Supervisors that do not contain an Aux port (or, in the case of the Catalyst 5000 Supervisor III, where the Aux port is not enabled).

TIP   The **session** command opens a Telnet session across the Catalyst's backplane. The destination address is 127.0.0.slot_number + 1. For example, slot 3 uses 127.0.0.4. Some versions (but unfortunately not all) of the RSM code allow you to enter **telnet 127.0.0.2** to Telnet from the RSM to the Supervisor in slot 1 (or 127.0.0.3 for slot 2). This can very useful when accessing the box from a modem connected to the RSM's auxiliary port. If the code on your RSM does not permit the use of the 127.0.0.X addresses, use normal IP addresses assigned to both SC0 and an RSM interface. However, this obviously requires a valid configuration on the Supervisor *before* you remotely dial into the RSM.

Just as the auxiliary port is useful for connecting a modem to the Catalyst, the RSM's console port is useful for password recovery operations.

TIP   RSM password recovery is identical to normal Cisco router password recovery. See the IOS "System Management" documentation for more details.

RSM Interfaces

The RSM uses interfaces just as any Cisco router does. However, instead of using the usual Ethernet0 and Fast Ethernet1/0, the RSM uses virtual interfaces that correspond to VLANs. For example, **interface vlan 1** and **interface vlan 2** can be used to create interfaces for VLANs 1 and 2, respectively. These virtual interfaces are automatically linked to all ports configured in that VLAN on the Catalyst Supervisor. This creates a very flexible and intuitive routing platform. Simply use the **set vlan** *vlan_number port_list* command on the Supervisor to make VLAN assignments at will, and the RSM automatically reflects these changes.

TIP   RSMs do not use subinterfaces for VLAN configuration. Instead, the RSM uses virtual VLAN interfaces (that function as major interfaces). In fact, these VLAN interfaces currently do not support subinterfaces.

Except for the earliest versions of RSM code, RSM virtual interfaces only become active if the Supervisor detects active ports that have been assigned to that VLAN. For example, if VLAN 3 has no ports currently active, a **show interface vlan 3** command on the RSM shows in the interface in the down state. If a device in VLAN 3 boots, the RSM's VLAN 3 interface enters the up state. This value-added feature further reflects the tight integration between the Supervisor and RSM and is useful for avoiding black hole routing situations.

TIP   You cannot activate an RSM interface until the corresponding VLAN has one or more active ports.

This black hole prevention feature can be controlled through the use of the **set rsmautostate** [**enable** | **disable**] Supervisor command. In modern Catalyst images, this feature is enabled by default.

The RSM contains no VLANs by default. The VLAN virtual interfaces are created as **interface vlan** commands are first entered. Each VLAN interface can then be configured with the addressing and other parameters associated with that VLAN. For example, the code sample in Example 11-3 creates three interfaces that correspond to three VLANs.

Example 11-3 *RSM Configuration*

```
interface Vlan1
 ip address 10.1.1.1 255.255.255.0
 !
interface Vlan2
 ip address 10.1.2.1 255.255.255.0
 ipx network 2
 !
interface Vlan3
 ip address 10.1.3.1 255.255.255.0
 appletalk cable-range 300-310 304.101
 appletalk zone ZonedOut
 ipx network 3
```

As with the earlier examples, Vlan1 is only used for IP traffic. Vlan2 adds support for IPX routing, and Vlan3 is running IP, IPX, and AppleTalk services.

TIP   RSM interfaces are in a shutdown state when they are first created. Don't forget to use the **no shutdown** command to enable them.

Troubleshooting with the RSM

The usefulness of an RSM can go way beyond being a tightly integrated router—it can be a very powerful troubleshooting tool. Because the RSM uses the full IOS, you have access to all of the **debug** and **show** commands normally present on any Cisco router. Extended **ping** and **trace** can be very useful when the more limited capabilities of the Supervisor's tools have failed to reveal the problem. For example, Example 11-4 shows some of the extended **ping** options.

Example 11-4 *Using the RSM for Extended pings*

```
RSM# ping
Protocol [ip]:
Target IP address: 10.1.1.55
Repeat count [5]: 100000
Datagram size [100]: 1024
Timeout in seconds [2]:
Extended commands [n]: y
Source address or interface:
Type of service [0]:
Set DF bit in IP header? [no]: y
Validate reply data? [no]: y
Data pattern [0xABCD]: 0000
Loose, Strict, Record, Timestamp, Verbose[none]:
Sweep range of sizes [n]:
Type escape sequence to abort.
Sending 100000, 1024-byte ICMP Echos to 10.1.6.100, timeout is 2 seconds:
Packet has data pattern 0x0000
!!!!!!!!!!!!!!!!!!!!!!!!!!!!!!!!!!!!!!!!!!!!!!!!!!!!!!!!!!!!!!!
```

Example 11-4 illustrates the use of the repeat count, datagram size, and data pattern options. Respectively, these can be useful when trying to create a sustained stream of rapid-fire **ping**s, to probe for maximum transmission unit (MTU) problems, and to detect ones-density problems on serial links.

However, the most powerful troubleshooting advantage to the RSM is debug. For example, **debug ip icmp** or **debug ip packet** [*access-list-number*] can be extremely useful when trying to track down the reason why some **ping** operation mysteriously fails.

The usual caveats about **debug** output volumes apply, though. Be very careful, especially when using commands such as **debug ip packet** in production networks. It is almost always advisable to use the *access-list-number* parameter to very specifically limit the amount of output. Also, because the RSM automatically sends **debug** output to a connection made via the **session** command, the **terminal monitor** command is not necessary.

TIP

To make it easier to enter commands while the router is generating **debug** or informational output, use the **logging synchronous** line command. For the RSM, it is most useful to enter this under **line vty 0 4**. However, this command can be useful on all of Cisco's router platforms running 10.2+ code (in which case it should also be applied to **line con 0** and **line aux 0**).

When to Use the RSM

Using an RSM in conjunction with a Catalyst 5000 can be a very effective combination for medium-sized networks with moderate Layer 3 bandwidth requirements. Although it is faster than most router-on-a-stick implementations, its speed is not enough for many larger campus backbone applications. Instead, it is the RSMs integration into the Catalyst 5000 architecture that makes it most appealing. Features such as ease of configuration, an intuitive interface, a wide range of supported capabilities, and troubleshooting capabilities are its strengths.

The RSM can also be extremely useful for organizations deploying switched infrastructures in remote offices. This requirement can be met by utilizing the Versatile Interface Processor (VIP) option for the RSM. This is a separate card that literally bolts on top of the RSM to become a two-slot card in the Catalyst. The RSM and the VIP do not communicate over the Catalyst backplane. Instead, a pair of ribbon cables are used to create miniature CyBuses as are used in a 7500-style router. The VIP then accepts a wide variety of 7200-style Port Adapters. This can allow wide-area serial and ATM links to be directly connected to the Catalyst chassis. Therefore, the RSM can not only provide inter-VLAN routing, it can also perform WAN routing duties.

TIP	Be careful when using the HSSI port adapter (typically used for T3 connections) with the RSM VIP because it can overload the power supplies on some models. Check the current release notes for the latest list of models that are affected by this.

As discussed earlier, the RSM is a software-based routing device that cannot provide enough Layer 3 performance for larger campus networks on its own. However, another appealing benefit to the RSM is that it can be easily upgraded to provide hardware-based forwarding via MLS, the subject of the next section.

MLS

Multilayer Switching (MLS) is Cisco's Ethernet-based routing switch technology. MLS is currently supported in two platforms: the Catalyst 5000 and the Catalyst 6000. The Catalyst 5000 makes use of the NetFlow Feature Card (NFFC) I or II to provide hardware-assisted routing. The Catalyst 6000 performs the same operations using the Multilayer Switch Feature Card (MSFC) in conjunction with the Policy Feature Card (PFC). In keeping with the chronological presentation of this chapter, this section focuses on the Catalyst 5000's implementation of MLS. The Catalyst 6000's Layer 3 capabilities are discussed in the "Catalyst 6000 Layer 3 Switching" section later in the chapter and in Chapter 18, "Layer 3 Switching and the Catalyst 6000/6500s." Also, although MLS supports both IP and IPX traffic, this section focuses on IP.

NOTE	IPX MLS is supported on all Catalyst 6000s using a Multilayer Switch Feature Card (MSFC, discussed later in the chapter). IPX MLS is supported on Catalyst 5000s using a NFFC II and 5.1+ software.

In its most basic sense, the NFFC is a pattern-matching engine. This allows the Catalyst to recognize a wide variety of different packets. By matching on various combinations of addresses and port numbers, the routing switch form of Layer 3 switching can be performed. However, a host of other features are also possible. By matching on Layer 3 protocol type, a feature called Protocol Filtering can be implemented. By matching on Internet Group Management Protocol (IGMP) packets, the Catalyst can perform IGMP Snooping to dynamically build efficient multicast forwarding tables. Finally, by matching on Layer 2 and Layer 3 QoS and COS information, traffic classification and differentiation can be performed.

This section initially only considers the Layer 3 switching aspects of the NFFC. The other capabilities are addressed at the end of the section (as well as in other chapters such as Chapter 13, "Multicast and Broadcast Services").

One of the important things to keep in mind when discussing MLS is that, like all shortcut switching mechanisms, it is a caching technique. *The NFFC does not run any routing protocols such as OSPF, EIGRP, or BGP.*

It is also important to realize that MLS, formerly known as NetFlow LAN Switching, is a completely different mechanism than the NetFlow switching on Cisco's software-based routers. In its current implementation, NetFlow on the routers is targeted as a powerful data collection tool via NetFlow Data Export (although it can also be used to reduce the overhead associated with things like complex access lists). Although MLS also supports NetFlow Data Export (NDE), its primary mission is something very different—Layer 3 switching.

Because the NFFC does not run any routing protocols, it must rely on its pattern-matching capabilities to discover packets that have been sent to a router (notice *this* is the device running protocols such as OSPF) and then sent back to the same Catalyst. It then allows the NFFC to shortcut future packets in a manner that bypasses the router. In effect, the NFFC notices that it sent a particular packet to the router, only to have the router send it right back. It then says to itself, "Boy, that was a waste of time!" and starts shortcutting all remaining packets following this same path (or flow).

NOTE	NetFlow defines a flow as being unidirectional. Therefore, when two nodes communicate via a bi-directional protocol such as Telnet, two flows are created.

Although MLS is fundamentally a very simple technique, there are many details involved. The following section presents an in-depth account of the entire MLS mechanism. Later sections examine how to configure and use MLS.

Detailed MLS Theory of Operations

MLS makes use of three components:

- MLS Route Processor (MLS-RP)
- MLS Switching Engine (MLS-SE)
- Multilayer Switching Protocol (MLSP)

The MLS-RP acts as the router in the network (note that more than one can be used). This device handles the first packet in every flow, allowing the MLS-SE to build shortcut entries in a Layer 3 CAM table. The MLSP is a lightweight protocol used by the MLS-RP to initialize the MLS-SE and notify it of changes in the Layer 3 topology or security requirements. For simplicity, this chapter usually refers to the MLS-RP as the router and the MLS-SE as the NFFC.

MLS uses a four-step process:

Step 1   MLSP hello packets are sent by the router

Step 2   The NFFC identifies candidate packets

Step 3   The NFFC identifies enable packets

Step 4   The NFFC shortcuts future packets

The following sections describe each of these steps using the sample network shown in Figure 11-4.

Figure 11-4 *Sample MLS Network*

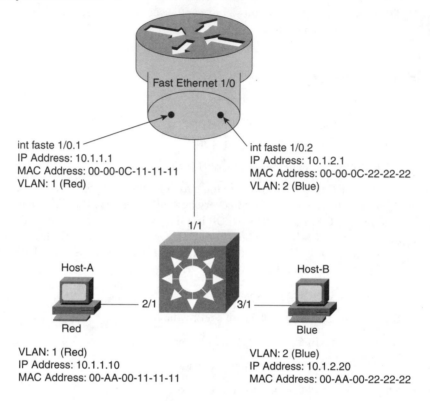

This network consists of two VLANs, VLAN 1 (Red) and VLAN 2 (Blue). Two end stations have been shown. Host-A has been assigned to the Red VLAN, and Host-B has been assigned to the Blue VLAN. An ISL-attached router has also been included. Its single Fast Ethernet interface (Fast Ethernet1/0) has been logically partitioned into two subinterfaces, one per VLAN. The IP and MAC addresses for all devices and subinterfaces are shown.

Figure 11-4 portrays the router as an ISL-attached external device using the router-on-a-stick configuration. Other possibilities include an RSM or a one-interface-per-VLAN attached router.

Step 1: MLSP Hello Packets Are Sent by the Router

When the router first boots, it begins sending MLSP hello packets every 15 seconds. These packets contain information on the VLANs and MAC addresses in use on the router. By listening for these hello packets, the NFFC can learn the attributes of any MLS-capable routers in the Layer 2 network. The NFFC associates a single XTAG value with every MLS router that it identifies. Because the MLSP hellos are periodic in nature, they allow routers and Catalysts to boot at random times while also serving as a router keepalive mechanism for the NFFC (if a router goes offline, its cache entries are purged).

There is one XTAG per MLS-capable router. The XTAG serves as a single handle for a router's multiple MAC addresses (each interface/VLAN could be using a different MAC address). XTAGs are locally significant (different NFFCs can refer to the same router with different XTAGs).

Figure 11-5 illustrates the MLS hello process.

Figure 11-5 *MLS Hello Process*

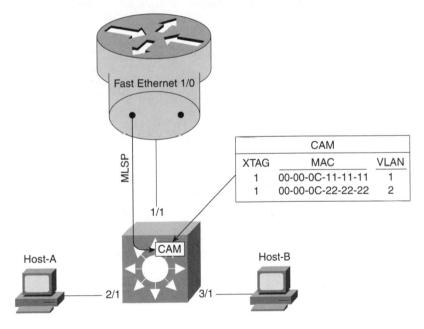

As shown in Figure 11-5, the MLSP packets are sourced from subinterface Fast Ethernet1/0.1 on the router (this is a configurable option; the router commands are presented later). These packets are then used to populate the Layer 2 CAM table (a form of bridging table commonly used in modern switches) with special entries that are used to identify packets going to or coming from a router interface (the **show cam** Catalyst command places an **R** next to these entries). Each router is also assigned a unique XTAG value. If a second router were present in Figure 11-5, it would receive a different XTAG number than the value of 1 assigned to the first router. However, notice that all MAC addresses and VLANs for a single router are associated with a single XTAG value.

Although it is not illustrated in Figure 11-5, the MLSP hello packets flow throughout the Layer 2 network. Because they are sent using a multicast address (01-00-0C-DD-DD-DD, the same address used by CGMP), non-MLS-aware switches simply flood the hello packets to every segment in VLAN 1. In this way, all MLS switches learn about all MLS-capable routers.

Step 2: The NFFC Identifies Candidate Packets

After Step 1 has allowed the NFFC to acquire the addresses of the MLS-capable routers, the NFFC starts using its pattern-matching capabilities to look for packets that are destined to these addresses. If a packet is headed to the router and does not have an existing shortcut entry (if it did have a shortcut entry, it would skip this step and be shortcut switched), it is classified as a *candidate packet*. The packet uses the normal Catalyst Layer 2 forwarding process and gets forwarded out the port connected to the router.

NOTE   Candidate packets must meet the following criteria:

- They have a destination address equal to one of the router MAC addresses learned via MLSP.

- They do not have an existing shortcut entry.

For example, refer to Figure 11-6 and assume that Host-A Telnets to Host-B. Recognizing that Host-B is in a different subnet, Host-A sends the packets to its default gateway, subinterface 1/0.1 on the router.

Figure 11-6 *A Candidate Packet*

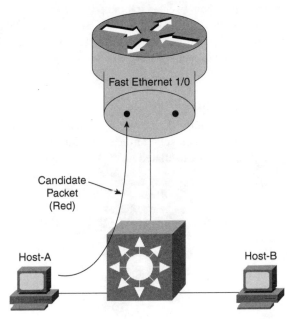

Figure 11-7 illustrates the relevant fields in this packet as it traverses the ISL link to the router.

Figure 11-7 *Candidate Packet Fields*

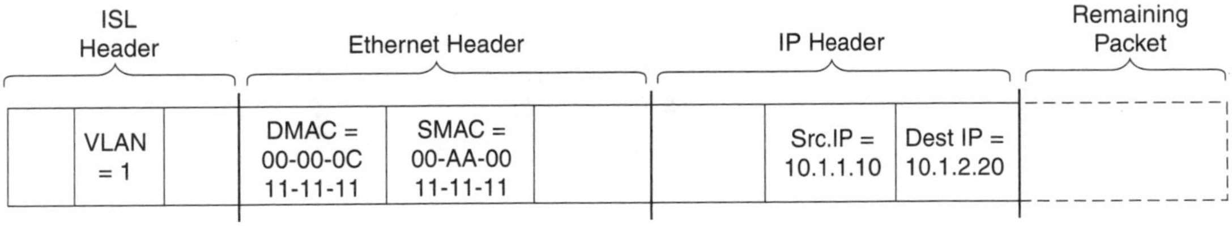

ISL Header		Ethernet Header				IP Header		Remaining Packet
VLAN = 1		DMAC = 00-00-0C 11-11-11	SMAC = 00-AA-00 11-11-11			Src.IP = 10.1.1.10	Dest IP = 10.1.2.20	

The ISL header contains a VLAN ID of 1. The Ethernet header contains a source MAC address equal to Host-A and a destination MAC address equal to 00-00-0C-11-11-11, the MAC address of subinterface 1/0.1 on the router. The source and destination IP addresses belong to Host-A and Host-B, respectively. The switch uses the destination MAC address to perform two actions:

- It forwards the packet out Port 1/1 toward the router using Layer 2 switching.

- It recognizes the MAC address destination address as one of the router's addresses learned in Step 1. This triggers a lookup for an existing Layer 3 shortcut entry based on the destination IP address (other options are available, but these are discussed later). Assuming that a shortcut does not exist (it is a new flow), the packet is flagged as a candidate packet and a partial shortcut entry is created.

Step 3: The NFFC Identifies Enable Packets

The router receives and routes the packet as normal. Recognizing the destination address as being directly connected on subinterface Fast Ethernet1/0.2, the router sends the packet back across the ISL link encapsulated in VLAN 2 as illustrated in Figure 11-8.

Figure 11-8 *An Enable Packet*

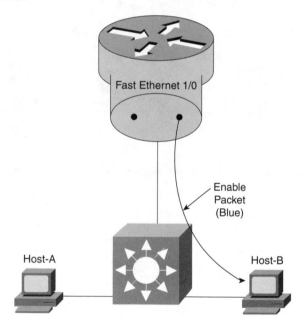

Figure 11-9 shows the relevant fields contained in the packet as it crosses the ISL link between the router and switch.

Figure 11-9 *Enable Packet Fields*

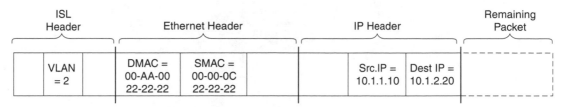

The router has rewritten the Layer 2 header. Not only has it changed the VLAN number in the ISL header, it has modified both MAC addresses. The source MAC address is now equal to 00-00-0C-22-22-22, the MAC address used on the router's Fast Ethernet1/0.2 subinterface, and the destination address is set to Host-B. Although the IP addresses have not been changed, the router must modify the IP header by decrementing the Time To Live (TTL) field and update the IP checksum.

As the packet traverses the Catalyst on its way from the router to Host-B, five functions are performed:

1 The destination MAC address is used to Layer 2 switch the packet out Port 3/1.

2 The NFFC recognizes the source MAC address as one of the entries created in Step 1 via the hello process.

3 The NFFC uses the destination IP address to look up the existing partial shortcut entry created in Step 2.

4 The NFFC compares the XTAG values associated with the source MAC address of this packet and the partial shortcut entry. Because they match, the NFFC knows that this is the enable packet coming from the same router targeted by the candidate packet.

5 The NFFC completes the shortcut entry. This entry will contain all of the information necessary to rewrite the header of future packets (in other words, the fields shown in Figure 11-9).

Step 4: The NFFC Shortcuts Future Packets

As future packets are sent by Host-A, the NFFC uses the destination IP address to look up the completed shortcut entry created in Step 3. Finding a match, it uses a rewrite engine to modify the necessary header information and then sends the packet directly to Host-B (the packet is *not* forwarded to the router). The rewrite operation modifies all of the same fields initially modified by the router for the first packet. From Host-B's perspective, it has no idea that the NFFC has intercepted the packet. Figure 11-10 illustrates this operation.

Figure 11-10 *A Shortcut Packet*

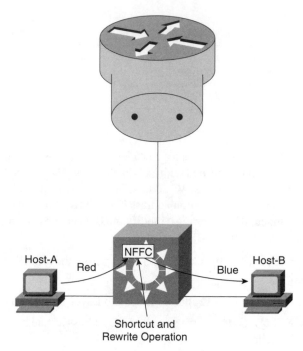

The rewrite mechanism can modify the following fields:

- Source and Destination MAC address
- VLAN ID
- TTL
- Encapsulation (for example, ARPA to SNAP)
- Checksums
- ToS/COS

NOTE   It is important to understand that, although MLS is a Cisco-specific feature, it is entirely standards compliant. Unlike some other shortcut and cut-through mechanisms, MLS makes all of the modifications that a normal router makes to an IP and IPX packet. In fact, if you were to use a protocol analyzer to capture traffic going through MLS and a normal router, you would not be able to tell the difference.

There are two options that MLS can use to rewrite the packet. In the first option, the NFFC card itself is used to rewrite the packet. The NFFC actually contains three rewrite engines, one per Catalyst 5500 bus. These rewrite engines are referred to as *central rewrite engines*. The downside of using a central rewrite engine is that it requires the packet to traverse the bus twice. For example, in Figure 11-10, the packet first arrives through Port 2/1 and is flooded across the backplane as a VLAN 1 frame. The NFFC is treated as the destination output port. After the NFFC has completed the shortcut lookup operation, it uses the rewrite information contained in the Layer 3 CAM table to update the packet appropriately. *It then sends the rewritten packet back across the bus* as a VLAN 2 frame, where the Layer 2 CAM table is used to forward it out Port 3/1. In other words, it crosses the bus first as a packet in the Red VLAN and again as a packet in the Blue VLAN. As a result, performance is limited to approximately 750,000 pps (on Catalyst 5000s).

The second rewrite option uses a feature called *inline rewrite* to optimize this flow. When using Catalyst modules that support this feature, the rewrite operation can be performed on the output module itself, allowing the packet to cross the bus a single time. Figure 11-11 illustrates the inline rewrite operation.

Figure 11-11 *Inline Rewrite*

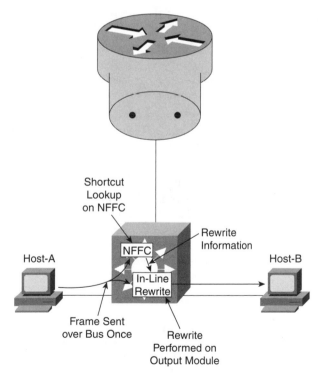

When the packet comes in from Host-A, it is flooded across the bus. All ports make a copy of the frame, including the destination Port 3/1 and the NFFC. The NFFC looks up the existing shortcut entry and sends just the rewrite information to Module 3 (this occurs on a separate bus from the data bus). Module 3 uses its local rewrite engine to modify the packet and immediately forwards it out Port 3/1. Because the frame only traversed the bus once, throughput is doubled to approximately 1,500,000 pps.

NOTE	The central rewrite versus inline rewrite issue is not a problem on the Calayst 6000 because all of its Ethernet line cards support inline rewrite.

Cache Aging

To prevent the MLS cache from overflowing, an aging process must be run. This is a software-controlled operation that runs in the background. Although the architecture of current NFFCs can theoretically hold 128,000 entries, it is recommended to keep the total number of entries below 32,000 on current versions of the card. MLS supports three separate aging times:

- Quick
- Normal
- Fast

Quick aging is utilized to age out partial shortcut entries that never get completed by an enable packet. The aging period for these entries is fixed at five seconds.

Normal aging is used for the typical sort of data transfer flow. This is a user-configurable interval that can range from 64 to 1,920 seconds with the **set mls agingtime** [*agingtime*] command. The default is 256 seconds. When changing the default value, it is rounded to the nearest multiple of 64 seconds.

Fast aging is used to age short-term data flows such as DNS, ping, and TFTP. The Fast aging time can be adjusted with the **set mls agingtime fast** [*fastagingtime*] [*pkt_threshold*] command. If the entry does not have more than *pkt_threshold* packets within *fastagingtime* seconds, the entry is removed. By default, Fast aging is not enabled because the *fastagingtimeme* parameter is set to 0. The possible *fastagingtime* values are 0, 32, 64, 96, and 128 seconds (it uses the nearest value if you enter a different value). The *pkt_threshold* parameter can be set to 0, 1, 3, 7, 15, 31, or 63 (again, you can enter other values and it uses the closest possible value).

Access Lists and Flow Masks

One of the best features of MLS is that it supports access lists. Both standard and extended output IP access lists are available. This support relies on three mechanisms:

- The assumption that if a candidate packet fails an access list, the router never sends an enable packet to complete the shortcut

- The MLSP protocol to notify the NFFC to flush all shortcut entries if the access list is modified
- A flow mask

The first mechanism handles the case where a packet is forwarded to the router and never returned to any Catalyst because it failed an access list. As a result, MLS can be a safe and effective technique.

The MLSP flush mechanism provides important integration between the router and the NFFC. If the router is configured with an access list, the MLSP protocol can be used to cause all cache entries to be flushed (forcing new entries to be processed by the access list). The flush mechanism is also used to remove cache entries after a routing table change.

The flow mask is used to set the granularity with which the NFFC determines what constitutes a flow. In all, three flow masks are possible:

- Destination flow mask
- Destination-source flow mask
- Full flow mask

A destination flow mask enables flows based on Layer 3 destination addresses only. A single shortcut is created and used for all packets headed to a specific destination IP (or IPX) address, regardless of the source node or application. This flow mask is used if no access lists are configured on the router.

A destination-source flow mask uses both the source and destination Layer 3 addresses. As a result, each pair of communicating nodes uses a unique shortcut entry. However, all of the applications flowing between each pair of nodes uses the same shortcut entry. This flow mask is used if a standard access list or a simple extended access list without port numbers is in use on the router.

A full flow mask uses Layer 4 port numbers in addition to source and destination Layer 3 addresses. This creates a separate shortcut for every application flowing between every pair of nodes. By doing so, a full flow mask provides the highest level of control and allows the NFFC to perform Layer 4 switching. Because it tracks flows at the application level, it can also be used to provide very detailed traffic statistics via NetFlow Data Export (NDE), a feature that is discussed in more detail later. The full flow mask is applied if extended access lists referencing port numbers are in use.

For example, consider the network shown in Figure 11-12.

Figure 11-12   *A Sample MLS Network*

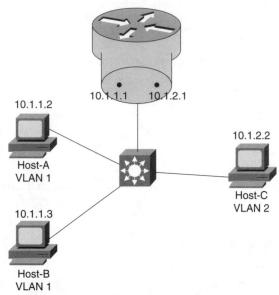

Host-A and Host-B are assigned to VLAN 1, whereas Host-C is in VLAN 2. The Catalyst and the router have been correctly configured for MLS. Example 11-5 shows the output of the **show mls entry** command when using a destination flow mask.

Example 11-5   *Sample* **show mls entry** *Output When Using a Destination Flow Mask*

```
Cat-A> (enable) show mls entry
                  Last Used       Last    Used
Destination IP  Source IP        Prot DstPrt SrcPrt Destination Mac    Vlan Port
--------------- ---------------- ---- ------ ------ ----------------- ---- -----
MLS-RP 10.1.1.1:
10.1.1.2        10.1.2.2         TCP  11000  Telnet 00-00-0c-7c-3c-90 1    2/16
10.1.1.3        10.1.2.2         ICMP -      -      00-60-3e-26-96-00 1    2/15
10.1.2.2        10.1.1.3         ICMP -      -      00-00-0c-5d-0b-f4 2    2/17
```

Because only three destination IP addresses exist between the two VLANs in this network, only three lines are displayed with a destination flow mask. Notice that all of the traffic flowing to a single destination address uses a single shortcut entry. Therefore, each line in the output only shows information on the *most recent* packet going to each destination. This fact is reflected in the column headers that use names such as Last Used Source IP.

Example 11-6 shows the same output after a destination-source flow mask has been configured.

Example 11-6 *Sample* **show mls entry** *Output When Using a Destination-Source Flow Mask*

```
Cat-A> (enable) show mls entry
                                Last    Used
Destination IP   Source IP      Prot DstPrt SrcPrt Destination Mac    Vlan Port
---------------  ---------------  ----  ------  ------  ----------------  ----  -----
MLS-RP 10.1.1.1:
10.1.1.3         10.1.2.2        ICMP -       -       00-60-3e-26-96-00 1    2/15
10.1.2.2         10.1.1.3        ICMP -       -       00-00-0c-5d-0b-f4 2    2/17
10.1.1.2         10.1.2.2        TCP  61954   Telnet  00-00-0c-7c-3c-90 1    2/16
10.1.2.2         10.1.1.2        TCP  Telnet  61954   00-00-0c-5d-0b-f4 2    2/17
```

Example 11-6 displays two lines of output for every pair of nodes that communicate through the router (one for each direction). For example, the first two lines indicate that the last packets to travel between **10.1.1.3** and **10.1.2.2** was a ping (the first line shows the flow from **10.1.1.3** to **10.1.2.2**, and the second line shows the flow in the opposite direction). The last two lines show the two sides of a Telnet session between **10.1.1.2** and **10.1.2.2** (notice how the source and destination port number numbers are swapped). Notice that traffic between **10.1.1.2** and **10.1.1.3** do not show up (this information is Layer 2 switched and does not use MLS). Also notice that the "Last Used" header only applies to the **Prot** (protocol), **DstPrt** (destination port), and **SrcPrt** (source port) fields. It no longer applies to the Source IP field because every new source addresses creates a new shortcut entry.

Finally, Example 11-7 displays sample output after configuring a full flow mask.

Example 11-7 *Sample* **show mls entry** *Output When Using a Full Flow Mask*

```
Cat-A> (enable) show mls entry
Destination IP   Source IP      Prot DstPrt SrcPrt Destination Mac    Vlan Port
---------------  ---------------  ----  ------  ------  ----------------  ----  -----
MLS-RP 10.0.1.1:
10.0.1.2         10.0.2.2        TCP  11778   69      00-00-0c-7c-3c-90 1    2/16
10.0.2.2         10.0.1.3        TCP  110     11004   00-00-0c-5d-0b-f4 2    2/17
10.0.2.2         10.0.1.2        TCP  69      11778   00-00-0c-5d-0b-f4 2    2/17
10.0.1.2         10.0.2.2        TCP  65026   SMTP    00-00-0c-7c-3c-90 1    2/16
10.0.1.3         10.0.2.2        TCP  11002   Telnet  00-60-3e-26-96-00 1    2/15
10.0.1.2         10.0.2.2        TCP  12290   110     00-00-0c-7c-3c-90 1    2/16
10.0.1.2         10.0.2.2        TCP  11266   WWW     00-00-0c-7c-3c-90 1    2/16
10.0.1.2         10.0.2.2        TCP  64514   FTP     00-00-0c-7c-3c-90 1    2/16
10.0.2.2         10.0.1.2        TCP  FTP     64514   00-00-0c-5d-0b-f4 2    2/17
10.0.2.2         10.0.1.3        TCP  69      11005   00-00-0c-5d-0b-f4 2    2/17
10.0.2.2         10.0.1.2        TCP  WWW     63490   00-00-0c-5d-0b-f4 2    2/17
10.0.2.2         10.0.1.3        TCP  9       11001   00-00-0c-5d-0b-f4 2    2/17
10.0.2.2         10.0.1.3        ICMP -       -       00-00-0c-5d-0b-f4 2    2/17
10.0.1.2         10.0.2.2        TCP  62978   9       00-00-0c-7c-3c-90 1    2/16
10.0.1.2         10.0.2.2        TCP  64002   20      00-00-0c-7c-3c-90 1    2/16
10.0.2.2         10.0.1.2        TCP  Telnet  62466   00-00-0c-5d-0b-f4 2    2/17
10.0.1.2         10.0.2.2        TCP  63490   WWW     00-00-0c-7c-3c-90 1    2/16
10.0.1.2         10.0.2.2        TCP  62466   Telnet  00-00-0c-7c-3c-90 1    2/16
```

continues

Example 11-7 *Sample* **show mls entry** *Output When Using a Full Flow Mask (Continued)*

```
10.0.2.2       10.0.1.3       TCP  Telnet 11002  00-00-0c-5d-0b-f4 2   2/17
10.0.2.2       10.0.1.2       TCP  WWW    11266  00-00-0c-5d-0b-f4 2   2/17
10.0.1.3       10.0.2.2       TCP  11004  110    00-60-3e-26-96-00 1   2/15
10.0.2.2       10.0.1.2       TCP  SMTP   65026  00-00-0c-5d-0b-f4 2   2/17
10.0.1.3       10.0.2.2       TCP  11005  69     00-60-3e-26-96-00 1   2/15
10.0.2.2       10.0.1.2       TCP  110    12290  00-00-0c-5d-0b-f4 2   2/17
10.0.2.2       10.0.1.3       TCP  WWW    11003  00-00-0c-5d-0b-f4 2   2/17
10.0.1.3       10.0.2.2       TCP  11003  WWW    00-60-3e-26-96-00 1   2/15
10.0.2.2       10.0.1.2       TCP  20     64002  00-00-0c-5d-0b-f4 2   2/17
10.0.1.3       10.0.2.2       ICMP -      -      00-60-3e-26-96-00 1   2/15
10.0.1.3       10.0.2.2       TCP  11001  9      00-60-3e-26-96-00 1   2/15
10.0.2.2       10.0.1.2       TCP  9      62978  00-00-0c-5d-0b-f4 2   2/17
```

Notice that Example 11-7 includes every pair of communicating *applications* (both IP addresses and port numbers are considered). Also notice that none of the fields include a Last Used header because all of the individual flows are fully accounted for.

The multiple flow masks allow the NFFC to track information at a sufficient level of granularity to ensure that denied packets do not slip through using a pre-existing shortcut entry. However, to be truly secure, input access lists need to process every packet. As a result, configuring an input access on the router disables MLS on that interface. However, an optional parameter was introduced in 12.0 IOS images to allow input access lists at the expense of some security risk. To enable this feature, specify the **input-acl** parameter on the end of the **mls rp ip** global router command (Step 1 in the five-step router configuration process discussed later).

TIP	The **mls rp ip input-acl** command can be used to enable input access lists at the expense of some fairly minor security risks.

If multiple routers are in use with different flow masks, all MLS-capable Catalysts use the most granular (longest) flow mask. In other words, if there are two routers without access lists and a third router with a standard access list, the destination-source flow mask is used.

If you are not using access lists but you want to use a source-destination or full flow mask, you can use the **set mls {flow destination | destination-source | full}** command to set a minimum flow mask. For example, by forcing the flow mask to full, you can collect detailed traffic statistics (see the "Using MLS" section).

Configuring MLS

Although the theory behind MLS is somewhat involved, it is fairly easy to configure. To fully implement MLS, you must separately configure the router and the Catalyst Supervisor.

MLS Router Configuration

To configure a Cisco router for MLS, use the following five-step process:

Step 1   Globally enable MLS on the router. To do this, use the **mls rp ip** command. This command must be entered from the global configuration mode (in other words, not on a particular interface or subinterface).

Step 2   Configure a VLAN Trunking Protocol (VTP) domain for each interface using the **mls rp vtp-domain** *domain_name* command. This is an interface configuration command. For ISL interfaces, it can only be entered on the major interface (all of the subinterfaces inherit the same VTP domain name). The **vtp-domain** command should be entered prior to completing the remaining steps. However, if no VTP domain has been assigned to the switches in your network, this step can be skipped.

Step 3   If a non-trunk interface is used on an external router, the **mls rp vlan-id** *vlan_number* command must be used to tell the router about VLAN assignments. This command must be entered before the remaining steps can be completed. On an ISL interface, this command is not required because the **encap isl** *vlan_number* command performs the same function. In the case of an RSM, this command is also not required because the RSM automatically receives VLAN information.

Step 4   Enable each MLS interface using the **mls rp ip** command. This is an interface or subinterface configuration command.

Step 5   Select one or more router interfaces to send MLSP packets using the **mls rp management-interface** command. Again, this is an interface or subinterface command. In general, you only enter it on a single interface. Choose an interface connected to a VLAN that reaches all of the MLS-capable Catalysts in your network. If the command is not entered at all, no MLSP packets are sent, preventing MLS from functioning.

TIP   If no VTP domain has been specified on the Catalysts (check this with **show vtp domain**), you do not need to set one on the router (in other words, the Null domain is used). If you use the **mls rp ip** or **mls rp management-interface** commands before specifying a VTP domain, the interface is automatically assigned to the Null domain. To change the domain name to something else, *you need to remove all* **mls rp** *commands from that interface and start reconfiguring it from scratch* (current versions automatically remove the **mls rp** commands when you enter **no mls rp vtp-domain** *domain_name*).

Example 11-8 illustrates a router MLS configuration that is appropriate for the example presented in Figures 11-4 through Figure 11-11.

Example 11-8 *External Router MLS Configuration*

```
mls rp ip
!
interface FastEthernet1/0
 mls rp vtp-domain Skinner
!
interface FastEthernet1/0.1
 ip address 10.1.1.1 255.255.255.0
 mls rp management-interface
 mls rp ip
!
interface FastEthernet1/0.2
 ip address 10.1.2.1 255.255.255.0
 mls rp ip
```

The corresponding RSM configuration appears as in Example 11-9.

Example 11-9 *RSM Router MLS Configuration*

```
mls rp ip
!
interface Vlan1
 ip address 10.1.1.1 255.255.255.0
 mls rp vtp-domain Skinner
 mls rp management-interface
 mls rp ip
!
interface Vlan2
 ip address 10.1.2.1 255.255.255.0
 mls rp vtp-domain Skinner
 mls rp ip
```

And finally, the same configuration running on a router using two Ethernet ports looks like Example 11-10.

Example 11-10   *External Router MLS Configuration for Multiple Ethernet   rts*

```
mls rp ip
!
interface Ethernet0
 ip address 10.1.1.1 255.255.255.0
 mls rp vtp-domain Skinner
 mls rp vlan-id 1
 mls rp management-interface
 mls rp ip
!
interface Ethernet1
 ip address 10.1.2.1 255.255.255.0
 mls rp vtp-domain Skinner
 mls rp vlan-id 2
 mls rp ip
```

MLS Switch Configuration

The switch configuration is considerably more straightforward. In fact, if you are using MLS in conjunction with an RSM that is located in the same chassis, no configuration is necessary on the Catalyst Supervisor. However, you must specify each MLS-capable router when using external routers. To do this, use the **set mls include** {*route_processor_ip* | *route_processor_name*} command. For example, to include an external router using the IP address **10.1.1.1**, you should enter **set mls include 10.1.1.1**. Only include the IP address associated with the first MLS interface on the router.

TIP   The address to include is displayed on the **mls ip address** field of the **show mls rp** router command. Be sure to enter **show mls rp** on the router, not the Catalyst Supervisor.

The switch supports a **set mls [enable | disable]**. However, because MLS is enabled by default (given that you have the proper hardware and software), this command is not necessary.

Using MLS

Because the routing switch form of Layer 3 switching is a fairly new technique to most network administrators, this section takes a look at some of the more important MLS commands.

The **show mls** Command

One of the most important commands is the **show mls** Catalyst command. Several options are available for this command. In its basic form, **show mls** displays output similar to that included in Example 11-11.

Example 11-11 *Output of* **show mls** *on the Catalyst Supervisor*

```
Cat-A> (enable) show mls
Multilayer switching enabled
Multilayer switching aging time = 256 seconds
Multilayer switching fast aging time = 0 seconds, packet threshold = 0
Current flow mask is Destination flow
Configured flow mask is Destination flow
Total packets switched = 0
Active shortcuts = 0
Netflow Data Export disabled
Netflow Data Export port/host is not configured.
Total packets exported = 0


MLS-RP IP        MLS-RP ID      XTAG MLS-RP MAC-Vlans
---------------  ------------   ---- --------------------------------
10.1.1.1         00000c111111     2 00-00-0c-11-11-11  1
                                    00-00-0c-22-22-22  2
```

The first three lines after the initial prompt tell you if MLS is enabled on this Catalyst and the configured aging timers. The next two lines indicate the flow mask currently in use and if a minimum flow mask has been configured. The **Total packets switched** and **Active shortcuts** lines can be very useful for keeping track of the amount of shortcut switching being performed and the size of your shortcut cache (as mentioned earlier, it is best to keep this value below 32,000 entries or current versions of the NFFC). The next three lines report the status of NetFlow Data Export, a feature that is discussed later. The bottom section lists all of the known routers, their XTAG values, and a list of the MAC addresses and VLANs.

The **show mls entry** Command

The **show mls entry** command is very useful when you want to examine the shortcut cache entries. Example 11-12 shows some sample output for the **show mls entry** command.

Example 11-12 *Output of* **show mls entry**

```
Cat-A> (enable) sh mls entry
                    Last Used       Last   Used
Destination IP  Source IP        Prot DstPrt SrcPrt Destination Mac   Vlan Port
--------------  ---------------  ---- ------ ------ ----------------  ---- -----
MLS-RP 10.1.1.1:
10.1.1.9        10.1.2.99        TCP  1293   5001   00-60-08-b6-49-84 1    3/9
10.1.1.7        10.1.2.99        ICMP -      -      00-60-08-b6-4a-49 1    3/13
10.1.2.99       10.1.1.7         ICMP -      -      00-10-7b-3a-7b-97 2    3/18
```

Because the flow mask is set to destination, the cache only creates a single entry per destination address. Each cache entry is shown on a separate line. The Last Used Source IP, Protocol, Destination Port, and Source Port Fields show the characteristics of the packet that most recently used this shortcut entry. Because a single entry exists for all source nodes, protocols, and applications targeted to the destination address listed in the first column, it cannot list every type of packet individually (use a full flow mask for that level of detail).

If your cache is large, you probably want to use one of the options to filter the output. The full syntax for the **show mls entry** command is:

```
show mls entry {[destination ip_addr_spec] [source ip_addr_spec] | [flow  protocol
[ccc] src_port dst_port]} [rp ip_addr]
```

For example, **show mls entry rp 10.1.1.1** lists all of the cache entries created from router **10.1.1.1**. **show mls entry destination 10.1.2.20** lists the entries created for packets containing a destination IP address of **10.1.2.20**.

The **show mls statistics entry** Command

Packet and byte counts for each entry can be listed with **show mls statistics entry**. The output is similar to that of **show mls entry** except it includes two new fields at the end of each line as shown in Example 11-13.

Example 11-13 *Output of* **show mls statistics entry**

```
Cat-A> (enable) show mls statistics entry
Destination IP  Source IP        Prot DstPrt SrcPrt Stat-Pkts  Stat-Bytes
--------------- ---------------  ---- ------ ------ ---------- ---------------

MLS-RP 10.1.1.1:
10.1.2.99       10.1.1.7         ICMP -      -      6          456
10.1.1.9        10.1.2.99        ICMP -      -      8          824
10.1.1.7        10.1.2.99        TCP  1037   Telnet 11         802
```

The **show mls statistics protocol** Command

If you are using a full flow mask, the **show mls statistics protocol** command can provide extremely useful application layer information such as that displayed in Example 11-14.

Example 11-14 *Output of* **show mls statistics protocol**

```
Cat-A> (enable) show mls statistics protocol
Protocol    TotalFlows  TotalPackets  TotalBytes
----------  ----------  ------------  ---------------
Telnet      6                     24          1641
FTP         2                      6           390
WWW         8                     30          5219
SMTP        2                      6           390
X           0                      0             0
DNS         2                      6           390
Others      12                 11543       9093664
Total       32                 11615       9101694
```

This information is very similar to the output of the **show ip cache flow** router command. By listing traffic volumes by both packet and byte counts, it can be very useful for profiling your network.

The **debug mls rp** Command

On the router, **debug mls rp** commands can be used to troubleshoot various issues. Example 11-15 displays the available options.

Example 11-15 *Available Options for the* **debug mls rp** *Command*

```
Router# debug mls rp ?
  all               mls all
  error             mls errors
  events            mls events
  ip                mls ip events
  locator           mls locator
  packets           mls packets
  verbose packets   mls verbose packets
```

As always, you should be very careful when using **debug** on production networks.

MLS Design Considerations

As discussed earlier, MLS can be characterized as a mechanism that caches "to the router and back" flows. Although this is a simple concept, it can be tricky to achieve in certain topologies and networks.

TIP

Note in advance that almost all of the issues discussed in this section can be avoided by simply making sure that every NFFC is paired with its own "internal router" such as the RSM (or RSFC). Because this automatically creates a "to the router and back" set of flows (across the blackplane of the Catalyst), it can dramatically simply your overall design considerations.

WAN Links

For example, MLS currently cannot be used on WAN links. Consider the network illustrated in Figure 11-13.

Figure 11-13 *WAN Flows Defeat MLS*

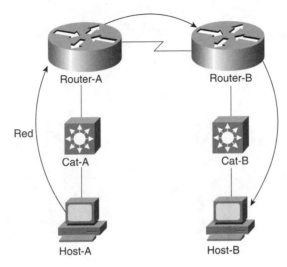

As with the earlier examples, Host-A is sending packets to Host-B. Recognizing that Host-B is on a different subnet, Host-A forwards all of the traffic to its default gateway, Router-A. The NFFC in Cat-A recognizes the first packet as a candidate packet and creates a partial shortcut entry. However, an enable packet is never received by Cat-A because the traffic is forwarded directly out the router's serial interface. The to the router and back flow necessary for MLS is not present. Because the shortcut entry is never completed, it ages out using the five-second quick aging scheme.

Using Multiple Router Ports

Although it is fairly obvious why MLS is not suitable for situations such as Figure 11-13, other situations can be far more subtle. The rule to remember is that *the same NFFC must see the flow traveling to and from the router.* For this to happen, the Catalyst performing MLS needs to participate in both VLANs/subnets. For example, the Catalysts shown in Figure 11-14 only contain a single VLAN.

Figure 11-14 *Each Catalyst Contains Only a Single VLAN*

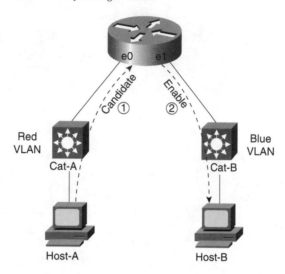

The results in Figure 11-14 are very similar to those in Figure 11-13. Cat-A sees the candidate packet, but only Cat-B sees the enable packet. Shortcut switching is not possible.

<table>
<tr><td>**TIP**</td><td>MLS requires that the same NFFC or MSFC/PFC must see the flow traveling to and from the router. This can require careful planning and design work in certain situations.</td></tr>
</table>

However, simply placing both VLANs on both switches does not necessarily solve the problem. In Figure 11-15, both Cat-A and Cat-B contain the Red and Blue VLANs. An ISL trunk has even been provided to create a contiguous set of Layer 2 bridge domains.

Figure 11-15 *Although Both Switches Contain Both VLANs, MLS Is Not Possible*

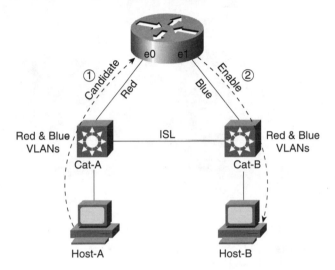

However, because non-trunk links are used to connect the router, the router only sends and receives traffic for the Red VLAN to/from Cat-A, whereas all Blue traffic flows to/from Cat-B. The effect of this is the same as in the previous two examples: Cat-A only sees the candidate packet because the enable packet is sent to Cat-B.

A Solution for Using Multiple Router Ports

Although several alternatives are available to fix this configuration, the simplest option involves connecting the router to a single Catalyst. At this point, the one-link-per-VLAN or the trunk-connected router designs are appropriate. For example, Figure 11-16 simply swings the interface Ethernet1 router link from Cat-B to Cat-A to employ the one-link-per-VLAN design.

Figure 11-16 *Connecting the Router to a Single Catalyst Permits MLS*

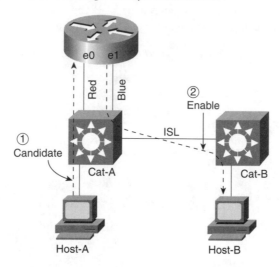

As shown in Figure 11-16, this forces all inter-VLAN traffic to flow through Cat-A and, therefore, makes shortcut switching possible.

The Spanning-Tree Protocol and MLS

But what if additional switches are added so that additional Layer 2 loops are introduced? For example, consider the network shown in Figure 11-17 (assume all three Catalysts are MLS-capable and the router is connected via an ISL link).

Figure 11-17 *A More Complex Network Using MLS*

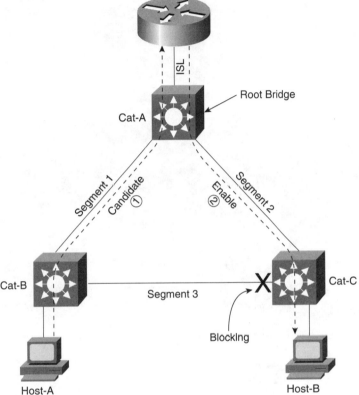

Because this is a redundant (that is, looped) Layer 2 topology, the Spanning-Tree Protocol becomes involved. Figure 11-17 assumes that Cat-A is functioning as the Root Bridge for all VLANs. This places one of the ports on Segment 3 in the Spanning Tree Blocking state. As a result, traffic flowing in the Red VLAN from Host-A to the router uses Segment 1. Both Cat-B and Cat-A recognize this as a candidate packet and create a partial shortcut entry. However, because traffic flowing from the router to Host-B uses Segment 2, only Cat-A sees the enable packet and creates a full shortcut entry. Cat-B's partial shortcut entry ages out in five seconds.

Consider what happens if Cat-B becomes the Spanning Tree Root Bridge. Figure 11-18 provides a diagram for this situation.

Figure 11-18 *Cat-B Is the Spanning Tree Root Bridge*

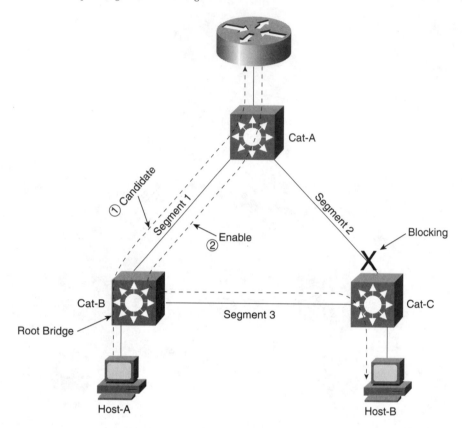

This causes Spanning Tree to reconverge to a logical topology where one of the ports on Segment 2 is Blocking. This allows the traffic from Host-A to the router to follow the same path as in Figure 11-17. Both Cat-A and Cat-B recognize the first packet as a candidate packet and create a partial shortcut entry. However, the traffic flowing from the router to Host-B cannot use Segment 2 because it is blocked. Instead, the traffic flows back through Cat-B and uses Segment 1 and Segment 3. Notice that this causes both Cat-A and Cat-B to see the Enable Packet and complete the shortcut entry.

When the second packet is sent from Host-A to Host-B, Cat-B uses its shortcut entry to Layer 3 switch the packet directly onto Segment 3, bypassing the router. Because Cat-A does not see any traffic for the shortcut entry it created, the entry ages out in 256 seconds by default. Although this *allows* MLS to function (in fact, it creates a more efficient flow in this case), it can be disconcerting to see the shortcut switching operation move from Cat-A to Cat-B only because of Spanning Tree. Obviously, the interaction between MLS and

Spanning Tree can get very complex in large and very flat campus networks (yet one more reason to avoid the flat earth approach to campus design; see Chapters 14 and 15 for more information).

Using MLS on a Subset of Your Switches

Figures 11-17 and 11-18 assumed that all three Catalysts supported MLS. Subtleties can also arise if this is not the case. For example, what if Cat-A did not support MLS? In Figure 11-17, MLS would not be possible. Because Cat-A was the only switch to see both sides of the flow, it is the only device capable of performing MLS in this topology. However, MLS *is* possible in Figure 11-18, even if Cat-A is not MLS capable. Because of the Spanning Tree reconvergence performed in Figure 11-18, Cat-B now sees both sides of the flow and can perform shortcut switching in the same manner as already explained.

Using Stacks of MLS Devices

This section considers the case where stacks of MLS-capable devices connect multiple end stations and Catalysts as shown in Figure 11-19.

Figure 11-19 *Host-A Communicating with Host-B via MLS*

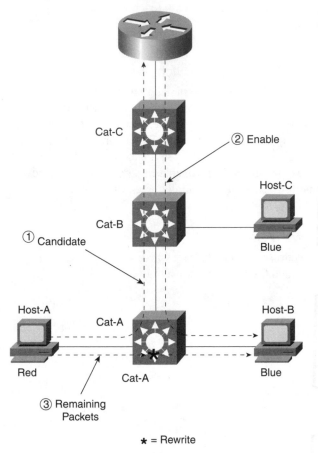

★ = Rewrite

First, look at the case of Host-A sending traffic to Host-B. The traffic from Host-A to the router travels up the ISL links connecting the Catalysts and the router to each other. As the first packet hits the NFFC in each Catalyst, it is recognized as a candidate packet and three partial shortcut entries are created (one per Catalyst). As the packet travels back down from the router to reach Host-B, all three NFFC cards see the enable packet and complete the shortcut entries. However, as additional packets travel from Host-A to Host-B, Cat-A shortcut switches them directly to Host-B. The shortcut entries in Cat-B and Cat-C simply age out in 256 seconds (by default).

Now consider the flow from Host-A to Host-C. Again, all three NFFCs see the initial packet as a candidate packet. However, the return packet only passes through Cat-C and Cat-B. The partial shortcut entry in Cat-A ages out in five seconds. As Host-A sends additional packets, Cat-A uses normal Layer 2 switching to send the packets towards the MAC address of the router. When Cat-B receives the packets, it recognizes that it has a completed shortcut for this flow and shortcut switches the packets directly to Host-C. Cat-C's shortcut entry is not used and therefore ages out in 256 seconds. Figure 11-20 illustrates this sequence.

Figure 11-20 *Host-A Communicating with Host-C via MLS*

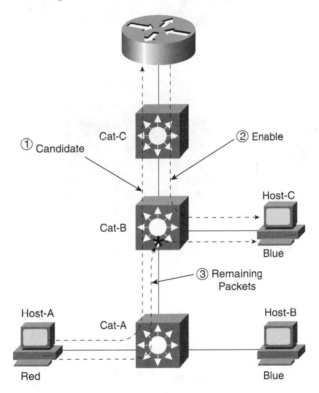

★ = Rewrite

Using Multiple Routers with a Single MLS-Capable Catalyst

Finally, consider the case of multiple MLS-capable routers and a single MLS switch shown in Figure 11-21.

Figure 11-21 *Two MLS Routers and One MLS Switch*

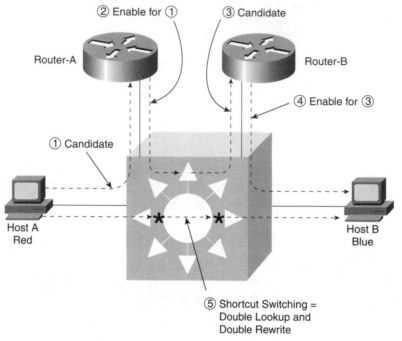

Here, Host-A is still located in the Red VLAN and Host-B is still located in the Blue VLAN. However, a new VLAN has been created between the two routers (call it the Purple VLAN). Host-A still sends traffic destined to Host-B to its default gateway using the Red VLAN. As the first packet passes through the Catalyst, the NFFC recognizes it as a candidate packet and creates a partial shortcut entry (labeled Step 1 in Figure 11-21). Router-A then forwards the traffic over the Purple VLAN to Router-B. As the packet passes back through the Catalyst, the NFFC recognizes the packet as an enable packet and completes the shortcut entry (Step 2 in Figure 11-21). However, it also recognizes the destination MAC address as that of Router-B and therefore sees this packet as another candidate packet (Step 3 in Figure 11-21). Router-B then routes the packet normally and forwards it to Host-B over the Blue VLAN. As the packet passes back through the Catalyst for the third time, it is identified as an enable packet for the partial entry created in Step 3. A second shortcut entry is created (Step 4 Figure 11-21).

When additional traffic flows from Host-A to Host-B (Step 5 in Figure 11-21), two sets of shortcut lookups and rewrite operations are performed. As a result, the additional packets are not sent to either router. Neat!

Other MLS Capabilities

One of the nicest things about using the NFFC for MLS is that it enables many other applications that extend beyond accelerated Layer 3 routing. Because the NFFC is at its most basic level a pattern-matching engine, these pattern-matching capabilities can be used to provide many interesting and powerful features as detailed in the following sections.

Protocol Filtering

Protocol Filtering is the capability of the NFFC to limit broadcast and multicast traffic on a per-port and per-protocol basis. As discussed in Chapter 5, "VLANs," it allows a group of nodes to be placed in a single VLAN and only receive traffic associated with the protocols they are actually running. Four groupings of protocols exist: IP, IPX, a combined group of AppleTalk and DECnet (some platforms also include VINES here), and a final group that contains all other protocols. By pattern matching on the protocol type information contained in the Layer 2 header, the NFFC can, for example, filter IPX SAPs on ports that are only using IP.

Protocol Filtering is disabled by default. To enable this feature, use the **set protocolfilter enable** command. To configure Protocol Filtering, use the **set port protocol** command:

```
set port protocol mod_num/port_num {ip|ipx|group} {on|off|auto}
```

The **group** parameter corresponds to AppleTalk and DECnet (and, in some cases, VINES). The **on** state forces that port to send broadcasts of the specified type. The **off** state forces that port to not send broadcasts of the specified type. The **auto** state only send broadcasts for the specified protocol if that protocol is detected coming in that port. This creates a dynamic configuration where the Catalyst is detecting the protocols being run on each port and only sending the appropriate broadcasts in response. IP defaults to the **on** state, and the other protocol categories (IPX and "group") default to **auto**.

The **show protocolfilter** command can be used to determine if Protocol Filtering is running on a device. The **show port protocol** command can be used to view the configuration on a per-port basis (including the number of nodes detected on a per port and per protocol basis). For ports and protocols in the **auto** state, **auto-on** and **auto-off** are used to indicate the dynamically selected setting currently in use. Trunk ports are excluded from Protocol Filtering.

Multicast Switching and IGMP Snooping

Traditional transparent bridges (and, therefore, most Layer 2 switches) do not have a mechanism to learn multicast MAC address. As a result, these Layer 2 bridging and switching devices treat multicast frames as if they were broadcast frames. Although this does allow multicast applications to function, it has the highly undesirable side effect of wasting lots of bandwidth (it can also waste CPU cycles on end stations).

One solution to this problem is the use of static CAM entries. However, given the growing popularity of multicast usage, this can rapidly become a huge management problem. For example, every time a user wants to join or leave a multicast group, it requires manual intervention by the network administrators. In a large network, this can easily amount to hundreds of entries and adjustments per day.

Clearly some sort of dynamic process is required. Three options are available for dynamically building multicast forwarding tables: CGMP, GMRP, and IGMP Snooping. This section briefly discusses these three options, especially as they pertain to the NFFC. For a more thorough discussion, please see Chapter 13.

Of these techniques, Cisco developed the Cisco Group Management Protocol (CGMP) first. This allows routers running the Internet Group Management Protocol (IGMP) to update the Catalyst Layer 2 CAM table. IGMP is a protocol that allows end stations to request that routers send them a copy of certain multicast streams. However, because it is a Layer 3 protocol, it is difficult for a Layer 2 switch to speak this protocol. Therefore, Cisco developed CGMP. Think of it as a mechanism that allows a Layer 3 router to tell a Layer 2 Catalyst about multicast group membership. As a result, the Layer 2 Catalyst forwards IP multicast traffic only to end-station ports that are actually interested.

Configuring CGMP on a Catalyst is simple. It runs by default on most Catalysts, requiring no configuration whatsoever. Other Catalysts, such as the 5000, require the **set cgmp enable** command. The **show multicast group cgmp** command can be used to display the multicast MAC address to port mappings created via the CGMP protocol. To configure CGMP on the router, the **ip cgmp** command must be configured on the interfaces where CGMP support is desired. In addition, some sort of multicast routing protocol must be configured (PIM dense-mode is the simplest option).

In the future, the GARP Multicast Registration Protocol (GMRP) might become a commonly used approach. GMRP uses the Generic Attributed Registration Protocol (GARP) specified in 802.1p to provide registration services for multicast MAC addresses. However, because work is still ongoing in the development of GMRP, this is not a suitable option today.

The third option, IGMP Snooping, is a standards-based alternative to the Cisco Group Management Protocol (CGMP). This relies on the pattern-matching capabilities of the NFFC to listen for IGMP packets as they flow between the router and the end stations. By inspecting these packets, the Catalyst can learn which ports have end stations interested in which multicast groups.

Some vendors have implemented IGMP Snooping using general-purpose CPUs. However, without some sort of hardware-based support, this approach suffers from extreme scaling problems. This situation arises because IGMP messages are intermixed with data in literally every multicast flow in the network. In short, vendors cannot simply point a single IGMP multicast MAC address at the CPU. Instead, the switch must sort through every packet of every multicast stream looking for and processing IGMP packets. Do not try this on a general-purpose CPU!

NOTE   This also suggests that IGMP is not a replacement for CGMP. IGMP is suitable for high-end devices that contain ASIC-based pattern-matching capabilities. However, low-end devices without this support still require the services of CGMP. In fact, many multicast networks require both.

The good news is that IGMP Snooping is extremely easy to configure. Because IGMP Snooping is a passive listening process much like **routed** running in quiet mode on a UNIX box, no configuration is required on the router (although it still needs to be running a multicast routing protocol). On the Catalyst, simply enter the **sct igmp cnable** command. Use the **show multicast group igmp** command to display the list of multicast MAC address to port mappings created via the IGMP Snooping process.

Quality of Service

Although the initial version of the NFFC (NFFC I) did not support Quality of Service (QoS) and Class of Service (COS), more recent versions (NFFC II and MSFC/PFC) have included this feature. This capability is targeted at being able to reclassify traffic in the wiring closet at the edge of the network. This can allow mission critical traffic to be flagged as such using Layer 3 IP Type of Service (ToS) bits or Layer 2 capabilities such as 802.1p and ISL (the ISL header contains 3 bits for COS). Devices that support sophisticated queuing and scheduling algorithms such as the Catalyst 8500 can then act on these QoS/COS fields to provide differentiated service levels. Because these capabilities are still evolving at the time this book goes to press, they are not discussed here.

NetFlow Data Export

Just as MLS **show** commands such as **show mls entry** and **show mls statistics protocol** provide incredibly detailed information on protocol flows in the network, this information can be captured on an ongoing basis with NetFlow Data Export (NDE). NDE ships information on each flow to a NetFlow collection device (such as Cisco's NetFlow FlowCollector). These collection stations then massage the data to eliminate duplicate information (a single flow could have traversed and therefore been reported by several devices) and output information such as reports and billing information. First enable NDE with **set mls nde enable**. Then specify the IP address and port number of the collector station with **set mls nde** {*collector_address | collector_name*} *port_number*.

TIP   The **set mls nde flow** command can be used to filter the amount of information collected by NDE. For example, **set mls nde flow destination 10.1.1.1/32 source 10.1.1.2/32** collects information flowing only from **10.1.1.2** to **10.1.1.1**.

When to Use MLS

MLS's hardware-assisted approach to routing can be very useful when the RSM and router-on-a-stick techniques do not have enough capacity. In fact, one of the most appealing benefits to MLS is that it can be easily added to an existing network to turbocharge the routing performance. Therefore, the most common argument for using MLS is throughput. The additional capabilities of the NFFC to handle tasks such as Protocol Filtering, IGMP Snooping, NetFlow data collection, and QoS can make MLS an even more attractive option than simply using it for go fast routing. However, to fully discuss the pros and cons of MLS, 8500-style routing must be considered.

Switching Routers

Whereas MLS relies on hardware-based caching to perform shortcut switching, the Catalyst 8500 relies on hardware to perform the same tasks as a traditional router, only faster. To accomplish the extremely high throughput required in modern campus backbones, the 8500s split routing tasks into two functional groups. The job of running routing protocols such as OSPF and EIGRP for purposes of topology discovery and path determination are handled by a general-purpose, RISC-based CPU (these are often referred to as "control plane" activities). The job of doing routing table lookups and data forwarding is handled by high-speed ASICs (this if often called the "data plane"). Combined, these create a very fast but feature-rich and flexible platform.

NOTE   The "*Native IOS Mode*" of the Catalyst 6000 can also be used to implement the "switching router" style of Layer 3 switching. This will be discussed later in this chapter, as well as in Chapter 18.

In the case of the Catalyst 8510, Cisco's first switching router targeted at the campus market, the routing functions are performed by a Switch Route Processor (SRP). From a hardware perspective, the SRP is essentially the same as the ATM Switch Processor (ASP) from a Lightstream 1010 ATM switch. However, rather than running ATM routing protocols such as PNNI, the SRP is used to run datagram routing protocols such as RIP and OSPF.

After the routing protocol has been used to build a routing table, the CPU uses this information to create what is called a Cisco Express Forwarding (CEF) table. Just as the routing table lists all of the possible locations this router can deliver packets to, the CEF table contains an entry indicating how to reach every known location in the network. However, unlike a routing table, which is limited to very basic information such as destination route, next hop, and routing metric, the CEF table can be used to store a variety of information that pertains to features such as Queuing and QoS/COS. Furthermore, because it is stored in a format that provides extremely efficient longest-match lookups, it is very fast. CEF fulfills the competing goals of speed and functionality and represents an important step forward in routing technology. Cisco has been using CEF with great success in their high-end, Internet-oriented routing platforms since 1997 and has introduced it to the entire line of routers starting in IOS 12.0.

Although the basic concept of CEF is available throughout Cisco's product line, the 8510 introduced a new use of this technology. The CPU located on the SRP is used to create the CEF table, but it is not used to make forwarding decisions. Instead, the CPU downloads a copy of the CEF table to every line card. The line cards then contain ASICs that perform the actual CEF lookups at wire-rate speeds. From the point of view of the ingress port on the 8510, it has a bunch of ATM-like virtual circuits that connect it to every other port in the box (there are multiple virtual circuits [VCs] between all of the ports to facilitate QoS). You can think of these VCs as tubes that the input port can use to send data to each output port. If you then think of the incoming data as marbles, each input port simply uses the CEF to determine which marble gets dropped in which tube. The result is a mechanism that builds an efficient and flexible forwarding table centrally using a general-purpose CPU, but uses a distributed set of high-speed ASICs to handle the resource intensive process of determining how to move frames through the box. When this is combined with the fact that 8500 switches are based on ATM technology internally and therefore support sophisticated QoS mechanisms, the benefits of CEF become extremely compelling.

The 8540, Cisco's next switching router, uses the same technique but with different hardware. The primary differences are a new set of control and line cards and a larger chassis that supports more interfaces and a higher-speed backplane/fabric (because the 8500s use ATM technology internally, they have more of a fabric than a backplane). In the 8540, the single SRP of the 8510 has been split into the Route Processor (RP) and the Switch Processor (SP). The RP handles functions such as running routing protocols and building the CEF tables (control plane). The line cards still contain ASICs that use a local copy of the CEF table to make forwarding decisions (data plane). However, to move data across the backplane/fabric, the line cards must use the services of the SP.

In most respects, another advantage to the 8500's approach to Layer 3 switching is that the CPU runs the full IOS. Not only does this result in a more mature implementation of routing protocols and other features, it makes configuration a breeze for anyone familiar with Cisco's traditional router platform. Simply perform the normal **conf t**, **int fa X/X/X**, and **router ospf 1** sequence of commands and you are ready to roll in most situations. For example, consider the network illustrated in Figure 11-22.

Figure 11-22 *A Sample Catalyst 8500 Network*

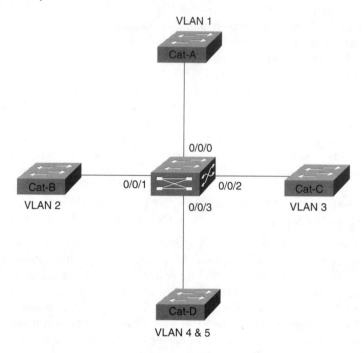

Cat-A, Cat-B, Cat-C, and Cat-D are Catalyst 5000 devices performing the usual Layer 2 switching. Each of these has a single VLAN except Cat-D which has two VLANs. All of the Catalyst 5000s are connected to a central 8500 for Layer 3 routing services. Example 11-16 shows a possible configuration for the 8500.

Example 11-16 *Sample Catalyst 8500 Series Configuration*

```
ipx routing 0000.0000.1001
!
interface FastEthernet0/0/0
 description VLAN 1
 ip address 10.1.1.1 255.255.255.0
!
interface FastEthernet0/0/1
 description VLAN 2
 ip address 10.1.2.1 255.255.255.0
 ipx network 2
!
interface FastEthernet0/0/2
 description VLAN 3
 ip address 10.1.3.1 255.255.255.0
 ipx encapsulation ARPA
 ipx network 3
!
interface FastEthernet0/0/3
 no ip address
!
interface FastEthernet0/0/3.4
 description VLAN 4
 encapsulation isl 4
 ip address 10.1.4.1 255.255.255.0
 ipx network 4
!
interface FastEthernet0/0/3.5
 description VLAN 5
 encapsulation isl 5
 ip address 10.1.5.1 255.255.255.0
 ipx network 5
!
router eigrp 1
 network 10.0.0.0
```

All VLANs are configured for both IP and IPX traffic except VLAN 1 which is only using IP. All of the IPX interfaces are using the default Ethernet encapsulation of **novell_ether** except Fast Ethernet0/0/2 which is using **ARPA** (DIX V2). Also, because Cat-D is using two VLANs, Fast Ethernet0/0/3 is configured for ISL. As with the ISL router-on-a-stick examples earlier, each VLAN is configured on a separate subinterface.

TIP   The **show vlan** command on the 8500 can be very useful for getting a quick overview of which VLANs have been configured on which ports.

EtherChannel

One feature that deserves special mention is EtherChannel. The 8500s support both Fast and Gigabit EtherChannel. When configuring EtherChannel on any Cisco router (including the 8500s), the configuration centers around a virtual interface known as the *Port-Channel interface*. Your IP and IPX configurations are placed on this interface. The real Ethernet interfaces are then included in the channel by using the **channel-group** command. For example, the partial configuration in Example 11-17 converts Cat-D in Figure 11-22 to use EtherChannel on Ports 0/0/3 and 0/0/4.

Example 11-17 *Configuring EtherChannel on the Catalyst 8500 and Cisco Routers*

```
interface Port-Channel1
 description To Cat-D
 no ip address
!
interface Port-Channel1.4
 description VLAN 4
 encapsulation isl 4
 ip address 10.1.4.1 255.255.255.0
 ipx network 4
!
interface Port-Channel1.5
 description VLAN 5
 encapsulation isl 5
 ip address 10.1.5.1 255.255.255.0
 ipx network 5
!
interface FastEthernet0/0/3
 no ip address
 channel-group 1
!
interface FastEthernet0/0/4
 no ip address
 channel-group 1
```

Notice that the ISL subinterfaces are created under the Port-Channel interface, not under the real Fast Ethernet interfaces.

MLS versus 8500s

Which method of Layer 3 switching is better, switching routers (8500s) or routing switches (MLS)? Well, as you can imagine, the real answer is, it depends. Neither option is technically superior to the other. Neither option is newer. In fact, both were released in the same month (June, 1998). Neither option is inherently faster than the other option (although in the first several revisions of both products, the 8500s have had higher throughput). Many people have therefore come to the conclusion that MLS and 8500s are interchangeable options. However, the opposite view is much closer to the truth.

From a design perspective, MLS and 8500s approach the same problem (Layer 3 switching) from completely different angles. On one hand, MLS is a technique that adds Layer 3 capabilities into predominately Layer 2 Catalysts. Think of MLS as enabling Layer 2 Catalyst Supervisors to move up into Layer 3 processing. On the other hand, the 8500s function as a pure router that, like all Cisco routers, happens to also support bridging functionality. It is not an issue of which device can or cannot do Layer 3 processing—after all, both devices can do both Layer 2 and Layer 3. Instead, the issue is what layer a device is most comfortable with (or what the device does by default).

TIP   Routing switches and switching routers both support Layer 3 switching, but they approach it from opposite directions. Routing switches are predominately Layer 2 devices that have moved up into the Layer 3 arena. Conversely, switching routers are predominately Layer 3 devices that also happen to support Layer 2 bridging.

Routing Switch Applications

From the perspective discussed in the previous paragraphs, it becomes clear that MLS is most comfortable in a more Layer 2-oriented world. Although its Layer 3 performance is very respectable, this is not what sets MLS apart from the 8500s. What does differentiate MLS is its capability to very tightly integrate Layer 2 and Layer 3 processing.

For example, designs utilizing campus-wide VLANs can benefit greatly from MLS support. Although Chapter 14 argues that campus-wide VLANs are not the best approach for most networks, they can be very effective in certain situations (for example, when specific user mobility and security issues exist). Given the router-oriented nature of the 8500s, it can be tedious to mix Layer 2 and Layer 3 processing in more than the simplest configurations (this point is discussed in more detail in the section on Integrated Routing and Bridging [IRB] at the end of the chapter).

Designs utilizing a more hierarchical approach (such as the "multilayer model" discussed in Chapter 14) can also benefit from MLS. Not only can it be used to implement the Layer 3 switching component required by this design, it can do it with considerable flexibility. One case where this flexibility can be advantageous is where the user requirements are such that you would like to have VLANs (in other words, IP subnets and IPX networks) that traverse multiple MDF switches in order to reach multiple IDF switches. For example, both a user connected to IDF-1 and another user connected to IDF-2 could be placed in the "Marketing" VLAN and have IP addresses on the same subnet.

As will be discussed later in this section, it turns out that the 8500s make it fairly difficult to implement VLANs that span multiple IDF switches. Under the 8500 approach, the recommendation is to use *different VLANs on **every** IDF*. This design looks at things from the point of view "Why do they need to be in the same VLAN/subnet?" Simply put both users in different VLANs/subnets and let the wire-speed Layer 3 performance of the 8500 route all packets between these two nodes (after all, it essentially routes and bridges at the same speed). Also, DHCP can be used to handle user-mobility problems, further minimizing the need to place these two devices in the same subnet.

Another case where MLS' strengths shine is in the wiring closet where port densities and cost are very important issues. Placing a switching router in the wiring closet is usually cost prohibitive. Instead, high-density and cost-effective Catalyst 5000s and 6000s can be used. Where local traffic can be shortcut switched, MLS can offload processing from the backbone routers. Furthermore, the NFFC's additional capabilities such as Protocol Filtering, IGMP Snooping, and QoS classification can be extremely useful in wiring-closet applications (in fact, this is where they are most useful).

TIP The primary advantage of a routing switch (MLS) is its unique capability to blend Layer 2 and Layer 3 technology.

On the other hand, MLS requires that you take specific actions to fully realize the scalability benefits of Layer 3 processing. For example, Chapter 7 discussed the importance of using Layer 3 processing to break large campus networks into smaller Spanning Tree domains. However, just blindly installing MLS-capable switches does not do this. Figure 11-23 illustrates a large network containing 50 MLS-capable switches with RSMs (for simplicity, not all are shown) and 50 VLANs.

Figure 11-23 *A Large MLS Network*

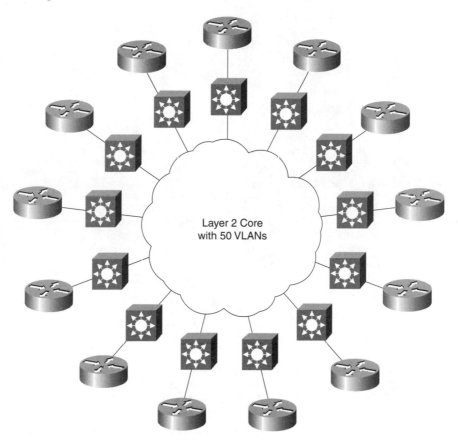

As you can see, the net effect is a huge, flat network with lots of routers sitting on the perimeter. The RSM and the MLS processing are not creating any Layer 3 barriers. The VLAN Trunking Protocol (VTP) discussed in Chapter 12, "VLAN Trunking Protocol," automatically puts all 50 VLANs on all 50 switches by default (even if every switch only uses two or three VLANs). Every switch then starts running 50 instances of the Spanning-Tree Protocol. If a problem develops in a single VLAN on a single switch, the entire network can quickly collapse.

Creating Layer 3 partitions when using the MLS-style of Layer 3 switching requires careful design and planning of VLANs and trunk links. Figure 11-24 illustrates one approach.

Figure 11-24 *Using MLS to Create Layer 3 Partitions*

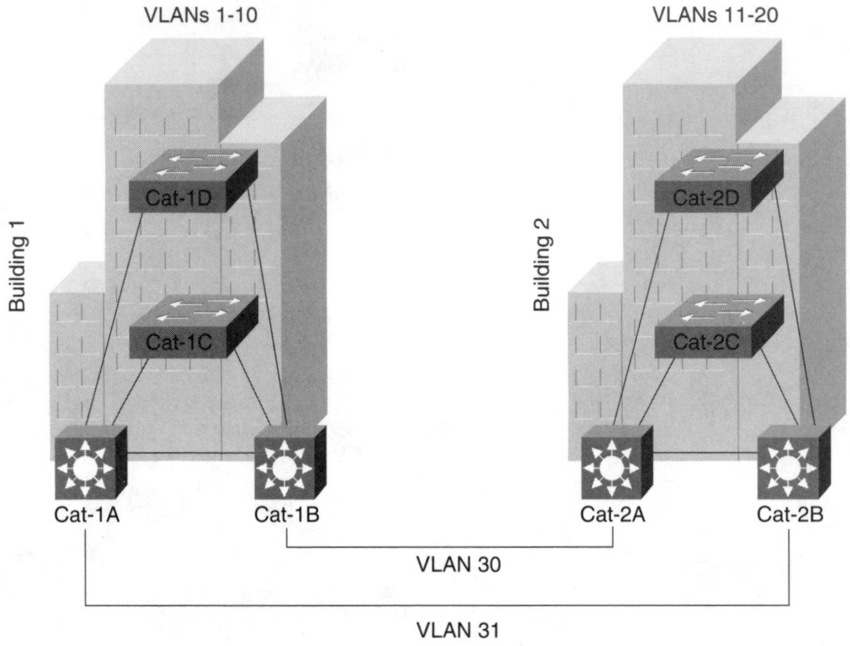

In this case, VLANs have not been allowed to spread throughout the campus. Assume that that the campus represents two buildings. VLANs 1–10 have been contained with Building 1. VLANs 11–20 have been placed in Building 2. A pair of links connects the two buildings. Rather than simply creating ISL links that trunk all VLANs across to the other building, non-trunk links have been used. By placing each of these links in a unique VLAN, you are forcing the traffic to utilize Layer 3 switching before it can exit a building. Also, because VTP advertisements are sent only on trunk links, this prevents VTP's default tendency of spreading every VLAN to every switch.

TIP   Another strategy that helps create Layer 3 barriers in an MLS network is assigning a unique VTP domain to each building. VTP advertisements are only shared between Catalysts that have matching VTP domain names. If each building has a different VTP domain name, the VLANs are contained.

Switching Router Applications

Although it is certainly possible to create Layer 3 partitions using MLS technology with techniques like that shown in Figure 11-24, it is not the default behavior, and it can get tricky in certain topologies. This is where the switching router approach of the 8500s excels. Because 8500s are simply a faster version of the traditional Cisco router, they automatically create Layer 3 barriers that are the key to network stability and scalability. For example, 8500s do not run the Spanning-Tree Protocol unless bridging is specifically enabled. Similarly, the 8500s do not pass VLANs by default. Instead, they terminate VLANs and then route them into other VLANs. Therefore, you *must* take specific steps (such as enabling bridging) on an 8500 to *not* get the benefits of Layer 3 partitions. Figure 11-25 illustrates this point.

Figure 11-25 *Using an 8500 to Link Layer 2 Catalysts*

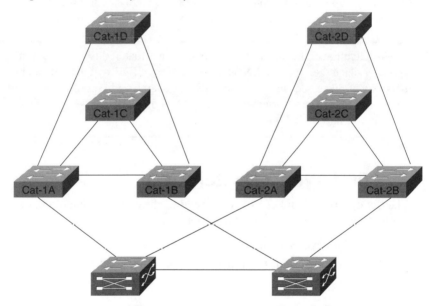

Without any special effort on the part of the Catalyst 5000s, the 8500s automatically isolate each building behind a Layer 3 barrier. This provides many benefits such as improved Spanning Tree stability and performance, easier configuration management, and improved multicast performance.

TIP	The primary advantage of switching routers (8500s) is simplicity. They allow a network to be as simple as the old router and hub design while also having the performance of modern-day switching.

Notice that the Catalyst 8500 is such a Layer 3-oriented box that it essentially has no concept of a VLAN. Yes, it does support bridge groups, an alternate means of creating multiple broadcast domains. However, it currently does not directly support VLANs and all of the VLAN-related features you find on more Layer 2-oriented platforms such as the Catalyst 5000 and 6000 (such as VTP and Dynamic VLANs). This essentially brings the discussion full circle to the opening point of this section: if you need a box with sophisticated Layer 2 features such as VLANs, VTP, and DISL/DTP, but you also need high-performance Layer 3 switching, go with MLS. If, on the other hand, you desire the simplicity of a traditional router-based network, 8500s are the solution of choice.

TIP   One implication of the discussion in this section is that 8500s virtually require a design that does *not* place the same VLAN/subnet on different IDF switches (it can be done through IRB, but, as discussed early, the use of IRB on a large scale should be avoided). On the other hand, the more Layer 2-oriented nature of MLS makes it fairly easy to have a single VLAN connect to multiple IDF switches.

Catalyst 6000 Layer 3 Switching

The Catalyst 6000 family of switches build on the existing technologies introduced by Cisco. From a Layer 3 switching perspective, two options are available:

- The Multilayer Switch Module (MSM)
- MLS using the Multilayer Switch Feature Card (MSFC)

NOTE   In a Catalyst 6000, the NFFC functionality is technically handled by an additional card known as the Policy Feature Card (PFC). However, because current implementations require an MSFC to allow a PFC to perform *Layer 3 switching* (alone, the PFC can provide QoS and access list features), this text will simply refer to the MSFC.

The MSM was the initial Layer 3 offering for the Catalyst 6000s. Based on the 8510 SRP, this card offers approximately 5 million pps for IP and IPX routing. From a configuration standpoint, it uses four Gigabit Ethernet connections to the backplane. Each of these ports can be used in a separate VLAN. Or, by enabling Gigabit EtherChannel on these ports, it can be used as a single interface supporting any number of VLANs. As with the router-on-a-stick approach discussed earlier, each VLAN can then be configured on a separate subinterface.

The second phase of Layer 3 switching for the Catalyst 6000s introduced the MSFC. This brings NFFC II functionality to the Catalyst 6000s, allowing full MLS support at 15 million pps for both IP and IPX. This also provides software-based routing services via technology derived from the 7200 router NPEs. By doing so, it completely eliminates the need for also having an MSM in the same chassis. The on-board router uses software routing to handle the first packet of every IP or IPX flow. The remaining packets are then handled in hardware by MLS. Finally, the on-board router can also be used to provide full software-based multiprotocol routing for protocols such as AppleTalk, DECnet, and VINEs at approximately 100,000 pps (Fast-Switched speeds).

One of the most interesting features of the MSFC, is that its configuration and management characteristics can be completely changed by using one of two different software images. Under the first option, the software-based router uses a traditional IOS image while the Supervisor uses the traditional XDI/CatOS image. This results in a user-interface and configuration process that is virtually identical to that discussed in the "MLS" section earlier in the chapter. This is referred to as the MSFC "Hybrid Mode." In the second option, the MSFC "Native IOS Mode" both the software-based router *and* the Supervisor run full IOS images. This creates an extremely integrated user interface. In short, by simply modifying the software on your Catalyst you can convert a very switch-like device into a full-blown router! For more information, see Chapter 18, "Layer 3 Switching and the Catalyst 6000/6500s."

HSRP

Cisco's Hot Standby Router Protocol (HSRP) plays an important role in most campus networks. The primary mission of HSRP is providing a redundant default gateway for end stations. However, it can also be used to provide load balancing. This section discusses both of these issues.

Many end stations allow only a single default gateway. Normally, this makes these hosts totally dependent on one router when communicating with all nodes off the local subnet. To avoid this limitation, HSRP provides a mechanism to allow this single IP address to be shared by two or more routers as illustrated in Figure 11-26.

Figure 11-26 *HSRP Allows Multiple Routers to Share IP and MAC Addresses*

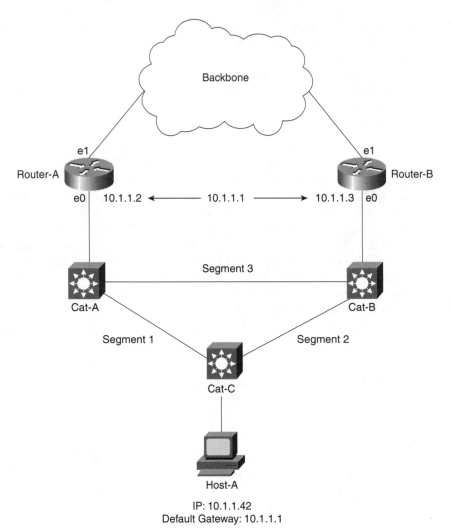

Although both routers are assigned unique IP addresses as normal (**10.1.1.2** and **10.1.1.3**), HSRP provides a third address that both routers share. The two routers exchange periodic hello messages (every three seconds by default) to monitor the status of each other. One router is elected the active HSRP peer and handles all router responsibilities for the shared address. The other node then acts as the standby HSRP peer. If the standby peer misses three HSRP hellos, it then assumes that the active peer has failed and takes over the role of the active peer.

One of the subtleties of HSRP is that the routers do not just share an IP address. To create a truly transparent failover mechanism, they must also share a MAC address. The routers therefore use an algorithm to create a shared virtual MAC address. As with the shared IP address, the active peer is the only node using the derived MAC address. However, if the active peer fails, the other device not only adopts the shared IP address, but also the shared MAC address. By doing so, the ARP cache located in every end station on the network does not require updating after a failover situation.

TIP   Although the shared MAC address prevents ARP cache problems during an HSRP failover scenario, it can be a problem when initially testing HSRP. For example, assume that you convert an existing router using the **10.1.1.1** address into an HSRP configuration where **10.1.1.1** becomes the shared IP address. At this point, the end stations still have the *real* MAC address associated with the original router, not the *virtual* MAC address created by HSRP. To solve this problem, reboot the end stations or clear their ARP caches.

Note that HSRP can be useful even in cases where the TCP/IP stack running on your clients supports multiple default gateways. In some cases, the mechanisms used by these stacks to failover to an alternate default gateway do not work reliably. In other cases, such as with current Microsoft stacks, the redundancy feature only works for certain protocols (such as TCP, but not UDP). In either case, most organizations do not want to leave default gateway reliability to chance and instead implement HSRP.

TIP   HSRP is useful even if your TCP/IP stack allows multiple default gateways.

Example 11-18 presents a sample HSRP configuration for the Router-A in Figure 11-26.

Example 11-18 *HSRP Configuration for Router-A*

```
interface Ethernet0
 description Link to wiring closet Catalysts
 ip address 10.1.1.2 255.255.255.0
 standby 1 priority 110
 standby 1 preempt
 standby 1 ip 10.1.1.1
 standby 1 track Ethernet1 15
!
interface Ethernet1
 description Link to backbone
 ip address 10.1.2.2 255.255.255.0
```

The real IP address is assigned with the usual **ip address** command. HSRP parameters are then configured using various **standby** commands. The shared IP address is added with **standby** *group_number* **ip** *ip_address* command. This command needs to be entered on both routers.

The *group_number* parameters on both routers must match.

In most campus designs, some thought should be given as to the proper placement of the active peer. In general, the following guidelines should be used:

- The active HSRP peer should be located near or at the Spanning Tree Root Bridge.
- A router should relinquish its role as the active HSRP peer if it looses its connection to the backbone.

In networks that contain Layer 2 loops, the Spanning Tree Root Bridge acts as the center of the universe. Other bridges then look for the most efficient path to this device. By placing the active HSRP peer at or near the Root Bridge, the Spanning-Tree Protocol automatically helps end-user traffic follow the best path to the default gateway. For example, if Router-A is the active HSRP peer in Figure 11-26 but Cat-B is the Spanning Tree Root Bridge, Segment-1 has a port in the Blocking state. This forces all of the default gateway traffic to take an inefficient path through Cat-B (using Segment 2 and Segment 3). By co-locating the active HSRP peer and the Root Bridge at Cat-A and Router-A, this unnecessary bridge hop can be eliminated.

To force Cat-A to be the Root Bridge, the **set spantree root** or **set spantree priority** commands discussed in Chapter 6 can be used. To force Router-A to the active HSRP peer, the **standby** *group_number* **priority** *priority_value* command can be used. The peer with the highest *priority_value* becomes the active peer (the default is 100). In this case, Router-A has a configured priority of 110, making it win the active peer election. However, if Router-A boots after Router-B, it does not supercede Router-B by default (it waits for Router-B to fail first), creating the same inefficient pattern discussed earlier. This can be avoided by configuring the **standby** *group_number* **preempt** command. This causes a router to instantly take over as soon as it has the highest priority.

Unlike the Spanning-Tree Protocol where lower values are always preferred, HSRP prefers *higher* values.

The second guideline speaks to a situation where a router has the highest priority, but it has lost its connection to the rest of the network. For example, Router-A is the active HSRP peer but its Ethernet1 link goes down. Although this does not prevent traffic from reaching the backbone (Router-A can use its Ethernet0 interface to send traffic to the backbone through Router-B), it does lead to an inefficient flow. To prevent this situation, the **standby track** option can be used as shown in Example 11-18. The value indicated by the **standby track** command is the value that gets *decremented* from the node's priority if the specified interface goes down. Multiple **standby track** commands can be used to list multiple interfaces to track (if more than one interface goes down, the decrement values are cumulative). In this example, if Router-A loses interface Ethernet1, the priority is lowered to 95. Because this is lower than the default priority of 100 being used by Router-B, Router-B takes over as the active peer and provides a more optimal flow to the backbone.

Although the configuration discussed in this section does provide a redundant default gateway for the end stations connected to Cat-C, it does suffer from one limitation: Router-A is handling all of the traffic. To eliminate this problem, multiple VLANs should be created on Cat-C. Each VLAN uses a separate *group_number* on the **standby** command. Then, the VLANs should alternate active peers between the two routers. For example, Router-A could be the active peer for all odd-numbered VLANs, and Router-B could be the active peer for all even-numbered VLANs. Example 11-19 presents a sample configuration for Router-A (two VLANs and an ISL interface are used).

Example 11-19 *ISL HSRP Configuration for Router-A*

```
interface FastEthernet0/0/0
 description Link to wiring closet Catalyst
 no ip address
!
interface FastEthernet0/0/0.1
 encapsulation isl 1
 ip address 10.1.1.3 255.255.255.0
 standby 1 priority 110
 standby 1 preempt
 standby 1 ip 10.1.1.1
 standby 1 track FastEthernet0/0/1 15
!
interface FastEthernet0/0/0.2
 encapsulation isl 2
 ip address 10.1.2.2 255.255.255.0
 standby 2 priority 100
 standby 2 preempt
 standby 2 ip 10.1.2.1
!
interface Ethernet0/0/1
 description Link to backbone
 ip address 10.1.3.2 255.255.255.0
```

Example 11-20 shows the corresponding configuration for Router-B.

Example 11-20 *ISL HSRP Configuration for Router-B*

```
interface FastEthernet0/0/0
 description Link to wiring closet Catalyst
 no ip address
!
interface FastEthernet0/0/0.1
 encapsulation isl 1
 ip address 10.1.1.4 255.255.255.0
 standby 1 ip 10.1.1.1
 standby 1 priority 100
 standby 1 preempt
!
interface FastEthernet0/0/0.2
 encapsulation isl 2
 ip address 10.1.2.3 255.255.255.0
 standby 2 ip 10.1.2.1
 standby 2 priority 110
 standby 2 track FastEthernet0/0/1 15
 standby 2 preempt
!
interface Ethernet0/0/1
 description Link to backbone
 ip address 10.1.3.3 255.255.255.0
```

TIP   Alternate HSRP active peers for different VLANs between a pair of routers. This provides load balancing in addition to redundancy.

As discussed earlier, alternating HSRP active peer placements should obviously be coordinated with the Spanning Tree Root Bridge configuration. Cat-A should be the Root Bridge for the odd VLANs, and Cat-B should be the Root Bridge for the even VLANs.

TIP   The HSRP syntax allows a single standby group to be created without specifying the *group_number* parameter. However, I recommended that you always specify this parameter so that it is much easier to add other standby groups in the future. Also, using the default standby group can lead to very strange behavior if you accidentally use it in an attempt to configure HSRP for multiple VLANs.

Load Balancing with MHSRP

Using Spanning Tree and multiple VLANs can be effective if Layer 2 loops and multiple VLANs exist on Cat-C, the wiring closet switch. However, this is not always the case. Many network designers want to deploy networks similar to the one illustrated in Figure 11-27.

Figure 11-27 *A Network Using a Single VLAN in the Wiring Closet*

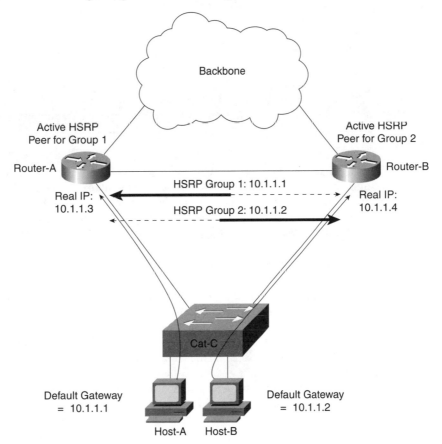

The design in Figure 11-27 has the wiring closet switch directly connected to a pair of switching routers such as the Catalyst 8500. This eliminates all Layer 2 loops and removes Spanning Tree from the equation (although there is a link between the two routers, it is a separate subnet). Furthermore, because a single VLAN is in use on Cat-C, the wiring closet switch, the alternating VLANs trick cannot be used.

In this case, the most effective solution is the use of Multigroup HSRP (MHSRP). This feature allows multiple HSRP *group_numbers* to be used on a single interface. For example, Example 11-21 shows a possible configuration for Router-A.

Example 11-21 *MHSRP Configuration on a Catalyst 8500*

```
interface FastEthernet0/0/0
 description Link to wiring closet Catalyst
 ip address 10.1.1.3 255.255.255.0
 standby 1 ip 10.1.1.1
 standby 1 priority 110
 standby 1 track FastEthernet0/0/1 15
 standby 1 preempt
 standby 2 ip 10.1.1.2
 standby 2 priority 100
 standby 2 preempt
```

NOTE   Some of the low-end routers use a Lance Ethernet chipset that does not support MHSRP. However, all of the devices suitable for campus backbone use do support MHSRP.

The code in Example 11-21 creates two shared addresses between Router-A and Router-B for a single subnet. Load balancing can then be implemented by having half of the hosts on Cat-C use **10.1.1.1** as a default gateway and the other half use **10.1.1.2**. The potential downside is that you have to come up with some way of configuring different hosts to use different default gateways. Fortunately, DHCP provides a simple and effective technique to accomplish this.

Because existing DHCP standards do not provide for server-to-server communication, organizations are forced to divide every scope (a scope can be loosely defined as a subnet's worth of DHCP addresses) of addresses into two blocks (assuming they want redundant DHCP servers). Each of two redundant DHCP servers receives one half of each scope. For example, a /24 subnet with 54 addresses reserved for fixed configuration leaves 200 addresses available for DHCP. 100 of these addresses can be placed on the first DHCP server and the other 100 are placed on the second DHCP server. If one of the DHCP servers fails, the other can provide addresses for clients on the network (assuming that no more than 100 new addresses are required). Because each server has its own block of globally unique addresses for every server, the lack of a server-to-server protocol is not a problem.

DHCP supports a variety of options that can be used to configure client stations. The DHCP Option 3 allows DHCP servers to provide a default gateway (or a list of default gateways) to clients. Simply configure one DHCP server with the first shared HSRP address (**10.1.1.1** in Figure 11-26) and the other DHCP server with the second shared HSRP address (**10.1.1.2**).

For this technique to work, it requires a fairly random distribution of leases between the two DHCP servers. If one server ends up issuing 90 percent of the leases, one of the routers likely receives 90 percent of the traffic. To help ensure a random distribution, you should place the two DHCP servers close to each other (generally in the same server farm). You can also alternate the order of **ip helper-address** statements between the two routers. For example, assuming that the DHCP servers have the addresses **10.1.55.10** and **10.1.55.11**, Router-A might use the **ip helper-address** configuration in Example 11-22.

Example 11-22 *IP Helper Address Configuration for Router-A*

```
interface FastEthernet0/0/0
 ip helper-address 10.1.55.10
 ip helper-address 10.1.55.11
```

Conversely, Router-B can then use the opposite order as demonstrated in Example 11-23.

Example 11-23 *IP Helper Address Configuration for Router-B*

```
interface FastEthernet0/0/0
 ip helper-address 10.1.55.11
 ip helper-address 10.1.55.10
```

This causes Router-A to give a slight advantage to the DHCP server located as **10.1.55.10**, but Router-B gives an advantage to the other DHCP server. In general, both servers have an equal chance of responding first to the DHCP_DISCOVER packets that clients use to request a lease.

TIP

If this DHCP and MHSRP trick is not to your liking, consider placing a Layer 3 switch in the IDF wiring closet. Although this can be cost-prohibitive, it allows all devices connected to that IDF to use the IDF switch itself as a default gateway. The Layer 3 routing capabilities in the IDF switch can then choose the best path to use into the campus backbone and automatically balance the load over both uplinks. However, I should also point out that this can be difficult to implement with routing switch (MLS) devices. In general, it is much easier to accomplish with switching router designs such as the Catalyst 8500 and the native IOS router mode of the 6000.

Integration between Routing and Bridging

The section "MLS versus 8500s" discussed the advantages of having Layer 3 barriers or partitions in your network (this issue is also discussed extensively in Chapters 14, 15, and 17). However, for a variety of reasons, many people want to avoid the "hard barriers" formed by this approach. Instead, they seek "softer barriers" where some protocols or VLANs are terminated while others pass through. This requires a mixture of routing (that is, Layer 3 switching) and bridging (that is, Layer 2 switching). The next two sections look at the two most common forms of mixing routing and bridging.

NOTE

A third technique is possible using the Catalyst 6000 Native IOS Mode. This will be discussed in Chapter 18.

Bridging between VLANs

One of the simplest ways of avoiding the "hardness" of a Layer 3 barrier is bridging between multiple VLANs. Many network designers want to do this when they have two separate VLANs that need to share some non-routable protocol such as local-area transport (LAT) or NetBIOS/NetBEUI.

TIP   Other network designers cringe at this thought because it no longer keeps the VLANs separate.

This sort of bridging can be easily configured using the same **bridge-group** technology that Cisco routers have supported for many years. For example, the configuration in Example 11-24 enables bridging between VLANs 2 and 3 on an 8500.

Example 11-24 *Using Bridge Groups to Bridge between VLANs*

```
interface FastEthernet0/0/0
 no ip address
!
interface FastEthernet0/0/0.1
 encapsulation isl 1
 ip address 10.1.1.1 255.255.255.0
!
interface FastEthernet0/0/0.2
 encapsulation isl 2
 ip address 10.1.2.1 255.255.255.0
 ipx network 2
 bridge-group 1
!
interface FastEthernet0/0/0.3
 encapsulation isl 3
 ip address 10.1.3.1 255.255.255.0
 ipx network 3
 bridge-group 1
!
interface FastEthernet0/0/0.4
 encapsulation isl 4
 ip address 10.1.4.1 255.255.255.0
 ipx network 4
!
bridge 1 protocol ieee
```

The configuration in Example 11-24 results in IP and IPX traffic being routed between subinterfaces Fast Ethernet1/0.2 and 1/0.3 while all other protocols are bridged. No bridging is performed on subinterfaces Fast Ethernet1/0.1 and 1/0.4. Notice that this requires IP users in VLANs 2 and 3 to use different IP subnets (and IPX networks) but the same AppleTalk cable range.

TIP   When using bridge-groups, remember that protocols configured with a Layer 3 address will be *routed* while all other protocols will be *bridged*. For example, if you only configure an IP address on a given interface, IP will be routed and all other protocols (IPX, AppleTalk, DECnet, and so on) will be bridged.

This technique is applicable as long as a particular protocol is either bridged or routed on a specific device. For instance, the previous example routed IP and IPX on *every* interface. Also, AppleTalk was only bridged on this device. Normal bridge-group processing does not allow you to bridge IP between two interfaces and route it between two other interfaces. To do so requires a feature called Integrated Routing and Bridging (IRB).

IRB

Integrated Routing and Bridging (IRB) is a technique Cisco introduced in IOS 11.2 to allow a single protocol to be both bridged and routed on the same box. IOS 11.1 introduced a precursor to IRB called Concurrent Routing and Bridging (CRB). This allowed a particular protocol such as IP to be both bridged and routed on the same device. It allowed all of the routed interfaces using this protocol to communicate and all of the bridged interfaces to communicate. However, CRB did not let routed interfaces communicate with the bridged interfaces. In other words, the routed and bridged worlds for the configured protocol were treated as two separate islands. Most people were not looking for this functionality.

IRB filled this gap by allowing communication between these two islands. This enabled configurations such as those shown in Figure 11-28.

Figure 11-28 *A Sample IRB Configuration*

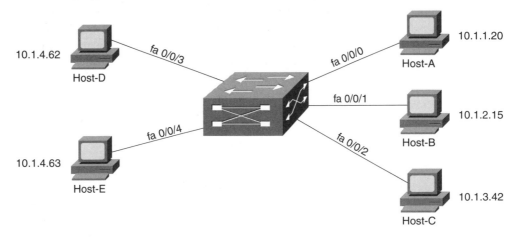

The interfaces on the right side of the router (fa0/0/0, fa0/0/1, and fa0/0/2) all use IP addresses on separate IP subnets. Conversely, the interfaces on the left (fa0/0/3 and fa0/0/4) both fall on the *same subnet*. And, because IRB is in use, **10.1.4.62** could **ping 10.1.1.20** (this is not possible in CRB).

To create a link between the routed and bridged domains, Cisco created a special virtual interface known as a Bridged Virtual Interface (BVI). The BVI can be configured with Layer 3 addresses (it cannot be configured with bridging statements) and acts as a routed interface into the rest of the box. For example, the BVI in Figure 11-28 might use an IP address of 10.1.4.1, as illustrated in Figure 11-29.

Figure 11-29 *A Logical Representation of a BVI*

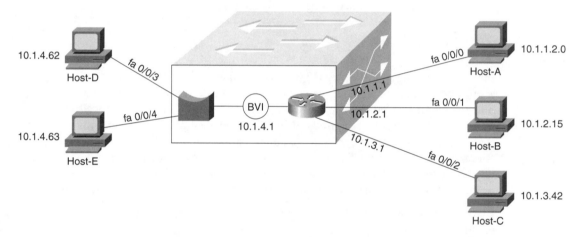

If interface fa0/0/4 receives a frame with Host-D's MAC address, it bridges it out interface fa0/0/3. However, if Host-D **ping**s Host-A, Host-D sends the IP packet to its default gateway, address **10.1.4.1** (the BVI's address). If necessary, Host-D ARPs for **10.1.4.1** to learn the BVI's MAC address. When interface fa0/0/4 receives the traffic with a MAC address that belongs to the BVI, it knows to route, not bridge, the traffic. The normal routing process then sends the traffic out interface fa0/0/0.

The BVI essentially acts as a single routed interface on behalf of all of the bridged interfaces in a particular VLAN. In Figure 11-29, the BVI communicates with the right side of the box through routing, whereas the left side uses bridging.

TIP You need one BVI interface for each VLAN that contains two or more interfaces on a single IOS-based router (except for the ports that make up an individual EtherChannel bundle).

Example 11-25 shows sample configuration for the network illustrated in Figures 11-28 and 11-29.

Example 11-25 *IRB Configuration*

```
interface FastEthernet0/0/0
 ip address 10.1.1.1 255.255.255.0
!
interface FastEthernet0/0/1
 ip address 10.1.2.1 255.255.255.0
!
interface FastEthernet0/0/2
 ip address 10.1.3.1 255.255.255.0
!
interface FastEthernet0/0/3
 no ip address
 bridge-group 1
!
interface FastEthernet0/0/4
 no ip address
 brige-group 1
!
interface BVI 1
 ip address 10.1.4.1 255.255.255.0
!
bridge 1 protocol ieee
bridge 1 protocol ieee
 bridge 1 route ip
```

TIP   The BVI interface number must match the bridge group number.

IRB is an important feature on platforms such as the Catalyst 8500. For instance, consider the case where you want to directly connect 10 servers to an 8540 along with 20 trunks that lead to separate wiring closet switches. Assume the servers are going to all be placed in the same subnet (therefore bridging IP traffic), whereas each wiring closet switch uses a separate subnet (therefore routing IP). Without IRB, it is not possible to both route and bridge the IP traffic in one device. In other words, IRB allows you to route IP subnets while also extending the server farm VLAN through the router. Another advantage to IRB is that it is performed at nearly wire speed in the 8500 (IRB is Fast-Switched in software-based routers).

However, IRB does have its downsides. Most importantly, the extensive use of IRB can create configuration nightmares. For example, consider an 8540 with 100+ interfaces and 30 or 40 BVIs (one for every VLAN that needs to mix routing and bridging). Also, it can quickly deplete the number of available logical interfaces supported by the IOS. To avoid these issues, IRB should be used to solve specific and narrowly defined problems. Do not try to build your entire network on IRB.

TIP A single BVI that contains many interfaces does not present configuration challenges. However, a design that uses many BVIs can lead to problems and confusion.

Issues and Caveats with Bridging between VLANs

Regardless of which approach is used, bridging between VLANs can create a wide variety of problems. One of the most common problems is that of throughput and switching speed. Many organizations have used software-based routers to rely on bridge groups and possibly BVIs to allow non-routable traffic to cross VLAN boundaries. However, software-based bridges perform these bridging functions at IOS Fast-Switching speeds. This creates a situation where traffic gets Layer 2 switched at millions of packets per second only to slam into a software-based bridging process often running at less than 100,000 pps. Talk about having the Autobahn suddenly turn into a dirt road!

NOTE As discussed earlier, switching router platforms such as the 8500s do not suffer from this drawback because they perform both Layer 2 and Layer 3 forwarding at essentially the same speed.

However, even if the throughput problem is not an issue in your network, there is another problem that can surface. Assume that you link two Layer 2 domains with the configuration in Example 11-26.

Example 11-26 *Routing IP and IPX While Bridging All Other Protocols*

```
interface FastEthernet0/0/0
 no ip address
!
interface FastEthernet0/0/0.1
 encapsulation isl 1
 ip address 10.1.1.1 255.255.255.0
 ipx network 1
 bridge-group 1
!
interface FastEthernet0/0/0.2
 encapsulation isl 2
 ip address 10.1.2.1 255.255.255.0
 ipx network 2
 bridge-group 1
!
bridge 1 protocol ieee
```

The configuration in Example 11-26 routes IP and IPX between VLANs 1 and 2 but also allows non-routable traffic such as NetBIOS/NetBEUI to be bridged through the router. However, this also merges the Spanning Trees in VLAN 1 and 2. This introduces two significant problems:

- **Scalability problems**—When two (or more) Spanning Trees are merged into a single tree, all of the Spanning Tree scalability benefits created by introducing routers disappear. A single Root Bridge is established between both VLANs. A single set of least-cost paths is found to this Root Bridge. Spanning Tree instability can easily and quickly spread throughout both VLANs and create network-wide outages.

- **Defeats Spanning Tree load balancing**—Recall from Chapter 7 that Spanning Tree load balancing uses multiple VLANs to create different logical topologies between VLANs. For example, VLAN 1 can use Trunk-1 and VLAN 2 can use Trunk-2. However, if the Spanning Trees are merged because of inter-VLAN bridging, both VLANs are forced to use a single trunk. This cuts your available bandwidth in half!

Even if you find a way to avoid the issues previously discussed, you must plan very carefully to avoid a third problem that I refer to as the Broken Subnet Problem. Figure 11-30 illustrates this issue.

Figure 11-30 *The Broken Subnet Problem*

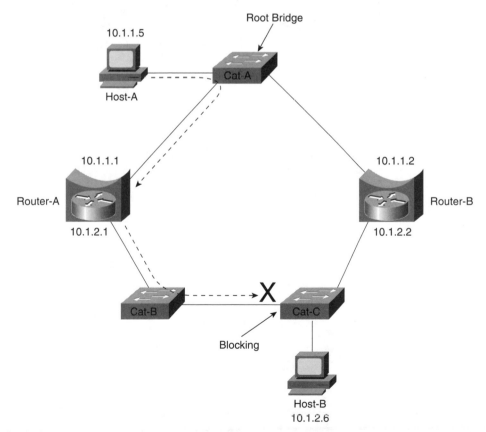

Three Layer 2 Catalysts and two routers have been used to form a ring. Router-A and Router-B have been configured to route IP and bridge all other protocols using a **bridge-group 1** command on both Ethernet interfaces. As a result, IP sees the topology shown in Figure 11-31.

Figure 11-31 *IP's View of the Network Shown in Figure 11-30*

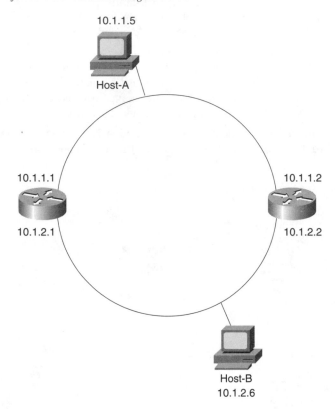

In other words, IP has divided the network into two subnets. However, the Spanning-Tree Protocol has a very different view of the world. Spanning Tree knows nothing about IP's interpretation. Instead, it sees only a ring of five Layer 2 devices. Assuming that Cat-A becomes the Root Bridge, Spanning Tree creates the topology shown in Figure 11-32 (see Chapter 6 for information on DP, RP, F, and B).

Figure 11-32 *Spanning Tree's View of the Network Shown in Figure 11-29*

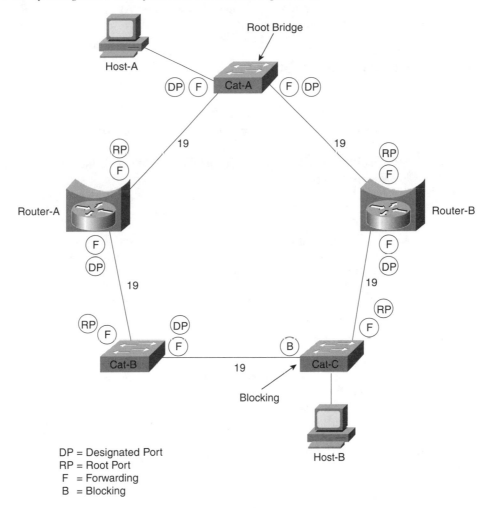

DP = Designated Port
RP = Root Port
F = Forwarding
B = Blocking

Unfortunately, this can create a very subtle problem. Consider what happens if Host-A tries to send IP data to Host-B. Host-A recognizes that Host-B is in a different subnet and forwards the traffic to Router-A, its default gateway. Router-A does the normal IP routing thing and forwards the traffic out its interface E1. However, the traffic cannot be delivered to Host-B because the Layer 2 switches have blocked the path (remember that Spanning Tree blocks all traffic on a Catalyst, not just non-routable traffic)! The dashed line in Figure 11-30 shows this path.

The Broken Subnet Problem can be extremely difficult to troubleshoot and diagnose. In many cases, only a very small number of nodes experience problems communicating with each other. For example, Host-A cannot reach Host-B, but it might be able to reach every other address in the network. If your network has Spanning Tree stability problems, the broken link is constantly shifting locations. Furthermore, the failure is protocol specific. If Host-A tries to reach Host-B using any protocol other than IP, it succeeds. All of these issues can lead to many extremely long days of troubleshooting before the actual problem is discovered.

How to Fix the Broken Subnet Problem

In general, there are three ways to fix the Broken Subnet Problem:

- Disable the inter-VLAN bridging on at least one bridge.
- Manipulate the Spanning Tree parameters to move the Blocking port to one of the router ports.
- Run a different version of the Spanning-Tree Protocol on the routers than on the Layer 2 switches.

Disable Inter-VLAN Bridging

The simplest and most effective solution to the Broken Subnet Problem is to disable inter-VLAN bridging on at least one of the routers (by removing the **bridge-group** commands from the interfaces). Because this creates a loop-free Layer 2 configuration, it prevents any of the ports in Figure 11-30 from Blocking. However, it also removes redundancy from the inter-VLAN bridging and, therefore, might not be appropriate for all networks.

Manipulating Spanning Tree Parameters

By tuning a variety of Spanning Tree parameters, the blocked port can be moved to one of the ports on the router. By doing so, the router can have full access to the network for routable protocols but also prevent Layer 2 loops within the non-routable protocols. In short, this allows the router to create a protocol-specific Blocking port. For routable protocols, the Spanning Tree Blocking port is ignored. However, for protocols the router does not route, the Blocking port is enforced. In general, there are three options for moving the Blocking port (see Table 11-1).

Table 11-1 *Moving the Spanning Tree Blocking Port to a Router*

Option	Description
Path Cost	Increases or decreases the STP path cost parameter to influence the election of Designated and non-Designated Ports.
Root Bridge placement	Moves the STP Root Bridge such that the Blocking port is forced to a router interface.
Multiple Spanning Trees	Uses IEEE STP on the Layer 2 Catalysts and DEC or VLAN-Bridge on the routers. See the section "Using Different Spanning-Tree Protocols."

Figure 11-33 shows how this can be done by increasing the cost of the link between Cat-A and Router-A to 1000 (the cost actually needs to be increased on the Router, not Cat-A, because Cat-A is the Root Bridge).

Figure 11-33 *Moving the Blocking Port to a Router Interface*

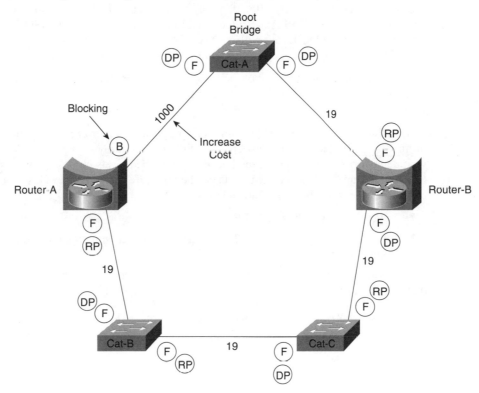

Another option is to move the Root Bridge to Router-B. When using this approach, Bridge Priorities or Path Costs might also have to be adjusted to force the Blocking port to the router-end of the link to Cat-B.

Using Different Spanning-Tree Protocols

The most complex and creative solution involves using a different version of the Spanning-Tree Protocol on the Layer 2 bridges than on the routers. Layer 2 Catalysts such as the Catalyst 6000 and Catalyst 5000 only use the IEEE version of the Spanning-Tree Protocol. Meanwhile, devices that run the full IOS, such as a 7500 router or a Catalyst 8500, can use one of three versions of the Spanning-Tree Protocol for transparent bridging (very early 8500 images only support IEEE, and VLAN-Bridge requires IOS 12.0+):

- IEEE
- DEC
- VLAN-Bridge

As discussed in Chapter 6, Radia Perlman created the DEC version of the Spanning-Tree Protocol, which was initially offered on DEC equipment. The IEEE version was the one standardized in 802.1D. VLAN-Bridge is a Cisco-specific extension to the IEEE protocol (it uses the same BPDU layout with a SNAP header). It was created to provide exactly the sort of feature being discussed in this section.

For example, in Figure 11-30, the Catalysts Cat-A, Cat-B, and Cat-C are using the IEEE Spanning-Tree Protocol, and Router-A and Router-B are using the DEC Spanning-Tree Protocol.

At first thought, this sounds like a dangerous proposition. After all, mixing the two protocols can lead to situations where one of the protocols does not detect a loop and the whole network collapses. However, because Layer 2 Catalysts process BPDUs slightly differently than IOS routers, the results can be both safe and effective. This is possible because of the following two characteristics:

- Layer 2 Catalysts flood DEC BPDUs
- IOS routers swallow IEEE BPDUs if they are only running the DEC variation of the Spanning-Tree Protocol

As a result, the IEEE BPDUs are blocked by the routers, creating a topology that resembles that shown in Figure 11-34.

Figure 11-34 *IEEE Topology When Running Two Versions of the Spanning-Tree Protocol*

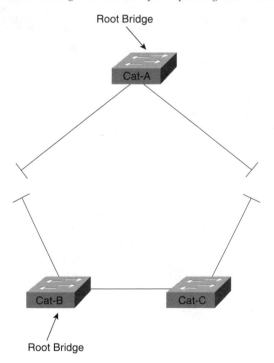

The IEEE Spanning-Tree Protocol views the network as being partitioned into two separate halves. Each half elects its own Root Bridge.

On the other hand, the DEC Spanning-Tree Protocol running on the routers sees a very different view of the network. From the DEC perspective, the Layer 2 Catalysts do not exist because DEC BPDUs are flooded without alteration by Cat-A, Cat-B, and Cat-C. This creates the logical topology diagrammed in Figure 11-35.

Figure 11-35 *DEC Topology When Running Two Versions of the Spanning-Tree Protocol*

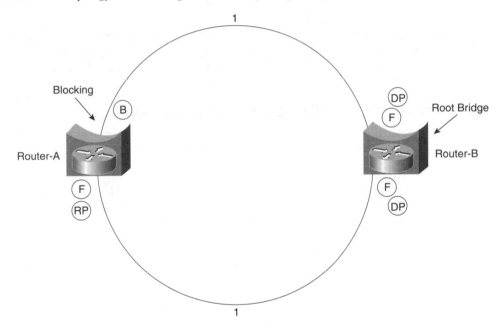

NOTE   Notice that the DEC Spanning-Tree Protocol uses a cost of 1 for Fast Ethernet links.

As a result, the two Spanning-Tree Protocols work together to provide connectivity throughout the network. The IEEE Spanning Trees are used to make sure that Layer 2 loops are not formed between the routers. Because each IEEE Spanning Tree provides full connectivity between all of the routers it touches, this avoids the Broken Subnet Problem. The DEC protocol is then used to detect if these pockets of IEEE Spanning Tree are interconnected in a looped topology. In the case of this example, it detects that a loop has been formed and blocks a port running the DEC Spanning-Tree Protocol. Assume that Router-B is acting as the Root Bridge of the DEC Spanning Tree in Figure 11-35. This causes the upper interface on Router-A to enter the Blocking state.

NOTE	As a minor detail, this assumes that the upper interface on Router-B has a lower Port ID. See the "Port/VLAN Priority Load Balancing" section of Chapter 7 for more detail.

Although this can hardly be called the most intuitive approach, it can be very useful in networks that need to mix routing and bridging technology.

TIP	Use multiple versions of the Spanning-Tree Protocol to avoid the Broken Subnet Problem where the simpler techniques discussed in the previous two sections are not an option.

Recommendations on Mixing Bridging and Routing

In general, the best advice is to avoid inter-VLAN bridging wherever possible. Not only does it create the obvious problem of potentially excessive broadcast radiation, it introduces a wide variety of scalability issues.

The simplest way to avoid inter-VLAN bridging is by putting all nodes that need to communicate via non-routable protocols in a single VLAN. If this VLAN needs to span multiple switching routers in the network's core, a single BVI interface can be created without significant problems. If more than one VLAN needs to be used for non-routable traffic, strive to limit them as much as possible. Also consider migrating to routable alternatives. For example, organizations using NetBIOS/NetBEUI for Microsoft's networking features can enable WINS and use NetBIOS over TCP/IP (NBT).

Finally, remember the unique benefits provided by the combination of MLS and Catalyst-based routers such as the RSM. The Catalyst's feature-rich Layer 2 architecture makes it very easy to group various combinations of ports into multiple VLANs. The RSM's unique design that treats all of the ports in a VLAN as a single router interface (**interface Vlan X**) also makes it very easy to route between these VLANs. This approach is considerably simpler and more scalable (at least from a configuration standpoint) than IRB. You can obtain similar benefits by using the Native IOS Mode routing feature of the Catalyts 6000 (see Chapter 18).

Review Questions

This section includes a variety of questions on the topic of this chapter—Layer 3 switching. By completing these, you can test your mastery of the material included in this chapter as well as help prepare yourself for the CCIE written and lab tests.

1 What is the difference between routing and Layer 3 switching?

2 Can the router-on-a-stick approach to inter-VLAN routing also support inter-VLAN bridging?

3 How can the RSM be especially useful in remote office designs?

4 What are the strengths of the RSM approach to Layer 3 switching?

5 Does MLS eliminate the need for a router?

6 Does MLS require a router that runs the router-based NetFlow mechanism?

7 In MLS, does the router create the shortcut entry and download it to the Layer 3 CAM table located in the Catalyst's NFFC or MSFC/PFC?

8 What is a flow mask?

9 How does the Catalyst 8500 make routing decisions?

10 What are the two routing options offered for the Catalyst 6000 family? From a conceptual standpoint, how do they differ?

11 What is MHSRP? How is it useful?

12 What is the difference between CRB and IRB?

13 When is IRB useful?

14 What are some of the dangers associated with mixing bridging and routing?

15 What is the benefit of using the IEEE and DEC Spanning-Tree Protocols at the same time? Where should each be run?

This chapter covers the following key topics:

- **Understanding VTP**—Explains what VTP is and why it is used.

- **VTP Modes**—Compares and demonstrates VTP server, client and transparent modes.

- **The Working Mechanics of VTP**—Describes the various VTP messages such as summary and subset advertisements, advertisement requests, and pruning messages.

- **Configuring VTP Mode**—Provides various configuration examples that illustrate VTP operations and troubleshooting tools.

- **VTP Pruning: Advanced Traffic Management**—Explains how VTP pruning works, and how to configure it.

CHAPTER 12

VLAN Trunking Protocol

A number of Catalyst 5000/6000 features are specific to Cisco's LAN switching products. For example, this includes VLAN Trunking Protocol (VTP) described in this chapter as well as features described in other chapters. These features enhance how the Catalyst performs in the network and ease administrative burdens inherent in large LAN implementations. The Catalyst can operate without many, if not all, of the advanced features detailed in this and other chapters. You will, however, find administering and configuring your network cumbersome without them.

For example, the steps for creating a VLAN are to assign a Catalyst to a management domain, create the VLAN, and assign ports to the VLAN. One of the features covered in this chapter, VLAN Trunking Protocol (VTP), helps to minimize configuration efforts by helping with the first two steps. Without VTP, you need to perform these steps in every Catalyst in your network. With VTP, you only need to perform the first two steps at selected devices. This chapter details how VTP operates and how to configure it in your network and provides guidelines on when to exercise some of its features and when not to.

Dynamic VLANs are another feature intended to ease administrative burdens. Dynamic VLANs enable the Catalyst to configure ports to a VLAN automatically based upon the MAC address of the attached device. Chapter 5, "VLANs," covers dynamic VLANs and the VMPS server and client and details how to configure it.

Some advanced features in the Catalyst provide network performance enhancements by reducing the amount of flooded traffic in your network. A bridge deals with certain kinds of traffic, broadcast, multicast, and unknown unicast traffic, by flooding it throughout the bridged network. The Catalyst is a bridge, and, therefore, floods this traffic too. This chapter describes a mechanism for controlling flooded traffic in your network: VTP pruning. VTP pruning eliminates flooding by only flooding VLAN traffic over a trunk port if it *needs to*. VTP helps the Catalyst make the *need to* determination. This chapter describes the feature and details how to configure it on the 5000/6000 models.

Understanding VTP

VTP is a Cisco proprietary, Layer 2 multicast messaging protocol that can ease some of the administrative burden associated with maintaining VLANs. VTP maps VLANs across all media types and VLAN tagging methods between switches, enabling VLAN configuration consistency throughout a network. VTP reduces manual configuration steps required at each switch to add a VLAN when the VLAN extends to other switches in the network. Further, VTP minimizes potential configuration mismatches and manages the addition, deletion, and renaming of a VLAN in a more secure fashion than making manual changes at every switch. VTP is a value-add software feature specific to Cisco Catalyst switch products such as the 1900, 2820, 2948G, 3000, 4003, 5000 family, and 6000 family.

Not infrequently, users confuse the difference between VTP, ISL, 802.1Q, DISL, and DTP. All of these protocols involve trunks, but have different purposes. Table 12-1 compares these protocols.

Table 12-1 *Summary of Trunk-Related Protocols*

Protocol	Description
ISL	Cisco's proprietary trunk encapsulation method for carrying VLANs over FE or GE interfaces
802.1Q	An IEEE standard for carrying VLANs over FE or GE trunks that is essentially a subset of Cisco's current implementation of 802.1Q, which uses a Per-VLAN Spanning Tree implementation like ISL Trunk Protocol
DISL	Cisco's first generation trunk establishment protocol provides several options to enable the configuration of trunks at the other end of a switch link(s)
DTP	Cisco's second generation trunk establishment protocol establishes trunk negotiation options with links that may be using either 802.1Q or ISL as the trunk encapsulation type
VTP	Cisco's method of distributing VLAN information

ISL and 802.1Q specify how to encapsulate or tag data transported over trunk ports. The encapsulation and tagging methods identify a packet's source VLAN. This enables the switches to multiplex the traffic from multiple VLANs over a common trunk link. Chapter 8, "Trunking Technologies and Applications" describes these two methods and how they function.

DISL and DTP help Catalysts to automatically negotiate whether to enable a common link as a trunk or not. The Catalyst software included DISL until Cisco incorporated support for 802.1Q. When 802.1Q was introduced, the protocol needed to negotiate whether to use ISL or 802.1Q encapsulation. Therefore, Cisco introduced the second generation trunk negotiation protocol, DTP. DISL and DTP are described in Chapter 8.

VTP provides a communication protocol between Catalysts over trunks. The protocol allows Catalysts to share information about VLANs in the VTP management domain. VTP operates only after DISL/DTP complete the trunk negotiation process and functions as a payload of ISL/802.1Q. VTP does not work over non-trunk ports. Therefore, it cannot send/receive any messages until DISL or DTP negotiate a link into trunk status. VTP works separately from ISL and 802.1Q in that VTP messages transport configuration data, whereas ISL and 802.1Q specify encapsulation methods. If you have a protocol analyzer capable of decoding these protocols and set it up to capture trunk traffic, it displays VTP as encapsulated within an ISL or 802.1Q frame. Figure 12-12, discussed later in this chapter, shows a VTP frame encapsulated in ISL.

VTP primarily distributes VLAN information. You must configure VTP before you can configure any VLANs. Chapter 5 presented the three steps for creating a VLAN. Specifically, the steps include:

Step 1   Assign the Catalyst to a VTP domain (unless the Catalyst is configured in VTP transparent mode, discussed later.)

Step 2   Create the VLAN.

Step 3   Associate ports to the VLAN.

Chapter 5 described the details of the last two steps, but deferred the discussion about VTP domains to this chapter.

A VTP domain associates Catalysts with a common configuration interest. Catalysts within a VTP domain share VLAN information with each other. If an administrator on a Catalyst creates or deletes a VLAN, the other Catalysts in the VTP domain automatically become aware of the change in the list of VLANs. This helps to ensure administrative conformity between the Catalysts. Without configuration uniformity, Spanning Tree might not, for example, converge upon an optimal topology for the VLANs. VTP also serves to eliminate configuration steps for you. Without VTP, you need to manually create and delete VLANs in each Catalyst. But with VTP, VLANs automatically propagate to all other Catalysts throughout the VTP management domain. This is the principle benefit of VTP. Although this might not sound significant in a small network, it becomes particularly beneficial in larger networks.

A parallel benefit of the management domain limits the extent to which changes can be propagated. Figure 12-1 shows a Catalyst system with two management domains *wally* and *world*. Domain *wally* has VLANs 1, 2, 3, and 4 configured, and domain *world* has VLANs 1, 2, 3, and 10 configured. Assuming there are no Layer 3 issues, workstations assigned to the same VLAN can communicate with each other even though they are in different management domains. A station in VLAN 2 in *wally* belongs to the same broadcast domain as a station in VLAN 2 in *world*.

Figure 12-1 *VLAN Distribution in a Catalyst Network*

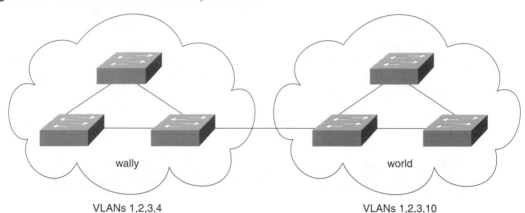

VLANs 1,2,3,4   VLANs 1,2,3,10

Suppose a network administrator decides to add a VLAN 5 to both domains. If you create VLAN 5 in *wally*, VTP propagates the new VLAN throughout the domain *wally*. When the VTP announcement reaches the border Catalyst in *world*, that Catalyst ignores the information from *wally*. The administrator needs to also create VLAN 5 in *world* to spread the VLAN existence.

Suppose the administrator decides to remove VLAN 3 from *world*. At a Catalyst in domain *world*, the administrator clears VLAN 3. What happens to VLAN 3 in *wally*? Nothing. When the border Catalyst in *world* advertises a VTP announcement to the Catalyst in *wally*, the *wally* border Catalyst ignores the information and retains VLAN 3.

TIP   In this case where the administrator deletes a VLAN, VTP propagates the deletion information to the other Catalysts in the management domain. Any hosts attached to ports in the deleted VLAN lose network connectivity because all Catalyst ports in the domain assigned to the VLAN become disabled.

At times, network administrators get new equipment. The equipment, of course, arrives with no configuration. But you cannot immediately start to create VLANs. You must first define a VTP domain. If your Catalyst is configured in the default server VTP mode and you do not assign a Catalyst to a VTP domain, the Catalyst does not let you create a VLAN as demonstrated in Example 12-1. Note that the Catalyst posts a message to the console stating that it refuses to change any VLAN status until it has a domain name. The message also references a VTP server. This is described in more detail later in the section "Configuring VTP Mode."

Example 12-1 *Creating a VLAN with No VTP Domain Configured*

```
Console> (enable) set vlan 10 name willitwork
Cannot add/modify VLANs on a VTP server without a domain name.
Console> (enable)
```

What constitutes a VTP domain? Three required conditions associate Catalysts to a common VTP domain:

- The Catalysts must have the same VTP domain name.

- They must be adjacent.

- Trunking must be enabled between the Catalysts.

The first prerequisite for VTP domain membership involves the management domain name. Catalysts identify their VTP management domain membership through the domain name. All Catalysts that you want to be in the same domain must have the same management domain name. Catalysts initially obtain their VTP management domain name either through command-line configuration or configuration file, or, if trunks are enabled, automatically from a neighbor Catalyst. To manually configure a Catalyst into a management domain, use the **set vtp domain** *name* command. Full usage is shown in Example 12-2.

Example 12-2 **set vtp** *Usage*

```
cat6> (enable) set vtp ?
Usage: set vtp [domain <name>] [mode <mode>] [passwd <passwd>]
               [pruning <enable¦disable>] [v2 <enable¦disable>
        (mode = client¦server¦transparent
         Use passwd '0' to clear vtp password)
Usage: set vtp pruneeligible <vlans>
        (vlans = 2..1005
         An example of vlans is 2-10,1005)
```

The Catalyst accepts domain names up to 32 characters long. Example 12-3 shows a VTP domain name configuration example. The administrator configures the Catalyst as a member of the VTP domain *wally*.

Example 12-3 **set vtp domain** *Example*

```
Console> (enable) set vtp domain wally
VTP domain wally modified
Console> (enable)
```

What domain and VLAN do the Catalysts belong to when they have a clean configuration? If no VTP domain is assigned to the Catalysts, the domain is NULL. All ports belong to VLAN 1. Use the command **show vtp domain** any time to discover what VTP domain a Catalyst belongs to as illustrated in Example 12-4.

Example 12-4 show vtp domain *Output*

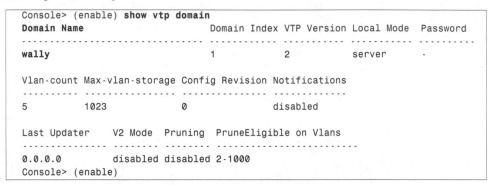

```
Console> (enable) show vtp domain
Domain Name                         Domain Index VTP Version Local Mode  Password
--------------------------------    ------------ ----------- ----------- ----------
wally                               1            2           server      -

Vlan-count Max-vlan-storage Config Revision Notifications
---------- ---------------- --------------- ------------
5          1023             0               disabled

Last Updater    V2 Mode  Pruning  PruneEligible on Vlans
--------------  -------- -------- -----------------------------
0.0.0.0         disabled disabled 2-1000
Console> (enable)
```

For example, in the highlighted portion of Example 12-4, the Catalyst's display indicates that it belongs to the domain *wally*. If the **Domain Name** field is blank, the domain is *NULL*.

TIP   VTP domain names are case sensitive. A VTP domain name *San Jose* is not the same as *san jose*. Catalysts with the former domain name cannot exchange VLAN configuration information with Catalysts configured with the later domain name.

As an example of how Catalysts obtain VTP membership, consider the Catalyst system in Figure 12-2 where multiple Catalysts interconnect over trunks, but no management domain is assigned.

Figure 12-2 *A Catalyst VTP Domain Example*

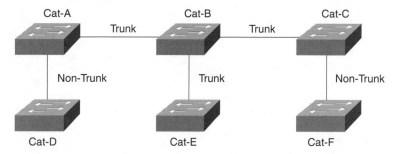

Cat-A, Cat-B, Cat-C, and Cat-E all have trunk connections to other Catalysts, whereas Cat-D and Cat-F only attach through access ports. This prevents Cat-D and Cat-F from receiving VTP messages from any of the other Catalysts. Entering the command **show vtp domain** reveals an output similar to that seen in Example 12-4, but with no domain name assigned on any unit. Assume that you attach to Cat-A's console port to make configurations, and you enter the command **set vtp domain wally**. What happens to the other Catalysts in the network? You examine the VTP status on each Catalyst with the **show vtp domain** command, and you discover that Cat-A, Cat-B, Cat-C, and Cat-E all learn about the management domain, but not Cat-D and Cat-F. Cat-D and Cat-F fail to learn about the management domain because they do not have trunk ports on which to receive VTP updates.

By setting the VTP domain in one unit, all other Catalysts attached with trunk ports automatically learn about VTP domain *wally* and configure themselves as part of the domain. This works because Cat-B, Cat-C, and Cat-E had trunk connections and did not already belong to a VTP domain. If however, you had previously associated them with a different domain, they would ignore the VTP announcement for *wally*.

At this point, you can create new VLANs in Cat-A, Cat-B, Cat-C, and Cat-E, but not Cat-D and Cat-F. You can only create VLANs in Catalysts configured with a VTP domain name (as mentioned earlier, this assumes the default setting of VTP Server Mode as discussed in the next section). Because D and F do not have a domain name, you cannot create VLANs in them. So how do you add VLANs to Cat-D and Cat-F? You need to manually enter a VTP domain name in these two units before you can create any VLANs in them. When you assign them to a domain, they do not make any VTP announcements because there is no trunk link. But they do belong to a management domain. Alternatively, you can enable the links between Cat-A and Cat-D and Cat-C and Cat-F as trunks. When they are enabled as trunks, Cat-D and Cat-F can then receive VTP updates and become members of the management domain *wally*.

The requirements for defining a VTP domain are listed earlier. One of the requirements is that Catalysts with the same VTP domain name must be adjacent to belong to the same management domain. In Figure 12-3, Catalysts interconnect with trunk links and belong to several management domains. Two of the domains have the same name, but are separated by other domains. Even though the Catalysts in the first and last domain have the same management domain name, they actually belong to two different domains from a system point of view.

Figure 12-3 *A Multiple VTP Domain Network*

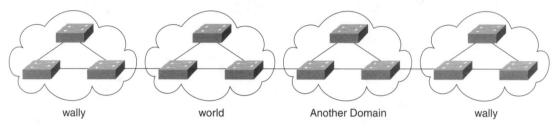

| wally | world | Another Domain | wally |

Whenever a Catalyst makes a VTP announcement, it includes the VTP domain name. If the receiving Catalyst belongs to a different management domain, it ignores the announcement. Therefore, VTP announcements from the *wally* domain on the left of the drawing are never seen by the Catalysts in the *wally* domain on the right of the drawing.

TIP   If you are installing a domain border switch that connects two domains, it becomes a member of the management domain that it first hears from. Therefore, be sure to attach it to the domain that you want it to belong to first. Make sure that it acquires the VTP domain name, and then attach it to the other domain. Otherwise, you need to manually configure the domain name.

WARNING   A side effect of VTP domains can prevent an ISL trunk link from negotiating correctly with dynamic ISL (DISL). When DISL initiates trunk negotiation, it includes the VTP domain name in the message. If the two ends of the link belong to different domains, the trunk fails to establish automatically. To enable a trunk on border Catalysts between domains, set both ends of the trunk to *ON* or *nonegotiate*.

VTP Modes

Referencing the **set vtp ?** output of Example 12-2, notice that you have the option to configure a VTP mode. You can configure VTP to operate in one of three modes: server, client, or transparent. The three modes differ in how they source VTP messages and in how they respond when they receive VTP messages. Table 12-2 summarizes the differences between the three modes.

Table 12-2   *VTP Mode Comparisons*

Feature	Server	Client	Transparent
Source VTP Messages	Yes	Yes	No
Listen to VTP Messages	Yes	Yes	No
Create VLANs	Yes	No	Yes*
Remember VLANs	Yes	No	Yes*

*Locally significant only.

Source VTP Messages

Whenever you create a VLAN that you want VTP to automatically distribute to the other Catalysts in the management domain, you must create the VLAN on a Catalyst configured as a VTP server. After you create the VLAN, the VTP server automatically distributes the VLAN information through a VTP message called a *VTP subset advertisement*, which is described in more detail in the section, "Subset Advertisements." This message informs the other Catalysts in the management domain about the new VLAN. The Catalyst where you configure the new VLAN generates the initial subset advertisement which it sends out its trunk interfaces. Other servers and clients continue the propagation to other Catalysts in the network.

Catalysts configured in transparent mode, however, never generate VTP messages. When you create a VLAN on a transparent device, the VLAN information stays local and is not advertised to any other device—even if it has trunk connections to other Catalysts.

Listen to VTP Messages

Only Catalysts configured as server or client pay attention to VTP messages. Whenever they receive a message with the VTP multicast address **01-00-0C-CC-CC-CC** and an SNAP type value of **0x2003**, the receiving Catalyst sends the frame to the Supervisor module where it is processed. If the Supervisor determines that the information included in the update supercedes the information that it has, it updates the VLAN information and creates updated messages to other neighbor Catalysts. The Catalyst uses the VTP configuration revision number to recognize if it has older or current data. The configuration revision number usage is discussed later in this chapter.

When a Catalyst configured in transparent mode receives a VTP update, the Catalyst does not send the frame to the Supervisor. Rather, it locally ignores the frame. If, however, the Catalyst has other trunk links connected, it floods the frame out the other trunk ports. But the VTP message does not change the transparent Catalyst's configuration as it does for a server or client device.

Create VLANs

If you desire to create a VLAN, you must create it on a Catalyst configured in server or transparent mode. These are the only modes authorized to accept **set vlan** and **clear vlan** commands. The difference between them, though, is the behavior after you create the VLAN. In the case of the server mode, the Catalyst sends VTP advertisements out all trunk ports to neighbor Catalysts. Transparent mode Catalysts do not issue any type of VTP announcement when a VLAN is created. The new VLAN is only locally significant. If you build an entire network with Catalysts configured in transparent mode, you need to create new VLANs in each and every Catalyst as an individual command. Catalysts in transparent mode do not, for all intents and purposes, participate in VTP. To them, it is as if VTP does not exist. You do not need to assign the transparently configured Catalyst to a VTP domain before you can create any local VLANs. VTP transparent mode switches do not advertise changes or additions made for VLANs on the local switch, but they pass through VLAN additions or changes made elsewhere.

Catalysts configured as clients do not have the authority to create any VLANs. If you associate a client port to a VLAN that it does not know about, the Catalyst generates a message informing you that you must create a VLAN on a server before it can move the ports to the VLAN. If, after assigning the ports to the VLAN, you look at the VLAN status with the **show vlans** command, you might notice that the ports belong to the new but non-existent VLAN and are in a suspended state preventing the forwarding of frames in the VLAN. When you actually create the VLAN on a server in the same management domain as the client, the client eventually hears about the new VLAN and interprets this as authorization to activate ports in the new VLAN.

Similarly, you cannot delete VLANs in a client, only in a server or transparent device. Deleting a VLAN in a transparent device only affects the local device as opposed to when you delete a VLAN from a server. When deleting a VLAN from a server, you get a warning message from the Catalyst informing you that this action places any ports assigned to the VLAN within the management domain into a suspended mode, as shown in Example 12-5.

Example 12-5 *Clearing a VLAN in a Management Domain*

```
Console> (enable) clear vlan 10
This command will deactivate all ports on vlan 10
in the entire management domain
Do you want to continue(y/n) [n]?y
Vlan 10 deleted
Console> (enable)
```

TIP   Clearing a VLAN does not cause the ports in the management domain to reassign themselves to the default VLAN 1. Rather, the Catalysts keep the ports assigned to the previous VLAN, but in an inactive state. You need to reassign ports to an active VLAN before the attached devices can communicate again.

Remember VLANs

Whenever you create, delete, or suspend a VLAN in a server or transparent Catalyst, the Catalyst stores the configuration information in NVRAM so that on power up it can recover to the last known VLAN configuration. If the unit is a server, it also transmits configuration information to its Catalyst neighbors.

Clients, on the other hand, do not store VLAN information. When a Catalyst configured in client mode loses power, it forgets about all the VLANs it knew except for VLAN 1, the default VLAN. On power up, the client cannot locally activate any VLANs, except VLAN 1, until it hears from a VTP server authorizing a set of VLANs. Any ports assigned to VLANs other than VLAN 1 remain in a suspended state until they receive a VTP announcement from a server. When the client receives a VTP update from a server, it can then activate any ports assigned to VLANs included in the VTP announcement.

VTP VLAN Distribution Demonstrated

Consider Figure 12-4 to illustrate the differences between a server (Cat-A), client (Cat-C), and transparent (Cat-B) configuration, where one of each is linearly cascaded with a transparent device (Cat-B) in the middle.

Figure 12-4 *VLAN Distribution for VTP Modes Server, Client, and Transparent*

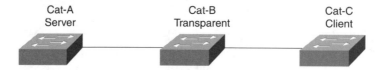

Cat-A
Server

Cat-B
Transparent

Cat-C
Client

Table 12-3 shows the starting condition and all subsequent conditions for Catalysts A, B, and C.

Table 12-3 *Status for Catalysts in Figure 12-4 Demonstrating Server, Client, and Transparent Mode*

		Configured VLANs for:		
Step #	**Event**	**Cat-A Server**	**Cat-B Transparent**	**Cat-C Client**
1	Starting Condition.	1	1	1
2	Create VLAN 2 in Cat-C.	1	1	1
3	Assign ports to VLAN 2 in Cat-C.	1	1	1
4	Create VLAN 2 in Cat-A.	1, 2	1	1, 2
5	Create VLAN 10 in Cat-B.	1, 2	1, 10	1, 2
6	Lose and restore power on Cat-A and Cat-B.	1, 2	1, 10	1, 2

continues

Table 12-3 *Status for Catalysts in Figure 12-4 Demonstrating Server, Client, and Transparent Mode (Continued)*

7	Lose power on Cat-A and Cat-C. Restore power to Cat-C only.	N/A	1, 10	1
8	Restore power on Cat-A.	1, 2	1, 10	1, 2
9	Create VLAN 20 on all three Catalysts.	1, 2, 20	1, 10, 20	1, 2, 20

In the starting configuration of Step 1, the Catalysts have a VTP domain name assigned to them. In reality, VTP in Cat-B isn't really participating and can be ignored for now. All three Catalysts start with only the default VLAN 1. In Step 2, the administrator starts work on the client and tries to create a new VLAN. But because Cat-C is a client, Cat-C rejects the command, posts an error to the console, and does not create any new VLAN. Only VLAN 1 remains in existence. The administrator assigns ports to VLAN 2 in Step 3 with the **set vlan** command. Even though VLAN 2 does not exist yet, Cat-C accepts the port assignment, moves ports to VLAN 2, and places them in the suspend state. However, Cat-C only knows about VLAN 1.

In Step 4, the administrator moves to Cat-A, a server, and creates VLAN 2 which then gets propagated to its neighbor, Cat-B. But Cat-B, configured in transparent mode, ignores the VTP announcement. It does not add VLAN 2 to its local VLAN configuration. Cat-B floods the VTP announcement out any other trunk ports to neighbor Catalysts. In this case, Cat-C receives the VTP update, checks the VTP management domain name, which matches, and adds VLAN 2 to its local list. Cat-C then activates any ports assigned to VLAN 2. Any devices attached to ports in VLAN 2 on Cat-A now belong to the same broadcast domain as ports assigned to VLAN 2 on Cat-C. If Layer 3 permits, these devices can now communicate with each other.

The administrator now moves (or Telnets) to Cat-B in Step 5 and creates a new broadcast domain, VLAN 10. As a Catalyst configured in transparent mode, the Catalyst is authorized to create VLAN 10. But Cat-B does not propagate any information about VLAN 10 to the other Catalysts. VLAN 10 remains local to Cat-B and is not a global VLAN.

A disaster occurs in Step 6 when the facility loses power to Cat-A and Cat-B. But, because you are a savvy network engineer, you configured them in server and transparent modes so they can remember their VLAN configuration information. Although Cat-A and Cat-B remain without power, Cat-C continues to operate based upon the last VLAN configuration it knew. All ports on Cat-C remain operational in their assigned VLANs. When power is restored to Cat-A and Cat-B, both Catalysts remember their authorized VLANs and enable them. Cat-A also issues VTP messages to neighbors. This does not affect the operations of Cat-B or Cat-C, though, because they both remember their configuration.

Now consider what happens if Cat-A and Cat-C lose power. In Step 7, this occurs, but power is restored to Cat-C before Cat-A. When Cat-C recovers, it starts with only VLAN 1 authorized. Ports in any other VLAN are disabled until Cat-C hears a VTP message from a server. If Cat-A takes one hour to recover, Cat-C remains in this state the entire time. When Cat-A finally restarts in Step 8, it sends VTP messages that then authorize Cat-C to enable any ports in VLANs included in the VTP announcement.

Finally, the administrator creates another VLAN for the entire management domain. In Step 9, the administrator creates VLAN 20. But this takes two configuration statements. The administrator must create the VLAN in Cat-A and in Cat-B. Now there are two global VLANs in the domain. Any devices in VLAN 20 belong to the same broadcast domain, regardless of which Catalyst they connect to. VLAN 1 is the other global broadcast domain. Any devices in VLAN 1 can also communicate with each other. But, devices in VLAN 1 cannot communicate with devices in VLAN 20 unless there is a router in the network.

The Working Mechanics of VTP

The VLAN Trunking Protocol developed by Cisco operates as a Layer 2 protocol for Catalyst products. When transmitting VTP messages to other Catalysts in a network, a Catalyst encapsulates the VTP message in a trunking protocol frame, such as ISL or 802.1Q. Figure 12-5 shows the generic encapsulation for VTP within an ISL frame. The ISL encapsulation starts with the header information detailed in Chapter 8, "Trunking Technologies and Applications." The VTP header varies depending upon the type of VTP message discussed, but generally, four items are found in all VTP messages:

- **VTP protocol version**—Either version 1 or 2
- **VTP message type**—Indicates one of four types
- **Management domain name length**—Indicates the size of the name that follows
- **Management domain name**—The name configured for the management domain

Additional details on the VTP messages are in the following sections. VTP messages always travel over the default VLAN for the media. For example, on an Ethernet trunk, VTP transports over VLAN 1; on FDDI, it transports over VLAN 1002; and over ATM, VTP transports over ELAN *default*. Because you cannot delete any of the default VLANs, VTP messages always propagate over LAN trunk ports. However, VTP does not always transport over ATM trunks. ELAN *default* must be enabled for VTP to cross ATM. But, this ELAN does not automatically exist. You must explicitly enable this ELAN if you want VTP messages to cross the ATM link.

Figure 12-5 *VTP Encapsulation over ISL Trunks*

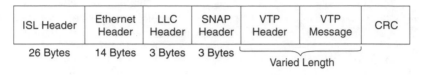

Although Cisco routers understand trunking protocols like ISL, LANE, and 802.1Q, they currently do not participate in VTP; routers ignore VTP messages and discard them at the router interface. Therefore, VTP messages propagate no further than a router interface, or to another Catalyst that belongs to a different VTP management domain. Figure 12-6 shows a system with three management domains isolated through varied domain assignments and through a router. Domain 1 has three management domain border points, one to the router and two into Domain 2.

Figure 12-6 *VTP Boundaries*

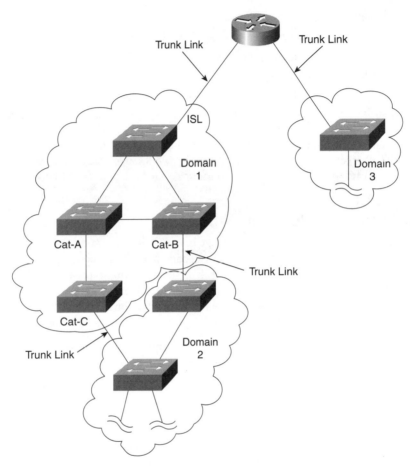

When Cat-A in Domain 1 issues a VTP message, the message gets distributed to all of the other Catalysts in the domain. Cat-B and Cat-C receive the message and forward it to the two Catalysts in Domain 2. However, these Catalysts see that the source domain differs from their own and, therefore, discard the VTP message.

The VTP message generated in Domain 1 also propagates to the router. But the router does not participate with VTP and discards the message.

Likewise, VTP messages generated in Domain 2 or Domain 3 never affect devices outside of their domain.

VTP defines four message types:

- Summary advertisements
- Subset advertisements
- Advertisement requests
- VTP join messages

The first three message types describe interactions between VTP servers and clients for the distribution of VLAN information. These messages occur by default whenever you enable a trunk between Catalysts configured as servers and/or clients. The fourth message is disabled by default and is only enabled whenever you turn on VTP pruning. The section in this chapter, "VTP Pruning: Advanced Traffic Management," describes VTP pruning; therefore, the discussion on the fourth message type is deferred until then.

VTP Configuration Revision Number

Whenever you make a VLAN change on a server Catalyst, the Catalyst issues VTP messages so that other Catalysts can update their VLAN configurations. It is, however, important that the Catalysts keep track of what information is newer than others. Therefore, VTP keeps a configuration revision number that increments whenever you add, delete, or suspend a VLAN. Catalysts in a management domain compare the revision number to determine if the announcement contains newer or obsolete information.

With a fresh configuration, the Catalyst has a revision number of zero. The revision number in the management domain continues to increment until it reaches 2,147,483,648, at which point the counter wraps back to zero.

TIP   You can quickly and easily reset the configuration revision number with the **set vtp domain** *name* command. Changing the domain name sets the configuration revision number to zero. Or, you can make 2,147,483,684 VLAN changes to your system to force the counter to roll back to zero. Unfortunately, this could take a very long time to accomplish.

Summary Advertisements

By default, server and client Catalysts issue summary advertisements every five minutes. Summary advertisements inform neighbor Catalysts what they believe to be the current VTP configuration revision number and management domain membership. The receiving Catalyst compares the domain names and, if they differ, ignores the message. If the domain names match, the receiving server or client Catalyst compares the configuration revision number. If the advertisement contains a higher revision number than the receiving Catalyst currently has, the receiving Catalyst issues an advertisement request for new VLAN information.

Figure 12-7 shows the protocol format for a summary advertisement.

Figure 12-7 *VTP Summary Advertisement Format*

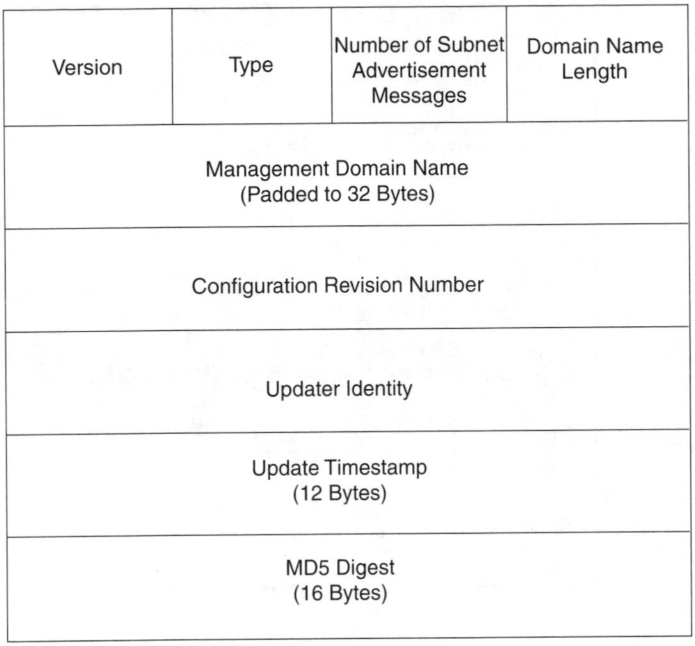

Version	Type	Number of Subnet Advertisement Messages	Domain Name Length
Management Domain Name (Padded to 32 Bytes)			
Configuration Revision Number			
Updater Identity			
Update Timestamp (12 Bytes)			
MD5 Digest (16 Bytes)			

Each row in Figure 12-7 is four octets long. The Version, Type, Number of Subnet Advertisement Messages, and Domain Name Length Fields are all one octet long. Some of the fields can extend beyond four octets and are indicated in the figure. A description of each of the fields follows the decode in Figure 12-8.

Figure 12-8 decodes a summary advertisement packet encapsulated in an ISL trunking protocol frame. If the trunk uses 802.1Q rather than ISL, the VTP message is exactly the same, only encapsulated in an 802.1Q frame.

Figure 12-8 *VTP Summary Advertisement Analyzer Decode*

```
ISL: ----- ISL Protocol Packet -----
  ISL:
  ISL: Destination Address        = 01000C0000
  ISL: Type                       = 0 (Ethernet)
  ISL: User                       = 0 (Normal)
  ISL: Source Address             = 00E0F756D501
  ISL: Length                     = 113
  ISL: Constant value             = 0xAAAA03
  ISL: Vendor ID                  = 0x01000C
  ISL: Virtual LAN ID (VLAN)      = 1
  ISL: Bridge Protocol Data Unit (BPDU)  = 1
  ISL: Port Index                 = 1
  ISL: Reserved
  ISL:
ETHER: ----- Ethernet Header -----
  ETHER:
  ETHER: Destination = Multicast 01000CCCCCCC
  ETHER: Source      = Station 00E0F756D8FB
  ETHER: 802.3 length = 83
  ETHER:
LLC: C D=AA S=AA UI
SNAP: ID=Cisco  Type=2003 (VTP)
VTP: ----- Cisco Virtual Trunk Protocol (VTP) Packet -----
  VTP:
  VTP: Version                    = 1
  VTP: Message type               = 0x01 (Summary-Advert)
  VTP: Number of Subset-Advert messages = 0
  VTP: Length of management domain name = 5
  VTP: Management domain name     = "Cisco"
  VTP: Number of Padding bytes    = 27
  VTP: Configuration revision number = 0x0000005
  VTP: Updater Identity IP address = 10.0.5.5
  VTP: Update Timestamp           = "980123153500"
  VTP: MD5 Digest value           = 0x0E7BF0F335F9B463
  VTP:                              0x298ADEB7FC55D65D
```

The decode starts with the SNAP header that follows the other headers shown in Figure 12-5. Although VTP uses the same Ethernet multicast address as CDP, the SNAP value differs between the two. CDP uses a SNAP value of 0x2000, but VTP uses a SNAP value of 0x2003. This allows the receiving Catalysts to distinguish the protocols.

The VTP header contains the VTP version in use. All Catalysts in the management domain must run the same version. In this case, they are running VTP version 1. If there are Token Ring switch ports in your domain, this would have to be VTP version 2. The message type value indicates which of the four VTP messages listed earlier was transmitted by the source Catalyst.

The following field, Number of Subset Advertisement Messages, indicates how many VTP type 2 messages follow the summary advertisement frame. This value can range from zero to 255. *Zero* indicates that no subset advertisements follow. A Catalyst only transmits the subset advertisement if there is a change in the system, or in response to an advertisement request message.

The domain length and name follows this field along with any padding bytes necessary to complete the Domain Name field.

The source also transmits the VTP configuration revision number and identifies itself through its IP address. Remember from the earlier section, "VTP Configuration Revision Number," that the receiving Catalyst compares the configuration revision number with its internal number to determine if the source has new configuration information or not.

The message includes a timestamp which indicates the time the configuration revision number incremented to its current value. The timestamp has the format of *yymmddhhmmss* which represents year/month/day and hour/minute/second.

Finally, the source performs an MD5 one-way hash on the header information. An MD5 (message digest type 5) hash algorithm is frequently used in security systems as a non-reversible encryption process. The receiving Catalyst also performs a hash and compares the result to detect any corruptions in the frame. If the hashes do not match, the receiving Catalyst discards the VTP message.

Subset Advertisements

Whenever you change a VLAN in the management domain, the server Catalyst where you configured the change issues a summary advertisement followed by one or more subset advertisement messages. Changes that trigger the subset advertisement include:

- Creating or deleting a VLAN
- Suspending or activating a VLAN
- Changing the name of a VLAN
- Changing the MTU of a VLAN

Figure 12-9 shows the VTP subset advertisement packet format.

Figure 12-9 *VTP Subset Advertisement Format*

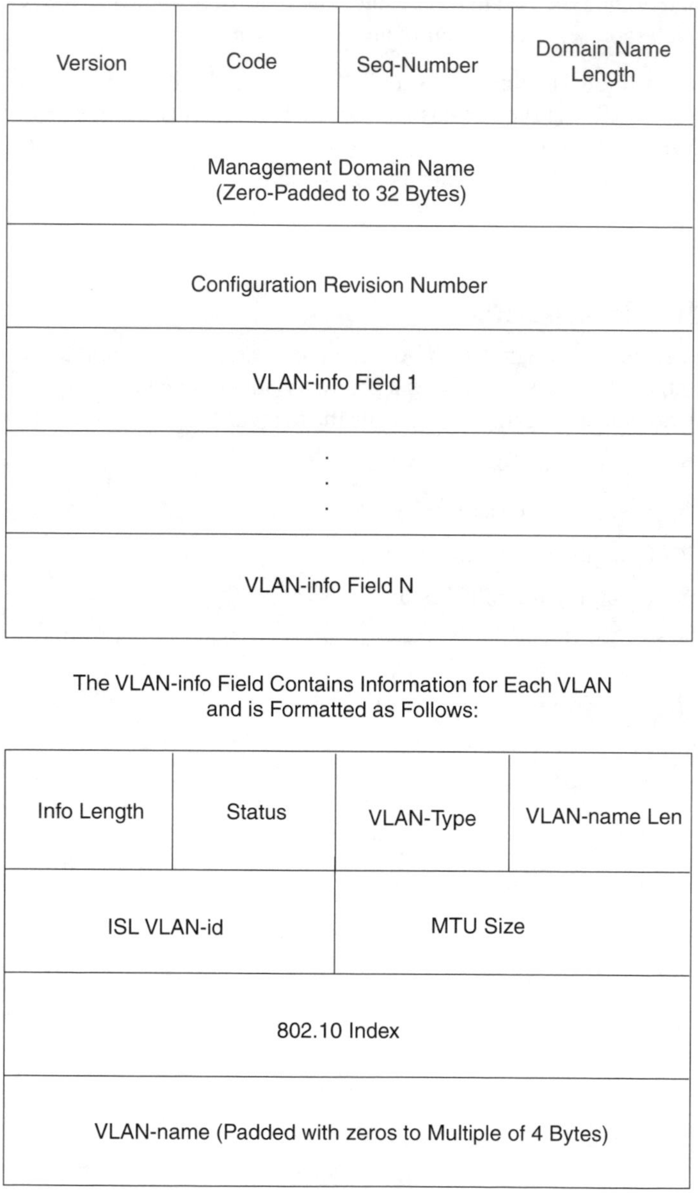

Version	Code	Seq-Number	Domain Name Length
Management Domain Name (Zero-Padded to 32 Bytes)			
Configuration Revision Number			
VLAN-info Field 1			
. . .			
VLAN-info Field N			

The VLAN-info Field Contains Information for Each VLAN
and is Formatted as Follows:

Info Length	Status	VLAN-Type	VLAN-name Len
ISL VLAN-id		MTU Size	
802.10 Index			
VLAN-name (Padded with zeros to Multiple of 4 Bytes)			

The summary advertisement has a *Seq-Number* field in the header indicating the number of subset advertisements that follow. If you have a long VLAN list, VTP might need to send the entire list over multiple subset advertisements.

Figure 12-10 shows a subset advertisement (partial listing). As with the summary advertisement, the message includes the VTP version type, the domain name and related fields, and the configuration revision number. The header sequence number indicates the identity of the subset advertisement. If multiple subset advertisements follow the summary advertisement, this number indicates the subset instance sent by the updater. The sequence numbering starts with *1*. The receiving Catalyst uses this value to ensure that it receives all subset advertisements and, if not, can request a resend starting with a specific subset advertisement.

Figure 12-10 *VTP Subset Advertisement Analyzer Decode*

```
ISL: VLAN=1 Type=0 (Ethernet) User=0 (Normal)
ETHER: 802.3 size=328 bytes
LLC: C D=AA S=AA UI
SNAP: ID=Cisco Type=2003 (VTP)
VTP: ------ Cisco Virtual Trunk Protocol (VTP) Packet ------
VTP:
VTP: Version                        = 1
VTP: Message type                   = 0x02 (Subset-Advert)
VTP: Sequence number                = 1
VTP: Management Domain Name length  = 5
VTP: Management Domain Name         = "Cisco"
VTP: Number of Padding bytes        = 27
VTP: Configuration revision number  = 0x00000006
VTP:
VTP: VLAN Information Field # 1:
VTP: VLAN information field length   = 20
VTP: VLAN status                     = 0x00
VTP: VLAN type                       = 1 (Ethernet)
VTP: Length of VLAN name             = 7
VTP: ISL VLAN-id                     = 1
VTP: MTU size                        = 1500
VTP: 802.10 SAID field               = 100001
VTP: VLAN Name                       = "default"
VTP: # padding bytes in VLAN Name    = 1
VTP:
VTP: VLAN Information Field # 2:
VTP: VLAN information field length   = 16
VTP: VLAN status                     = 0x00
VTP: VLAN type                       = 1 (Ethernet)
VTP: Length of VLAN name             = 2
VTP: ISL VLAN-id                     = 2
VTP: MTU size                        = 1500
VTP: 802.10 SAID field               = 100002
VTP: VLAN Name                       = "HR"
VTP: # padding bytes in VLAN Name    = 2
VTP:
VTP: VLAN Information Field # 3:
VTP: VLAN information field length   = 20
```

The summary advertisement then lists all of the VLANs in the management domain along with the following information for each:

- Length of the VLAN description field
- Status of the VLAN. The VLAN can be active or suspended
- VLAN type. Is it Ethernet, Token Ring, FDDI, or other?
- MTU (maximum transmission unit) for the VLAN. What is the maximum frame size supported on this VLAN?
- Length of the VLAN name
- The VLAN number for this named VLAN
- The SAID value to use if the frame is passed over an FDDI trunk
- The VLAN name

The VTP subset advertisement individually lists this information for each VLAN, even the default VLANs.

Advertisement Requests

A Catalyst issuing the third VTP message type, an *advertisement request*, solicits summary and subset advertisements from a server in the management domain. Catalysts transmit an advertisement request whenever you reset the Catalyst, whenever you change its VTP domain membership, or whenever it hears a VTP summary advertisement with a higher configuration revision number than it currently has. This can happen if a Catalyst is temporarily partitioned from the network and a change occurs in the domain.

Figure 12-11 shows a VTP advertisement request frame format.

Figure 12-11 *VTP Advertisement Request Format*

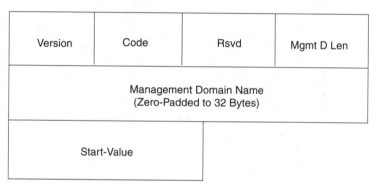

An advertisement request includes six fields. The **Version** field identifies the VTP version used by the device. The **Code** field identifies this as an advertisement request. The reserved *(Rsvd)* portion is set to zero. The **Management Domain Length** field (**MgmtD Len**) indicates the length of the domain name in the following field. These four fields are followed by the **Management Domain Name**. Finally, if the Catalyst expected to receive subset advertisements but failed to receive one or more, it can request a resend starting at a particular subset instance value. This is signaled in the **Start-Value** field. For example, if the Catalyst expected to see three subset advertisements but only received instances 1 and 3, it can request a resend starting at instance 2.

Figure 12-12 shows an advertisement request captured on an analyzer.

Figure 12-12 *VTP Advertisement Request Analyzer Decode*

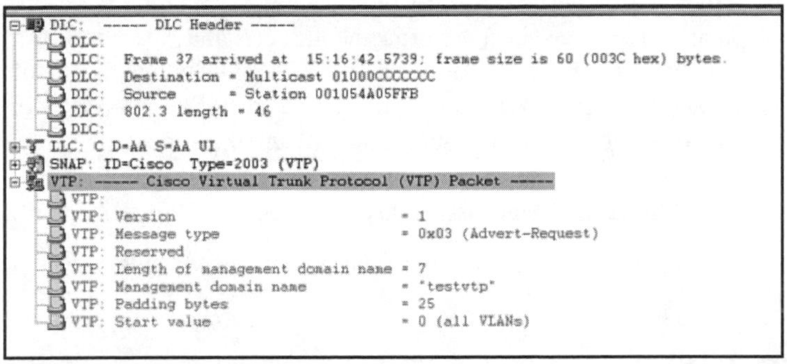

```
DLC:  ----- DLC Header -----
  DLC:
  DLC:  Frame 37 arrived at  15:16:42.5739; frame size is 60 (003C hex) bytes.
  DLC:  Destination = Multicast 01000CCCCCCC
  DLC:  Source      = Station 001054A05FFB
  DLC:  802.3 length = 46
  DLC:
LLC: C D=AA S=AA UI
SNAP: ID=Cisco  Type=2003 (VTP)
VTP: ----- Cisco Virtual Trunk Protocol (VTP) Packet -----
  VTP:
  VTP:  Version                      = 1
  VTP:  Message type                 = 0x03 (Advert-Request)
  VTP:  Reserved
  VTP:  Length of management domain name = 7
  VTP:  Management domain name       = "testvtp"
  VTP:  Padding bytes                = 25
  VTP:  Start value                  = 0 (all VLANs)
```

The advertisement request in Figure 12-12 requests all subset advertisements for the management domain *testvtp*. This is recognized because the *start value* is zero.

Configuring VTP Mode

Use the **set vtp mode {server|client|transparent}** to define the Catalyst's VTP mode. You have the option to specify the VTP mode when you specify the VTP domain name. If you do not specify a VTP mode, server is defined as the default.

Example 12-6 shows output for configuring a Catalyst into the client mode. Note the highlighted portion of the output indicating that the Catalyst is now configured as a client.

Example 12-6 *Setting VTP Mode to Client*

```
Console> (enable) set vtp mode client
VTP domain wally modified
Console> (enable) show vtp domain
Domain Name                      Domain Index VTP Version Local Mode  Password
-------------------------------- ------------ ----------- ----------- ----------
wally                            1            2           client      -
Vlan-count Max-vlan-storage Config Revision Notifications
---------- ---------------- --------------- -------------
10         1023             40              enabled
Last Updater    V2 Mode  Pruning  PruneEligible on Vlans
--------------- -------- -------- ------------------------
10.0.0.1        disabled disabled 2-1000
Console> (enable)
```

As illustrated in the section on decoding VTP subset advertisements, all VLAN information sent over the wire is cleartext. Anyone with an analyzer package can capture the VTP frame and decode it. A system attacker can use this information to disrupt your network. For example, an attacker can fabricate a false subset advertisement with a higher configuration revision number and delete the VLANs in your management domain.

As a security option, you can specify a password for VTP subset advertisements. If you specify a password, the Catalyst uses this as a key to generate an MD5 hash. Whenever a source Catalyst issues a subset advertisement, it calculates the hash for the advertisement message and uses the password as the key. VTP includes the hash result in the subset advertisement. The receiving Catalyst must also have the same password locally configured. When it receives the subset advertisement, it generates a hash using its password and compares the result with the received message. If they match, it accepts the advertisement as valid. Otherwise, it discards the subset advertisement.

You can configure a password using the command **set vtp passwd** *passwd*.

Tracking VTP Activity

The command **show vtp statistics** is a particularly useful command for tracking VTP activity such as the number and type of VTP messages sent and received from a Catalyst. Example 12-7 shows typical **show vtp statistics** output.

Example 12-7 show vtp statistics *Screen*

```
Cat-A > (enable) show vtp statistics

VTP statistics:
summary advts received         5392
subset  advts received         16
request advts received         3
summary advts transmitted      5280
subset  advts transmitted      7
request advts transmitted      0
No of config revision errors   0
No of config digest errors     0
VTP pruning statistics:
Trunk      Join Trasmitted  Join Received  Summary advts received from
                                           non-pruning-capable device
--------   ---------------  -------------  --------------------------
  1/1      0                0              0
  1/2      0                0              0
Cat-A > (enable)
```

Notice the highlighted line in Example 12-7. It lists the number of incidents where the received MD5 hash did not match the locally calculated value. This can indicate either a corruption of the frame from a physical layer problem or a security issue. If the problem stems from a physical layer issue, you might anticipate that other frames also have problems. If you do not experience other transmission errors, there might be an attack where the attacker is attempting to spoof a Catalyst and corrupt your management domain.

VTP: A Good or Bad Thing?

One of the primary advantages of VTP is its capability to distribute VLANs to other Catalysts to simplify your configuration tasks. As a result of VTP, you do not need to type the **set vlan** command nearly as often as you do without it. You only need to create the VLAN once in the management domain rather than at each switch. But, you still need to do a **set vlan** command to add the ports that will be assigned to that VLAN on a given switch. Deleting a VLAN in a domain is also easy because you only need to do it at one location.

However, there are some disadvantages to VTP and trunking that you need to consider as discussed in the sections that follow.

VLAN Table Deletion

Ironically, one of the disadvantages stems directly from the simplified configuration feature of VTP. Consider the network in Figure 12-13 where multiple Catalysts interconnect in a management domain.

Figure 12-13 *A Multiple Catalyst Network and VTP Synchronization Problem*

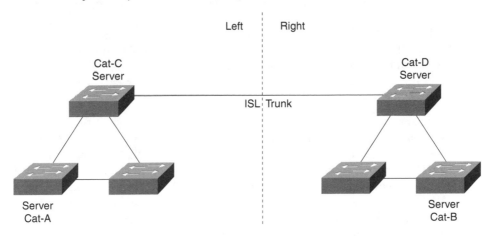

If you make any changes to the VLAN list on any server in the network, the change gets distributed to the other Catalysts in the management domain. But what happens if you make changes while the network is partitioned? For example, assume in Figure 12-13 that the trunk link between Cat-C and Cat-D servers isolate the three Catalysts on the left from the three on the right. All Catalysts should have the same VTP configuration revision number, *N*. See Table 12-4 for VLAN table and VTP configuration revision numbers for these steps.

Table 12-4 *Synchronization Problem with Partitioned Catalysts*

Step	Event	Left Catalysts		Right Catalysts	
		VLANs	**Rev.#**	**VLANs**	**Rev. #**
1	Initial state	1, 2, 3, 4, 5	N	1, 2, 3, 4, 5	N
2	Partition network between Cat-C and Cat-D	1, 2, 3, 4, 5	N	1, 2, 3, 4, 5	N
3	Create VLAN 10 in left portion	1, 2, 3, 4, 5, 10	N+1	1, 2, 3, 4, 5	N
4	Delete VLAN 5 in right portion	1, 2, 3, 4, 5, 10	N+1	1, 2, 3, 4	N+1
5	Restore link between Cat-C and Cat-D	1, 2, 3, 4, 5, 10	N+1	1, 2, 3, 4	N+1
6	Delete VLAN 5 in left portion	1, 2, 3, 4, 10	N+2	1, 2, 3, 4, 10	N+2

While the network is partitioned, an administrator on the left creates a new VLAN thinking, "When the network recovers, the new VLAN will get distributed to the Catalysts on the right." At the same time, an administrator on the right makes a VLAN change by deleting a VLAN. This administrator thinks like the first administrator and expects VTP to propagate the deletion when the network recovers.

When the trunk link between Cat-C and Cat-D is restored, both Catalysts issue VTP summary advertisements announcing a configuration revision update of *N+1*. Catalysts in each half compare the number with their own values, see that they match, and never issue a VTP advertisement request. This leaves the two portions with unsynchronized VLAN tables as shown in Step 5. To resynchronize the tables, the administrator needs to enter a VLAN modification as in Step 6, which forces an increment in the revision number. The Catalyst where the configuration change was made then issues a VTP summary advertisement and a VTP subset advertisement. This information gets distributed to the other Catalysts in the network synchronizing the VLAN tables.

A more severe case can occur when two normally isolated portions merge. Suppose the three Catalysts on the left belong to one corporate department (Engineering) that doesn't like the corporate division using the three Catalysts on the right (Marketing). The Catalysts remain isolated until a higher level manager mandates that the two divisions need to connect their networks. It is decided ahead of time by the manager that the two groups will change their domain names to a new third name so that they all belong to the same management domain. The two groups now have a configuration as shown in Step 1 of Table 12-5. (The configuration revision number was arbitrarily selected for this example.)

Table 12-5   *A Catastrophic Merger of VTP Domains*

Step	Event	Left Catalysts		Right Catalysts	
		VLANs	Rev.#	VLANs	Rev.#
1	Initial state	1, 2, 3, 4, 5	32	1, 10, 20, 30	57
2	Merge domains	1, 10, 20, 30	57	1, 10, 20, 30	57

The big moment arrives when the two groups shake hands and join the networks. What happens? Disaster. Because the Marketing side has a higher configuration revision number than the Engineering side, VTP updates the Engineering VLAN tables to match the Marketing side. All of the Engineering users that were attached to VLANs 2, 3, 4, and 5 now attach to ports in suspended mode. Marketing just torpedoed the Engineering LAN! Now engineering is really mad at Marketing.

TIP   Before merging different domains, be sure to create a super set of VLANs in both domains to prevent VLAN table deletion problems. Make sure that all partitions have a complete list of all VLANs from each partition before joining them together.

Similarly, if you have a Catalyst dedicated to you for *playing around*, and you attach it to the production network, you might delete the VLANs in your production network if you are not careful. Make sure that you either **clear config all**, change the VTP domain name, or put it in transparent mode before attaching it to the production network.

TIP   Another real-world situation exists that could delete VLANs in your network. If you replace a failed Supervisor module on a Catalyst configured in the server mode, you run the possibility of deleting VLANs if the new module has a higher configuration revision number than the others in the domain. Be sure to reset the configuration revision number on the new module before activating it in the system.

Broadcast Flooding

Another issue involves trunks and VTP. Chapter 8 described trunks and the syntax to establish trunks. Whenever you enable a trunk, the trunk, by default, transports traffic for all VLANs. This includes all forwarded and flooded traffic. If you have a VLAN that generates a high volume of flooded traffic from broadcasts or multicasts, the frames flood throughout the entire network. They even cross VTP management domains. This can have a significant impact on your default management VLAN 1. Refer to Chapters 15, "Campus Design Implementation," and 17, "Case Studies: Implementing Switches," for discussions on cautions and suggestions regarding the management VLAN. In Figure 12-14, a Catalyst system has trunk and access links interconnecting them. PC-1 in the system attaches through an access link assigned to VLAN 2. This particular station generates multicast traffic for video distribution on VLAN 2. The network administrator dedicated VLAN 2 to this application to keep it separate from other user traffic. Although the administrator managed to keep any of the multicast traffic from touching Cat-A and Cat-B, it still touches all of the other Catalysts in the network, even though VLAN 2 is not active in Domain 2. Why doesn't the multicast traffic bother Cat-A and Cat-B? Cat-A and Cat-B do not see the traffic from PC-1 because all of the links to these units are access links on different VLANs.

Figure 12-14 *Flooding in a Multiple Domain Network*

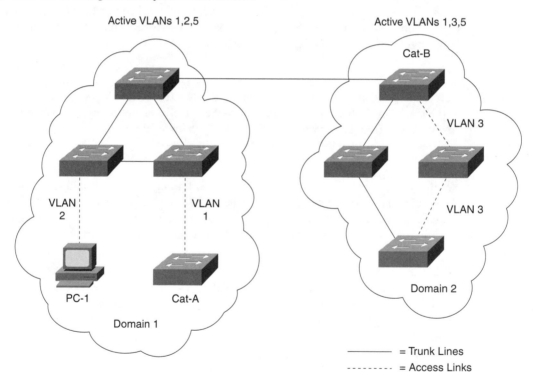

There are methods of controlling the distribution of flooded traffic throughout the network. These methods include the features of VTP pruning to control flooding, and modifications to the multicast behavior through Cisco Group Management Protocol (CGMP). VTP pruning is discussed in the section in this chapter, "VTP Pruning: Advanced Traffic Management." Details on controlling multicast with CGMP is described in Chapter 13, "Multicast and Broadcast Services."

Excessive STP

A related issue with VTP and trunking is the universal participation in Spanning Tree by all Catalysts in the network for all VLANs. Whenever you create a new VLAN, the Catalysts create a new instance of Spanning Tree for that VLAN. This feature, Per-VLAN Spanning Tree (PVST), allows you to optimize the Spanning Tree topology individually for each VLAN. All Catalysts, by default, participate in PVST. But as in the case of flooding traffic in the network, each additional instance of Spanning Tree creates additional Layer 2 background traffic. The additional traffic comes from the BPDUs distributed for each VLAN's instance of Spanning Tree. Not only does this add traffic to each link, it also requires more processing by each Catalyst. Each Catalyst must generate and receive hello messages at whatever interval is specified by the *hello timer*, which is every two seconds by default. And, each Catalyst must calculate a Spanning Tree topology for each VLAN whenever there is a Spanning Tree topology change. This, too, temporarily consumes CPU cycles with a complex Spanning Tree topology.

Bottom line: Controlling VTP in Large Networks

In large networks, these issues multiply and can develop into situations making you want to disable trunking, VTP, or other aspects of VLANs. Clearly, trunking remains as a necessary element of networking life. It is not practical to deploy a large network without trunks because of the number of resources that you consume with multiple access links. Therefore, trunks remain. However, as previously mentioned, we have methods of minimizing some of the negative side effects of trunking.

VTP is also an ever present part of networking with Catalysts whenever you enable trunks. You cannot disable VTP (the closest thing to an exception is Catalysts configured in transparent mode). Therefore, you need to be very careful in how you partition your management domains, who can modify the domains, what components listen to VTP, as well as in how many Catalyst switches are defined as VTP Servers in the network to limit the possibility of mistakes made by an administrator that might cause a major change in other Catalyst switches. As discussed previously, a major concern when deploying large Catalyst networks is the risk of VLAN table deletion. Intended to simplify configuration issues, it can turn against you if not carefully managed.

TIP   If you have a fairly static network where you are not adding or deleting globally significant VLANs, consider using the transparent mode to prevent erroneous actions from deleting your VLANs. However, setting up a unit in transparent mode does increase your administrative burden.

VTP V2

With the introduction of Token Ring switching in the Catalyst, Cisco updated the VTP protocol to version 2. By default, Catalysts disable VTP version 2 and use version 1. As an administrator, you need to select which version of VTP to use and ensure that all Catalysts in the VTP management domain run the same version.

VTP version 2 assists Token Ring VLANs by ensuring correct Token Ring VLAN configuration. *If you plan on doing Token Ring switching, you MUST use VTP version 2 so that processes like DRiP operate.* Chapter 3, "Bridging Technologies " describes DRiP in more detail.

TIP   VTP version 2 adds functionality over VTP version 1, but uses a modified form of the protocol. Version 1 and version 2 cannot coexist in the same management domain. All Catalysts in a management domain must run a homogenous VTP version to function correctly.

If you enable VTP version 2 on a Catalyst, all VTP version 2 capable Catalysts in the management domain automatically enable VTP version 2. Not all Catalysts support VTP version 2, nor do all releases of the Supervisor engine software. If you elect to use VTP version 2, ensure that all Catalysts in the domain are VTP version 2 capable.

Support for Token Ring is not the only feature added in VTP version 2, but it is the principle one.

To enable VTP version 2, use the command **set vtp v2 enable**.

Verify that you correctly changed it with the **show vtp domain** command.

Example 12-8 shows a Catalyst configured for VTP version 2 and the corresponding output from the **show vtp domain** command. Note the warning whenever you attempt to enable version 2 that all Catalysts in the management domain must support version 2. When you enable version 2, all Catalysts in the management domain enable version 2. Note in Figure 12-8 that there are two columns related to the VTP version. One column is titled **VTP Version** and the other **V2 Mode**. **VTP Version** identifies what version of VTP your code supports, but does not indicate what is currently in use. Even if you use VTP version 1, this value still shows a **2** because you have the possibility of enabling version 2. The other column on the other hand, **V2 Mode**, indicates what VTP version you currently enabled. If you have the default version 1 enabled, then this column indicates *disabled* as seen in Figure 12-6.

Example 12-8 *Configuring a Catalyst for VTP Version 2*

```
Console> (enable) set vtp v2 enable
This command will enable the version 2 function in the entire management domain.
All devices in the management domain should be version2-capable before enabling.
Do you want to continue (y/n) [n]? y
VTP domain wally modified
Console> (enable) show vtp domain
Domain Name                           Domain Index VTP Version Local Mode  Password
-------------------------------------- ------------ ----------- ----------- ----------
wally                                       1            2        server        -
Vlan-count Max-vlan-storage Config Revision Notifications
---------- ---------------- --------------- -------------
10           1023                1              enabled
Last Updater    V2 Mode   Pruning  PruneEligible on Vlans
--------------- --------  -------- ----------------------------
10.0.0.1        enabled   disabled 2-1000
Console> (enable)
```

VTP Pruning: Advanced Traffic Management

A transparent bridge handles LAN frames by filtering (dropping), forwarding, or flooding. Flooding occurs whenever the bridge receives a frame with a destination MAC address for which it has no entry in its bridging table. This happens whenever the bridge never hears from the destination and, therefore, has no entry in the bridge table. Or, no entry can exist because the bridge's aging timer expired for the MAC address. Frames in these scenarios are *unknown unicast*. Bridges also flood whenever they receive a frame with a broadcast or multicast destination address. Whenever the bridge floods, it transmits the frame to all ports in the broadcast domain (except for the source port) including trunk ports. Trunks by default transport traffic for all VLANs unless you restrict the authorized VLAN list with the **clear trunk** *VLAN#* command. This command statically defines the VLANs *not allowed* to transport over the trunk. The Catalyst has features to control flooding of unknown unicast, broadcast, and multicast frames. This section covers the control of unknown unicast and broadcast flooding. Chapter 13 discusses the control of multicast and broadcast flooding. The other bridging modes, forwarding and filtering, continue to operate in standard bridging fashion.

Bridges flood to increase the probability of the frame reaching the destination, even though the bridge doesn't know where the destination lives. (The other reason bridges flood is because the standards tell them to.) If the destination is alive and well in the broadcast domain, the frame should reach the destination.

Whenever the Catalyst floods the frame, it sends the frame out all trunk ports. Figure 12-15 shows a system with pruning disabled. When PC-1 generates a frame that Cat-A decides to flood, Cat-A sends the frame out all ports. The flooded frame reaches Cat-B which also decides to flood out all ports. Eventually, the flooded frame reaches all Catalysts in the trunk network including Cat-C. Note, however, that PC-1 belongs to VLAN 2. But there are no members of VLAN 2 in Cat-C; yet the flooded traffic crosses all of the trunks and eventually hits Cat-C. This consumes bandwidth on the trunks and consumes bandwidth in the Catalyst's backplane. (Cat-C discards the frame after the frame crosses the backplane.)

Figure 12-15 *Flooding in a Catalyst Network Without Pruning*

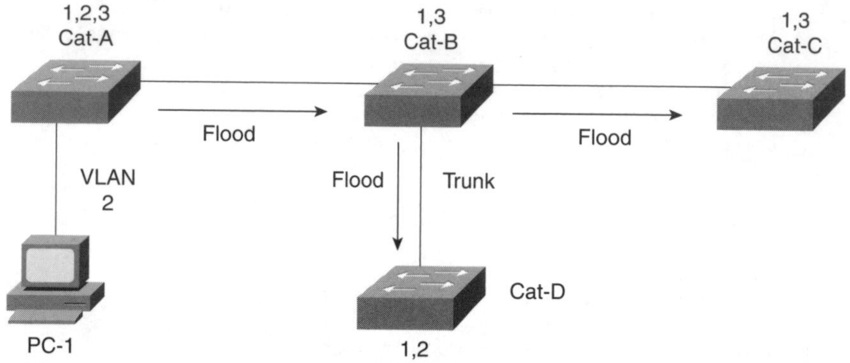

VTP pruning limits the distribution of the flooded frames to only those Catalysts that have members of VLAN 2. Otherwise, the sending Catalyst blocks flooded traffic from that VLAN.

Cisco introduced VTP pruning with Supervisor engine software release 2.1 as an extension to VTP version 1. VTP pruning defines a fourth VTP message type which announces VLAN membership. Whenever you associate Catalyst ports to a VLAN, the Catalyst sends a message to its neighbor Catalysts informing them that they are interested in receiving traffic for that VLAN. The neighbor Catalyst uses this information to decide if flooded traffic from a VLAN should transit the trunk or not.

An administrator enables pruning in Figure 12-16. When PC-1 generates a broadcast frame with pruning enabled in the Catalysts, the broadcast does not reach Cat-C as it did in Figure 12-15. Cat-B receives the broadcast and normally floods the frame to Cat-C. But Cat-C does not have any ports assigned to VLAN 2. Therefore, Cat-B does not flood the frame out the trunk toward Cat-C. This preserves bandwidth on the trunk and on the Catalyst's backplane.

Figure 12-16 *Flooding with VTP Pruning Enabled*

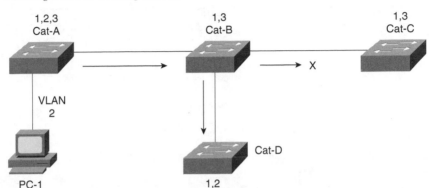

Configuring VTP Pruning

You can enable VTP pruning with the command **set vtp pruning enable**. By default, this enables the Catalyst to prune all VLANs. But you can elect to prune only a couple of VLANs. Then, you can modify the prune list by first clearing the list with the command **clear vtp pruneeligible** *vlan_range*. Next, you can specify which VLANs to prune with the related command, **set vtp pruneeligible** *vlan_range*.

Example 12-9 shows a session where an administrator enables pruning, but then modifies the list of pruning eligible VLANs. When you initially enable pruning, the Catalyst considers all VLANs as pruning eligible. The administrator then specifies VLANs 10-20 as pruning ineligible. This means that any flooded traffic in these VLANs propagate to all Catalysts, even if there is no member of the VLAN on the receiving Catalyst. Note that the default VLANs 1, 1001–1005 are always pruning ineligible. Finally, the administrator restores VLAN 15 as pruning eligible. The **show vtp domain** output in Example 12-9 confirms pruning as enabled and further confirms the list of pruning eligible VLANs. (See the highlighted fields on the output.)

Example 12-9 *Configuring VTP Pruning*

```
Console> (enable) set vtp pruning enable
This command will enable the pruning function in the entire management domain.
All devices in the management domain should be pruning-capable before enabling.
Do you want to continue (y/n) [n]? y
VTP domain wally modified
Console> (enable) clear vtp pruneeligible 10-20
Vlans 1,10-20,1001-1005 will not be pruned on this device.
VTP domain Lab_Network modified.
Console> (enable) set vtp pruneeligible 15
Vlans 2-9,15,21-1000 eligible for pruning on this device.
VTP domain Lab_Network modified.
```

Example 12-9 *Configuring VTP Pruning (Continued)*

```
Console> (enable) show vtp domain
Domain Name                           Domain Index VTP Version Local Mode  Password
-----------------------------------   ------------ ----------- ----------  ----------
wally                                      1            2          server       -

Vlan-count Max-vlan-storage Config Revision Notifications
---------- ---------------- --------------- -------------
4               1023              10             disabled

Last Updater    V2 Mode  Pruning  PruneEligible on Vlans
--------------  -------  -------  ----------------------
10.0.0.1        disabled enabled  2-9,15,21-1000
Console> (enable)
```

Review Questions

This section includes a variety of questions on the topic of this chapter—VTP. By completing these, you can test your mastery of the material included in this chapter as well as help prepare yourself for the CCIE written and lab tests.

Refer to Figure 12-17 for all review questions.

Figure 12-17 *For Review Questions 1–9*

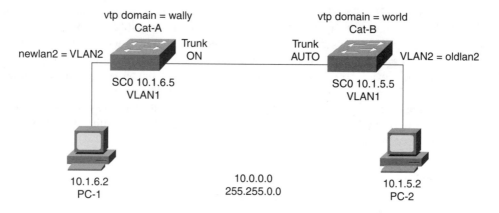

1 In what mode is the link between the two Catalysts?

2 Change both ends of the trunk to *ON*. Can PC-1 **ping** PC-2?

3 Can Cat-A **ping** Cat-B?

4 Can Cat-B **ping** PC-2?

5 VLAN 2 used to be called *oldlan2*. An administrator at Cat-A renames VLAN 2 to *newlan2*. Does Cat-B know about the new name, newlan2?

6 **Clear config all** on Cat-B. Reenter the IP address on sc0. Can Cat-B **ping** Cat-A?

7 Can PC-2 **ping** PC-1?

8 Does Cat-B know about newlan2?

9 Can Cat-B remove newlan2?

This chapter covers the following key topics:

- **CGMP/IGMP: Advanced Traffic Management**—Covers the protocol operations, message formats, and options in addition to how CGMP and IGMP work in routed and switched environments. This section also provides details on the steps necessary to make these protocols active in your Catalysts and routers.

- **IGMP Snooping: Advanced Traffic Management**—Covers another method of controlling multicasts in a Catalyst network.

- **Broadcast Suppression: Advanced Traffic Management**—Explains broadcast suppression methods in a Catalyst network.

CHAPTER 13

Multicast and Broadcast Services

Many corporations and industries now realize the potential of multimedia applications. Video and voice conference applications generate much of the multicast traffic today. Many Web sites offer video streams that transmit multicast traffic. Organizations, therefore, are experiencing an increase in multicast traffic from internal users and from Web downloads. If you do not see much multicast traffic in your system today, be prepared because you soon will. As a result of the proliferation of multicast applications, network administrators have to plan and deal with multicast traffic loads in more frequency than in the past. Many network plans deal efficiently with unicast traffic, but neglect the impact of multicast services in the network. Unfortunately, this severely impacts the well-thought-out unicast network.

With multicast traffic present in networks, wisdom dictates that you should proactively control the distribution of multicast throughout your network. The default behavior of a switch floods the frame everywhere in the broadcast domain. This is usually not necessary, but happens because of bridge rules. Cisco implements the proprietary Cisco Group Management Protocol (CGMP) to help you administer multicast in your network. CGMP works in a Catalyst and router along with Internet Group Membership Protocol (IGMP) in a router to control the flooding of multicast traffic in a network. The Catalyst 5000, 6000, 4000, 2948G, 2926G, and 2926 models support multicast suppression through CGMP.

Although this chapter does not intend to be a definitive source for multicast issues, a brief overview of multicast usage, addressing, IGMP operations (both version 1 and version 2), and CGMP is germane to the Catalyst. The following sections, therefore, provide background information on these topics.

CGMP/IGMP: Advanced Traffic Management

Multicast traffic originates at sources desiring to distribute the same information to multiple recipients. When a source creates multicast traffic, it uses special Layer 2 and Layer 3 addresses so that routers and bridges know how to disperse the frame. By default, routers do not forward multicast traffic unless they are multicast capable and have a multicast routing protocol such as DVMRP (distance vector multicast routing protocol) or PIM (protocol independent multicast) enabled. DVMRP and PIM are inter-router protocols. Therefore, hosts and switches do not participate in messages for these protocols.

A LAN switch is not a router (although a router can be incorporated, such as the RSM). What happens, then, to multicast traffic in a switched network? By default, a switch (bridge) floods multicast traffic within a broadcast domain. This consumes bandwidth on access links and trunk links. Depending upon the host's TCP/IP stack implementation and network interface card (NIC) attributes, the multicast frame can cause a CPU interrupt. Why does a switch flood multicast traffic? A switch floods multicast traffic because it has no entry in the bridge table for the destination address. Multicast addresses never appear as source addresses, therefore the bridge/switch cannot dynamically learn multicast addresses. You can manually configure an entry with the **set cam static** command.

IGMP is a multicast protocol that directly affects hosts. IGMP allows hosts to inform routers that they want to receive multicast traffic for a specific multicast group address.

Current Catalysts don't understand IGMP messages (unless you have the NetFlow Feature Card [NFFC]). IGMP messages appear to a Catalyst like any other multicast frames. Cisco developed the proprietary CGMP that enables routers to inform Catalysts about hosts and their interest in receiving multicast traffic. This modifies the Catalyst's default behavior of flooding the multicast frame to all hosts in the broadcast domain. Rather than flooding the frame to all hosts, the Catalyst limits the flooding scope to only those hosts in the broadcast domain that registered with the router through IGMP. If a host does not register with the router, it does not receive a copy of the multicast frame. This preserves access link bandwidth.

Multicast Addresses

Whenever an application needs to send data to more than one station, but wants to restrict the distribution to only stations interested in receiving the traffic, the application typically uses a multicast destination address. Multicast addresses target a *subset* of all stations in the network. The other two transmission choices for a transmitting device are unicast or broadcast frames. If the source uses a broadcast address, all stations in the broadcast domain must process the frame, even if they are not interested in the information. If the source transmits unicast frames, it must send multiple copies of the frame, one addressed to each intended receiver. This is a very inefficient use of network resources and does not scale well as the number of receivers increases.

By using multicast addresses, the source transmits only one copy of the frame onto the wire and routers distribute the multicast message to the other segments where interested receivers reside. Multicast addresses appear at Layer 2 and at Layer 3. A network administrator assigns the multicast Layer 3 address for an application. The Layer 2 multicast address is then calculated from the Layer 3 multicast address. This is shown in the section, "Layer 2 Multicast Addresses." When you configure a multicast application, the NIC adds the multicast address to its list of valid MAC addresses. Usually this list consists of the built-in MAC address plus any user configured addresses. Whenever the station receives a frame with a matching multicast destination address, the receiver sends the frame to the CPU.

The router examines multicast addresses at both Layer 2 and Layer 3, whereas a switch examines the Layer 2 address. If the switch has hardware such as a Catalyst 5000 Supervisor III module with an NFFC, the Catalyst can examine the Layer 3 addresses as well. (The advantage of this is seen in the section, "IGMP Snooping: Advanced Traffic Management," later in the chapter). Otherwise, the Catalyst simply examines the MAC address in the frame.

Layer 3 Multicast Addresses

IP multicast addresses at Layer 3 are characterized as *class D* addresses. The first four bits of IP class D addresses are 1110. This means that IP multicast addresses have a valid range from 224.0.0.0 to 239.255.255.255. Note that multicast addresses from 224.0.0.0 to 224.0.0.255 are reserved. The following three reserved addresses are specifically interesting to this discussion:

- **224.0.0.1**—All multicast capable hosts on the segment
- **224.0.0.2**—All multicast capable routers on the segment
- **224.0.0.4**—All DVMRP routers on the segment

Usually, a network administrator assigns a multicast address to the application and must select an address not used by other applications or processes. The administrator should not use a multicast address in the reserved range.

Layer 2 Multicast Addresses

When you assign a Layer 3 multicast address, a Layer 2 address is automatically generated from the IP address. Figure 13-1 shows how a MAC multicast address is derived from an IP multicast address. To calculate the Layer 2 address, the host copies the last 23 bits of the IP address into the last 24 bits of the MAC address. The high order bit is set to 0.

The first 3 bytes (24 bits) of the multicast MAC address are 0x01-00-5E. This is a reserved OUI value indicating a multicast application.

Figure 13-1 *Calculating a Multicast MAC Address*

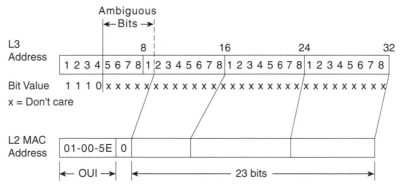

Consider an example. The IP address 224.1.10.10, assigned by an administrator, has a low 23-bit value of 1.10.10. In hexadecimal format, this is 0x01-0A-0A. The MAC address takes the last 23 of the 24 bits and places them into the MAC field. The complete MAC address in this case is 01-00-5E-01-0A-0A.

What happens if the IP multicast address is 225.1.10.10? A side effect of this scheme is address ambiguity. Although a different IP multicast group is identified at Layer 3, the Layer 2 address is the same as for 224.1.10.10. Layer 2 devices cannot distinguish the two multicast groups and receive frames from both multicast groups. The user application needs to filter the two streams and discard the unwanted multicast frames. Any bit value combination for the 5 bits in Figure 13-1 identified as ambiguous generates the same Layer 2 MAC multicast address. Five bits means that there are 2^5 combinations, or 32 Layer 3 addresses that create the same Layer 2 address.

TIP   When assigning multicast addresses, be sure to remember the 32:1 ambiguity and try to avoid multicast overlaps. This helps to preserve bandwidth on access and trunk links. The end station discards the unwanted multicast at Layer 3, after it interrupts the CPU.

IGMP

IGMP defines a protocol for hosts to register with a router to receive multicast traffic for a specific multicast group. Two versions of IGMP exist: version 1, specified in RFC 1112, and version 2, specified in RFC 2236. Version 2 added significant features to version 1 making it more efficient and enabling hosts to explicitly leave a multicast group. These features are described in the section on IGMP version 2.

IGMP Version 1

Figure 13-2 shows the 8-octet IGMP version 1 frame format.

Figure 13-2 *IGMP Version 1 Frame Format*

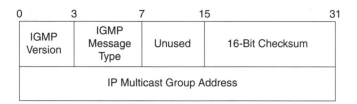

The first field of the frame indicates what version of IGMP generated the frame. For version 1, this value must be 1. The next field specifies the message type. Version 1 defines two messages: a host membership query and a host membership report. The Checksum field carries the checksum computed by the source. The receiving device examines the checksum value to determine if the frame was corrupt during transmission. If the checksum value doesn't match, the receiver discards the frame. The source computes the checksum for the entire IGMP message. The final field indicates the multicast destination group address targeted by the message.

In Figure 13-3, several hosts and a router share a LAN segment. When a host on the segment wants to receive multicast traffic, it issues an unsolicited host membership report targeting the intended multicast group.

Figure 13-3 *A Router and Hosts Using IGMP*

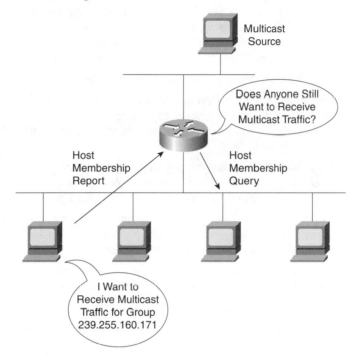

Note the membership report shown in Figure 13-4.

Figure 13-4 *IGMPv1 Multicast Host Membership Report*

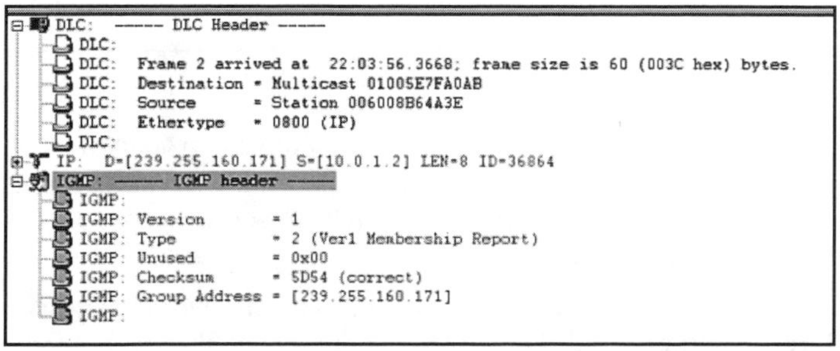

```
□ ■♥ DLC:  ------ DLC Header ------
  └─🗎 DLC:
  └─🗎 DLC:   Frame 2 arrived at  22:03:56.3668; frame size is 60 (003C hex) bytes.
  └─🗎 DLC:   Destination = Multicast 01005E7FA0AB
  └─🗎 DLC:   Source      = Station 006008B64A3E
  └─🗎 DLC:   Ethertype   = 0800 (IP)
  └─🗎 DLC:
⊕🟔 IP:  D=[239.255.160.171] S=[10.0.1.2] LEN=8 ID=36864
□ 🗐 IGMP:  ------ IGMP header ------
  └─🗎 IGMP:
  └─🗎 IGMP:  Version      = 1
  └─🗎 IGMP:  Type         = 2 (Ver1 Membership Report)
  └─🗎 IGMP:  Unused       = 0x00
  └─🗎 IGMP:  Checksum     = 5D54 (correct)
  └─🗎 IGMP:  Group Address = [239.255.160.171]
  └─🗎 IGMP:
```

The destination MAC address targets the multicast group it intends to join. If this were the only information in the frame to identify the group, any of 32 groups might be desired due to the address ambiguity discussed earlier. However, the Layer 3 address is included in both the IP header and in the IGMP header. The Layer 3 multicast group desired by the host is 239.255.160.171. This translates to a MAC address of 01-00-5E-7F-A0-AB. All multicast-capable devices on the shared media receive the membership report. In this situation, however, only the router is interested in the frame. The frame tells the router, "I want to receive any messages for this multicast group." The router now knows that it needs to forward a copy of any frames with this multicast address to the segment where the host that issued the report lives.

A device issues an IGMP membership report under two conditions:

- **Whenever the device first intends to receive a multicast stream**—When you enable the multicast application, the device configures the NIC, and the built-in IGMP processes send an *unsolicited* membership report to the router requesting copies of the multicast frames.

- **In response to a membership query from the router**—This is a *solicited* membership report and helps the router to confirm that hosts on the segment still want to receive multicast traffic for a particular multicast group.

Routers periodically issue host membership queries. You can configure the router query period from 0 seconds to a maximum of 65,535 seconds with the router command **ip igmp query-interval** *seconds*. The default is 60 seconds.

The host membership query message in Figure 13-5 interrogates the segment to determine if hosts on the segment still desire to receive multicast frames.

Figure 13-5 *An IGMPv1 Multicast Host Membership Query*

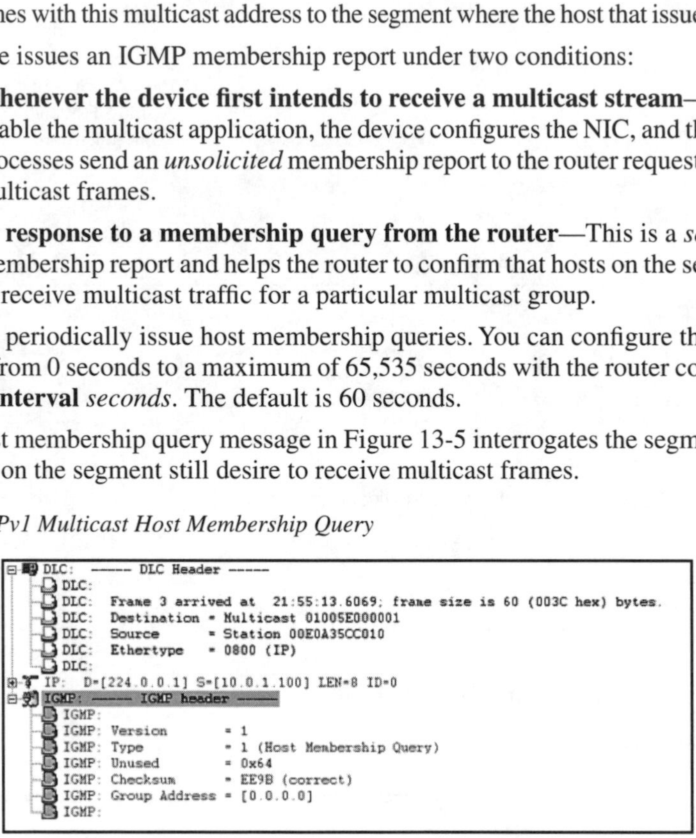

Only one router on each segment issues the membership query message. If the segment uses IGMP version 1, the designated router for the multicast routing protocol issues the query. If the segment uses IGMP version 2, the multicast router with the lowest IP address on the segment issues the queries.

The host membership query message targets the *all multicast hosts* address, 224.0.0.1, in the Layer 3 address field. The Layer 2 address is 01-00-5E-00-00-01. The IGMP header uses a group address of 0.0.0.0. This translates to a query for all multicast hosts on all groups on the segment.

A host for each active multicast group must respond to this message. When multicast hosts receive the host membership query, and if the host wants to continue to receive multicast frames for a multicast group, the multicast host starts an internal random timer with an upper range of 10 seconds. The host waits for the timer to expire and then it sends a membership report for each multicast group that it wants to continue to receive.

If another station sends a membership report before the local timer expires, the host cancels the timer and suppresses the report. This behavior prevents a segment and a router from experiencing host membership report floods. Only one station from each multicast group needs to respond for each group on the segment.

If the router does not receive a membership report for a particular multicast group for three query intervals, the router assumes no hosts remain that are interested in that group multicast stream. The router stops forwarding the multicast packets for this group and informs upstream routers to stop sending frames.

This process defines an *implicit* leave from the multicast group. A host using IGMP version 1 cannot explicitly inform a router that it left the multicast group. A router learns this from repeated queries that receive no responses.

IGMP Version 2

Figure 13-6 shows the construction of a frame per the version 2 document, RFC 2236. Note that the version number disappeared, but the message type field expanded in length and new values allow a version 1 device to receive a version 2 frame for backwards compatibility. Another field added and not found in IGMP version 1 is the *Maximum Response Time*. This is explained later in this section.

Figure 13-6 *IGMP Version 2 Frame Format*

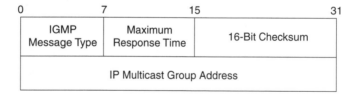

IGMP version 2 adds two messages not found in IGMP version 1 to streamline the join and leave process. RFC 2236 added a version 2 membership report and a leave group message. The complete list of messages now consists of the following:

0x11—Membership query
0x12—Version 1 membership report
0x16—Version 2 membership report
0x17—Leave group

The membership query and version 1 membership report carry over from IGMP version 1. However, the membership query can now target specific multicast groups. In version 1, the query message is a general query with the group address set to 0.0.0.0. All active groups respond to the general query. Version 2 allows a multicast query router to target a specific multicast group. When it sends this type of message, a multicast host, if it is running version 2, responds with a version 2 membership report. Other multicast groups ignore the group specific query if it is not directed to their group. The group specific membership query only works for version 2 systems.

If a version 2 host leaves a multicast group, it sends an unsolicited leave group message to inform the query router that it no longer desires to receive the multicast stream. The router maintains a table of all hosts in the multicast group on the segment. If other hosts still want to receive the multicast stream, the router continues to send the multicast frames onto the segment. If, however, the membership report arrives from the last host on the segment for the multicast group, the router terminates the multicast stream for that group.

Consider the multicast group shown in Figure 13-7. Two hosts belong to the multicast group 224.1.10.10, and one host belongs to the group 224.2.20.20.

Figure 13-7 *An IGMP Version 2 Leave Demonstrated*

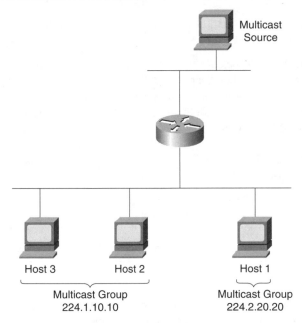

The router currently forwards frames for both groups on the segment. The host currently subscribed to 224.2.20.20 decides that it no longer wants to receive the multicast stream for this group, so it transmits a leave message. The router receives this message and checks its multicast table to see if there are any other hosts on the segment that want the stream. In this example, there are no other hosts in the group. The router sends a group specific query message to the group 224.2.20.20 to make sure. If the router does not receive a membership report, it stops the 224.2.20.20 stream.

Continuing the example, assume that sometime later, Host 3 decides to leave the group 224.1.10.10 and issues a leave message. The router receives the leave message, sends a group specific query, and realizes that additional hosts on the segment still want to receive the multicast stream. Therefore, it continues to transmit all multicast frames for this group.

If at any time the router wants to confirm its need to send the stream, it can transmit a general or group specific query onto the segment. If it does not receive any responses to a couple of query messages, the router assumes no more hosts want the stream.

Another feature of IGMP version 2 affects the method for selecting the query router. In version 1, the query router is selected by the multicast routing protocol. The designated router for the protocol becomes the querier. In version 2, the IP address determines the query router. The multicast router with the lowest IP address becomes the query router. All routers initially assume that they are the query router and send a query message. If a router hears a query message from another multicast router with a lower IP address, the router becomes a non-querier router.

A final feature added to IGMP version 2 is the capability for the multicast router to specify the hosts' response timer range. Remember that when a host receives a membership query, the host starts a random timer. The timer value is in the range of 0 to *maximum response time*, with the maximum response time specified in the router's query message. Version 2 allows you to configure the upper range of the timer to a maximum of 25 seconds. The default in a Cisco router is 10 seconds.

TIP   If there are many groups on a segment, you might want to use a larger timer to spread out the responses. This helps to smooth out any membership report bursts on the segment. If you have fewer groups, you might want to lower the value so that a router can terminate a multicast flow stream sooner.

IGMP Version 1 and Version 2 Interoperability

The preceding two sections describe operations whenever the IGMP hosts and routers all run the same version. This represents a homogenous system. But what if you have a mixture of versions in your system?

The first possible combination of versions might involve hosts with a mix of versions as in Figure 13-8, but with a version 1 query router. All IGMP operations in this scenario are driven by the version that the query router uses. When there is such a combination, the hosts must use version 1 messages. The router does not understand version 2 membership reports, nor does it understand version 2 leave messages.

Figure 13-8 *IGMPv1 and IGMPv2 Hosts with an IGMPv1 Router*

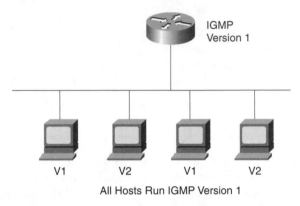

All Hosts Run IGMP Version 1

A second case exists when the router supports IGMP version 2, but hosts use IGMP version 1. Although the router understands more message types than the hosts, it ultimately uses only version 1 messages. When the version 2 router receives the version 1 membership report, it remembers that they are present and only uses version 1 membership queries. Version 1 queries use the group address 0.0.0.0 and does not generate group specific queries. If it generated group specific queries, the version 1 hosts would not recognize the message and would not know how to respond.

What if there are both version 1 and version 2 hosts on the segment with the version 2 router as in Figure 13-9? As in the previous case, the router must remember that there are version 1 hosts and must, therefore, issue version 1 membership queries. Additionally, if any of the version 2 hosts send a leave message, the router must ignore the leave notification. It ignores the message because it must still issue general queries in case a version 1 member is still active on the segment.

Figure 13-9 *IGMPv1 and IGMPv2 Hosts with an IGMPv2 Router*

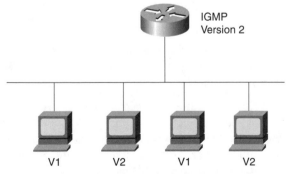

Hosts Run Either IGMP Version 1 or IGMP Version 2

If two routers attach to the segment where one supports version 1 and the other version 2, the version 2 router must be administratively configured as a version 1 router. The version 1 router has no way to detect the presence of the version 2 router. Because the two versions use different methods of selecting the query router, they might not reliably agree on the query router.

IGMP in a Switched Environment

Switches, by default, flood multicast traffic. The network in Figure 13-10 has multicast hosts and routers attached to a LAN switch. All of the ports belong to one VLAN. Some of the hosts attached to the switch, such as PC-3, do not participate in multicast traffic. When multicast host PC-1 sends a membership report, the switch floods the multicast frame to all ports, even to the hosts that do not want multicast traffic.

Figure 13-10 *Switches and Multicast Traffic*

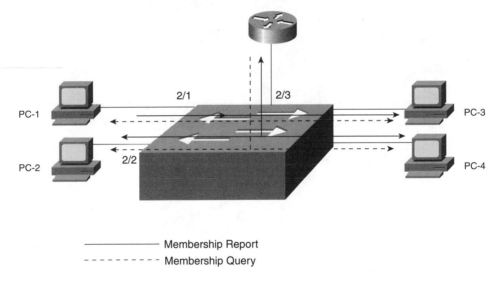

When the router sends a general membership query, it uses the MAC multicast address 01-00-5E-00-00-01. This multicast address forces the switch to send the frame to all ports. When a host responds to the query with a report, the report goes to all ports.

Clearly, though, it would be nice to restrict the distribution of multicast frames in the switched network to only those hosts that really want the traffic. In a Catalyst, you have three potential ways of limiting the multicast scope: static configurations, CGMP, and IGMP Snooping, each of which is covered later in the chapter.

Configuring IGMP on a Router

Basic IGMP router configuration requires you to enable a multicast routing protocol and then to configure optional IGMP features if desired. For example, you can select the IGMP version to use. The router enables IGMP version 2 by default. If you enable version 2, you can adjust various timers if the hosts on the segment support version 2. Example 13-1 shows a partial configuration. Other unrelated router command lines were deleted for brevity. However, it shows the significant IGMP and multicast routing commands.

Another command present in the example output enables CGMP, which is described in more detail in a later section.

Example 13-1 *Partial Router Configuration for IGMP/CGMP*

```
!
ip multicast-routing
ip dvmrp route-limit 7000
!
!
interface Ethernet0
 ip address 193.10.2.33 255.255.255.224
 ip pim dense-mode
 ip cgmp
```

This router uses PIM for the multicast routing. Notice the global configuration statement **ip multicast-routing**. This is mandatory to enable the routing. If you do not enter this statement, neither CGMP nor PIM functions.

To check the operation of your multicast router, use the **show ip igmp interface** command as demonstrated in Example 13-2.

Example 13-2 *show ip igmp interface* *Output*

```
Router3-gateway#show ip igmp interface e0
Ethernet0 is up, line protocol is up
  Internet address is 193.10.2.33/27
  IGMP is enabled on interface
  Current IGMP version is 2
  CGMP is enabled on interface
  IGMP query interval is 60 seconds
  IGMP querier timeout is 120 seconds
  IGMP max query response time is 10 seconds
  Inbound IGMP access group is not set
  IGMP activity: 3 joins, 2 leaves
  Multicast routing is enabled on interface
  Multicast TTL threshold is 0
  Multicast designated router (DR) is 193.10.2.33 (this system)
  IGMP querying router is 193.10.2.33 (this system)
  Multicast groups joined: 224.0.1.40
Router3-gateway#
```

The output of Example 13-2 verifies that IGMP is enabled and the version number. It also displays the timer values and the identity of the query router. In this case, this router is the query router.

Static Multicast Configurations

One tool that you have to control the distribution of multicast frames modifies the bridge table. You can statically define which ports should receive what multicast traffic. For example, suppose that PC-1 and PC-2 in Figure 13-10 belong to multicast group 224.1.10.10. You can manually modify the bridge table specifying that the ports they attach to should receive any frames with a destination address of 01-00-5E-01-0A-0A. You can do this with the Catalyst command **set cam** {**static** | **permanent**} *multicast_mac mod/ports.. VLAN.* (CAM means *content addressable memory* and refers to the hardware portion containing the bridge table.) You can enter the multicast address *multicast_MAC* to the bridge table as a static or permanent entry. A static entry modifies the table until you reset the Catalyst. Normal bridge aging processes are suspended for static entries. But the Catalyst does not remember the entry across power cycles or resets. On the other hand, you can make the change permanent. A permanent entry stores the address in NVRAM so that the Catalyst restores the configuration after a reset or power cycle.

Modifying the configuration of Figure 13-10 can be accomplished through the command entry shown in Example 13-3.

Example 13-3 *Creating a Permanent CAM Entry*

```
Console> (enable) set cam permanent 01-00-5E-01-0A-0A 2/1-3 30
Permanent multicast entry added to CAM table.
Console> (enable)
```

Note that the configuration includes the router port. If you exclude the router from the command, the router never receives a membership report from a host. When the host transmits the multicast frame with the address in the configuration, the switch looks at the destination address and checks the bridge table. The properly configured bridge table in this case has three ports eligible to receive the multicast frame. The Catalyst does not forward the frame to any ports without the multicast configuration.

This is a reliable method of modifying the CAM table. But, it is completely manual. If you need to add or delete a multicast group, or if you need to add or move a host, you need to change the configuration in the switch. Manually modifying the CAM table does not scale well if you have many hosts and many multicast groups.

The Catalyst has two dynamic tools for modifying the bridge tables in a multicast environment. These methods, CGMP and IGMP Snooping, eliminate the need for manual configuration and become very attractive in dynamic multicast environments. The following sections describe both dynamic processes.

CGMP

The Cisco proprietary CGMP protocol interacts with IGMP to dynamically modify bridge tables. Because CGMP is Cisco proprietary, you must use Cisco routers and Catalyst switches for it to be effective. When a host sends IGMP membership reports to a CGMP-capable router, the router sends configuration information, via CGMP, to the Catalyst. The Catalyst modifies its local bridge table based upon the information contained in the CGMP message. Figure 13-11 shows a multicast system with two Catalysts cascaded together and a router attached to one of them. PCs attach to the Catalysts and desire to receive a multicast stream.

Figure 13-11 *CGMP Operation Example*

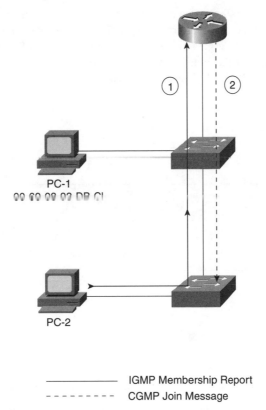

PC-1
00 60 08 93 DB C1

PC-2

—————————— IGMP Membership Report
— — — — — — — — CGMP Join Message

In Figure 13-11, a Cisco router receives IGMP membership reports from PC-1 and PC-2. The router sends a CGMP configuration message to the Catalyst telling it about the source MAC address of the host and the multicast group from which it wants to receive traffic. For example, PC-1 asks to join 224.1.10.10. The router tells the Catalyst to send multicast traffic with the destination MAC address of 01-00-5E-01-0A-0A to the host with the source MAC address 00-60-08-93-DB-C1. The Catalyst searches its bridge table for the corresponding unicast address and adds the multicast group address to the port the host attaches to. Any frames that the Catalyst sees with the multicast address gets forwarded to the port without bothering other ports. It is possible that many hosts belong to the multicast group. Each host individually registers with the router, and the router updates the Catalyst.

Notice two things about the CGMP operations. First, CGMP does not require any modifications to the host. CGMP operates independently of the hosts and only involves the router and the switch. Secondly, CGMP messages flow from the router to the switch, never from the switch to the router.

CGMP Frame Format

CGMP defines a single frame format, but the content of it varies depending upon the operation that the router attempts to perform. When the router transmits the CGMP frame, the data link layer targets the destination MAC address of 0x01-00-0C-DD-DD-DD. The SNAP header uses a value of 0x2001. Figure 13-12 illustrates the CGMP frame format, excluding the DLC, LLC, and SNAP header.

Figure 13-12 *CGMP Frame Format*

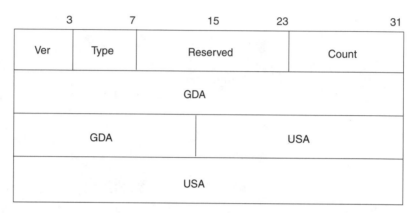

Several fields comprise the CGMP frame of Figure 13-12 as detailed in the following list:

- **Version**—Describes the version of CGMP sending this message.
- **Message Type**—Two messages defined: join or leave.
- **Reserved**—Not used, set to 0.
- **Count**—Indicates number of multicast/unicast address pairs contained in this CGMP message.
- **Group Multicast Address**—Indicates multicast address to be modified. Referred to as *Group Destination Address* (GDA).
- **Source Unicast Address**—Indicates the source address of the device joining or leaving the multicast group. Referred to as the *Unicast Source Address* (USA).

The **Version Number** indicates the version of CGMP that the transmitting router is using. Currently, only one version exists. Therefore, this 4-bit field has a value of *1*.

The **Message Type** might have one of two values. The message is either a *join* message with a type value of *0*, or a *leave* message with a type value of *1*.

The **Reserved** field is currently unused and sets all bits in the field to *0*.

When the router sends a CGMP message to the switch, it includes address pairs of hosts and the multicast address the host wants to receive. The router can include more than one pair in the CGMP message. The **Count** field tells the switch how many address pairs are included in the CGMP message.

CGMP refers to the **Multicast Group Address** as a *Group Destination Address* (GDA). Many of the **show** statements display values labeled as the GDA. The first three octets of this field value should be 0x01-00-5E.

Finally, the **Unicast Source Address** (USA) appears in the list. It helps the Catalyst recognize the specific host desiring to receive the multicast stream. The GDA/USA forms an address pair. A router can include many address pairs in the CGMP frame when it sends configuration information to the switch.

You might see several combinations of GDAs and USAs in a CGMP message decode. Table 13-1 shows possible combinations and describes the meaning of each.

Table 13-1   *CGMP Message Combinations*

GDA	USA	Message Type	Description
Multicast	Device	Join	Add USA port to group
Multicast	Device	Leave	Delete USA port from group
0000.0000.0000	Router	Join	Learn CGMP router and port
0000.0000.0000	Router	Leave	Forget CGMP router and port
Multicast	0000.0000.0000	Leave	Delete multicast group from bridge table
0000.0000.0000	0000.0000.0000	Leave	Delete all multicast groups from bridge table

The first two messages of Table 13-1 represent typical messages because the router sends these when it instructs the Catalyst to add or delete a host or set of hosts from the multicast group specified in the GDA field. When the Catalyst receives this message, it correspondingly modifies the bridge table to correctly forward or filter group multicast traffic to the port.

The Catalyst needs to learn where a CGMP-capable router resides. You can manually configure the information in the switch. However, a CGMP discovery process enables a router to announce itself to a switch. A router can also tell the switch that it no longer participates in CGMP by sending a leave message with its MAC address and an all zeros GDA value.

Finally, the router can inform a switch to forget about a specific multicast group and to remove any entries for this group. Or, it can send a flush to delete all multicast entries for all multicast groups from the bridge table. Figure 13-13 shows a decoded CGMP join message for a specific host. What multicast group does this client want to join?

Figure 13-13 *A CGMP Join Message Analyzer Decode*

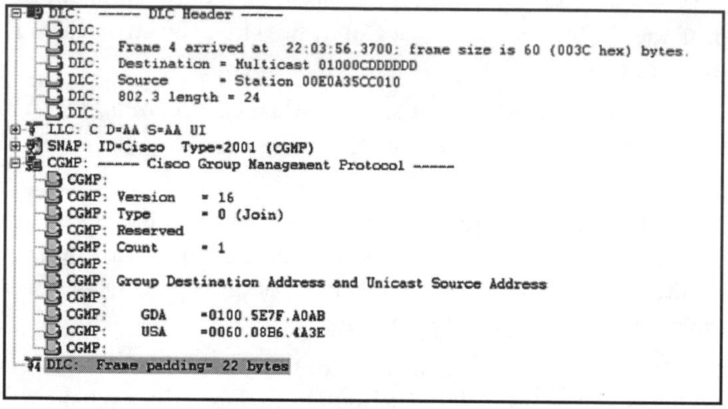

```
DLC: ------ DLC Header ------
   DLC:
   DLC:  Frame 4 arrived at  22:03:56.3700; frame size is 60 (003C hex) bytes.
   DLC:  Destination = Multicast 01000CDDDDDD
   DLC:  Source      = Station 00E0A35CC010
   DLC:  802.3 length = 24
   DLC:
  LLC: C D=AA S=AA UI
  SNAP: ID=Cisco  Type=2001 (CGMP)
  CGMP: ------ Cisco Group Management Protocol ------
   CGMP:
   CGMP: Version  = 16
   CGMP: Type     = 0 (Join)
   CGMP: Reserved
   CGMP: Count    = 1
   CGMP:
   CGMP: Group Destination Address and Unicast Source Address
   CGMP:
   CGMP:   GDA   =0100.5E7F.A0AB
   CGMP:   USA   =0060.08B6.4A3E
   CGMP:
  DLC:  Frame padding= 22 bytes
```

You cannot tell exactly which multicast group the client wants to join, because there are no
Layer 3 addresses in the message. If you could capture the IGMP join message that
spawned the CGMP join, you could know for certain the desired multicast group. From the
CGMP decode, the only thing you can tell about the multicast group is the last 23 bits of
the address. These bits translate to a decimal address representation of xxx.127.160.171.
You cannot determine the first octet due to the address ambiguity issue.

The GDA 0100.5E00.0128 is for the multicast routing protocol. The router indicates to the
switch that it wants to receive any multicast frames belonging to this group to ensure that
it receives multicast route updates. Examine the network in Figure 13-14. Multiple hosts
desire to receive a multicast stream from a single multicast group group.

Figure 13-14 *A Detailed CGMP Exchange*

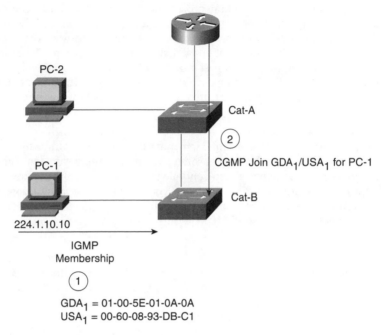

GDA$_1$ = 01-00-5E-01-0A-0A
USA$_1$ = 00-60-08-93-DB-C1

PC-1 wants to join multicast group 224.1.10.10. It sends an IGMP membership report informing routers that it wants to see these frames. The router creates a CGMP join message with a GDA of 01-00-5E-01-0A-0A and a USA with PC-1's source address. The router sends the frame as a CGMP multicast (01-00-0C-DD-DD-DD). The Catalyst detects the CGMP join message, looks in its bridge table for the host, adds the GDA to the port bridge table, and starts to forward any frames for this GDA to PC-1. The CGMP join message from the router causes both Cat-A and Cat-B to modify their bridge tables. Cat-A modifies its bridge table so that the multicast frame forwards to Cat-B. This works if the port is an access or trunk link. In either case, the multicast frame stays within the VLAN boundaries. If PC-2 decides to join the multicast group too, the process repeats, but with PC-2's USA.

The multicast query router occasionally issues a general query that both hosts receive. They both start random timers to determine when to issue a solicited membership report. The report suppression mechanism works here, because the report frame has the GDA in the MAC layer destination field. The switch forwards this to all ports with members of the group. When the other host receives the membership report, it cancels its timer and does not send another membership report for that group.

After some period of time, PC-1 decides it wants to leave the group. In an IGMP version 1 environment, PC-1 does nothing proactively to announce its leave, so the router does not know explicitly. However, at some point in time, the query router issues a general query. PC-2 responds to the query and the router continues to forward multicast traffic for the group. The router still does not know that PC-1 left the group. Therefore, the switch continues to forward the multicast traffic to PC-1 even though it no longer wants to receive the frame. In fact, PC-1 continues to receive the group traffic until all hosts leave the group and the router detects that there are no more members in the group.

TIP

In an IGMP version 1 environment, members of a group continue to receive traffic until all members of the group leave. If at some point in time there were ten members, but only one currently remains active, all ten continue to receive the multicast stream. IGMP version 2 improves this situation. If all clients on your segments (broadcast domain) support IGMP version 2, it is wise to set them up to run the later version and gain bandwidth efficiencies that are not possible with IGMP version 1.

Eventually, PC-2 decides that it no longer wants to receive the multicast stream. When the query router issues a membership query, no hosts respond for this group. The multicast query router stops forwarding the multicast frames after it fails to see a solicited membership report for at least two queries. At this point, the router stops forwarding the multicast traffic and sends a CGMP group leave message to the switch. The group leave message has the GDA for the group and a USA of 0000.0000.0000. This forces the Catalyst to flush all entries in the bridge table for this group.

TIP

Note that the Catalyst does not prune all multicast addresses. For example, the switch forwards reserved multicast addresses such as 224.0.0.5 and 224.0.0.6. These are used by Open Shortest Path First (OSPF) routing. If the switch pruned traffic for these multicast groups, the protocols would break.

TIP

Enabling CGMP Fast Leave processing on a Catalyst switch forces the switch to capture all IGMP leave messages sent to the IP multicast address 224.0.0.2 (all routers multicast). This is the same address used for the Cisco protocol Hot Standby Router Protocol (HSRP) and translates to a multicast MAC address of 01-00-5E-00-00-02. To capture the IGMP leave message, the Enhanced Address Recognition Logic (EARL) table has static entries for this MAC address causing the switch to absorb the leave message. This results in the switch also consuming HSRP frames. Normally the switch does not forward absorbed frames (such as CDP) to any other ports, and would break HSRP. However, the switch behavior is modified in the supervisor code so that the switch Supervisor module recognizes non-IGMP frames and floods them out all router ports and the Spanning Tree Root Port, preserving HSRP functionality.

Configuring CGMP

Enabling CGMP requires configurations on both the router and the Catalyst. By default, CGMP is disabled on both. Note that if you are using IGMP Snooping (described in the next section) on a Catalyst, you cannot use CGMP. CGMP and IGMP are mutually exclusive.

Catalyst configurations for CGMP include three **set** commands. The **set cgmp enable** command enables CGMP. This command was introduced in switch supervisor code version 2.2. Ensure that you have at least this revision before trying to use CGMP. The **set multicast router** *mod_num/port_num* command is an optional command that statically configures a multicast router. Normally, the router announces itself, enabling the switch to dynamically learn the presence of the multicast router. You can, however, elect to statically configure this so that your Catalyst does not need to wait to learn this information. Finally, you can use the **set cgmp leave enable** command in an IGMP version 2 environment to enable the Catalyst to look for IGMP version 2 leave messages. If the Catalyst sees a leave message from a host, it waits to see if any join messages appear on the interface. If not, the Catalyst prunes the port from the multicast group without sending the leave message to the router. Without this feature, the Catalyst waits to see a CGMP leave message from the router.

You must also turn on CGMP in the router. Use the **ip cgmp** interface configuration command to enable CGMP. You need to enter this command on all router ports participating in CGMP. The router output in Example 13-4 shows a router announcing itself with CGMP to any switches listening on the interface.

Example 13-4 *Router **debug** for CGMP Hello Message*

```
Router3-gateway#debug ip cgmp
CGMP debugging is on
Router3-gateway#
02:03:09: CGMP: Sending self Join on Ethernet0
02:03:09:       GDA 0000.0000.0000, USA 0010.7b3a.d4bb
02:03:19: CGMP: Sending self Join on Ethernet0
02:03:19:       GDA 0100.5e00.0128, USA 0010.7b3a.d4bb
Router3-gateway#
```

Notice that the GDA value targets the all groups address, whereas the USA value reflects the router's built-in MAC address on the Ethernet interface.

The router output comes from the router with the configuration shown in Example 13-2. The router also announces itself as a member of GDA 0100.5e00.0128. Where did this group come from?

The GDA 0100.5E00.0128 is for the multicast routing protocol. The router indicates to the switch that it wants to receive any multicast frames belonging to this group to ensure that it receives multicast route updates.

IGMP Snooping: Advanced Traffic Management

Life isn't perfect. Therefore, not everyone uses Cisco routers, even though they might use Cisco switches. What do you do if the user has non-Cisco routers in the system along with Catalysts? Or for that matter, what do other vendor products do with multicast frames? You cannot use CGMP in a non-Cisco environment because it is a Cisco proprietary feature.

Many other vendors use a software feature where the switch processor examines each frame transferred through the switch. The processor software looks for IGMP join and leave messages. If the processor sees such a message, it modifies its local bridge table. Too often, though, the processor is underpowered to keep up with an active multicast environment.

Cisco has a similar feature, but one that does not depend upon the switch processor. If you have a NetFlow Feature Card (NFFC) installed in your Catalyst with a Supervisor III module, you can use the IGMP Snooping feature. Because Cisco's IGMP Snooping occurs on the NFFC, it can keep up with busy multicast systems without impairing switching performance. The NFFC offloads the snooping activities from the Supervisor processor.

In the multicast environments described in previous sections, a router participates in the IGMP messages and informs Catalyst switches, through CGMP, about any necessary modifications to the bridge tables. With IGMP Snooping, the Catalyst monitors the IGMP exchanges between routers and workstations, and autonomously determines any need to modify the bridge tables.

If you have a Catalyst 5000 Supervisor III engine card with an NFFC installed, and are running Supervisor engine software release 4.1 or later, you can enable IGMP Snooping. This is useful if you have non-Cisco routers in your system, but still want to control multicast distribution in your network. Further, you must have the Catalyst attached to a multicast router either directly or indirectly.

To enable IGMP Snooping, make sure that you disable CGMP first. You cannot have both CGMP and IGMP Snooping operating concurrently in a Catalyst. Use the command **set igmp enable** to enable IGMP Snooping. As with CGMP, the switch needs to know about the multicast router. But with IGMP Snooping, you must manually configure the setting with the **set multicast router** *mod_num/port_num* command. This is necessary because the routers are not issuing CGMP announcements for the switch to automatically discover the multicast router. The Catalyst needs to know where the router is so that it can forward multicast source data and IGMP membership reports to all multicast routers on the segment. Use the **show igmp statistics** [*vlan number*] command to see how many of what IGMP packet type the Catalyst received and transmitted.

Broadcast Suppression: Advanced Traffic Management

Some members of the Catalyst family support a feature intended to minimize the transfer of broadcast and multicast frames sourced from a port. The broadcast/multicast suppression feature measures the broadcast and multicast traffic coming from a device and restricts the flow of the frames across the Catalyst switch fabric if the amount of the traffic exceeds a configurable threshold.

Depending upon your version of Catalyst, you have two methods to measure the broadcast and multicast frames. One method measures the amount of port bandwidth consumed by multicasts and broadcasts (hardware-based broadcast suppression). The other method measures the number of broadcast and multicast frames (software-based broadcast suppression). Both metrics integrate over a 1-second interval. The effect of the two varies, though.

Hardware-Based Broadcast Suppression

Hardware-based broadcast suppression measures the percentage of port bandwidth consumed by incoming broadcast/multicast frames every second. If the load crosses a threshold that you configure, the Catalyst drops the balance of the broadcast frames for the remainder of the 1-second interval, but passes normal unicast frames.

Figure 13-15 shows the results of hardware suppression over several 1-second intervals. In the first interval, both the broadcast and unicast traffic stay under the configured threshold. The Catalyst passes all of the frames. In the second case, the broadcast frames stay under the threshold, but the unicast frames exceed it. Again, the Catalyst passes all frames because it only measures the broadcast and multicast frames and ignores the unicast level. In the third interval, the unicast does not exceed threshold, but the broadcast frames do. When the broadcast level exceeds the threshold, the Catalyst drops all of the broadcast frames for the remainder of the 1-second interval, but continues to pass the unicast frames. In the fourth interval, both cross the threshold, but the Catalyst drops only the broadcast frames, even though the broadcast level drops back below the threshold during the interval. After the Catalyst measures a broadcast excess, it drops all of the broadcast frames for the rest of the interval.

Figure 13-15 *Hardware-Based Broadcast Suppression*

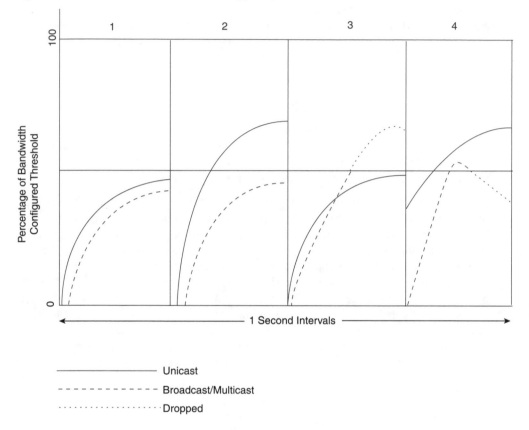

To configure hardware-based suppression, use the command **set port broadcast** *mod_num/ port_num threshold%*. Note the percent sign at the end of the command. You must include this for the Catalyst to distinguish the value as a bandwidth threshold rather than a packet count threshold.

Software-Based Broadcast Suppression

Software-based broadcast suppression differs from the hardware-based broadcast suppression in its metric and its effect. Software-based broadcast suppression measures the actual number of incoming broadcast/multicast frames on an interface over a 1-second interval. If the absolute value of frames exceeds the threshold, the Catalyst drops *all* frames for the balance of the 1-second interval.

In Figure 13-16, a Catalyst reacts to frames during three time intervals. In the first interval, both the unicast and broadcast frames remain below the configured threshold. Therefore, the Catalyst forwards all frames. In the second interval, unicast frames exceed the threshold, whereas the broadcast level remains below the threshold. The Catalyst forwards all frames. In the third interval, the broadcast level exceeds the threshold. At the point in the interval when this occurrs, the Catalyst drops all frames (both broadcast and unicast) for the rest of the time interval.

Figure 13-16 *Software-Based Broadcast Suppression*

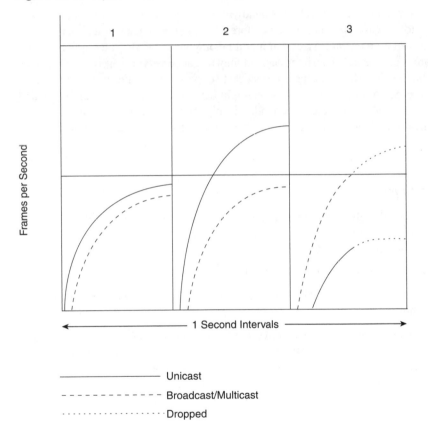

To enable software-based broadcast suppression on your Catalyst, use the **set port broadcast** *mod_num/port_num threshold* command. Note the absence of the percent sign. This instructs the Catalyst to use software-based broadcast suppression.

Determining Whether to Use Hardware- or Software-Based Broadcast Suppression

There is a significant difference in the behavior between hardware- and software-based broadcast suppression. Not all Catalyst models support hardware-based broadcast suppression. In fact, some models support no broadcast suppression, yet others support hardware- but not software-based broadcast suppression. Therefore, you might not have a choice as to which to use. Use the **show port capabilities** command to determine what your Catalyst can do.

When you do have a choice, generally the bandwidth-based (hardware-based) approach excels. Bandwidth measurements tend to be more accurate than packet count methods because of the variation in frame sizes that might be on your network. You might have few broadcast frames per second on an interface, but they might be very large, consuming much of your port bandwidth. Hardware-based broadcast suppression catches this situation and reacts. Software-based broadcast suppression might never trigger if the frames per second stays below your threshold. On the other hand, this might be normal and desirable behavior for your applications. In which case, you might want to use software rather than hardware triggers.

Review Questions

1 IGMP version 2 includes an explicit leave message for hosts to transmit whenever they no longer want to receive a multicast stream. Why, then, does version 2 include the query message?

2 Why doesn't a Catalyst normally learn multicast addresses?

3 What Layer 2, Layer 3, and IGMP information does a multicast device transmit for a membership report?

4 Assume that you have a switched network with devices running IGMP version 1 and the switches/routers have CGMP enabled. One of the multicast devices surfs the Web looking for a particular multicast stream. The user first connects to group 1 and finds it isn't the group that he wants. So he tries group 2, and then group 3, until he finally finds what he wants in group 4. Meanwhile, another user belongs to groups 1, 2, and 3. What happens to this user's link?

Real-World Campus Design and Implementation

This chapter covers the following key topics:

- **Changing Traffic Patterns**—The rise of client/server computing, server farms, and Internet-based technology has dramatically changed most campus traffic patterns. This chapter looks at some of the challenging issues that this has created for campus network designers.

- **Campus Design Terminology**—Explains IDF/MDF and access/distribution/core terminology, the two most common ways of explaining and discussing campus designs.

- **Key Requirements of Campus Designs**—Looks at the attributes of the ideal campus design.

- **Advantages of Routing**—The recommended approach to campus design makes extensive use of Layer 3 switching (routing) technology. The important benefits of this approach are discussed.

- **Campus Design Models**—Three of the most common campus design models are discussed: the router and hub model, the campus-wide VLANs model, and the multilayer model.

- **General Recommendation: Multilayer Model**—Some specific considerations and issues associated with the multilayer model, the recommended approach to campus design, are discussed.

- **Distribution Blocks**—Discusses issues related to distribution blocks (usually a set of switches contained within a single building) for the multilayer design model.

- **Core**—Explains issues related to designing a core for a multilayer network.

CHAPTER 14

Campus Design Models

This chapter looks at several important models that can be used for campus designs. The discussion begins with a look at two sets of terminology used to describe and discuss network designs. Then, the three main approaches to campus design are presented:

- First, the traditional router and hub model is covered. Although this design is not suitable for use in modern campus networks, the proven advantages of this design are highlighted.

- Second, the chapter discusses the campus-wide VLANs or "flat earth" design. This is the design most people think of when the subject of a switched campus network comes up. Although it can be very useful for certain requirements, in general, it has many drawbacks and downsides.

- Third, the multilayer model is presented. This model is designed to blend Layer 2 and Layer 3 processing into a cohesive whole. The last half of the chapter elaborates on some issues that are specific to the multilayer architecture.

Whereas this chapter focuses on overall design architectures and paradigms, Chapter 15, "Campus Design Implementation," looks at specific strategies associated with campus designs. For example, this chapter points out the advantages of the multilayer model for the Spanning-Tree Protocol (STP), and Chapter 15 discusses STP best practices and makes specific STP recommendations.

Finally, please note that the intent of this chapter is not to create a survey of every campus design ever conceived. Instead, this text is oriented toward the design *process*. It explores several of the more popular and widely applicable designs in an attempt to discuss good design practices, as well as the pros and cons of various approaches to campus design.

Changing Traffic Patterns

Any effective campus design must take traffic patterns into account. Otherwise, switching and link bandwidth are almost certainly wasted. The good news is that most modern campus networks follow several trends that create unmistakable flows. This section discusses the traditional campus traffic patterns and shows how popular new technologies have drastically changed this.

The earliest seeds of today's campus networks began with departmental servers. In the mid-1980s, the growth of inexpensive PCs led many organizations to install small networks utilizing Ethernet, ArcNet, Token Ring, LocalTalk, and a variety of proprietary solutions. Many of these networks utilized PC-based server platforms such as Novell's Netware. Not only did this promote the sharing of information, it allowed expensive hardware such as laser printers to be shared.

Throughout the late-1980s, these small networks began to pop up throughout most corporations. Each network was built to serve a single workgroup or department. For example, the finance department would have a separate network from the human resources department. Most of these networks were extremely decentralized. In many cases, they were installed by non-technical people employed by the local workgroup (or outside consultants hired by the workgroup). Although some companies provided centralized support and guidelines for deploying these departmental servers, few companies provided links between these pockets of network computing.

In the early 1990s, multiprotocol routers began to change all of this. Routers suddenly provided the flexibility and scalability to begin hooking all of these "network islands" into one unified whole. Although routers allowed media-independent communication across the many different types of data links deployed in these departmental networks, Ethernet and Token Ring became the media of choice. Routers were also used to provide seamless communication across wide-area links.

Early routers were obviously extremely bandwidth-limited compared to today's products. How then did these networks function when the Gigabit networks of today strain to keep up? There are two main factors: the *quantity* of traffic and the *type* of traffic.

First, there was considerably less traffic in campus networks at the time early router-based campus networks were popular. Simply put, fewer people used the network. And those who did use it tended to use less network-intensive applications.

However, this is not to say that early networks were like a 15-lane highway with only three cars on it. Given the lower available bandwidth of these networks, many had very high average and peak utilization levels. For instance, before the rise of client/server computing, many databases utilized file servers as a simple "hard drive at the end of a long wire." Thousands of dBase and Paradox applications were deployed that essentially pulled the entire database across the wire for each query. Therefore, although the *quantity* of traffic has grown dramatically, another factor is required to explain the success of these older, bandwidth-limited networks.

To explain this difference, the *type* of traffic must be considered. Although central MIS organizations used routers and hubs to merge the network into a unified whole, most of the traffic remained on the local segment. In other words, although the networks were linked together, the workgroup servers remained within the workgroups they served. For example, a custom financial application developed in dBase needed to use only the finance department's server; it never needed to access the human resource server. The growing amount of file and printer server traffic also tended to follow the same patterns.

These well-established and localized traffic flows allowed designers to utilize the popular 80/20 rule. Eighty (or even 90+) percent of the traffic in these networks remained on the local segment. Hubs (or possibly early "switching hubs") could support this traffic with relative ease. Because only 20 (or even less than 10) percent of the traffic needed to cross the router, the limited performance of these routers did not pose significant problems.

With blinding speed, all of this began to change in the mid-1990s. First, enterprise databases were deployed. These were typically large client/server systems that utilized a small number of highly centralized servers. On one hand, this dramatically cut the amount of traffic on networks. Instead of pulling the entire database across the wire, the application used technologies such as Structured Query Language (SQL) to allow intelligent database servers to first filter the data before it was transmitted back to the client. In practice, though, client/server systems began to significantly increase the utilization of network resources for a variety of reasons. First, the use of client/server technology grew at a staggering rate. Although each query might only generate one fourth of the traffic of earlier systems, many organizations saw the number of transactions increase by a factor of 10–100. Second, the centralized nature of these applications completely violated the 80/20 rule. In the case of this traffic component, 100 percent needs to cross the router and leave the local segment.

Although client/server applications began to tax traditional network designs, it took the rise of Internet and intranet technologies to completely outstrip available router (and hub) capacity. With Internet-based technology, almost 100 percent of the traffic was destined to centralized servers. Web and e-mail traffic generally went to a small handful of large UNIX boxes running HTTP, Simple Mail Transfer Protocol (SMTP), and Post Office Protocol (POP) daemons. Internet-bound traffic was just as centralized because it needed to funnel through a single firewall device (or bank of redundant devices). This trend of centralization was further accelerated with the rise of server farms that began to consolidate workgroup servers. Instead of high-volume file and print server traffic remaining on the local wire, everything began to flow across the corporate backbone.

As a result, the traditional 80/20 rule has become inverted. In fact, most modern networks have less than five percent of their traffic constrained to the local segment. When this is combined with the fact that these new Internet-based technologies are wildly popular, it is clear that the traditional router and hub design is no longer appropriate.

TIP   Be sure to consider changing traffic patterns when designing a campus backbone. In doing so, try to incorporate future growth and provide adequate routing performance.

Campus Design Terminology

This section explains some of the terminology that is commonly used to describe network designs. The discussion begins with a review of the Intermediate Distribution Frame/Main Distribution Frame (IDF/MDF) terminology that has been borrowed from the telephone industry. It then looks at a three-level paradigm that can be very useful.

IDF/MDF

For years, the telephone industry has used the terms Intermediate Distribution Frame (IDF) and Main Distribution Frame (MDF) to refer to various elements of structured cabling. As structured cabling has grown in popularity within data-communication circles, this IDF/MDF terminology has also become common.

The following sections discuss some of the unique requirements of switches placed in IDF and MDF closets. In addition to these specialized requirements, some features should be shared across all of the switches. For new installations, all of the switches should offer a wide variety of media types that include the various Ethernet speeds and ATM. FDDI and Token Ring support can be important when migrating older networks. Also, because modern switched campus infrastructures are too complex for the "plug-it-in-and-forget-it" approach, comprehensive management capabilities are a must.

IDF

IDF wiring closets are used to connect end-station devices such as PCs and terminals to the network. This "horizontal wiring" connects to wall-plate jacks at one end and typically consists of unshielded twisted-pair (UTP) cabling that forms a star pattern back to the IDF wiring closet. As shown in Figure 14-1, each floor of a building generally contains one or more IDF switches. Each end station connects back to the nearest IDF wiring closet. All of the IDFs in a building generally connect back to a pair of MDF devices often located in the building's basement or ground floor.

Figure 14-1   *Multiple IDF Wiring Closets*

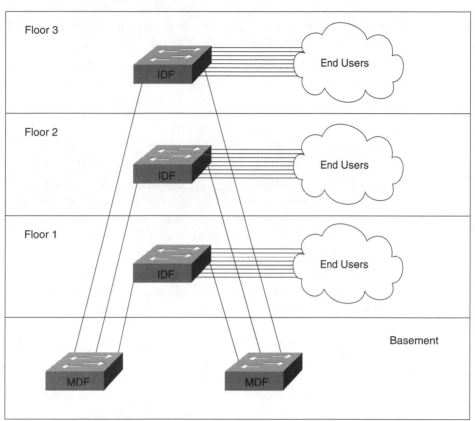

Given the role that they perform, IDF wiring closets have several specific requirements:

- **Port density**—Because large numbers of end stations need to connect to each IDF, high port density is a must.

- **Cost per port**—Given the high port density found in the typical IDF, cost per port must be reasonable.

- **Redundancy**—Because several hundred devices often connect back to each IDF device, a single IDF failure can create a significant outage.

- **Reliability**—This point is obviously related to the previous point, however, it highlights the fact that an IDF device is usually an end station's only link to the rest of the world.

- **Ease of management**—The high number of connections requires that per-port administration be kept to a minimum.

Because of the numerous directly connected end users, redundancy and reliability are critical to the IDF's role. As a result, IDFs should not only utilize redundant hardware such as dual Supervisors and power supplies, they should have multiple links to MDF devices. Fast failover of these redundant components is also critical.

IDF reliability brings up an interesting point about end-station connections. Outside of limited environments such as financial trading floors, it is generally not cost-effect to have end stations connected to more than one IDF device. Therefore, the horizontal cabling serves as a single point of failure for most networks. However, note that these failures generally affect only one end station. This is several orders of magnitude less disruptive than losing an entire switch. For important end stations such as servers, dual-port network interface cards (NICs) can be utilized with multiple links to redundant server farm switches.

The traditional device for use in IDF wiring closets is a hub. Because most hubs are fairly simple devices, the price per port can be very attractive. However, the shared nature of hubs obviously provides less available bandwidth. On the other hand, routers and Layer 3 switches can provide extremely intelligent bandwidth sharing decisions. On the downside, these devices can be very expensive and generally have limited port densities.

To strike a balance between cost, available bandwidth, and port densities, almost all recently deployed campus networks use Layer 2 switches in the IDF. This can be a very cost-effective way to provide 500 or more end stations with high-speed access into the campus backbone.

However, this is not to say that some Layer 3 technologies are not appropriate for the wiring closet. Cisco has introduced several IDF-oriented features that use the Layer 3 and 4 capabilities of the NetFlow Feature Card (NFFC). As discussed in Chapter 5, "VLANs," and Chapter 11, "Layer 3 Switching," Protocol Filtering can be an effective way to limit the impact of broadcasts on end stations. By allowing a port to only output broadcasts for the Layer 3 protocols that are actually in use, valuable CPU cycles can be saved. For example, a broadcast-efficient TCP/IP node in VLAN 2 can be spared from being burdened with IPX SAP updates. IGMP Snooping is another feature that utilizes the NFFC to inspect Layer 3 information. By allowing the Catalyst to prune ports from receiving certain multicast addresses, this feature can save significant bandwidth in networks that make extensive use of multicast applications. Finally, the NFFC can be used to classify traffic for Quality of Service/Class of Service (QoS/COS) purposes.

TIP   The most important IDF concerns are cost, port densities, and redundancy.

MDF

IDF devices collapse back to one or more Main Distribution Frame (MDF) devices in a star-like fashion. Each IDF usually connects to two different MDF devices to provide adequate redundancy. Some organizations place both MDF devices in the same physical closet and rely on disparate routing of the vertical cabling for redundancy. Other organizations prefer to place the MDF devices in separate closets altogether. The relationship between buildings and MDFs is not a hard rule—larger buildings might have more than two MDF switches, whereas a pair of redundant MDF devices might be able to carry multiple buildings that are smaller in size.

Figure 14-2 shows three buildings with MDF closets. To meet redundancy requirements, each building generally houses two MDF devices. The MDF devices can also be used to interconnect the three buildings (other designs are discussed later).

Figure 14-2   *MDF Closets*

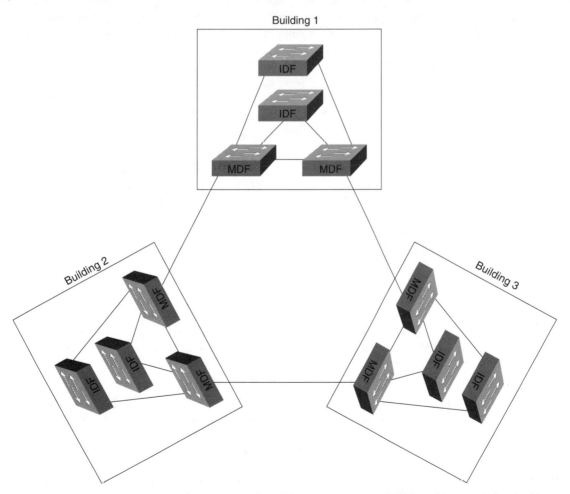

MDF closets have a different set of requirements and concerns than IDF closets:

- Throughput
- High availability
- Routing capabilities

Given that they act as concentration points for IDF traffic, MDF devices must be able to carry extremely high levels of traffic. In the case of a Layer 2 switch, this bandwidth is inexpensive and readily available. However, as is discussed later in this chapter, many of the strategies to achieve robust and scalable designs require routing in the MDF. Achieving this level of Layer 3 performance can require some careful planning. For more information on Layer 3 switching, see Chapter 11. Issues associated with Layer 3 switching are also addressed later in this chapter and in Chapter 15.

High availability is an important requirement for MDF devices. Although the failure of either an MDF or IDF switch potentially affects many users, there is a substantial distinction between these two situations. As discussed in the previous section, the failure of an IDF device completely disables the several hundred attached end stations. On the other hand, because MDFs are almost always deployed in pairs, failures rarely result in a complete loss of connectivity. However, this is not to say that MDF failures are inconsequential. To the contrary, MDF failures often affect thousands of users, many more than with an IDF failure. This requires as many features as possible that transparently reroute traffic around MDF problems.

In addition to the raw Layer 3 performance discussed earlier, other routing features can be important in MDF situations. For example, the issue of what Layer 3 protocols the router handles can be important (IP, IPX, AppleTalk, and so forth). Routing protocol support (OSPF, RIP, EIGRP, IS-IS, and so on) can also be a factor. Support for features such as DHCP relay and HSRP can be critical.

Three types of devices can be utilized in MDF closets:

- Layer 2 switches
- Hybrid, "routing switches" such as MLS
- "Switching routers" such as the Catalyst 8500

The first of these is also the simplest—a Layer 2 switch. The moderate cost and high throughput of these devices can make them very attractive options. Examples of these devices include current Catalyst 4000 models and traditional Catalyst 5000 switches without a Route Switch Module (RSM) or NFFC.

However, as mentioned earlier, there are compelling reasons to use Layer 3 processing in the MDF. This leads many network designs to utilize the third option, a Layer 3 switch that is functioning as a hardware-based router, what Chapter 11 referred to as a switching router. The Catalyst 8500 is an excellent example of this sort of device.

Cisco also offers another approach, Multilayer Switching (MLS), that lies between the previous two. MLS is a hybrid approach that allows the Layer 2-oriented Supervisors to cache Layer 3 information. It allows Catalysts to operate under the routing switch form of Layer 3 switching discussed in Chapter 11. A Catalyst 5000 with an RSM and NFFC is an example of an MLS switch. Other examples include the Catalyst 5000 Route Switch Feature Card (RSFC) and the Catalyst 6000 Multilayer Switch Feature Card (MSFC).

NOTE   It is important to understand the differences between the routing switch (MLS) and switching router (Catalyst 8500) styles of Layer 3 switching. These concepts are discussed in detail in Chapter 11.

Although the switching router (8500) and routing switch (MLS) options both offer very high throughput at Layer 3 and/or 4, there are important differences. For a thorough discussion of the technical differences, please see Chapter 11. This chapter and Chapter 15 focus on the important design implications of these differences.

TIP   The most important MDF factors are availability and Layer 3 throughput and capabilities.

Three-Layer Campus Network Model: Access, Distribution, Core

The IDF/MDF terminology discussed in the previous section describes the world in terms of two layers. However, MDF interconnections can often be better described with a third layer. For this reason, it is often useful to describe campus (and WAN) networks in terms of a three-layer model that more accurately describes the unique requirements of the inter-MDF connections. Geoff Haviland's excellent Cisco Internetwork Design (CID) course has popularized the use of the terms access, distribution, and core to describe these three layers. Figure 14-3 illustrates the three-layer model.

Figure 14-3 *The Three-Layer Design Model*

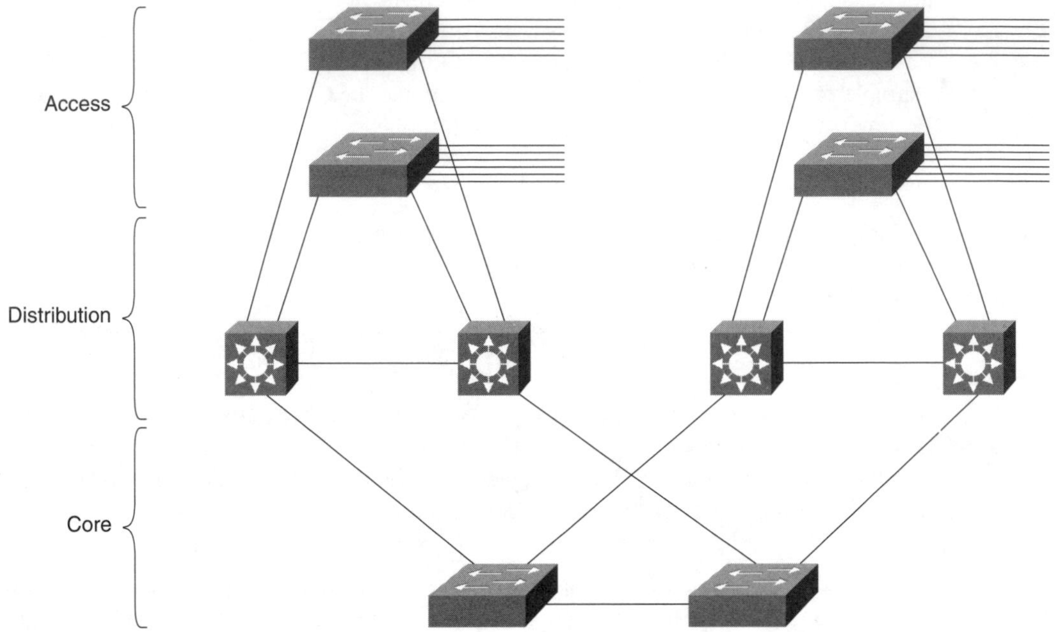

Each of these layers is briefly discussed in the following three sections.

Access Layer

The IDF closets are termed *access layer* closets under the three-layer model. The idea is that the devices deployed in these closets should be optimized for end-user access. Access layer requirements here are the same as those discussed in the IDF section: port density, cost, resiliency, and ease of management.

Distribution Layer

Under the three-layer model, MDF devices become *distribution layer* devices. The requirement for high Layer 3 throughput and functionality is especially important here.

TIP	In campus networks, the term *access layer* is synonymous with IDF, and *distribution layer* is equivalent to MDF.

Core Layer

The connections between the MDF switches become the *core layer* under the three-layer model. As is discussed in detail later, some networks have a very simple core consisting of several inter-MDF links or a pair of Layer 2 switches. In other cases, the size of the network might require Layer 3 switching within the core. Many networks utilize an Ethernet-based core; others might use ATM technology.

NOTE   In general, the terms *access layer* and *distribution layer* are used interchangeably with IDF and MDF. However, the IDF/MDF terms are used most often when discussing two-layer network designs; the access/distribution/core terminology is used when explaining three-layer topologies.

Key Requirements of Campus Designs

The "ideal" campus network should strive to achieve certain objectives. Some of these aspects have already been mentioned, but several new and important issues are introduced here (the new points are mentioned first):

- **Load balancing**—Given redundant paths, load balancing allows you to utilize all of the bandwidth you paid for. As is discussed in more detail in Chapter 15, flexibility, intelligence, and ease of configuration can be critical factors when utilizing this important feature.

- **Deterministic traffic patterns**—Traffic that flows in predictable ways can be crucial to network performance and troubleshooting. This can be especially true during network failure and recovery situations.

- **Consistent number of hops**—One of the principle factors contributing to deterministic traffic flows is a consistent number of hops throughout the network. As is discussed later in the chapter, this can best be achieved through a modular and consistent design.

- **Ease of configuration**—The network should not be excessively difficult to initially configure.

- **Ease of maintenance**—Ongoing maintenance tasks should be minimized. Where required, the tasks should follow well-established patterns that allow "cookie cutter" configurations.

- **Ease of troubleshooting**—Some designs can appear extremely appealing on paper, but they are a nightmare to troubleshoot (for example, extremely flat networks). A good design utilizes scalable modules or building blocks to promote easy troubleshooting through consistency and predictability.

- **Redundancy**—A 10–20 percent increase in hardware costs can increase network reliability by several hundred percent.

- **Cost**—Cost per port is especially important for high-density IDF devices.

Advantages of Routing

One of the key themes that is developed throughout this chapter is the idea that routing is critical to scalable network design. Hopefully, this is not news to you. However, given the recent popularity and focus on extremely flat, "avoid-the-router" designs, a fair amount of attention is devoted to this subject. Many people are convinced that the key objective in campus network design is to eliminate as many routers as possible. On the contrary, my experience suggests that this is exactly the wrong aim—routers have a proven track record of being the key to achieving the requirements of campus design discussed in the previous section.

- **Scalable bandwidth**—Routers have traditionally been considered slower than other approaches used for data forwarding. However, because a routed network uses a very decentralized algorithm, higher aggregate rates can be achieved than with less intelligent and more centralized Layer 2 forwarding schemes. Combine this fact with newer hardware-based routers (Layer 3 switches) and routing can offer extraordinary forwarding performance.

- **Broadcast filtering**—One of the Achilles heels of Layer 2 switching is broadcast containment. Vendors introduced VLANs as a partial solution to this problem, but key issues remain. Not only do broadcasts rob critical bandwidth resources, they also starve out CPU resources. Techniques such as ISL and LANE NICs that allow servers to connect to multiple VLANs in an attempt to build flat networks with a minimal use of routers only make this situation much worse—now the server must process the broadcasts for 10 or 20 VLANs! On the other hand, the more intelligent forwarding algorithms used by Layer 3 devices allow broadcasts to be contained while still maintaining full connectivity.

- **Superior multicast handling**—Although progress is being made to improve multicast support for Layer 2 devices through schemes such as IGMP Snooping, CGMP, and 802.1p (see Chapter 13, "Multicast and Broadcast Services"), it is extremely unlikely that these efforts will ever provide the comprehensive set of features offered by Layer 3. By running Layer 3 multicast protocols such as PIM, routers always provide a vast improvement in multicast efficiency and scalability. Given the predictions for dramatic multicast growth, this performance will likely be critical to the future (or current) success of your network.

- **Optimal path selection**—Because of their sophisticated metrics and path determination algorithms, routing protocols offer much better path selection capabilities than Layer 2 switches. As discussed in the Spanning Tree chapters, Layer 2 devices can easily send traffic through many unnecessary bridge hops.

- **Fast convergence**—Not only do routing protocols pick optimal paths; they do it very quickly. Modern Layer 3 routing protocols generally converge in 5–10 seconds. On the other hand, Layer 2 Spanning-Tree Protocol (STP) convergence takes 30–50 seconds by default. Although it is possible to change the default STP timers and to make use of optimizations such as UplinkFast in certain topologies, it is very difficult to obtain the consistently speedy results offered by Layer 3 routing protocols.

- **Load balancing**—Routing protocols also have sophisticated load balancing mechanisms. Layer 3 load balancing is flexible, easy to configure, and supports many simultaneous paths. On the other hand, Layer 2 load balancing techniques such as the STP load balancing described in Chapter 7, "Advanced Spanning Tree," can be extremely cumbersome and difficult to use.

- **Flexible path selection**—In addition to all of the other path selection benefits offered by routers, Cisco routers offer a wide variety of tools to manipulate path selections. Distribute lists, route maps, static routes, flexible metrics, and administrative distances are all examples of such mechanisms. These tools provide very granular control in a Layer 3 network.

- **Summarized addressing**—Layer 2 addresses use a flat address space. There is nothing about a MAC address that indicates physical location (it is much like a Social Security number). As a result, every bridging table in a flat network must contain an address for every node. On the other hand, Layer 3 addresses indicate location much like a ZIP code (postal code) or a telephone number's area code. By allowing addresses to be summarized, this hierarchical approach can allow *much* larger networks to be built. As a result, forwarding tables not only shrink dramatically in size, the address learning or routing table update process becomes much easier. Finally, lookups in the forwarding tables can be much faster.

- **Policy and access lists**—Most Layer 2 switches have very limited, if any, filtering capabilities. When filtering or access lists are supported, they use MAC addresses, hardly an efficient way to implement policy. On the other hand, routers can be used to provide complex access lists that function on Layer 3 and 4 information. This is much more useful from a policy implementation perspective. Hardware-based access lists are becoming increasingly common and flexible in Layer 3 switches.

- **Value-added features**—Although it is unlikely that the switching router Layer 3 devices such as the Catalyst 8500 will support "high touch" WAN-oriented services such as DLSw+ and protocol translation, there are still a large number of extremely important features that are offered by these platforms. For example, technologies such as DHCP relay, proxy ARP, debug, and proxy GNS can be critical router-based features in campus networks. (Note that some Layer 3 platforms can perform "high touch" services by running them in software. For example, MLS using an RSM could do DLSw+ on the RSM. The native IP traffic uses the NFFC for wire-speed forwarding; the DLSw+ is dependent on slower software-based forwarding.)

TIP   Large networks almost always benefit from scalability, flexibility, and intelligence of routing. Try to build routing (Layer 3 switching) into your campus design.

Campus Design Models

Although a myriad of permutations and variations exist, most campus designs can be grouped into three categories:

- Traditional router and hub model
- Campus-wide VLANs model (also known as flat earth and end-to-end VLANs)
- Multilayer model

The sections that follow go into more detail on each of these campus design models.

Router and Hub Model

Figure 14-4 illustrates the traditional router and hub model.

Figure 14-4   *Router and Hub Model*

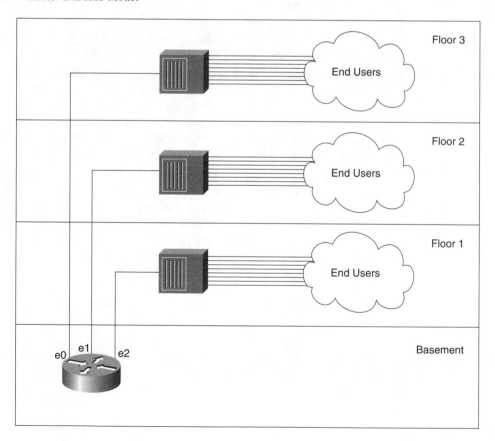

The traditional router and hub model uses Layer 1 hubs in IDF/access wiring closets. These connect back to unique ports on routers located in MDF/distribution closets. Several options are available for the campus core. In one approach, the distribution layer routers directly interconnect to form the network core/backbone. Because of its reliability and performance, an FDDI ring has traditionally been the media of choice for these connections. In other cases, some network designers prefer to form a collapsed backbone with a hub or router.

There are several advantages to the router and hub model as well as several reasons why most new designs have shied away from this approach. Table 14-1 lists the advantages and disadvantages of the router and hub model.

Table 14-1   *Advantages and Disadvantages of the Router and Hub Model*

Advantage	Disadvantage
Its reliance on routers makes for very good broadcast and multicast control.	Shared-media hubs do not offer enough bandwidth for modern applications. For example, in Figure 14-2, each floor must share a single 10 Megabit segment (factor in normal Ethernet overhead and these segments become extremely slow).
Because each hub represents a unique IP subnet or IPX network, administration is straightforward and easy to understand.	This design generally uses software-based routers that cannot keep up with increasing traffic levels.
Given moderate levels of traffic and departmental servers located on the local segment, the router and hub model can yield adequate performance.	Traffic patterns have changed, invalidating the assumption that most traffic would remain local. As a result, the campus-wide VLANs model became popular.
The hardware for this model is readily available and inexpensive.	

The chief advantage of this approach is the simplicity and familiarity that it brings to campus network design and management. The primary disadvantage is the limited bandwidth that this shared-media approach offers. The multilayer design model discussed later attempts to capitalize on the simplicity of the router and hub model while completely avoiding the limited bandwidth issue through the use of Layer 2 and 3 switching technology.

Campus-Wide VLANs Model

As people began to notice their router and hub networks struggling to keep up with traffic demands, they looked for alternate approaches. Many of these organizations decided to implement campus-wide VLANs, also known as the flat earth and end-to-end VLAN approach to network design.

Campus-wide VLANs strive to eliminate the use of routers. Because routers had become a significant bottleneck in campus networks, people looked for ways to minimize their use. Because broadcast domains still needed to be held to a reasonable size, VLANs were used to create logical barriers to broadcasts. Figure 14-5 illustrates a typical campus-wide VLANs design.

Figure 14-5   *Campus-Wide VLAN Model*

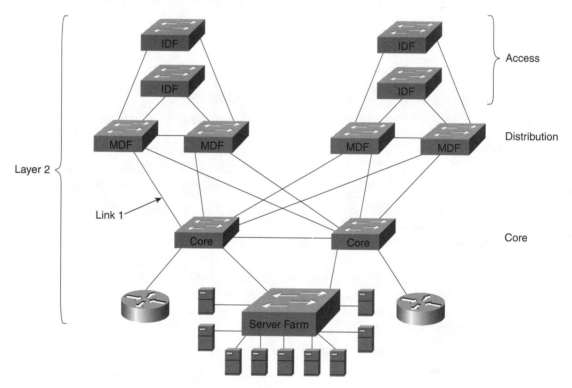

Figure 14-5 uses Layer 2 switching throughout the entire network. To provide communication between VLANs, two routers have been provided using the router-on-a-stick configuration (see Chapter 11).

Advantages of Campus-Wide VLANs

As the paragraphs that follow attest, there are some alluring aspects to the flat earth approach.

First, the campus-wide VLANs model allows network designers to create a direct Layer 2 path from end stations to the most commonly used servers. By deploying Layer 2 switching in all three layers of the access/distribution/core model, campus-wide VLANs should dramatically increase available bandwidth.

The second advantage of the campus-wide VLANs model is that VLANs can be used to provide logical control over broadcast domains and, therefore, subnets. Some platforms allow the switches to automatically detect what VLAN an end station should be assigned to, requiring no administration for adds, moves, and changes. Other schemes allow for more centralized control over VLAN assignments and strive to make the administration as easy as possible. For example, vendors can provide demos of glitzy products that allow you to drag-and-drop end users into VLANs. Other examples include Cisco's Virtual Management Policy Server (VMPS) that makes VLAN assignments based on MAC addresses and User Registration Tool (URT) that uses NT directory services (VMPS and URT are discussed in the section "VMPS and Dynamic VLANs: Advanced Administration" of Chapter 5, "VLANs").

The third advantage of campus-wide VLANs is that traffic only goes through a router if it needs to cross VLAN boundaries. If a user in the Finance VLAN needs to access the Finance server (located in the same VLAN), no routers are involved. However, if this user needs to occasionally access a server in the Marketing VLAN, a router is used. Servers can even be directly connected to multiple VLANs through the use of ISL or LANE NICs, further reducing the requirement for routers. For example, the server in the Marketing VLAN can be fitted with an ISL NIC to allow direct, Layer 2 access from the Finance VLAN.

Finally, this centralized use of routing can make it much easier to configure access lists and security in the network. For example, consider the case of a college network where two VLANs exist: students and professors. These two VLANs might span dozens of buildings, but because of the centralized routing typically used with campus-wide VLANs, access lists might only need to be configured on a pair of routers. On the other hand, if every building on campus connected to the campus backbone through a router, the network might require hundreds of access lists scattered across many dozens of routers.

The end result: you have the speed of Layer 2, the flexibility of VLANs, and you have avoided the "slowness" of the router.

Disadvantages of Campus-Wide VLANs

There are also some significant downsides to the campus-wide VLANs model:

- Management difficulties
- Lack of logical structure
- Large and overlapping Spanning Tree domains
- It is easy for a problem in one VLAN to deplete bandwidth in all VLANs across trunk links
- Many networks using campus-wide VLANs must resort to eliminating all redundancy to achieve network stability

- Lack of scalability
- Most modern traffic violates the "stay in one subnet" rule employed by the campus-wide VLAN model
- Modern routers are not a bottleneck

The paragraphs that follow provide more detailed coverage of each of these disadvantages.

Management of these networks can be much more difficult and tedious than originally expected. The router and hub design had the logical clarity of one subnet per wiring closet. Conversely, many networks using campus-wide VLANs have developed into a confusing mess of VLAN and Layer 3 address assignments.

Another downside to campus-wide VLANs is that the lack of logical structure can be problematic, especially when it comes to troubleshooting. Without a clearly defined hierarchy, it is very difficult to narrow down the source of each problem. Before each troubleshooting session, valuable time can be wasted trying to understand the constantly changing VLAN structure.

Also, campus-wide VLANs result in large and overlapping Spanning Tree domains. As discussed in Chapter 6, "Understanding Spanning Tree," and Chapter 7, "Advanced Spanning Tree," STP uses a complex set of evaluations that elect one central device (the Root Bridge) for every VLAN. Other bridges and switches then locate the shortest path to this central bridge/switch and use this path for all data forwarding. The Spanning-Tree Protocol is extremely dynamic—if the Root Bridge (or a link to the Root Bridge) is "flapping," the network continuously vacillates between the two switches acting as the Root Bridge (disrupting traffic every time it does so). Large Spanning Tree domains must use very conservative timer values, resulting in frustratingly slow failover performance. Also, as the size and number of the Spanning Tree domains grow, the possibility of CPU overload increases. If a single device in a single VLAN falls behind and opens up a loop, this can quickly overload every device connected to every VLAN. The result: network outages that last for days and are difficult to troubleshoot.

Yet another downside to campus-wide VLANs is that the wide use of trunk links that carry multiple VLANs makes the Spanning Tree problems even worse. For example, consider Link 1 in Figure 14-5, a Fast Ethernet link carrying VLANs 1–15. Assume that the CPU in a single switch in VLAN 1 becomes overloaded and opens up a bridging loop. Although the loop might be limited to VLAN 1, this VLAN's traffic can consume all of the trunk's capacity and starve out all other VLANs. This problem is even worse if you further assume that VLAN 1 is the management VLAN. In this case, the broadcasts caught in the bridging loop devour 100 percent of switch's CPU horsepower throughout the network. As more and more switch CPUs become overloaded, more and more VLANs experience bridging loops. Within a matter of seconds, the entire network "melts down."

An additional problem with the campus-wide VLAN model is that, to avoid these Spanning Tree and trunking problems, many campus-wide VLAN networks have had to resort to eliminating all redundant paths just to achieve stability. To solve this problem, redundant links can be physically disconnected or trunks can be pruned in such a way that a loop-free Spanning Tree is manually created. In either case, this makes every device in the network a single point of failure. Most network designers never intend to make this sort of sacrifice when they sign up for a flat earth design. Without routers, there are no Layer 3 "barriers" in the network and it becomes very easy for problems to spread throughout the entire campus.

Furthermore, campus-wide VLANs are not scalable. Many small networks have been successfully deployed using the campus-wide VLAN design. Initially, the users of these networks are usually very happy with both the utility and the bandwidth of their new infrastructure. However, as the network begins to grow in size, the previously mentioned problems become more and more chronic.

Yet another downside to campus-wide VLANs is that it is harder and harder to bypass routers, the very premise that the entire campus-wide VLANs scheme was built upon. As traffic patterns have evolved from departmental servers on the local segment to enterprise servers located in a centralized server farm, it has become very difficult to remove routers from this geographically dispersed path. For example, it can be difficult to connect an enterprise web server to 20 or more VLANs (subnets) without going through a router. A variety of solutions such as ISL, 802.1Q, and LANE NICs have become available; however, these have generally produced very disappointing performance. And, as mentioned earlier, these NICs request the server to process all broadcasts for all VLANs, robbing it of valuable and expensive CPU cycles. Also, the multiple-VLAN NICs have been fraught with other problems such as slow initialization time, a limited number of VLANs, and unexpected server behavior.

Finally, another basic premise of the campus-wide VLAN strategy is no longer true. Specifically, routers are now as fast (or nearly as fast) as Layer 2 switches. Although this equivalent performance generally comes at a price premium, it is no longer worthwhile to go to such great lengths to avoid Layer 3 routing.

Practical Advice Regarding Campus-Wide VLANs

I have implemented several networks utilizing the campus-wide VLAN approach. Prior to 1998, routers were simply too slow to place them in the middle of burgeoning campus traffic levels. Although I often had this nagging feeling about the lack of Layer 3 hierarchy, I jumped on the bandwagon with everyone else. In short, there simply didn't seem to be another option. However, with the advent of Layer 3 switching, I see fewer and fewer compelling uses for campus-wide VLANs.

Before leaving you with the feeling that everyone using campus-wide VLANs hates it, I should also point out that there are some fairly large networks utilizing this model with great success. Whether it is because their traffic patterns still adhere to the 80/20 rule or they like to take advantage of the drag-and-drop approach to VLANs, some network administrators firmly support this style of network design.

However, I have talked to far more clients that have struggled to produce stable and scalable networks using this model. For many users, the disadvantages discussed earlier are far too debilitating to justify the advantages of the campus-wide VLAN design.

Multilayer Model

The multilayer model strives to provide the stability and scalability of the router and hub
model while also capturing the performance of the campus-wide VLANs model. This
approach takes full advantage of hardware-based routing, Layer 3 switching, to put routing
back into its rightful place. However, it does not ignore Layer 2 switching. In fact, it seeks
to strike the optimal balance—Layer 3 switching is used for control, whereas Layer 2
switching is used for cost-effective data forwarding.

Figure 14-6 illustrates a sample network using the multilayer model.

Figure 14-6   *Multilayer Model*

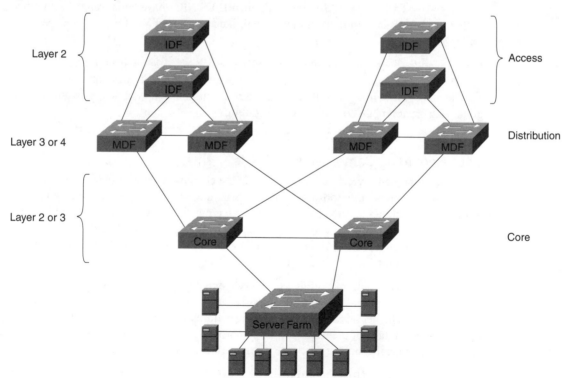

Each IDF/MDF cluster forms a separate module in the design. Figure 14-6 shows two modules. The access layer IDF switches use Layer 2 forwarding to provide large amounts of cost-effective bandwidth. The distribution layer MDF switches provide the Layer 3 control that is required in all large networks. These IDF/MDF modules then connect through a variety of Layer 2 or Layer 3 cores.

TIP	The multilayer model combines Layer 2 and Layer 3 processing into a cohesive whole. This design has proven to be highly flexible and scalable.

In general, the multilayer model is the recommended approach for enterprise campus design for several reasons.

First, the use of routers provides adequate Layer 3 control. In short, this allows all of the benefits discussed in the "Advantages of Routing" section to accrue to your network. Without listing all of these advantages again, a multilayer design is scalable, flexible, high performance, and easy to manage.

Second, as its name suggests, the multilayer model offers hierarchy. In hierarchical networks, layers with specific roles are defined to allow large and consistent designs. As the next section discusses, this allows each layer of the access/distribution/core model to meet unique and specific requirements.

Third, this approach is very modular. There are many benefits to a modular design, including the following:

- It is easy to grow the network.
- The total available bandwidth scales as additional modules are added.
- Modular networks are easier to understand, troubleshoot, and maintain.
- The network can use cookie cutter configurations. This consistency saves administrative headaches while also reducing the chance of configuration errors.
- It is easier to migrate to a modular network. The old network can appear as another module (although it does not have the consistent layout and configurations of modules in the new network).
- Modular networks allow consistent and deterministic traffic patterns.
- Modular designs promote load balancing and redundancy.
- It is much easier to provide fast failover in a consistent, modular design than it is in less structured designs. Because the topology is constrained and well defined, both Layer 2 and Layer 3 convergence benefit.
- Modular networks allow technologies to be easily substituted for one another. Not only does this allow organizations more freedom in the initial design (for example, the core can be either Ethernet or ATM), it makes it easier to upgrade the network in the long run.

General Recommendation: Multilayer Model

As discussed in the previous section, the multilayer model is the most appropriate approach for most modern campus networks for a variety of reasons. This section explains some specific considerations of this model.

Distribution Blocks

A large part of the benefit of the multilayer model centers around the concept of a modular approach to access (IDF) and distribution (MDF) switches. Given a pair of redundant MDF switches, each IDF/access layer switch forms a triangle of connectivity as shown in Figure 14-7. If there are ten IDF switches connected to a given set of MDF switches, ten triangles are formed (such as might be the case in a ten-story building). The collection of all triangles formed by two MDF switches is referred to as a *distribution block*. Most commonly, a distribution block equates to all of the IDF and MDF switches located in a single building.

Figure 14-7   *Triangles of Connectivity within a Distribution Block*

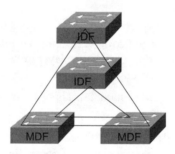

Because of its simplicity, the triangle creates the ideal building block for a campus network. By having two vertical links (IDF uplink connections), it automatically provides redundancy. Because the redundancy is formed in a predictable, consistent, and uncomplicated fashion, it is much easier to provide uniformly fast failover performance.

TIP   Use the concept of a distribution block to simplify the design and maintenance of your network.

The multilayer model does not take a dogmatic stance on Layer 2 versus Layer 3 switching (although it is based around the theme that *some* Layer 3 processing is a requirement in large networks). Instead, it seeks to create the optimal blend of both Layer 2 and Layer 3 technology to achieve the competing goals of low cost, high performance, and scalability.

To provide cost-effective bandwidth, Layer 2 switches are generally used in the IDF (access layer) wiring closets. As discussed earlier, the NetFlow Feature Card can add significant value in the wiring closet with features such as Protocol Filtering and IGMP Snooping.

To provide control, Layer 3 switching should be deployed in the MDF (distribution layer) closets. This is probably the single-most important aspect of the entire design. Without the Layer 3 component, the distribution blocks are no longer self-contained units. A lack of Layer 3 processing in the distribution layer causes Spanning Tree, VLANs, and broadcast domains to spread throughout the entire network. This increases the interdependency of various pieces of the network, making the network far less scalable and far more likely to suffer a network-wide outage.

By making use of Layer 3 switching, each distribution block becomes an independent switching system. The benefits discussed in the "Advantages of Routing" section are baked into the network. Problems that develop in one part of the network are prevented from spreading to other parts of the network.

You should also be careful to not circumvent the modularity of the distribution block concept with random links. For example, Links 1 and 2 in Figure 14-8 break the modularity of the multilayer model.

Figure 14-8   *Links 1 and 2 Break the Modularity of the Multilayer Design*

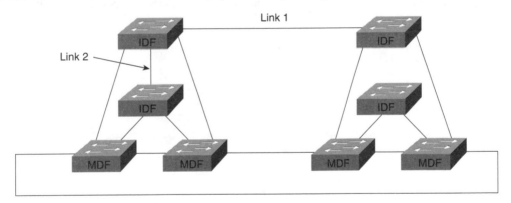

The intent here was good: provide a direct, Layer 2 path between three IDF switches containing users in the same workgroup. Although this does eliminate one or two router hops from the paths between these IDF switches, it causes the entire design to start falling apart. Soon another exception is made, then another, and so on. Before long, the entire network begins to resemble an interconnected mess more like a bowl of spaghetti than a carefully planned campus network. Just remember that the scalability and long-term health of the network are more important than a short-term boost in bandwidth. Avoid "spaghetti networks" at all costs.

TIP	Be certain to maintain the modularity of distribution blocks. Do not add links or inter-VLAN bridging that violate the Layer 3 barrier that the multilayer model uses in the distribution layer.

Without descending too far into "marketing speak," it is useful to note the potential application of Layer 4 switching in the distribution layer. By considering transport layer port numbers in addition to network layer addressing, Layer 4 switching can more easily facilitate policy-based networking. However, from a scalability and performance standpoint, Layer 4 switching does not have a major impact on the overall multilayer model—it still creates the all-important Layer 3 barrier at the MDF switches.

On the other hand, the choice of Layer 3 switching technology can make a difference in matters such as addressing and load balancing.

Switching Router (8500) MDFs

In the case of 8500-style switching routers, the MDF switches make a complete break in the Layer 2 topology by default. As a result, the triangles of connectivity appear as two unique subnets—one that crosses the IDF switch and one that sits between the MDF switches as illustrated in Figure 14-9.

Figure 14-9   *Switching Router MDF Switches Break the Network into Two Subnets*

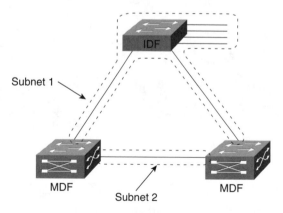

The resulting network is completely free of Layer 2 loops. Although some network designers have viewed this as an opportunity to completely disable the Spanning-Tree Protocol, this is generally not advisable because misconfiguration errors can easily create loops in the IDF wiring closet or end-user work areas (therefore possibly taking down the entire IDF). However, it does mean that STP load balancing cannot be used. Recall from Chapter 7 that STP load balancing requires two characteristics to be present in the network. First, it requires redundant paths, something that exists in Figure 14-9. Second, it requires that these redundant paths form Layer 2 loops, something that the routers in Figure 14-9 prevent. Therefore, some other load balancing technique must be employed.

NOTE   The decision of whether or not the Spanning-Tree Protocol should be disabled can be complex. This book recommends leaving Spanning Tree enabled (even in Layer 2 loop-free networks such as the one in Figure 14-9) because it provides a safety net for any loops that might be accidentally formed through the end-user ports. Currently, most organizations building large-scale campus networks want to take this conservative stance. This choice seems especially wise when you consider that Spanning Tree does not impose any failover delay for important topology changes such as a broken IDF uplink. In other words, the use of Spanning Tree in this environment provides an important benefit while having very few downsides.

For more discussion on the technical intricacies of the Spanning-Tree Protocol, see Chapters 6 and 7. For more detailed and specific recommendations on using the Spanning-Tree Protocol in networks utilizing the various forms of Layer 3 switching, see Chapter 15.

In general, some form of HSRP load balancing is the most effective solution. As discussed in the "HSRP" section of Chapter 11, if the IDF switch contains multiple end-user VLANs, the VLANs can be configured to alternate active HSRP peers between the MDF switches. For example, the left switch in Figure 14-9 could be configured as the active HSRP peer for the odd VLANs, whereas the right switch would handle the even VLANs. However, if the network only contains a single VLAN on the IDF switch (this is often done to simplify network administration by making it more like the router and hub model), the Multigroup HSRP (MHSRP) technique is usually the most appropriate technology. Figure 14-10 illustrates the MHSRP approach.

Figure 14-10 *MHSRP Load Balancing*

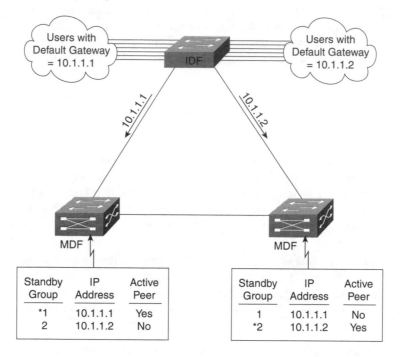

In Figure 14-10, two HSRP groups are created for a single subnet/VLAN. The first group uses the address **10.1.1.1**, whereas the second group uses **10.1.1.2**. Notice that both addresses intentionally fall within the same subnet. Half of the end stations connected to the IDF switch are then configured to use a primary default gateway of **10.1.1.1**, and the other half use **10.1.1.2** (this can be automated with DHCP). For more information on this technique, see the "MHSRP" section of Chapter 11 and the "Use DHCP to Solve User Mobility Problems" section of Chapter 15.

TIP

In general, implementing load balancing while using switching routers in the distribution layer requires multiple IDF VLANs (each with a separate HSRP standby group) or MHSRP for a single IDF VLAN.

Routing Services (MLS) MDFs

However, if the MDF switches are using routing switch MLS-style Layer 3 switching, the design might be very different. In this case, it is entirely possible to have Layer 2 loops. Rather than being pure routers as with the switching router approach, the MDF switches are normal Layer 2 devices that have been enhanced with Layer 3 caching technology. Therefore, MLS devices pass Layer 2 traffic by default (this default can be changed). For example, Figure 14-11 illustrates the Layer 2 loops that commonly result when MLS is in use.

Figure 14-11   *MLS Often Creates Layer 2 Loops that Require STP Load Balancing*

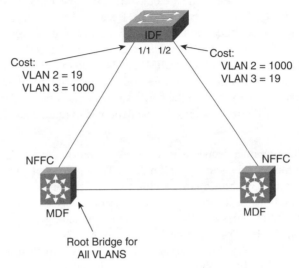

Both VLANs 2 and 3 are assigned to all three trunk links, forming a Layer 2 loop. In this case, STP load balancing is required. As shown in Figure 14-11, the cost for VLAN 3 on the 1/1 IDF port can be increased to 1000, and the same can be done for VLAN 2 on Port 1/2. For more detailed information on STP load balancing, please see Chapter 7.

TIP   The Layer 2/3 hybrid nature of MLS generally requires STP load balancing.

Core

Designing the core of a multilayer network is one of the areas where creativity and careful planning can come into play. Unlike the distribution blocks, there is no set design for a multilayer core. This section discusses some of the design factors that should be taken into consideration.

One of the primary concerns when designing a campus core backbone should be fast failover and convergence behavior. Because of the reliance on Layer 3 processing in the MLS design, fast-converging routing protocols can be used instead of the slower Spanning-Tree Protocol. However, one must be careful to avoid unexpected Spanning Tree slowdowns within the core itself.

Another concern is that of VLANs. In some cases, the core can utilize a single flat VLAN that spans one or more Layer 2 core switches. In other cases, traffic can be segregated into

VLANs for a variety of reasons. For example, multiple VLANs can be used for policy reasons or to separate the different Layer 3 protocols. A separate management VLAN is also desirable when using Layer 2-oriented switches.

Broadcast and multicast traffic are other areas of concern. As much as possible, broadcasts should be kept off of the network's core. Because the multilayer model uses Layer 3 switching in the MDF devices, this usually isn't an issue. Likewise, multicast traffic also benefits from the use of routers in the multilayer model. If the core makes use of routing, Protocol Independent Multicast (PIM) can be used to dynamically build optimized multicast distribution trees. If sparse-mode PIM is used, the rendezvous point (RP) can be placed on a Layer 3 switch in the core. If the core is comprised of Layer 2 switches only, then CGMP or IGMP Snooping can be deployed to reduce multicast flooding within the core.

One of the important decisions facing every campus network designer has to do with the choice of media and switching technology. The majority of campus networks currently utilize Fast and Gigabit Ethernet within the core. However, ATM can be a viable choice in many cases. Because it supports a wide range of services, can integrate well with wide area networks, and provides extremely low-latency switching, ATM has many appealing aspects. Also, MultiProtocol Label Swapping (MPLS, also known as Tag Switching), traditionally seen as a WAN-only technology, is likely to become increasingly common in very large campus backbones. Because it provides excellent traffic engineering capabilities and very tight integration between Layer 2 and 3, MPLS can be extremely useful in all sorts of network designs.

However, the most critical decision has to do with the switching characteristics of the core. In some cases, a Layer 2 core is optimal; other networks benefit from a Layer 3 core. The following sections discuss issues particular to each.

Layer 2 Core

Figure 14-12 depicts the typical Layer 2 core in a multilayer network.

Figure 14-12 *A Layer 2 Core*

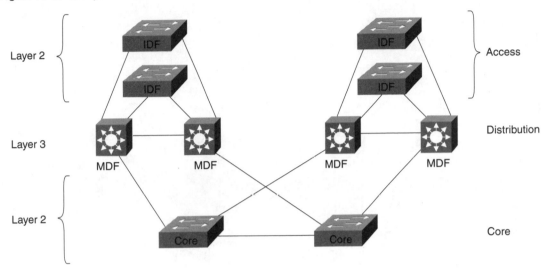

This creates a L2/L3/L2 profile throughout the network. The network's intelligence is contained in the distribution-layer MDF switches. Both the access (IDF) and core switches utilize Layer 2 switching to maintain a high price/performance ratio. To provide redundancy, a pair of switches form the core. Because the core uses Layer 2 processing, this approach is most suitable for small to medium campus backbones.

When building a Layer 2 core, Spanning Tree failover performance should be closely analyzed. Otherwise, the entire network can suffer from excessively slow reconvergence. Because the equipment comprising the campus core should be housed in tightly controlled locations, it is often desirable to disable Spanning Tree entirely within the core of the network.

TIP

I recommend that you only disable Spanning Tree in the core if you are using switching routers in the distribution layer. If MLS is in use, its Layer 2 orientation makes it too easy to misconfigure a distribution switch and create a bridging loop.

One way to accomplish this is through the use of multiple VLANs that have been carefully assigned to links in a manner that create a loop-free topology within each VLAN. An alternate approach consists of physically removing cables that create Layer 2 loops. For example, consider Figure 14-13.

Figure 14-13 *A Loop-Free Core*

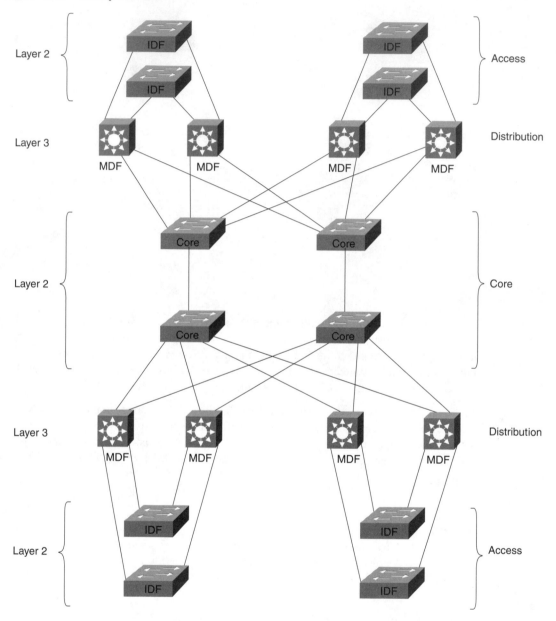

In Figure 14-13, the four Layer 2 switches forming the core have been kept loop free at Layer 2. Although a redundant path does exist through each distribution (MDF) switch, the pure routing behavior of these nodes prevents any Layer 2 loops from forming.

If Spanning Tree is required within the core, blocked ports should be closely analyzed. Because STP load balancing can be very tricky to implement in the network core, compromises might be necessary.

In addition to Spanning Tree, there are several other issues to look for in a Layer 2 core. First, be careful that multicast flooding is not a problem. As mentioned earlier, IGMP Snooping and CGMP can be useful tools in this situation (also see Chapter 13). Second, keep an eye on router peering limits as the network grows. Because each MDF switch is a router under the multilayer model, a Layer 2 core creates the appearance of many routers sitting around a single subnet. If the number of routers becomes too large, this can easily lead to excessive state information, erratic behavior, and slow convergence. In this case, it can be desirable to break the network into multiple VLANs that reduce peering.

TIP	Be careful to avoid excessive router peering when using Catalyst 8500s. One of the easiest ways to accomplish this is through the use of a Layer 3 core (see the next section).

A Layer 2 core can provide a very useful campus backbone. However, because of the potential issues and scaling limits, it is most appropriate in small to medium campus networks.

TIP	A Layer 2 core can be a cost-effective solution for smaller campus networks.

Layer 3 Core

Figure 14-14 redraws Figure 14-12 with a Layer 3 core.

Figure 14-14 *A Layer 3 Core*

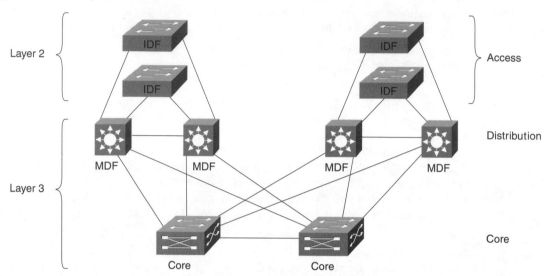

Although Figure 14-12 and Figure 14-14 look very similar, the use of Layer 3 switching within the core makes several important changes to the network.

First, the path determination is no longer contained only within the distribution layer switches. With a Layer 3 core, the path determination is spread throughout the distribution and core layer switches. This more decentralized approach can provide many benefits:

- Higher aggregate forwarding capacity
- Superior multicast control
- Flexible and easy to configure load balancing
- Scalability
- Router peering is reduced
- IOS feature throughout a large percentage of the network

In short, the power and flexibility of Layer 3 processing eliminates many of the issues discussed concerning Layer 2 backbones. For example, the switches can be connected in a wide variety of looped configurations without concern for bridging loops or STP performance. By cross-linking core switches, redundancy *and* performance can be maximized. Also, placing routing nodes within campus core, router mesh and peering between the distribution switches can be dramatically reduced (however, it is still advisable to consider areas of excessive router peering).

Notice that a Layer 3 core does add additional hops to the path of most traffic. In the case of a Layer 2 core, most traffic requires two hops, one through the end user's MDF switch and the other through the server farm's MDF switch. In the case of a Layer 3 core, an additional hop (or two) is added. However, several factors minimize this concern:

- The consistent and modular design of the multilayer model guarantees a consistent and small number of router hops. In general, no more than four router hops within the campus should ever be necessary.

- Many Layer 3 switches have latencies comparable to Layer 2 switches.

- Windowing protocols (such as TCP or IPX Burst Mode) reduce impact of latency for most applications.

- Switching latency is often a very small part of overall latency. In other words, latency is not as big an issue as most people make it out to be.

- The scalability benefits of Layer 3 are generally far more important than any latency concerns.

TIP   Larger campus networks benefit from a Layer 3 core.

Server Farm Design

Server farm design is an important part of almost all modern networks. The multilayer model easily accommodates this requirement. First, the server farm can easily be treated as its own distribution block. A pair of redundant Layer 3 switches can be used to provide physical redundancy as well as network layer redundancy with protocols such as HSRP. In addition, the Layer 3 switches create an ideal place to apply server-related policy and access lists. Figure 14-15 illustrates a server farm distribution block.

Figure 14-15   *The Server Farm Can Form Another Distribution Block*

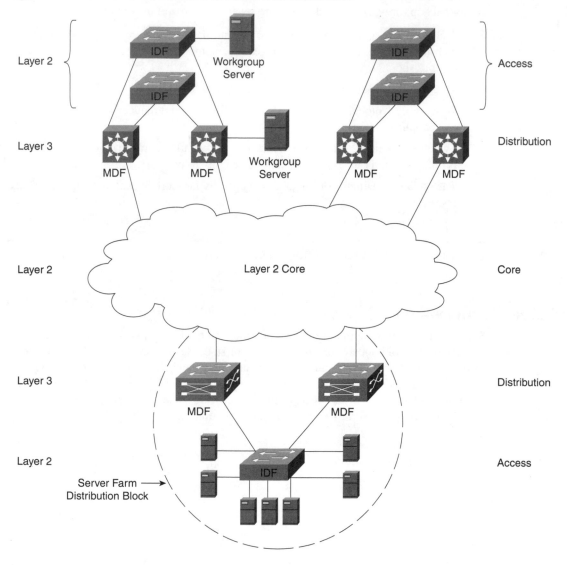

Although enterprise-wide servers should generally be deployed in a central location, workgroup servers can be attached directly to access or distribution level switches. Two examples of this are shown in Figure 14-15.

TIP

An enterprise server farm is usually best implemented as another distribution block that connects to the core.

Specific tips for server farm design are discussed in considerably more detail in the "Server Farms" section of Chapter 15.

Using a Unique VTP Domain for Each Distribution Block

When using the MLS approach to Layer 3 switching in the MDF closets, it might be advantageous to make each distribution block a separate VTP domain. Because of the Layer 2 orientation to MLS, VLANs propagate throughout the entire network by default (see Chapter 12 for more information on VTP). However, the multilayer model is designed to constrain VLANs to an individual distribution block. By innocently using the default behavior, your network can become unnecessarily burdened by extraneous VLANs and STP computations.

Assigning a unique VTP domain name to each distribution block is a simple but effective way to have VLAN propagation mirror the intended design. When a new VLAN is added within a distribution block, it automatically is added to every other switch in that block. However, because other distribution blocks are using a different domain name, they do not learn about this new VLAN.

TIP   The MLS approach to Layer 3 switching can lead to excessive VLAN propagation. Use a different VTP domain name for each distribution block to overcome this default behavior.

When VTP domains are in use, it is usually best to make the names descriptive of the distribution block (for example, Building1 and Building 2).

TIP   Recall from Chapter 8 that when using trunk links between different VTP domains, the trunk state will need to be hard-coded to **on**. The use of **auto** and **desirable** will not work across VTP domain names (in other words, the DISL and DTP protocols check for matching VTP domain names).

IP Addressing

In a very large campus network, it is usually best to assign bitwise contiguous blocks of address spaces to each distribution block. This allows the routers in each distribution block to summarize all of the subnets within that block into a single advertisement that gets sent into the core backbone. For example, the single advertisement **10.1.16.0/20** (**/20** is a shorthand way to represent the subnet mask **255.255.240.0**) can summarize the entire range of 16 subnets from **10.1.16.0/24** to **10.1.31.0/24** (**/24** is equivalent to the subnet mask **255.255.255.0**). This is illustrated in Figure 14-16.

Figure 14-16 *Using IP Address Summarization*

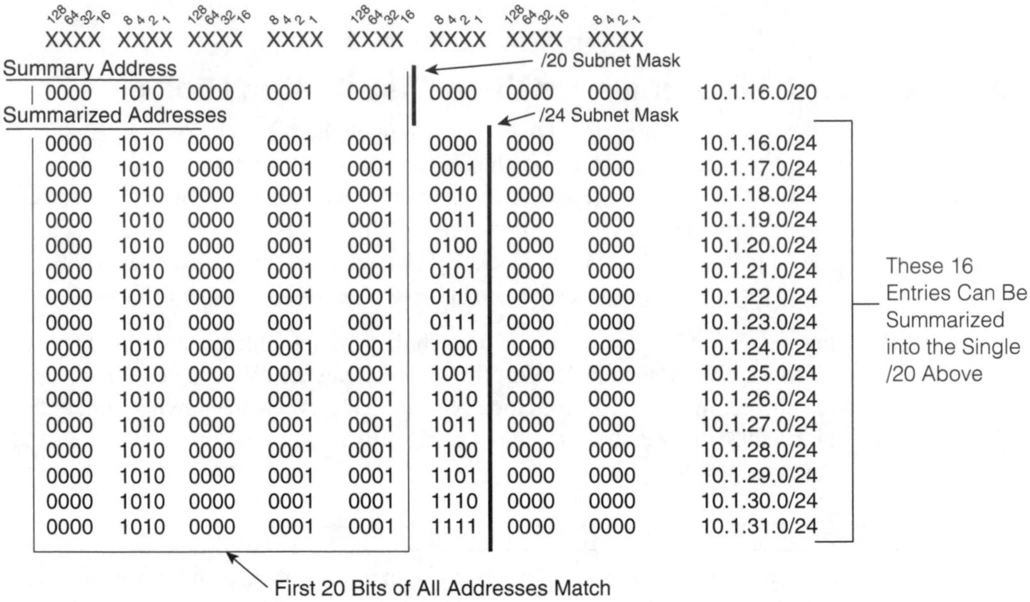

As shown in Figure 14-16, the **/20** and **/24** subnet masks (or network prefixes) differ by four bits (in other words, **/20** is four bits "shorter" than **/24**). These are the only four bits that differ between the 16 **/24** subnet addresses. In other words, because all 16 **/24** subnet addresses match in the first 20 bits, a single **/20** address can be used to summarize all of them.

In a real-world distribution block, the 16 individual **/24** subnets can be applied to 16 different end-user VLANs. However, outside the distribution block, a classless IP routing protocol can distribute the single **/20** route of **10.1.16.0/20**.

TIP   In very large campus networks, try to plan for future growth and address summarization by pre-allocating bitwise contiguous blocks of address space.

Scaling Link Bandwidth

Note that the modular nature of the multilayer model allows individual links to easily scale to higher bandwidth. Not only does the architecture accommodate entirely different media types, it is easy to add additional links and utilize Fast or Gigabit EtherChannel.

Network Migrations

Finally, the modularity of the multilayer model can make migrations much easier. In general, the entire old network can appear as a single distribution block to the rest of the new network (for example, imagine that the server farm distribution block in Figure 14-15 is the old network). Although the old network generally does not have all of the benefits of the multilayer model, it provides a redundant and routed linkage between the two networks. After the migration is complete, the old network can be disabled.

Exercises

This section includes a variety of questions on the topic of this chapter—campus design concepts and models. By completing these, you can test your mastery of the material included in this chapter as well as help prepare yourself for the CCIE written and lab tests.

Review Questions

1 What are some of the unique requirements of an IDF switch?

2 What are some of the unique requirements of an MDF switch?

3 Describe the access/distribution/core terminology.

4 Why is routing an important part of any large network design?

5 What networks work best with the router and hub model?

6 What are the benefits of the campus-wide VLANs model?

7 What are the downsides of the campus-wide VLANs model?

8 Describe the concept of a distribution block.

9 Why is it important to have modularity in a network?

10 What are the concerns that arise when using a Layer 2 core versus a Layer 3 core?

11 How should a server farm be implemented in the multilayer model?

Design Lab

Design two campus networks that meet the following requirements. The first design should employ the campus-wide VLANs model using Catalyst 5509 switches. The second design should implement the multilayer model by using Catalyst 8540 MDF switches and Catalyst 5509 IDF switches. Here are the requirements:

- The campus contains three buildings.

- Each building has four floors.

- Each floor has one IDF switch. (In reality there would be more, however, these can be eliminated from this exercise for simplicity.)

- Each building has two MDF switches in the basement.

- Each IDF has redundant links (one two each MDF switch).

- The MDF switches are fully or partially meshed (choose which one you feel is more appropriate) with Gigabit Ethernet links (in other words, the core does not use a third layer of switches).

- Each IDF switch should have a unique management VLAN where SC0 can be assigned.

- In the campus-wide VLANs design, assume there are 12 VLANs and that every IDF switch participates in every VLAN.

- In the multilayer design, assume that every IDF switch only participates in a single end-user VLAN (for administrative simplicity).

How many VLANs are required under both designs?

This chapter covers the following key topics:

- **VLANs**—The chapter begins with a range of virtual LAN (VLAN)-related topics from using VLANs to create a scalable design to pruning VLANs from trunk links.

- **Spanning Tree**—Covers important Spanning Tree issues that are essential to constructing a stable network.

- **Load Balancing**—Discusses the five techniques available for increasing campus network bandwidth.

- **Routing/Layer 3 Switching**—Discusses issues such as MLS (routing switches) and switching routers.

- **ATM**—Examines valid reasons for using ATM in your campus network and how to deploy it in a scalable fashion.

- **Campus Migrations**—Provides recommendations for migrating your campus network.

- **Server Farms**—Covers some basic server farm design principles.

- **Additional Campus Design Recommendations**—Discusses several other design issues such as VTP, port configurations, and passwords.

15

Campus Design Implementation

This chapter is designed to be a compendium of best practice for campus design. It draws on the collective wisdom of many people and many attempts at achieving the elusive goal of a perfect campus design. It is intended to be a concentrated shot of what has been proven to work well, and what has been proven to be a flop. The hope is that it will serve not only as an eye-opener, but as something that you will return to whenever you face campus design decisions.

The material in other chapters has, in some form, implied many of the items discussed in this chapter. Therefore, this chapter does not attempt to fully explain the background of every point (that is the job of the previous 14 chapters!). Instead, each point is fairly concise and uses references and pointers to other chapters for more detail.

VLANs

When the word *switching* is brought up, the first thing that comes to most network engineer's minds is the subject of VLANs. The use of VLANs can make or break a campus design. This section discusses some of the most important issues to remember when designing and implementing VLANs in your network.

The Appropriate Use of VLANs

Given that VLANs are associated so closely with switching, people most often think of what Chapter 14, "Campus Design Models," referred to as campus-wide VLANs. Given the popularity of campus-wide VLANs as both a concept and a design, this section discusses its pro and cons, as well as an alternate design for consideration.

The popularity of campus-wide VLANs is due in large part to several well-publicized benefits to this approach. First, it can allow direct Layer 2 paths between all of the devices located in the same community of interest. By doing so, this can remove routers from the path of high-volume traffic such as that going to a departmental file server. Assuming that software-based routers are in use, there is the potential for a tremendous increase in available bandwidth.

Second, campus-wide VLANs make it possible to use technology like Cisco's User Registration Tool (URT). By functioning as a sophisticated extension to the VLAN membership policy server (VMPS) technology discussed in Chapter 5, "VLANs," URT allows VLAN placement to be transparently determined by authentication servers such as Windows NT Domain Controllers and NetWare Directory Services (NDS). Organizations such as universities have found this feature very appealing because they can create one or more VLANs for professors and administrative staff while creating separate VLANs for students. Consequently, the same physical campus infrastructure can be used to logically segregate the student traffic while still allowing the use of roving laptop users.

The third benefit of campus-wide VLANs is actually implied by the second benefit—campus-wide VLANs allow these roving users to be controlled by a centralized set of access lists. For example, a university using campus-wide VLANs might utilize a pair of 7500 routers located in the data center for all inter-VLAN routing. As a result, access lists between the VLANs only need to be configured in two places. Consider the alternative where routers (or Layer 3 switches) might be deployed in every building on campus. To maintain user mobility, each of these routers needs to be configured with all of the VLANs and access lists used throughout the entire campus. This can obviously lead to a situation where potentially hundreds of access lists must be maintained.

TIP　　　Although campus-wide VLANs have several well-publicized benefits and are quite popular, they create many network design and management issues. Try to avoid using campus-wide VLANs.

Although these advantages are very alluring, many organizations that implement this approach quickly discover their downsides. Most of the disadvantages are the result of one characteristic of campus-wide VLANs: a lack of hierarchy. Specifically, this lack of hierarchy creates significant scalability problems that can affect the network's stability and maintainability. Furthermore, these problems are often difficult to troubleshoot because of the dynamic and non-deterministic nature of campus-wide VLANs (not to mention that it can be difficult to know where to start troubleshooting in a flat network). For more information on these issues, please refer to Chapter 14, "Campus Design Models," Chapter 11, "Layer 3 Switching," and Chapter 17, "Case Studies: Implementing Switches."

Although many books and vendors discuss campus-wide VLANs as simply the way to use switching, Layer 3 switching introduces a completely different approach that is definitely worthy of consideration. Chapter 14 discussed these Layer 3 approaches under the heading of the multilayer campus design model. Although this approach cannot match the support for centralized access lists available under campus-wide VLANs, it can allow you to build and maintain much larger networks than is typically possible with campus-wide VLANs. Layer 3 switching can also be used with the Dynamic Host Control Protocol (DHCP), a very proven and scalable technique for handling user mobility (see the next section). Therefore, as a general rule of thumb, use the multilayer model as your default design choice and only use flat earth designs if there is a compelling reason to justify the risks. For more information on the advantages and implementation details of the multilayer model, see Chapter 11, Chapter 14, and Chapter 17.

Note that this implies a fundamental difference in how VLANs are used between the two design models. In the case of campus-wide VLANs, VLANs are used to create logical partitions unique to the entire campus network. In the case of the multilayer model, they are used to create logical partitions that may be unique to a single IDF/access layer wiring closet.

TIP   The multilayer design model uses VLANs in a completely different fashion from the campus-wide VLANs model. In the multilayer model, VLANs are very often only unique to a single IDF device whereas campus-wide VLANs are globally unique.

Use DHCP to Solve User Mobility Problems

Many network engineers feel that campus-wide VLANs are the only way to handle mobile users and unwittingly saddle themselves with a flat network that requires high maintenance. As mentioned in the previous section, many user-mobility problems can be solved with DHCP. Because DHCP fits well into hierarchical designs that utilize Layer 3 processing for scalability, it can be a much safer choice than using campus-wide VLANs. As discussed in Chapter 11 and Chapter 17, the use of DHCP simply requires one or more **ip helper-address** statements on each router (or Layer 3 switch) interface. When using IP helper addresses for DHCP, consider using the **no ip forward-protocol** command to disable the forwarding of unwanted traffic types that are enabled by default (the **ip helper-address** command automatically enables forwarding of the following UDP ports: 37, 49, 53, 67, 68, 69, 137, and 138). Most commonly, UDP ports 137 and 138 are removed to prevent excessive forwarding of NetBIOS name registration traffic.

TIP   Be careful to not simply enter **no ip forward-protocol upd**. Prior to 12.0, entering this command disabled *all* of the default UDP ports, including ports 67 and 68 that are used by DHCP. Although **no ip forward-protocol upd** does not disable DHCP in early releases of 12.0, proceed with caution. For an example of **ip helper-address** and **no ip forward-protocol**, see Chapter 17.

VLAN Numbering

Although VLAN numbering is a very simple task, having a well thought-out plan can help make the network easier to understand and manage in the long run. In general, there are two approaches to VLAN numbering:

- Globally-unique VLAN numbers
- Pattern-based VLAN numbers

In globally-unique VLAN numbers, every VLAN has a unique numeric identifier. For example, consider the network shown in Figure 15-1. Here, the VLANs in Building 1 use numbers 10–13, Building 2 uses 20–23, and Building 3 uses 30–33.

Figure 15-1 *Globally-Unique VLANs*

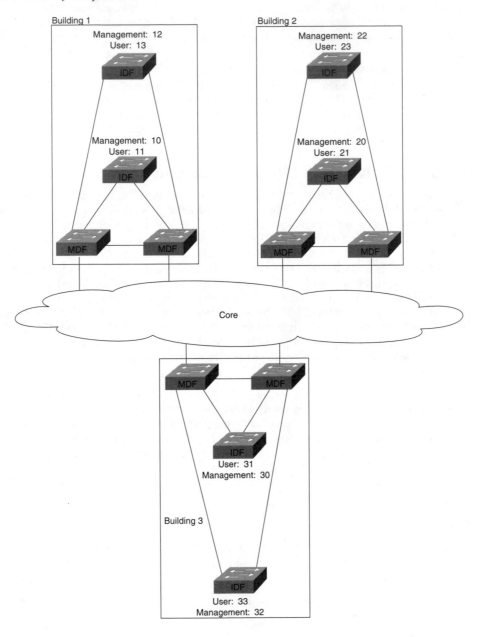

TIP   When using globally-unique VLANs, try to establish an easily remembered scheme such as the one used in Figure 15-1 (Building 1 uses VLANs 1X, Building 2 uses 2X, and so on).

In the case of pattern-based VLAN numbers, the same VLAN number is used for the same purpose in each building. For example, Figure 15-2 shows a network where the management VLAN is always 1, the first end user VLAN is 2, the second end user VLAN is 3, and so on.

Figure 15-2 *Pattern-Based VLANs*

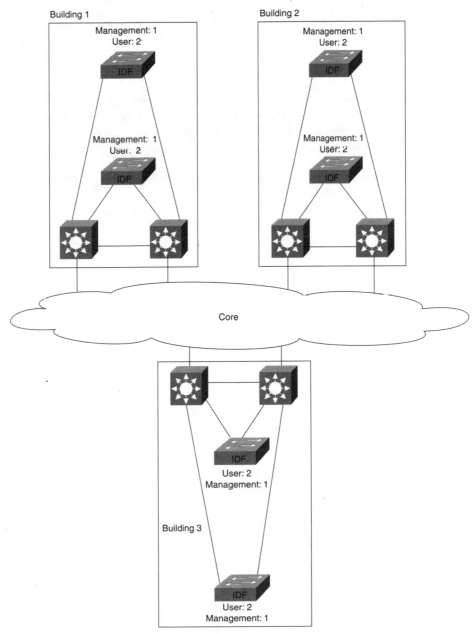

Which approach you use is primarily driven by what type of design model you adopt. If you have utilized the campus-wide VLANs model, you are essentially forced to use globally-unique VLAN numbers. Although there are special cases and "hacks" where this may not be true, not using unique VLANs in flat designs can lead to cross-mapped VLANs and widespread connectivity problems.

TIP   Use globally-unique VLAN numbers with campus-wide VLANs.

If you are using the multilayer model, either numbering scheme can be adopted. Because VLANs are terminated at MDF/distribution layer switches, there is no underlying technical requirement that the VLAN numbers must match (this is especially true when using using switching router platforms such as the Catalyst 8500). In fact, even if the VLAN numbers do match, they are still maintained as completely separate broadcast domains because of Layer 3 switching/routing. If you like the simplicity of knowing that the management VLAN is always VLAN 1, the pattern-based approach might be more appropriate. On the other hand, some organizations prefer to keep every VLAN number unique just as every IP subnet is unique (this approach often ties the VLAN number to the subnet number—for example, VLAN 25 might be 10.1.25.0/24). In other cases, a blend of the two numbering schemes works best. Here, organizations typically adopt a single number for use in all management VLANs but use unique numbers for end-user VLANs.

TIP   The multilayer model can be used with both globally-unique VLANs and pattern-based VLANs.

Use Meaningful VLAN Names

Although common sense dictates that clearly-named VLANs serve as a form of documentation, networks are frequently built with useless VLAN names. Recall from Chapter 5 that if you do not specify a VLAN name, the Catalysts use a very creative name such as VLAN0002 for VLAN 2 and VLAN0003 for VLAN3. In other cases, organizations do specify a VLAN name as a parameter to the **set vlan** command, but the names are cryptic or poorly maintained.

It is usually a far better choice to create VLAN names that actually describe the function of that broadcast domain. This is especially true when using campus-wide VLANs and globally-unique VLAN numbers. The dynamic and non-hierarchical nature of these networks makes troubleshooting challenging enough without having to waste time trying to determine what VLAN a problem involves. Having clearly-defined and descriptive VLAN names can save critical time during a network outage (as well as avoiding the confusion that might cause an administrator to misconfigure a device and thus *create* a network outage).

TIP   Descriptive VLAN names are especially important when using campus-wide VLANs.

Although VLAN names are less important when the multilayer design model is in use, the names should at least differentiate management and end-user traffic. Try to include the name of the department or IDF/access layer closet where the VLAN is used. Also, some organizations like to include the IP subnet number in the VLAN name.

Use Separate Management VLANs

When first exposed to VLANs, many network administrators find them confusing and therefore decide to adopt a policy of placing only a single VLAN on every switch. Although this can have an appealing simplicity, it can seriously destabilize your network. In short, you want to always use at least two VLANs on every Layer 2 Catalyst switch. At a minimum, you want one VLAN for management traffic and a separate VLAN for end-user traffic.

TIP   Make sure every Layer 2 switch participates in at least two VLANs: one that functions as the management VLAN and one or more for end-user VLANs.

However, this is not to suggest that having more than two VLANs is a good idea. To the contrary, the simplicity of maintaining a single end-user VLAN (or at least a small number) can be very beneficial for network maintenance.

Why, then, is it so important to have at least two VLANs? Think back to the material discussed in Chapter 5 regarding the impact of broadcasts on end stations. Because broadcasts are not filtered by hardware on-board the network interface card (NIC), every broadcast is passed up to Layer 3 using an interrupt to the central CPU. The more time that the CPU spends looking at unwanted broadcast packets, the less time it has for more useful tasks (like playing Doom!).

Well, the CPU on a Catalyst's Supervisor is no different. The CPU must inspect every broadcast packet to determine if it is an ARP destined for its IP address or some other interesting broadcast packet. However, if the level of uninteresting traffic becomes too large, the CPU can become overwhelmed and start dropping packets. If it drops Doom packets, no harm is done. On the other hand, if it drops Spanning Tree BPDUs, the whole network could destabilize.

NOTE Note that this section is referring to Layer 2 Catalysts such as the 2900s, 4000s, 5000s, and 6000s. Because these devices currently have one IP address that is only assigned to a single VLAN, the selection of this VLAN can be important. On the other hand, this point generally does not apply to router-like Catalysts such as the 8500. Because these platforms generally have an IP address assigned to *every* VLAN, trying to pick the best VLAN for an IP address obviously becomes irrelevant. For more information on the Catalyst 8500, see Chapter 11.

In fact, this Spanning Tree problem is one of the more common issues in flat earth campus networks. The story usually goes something like this: The network is humming along fine until a burst of broadcast data in the management VLAN causes a switch to become overwhelmed to the point where is starts dropping packets. Because some of these packets are BPDUs, the switch falls behind in its Spanning Tree information and inadvertently creates a Layer 2 loop in the network. At this point, the broadcasts in the network go into a full feedback loop as discussed in Chapter 6, "Understanding Spanning Tree."

If this loop occurs in one or more VLANs other than the management VLAN, it can quickly starve out all remaining trunk bandwidth throughout the entire campus in a flat network. However, the Supervisor CPUs are insulated by the VLAN switching ASICs and continue operating normally (recall that all data forwarding is handled by ASICs in Catalyst gear).

On the other hand, if the loop occurs in the management VLAN (the VLAN where SC0 is assigned), the results can be truly catastrophic. Suddenly, every switch CPU is hit with a tidal wave of broadcast traffic, completely crushing every switch in a downward spiral that virtually eliminates any chance of the network recovering from this problem. If a network is utilizing campus-wide VLANs, this problem can spread to every switch within a matter of seconds.

NOTE Recall that SC0 is the management interface used in Catalyst switches such as the 4000s, 5000s, and 6000s. This is where the management IP address is assigned to a Catalyst Supervisor. Because the CPU processes all broadcast packets (and some multicast packets) received on this interface, it is important to not overwhelm the CPU.

How do you know if your CPU is struggling to keep up with traffic in the network? First, you can use the Catalyst 5000 **show inband** command (this is used for Supervisor IIIs; use **show biga** on Supervisor Is and IIs [biga stands for Backplane Interface Gate Array]) to display low-level statistics for the device. Look under the **Receive** section for the **RsrcErrors** field. This lists the number of received frames that were dropped by the CPU. Second, to view the load directly on the CPU, use the undocumented command **ps -c**. The final line of this display lists the CPU *idle* time (subtract from 100 to calculate the load). Note that **ps-c** has been replaced by **show proc cpu** in newer images.

TIP Use the **show inband**, **show biga**, **ps -c**, and **show proc cpu** commands to determine if your CPU is overloaded.

If you find that you are facing a problem of CPU overload, also read the section "Consider Using Loop-Free Management VLANs" later in this chapter.

Deciding What Number Should be Used for the Management VLAN

A common question surrounds the issue of VLAN numbering for the management VLAN. To appropriately answer this question, you must consider the three types of traffic that pass through Catalyst switches:

- Control traffic
- Management traffic
- End-user traffic

Control traffic encompasses plug and play-oriented protocols such as DISL/DTP (used for trunk state negotiation), CDP, PAgP, and VTP. *These protocols always use VLAN 1.*

Management traffic includes end-to-end and IP-based protocols such as Telnet, SNMP, and VQP (the protocol used by VMPS). *These protocols always use the VLAN assign to SC0.*

End-user traffic is all of the remaining traffic on your network. Obviously, this represents the majority of traffic on most networks.

The overriding principle concerning Management VLAN design is to *never mix end-user traffic with the control and management traffic.* Failing to abide by this rule will open your network up to the sort of network meltdown scenarios discussed in the previous section.

TIP   Never mix end-user traffic with control and management traffic.

When implementing this principle, you must generally choose one of two designs:

- Use VLAN 1 for all control *and* management traffic while placing end-user traffic in other VLANs (VLANs 2–1000).
- Use VLAN 1 for control traffic, another VLAN (such as VLAN 2) for management traffic, and the remaining VLAN for end-user traffic (such as VLAN 3–1000).

The first option combines control and management traffic in VLAN 1. The advantage of this approach is management simplicity (it is the default setting and uses a single VLAN). The primary disadvantage of this approach centers around the default behavior of VLAN 1— because VLAN 1 cannot currently be removed from trunk links, it is easy for this VLAN to become extremely large. For example, the use of Ethernet trunks throughout a network along with MLS Layer 3 switching in the MDF/distribution layer will result in VLAN 1 spanning *every* link and every switch in the campus, exactly what you do *not* want for your all-important management VLAN. Therefore, placing SC0 in such as large and flat VLAN can be risky.

NOTE   Although VLAN 1 cannot be removed from Ethernet trunks in current versions of Catalyst code, Cisco is developing a feature that will provide this capability in the future. In short, this feature is expected to allow VLAN 1 to be removed from both trunk links and the VTP VLAN database. Therefore, from a user-interface perspective, enabling this feature effectively removes VLAN 1 from the device. However, from the point of view of the Catalyst internals, the VLAN will actually remain in use, but only for control traffic such as VTP and CDP (for example, a Sniffer will reveal these packets tagged with a VLAN 1 header on trunk links). In other words, this feature will essentially convert VLAN 1 into a "reserved" VLAN than can only be used for control traffic.

This risk can be avoided with the second option where the control and management traffic are separated. Whereas the control traffic must use VLAN 1, the management traffic is relocated to a different VLAN (many organizations choose to use VLAN 2, 999, or 1000). As a result, SC0 and the CPU will be insulated from potential broadcast problems in VLAN 1. This optimization can be particularly important in extremely large campus networks that are lacking in Layer 3 hierarchy.

TIP   For the most conservative management/control VLAN design, only use VLAN 1 for control traffic while placing SC0 in its own VLAN (in other words, no end-user traffic will use this VLAN).

Also, when using the upcoming feature that "removes" VLAN 1 from a Catalyst, you are effectively forced to use this approach.

Be Careful When Moving SC0's VLAN

Although some traffic always uses VLAN 1, other management traffic changes VLANs as SC0 is reassigned. This includes all of the end-to-end protocols (as opposed to the link-by-link protocols that only use VLAN 1) such as:

- Telnet
- SNMP
- The VQP protocol used by VMPS
- Syslog
- Ping

For these protocols to function, SC0 must be assigned to the correct VLAN with a valid IP address and one or more functioning default gateways to reach the rest of the network. The most common problem here is that people often move SC0 to a different VLAN for troubleshooting purposes and forget to move it back when they are done. Although this can help troubleshoot the immediate problem, it is almost guaranteed to create more problems! Another common problem is failing to use an IP address that is appropriate for the VLAN assigned to SC0.

TIP	If you reconfigure SC0 for troubleshooting (or other) purposes, be sure to return it to its original state.

Prune VLANs from Trunks

Two generic technologies are available for creating trunks that share multiple VLANs:

- Implicit tagging
- Explicit tagging

When using implicit tagging, some information already contained in the frame serves as an indicator of VLAN membership. Many vendors have created equipment that uses MAC addresses for this purpose (other possibilities include Layer 3 addresses or Layer 4 port numbers). The downside of this approach is that you must devise some technique for sharing these tags. For example, when using MAC addresses, all of the switches must be told what VLAN every MAC address has been assigned to. Maintaining and synchronizing these potentially huge tables can be a real problem.

To avoid these synchronization issues, Cisco has adopted the approach of using explicit tagging through ISL and 802.1Q. There are two advantages to explicit tagging. First, because the tag is carried in an extra header field that is added to the original frame, VLAN membership becomes completely unambiguous (therefore preventing problems associated with frames bleeding through between VLANs). Second, each switch needs to know only the VLAN assignments of its directly-connected ports (in implicit tagging, the shared tables require every switch to maintain knowledge of every MAC address/end station). As a result, the amount of state information required by each switch is dramatically reduced.

NOTE	Cisco's use of explicit tagging creates significant scalability benefits.

However, there is a hidden downside to the advantage of every switch not needing to know what VLANs other switches are using—flooded traffic must be sent to every switch in the Layer 2 network. In other words, by default, one copy of every broadcast, multicast, and unknown unicast frame is flooded across every trunk link in a Layer 2 domain.

Two approaches can be used to reduce the impact of this flooding. First, note that if you are using campus-wide VLANs, this flooding problem also becomes campus-wide. Therefore, one of the simplest and most scalable ways to reduce this flooding is to partition the network with several Layer 3 barriers that utilize routing (Layer 3 switching) technology. This breaks the network into smaller Layer 2 pockets and constrains the flooding to each pocket.

Where Layer 3 switching cannot prevent unnecessary flooding (such as with campus-wide VLANs or within each of the Layer 2 pockets created by Layer 3 switching), a second technique of VLAN pruning can be employed. By using the **clear trunk** command discussed in Chapter 8, "Trunking Technologies and Applications," unused VLANs can be manually pruned from a trunk. Therefore, when a given switch needs to flood a frame, it only sends it out access ports locally assigned to the source VLAN and trunk links that have not been pruned of this VLAN. For example, an MDF switch can be configured to flood frames only for VLANs 1 and 2 to a given IDF switch if the switch only participates in these two VLANs. To automate the process of pruning, VTP pruning can be used. For more information on VTP pruning, please refer to Chapter 12, "VLAN Trunking Protocol."

One of the most important uses of manual VLAN pruning involves the use of a Layer 2 campus core, the subject of the next section.

TIP   VLAN pruning on trunk lines is one of the most important keys to the successful implementation of a network containing Layer 2 Catalyst switching.

Make Layer 2 Cores Loop Free

When using a Layer 2 core in association with the multilayer model, strive to eliminate links that create loops. On one hand, this sounds completely counter-intuitive. After all, most network engineers spend countless hours trying to improve the resiliency of their network's core. However, by carefully pruning your network of certain links and VLANs, you can eliminate Spanning Tree convergence delays while still maintaining a high degree of redundancy and network resiliency. In other words, simply throwing more links (and VLANs) at a Layer 2 core can actually *degrade* network reliability by introducing Spanning Tree delays.

Furthermore, there is another advantage to using loop-free Layer 2 cores. When loops exist, Spanning Tree automatically places ports in the Blocking state and therefore reduces the capability to load balance across the core. By eliminating loops and therefore removing Spanning Tree Blocking ports, every path through the core can be utilized to maximize available bandwidth in this important area of the network.

For example, consider the collapsed Layer 2 backbone illustrated in Figure 15-3.

Figure 15-3 *A Loop-Free Collapsed Layer 2 Core*

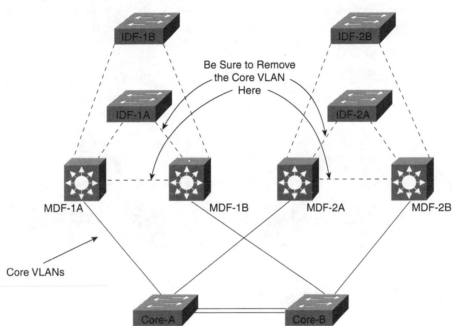

The core in Figure 15-3 is formed by a pair of redundant Layer 2 switches each carrying a single VLAN. All four of the MDF switches connect to one of the core switches (Core-A or Core-B), allowing any single link or switch to fail without creating a permanent outage. If the four MDF switches are configured with Catalyst 8500-style switching routers, then this will automatically result in a loop-free core. On the other hand, the use of Layer 3 router switching (MLS) in the MDF devices requires more careful planning. Specially, the core VLAN must be removed from the links to IDF switches as well as on the link between MDF switches.

TIP   When using MLS (and other forms of routing switches), be certain that you remove the core VLAN from links within the distribution block (the triangles of connectivity formed by MDF and IDF switches).

Larger Layer 2 campus cores require even more careful planning. For example, Figure 15-4 shows a network that covers a larger geographic area and therefore uses four Layer 2 switches within the core. This design is often referred to as a "split Layer 2" core.

Figure 15-4 *A Split Layer 2 Core*

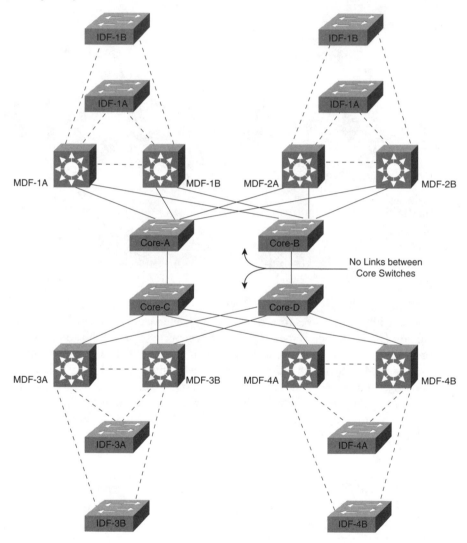

In this case, the key to creating a fast-converging and resilient core is to actually partition the core into two separate VLANs and not cross-link the switches to each other. The first core VLAN is used for the pair of switches on the left, and the second VLAN is used for the pair of switches on the right. If the core switches in Figure 15-4 were cross-linked or fully meshed and a single VLAN were deployed, Spanning Tree convergence and load balancing issues would become a problem.

Finally, notice that creating a loop-free core requires the use of Layer 3 switching in the MDF/distribution layer closets. When using campus-wide VLANs, the only way to achieve a loop-free core is to remove all loops from the *entire* network, obviously a risky endeavor if you are at all concerned about redundancy. Again, follow the suggestion of this chapter's first section and try to always use the multilayer model and the scalability benefits it achieves through the use of Layer 3 switching.

TIP
When using split Layer 2 cores, some network designers chose to use this to segregate the traffic by protocol to provide additional control. For example, the Core-A and Core-C switches could be used for IP traffic while the Core-B and Core-D can carry IPX traffic. This can be a useful way of guaranteeing a certain amount of bandwidth for each protocol.

It is especially useful when you have non-routable protocols that require bridging throughout a large section of the network. This will allow one half of the core to carry the non-routable/bridged traffic while the other half carries the multiprotocol routed traffic.

This section has repeatedly discussed the pruning of VLANs from links. Obviously, one way to accomplish this is to use the **clear trunk** command discussed in the "Restricting VLANs on a Trunk" section of Chapter 8. However, the simplest and most effective approach for removing VLANs from a campus core is to just use non-trunk links. By merely assigning these ports to the core VLAN, you will automatically prevent VLANs from spanning the core and creating flat earth VLANs.

TIP
Use non-trunk links in the campus core to avoid campus-wide end-user VLANs.

In fact, this technique is also the most effective method of removing VLAN 1 from the core. Recall that current versions of Catalyst code do not allow you to prune VLAN 1 from Ethernet trunks. Therefore, as discussed earlier, this can result in a single campus-wide VLAN in the all-important VLAN 1 (the *last* place you want to have loops and broadcast problems).

TIP
Use non-trunk links in the campus core to avoid a campus-wide VLAN in VLAN 1 (this is where you least want a flat earth VLAN, especially if SC0 is assign to VLAN 1).

Don't Forget PLANs

When creating a new design or when your first one or two attempts at solving a particular problem fail, redraw your VLAN design using physical LANs (PLANs). In other words, take the logical topology created through the use of virtual LANs and redraw it using PLANs.

PLAN is a somewhat tongue-in-cheek term the author coined to describe a very serious issue. For some reason, the human brain is almost guaranteed to forget all knowledge of IP subnetting when faced with virtual LANs. People spend days looking at Sniffer traces of complex things like ISL trunks and Spanning Tree to only learn in the end that someone "fat fingered" one digit in an IP address.

So, you ask, what the heck is a PLAN? To answer this mystery, first consider Figure 15-5, a drawing of a typical network using VLANs.

Figure 15-5 *Virtual LANs (VLANs)*

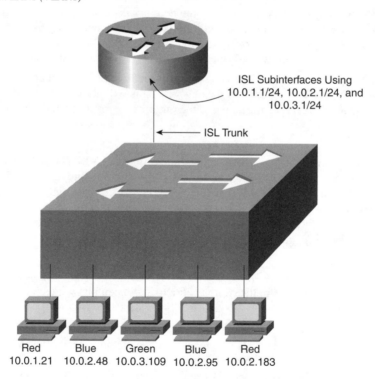

Figure 15-6 redraws Figure 15-5 using PLANs.

Figure 15-6 *Physical LANs (PLANs)*

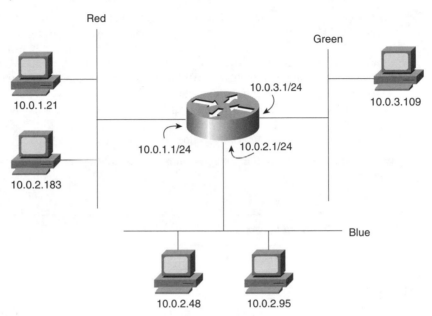

Each VLAN in Figure 15-6 has been redrawn as a separate segment connected to a different router interface. It depicts the logical separation of VLANs with the physical separation used in traditional router and hub designs. However, from a Layer 3 perspective, both networks are identical.

By doing this, it makes the network extremely easy to understand. In fact, it makes it painfully obvious that this network contains a problem—the host using 10.0.2.183 is located on the wrong segment/VLAN (it should be on the Blue VLAN).

Although this might seem like a simple example, simple addressing issues trip up even the best of us from time to time. Why not use a technique that removes VLANs as an extra layer of obfuscation? However, PLANs can be useful in many situations other than for your own troubleshooting. Even if you understand why a network is having a problem, PLANs can be useful for explaining it to other people who might not see the problem as clearly. PLANs can also be used to simplify a new design and help you better analyze the traffic flows and any potential problems.

TIP   PLANs are no joke—use them to help troubleshoot and explain your network.

How to Handle Non-Routable Protocols

Chapter 11 discussed various approaches to integrating Layer 3 routing with Layer 2 bridging, including options such as bridging between VLANs, Concurrent Routing and Bridging (CRB), and Integrated Routing and Bridging (IRB). Most organizations utilize one of these techniques because of the need to have users in two different VLANs communicate via a non-routable protocol such as NetBEUI or LAT. Although the techniques discussed in Chapter 11 can provide relief in limited situations, it is almost always better to avoid their use entirely. Instead, try to place all users of a particular non-routable protocol in a single VLAN. In situations where Catalyst 8500-style switching routers are in use, this might require IRB to be enabled (the Layer 2 nature of MLS does not require the use of IRB).

For more information, see the "Integration Between Routing and Bridging" section of Chapter 11.

TIP   Try to avoid "bridging between VLANs" at all costs.

Spanning Tree

Intertwined with the issue of VLANs is the subject of the Spanning-Tree Protocol. In fact, it is the inappropriate use of VLANs (the flat earth theory) that most often leads to Spanning Tree problems in the first place. This section discusses some of the dos and don'ts of the Spanning-Tree Protocol.

One of the primary themes developed throughout this section is that although Spanning Tree can be quite manageable when used in conjunction with Layer 3 switching, it can also become very complex when used in large, flat designs like campus-wide VLANs. Combining good Spanning Tree knowledge with a good design is the key to success.

Keep Spanning Tree Domains Small

One of the most effective techniques for minimizing Spanning Tree problems is keeping Spanning Tree domains small in size. The easiest way to accomplish this is to use the multilayer design model. By automatically creating Layer 3 barriers that partition the network from a Spanning Tree point of view, most of the typical Spanning Tree problems become non-issues.

There are many benefits to constricting Spanning Tree to small pockets within your network, including the following:

- It allows you to safely tune the Spanning Tree timers.
- As a result, Spanning Tree convergence time can be significantly improved.
- It becomes very difficult for Spanning Tree problems in one section of the network to spread to other sections of the network.

- When using the switching router (Catalyst 8500) form of the multilayer design model, Spanning Tree load balancing can be eliminated. In this case, the IDF traffic creates *Layer 2 V's* that are inherently loop free and therefore do not require the Spanning-Tree Protocol, although I recommend that you don't disable Spanning Tree; see the next section.

Note   If you enable bridging and/or IRB on Catalyst 8500 devices, they will starting bridging traffic and convert the Layer 2 V's that they produce by default into Layer 2 triangles. This will obviously require the use of Spanning Tree (use of the Root Bridge placement technique discussed in the following bullet point is recommended).

- When using the routing switch (MLS) form of the multilayer design model, Spanning Tree load balancing can be dramatically simplified through the use of the Root Bridge placement technique. When using MLS and the multilayer model, each IDF and a pair of MDFs create *Layer 2 triangles* that, although not loop free, are easy to manage. For more information on the Root Bridge placement approach to Spanning Tree load balancing, see Chapter 7, "Advanced Spanning Tree," and Chapter 17.
- Spanning Tree becomes much simpler to design, document, and understand.
- Troubleshooting becomes much easier.

Figure 15-7 illustrates the Layer 2 triangles created by MLS (Part A) and the Layer 2 V's created by switching routers. Although MLS very often uses route-switch modules (RSMs), a logical representation has been used for Part A.

Figure 15-7 *Layer 2 Topologies under Routing Switches (MLS) and Switching Routers*

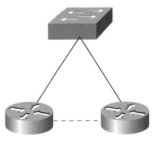

NOTE   It is important to realize that both routing switches (MLS) and switching routers (8500s) can be used to create the designs shown in Figure 15-7. This section is merely trying to point out the *default* behavior and most common use of these platforms.

When using campus-wide VLANs, it is often possible to achieve some of the benefits listed in this section by manually pruning VLANs from selected trunks. However, it is not possible to create the simplicity and scalability that are available when using Layer 3 switching. Also, the pruning action can often reduce redundancy in the network.

The multilayer model allows the benefits listed in this section to be easily designed into the network. When using routing switches (MLS) as shown in Part A, this can be accomplished by pruning selected VLANs from key trunk links (such as links in the core and between MDF switches). When using switching routers such as the 8500 as shown in Part B, the benefits of having small Spanning Tree domains accrue by default.

Don't Disable Spanning Tree

In frustration, many organizations disable the Spanning-Tree Protocol to achieve network stability (especially when using flat earth designs). However, when this is done at the expense of redundancy, it obviously introduces a whole new set of problems.

When Spanning Tree is disabled, you are not protected from the inevitable configuration mistakes that create Layer 2 loops in the network. As discussed in Chapter 6, Layer 2 protocols have no way of recovering from feedback loops without a protocol such as Spanning Tree (there is no Time To Live [TTL] field in Layer 2 headers)—the loop continues until you manually intervene.

Typically, Spanning Tree is disabled in one of three situations:

- **As a last resort to achieve network stability under the campus-wide VLANs design model**—However, because this also requires that redundancy be eliminated, this is not recommended.

- **When using Catalyst 8500-style switching routers in the MDF/distribution layer closets**—Because switching routers result in loop-free Layer 2 V's (as shown in Part B of Figure 15-7), Spanning Tree is no longer required—at least for the intended topology. However, loops can be formed unintentionally through configuration and cabling mistakes on the part of network administrators or because end users installed devices such as hubs or switches. Therefore, an element of risk remains with this approach.

- **When using a LANE backbone**—Because LANE automatically creates a loop-free topology *within the ATM core itself*, Spanning Tree can be disabled. In fact, ATM-centric vendors such as Fore Systems disable Spanning Tree for LANE by default. However, you must be careful to not create Layer 2 loops *outside* the LANE backbone. Not only does this include the examples discussed in the previous bullet, it also includes such practices as using redundant Ethernet links to extend the ATM backbone to IDF wiring closets.

In general, it is better to use scalable design techniques and Spanning Tree tuning rather than to disable the Spanning-Tree Protocol altogether. As discussed in the previous section, designs such as the multilayer model can achieve network stability without having to resort to disabling Spanning Tree. Also, a carefully planned design can then allow Spanning Tree to be tuned for better performance.

Evaluate Spanning Tree Patterns

As discussed in Chapter 11 and Chapter 14, using Layer 3 switching and the multilayer design model generally results in networks that are comprised of many small "triangles" and "V's" of Layer 2 connectivity.

As this material discussed, switching router platforms such as the Catalyst 8500s produce Layer 2 V's by default. Although bridging and IRB can be enabled to convert these V's into Layer 2 triangles, it is generally advisable to avoid widespread deployment of these features (see the section "Integration between Routing and Bridging" in Chapter 11). Therefore, you will usually see Layer 2 V's in conjunction with switching router technology.

From a Spanning Tree perspective, it is important to note that these V's are loop-free and therefore do not place any ports in the blocking state. As a result, Spanning Tree will not impact your failover performance.

NOTE	Although Spanning Tree will not impact failover performance of the IDF uplink ports when using Layer 2 Vs, it is still enabled by default and may impact end-user devices. Therefore, you may wish to configure PortFast on end-user ports to facilitate start-up protocols such as DHCP and NetWare authentication.

Unlike 8500s where Layer 2 V's are far more common, MLS (and routing switches) allow you to easily configure either Layer 2 triangles *or* V's. By default, MLS allows all VLANs to transit the switch. Therefore, assuming that you have removed end-user VLANs from the network core, you will be left with Layer 2 triangles by default (Part A of Figure 15-7). However, by pruning a given VLAN from the link between the MDF/distribution switches, this VLAN can easily be converted into a V (Part B of Figure 15-7). In other words, by simply pruning the VLAN from the triangle's base, it is converted into a V.

From a Spanning Tree perspective, it is important to evaluate the differences that this brings to your network. If you opt for using triangles, then Spanning Tree will be in full effect. The Root Bridge placement form of load balancing and features such as UplinkFast will be important. If you opt for the Layer 2 V's, you will be left with the same "almost Spanning Tree free" situation described several paragraphs earlier in connection with the 8500s.

Be sure to consider the impact and performance of Spanning Tree where you have Layer 2 triangles in your campus network.

Consider Using Switching Routers to Virtually Eliminate Spanning Tree

Because Catalyst 8500-style switching routers in the MDF/distribution layer closets eliminates loops through the IDF switches, this results in Layer 2 V's. Therefore, Spanning Tree can be much simpler to design, maintain, and troubleshoot. The IDF switch automatically elects itself as the Root Bridge of a one-bridge network (the Layer 3 switches prevent the bridges from learning about each other and keep the Spanning Tree separate). Timer values can be fairly aggressively tuned without risk (use the **set spantree root** command with a diameter of 2 or 3 hops). Also, Spanning Tree load balancing is no longer necessary.

NOTE   Note that Layer 2 V's can also be created with routing switch (MLS) platforms by pruning VLAN from selected links (in this case, the base of the triangle—the MDF-to-MDF link).

Consider Using Loop-Free Management VLANs

As discussed in the section "Use Separate Management VLANs," exposing a Layer 2 Catalyst Supervisor to excessive broadcast traffic can lead to network-wide outages. This section recommended using a management VLAN to isolate the Catalyst SC0 interface from end-user broadcast traffic. However, even when using a separate management VLAN, some risk remains. If a loop were to form in the management VLAN itself, the Supervisors could once again find themselves crushed by a wave of traffic.

TIP   Make certain that your design minimizes the risk of braodcast storms occurring in the management VLAN.

Therefore, ensuring that the management VLAN itself is loop free can provide an additional layer of protection. In general, two techniques can be used to create a loop-free management VLAN:

- The use of Catalyst 8500-style switching routers in the MDF/distribution layer automatically creates loop-free management VLANs on the IDF/access devices by default. Notice that this also implies that you should not use IRB to merge the management VLANs back into a single VLAN. Although this can appear to simplify the management of your network by placing all of the switches in a single VLAN, it can create management problems in the long term by adding loops into the management VLAN.

- Campus-wide VLANs often require the use of an out-of-band management network. Because it is very difficult to maintain a loop free and stable environment when campus-wide VLANs are in use, you often have to resort to running separate Ethernet links from routers to a port on each Catalyst. By then assigning only this Ethernet port to the management VLAN used for SC0, a loop-free topology can be created. The ME1 (Management Ethernet) ports available on some Catalyst devices can also be used to create an out-of-band management network.

Figure 15-8 illustrates a typical network using the out-of-band approach to creating loop-free management VLANs. Assume that because the switches are deployed in a haphazard manner, it is not feasible to create loop-free management VLANs using the existing infrastructure. Instead, separate Ethernet links are pulled from the nearest available router port. Where possible, hubs can be used to reduce the number of router ports required.

Figure 15-8 *Creating Loop-Free Management VLANs with an Out-Of-Band Network*

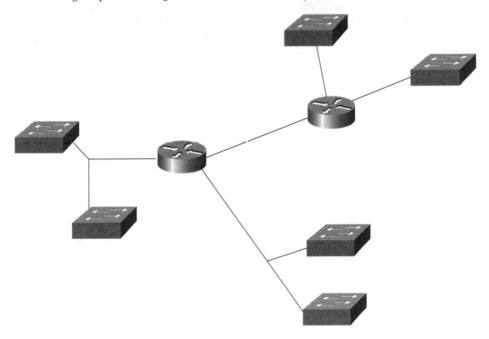

As discussed in the section "Make Layer 2 Cores Loop-Free," you should also keep an eye on VLAN 1. Although you may have carefully used Layer 3 switching to create hierarchy in your network, you can still be left with a campus-wide VLAN in VLAN 1 (especially if you are using MLS Layer 3 switching). Note that this will be true even if you followed the earlier advice (see the section "Prune VLANs from Trunks") of pruning VLANs core VLANs from the wiring closet trunks and wiring closet VLANs from the core trunks (recall that VLAN 1 *cannot be deleted* and *cannot be pruned* from Ethernet trunk links in current code images).

Because VLAN 1 is given special priority because of the control traffic discussed in the section "Deciding What Number Should be Used for the Management VLAN," a broadcast loop in this VLAN can be devastating to the health of your network. How, then, are you supposed to control this situation? In general, organizations have used one or more of the following techniques:

- Probably the simplest and most effective option involves using non-trunk links in the core. By assigning each of these core links to a single VLAN (do *not* use VLAN 1 here!), the core will block the transmission of VLAN 1 information.

- Use "switching routers" such as the Catalyst 8500s that do not forward VLAN 1 by default.
- Once it is available, use the upcoming feature that will allow VLAN 1 to be removed from trunk links (see the section "Deciding What Number Should be Used for the Management VLAN").
- If you are using an ATM core, VLAN 1 *can* be removed from this portion of the network (see Chapter 9).

NOTE   For the record, heavy broadcast traffic can also be a problem for routers. They are no different from other devices—all broadcasts must be processed to see if they are "interesting" or not. In fact, this phenomenon can be worse for routers because, by definition, they are connected to multiple subnets and therefore must process the broadcasts from every subnet.

However, with this being said, routers (and Layer 3 switches) are still the best tools for handling broadcast problems. Although the routers themselves can be susceptible to broadcast storms, their very use can greatly reduce the risk of Layer 2 loops ever forming. The multilayer model is designed to maximize this benefit by reducing Layer 2 connectivity to many small triangles and V's. Furthermore, although a broadcast loop can overload any directly-connected routers, the problem does not spread to other sections of the network, a huge improvement over the problems described earlier in this section and in the section "Use Separate Management VLANs."

Always Specify Your Root Bridges

Chapter 6 discussed the problems that can arise when you do not manually specify Root Bridge locations in your network. It is highly possible (even probable if using older Cisco equipment) that a suboptimal bridge or switch wins the Root War election. Rather than leaving it to chance, always specify both a primary and a secondary Root Bridge for every VLAN (in a large and very flat network, it might be beneficial to also specify a tertiary Root Bridge). By manually setting the Root Bridges, it can not only optimize the data path, but it makes the network more deterministic and improves its stability, maintainability, and ease of troubleshooting.

TIP	All networks using groups of contiguous Layer 2 switches or transparent bridges should specify a primary and a backup Root Bridge.

Try to Use Root Bridge Placement Load Balancing

As discussed in Chapter 7, the Root Bridge placement form of Spanning Tree load balancing can be extremely effective and easy to implement if the topology supports it. In most networks that utilize campus-wide VLANs and a centralized server farm, it is very difficult to obtain any degree of load balancing with this technique.

However, when using the multilayer model in conjunction with MLS (and other types of routing switches), this form of load balancing is highly recommended. Because the multilayer model and MLS reduce the network to a series of many small Layer 2 triangles that span each IDF switch and the corresponding pair of MDF switches, the Layer 2 topology is constrained, well-defined, and deterministic. Consequently, it is easy to make one MDF switch the Root Bridge for approximately half of the VLANs contained in that distribution block while the other switch is configured as the Root Bridge for the remaining VLANs. (As a reminder, a distribution block is comprised of a pair of MDF switches and their associated collection of IDF switches—typically this is contained within a single building.) For example, Figure 15-9 illustrates a typical distribution block where MDF-A is the Root Bridge for the odd-numbered VLANs and MDF-B is the Root Bridge for the even-numbered VLANs.

Figure 15-9 *Root Bridge Placement Spanning Tree Load Balancing*

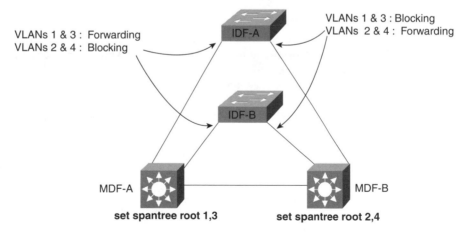

This causes the odd VLANs to use the left riser link (the right IDF port is Blocking for these VLANs), whereas the even VLANs use the right link (the left IDF port is Blocking). As discussed in the following section and Chapter 11, this should be coordinated with any Hot

Standby Routing Protocol (HSRP) load balancing being performed by your MDF/distribution layer devices.

Root Bridge Placement Considerations

Besides influencing traffic distribution through load balancing, several other factors should be considered when determining where Root Bridges should be located. Some of the more important considerations are mentioned in the following list:

- **Place the Root Bridge in the path of high-bandwidth data flows**—This point is discussed in more detail in the following section.
- **Use a device that is very stable**—Because Spanning Tree is a protocol that constantly seeks out the most attractive Root Bridge, placing the Root Bridge on a device that reboots or fails frequently can disturb the entire network unnecessarily.
- **Use a device that can carry the load**—Because the Root Bridge functions as a central switching node for all of the branches of the Spanning Tree, it must be able to handle the potentially high aggregate load.

When implementing a Spanning Tree design, most organizations adopt one of two strategies:

- Distributed Root Bridges
- Centralized Root Bridges

Distributed Root Bridge placement is useful in situations where network designers want to spread the centralized switching load over more than one bridge. Besides increasing the overall available bandwidth, this technique can also improve network stability by not forcing the entire network to depend on one or two switches for Root Bridge services. However, distributing the Root Bridges can significantly increase troubleshooting complexity in your network by creating a different logical topology for every VLAN.

TIP   In general, distributed Root Bridges can add more complexity to the network than they are worth.

Centralized Root Bridges are useful in situations where the traffic flows are highly concentrated (such as in the case of a centralized server farm). Another advantage of this approach is that it can ease troubleshooting by creating identical (or at least very similar) logical topologies in all VLANs. Overall, centralized Root Bridges are more common.

Where to Put Root Bridges

In general, the most important consideration is placing Root Bridges in the path of high-bandwidth data flows. The goal is to have the Spanning Tree logical topology mirror the natural flow of traffic in your network. To do otherwise implies an inefficient path for the most bandwidth-intensive flows. As discussed in Chapter 6, this optimization is most often achieved in one of two ways:

- When using very flat designs such as campus-wide VLANs, the Root Bridges should generally be placed at the point where the server farm connects to the campus core. Assuming that a pair of switches is used to link the server farm to the core (this provides redundancy as well as additional bandwidth), the Root Bridges can be alternated on a per-VLAN basis.

- When using routing switches (MLS) with the multilayer model, the Root Bridge should be located in the switch that contains (or, in the case of an external router, links to) the active HSRP peer for a given VLAN. Therefore, if an MDF switch is acting as the active HSRP peer for the odd-numbered VLANs, it should also be the primary Root Bridge for these VLANs.

Timer Tuning

Your decision to utilize Spanning Tree timer tuning should be based primarily on your campus architecture. If you have utilized the campus-wide VLAN model, timer tuning is almost always an exercise in futility and frustration. Because campus-wide VLANs lead to very large Spanning Tree domains, timer tuning usually results in a network plagued by instability.

TIP	Do not attempt Spanning Tree timer tuning if your network uses the campus-wide VLAN model.

On the other hand, the Layer 3 barriers created by the multilayer model make timer tuning a very attractive option for most networks. When performing timer tuning, it is usually best to use the **set spantree root** macro discussed in the "Using A Macro: **set spantree root**" section of Chapter 6. In general, the values in Table 15-1 have been shown to be a good compromise between network stability and speed of convergence (for more information on the details of these timer values, refer to Chapters 6 and 7).

Table 15-1 *Recommended Spanning Tree Timer Values*

Network Design	Specified Diameter	Specified Hello Time	Resulting Max Age	Resulting Forward Delay
Campus-wide VLANs	N/A	N/A	Default (20 secs)	Default (15 secs)
Multilayer and routing switches (MLS)	3 hops	2 secs	12 secs	9 secs
Multilayer and switching routers (8500s)	2 hops	2 secs	10 secs	7 secs

Because timer tuning is not recommended for campus-wide VLANs and should therefore not be specified on the **set spantree root** command, these values have been omitted from Table 15-1. (Although, as discussed in Chapter 7, 802.1D assumes a diameter of 7 hops and the Hello Time defaults to 2 seconds.) The routing switch (MLS) and switching router values are based on fairly conservative assumptions about link failures and the possibility of additional bridging devices being attached to the network (these values are also used and discussed in the case studies covered in Chapter 17).

Also, if you are willing and able to incur the extra load of Spanning Tree BPDUs, the Hello Time can be reduced to 1 second to further improve convergence times. However, notice that this doubles the bandwidth consumed by BPDUs, and, more importantly, the load on the supervisor CPUs. Therefore, if each device only participates in a small number of VLANs, Hello tuning can successfully improve Spanning Tree convergence times with minimal impact on the CPU. Conversely, if your devices participate in a large number of VLANs, changing the Hello Time can overload your CPUs. When using a large number of VLANs, only lower the Hello Time for a subset of the VLANs where you need the improved convergence time as a compromise. If lowering the Hello Time to one second, consider using the values specified in Table 15-2.

Table 15-2 *Spanning Tree Timer Values When Using a Hello Time of 1 Second*

Network Design	Specified Diameter	Specified Hello Time	Resulting Max Age	Resulting Forward Delay
Multilayer and routing switches (MLS)	3 hops	1 secs	7 secs	5 secs
Multilayer and switching routers (8500s)	2 hops	1 secs	5 secs	4 secs

Finally, be certain that you set the chosen timer values on both the primary and backup Root Bridges. You can set the values on other bridges/switches, but it has no effect (for simplicity, some organizations simply set the values on every device).

Spanning Tree and the Management VLAN

The point made earlier in the "Consider Using Loop-Free Management VLANs" section bears repeating—Layer 2 loops in the management VLAN can lead to catastrophic network failures. You should consider implementing loop-free VLANs for your management networks, especially if using a flat earth network topology.

Study Your Spanning Tree Logical Topology

The time to be learning your Spanning Tree logical topology is not during the middle of a major network outage. Instead, it is advisable to create maps of both your primary and backup Spanning Tree topologies beforehand. Most organizations are accustomed to making extensive use of diagrams that reveal the Layer 3 topology of their network (often using tools such as HP OpenView). However, very few of these same organizations go through the exercise of creating and distributing Layer 2 maps.

TIP   A picture is worth a thousand words... diagram your Layer 2 topologies (including Spanning Tree).

At a minimum, these diagrams should illustrate the extent of each VLAN, the location of the Root Bridge, and which switch-to-switch ports are Blocking or Forwarding (diagramming end-user ports is rarely beneficial). In addition, it might be useful to label the Forwarding ports as either Designated Ports or Root Ports. See Chapters 6 and 7 for more information on these ports.

TIP   CiscoWorks 2000 can create basic Spanning Tree maps.

The importance of having Layer 2 diagrams is influenced by, once again, the choice of the network's design. They are especially important in the case of campus-wide VLANs where the combination of many VLANs and Blocking/Forwarding ports can become very complex. Fortunately, another benefit of the multilayer model is that it reduces the need for diagrams. First, the Layer 3 hierarchy created by this design makes the traditional Layer 3 maps much more useful. Second, the simplistic Layer 2 triangles and V's created by this design allow two or three template drawings to be used to document the entire Layer 2 network.

When to Use UplinkFast and BackboneFast

Both UplinkFast and BackboneFast are significant Cisco enhancements to the Spanning-Tree Protocol. It is important to know when and when not to use them. In general, neither feature is particularly useful in a network that contains a very strong Layer 3 switching component. Because this tends to break the network into a large number of loop-free paths, there are no Blocking ports for UplinkFast and BackboneFast to perform their magic.

TIP	Don't waste your time designing lots of Spanning Tree optimizations (such as UplinkFast and BackboneFast) into a heavily Layer 3-oriented network—they will have little or no effect.

On the other hand, UplinkFast and BackboneFast can be extremely useful in more Layer 2-oriented designs such as campus-wide VLANs and the multilayer model with routing switches (MLS). In either case, UplinkFast should be enabled only on IDF wiring closet switches while BackboneFast is enabled on every switch in each Spanning Tree domain. It is important to follow these guidelines. Although both protocols have been carefully engineered to not completely disable the network when they are used incorrectly, it causes the feature to either be completely ineffective (as is possible with BackboneFast) or to invalidate load balancing and Root Bridge placement (as is possible with UplinkFast). See Chapter 7 for more detailed information on BackboneFast and UplinkFast.

When to Use PortFast

PortFast is a tool that deserves consideration in every network. There are two main benefits to using PortFast:

- End stations and some servers that use fault-tolerant NICs can gain immediate access to the network. In the case of end stations, this can help with protocols such as DHCP and initial server or directory authentication. For servers using fault-tolerant NICs that toggle link-state, PortFast can mean the difference between transparent failover and a 30–50 second outage (however, most fault-tolerant NICs do *not* toggle link). When using PortFast with server connections, be sure to disable PAgP on EtherChannel-capable ports. Otherwise PortFast still takes approximately 20 seconds to enable the link. For more information, please refer to the section "Disabling Port Aggregation Protocol" in Chapter 7.

- Ports do not send Topology Change Notification (TCN) BPDUs when they are using PortFast. Because TCNs cause bridges and switches to use a shorter bridge aging period, an excess of these packets can destabilize a large campus network (especially with flat earth designs like campus-wide VLANs). By potentially eliminating tens of thousands of TCNs per day in the typical large campus network, the use of PortFast can have a significant impact.

Even though Catalysts allow you to enter the **set spantree portfast** *mod_num/port_num* **enable** command on a trunk link, the command is ignored. Despite this feature, it is best to leave PortFast disabled on trunk links and spare other administrators of the network some confusion when they see it enabled.

TIP   Although PortFast is extremely useful in Ethernet-only networks, you might wish to avoid its use in networks that employ a LANE core. Because PortFast suppresses TCN BPDUs, it can interfere with LANE's process of learning about devices/MAC addresses that have been relocated to a different LANE-attached switch. As a result, nodes that relocate may have to wait five minutes (by default) for their connectivity to be re-established if PortFast is in use.

By disabling PortFast, LANE will receive a TCN (both when the node is initially disconnected from the original switch *and* when it is reconnected to the new switch) that shortens the MAC aging process to the Spanning Tree Forward Delay timer (see Chapter 6). As an alternative you can manually (and permanently) lower the bridge table aging period using the **set cam agingtime** command. Both techniques will cause LANE to remove the MAC address to NSAP address mapping in the LES more quickly and force it to relearn the new mapping for a device that has been relocated. See Chapter 7 for more detailed information on the operation of LANE.

When One Spanning Tree Is Not Enough

Although many people complain that one Spanning Tree per VLAN is too complex for human comprehension (by the way, this is an exaggeration), there are times when you actually want to use more than one Spanning Tree per VLAN! Other than the corner-case of using PVST+ to tunnel multiple Spanning Trees through an 802.1Q region that only utilizes a single Spanning Tree, the primary use of multiple Spanning Trees per VLAN is to successfully integrate bridging and routing between VLANs. (See the "Per-VLAN Spanning Tree Plus" section of Chapter 7 for more information on PVST+). When combining bridging and routing, the situation can arise where IP subnets become partitioned and a partial loss of connectivity occurs—for example, when bridging protocols such as NetBIOS and LAT while simultaneously routing traffic such as IP. Chapter 11 referred to this as the broken subnet problem in the "Issues and Caveats with Bridging between VLANS" section and the "How to Fix the Broken Subnet Problem" section.

TIP   Watch out for the "broken subnet problem." It can create difficult to troubleshoot connectivity problems.

As detailed in Chapter 11, the solution is to use two versions of the Spanning-Tree Protocol. The Layer 2 Catalysts such as the 5000 and the 6000 only use the IEEE version of the Spanning-Tree Protocol. However, IOS-based devices such as the routers and Catalyst 8500s can either run the DEC version of Spanning Tree-Protocol or Cisco's proprietary VLAN-Bridge Spanning-Tree Protocol. In both cases, the BPDUs for these two protocols are treated as normal multicast data by the Layer 2 Catalysts and flooded normally. Conversely, the IOS-based devices swallow the IEEE BPDUs when they are running a different version of the Spanning-Tree Protocol. Consequently, the IOS-based devices partition the IEEE protocol into smaller pockets. Within each pocket, the IEEE Spanning-Tree Protocol ensures that the logical topology is loop free. The DEC or VLAN-Bridge version of the Spanning-Tree Protocol ensures that the collection of pockets remains loop free. The result is a network where both routed and non-routed protocols have full connectivity throughout the network. For more information, see the "Using Different Spanning-Tree Protocols" section in Chapter 11.

Load Balancing

Load balancing can be one of the telltale signs that indicate whether a network has been carefully planned or if it has grown up like weeds. By allowing redundant links to effectively double the available bandwidth, load balancing is something that every network should strive to implement.

This chapter briefly mentions the most popular alternatives available for implementing load balancing. As you go through this section, recognize that none of these accomplish round robin or per-packet load balancing. Therefore, although these techniques are most often referred to with the name load balancing, the name load sharing or load distribution might be more appropriate. However, do not get hung up with trying to achieve an exact 50/50 split when you implement load balancing over a pair of links. Just remember that any form of load balancing is preferable to the default operation of most campus protocols where only a single path is ever used.

Remember the Requirements for Load Balancing

Before diving into the details of various approaches to load balancing, it is worth pausing to examine some high-level considerations of load balancing. When thinking about load balancing, first look at the number of available paths. If you have only one set of paths through your network, load balancing (and, therefore, redundancy) is not possible. Most network designers strive to achieve two paths, as typically seen connected to an IDF/access layer switch. In some cases, especially inside a large campus core, more than two paths might be available.

Another consideration is the ease with which you can configure, manage, and troubleshoot a particular load balancing scheme. For example, the Root Bridge placement form of Spanning Tree load balancing is very easy to implement and troubleshoot.

Also, look at the flexibility of each style of load balancing. For instance, although Root Bridge placement scores very high on the simplicity scale, it can only be implemented in selected topologies (such as the Layer 2 triangles used by the multilayer model). By way of contrast, the **portvlancost** method of Spanning Tree load balancing is very flexible (however, it is also more complex).

Finally, consider the intelligence of a load balancing scheme. For example, some techniques such as EtherChannel use a very simple **XOR** algorithm on the low-order bits of IP or MAC address. On the other hand, Layer 3 routing protocols offer very sophisticated and tunable load balancing and, more importantly, path selection tools.

TIP   Important load balancing considerations include:

- Available paths

- Ease of configuration, management, and troubleshooting

- Flexibility

- Intelligence

Spanning Tree

Spanning Tree load balancing is useful within a redundant Layer 2 domain. As discussed in Chapter 7, there are four techniques available for load balancing under the Spanning-Tree Protocol:

- Root Bridge placement
- Port priority (**portvlanpri**)
- Bridge priority
- Port cost (**portvlancost**)

As discussed in Chapter 7 and earlier in this chapter, Root Bridge placement is the simplest and most effective technique if the network's traffic flows support it. Fortunately, the multilayer model with routing switches (MLS) automatically generates a topology where the Root Bridges can be alternated between redundant MDF switches within a distribution block.

TIP   When working with the Spanning-Tree Protocol, try not to use the Root Bridge placement form of Spanning Tree load balancing.

Root Bridge placement is not effective in less constrained topologies such as campus-wide VLANs. In these cases, it is best to use the **portvlancost** form of load balancing. Although **portvlancost** is harder to use than Root Bridge placement, it is useful in almost any redundant topology. Think of it as the Swiss army knife of Spanning Tree load balancing.

TIP   When working with the Spanning-Tree Protocol, use **portvlancost** load balancing when the use of Root Bridge placement is not possible.

HSRP

In situations where Layer 3 switching is being used, HSRP plays an important role. When using Layer 3 switching in networks that contain Layer 2 loops in the distribution block, such as with the multilayer model and routing switches (MLS), Spanning Tree and HSRP load balancing should be deployed in a coordinated fashion. For example, the network in Figure 15-9 modified the Spanning Tree parameters to force the odd VLANs to use the left link and the even VLANs to use the right link. HSRP should be added to this design by making MDF-A the active HSRP peer for the odd VLANs and MDF-B the active peer for the even VLANs.

TIP   Be sure to coordinate HSRP and Spanning Tree load balancing. This is usually required in networks employing routing switches and the multilayer model.

In cases where the switching router (8500) approach to the multilayer model is in use, HSRP might be the only option available for load balancing within each distribution block (there are no loops for Spanning Tree to be effective). Consequently, two HSRP groups should be used for each subnet. This configuration was discussed in Chapter 11 and is referred to as Multigroup HSRP (MHSRP). MHSRP can be used to load balance by alternating the HSRP priority values.

TIP   Use MHSRP load balancing for networks using switching router technology.

Figure 15-10 illustrates an example that provides load balancing for one subnet/VLAN on an IDF switch.

Figure 15-10 *MHSRP Load Balancing*

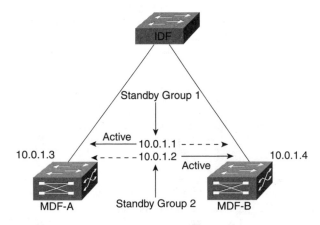

Both of the MDF switches are assigned two real IP addresses, 10.0.1.3 and 10.0.1.4. Rather than using a single standby group (which results in only one router and one riser link actively carrying traffic), two standby groups are configured. The first standby group uses an IP address of 10.0.1.1 and the priority of MDF-A has been increased to make it the active peer. The second standby group uses 10.0.1.2 and has MDF-B configured as the active peer. If both MDF switches are active, both riser links and both devices actively carry traffic. If either MDF device fails, the other MDF takes over with 100 percent of the load.

IP Routing

Another advantage in using Layer 3 switching is that IP routing protocols support very intelligent forwarding and path determination mechanisms. Whereas it can take considerable configuration to enable load balancing over two paths using techniques such as Spanning Tree load balancing and HSRP, Cisco routers automatically load balance up to six equal-cost paths (although Catalyst 8500s currently only load balance over two equal-cost paths because of the microcode memory limitations). Moreover, Layer 3 routing protocols support extensive path manipulation tools such as distribute lists and route maps.

Given that the multilayer design model focuses on Layer 3 switching in the MDF/distribution layer closets (and possibly the core), IP routing can be an extremely effective approach to load balancing across critical areas of the network such as the core (expensive WAN links are another area).

ATM

One of the benefits in using ATM in a campus environment is the sophistication of Private Network-Network Interface (PNNI) as an ATM routing and signaling protocol. Like IP, PNNI automatically load balances traffic over multiple paths. However, unlike IP, PNNI does not perform routing on every unit of information that it receives (cells). Instead, ATM only routes the initial call setup that is used to build the ATM connection. After the connection has been established, all remaining cells follow this single path. However, other calls between the same two ATM switches can use a different set of paths through a redundant ATM network (therefore, PNNI is said to do per connection load balancing). In this way, all of the paths within the ATM cloud are automatically utilized.

For more information on ATM, LANE, and PNNI, please consult Chapter 9, "Trunking with LAN Emulation."

EtherChannel

A final form of load balancing that can be useful for campus networks is EtherChannel. EtherChannel can only be used between a pair of back-to-back switches connected between two and eight links (although some platforms allow limited combinations). It uses an XOR algorithm on the low-order bits of MAC or IP addresses to assign frames to individual links. For more information, see Chapter 8, "Trunking Technologies and Applications."

TIP The 802.3ad committee of the IEEE is working on a standards-based protocol similar to Cisco's EtherChannel.

Routing/Layer 3 Switching

As this chapter has already mentioned many times, Layer 3 switching is a key ingredient in most successful large campus networks. This section elaborates on some issues specific to Layer 3 switching.

Strive for Modularity

One of the primary benefits of using Layer 3 technology is that it can create a high degree of modularity in a design. For instance, Figure 15-11 illustrates a typical two-building campus using the multilayer model.

Figure 15-11 *Using a Layer 3 Barrier to Create a Modular Design*

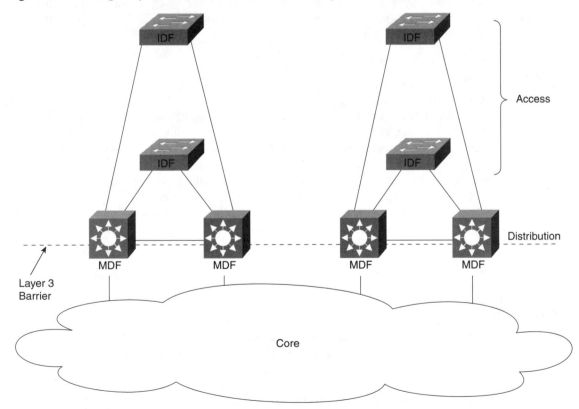

The Layer 3 barrier created by the routing function embedded in the MDF switches separates each building from the core. The primary benefits of this technique are:

- The modularity allows for cookie-cutter designs. Although the IP addresses (as well as other Layer 3 protocol addresses) change, each distribution block can be implemented with almost identical switch and router code.
- The network is very easy to understand and troubleshoot. Technicians can apply most of the same skills used for managing and troubleshooting router and hub networks.
- The network is highly scalable. As new buildings or server farms are added to the campus, they merely become new distribution blocks off the core.
- The network is very deterministic. As devices or links fail, the traffic will failover in clearly defined ways.

Although some degree of modularity can be created with more Layer 2-oriented designs such as campus-wide VLANs, it is much more difficult to get the separation required for true modularity. Without a Layer 3 barrier of scalability, the Layer 2 protocols tend to become intertwined and tightly coupled. Consequently, it becomes more difficult to grow and rearrange the network.

When to Use MLS (and Routing Switches)

The routing switch (MLS) form of the multilayer model is most appropriate when you want to maintain a strong Layer 2 component within each distribution block. By doing so, MLS allows the feature-rich Layer 2 Catalysts to flourish. Options such as VTP and PVST can all be very useful in this environment. Also, by maintaining this strong Layer 2 orientation, you can easily place a single VLAN on multiple IDF/access layer wiring closets (8500s require bridging/IRB to accomplish this). Furthermore, MLS has excellent support for multiprotocol routing, as well as combining routing and bridging within the same device. For more information on the specific benefits and configuration commands for MLS, see Chapter 11, Chapter 14, and Chapter 17.

When to Use Switching Routers (8500s)

Whereas MLS maintains a Layer 2 flavor within the distribution block, switching routers go to the opposite extreme. Switching routers such as the Catalyst 8540 are most easily configured and maintained when functioning as a pure router. Although they do support bridging through the use of IRB and bridge groups, extensive use of these features can lead to configurations that are difficult to maintain.

Instead, by using these devices as very high-speed routers, they can dramatically simplify network design. Issues and problems associated with Spanning Tree all but disappear. Traffic flows become highly deterministic. Support personnel accustomed to working in the traditional router and hub model find switching router designs easy to support and troubleshoot. The superior support of IP multicast technology at Layer 3 provides an excellent migration path to the future.

As with MLS, more information can be found on the pros and cons of switching routers in Chapters 11, 14, and 17.

When to Use IRB

In short, use IRB only when you have to. It is not that IRB is a bad feature. In fact, IRB is a very flexible technology for combining Layer 2 and Layer 3 traffic and it allows precise control over how both bridged and routed traffic is handled. The problem is more likely to be a human one—IRB can be difficult to understand, support, and design.

When considering the use of IRB, also take into account the following issues:

- An advantage to doing IRB on hardware-based platforms such as the Catalyst 8500 is that it can be performed at wire speed (the software-based routers are currently limited to fast-switching speeds).

- There is a limit to the number of Bridged Virtual Interfaces (BVIs) that the IOS supports (currently 64).

- Some features are not supported on BVIs. Because the list is constantly changing, check the release notes or place a call to Cisco's TAC.

When deciding where to utilize IRB, try to use it only as a tool for specific niche issues— for example, if you need to place several directly-connected servers into a single VLAN or if there is a VLAN that absolutely must transit a switching router.

TIP   If your design calls for the extensive use of IRB, consider using the Catalyst 6000 "Native IOS Mode" detailed in Chapter 18. In general, it will result in a network that is considerably easier to configure and maintain.

Limit Unnecessary Router Peering

When using routers in VLAN-based networks, it can be important to reduce unnecessary router peering. For example, consider cases such as those illustrated in Figure 15-7 and Figure 15-10. Assume that these routers connect to 30 wiring closet VLANs via ISL or 802.1Q trunks. By default, the routers will form 30 separate adjacencies, wasting valuable router memory and processor power. By listing all or most of these VLANs as passive interfaces for the routing protocol, this can dramatically reduce this unnecessary peering. For wiring closet VLANs where no other routers are located, all VLANs should be removed.

TIP   Reducing unnecessary peering can be especially important with Catalyst 8500 routers and the Catalyst 6000 MSM.

Load Balancing

As discussed in the Spanning Tree sections, the style of load balancing that is needed depends primarily on the type of Layer 3 switching that is in use. To summarize the earlier discussion, MLS generally requires that a combination of Spanning Tree and HSRP load balancing techniques be used within the distribution block. When using switching routers, MHSRP should be used.

Also, Layer 3 switches automatically load balance across the campus core if equal-cost paths are available.

Try to Use Only Routable Protocols

Unless it is absolutely necessary, try to pass only routable protocols through your Layer 3 switches. This is most often accomplished by relegating non-routable protocols to a single VLAN. If you are migrating to a new network infrastructure, consider leaving the non-routable traffic on the old infrastructure. The lagging performance of that network serves as an incentive for users of non-routable protocols to upgrade to an IP-based application.

ATM

As Layer 3 switching has grown in popularity, it has demonstrated that ATM is not the only technology capable of great speed. However, ATM does have its place in many campus networks. This section examines some of the more important issues associated with completing an ATM-based campus network design.

When to Use ATM

One of the first questions every network designer must face is should the design utilize ATM technology. In the past, ATM has been billed as the solution to every possible network problem. Although this might be true in terms of ATM's theoretical capabilities, it is not true in terms of how most organizations are using ATM. For example, in the mid-1990s, many network analysts foretold of the coming days where networks would use ATM on an end-to-end basis. Instead, Ethernet has continued to grow in popularity. When, then, is it best to use cell-based switching?

Traditionally, ATM has been touted for several unique benefits. The most commonly mentioned benefits include:

- **High bandwidth**—Because cells use fixed-size units of data with simple and predictable header formats, it is fairly easy to create high-speed hardware-based switching equipment.
- **Sophisticated bandwidth sharing**—Cells can be interleaved to allow multiple communication sessions to share a single link through an advanced form of statistical multiplexing. Because cells are all the same size, applications using large data transfer units do not create a log jam effect that slows down smaller and potentially more time-sensitive traffic.

- **Quality of Service (QoS)**—ATM has complex and sophisticated mechanisms to allow detailed traffic contracts to be specified and enforced.

- **Support for voice and video**—ATM's low latency and QoS benefit give it robust support for time-critical forms of communication such as voice and video.

- **Distance**—Unlike common campus technologies such as Ethernet, ATM can function over any distance.

- **Interoperability**—Because ATM is a global standard, a wide variety of devices can be purchased from different vendors.

Although many of these points remain true, advances in frame-based switching have significantly eroded ATMs edge in the following areas:

- Campus-oriented Gigabit Ethernet switches now match or exceed the speed of ATM switches. Although cell switching does maintain a theoretical advantage, ASIC-based Layer 2 and Layer 3 switches have become exceptionally fast. Furthermore, ATM has continued to struggle with the SAR boundary, the fastest speed that ATM's Segmentation And Reassembly function can be performed.

- Ethernet-based QoS (or at least Class of Service) schemes are becoming more available, more practical, and more effective. Although ATM holds a theoretical lead, ATM continues to suffer from a lack of applications that capitalize on its inherently superior capabilities. As a result, CoS-capable Gigabit Ethernet switches are rapidly growing in popularity.

- Although ATM does maintain a distinct advantage in its capability to handle isochronous (timing critical) applications, there is tremendous growth in non-isochronous mechanisms for sending voice and video traffic. Efforts such as voice over IP (VoIP) and H.323 videoconferencing are common examples. These technologies reduce the need for ATM's unique capabilities.

- Gigabit Ethernet distances are growing dramatically. As this book goes to press, a number of vendors are introducing 80–100 km Gigabit Ethernet products.

- All forms of Ethernet, including Gigabit Ethernet, have been perceived as being considerably more interoperable than ATM standards.

In addition, the complexity of ATM has become a significant issue for most organizations. Whereas Ethernet is considered easy and familiar, ATM is considered difficult and murky (and, to a significant extent, these perceptions are valid).

TIP   Although the growth of ATM in campus networks has slowed at the time this book goes to press, it is important to note that the use of ATM technology in the WAN continues to expand rapidly.

Where to Use ATM

Although there is considerable debate about the usefulness of ATM in a campus backbone, there is considerably less debate about where it is useful. Almost all analysts are in agreement that desktop connections will be Ethernet for the foreseeable future. Although 10/100 Ethernet sales continue to soar, sales of ATM to the desktop have staggered. When ATM is used, almost all agree that the ATM is best suited to the core of the network. In most cases, this means a LANE core connecting to Ethernet switches containing LANE uplink modules.

Although this issue has received fairly little debate, a second issue has been less clear-cut. The issue concerns the matter of how far the ATM backbone should reach. The debate surrounds two options.

Some vendors and network designers prefer to link only the MDF/distribution layer devices to the ATM core. Fast and Gigabit Ethernet links can then be used to connect to IDF switches as shown in Figure 15-12.

Figure 15-12 *Using Ethernet Links in Conjunction with an ATM Core*

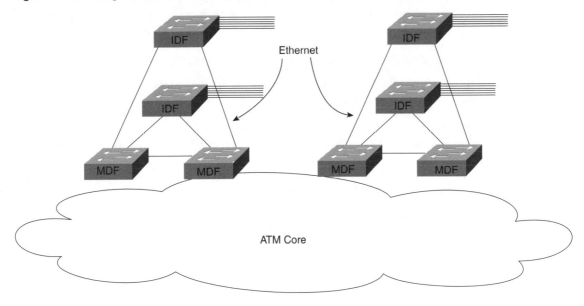

The advantage of this approach is that it uses cost-effective Ethernet technology in the potentially large number of IDF closets. This design is often deployed using the campus-wide VLAN model to extend the speed of ATM through the Ethernet links. The downside is that it creates a large number of Layer 2 loops where redundant MDF-to-IDF links are used. Unfortunately, these links have been shown to create Spanning Tree loops that can disable the entire campus network. Furthermore, it is harder to use ATM features such as QoS when the edges of the network use Ethernet.

The opposing view is that the ATM backbone should extend all the way to the IDF closets. Under this design, the entire network utilizes ATM except for the links that directly connect to end-user devices. This approach is illustrated in Figure 15-13.

Figure 15-13 *Extending the ATM Core to the IDF Switches*

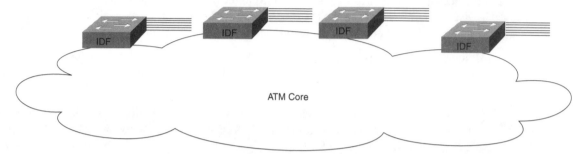

The downside of this alternative is a potentially higher cost because it requires more ATM uplink and switch ports. However, the major benefit of this design is that it eliminates the Layer 2 loops formed by the Ethernet links in the previous approach. Because LANE inherently creates a loop-free Layer 2 topology, the risk of Spanning Tree problems is considerably less (in fact, some vendors who promote this design leave Spanning Tree disabled by default, something many network engineers feel is a risky move).

Having worked with implementations using both designs, I feel that the answer should be driven by the use of Layer 3 switching (like many other things). If you are using the multilayer model to create hard Layer 3 barriers in the MDF/distribution layer devices, the MDF switches can be the attachment point to the ATM core and Ethernet links to the IDF devices can be safely used. However, when the campus-wide VLAN model is in use, extending the ATM backbone to the IDFs allows for the most stable and scalable design. Trying to use the MDF-attachment method with campus-wide VLANs results in Spanning Tree loops and network stability issues.

TIP   The use of Layer 3 switching in your network should drive the design of an ATM core.

Using SSRP

Until standards-based LANE redundancy mechanisms become widely available, Simple Server Redundancy Protocol (SSRP) will remain an important feature in almost any LANE-based core using Cisco ATM switches. Although SSRP allows more than one set of redundant devices, experience has shown that this can lead to scaling problems. See Chapter 9 for more information on SSRP.

BUS Placement

Always try to place your LANE Broadcast and Unknown Server (BUS) on a Catalyst LANE module. Because the BUS must handle every broadcast and multicast packet in the ELAN (at least in current versions of the protocols), the potential traffic volume can be extremely high. The Catalyst 5000 OC-3 and Catalyst 5000/6000 OC-12 LANE modules offer approximately 130 kpps and 450 kpps of BUS performance respectively, considerably more than any other Cisco device currently offered.

One decision faced by designers of large LANE cores involves whether a single BUS or multiple distributed BUSes should be utilized. The advantage of a single BUS is that every ELAN has the same logical topology (at least the primary topologies are the same, the backup SSRP topology is obviously different). The disadvantage is that the single BUS can more easily become a bottleneck.

Distributed BUSes allow each ELAN to have a different BUS. Although this can offer significantly higher aggregate BUS throughput, it can make the network harder to manage and troubleshoot. With the introduction of OC-12 LANE modules and their extremely high BUS performance, it is generally advisable to use a single BUS and capitalize on the simplicity of having a single logical topology for every ELAN.

TIP	With the high BUS throughput available with modern equipment, centralized BUS designs are most common today.

Chapter 9 contains additional information on BUS placement.

MPOA

Multiprotocol Over ATM (MPOA) can be a useful technology for improving Layer 3 performance. MPOA, as discussed in Chapter 10, "Trunking with Multiprotocol over ATM," allows shortcut virtual circuits to be created and avoids the use of routers for extended flows. When considering the use of MPOA, keep the following points in mind:

- MPOA can only create shortcuts in sections of the network that use ATM. Therefore, if the MDF devices attach to an ATM core but Ethernet is used to connect from the MDF to the IDF switches, MPOA is only useful within the core itself. If the core does not contain Layer 3 hops, MPOA offers no advantage over LANE. In general, MPOA is most useful when the ATM cloud extends to the IDF/access layer switches.

- Because MPOA is mainly designed for networks using ATM on an IDF-to-IDF basis, you must intentionally build Layer 3 barriers into the network. Without careful planning, MPOA can lead to flat earth networks and the associated scaling problems discussed earlier in this chapter and in Chapters 11, 14, and 17.

- At presstime, significant questions remain about the stability and scalability of MPOA.

TIP	MPOA only optimizes unicast traffic (however, related protocols such as a MARS can be used to improve multicast performance).

Hardware Changes

In most Catalyst equipment (such as the Catalyst 5000), both MPOA and LANE use MAC addresses from the chassis or Supervisor to automatically generate ATM NSAP addresses. For a detailed discussion of how NSAP addresses are created, refer to Chapter 9. When designing an ATM network, keep the following address-related points in mind:

- Devices with active backplanes such as the Catalyst 5500s use MAC addresses pulled from the backplane itself. Changing the chassis of one of these devices therefore changes the automatically-generated NSAP addresses.

- Devices with passive backplanes such as the Catalyst 5000 use MAC addresses from the Supervisor. Therefore, changing a Catalyst 5000 Supervisor module changes the pool of addresses used for automatically generating NSAP addresses.

- In both cases, 16 MAC addresses are assigned to each slot. Therefore, simply moving a LANE module to a different slot alters the automatically generated NSAP addresses.

- Because of these concerns, many organizations prefer to use hard-coded NSAP addresses. For more information, see the section "Using Hard-Coded Addresses" in Chapter 9.

TIP	Consider using hard-coded NSAP addresses in a large LANE network.

Campus Migrations

It can be very challenging to manage a campus migration. New devices are brought online as older equipment is decommissioned or redeployed. However, while the rollout is taking place, connectivity must be maintained between the two portions of the network. This section makes a few high-level recommendations.

Use the Overlay Approach

During a migration, many organizations attempt to intermingle old and new equipment on the same links to form a single network. Although this does appear appealing from the perspective of trying to maintain full connectivity during the migration, it can make the rollout extremely difficult. By intermingling the two sets of equipment, the new network can be dragged down by the old equipment. Problems such as excessive bridging for non-routable protocols and Spanning Tree issues can prevent the new network from living up to its full potential. Moreover, if two Gigabit-speed switches are forced to communicate through an existing software-based router, it is like trying to drive a 6000 hp dragster down a dirt road!

In general, the most effective solution for dealing with campus migrations is to use the overlay technique.

As shown in Figure 15-14, the overlay approach treats the two networks as totally separate. Rather than connecting the new devices to the existing links, a completely out-of-band set of new links are used. If old and new devices are located in the same wiring closet, both connect to separate links. Therefore, the new network is said to overlay the existing network.

Figure 15-14 *The Overlay Approach to Campus Migrations*

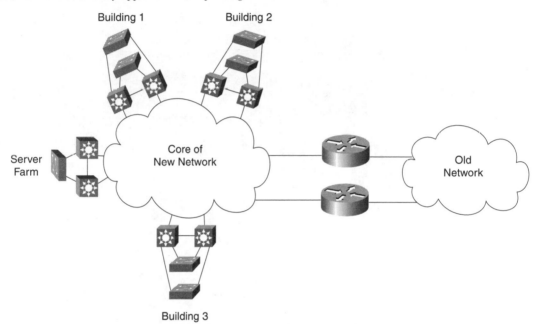

To maintain connectivity between the old and the new network, a pair of redundant routers is used. This provides a single line where the two networks meet. Issues such as route redistribution and access lists can be easily handled here. Also notice that this causes the old network to resemble just another distribution block connected to the core of the new network (another benefit of the modularity created by the multilayer model).

Server Farms

Servers play a critical role in modern networks. Given this importance, they should be considered early in the design process. This section discusses some common issues associated with server farm design.

Where to Place Servers

Most organizations are moving toward centralized server farms to allow better support and management of the servers themselves. Given this trend, it is generally best to position a centralized server farm as another distribution block attached to the campus core. This concept is illustrated in Figure 15-15.

Figure 15-15   *Centralized Server Farm*

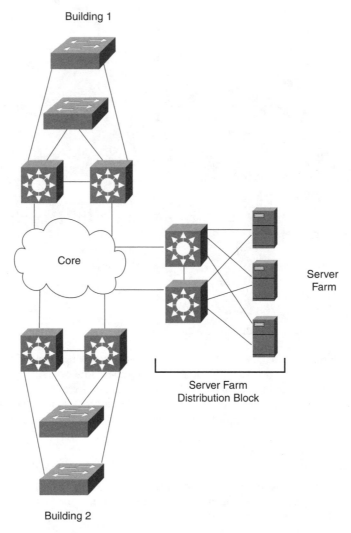

The servers in Figure 15-15 can be connected by a variety of means. The figure shows the servers directly connected to the pair of Layer 3 switches that link to the campus core. An alternative design is to use one or more Layer 2 switches within the server farm. These Layer 2 devices can then be connected to the Layer 3 switches through Gigabit Ethernet or Gigabit EtherChannel. Although some servers can connect to only a single switch, redundant NICs provide a measure of fault-tolerance.

The key to this design is the Layer 3 barrier created by the pair of Layer 3 switches that link the server farm to the core. Not only does this insulate the server farm from the core, but it also creates a much more modular design.

Some network designs directly connect the servers to the core as shown in Figure 15-16.

Figure 15-16 *Connecting Servers Directly to the Campus Core*

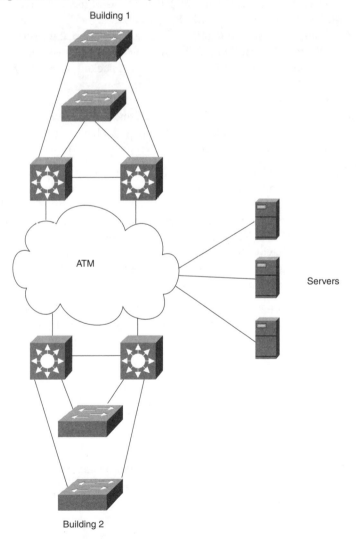

Figure 15-16 illustrates a popular method used for core-attached servers—using an ATM core. By installing LANE-capable ATM NICs in the servers, the servers can directly join the ELAN used in the campus core. A similar design could have been built using ISL or 802.1Q NICs in the servers.

Most organizations run into one of two problems when using servers directly connected to the campus core:

- Inefficient flows
- Poor performance

The first problem occurs with implementations of the multilayer model where the routing component contained in the MDF/distribution layer devices can lead to inefficient flows. For example, consider Figure 15-16. Assume that one of the servers needs to communicate with an end user in Building 1. When using default gateway technology, the server does not know which MDF Layer 3 switch to send the packets to. Some form of Layer 3 knowledge is required as packets leave the server farm. One way to achieve this is to run a routing protocol on the servers themselves. However, this can limit your choice of routing protocols throughout the remainder of the network, and many server administrators are reluctant to configure routing protocols on their servers. A cleaner approach is to simply position the entire server farm behind a pair of Layer 3 switches, as shown in Figure 15-15.

The second problem occurs with implementations of campus-wide VLANs where the servers can be made to participate in every VLAN used throughout the campus (for example, most LANE NICs allow multiple ELANs to be configured). Although this sounds extremely attractive on paper (it can eliminate most of the need for routers in the campus), these multi-VLAN NICs often have poor performance and are subject to frequent episodes of strange behavior (for example, browsing services in a Microsoft-based network). Moreover, this approach suffers from all of the scalability concerns discussed earlier in this chapter and in Chapters 14 and 17.

In general, it is best to always place a centralized server farm behind Layer 3 switches. Not only does this provide intelligent forwarding to the MDF switches located throughout the rest of the campus, but it also provides a variety of other benefits:

- This placement encourages fast convergence.
- Access lists can be configured on the Layer 3 switches to secure the server farm.
- Server-to-server traffic is kept off of the campus core. This can not only improve performance, but it can also improve security.
- It is highly scalable.
- Layer 3 switches have excellent multicast support, an important consideration for campuses making widespread use of multicast technology.

Consider Distributed Server Farms

Although centralized server farms are becoming increasingly common because they simplify server management, they do create problems from a bandwidth management perspective because the aggregate data rate can be extremely high. Although high-speed Layer 2 and Layer 3 switches have mitigated this problem to a certain extent, network designers should look for opportunities to intelligently distribute servers throughout the organization. Although this point is obviously true with regards to wide-area links, it can also be true of campus networks.

One occasion where servers can fairly easily be distributed is in the case of departmental servers (servers that are dedicated to a single organizational unit). These devices can be directly connected to the distribution block network they serve. In general, these servers are attached in one of two locations:

- They can be directly connected to the IDF switch that handles the given department.
- They can be attached to the MDF switches in that building or distribution block. This also presents the opportunity to create mini server farms in the MDF closets of every building. Departmental file and print servers can be attached here where enterprise and high-maintenance servers can be located in the centralized server farm.

Use Fault-Tolerant NICs

Many organizations spend numerous hours and millions of dollars creating highly redundant campus networks. However, much of this money and effort can go to waste unless the servers themselves are also redundant. A fairly simple way to improve a server's redundancy is to install some sort of redundant NICs.

Although using redundant NICs can be as simple as just installing two normal NICs in each server, this approach can lead to problems in the long run. Because most network operating systems require each of these NICs to use different addresses, clients need some mechanism to failover to the address assigned to the secondary NIC when the primary fails. This can be challenging to implement.

Instead, it is advisable to use special NICs that automatically support failover using a single MAC and Layer 3 address. In this case, the failover can be completely transparent to the end stations. A variety of these fault-tolerant NICs are available (some also support multiple modes of fault tolerance, allowing customization of network performance).

TIP   Fault-tolerant NICs allow two (or more) server NICs to share a single Layer 2 and Layer 3 address.

When selecting a fault-tolerant NIC, also consider what sort of load balancing it supports (some do no load balancing, and others only load balance in one direction). Finally, closely analyze the technique used by the NICs to inform the rest of the network that a change has occurred. For example, many NICs perform a gratuitous ARP to force an update in neighboring switches.

In some cases, this update process can be fairly complex and require a compromise of timer values. For example, when using fault-tolerant Ethernet NICs in conjunction with a LANE backbone, it is not enough to simply update the Layer 2 CAM tables and Layer 3 ARP tables. If redundant LANE modules are used to access the server farm, the LANE LE-ARP tables (containing MAC address to ATM NSAP address mappings) also need to be updated. When faced with this issue, you might be forced to disable PortFast and intentionally incur a Spanning Tree delay. The upside of this delay is that it triggers a LANE topology change message and forces the LE-ARP tables to update.

Obviously, redundant NICs should be carefully planned and thoroughly tested *before* a real network outage occurs.

TIP   You may need to disable PAgP on server ports using fault-tolerant NICs to support the binding protocols used by some of these NICs during initialization.

Use Secured VLANs in Server Farms

Cisco is developing a new model for VLANs to provide simple but effective security for applications such as very large server farms. Under this feature, one or more uplink ports are configured on each of the switches used to directly link the servers to one or more default gateways. These ports support two-way access to all servers within the VLAN. However, other ports within the VLAN designated as access or server ports cannot communicate with each other. This creates an easy-to-administer environment where the servers have full communication with the network's backbone/core but with no risk of the servers communicating with each other. This feature will be extremely useful in situations such as Internet service provider (ISP) web hosting facilities where communication between servers from different clients must be tightly controlled. Whereas earlier solutions generally involved creating hundreds of small VLANs and IP subnets, Cisco's new model of VLAN will be much easier to implement and maintain (all of the servers can use a single VLAN and IP subnet) while providing tight security.

NOTE   This feature had not received an official name at the time this book goes to press. Contact your Cisco sales team for additional information.

Additional Campus Design Recommendations

This section addresses a variety of other tips and best practices that do not fit in the previous sections or important points that deserve emphasis.

Access Layer Recommendations

When designing the IDF/access layer sections of the network, be sure to at least consider using the following features if NFFC/RSFC support is available in these devices:

- Protocol Filtering (see Chapter 11)
- IGMP Snooping (see Chapter 12)
- QoS classification

Distribution Layer Recommendations

The recommendation here is simple and has been clearly discussed earlier in the chapter. However, it is important enough to repeat: *Always try to form a Layer 3 barrier in the MDF/ distribution layer devices.*

Core Layer Recommendations

The primary thing to keep in mind is the point discussed in the Spanning Tree and VLAN sections: *Keep the core loop free when using a Layer 2 core.*

Watch Out for Discontiguous Subnets

Carefully scrutinize your designs for possible discontiguous subnets. One of the most common and subtle causes of this situation is created in scenarios such as that shown in Figure 15-17.

Figure 15-17 *Discontiguous Subnets*

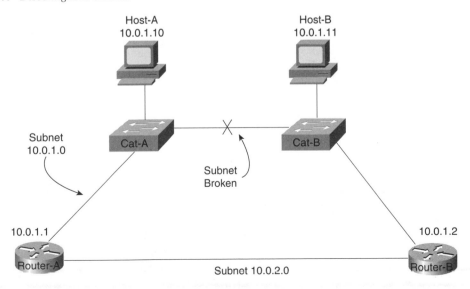

The link between Cat-A and Cat-B has failed, partitioning the 10.0.1.0 subnet into two halves. However, because neither router is aware of the failure, they are both trying to forward all traffic destined to this subnet out their upper interface. Therefore, Router-A will not be able to reach Host-B and Router-B will not be able to communicate with Host-A.

In general, there are two simple and effective ways to fix this problem:

- Utilize a mixture of Layer 2 and Layer 3 (such as with "routing switches"/MLS)

- Place only a single Layer 2 switch between routers (as well as between the "switching router" forms of Layer 3 switches)

Under the first approach, MLS is used to create a Layer 2 environment that, because it is redundant, remains contiguous even after the failure of any single link. Figure 15-18 illustrates this approach.

Figure 15-18 *Avoiding Discontiguous Subnets With A Routing Switch (MLS)*

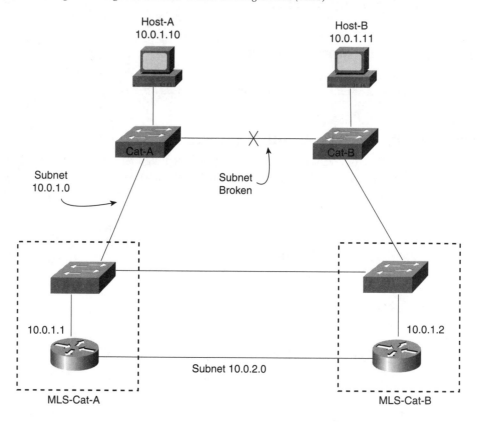

Figure 15-18 shows a logical representation of MLS devices where the Layer 2 and Layer 3 components are drawn separately in order to highlight the redundant Layer 2 configuration.

NOTE   The design in Figure 15-18 could also be implemented using switching router technology such as the Catalyst 8500s by utilizing bridging/IRB.

The second solution to the discontiguous subnet problem is to always use a single Layer 2 switch between routers, as shown in Figure 15-19.

Figure 15-19 *Avoiding Discontiguous Subnets By Using a Single Layer 2 Switch*

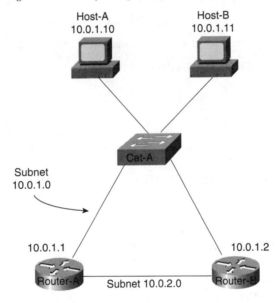

Because this eliminates the "chain" of Layer 2 switches shown in Figure 15-17, it allows any single link to fail without partitioning the subnet.

VTP

In some situations, the VLAN Trunking Protocol (VTP) can be useful for automatically distributing the list of VLANs to every switch in the campus. However, it is important to realize that this can automatically lead to campus-wide VLANs. Moreover, as discussed in Chapter 12, VTP can create significant network outages when it corrupts the global VLAN list.

When using VTP in large networks, consider overriding the default behavior using one of two techniques:

- VTP transparent mode
- Multiple VTP domains

First, many large networks essentially disable VTP by using the transparent mode of the protocol (there is no **set vtp disable** command). When using VTP transparent mode, you have absolute control over which VLANs are configured on each switch. This can allow you to prune back VLANs where they are not required to optimize your network.

Second, when organizations do decide to utilize VTP server and client mode, it is often beneficial to use a separate VTP domain name for each distribution block. This provides several benefits:

- It breaks the default behavior of spreading every VLAN to every switch (in other words, campus-wide VLANs).

- It constrains VTP problems to a single building.

- It allows the VTP protocol to better mirror the multilayer model.

- It can reduce Spanning Tree overhead.

Passwords

Because the XDI/CatOS-interface Catalysts (currently this includes 4000s, 5000s, and some 6000 configurations) automatically allow access by default, be sure to set user and privilege mode passwords. In addition, be certain to change the default SNMP community strings (unlike the routers, SNMP is enabled by default on XDI/CatOS-interface Catalysts).

Port Configurations

When configuring ports, especially important trunk links, hard-code as many parameters as possible. For example, relying on 10/100 speed and duplex negotiation protocols has been shown to occasionally fail. In addition, the state (**on** or **off**) and type (**isl** or **802.1Q**) of your Ethernet trunks should be hard-coded.

TIP   One exception to this rule concerns the use of PAgP, the Port Aggregation Protocol used to negotiate EtherChannel links. If PagP is hard-coded to the **on** state, this prevents the Catalyst from performing some value-added processing that can help in certain situations such as Spanning Tree failover.

Review Questions

This section includes a variety of questions on the topic of campus design implementation. By completing these, you can test your mastery of the material included in this chapter as well as help prepare yourself for the CCIE written and lab tests.

1   This chapter mentioned many advantages to using the multilayer model. List as many as possible.

2   This chapter also mentioned many disadvantages to using campus-wide VLANs. List as many as possible.

3   List some of the issues concerning management VLAN design.

4   What are some factors to be considered when determining where to place Root Bridges?

5   List five techniques that are available for campus load balancing.

6   What is the primary difference between using routing switches (MLS) and switching routers in MDF/distribution layer devices?

7   What are the pros and cons of using ATM?

This chapter covers the following key topics:

- **Troubleshooting Philosophies**—Describes philosophical approaches and practices to problem solving in a network. Lists probable areas where switched network problems can occur. Also covers using the OSI network model to organize troubleshooting thoughts.

- **Catalyst Troubleshooting Tools**—Describes various **show** commands and other facilities that provide further insight into network operations.

- **Logging**—Discusses how to use and configure Catalyst features to log significant events with your equipment.

CHAPTER 16

Troubleshooting

Throughout this book, you have seen suggestions on troubleshooting specific areas relevant to the chapter topic. This chapter differs in that it focuses on high level, structured troubleshooting techniques in the LAN switched environment and describes a number of resources and tools available to facilitate troubleshooting.

Troubleshooting Philosophies

Troubleshooting philosophies vary depending upon training, knowledge, ability, suspicions, system history, personal discipline, and how much heat you are getting from users and management. Many philosophies fall apart when pressure mounts from users screaming that they need network services now, and when managers apply even more pressure because they do not understand or appreciate the complexities of network troubleshooting. If you are susceptible to these pressures, this causes you to become unstructured in your approach and to depend upon random thoughts and clues. Ultimately, this increases the time to restore or deploy network services. Characteristics of a good troubleshooting philosophy, though, include structure, purpose, efficiency, and the discipline to follow the structure.

Two philosophical approaches are presented here to organize your thoughts. The first method to be discussed describes an approach recognizing problems based upon their probability of occurrence. They are then categorized into one of three "buckets" for the differing probabilities. This is the bucket approach to troubleshooting.

The second approach tackles network problems based upon the OSI model. Each layer represents a different network structure that you might need to examine to restore your network. This is the OSI model approach for troubleshooting.

The approaches really tackle problems in a very similar manner, but represent different methods of remembering the approach. The second method does differ, though, in its granularity. The bucket approach groups troubles into three buckets. Each bucket contains problems with similar characteristics and represents areas of probable problems. The second approach tackles problems through the OSI model. The model helps to think through symptoms and what high-level sources might cause the problems.

In reality, your troubleshooting technique probably uses a little of both. The bucket method lumps the OSI model, to some extent, into three areas.

Regardless of which approach you use, you must have one foundational piece to troubleshoot your network: documentation.

Keep and Maintain Network Documentation

One element for any troubleshooting philosophy to work is frequently absent: documentation. Many administrators neglect to document their network, or if they do, they do not keep the documentation up to date. Documentation provides the framework to answer fundamental questions such as, "What changed?" or "What connects to device X?" or "What Layer 2 paths exist from point A to point B?" Reconstructing the network topology documentation during a crisis does not lend itself to an efficient or structured troubleshooting approach. You are not doing yourself, your career, or your users any good when you have to take time during the crisis event to determine the network topology.

Document your network with both electronic media and old-fashioned paper. Electronically, use spreadsheets, graphics programs, network management tools, or any other means at your disposal to keep the documentation up to date. Electronic documentation has the advantage of portability; however, it has the disadvantage of limited access and vulnerability to outages. If you keep the documentation on your laptop or desktop, but make it inaccessible to others on your staff by either taking it with you or using passwords, they cannot use the documentation when you are not around. For security reasons (or to satisfy company politics), you might desire this, but in most cases this is not a good practice.

Paper versions offer non-dependence upon the electronic device, but frequently tend to be outdated through neglect. When you make an electronic change, make sure that the paper copy reflects the change as well.

Another underutilized documentation tool exists in your network equipment. Most equipment has built-in documentation features such as description strings for interfaces, modules, chassis, and so forth. Use these to prompt your memory for connectivity. It takes only a few seconds to put a description string on the port configuration. On the Catalyst 5000/6000, use the **set port name** *mod_num/port_num* [*port_name*] command to document interfaces with useful information. For example, you might indicate who or what attaches to the port. If the port is a trunk, indicate what Catalyst it connects to. As with previous documentation discussions, be sure to keep the descriptions current. You will see the port name if you use the **show port status** command as shown in Example 16-1. Here, Ports 1/1 and 3/1 have assigned names indicating the device the port attaches to.

Example 16-1 *Output from* **show port status**

```
Console> show port status
Port  Name               Status      Vlan       Level  Duplex Speed Type
----- ------------------ ----------- ---------- ------ ------ ----- -----------
 1/1  Cat-B              connected   523        normal half    100 100BaseTX
 1/2                     notconnect  1          normal half    100 100BaseTX
 2/1                     connected   trunk      normal half    400 Route Switch
 3/1  LS1010Switch12     notconnect  trunk      normal full    155 OC3 MMF ATM
```

Troubleshooting Philosophy 1: The Bucket Approach

The bucket approach to troubleshooting investigates likely problem areas based upon the probability of occurrence. It structures thoughts in terms of target areas for investigation. Specific problem areas frequently create the majority of situations you are likely to encounter. You can categorize these problems and place them into one of three buckets: cabling, configuration, and usage/implementation (other). The following sections describe the kinds of things to look for from each bucket. It is suggested that the probability of occurrence decreases for each bucket, as depicted by the size of the buckets in Figure 16-1. The first bucket, Cabling, is largest because it represents the highest probability of occurrence. You should check for problems from this bucket first in your network. The second bucket, Configuration, contains another group of problems, but typically has fewer instances in your network. Therefore, you check these problems after examining the cables. The last and smallest bucket, Other, contains all of the other problems that don't necessarily fall into either of the first two. Problems from this bucket occur the least and should be examined last in your system.

Each bucket is its own Pandora's Box. Unfortunately, no one stands over the bucket warning everyone to not spill the bucket. It happens. Your job in troubleshooting is to determine which bucket spilled its contents into your network.

Figure 16-1 *Three Buckets of Problems*

Bucket 1: Cabling   Bucket 2: Configuration   Bucket 3: Other

Bucket 1: Cabling

The bucket of cable problems contains issues such as wrong cables, broken cables, and incorrectly connected cables. Too often, administrators overlook cables as a trouble source. This is especially true whenever the system "was working." This causes troubleshooters to assume that because it was working, it must still be working. They then investigate other problem areas, only to return to cables after much frustration.

Common cable mistakes during installation generally include using the wrong cable type. One, for example, is the use of a crossover cable rather than a straight through cable, or vice versa. The following list summarizes many of the typical problems:

- Crossover rather than straight through, or vice versa
- Single-mode rather than multimode
- Connecting transmit to transmit
- Connecting to the wrong port
- Partially functional cables
- Cable works in simplex mode, but not full-duplex
- Cables too long or too short for the media

Remember that when attaching an MDI (media dependent interface) port to an MDI-X (media dependent crossover interface) port, you must use a straight through cable. All other combinations require a crossover cable type. Fortunately, using the wrong cable type keeps the link status light extinguished on equipment. This provides a clue that the cable needs to be examined. An extinguished link status light can result from the correct cable type, but a broken one. Be aware that an illuminated link status light does not guarantee that the cable is good either. The most that you can conclude from a status light is that you have the correct cable type and that both pieces of equipment detect each other. This does not, however, mean the cable is capable of passing data.

A form of partial cable failure can confuse some network operations like Spanning Tree. For example, if your cable works well in one direction, but not the other, your Catalyst might successfully transmit BPDUs, but not receive them. When this happens, the converged Spanning Tree topology might be incorrect and, therefore, dysfunctional.

NOTE   I have a box filled with cables that were healthy enough to illuminate the status light on equipment, but not good enough to transmit data. Consequently, I wasted much time investigating other areas only to circle back to cables. I should have stuck with my troubleshooting plans and checked the cables rather than bypassing it. Make sure that you have a cable tester handy—one capable of performing extensive tests on the cable, not just continuity checks.

Cisco introduced a feature in the Catalyst 6000 series called *Uni-Directional Link Detection* (UDLD), which checks the status of the cable in both directions, independently. If enabled, this detects a partial cable failure (in one direction or the other) and alerts you to the need for corrective action.

Another copper cable problem can arise where you fully expect a link to autonegotiate to 100 Mbps, but the link resolves to 10 Mbps. This can happen when multiple copper cables exist in the path, but are of different types. For example, one of the cable segments might be a Category 3 cable rather than a Category 5. Again, you should check your cables with a cable tester to detect such situations.

Another example of using a wrong cable type is the use of single-mode fiber rather than multimode, or multimode rather than single-mode. Use the correct fiber mode based upon the type of equipment you order. There are a couple of exceptions where you can use a different fiber mode than that present in your equipment, but these are very rare. Plan on using the correct fiber type. As with any copper installation, look for a status or carrier light to ensure that you don't have a broken fiber or that you didn't connect the transmit of one box to the transmit of the other box. And as with copper, a carrier light does not always ensure that the cable is suitable for data transport. You might have too much attenuation in your system for the receivers to decode data over the fiber. If using single-mode fiber, you might have too much light entering the receiver. Make sure that you have at least the minimal attenuation necessary to avoid saturating the optical receiver. Saturating the receiver prevents the equipment from properly decoding the equipment.

Unless there is a clearly obvious reason not to do so, particularly in an existing installation, check cables. Too often, troubleshooting processes start right into bucket 2 before eliminating cables as the culprit.

Bucket 2: Configuration

After confirming that cables are intact, you can start to suspect problems in your configuration. Usually, configuration problems occur during initial installations, upgrades, or modifications. For example, you might need to move a Catalyst from one location to another, but it doesn't work at the new location. Problems here can arise from not assigning ports to the correct VLAN, or forgetting to enable a trunk port. Additional configuration problems include Layer 3 subjects. Are routers enabled to get from one VLAN to another? Are routing protocols in place? Are correct Layer 3 addresses assigned to the devices? The following list summarizes some of the things to look for in this bucket:

- Wrong VLAN assignments on a port.
- Wrong addresses on a device or port.
- Incorrect link type configured. For example, the link might be set as a trunk rather than an access link, or vice versa.
- VTP domain name mismatches.

- VTP modes not set correctly.
- Poor selection of Spanning Tree parameters.
- Trunk/access port mismatches.
- EtherChannel mismatches.
- Routing protocols not enabled.
- Default paths not defined.

One of the most common configuration errors is wrong VLAN assignments. Administrators move a device to another port and forget to ensure that the VLAN assignment is consistent with the subnet assignment.

Other configuration errors arise from not modifying default parameters to enable a feature, or to change the behavior of a feature. For example, the trunk default mode is **auto**. If you leave the Catalyst ports at both ends of the link in the default state, the link does not automatically become a trunk. You might not realize that they are in the default setting and fail to realize the true reason for the link remaining as an access link.

The Catalyst PortFast feature, disabled by default, can correct many network problems when enabled. If you have clients failing to attach to the network or network services, you might need to enable PortFast to bypass the Spanning Tree convergence process and immediately reach the Forwarding state.

NOTE   You can enable PortFast on all ports except for trunk ports to alleviate the probability of client/server attachment problems. However, enable this feature with caution, as you can create temporary Layer 2 loops in certain situations. PortFast assumes the port is not a part of a loop and does not startup by looking for loops.

Bucket 3: Other

This bucket contains most other problem areas. The following list highlights typical problems:

- Hardware failures
- Software bugs
- Unrealistic user expectations
- PC application inadequacies

Sometimes, a user attempts to do things with his application program that it was not designed to do. When the user fails to make the program do what he thinks it should do, he blames the network. Of course, this is not a valid user complaint, but is an all-too-often scenario. Ensure that the user need is valid before launching into a troubleshooting session.

Unfortunately, you can discover another culprit in this bucket. Equipment designers and programmers are not perfect. You will encounter the occasional instance where a product does not live up to expectations due to a manufacturer's design flaw or programming errors. Most manufacturers do not intentionally deploy flawed designs or code, but it does occasionally happen. When corporate reputations are volatile and stockholder trust quickly evaporates, vendors work aggressively to protect their image. Vendors rarely have a chance to intervene reputation slams on the Internet because word spreads quickly. It is much more difficult for a vendor to recover a reputation than to maintain it. Therefore, vendors usually work under this philosophy and strive to avoid the introduction of bad products into the market.

As administrators, though, we tend to quickly blame the manufacturer whenever we experience odd network behavior that we cannot resolve. Although easy to do, it does not reflect the majority of problems in a network. We do this because of the disreputable companies that polluted the market and occasionally crop up today. Many networks fail to achieve their objectives due to unscrupulous vendors. As an industry, we now tend to overreact and assume that all companies operate that way. Do not be too quick to criticize the manufacturer.

NOTE   Yes. Even Cisco has occasional problems. Be sure to check the Cisco bug list on the Web or send an inquiry to Cisco's Technical Assistance Center (TAC) if you experience unusual network problems. This might be an unexpected "feature" of the software/hardware.

Troubleshooting Philosophy 2: Evaluate Layers of the OSI Model

The other troubleshooting philosophy looks at problems according to the OSI model that divide network technology into identifiable components. As you identify problems at each of the layers, you will find that you can place them into one of the three buckets discussed in the previous section. You can, for example, look at the physical layer. Problems at the physical layer relate to cables and media. Is there too much cable? Not enough? Did you connect the cable into the correct port? Clearly these problems easily fit into the first bucket.

What about the second layer of the OSI model, the data link layer? This layer describes the media access method. It defines how Token Ring and Ethernet operate. It also defines how the bridging methods work for these access methods. Spanning Tree and source route bridging operate at this layer. 802.1Q encapsulation is defined at Layer 2. If you misconfigure the native VLAN on the two ends of the link, the trunk port experiences errors.

At Layer 3, you must investigate routing issues. If you have problems communicating with devices in another VLAN, you need to determine if the Layer 3 is not routing correctly, or if there is something at Layer 1 or Layer 2 preventing the VLANs from functioning. Diagnostic approaches here test connectivity from a station to the router, and then across the router(s) interface. Figure 16-2 shows three VLANs interconnected with routers. Systematic troubleshooting determines if Layers 1 and 2 operate by attempting communication to each router interface.

Figure 16-2 *Testing Cross VLAN Connectivity*

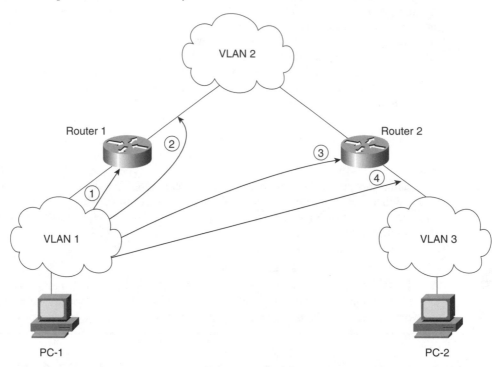

In Figure 16-2, PC-1 desires, but fails, to communicate with PC-2 in the figure. Assume that it is an IP environment. From one PC or the other, attempt to communicate (maybe with **ping**) to the first hop router. For example, you might first initiate a **ping** from PC-1 to the Router 1 interface (point 1 in the figure). Do this by **ping**ing the IP address of the ingress port of Router 1 which belongs to the same subnet as PC-1. Then, try the outbound interface on Router 1 (point 2 in the figure). Continue through the hops (points 3 and 4) until you reach PC-2. Probably, somewhere along the path, **ping**s fail. This is your problem area. Now, you need to determine if there is a routing problem preventing the echo request from reaching the router, or an echo reply from returning. For example, suppose the **ping** fails on the ingress port of Router 2 (point 3). To determine if the problem is at Layer 2, attempt to **ping** the router interface from another device in the VLAN. This might be another workstation or router in the broadcast domain. If the **ping** fails, you might reverse the process. Try **ping**ing from the router to other devices in the broadcast domain. Check the router's interface with the **show interface** command. On the other hand, you might need to check the Catalyst port to ensure that the port is active. You might need to check the following items for correctness:

- Is the port enabled?
- Is the port a trunk or access link?

- If not a trunk, is the port in the correct VLAN?
- Does the port speed and duplex match the settings on the attached device?

The Catalyst **show port** command provides this information. If all of these parameters look good, you probably have a Layer 3 issue preventing the router port from communicating. One further data point to investigate: Do any other protocols have a problem getting through/to this router? If they also have problems, this is a strong pointer to Layer 2 issues. If other protocols work, but IP does not, you need to seriously investigate Layer 3. Check the router's port address and mask to ensure that it belongs to the same subnet as the other devices in the broadcast domain.

Remember that you might need to redraw your network to show Layer 3 paths. Chapter 5, "VLANs," discussed how the physical drawing of your network docs provide good insight in how the data flows in your network. A drawing that shows how Catalysts interconnect provides some Layer 2 information about data flow, but certainly not any about Layer 3. For effective troubleshooting, you might need to show the Layer 2 and the Layer 3 paths in the network. For intra-VLAN troubleshooting, you need to draw the Layer 2 paths. This should include bridges and trunks so that you can examine your Spanning Tree topology. If you have problems with inter-VLAN connections, you might need to draw both layers. You might need to draw Layer 2 to ensure that you can get from a device to the next hop within the VLAN. Communication from router to router must cross a VLAN. Likewise, you might need to draw the Layer 3 pictures to ensure that you know what router paths the data transits so that you know what VLANs to examine.

Other Layer 3 issues might include access lists or routing table problems in routers. If you have an access list blocking certain stations or networks from communicating with each other, the system might *appear* to be broken, but in fact is behaving just like you told it to.

Be sure also to check workstation configurations. If the workstation has a wrong IP address for the VLAN it attaches to, it will fail to communicate with the rest of the world. Fortunately, IP utilities like DHCP minimize this, but occasionally some stations are manually configured and need to reflect the subnet for the VLAN.

Catalyst Troubleshooting Tools

Cisco built several mechanisms into the Catalyst to facilitate troubleshooting and diagnostics. Some standalone and others work in conjunction with external troubleshooting tools that you need to provide. These built-in tools help to troubleshoot Layer 1 and Layer 2. You usually need to do Layer 3 troubleshooting in your routers and workstations. Just make sure that Layer 1 or 2 isn't preventing Layer 3 from performing, as demonstrated in the previous section. The following sections examine key troubleshooting tools for evaluating the health of your switched network, including the following:

- Various **show** commands not discussed in previous chapters exist offering more insight into potential problem areas in your network.
- The Catalyst has extended SNMP MIB definitions and RMON (remote monitoring) capabilities to accumulate statistics on network performance and behavioral anomalies.

- A logging feature allows you to automatically record significant Catalyst events on a server. You can review the history of your Catalyst in the text file generated by the logging feature.
- An inherent capability to examine traffic in a Catalyst through a Switched Port Analyzer (SPAN) port. The SPAN port allows you to connect an external analyzer to the Catalyst and capture traffic from a port or VLAN within the Catalyst. You can look at both access and trunk links.

show Commands

Throughout this book, each chapter has presented **show** commands relevant to the chapter subject material. However, several additional **show** commands exist in the Catalyst to further enable you to diagnose your switched network environment.

show test Command

For example, you can obtain detailed information about the health of your Catalyst hardware through the **show test** command. It displays the results of the built-in hardware tests in the Catalyst. On power up, the Catalyst tests the power supply and components on the Supervisor module, including the bridging table memory and related chipsets. Example 16-2 shows an abbreviated output from the **show test** command.

Example 16-2   *Output from* **show test**

```
Console> show test
Environmental Status (. = Pass, F = Fail, U = Unknown)
  PS (3.3V):   .   PS (12V): .   PS (24V):   .   PS1: .    PS2: .
  Temperature: .   Fan:       .


Module 1 : 2-port 10/100BaseTX Supervisor
Network Management Processor (NMP) Status: (. = Pass, F = Fail, U = Unknown)
  ROM:   .   Flash-EEPROM: .   Ser-EEPROM: .   NVRAM:   .   MCP Comm: .

  EARL Status :
        NewLearnTest:           .
        IndexLearnTest:         .
        DontForwardTest:        .
        MonitorTest:            .
        DontLearn:              .
        FlushPacket:            .
        ConditionalLearn:       .
        EarlLearnDiscard:       .
        EarlTrapTest:           .


LCP Diag Status for Module 1  (. = Pass, F = Fail, N = N/A)
  CPU        : .    Sprom    : .    Bootcsum : .    Archsum  : .
  RAM        : .    LTL      : .    CBL      : .    DPRAM    : .    SAMBA : .
  Saints     : .    Pkt Bufs : .    Repeater : N    FLASH    : .
  Phoenix    : . TrafficMeter: . UplinkSprom : . PhoenixSprom: .
```

The first highlighted portion shows the results of the power supply tests. Because no **F** appears next to the supply entries, they passed the test. Other environmental test results are shown in this block. The second category tests the Enhanced Address Recognition Logic (EARL) functionality. The EARL manages the bridge tables. Again, only dots "." appear next to each test and therefore represent pass.

show port counters Command

Another command displays much information about Layer 2 media and access operations. Use the **show port counters** command to gain insight into the operations of the segment as shown in Example 16-3.

Example 16-3   *Output from* **show port counters**

```
Console> show port counters

Port  Align-Err  FCS-Err    Xmit-Err   Rcv-Err    UnderSize
----- ---------- ---------- ---------- ---------- ----------
 1/1       0          0          0          0          0
 1/2       0          0          0          0          0
 4/1       0          0          0          0          0
 4/2       0          0          0          0          0
 4/3       0          0          0          0          0
 4/4       0          0          0          0          0

Port  Single-Col Multi-Coll Late-Coll Excess-Col Carri-Sen Runts      Giants
----- ---------- ---------- --------- ---------- --------- ---------- ---------
 1/1      12          0          0          0          0         0          -
 1/2       0          0          0          0          0         0          0
 4/1       0          0          0          0          0         0          0
 4/2       0          0          0          0          0         0          0
 4/3       0          0          0          0          0         0          0
 4/4       0          0          0          0          0         0          0

                                      Ler
Port  CE-State Conn-State Type Neig Con Est Alm Cut Lem-Ct     Lem-Rej-Ct Tl-Min
----- -------- ---------- ---- ---- ----------------- ---------- ---------- ------
 3/1  isolated connecting A    U    no   9   9   7        0          0 102
 3/2  isolated connecting B    U    no   9   8   7        0          0 40
```

Several of these fields merit discussion as values in some columns can suggest areas to investigate. Values in the **Align-Err** and **FCS-Err** fields indicate that the media cable deteriorated or that the station NIC no longer operates correctly. These values increment whenever the received frame has errors in it. The errors are detected by the receiver with the CRC field on the frame. **Align-Err** further indicates that the frame had a bad number of octets in it. This can strongly point to a NIC failure.

The **Xmit-Err** and **Rcv-Err** fields indicate that the port buffers overflowed, causing the Catalyst to discard frames. This happens if the port experiences congestion preventing the Catalyst to forward frames onto the switching BUS, or out the interface onto the media. To help resolve the first case where the port cannot transfer the frame over the BUS (**Rcv-Err**), increase the port priority to *high* with the **set port priority** command. When set to high, the BUS arbiter grants the port access to the BUS at a rate five times more frequently than normal. This has the effect of emptying the buffer at a faster rate.

TIP   Do not set all ports to high priority as this effectively eliminates any advantage to it. Use this setting on your high volume servers.

If the Catalyst drops frames because it cannot place frames onto the media, this can indicate a congestion situation where there is not enough bandwidth on the media to support the amount of traffic trying to transmit through it. Figure 16-3 illustrates a switched network where multiple sources need to communicate with the same device.

Figure 16-3 *A LAN Congestion Situation*

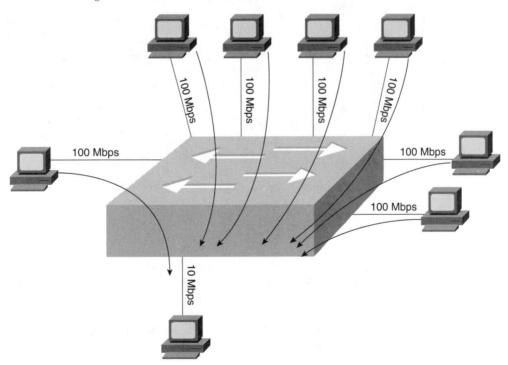

In Figure 16-3, the aggregate traffic from the sources exceeds the bandwidth available. The upper devices connect at 100 Mbps, but attempt to access a device running at 10 Mbps. If all of the stations transmit at the same time, they quickly overwhelm the 10 Mbps link. This forces the Catalyst to internally buffer the frames until bandwidth becomes available. Like any LAN device, however, the Catalyst does not hold onto the frame indefinitely. If it cannot transmit the frame in a fairly short period of time, the frame is discarded. This can happen if the Catalyst repeatedly experiences collisions when it attempts to transmit the frame. Like other LAN devices, the Catalyst attempts to transmit the frame up to 16 times. After 16 collisions, the Catalyst drops the frame. A Catalyst can also discard a frame if there is no more buffer space available. To fix this, you might need to increase the port bandwidth, or create multiple collision or broadcast domains on the egress side of the system.

Three fields indicate bad frame sizes: **UnderSize**, **Runts**, and **Giants**. The first two fields indicate frames that are less than a legal media frame size, whereas **Giants** indicates frames too large per the media specification. UnderSize and Giant frames usually mean that the frame format and CRC are valid, but the frame size falls outside of the media parameters. For example, a malfunctioning Ethernet station might create an Ethernet frame less than 64 bytes in length. Although the MAC header and CRC values are valid, they do not meet the Ethernet frame size requirements. The Catalyst discards any such frame. Runt frames differ from UnderSize frames in that they are usually a byproduct of a collision on a shared media. Runts, unlike UnderSize frames, do not carry valid CRC values. If you see the Runt counter continuously incrementing across periods of time, this can indicate that you either have too many devices contending for bandwidth in the collision domain or you have a media problem generating collisions and the runt byproduct. If the problem stems from bandwidth contention, break the segment into smaller collision domains. If the problem is from media (such as a 10BASE2 termination problem), fix it!

Four fields describe collision combinations: **Single-Coll**, **Multi-Coll**, **Excess-Col**, and **Late-Coll**. **Single-Coll** counts how many times the Catalyst wanted to transmit a frame, but experienced one and only one collision. After the collision, the Catalyst attempted to transmit again, but this time successfully. **Multi-Coll** counts collisions inclusively, from 2–15. The Catalyst attempted multiple times to transmit the frame, but experienced collisions when doing so. Eventually, it successfully transmitted the frame. **Excess-Col** counters increment whenever the Catalyst tries 16 times to transmit. When this counter increments, the Catalyst discards the frame. **Late-Coll** stands for late collision. A late collision occurs when the Catalyst detects a collision outside of the collision time domain described in Chapter 1, "Desktop Technologies." This means that the collision domain is too large. You either have too many cables or repeaters extending the end to end distance beyond the media timeslot specifications. Shorten the collision domain with bridges or by removing offending equipment.

show mac Command

The **show mac** command provides information on the number of frames transmitted and received on each Catalyst interface. Specifically, the **show mac** command provides a count of the total number of frames on the interface, the number of multicast frames, and the number of broadcast frames.

Although most of the column headers are fairly self explanatory, a couple deserve additional clarification. Example 16-4 shows a partial listing of the **show mac** output.

Example 16-4   *Partial* **show mac** *Output*

```
Console> show mac 3/4
MAC        Rcv-Frms   Xmit-Frms   Rcv-Multi   Xmit-Multi  Rcv-Broad   Xmit-Broad
--------   --------   ---------   ---------   ----------  ---------   ----------
  3/4            0           0           0            0           0            0

MAC        Dely-Exced MTU-Exced   In-Discard  Lrn-Discrd  In-Lost     Out-Lost
--------   --------   ---------   ---------   ----------  ---------   ----------
  3/4            0           0           0            0           0            0
```

The first line of the output shows the frame counters mentioned previously. The second line, highlighted in this example, counts other events. **Dely-Exced** indicates how many times that the Catalyst had to discard a frame when it wanted to transmit, but had to defer (wait to transmit) because the media was busy. The wait time was excessive because a source transmitted longer than what is expected for the media. This is sometimes referred to as *jabber* and is caused by a malfunctioning NIC in a shared media network. Rather than indefinitely holding the frame, the Catalyst discards the frame. Therefore, this counter displays the number of frames discarded because of the jabber. This should only occur when the port is attached to shared media.

MTU-Exced counts how many times the port received a frame where the frame exceeded the Maximum Transmission Unit (MTU) frame size configured on the interface. The size is set to the media maximum by default, but you can elect to reduce this value. You can do this when you have an FDDI source trying to communicate to an Ethernet source and want to ensure that any frames over the Ethernet MTU are discarded by the switch.

In-Discard reflects the number of times that the Catalyst discards a frame due to bridge filtering. This occurs when the source and destination reside on the same interface. See Chapter 3, "Bridging Technologies," for details on filtering.

Bridges (and Catalysts) have a finite amount of memory space for the bridge tables. The bridge fills the table through the bridge learning process described in Chapter 3. Depending upon the model of Catalyst you have, the Catalyst can remember up to 16,000 entries. But if you have a very large system where this memory space gets filled because of many stations, the Catalyst must replace existing entries until older entries are aged from the table to free space. The **Lrn-Discrd** counter tracks the number of unlearned addresses where the switch normally learns the source address, but cannot because the bridge table is already full.

In-Lost and **Out-Lost** represent the number of frames dropped by the Catalyst due to insufficient buffer space. **In-Lost** counts the frames coming into the port from the LAN. **Out-Lost** counts the frames to go out the port to the LAN.

show counters Command

The undocumented **show counters** command allows you to view a number of SNMP and RMON counters. For details on what each means, view appropriate RFCs for the media description.

SPAN

Sometimes you want to examine traffic flowing in and out of a port, or within a VLAN. In a shared network, you attach a network analyzer to an available port and your analyzer promiscuously listens to all traffic on the segment. Your analyzer can then decode the frames and provide you with a detailed analysis of the frame content. In a switched network, however, this is not nearly as simple as in a shared network. For one thing, a switch filters a frame from transmitting out a port unless the bridge table believes the destination is on the port, or unless the bridge needs to flood the frame. This is clearly inadequate for traffic analysis purposes. Therefore, the normal Catalyst behavior must be modified to capture traffic on other ports. The Catalyst feature called Switched Port Analyzer (SPAN) enables you to attach an analyzer on a switch port and capture traffic from other ports in the switch.

High performance analysis tools are also available such as the Network Analysis Module which provides enhanced RMON reporting to your network management station. This module plugs into a slot in your Catalyst and monitors traffic from a SPAN port or from NetFlow.

Another Cisco monitoring tool, the SwitchProbe, attaches externally to a Catalyst SPAN port or network segment and gathers RMON statistics that can then be retrieved by your network management station.

By default, this feature is disabled. You need to explicitly enable SPAN to capture traffic from other ports. When you enable SPAN, you need to specify what you want to monitor and where you want to monitor it.

What you can monitor includes:

- An individual port
- Multiple ports on the local Catalyst
- Local traffic for a VLAN
- Local traffic for multiple VLANs

Monitored traffic goes to a port on the local Catalyst. Figure 16-4 illustrates that the traffic from VLAN 100 is monitored and directed to the analyzer attached to Port 4/1.

Figure 16-4 *A SPAN VLAN Example*

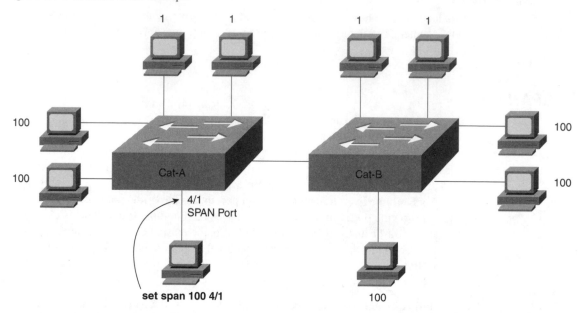

set span 100 4/1

Although the **set span 100 4/1** command says to monitor VLAN 100, note that only VLAN 100 traffic local to Cat-A is captured. If stations on Cat-B transmit unicast traffic to each other, and the frames are not flooded, the analyzer does not see that traffic. The only traffic that the analyzer can see is traffic flooded within VLAN 100, and any local unicast traffic.

TIP   Be careful when monitoring Gigabit Ethernet. The 9-port Gigabit Ethernet module provides local switching and cannot SPAN the switch backplane. If you have the 3-port Gigabit Ethernet module, this is not so. You can monitor all traffic within the Catalyst.

TIP   Although you can direct VLAN traffic to a SPAN port, the port sees only the local VLAN traffic. If a VLAN has a presence in multiple Catalysts, the SPAN port displays the VLAN traffic found in the local Catalyst where you enable SPAN. Therefore, you get all of the local traffic. You see VLAN traffic from other Catalysts only if the frame is forwarded or flooded to your local Catalyst. If a frame stays local in a remote Catalyst, your SPAN port does not detect this frame.

TIP   Be careful with the syntax for this command. It is very similar to the **set spantree** command. **set span** and **set spant** are the short forms of two different commands.

Destination Port Attributes

Depending upon the source traffic you are monitoring, you might need to be careful to avoid congestion on your SPAN port. For example, if you monitor a busy VLAN, the aggregate source traffic from the VLAN is sent to the SPAN port. You would not want, therefore, to monitor an entire VLAN and have the traffic sent to a 10 Mbps interface. This is especially true if the VLAN member ports are 100 Mbps interfaces. Make sure that your SPAN port has adequate bandwidth to effectively capture the traffic you want to monitor.

Logging

It is a good idea to maintain a log of significant events of your equipment. An automatic feature in your Catalyst can transmit information that you deem as important to a TFTP file server for you to evaluate at a later time. You might want this information for troubleshooting reasons or security reasons. You can use the file, for example, to answer questions such as "What was the last configuration?" or "Did any ports experience unusual conditions?"

A number of configuration commands modify the logging behavior. By default, logging is disabled. However, you can enable logging and direct the output to an internal buffer, to the console, or to a TFTP server. The following commands send events to the server:

set logging server {enable | disable}—This command enables or disables the log to server feature. You must enable it if you plan to automatically record events on the server.

set logging server *ip_addr*—Use this command to inform your Catalyst about the IP address for the TFTP server.

set logging server facility *server_facility_parameter*—A number of processes can be monitored and logged to the server. For example, significant VTP, CDP, VMPS, and security services can be monitored. Reference the Catalyst documentation for a detailed list.

set logging server severity *server_severity_level*—Various degrees of severity ranging in value from 0 through 7 describe the events. 0 indicates emergency situations, and 6 is informational. 7 is used for debugging levels. If you set the severity level to 6, you will have a lot of entries in the logging database because it provides information on trivial and significant events. If you set the level to 0, you will only get records when something catastrophic happens. An intermediate level is appropriate for most networks.

This chapter covers the following key topics:

- **Real-World Design Issues**—This chapter presents an opportunity to apply the skills learned in earlier chapters in two real-world designs.

- **Campus-Wide VLANs**—Considers the real-world downsides of flat earth designs.

- **MLS Design**—Discusses and analyzes the pros and cons of a campus design that uses Multilayer Switching (MLS) for Layer 3 switching.

- **Hardware-Based Routing Design**—Analyzes the benefits and unique characteristics of a campus design based on the Catalyst 8500-style of hardware-based routing.

- **Configuration Examples**—Looks at actual configurations for two different campus designs.

CHAPTER 17

Case Studies: Implementing Switches

Previous chapters have focused on building specific skills required to successfully understand and create scalable campus networks. This chapter steps back from specific campus skills and technologies to focus on the big picture.

In doing so, this chapter examines the design requirements for a rapidly growing campus network. To maximize the opportunity for analysis, two separate designs will be created for this single client requirement. Because of its proven advantages, both designs utilize Layer 3 switching in the distribution layer/Main Distribution Frame (MDF) devices. However, the first approach uses MLS to retain a distinct Layer 2 component at the distribution layer. The second design uses Catalyst 8500-style technology to create a hard Layer 3 barrier in the distribution layer.

Both designs also utilize a wide variety of other switching-related features. This presents a real-world environment where the pros and cons of different features and approaches can be discussed. Because, as a network designer, you are certain to face many of these same decisions, this chapter should serve as a useful template for your own campus designs.

Finally, do not focus on the specific products and models of equipment discussed in this chapter. Although the chapter mentions various products in an effort to be as precise and real world as possible, the main focus should be on campus design thought processes and methodologies. Although products are guaranteed to change at an ever-faster pace, the hallmarks of a good design rarely change (furthermore, the syntax shown in the configuration examples included in this chapter also rarely change signfiicanly).

The Design Scenario

The client for the network design is Happy Homes, Inc., a thriving builder of residential housing in the Eastern United States. In the past, Happy Homes has prided itself on a very decentralized management structure. The company has been divided into five geographic regions that have operated in a very autonomous fashion. However, with the recent retirement of Happy GoLucky, the company's charismatic founder, the new management team has decided that it must centralize leadership. As a result, the company's four regional headquarters will be relocated to the corporate headquarters outside Baltimore, Maryland.

Currently, the Baltimore campus consists of two three-story buildings (both also have basements to house utilities such as heating, plumbing, and, of course, network equipment). Building 1 has served as the company's headquarters for the last 15 years—the cornerstone was even laid by Mr. GoLucky himself. The building currently contains 371 employees. The sales department is located on the first floor, and the engineering and marketing departments share the second floor. Finance is located on the third floor.

From a network perspective, Building 1 consists of the chaotic mix of equipment shown in Figure 17-1.

Figure 17-1 *Building 1 of the Happy Homes, Inc. Headquarters*

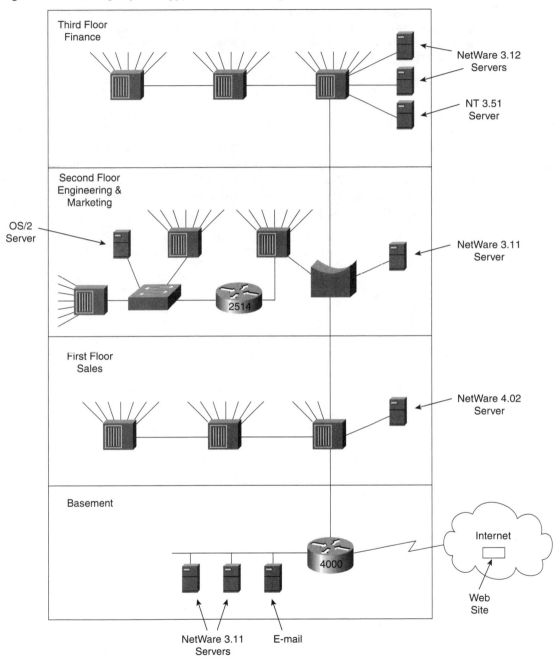

The basement of Building 1 contains a Cisco 4000 router that links the company to a local Internet service provider. The company currently has a Web site hosted by its ISP but wants to bring this function in-house. The Ethernet1 port of the router connects to a 10Base2 segment linked to two NetWare 3.11 servers and a NetBIOS-based e-mail server. The Ethernet0 port connects to a 10BaseT hub located in the sales department on the first floor. The sales department uses a total of three 48-port hubs in a daisy-chain configuration as well as a single NetWare 4.02 server. In all, 109 connections are in use on the first floor.

For the second floor, a four-port software-based bridge was purchased. Two ports are used to link to the first and third floors, and a third port links to the marketing department's NetWare 3.11 server. The fourth port connects to a 96-port hub that contains the end-user connections for the marketing department. Being more technically savvy, the engineering department has installed their own 2514 router and an 8-port Ethernet switch. The switch connects to two 48-port hubs and an OS/2 server running a CAD package. In total, there are 163 users on the second floor.

The finance department uses a series of 48-port hubs daisy chained off of the bridge on the second floor. The finance department has 99 end-user connections and three servers: two NetWare 3.12 servers and an NT 3.51 server.

Across the formal gardens from Building 1, Building 2 is in the final stages of construction. This building will be used to house the staff that replaces the regional office currently located in High Point, North Carolina. The engineering group will occupy the first floor, and the finance and marketing groups will use the second floor. The sales department has arranged mahogany offices on the third floor (they convinced senior management that the commanding view of Happy Home's growing headquarters would improve sales). Four hundred and thirty-one employees are expected to occupy Building 2.

As additional regional offices are closed and relocated to Baltimore, more buildings will be built. When these relocations are combined with Happy's ongoing success in the marketplace, they expect a total of six buildings and 2,600 employees within two years. Although the initial design should only include Buildings 1 and 2, the client has repeatedly stressed the importance of having a design that will easily scale to accommodate all six of the planned buildings.

Management is well aware of the drawbacks of the current network and wants to capitalize on technology as a competitive weapon. They want Happy to not only be known for building great houses, but also for being a technology leader. They recognize that a high speed and flexible campus network will play a key role in this. However, bandwidth alone will not be enough. Given the many outages experienced with the existing network, the new design must offer redundancy, stability, and high availability.

Should the Flat Earth Model Be Used?

Before running off to work on the design, a meeting was arranged with the key network personnel from Happy Homes. Knowing that many people associate switching with very flat networks, the design team wanted to get a feel for the client's expectations about the overall design.

Several members of the Happy team went to the white board and started drawing the network they envisioned. Their final drawing is reproduced in Figure 17-2.

Figure 17-2 *The Design Envisioned by the Happy Homes Staff*

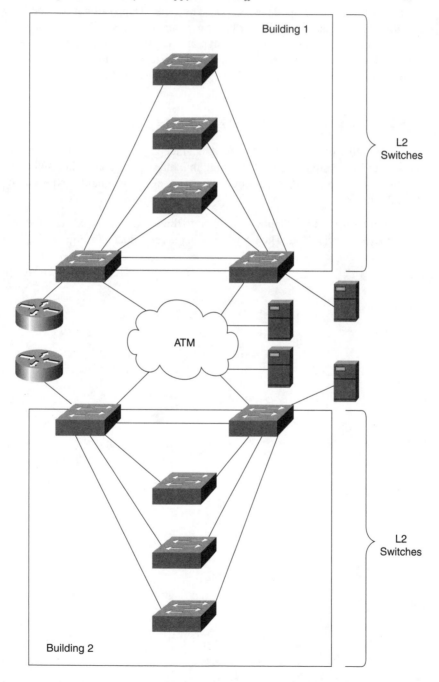

As the Happy staff described their design, it was clear that they subscribed to the campus-wide VLANs model discussed in Chapter 14, "Campus Design Models." Some of the key features they mentioned are included in the following list:

- Using 30 or 40 VLANs to create lots of communities of interest. This would provide fine-grained control over security and broadcast radiation.

- Because every VLAN would be configured on every switch, it would be easy to place users in different buildings and floors in the same subnet. This would allow traffic within the team to avoid the "slowness of routing."

- It would be easy to add a new user to any VLAN. A vendor had recently demonstrated a drag-and-drop VLAN assignment tool that had the whole team very excited.

- An ATM core could be used to trunk every VLAN between every building. The ATM core could also provide multiservice voice and video capabilities in the future.

- Servers could be attached to multiple VLANs/ELANs with LANE and ISL NICs. Again, this would provide a direct Layer 2 path from every user to every server and minimize the use of routers.

- VMPS could be used to dynamically assign VLANs to the rapidly growing number of laptop computer users. This would allow VLANs to follow the users as they moved between various offices and conference rooms. Their Cisco Sales Representative had also demonstrated a product called User Registration Tool (URT). This would allow VLAN assignments to be made based on NT Domain Controller authentication. The flexibility of this feature excited the Happy Homes network staff.

- The small amount of remaining inter-VLAN traffic could be handled by a pair of 7507 routers. These routers would use one HSRP group per VLAN to provide fault-tolerant routing for each VLAN.

The design crew had run into these sorts of expectations in the past. In fact, they had recommended almost this exact design to several clients one or two years earlier. At that time, the design team felt that avoid-the-router designs were necessary because software-based routers could not keep pace with the dramatic growth in campus bandwidth demands.

However, the results of these campus-wide VLANs created many unforeseen problems, including the following:

- Spanning Tree loops and instability were common. These frequent outages were often campus-wide and difficult to troubleshoot.

- Even when fast-converging protocols such as EIGRP, HSRP, and SSRP provided 5–10 second failover performance, Spanning Tree still created 30–50 second outages.

- Drag-and-drop VLAN assignment schemes were never as easy to use as everyone expected. Not only were some of the management platforms buggy, the VLANs-everywhere approach made it almost impossible to troubleshoot network problems. Instead of jumping in to solve the problem, network staff found themselves spending lots of time simply trying to comprehend the constantly changing VLAN layout.

- The performance of ISL and ATM NICs was disappointing and also led to unexplainable server behavior.

- It was becoming harder and harder to keep traffic within a single VLAN, the very premise of flat earth networks.

On the plus side, the design team did acknowledge that in certain situations, the advantages of the campus-wide VLAN model might outweigh its downsides. For example, the design team had recently worked on a large design for a university. The school wanted to create separate VLANs for students, professors, and administrative staff. Furthermore, they wanted these communities to be separate across each of the university's departments (for example, the biology department and physics department would use six VLANs: two for administrative staff, two for students, and two for professors). Because the school assigned a laptop to every student and professor, it was impossible to make static assignments to these VLANs. Campus-wide VLANs and URT/VMPS allowed students and university personnel to simply plug into any available outlet and receive the same connectivity throughout the entire campus. However, the inter-VLAN routing could still be centralized, allowing for much simpler access list configuration.

The design team mentioned that they also had some large hospital and government clients using similar designs. However, because the design team did not see the need for this sort of dynamic VLAN assignment and centralized access lists in the Happy Homes network, they recommended against this approach.

The discussion continued throughout the day. During this time, the design team brought up other issues discussed in Chapter 7, "Advanced Spanning Tree," Chapter 11, "Layer 3 Switching," Chapter 14, "Campus Design Models," and Chapter 15, "Campus Design Implementation." In the end, Happy Homes decided that the risks of the campus-wide VLAN approach were too great. They agreed that Layer 3 switching eliminated virtually all of the downsides they associated with traditional routers. Therefore, rather than striving to avoid Layer 3 routing, they decided to use it as a means to achieve stability, scalability, simplicity, and ease of management.

As the design team left at the end of the day, they agreed to return in several weeks with two separate designs for Happy Homes' consideration. Although both designs would utilize Layer 3 switching, one would blend Layer 2 and Layer 3 processing and the other would maximize the Layer 3 component. The results of their design efforts are presented in the following two sections.

Design 1: Using MLS to Blend Layer 2 and Layer 3 Processing

The first proposal presented to Happy Homes utilizes MLS for Layer 3 switching as illustrated in Figure 17-3.

Figure 17-3 *MLS Design*

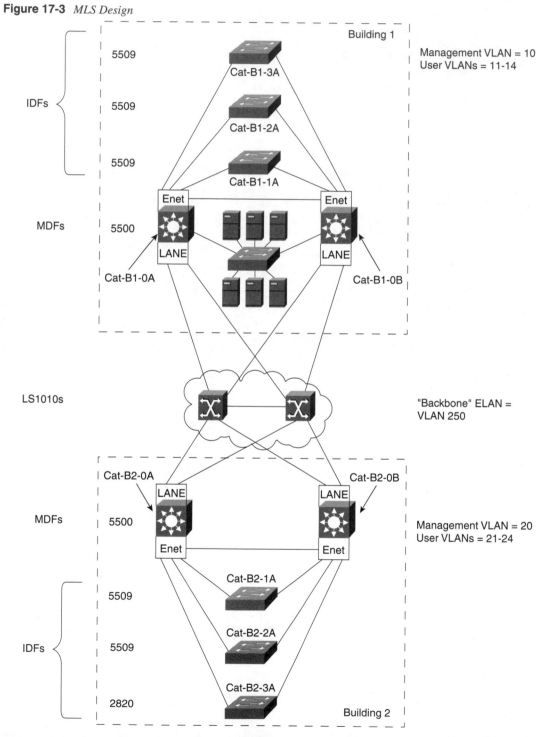

Design Discussion

This section introduces some of the design choices that were made for the first design. However, before diving into the specifics, it is worth pausing to look at the big picture of Design 1. As discussed earlier, both designs use Layer 3 switching in the MDF/distribution layer devices. This isolates each building behind a Layer 3 barrier to provide scalability and stability. By placing each building behind the safety of an intelligent Layer 3 router, it is much more difficult for problems to spread throughout the entire campus. Also, by providing a natural hierarchy, routers (Layer 3 switches) simplify the troubleshooting and maintenance of the network.

However, notice that Layer 2-oriented Catalysts, such as the Catalyst 5000s used in this design, do not automatically provide this Layer 3 barrier. In other words, simply plugging in a bunch of Catalyst 5000s or non-Native IOS Mode Catalyst 6000s (see Chapter 18, " Layer 3 Switching and the Catalyst 6000/6500s" for more information), add every VLAN to every switch (recall that VTP defaults to server mode). Only by manipulating VTP and carefully pruning selected VLANs from certain links can Layer 3 hierarchy be achieved when using technologies with a strong Layer 2 component (such as RSMs, MLS, and Catalyst 5000s and 6000s without any Layer 3 hardware/software).

For example, in this case the traffic from the end-user VLANs 11–14 and 21–24 could be forced through a separate VLAN in the core (VLAN 250) to create a true Layer 3 barrier. If left to the defaults where all of the devices are VTP servers in the same domain and therefore contain the full list of VLANs, routing might still be required between VLANs, but a Layer 3 barrier of scalability is not created. For more information on this point, see Chapter 14 and the section "MLS versus 8500s" in Chapter 11.

NOTE   It is extremely important to recognize that most of the devices in Cisco's product line can be used to build either Layer 2 or Layer 3 designs. This chapter is focusing on its relative strengths and **default** behavior. For example, as Chapter 11 pointed out, Catalyst 8500s can be used to build either Layer 2 or Layer 3 networks. However, by default, the 8500s function as switching routers, where every interface is a uniquely routed subnet/VLAN. Although you can use 8500s in Layer 2 designs, this generally involves the use of IRB, something that can easily become difficult to manage as the network grows.

Similarly, MLS can easily be used to build all of the Layer 3 topologies discussed in this chapter. However, many people are misled into believing that they automatically have Layer 3 hierarchy simply because they paid for some Layer 3 switching cards. As stated in the preceding text, this is not the case. Therefore, although MLS is suitable for almost all Layer 3 campus topologies, *it does not maximize the scalability benefits of Layer 3 switching* **by default** (you need to intervene to control VTP and implement selective VLAN pruning).

Finally, it is worth noting that the MSFC Native IOS Mode, discussed in Chapter 18, is equally adept at both designs. Consider it the multipurpose tool of Layer 3 campus switching.

Although both Design 1 and Design 2 create a Layer 3 barrier, for the reasons mentioned in previous paragraphs, the way in which the Layer 3 switching is implemented constitutes the primary difference between the two designs. In the case of Design 1, the Layer 3 barrier is created at the point where traffic enters and leaves the building. The result: traffic can continue to maintain a Layer 2 path within each building. In effect, Layer 3 switching has been implemented in such a way that *Layer 2 triangles* have been maintained within each building (the IDF switch represents one corner of the triangle with the other two corners being the MDF switches). By breaking the Layer 2 processing into clearly-defined and well-contained regions, this approach can provide a very scalable, high-performance, and cost-effective solution for campus networks.

By contrast, later sections of the chapter explore an alternate approach to Layer 3 switching used in Design 2. This design uses 8500-style hardware-based routing to implement routing both between *and within* the buildings. Although, as discussed in Chapter 11, Catalyst 8500s can be configured to provide a mixture of Layer 2 and Layer 3 switching, these devices are most comfortable as a pure Layer 3 device (this is from a configuration and maintenance standpoint, not from the standpoint of the data forwarding rate). This effectively chops off the bottom of the Layer 2 triangles in Design 1 to create *Layer 2 V's*.

NOTE   Note that MLS can also be used to create Layer 2 V's by simply pruning the MDF-to-MDF link of the IDF VLANs. Although this is a popular design choice successfully used by many organizations, this chapter does not utilize it in an attempt to maximize the differences between Design 1 and Design 2.

Although the difference between these two designs might seem trivial, it can be dramatic from a network implementation standpoint. By looking at specific configuration requirements and commands used by these two approaches, this chapter explores in detail the many implications of these two approaches to campus design.

Hardware Selection

Because of their high port densities and proven flexibility, Catalyst 5500s were chosen for the bulk of the devices used in Design 1. The horizontal wiring from end stations connect to an IDF/access layer switch located on each floor. Except for the third floor of Building 2, Catalyst 5509s have been selected as the IDF switches. Because the mahogany sales department offices on the third floor will take up considerably more space than other offices within Happy Homes, this will dramatically reduce the number of end stations located here. As a result, a Catalyst 2820 will be deployed on the third floor of Building 2.

The IDF switches will then connect via redundant links to a pair of MDF/distribution layer switches located in the basement of each building. Because they provide both ATM and Ethernet switching capabilities, Catalyst 5500s will be used in the MDFs. Route Switch Modules (RSMs) and MLS will also play a key role here.

The design also calls for a small server farm located in the basement of Building 1. This facility is designed to handle Happy Homes' server farm needs until construction can be completed on a separate data center building. The server farm will use a Catalyst 2948G switch to provide 10/100 Ethernet connectivity to the servers and Gigabit Ethernet uplinks to the Cat-B1-0A and Cat-B1-0B switches.

VLAN Design

The design utilizes five VLANs in each building plus an additional VLAN for the backbone. The first VLAN in each building is reserved for the management VLAN and only contains Catalyst SC0 interfaces (or ME1 interfaces on some models). The other four VLANs are used for end users: Sales, Marketing, Engineering, and Finance. Table 17-1 presents the VLAN names and numbers recommended by the design.

Table 17-1   *VLAN Names and Numbers*

Building 1		Building 2		Backbone	
Name	Number	Name	Number	Name	Number
Management	10	Management	20	Backbone	250
Sales	11	Sales	21		
Marketing	12	Marketing	22		
Engineering	13	Engineering	23		
Finance	14	Finance	24		

In other words, the first digit (or two digits in the case of the Backbone) of the VLAN number specifies the building number, and the last digit specifies the VLAN within the building.

The backbone VLAN, VLAN 250, corresponds to an ELAN named Backbone. Finally, notice that although the same five user communities exist in both buildings, separate broadcast domains are maintained because of the Layer 3 barrier created by MLS and the RSMs in the distribution layer.

Also note that this approach implements the recommendation made in Chapters 14 and 15 to separate end-user and management traffic. This is done to isolate the Catalyst CPU from the broadcast traffic that might be present in the end-user VLANs. By doing so, the stability of the network can be improved (for example, the CPU is not deprived of cycles for such important tasks as network management and the Spanning-Tree Protocol).

IP Addressing

Each VLAN utilizes a single IP subnet. Happy Homes will use network 10.0.0.0 with Network Address Translation (NAT) to reach the Internet. The design document calls for the following IP address scheme:

```
10.Building.VLAN.Node
```

The subnet mask will be /24 (or 255.255.255.0) for all links. For example, the thirtieth address on the Sales VLAN in Building 1 would be 10.1.11.30. Because HSRP will be in use, three node addresses are reserved for routers on each subnet. The .1 node address is reserved for the shared HSRP address, whereas .2 and .3 will be used for the real addresses associated with each router (.1 will be the default gateway address used by the end users).

This scheme results in the IP subnets presented in Table 17-2.

Table 17-2 *IP Subnets for Design 1*

Use	Building	VLAN	Subnet
Management	1	10	10.1.10.0
Sales	1	11	10.1.11.0
Marketing	1	12	10.1.12.0
Engineering	1	13	10.1.13.0
Finance	1	14	10.1.14.0
Management	2	20	10.2.20.0
Sales	2	21	10.2.21.0
Marketing	2	22	10.2.22.0
Engineering	2	23	10.2.23.0
Finance	2	24	10.2.24.0
Server Farm	N/A	100	10.100.100.0
Backbone	N/A	250	10.250.250.0

NOTE The server farm is listed with a building of N/A because it has its own addressing space that falls outside the 10.*Building*.*VLAN*.*Node* convention. This is also true because it will originally be located in basement of Building 1 and later be relocated to a separate building.

Happy Homes would like to start using DHCP in the new network. The first 20 addresses on each segment will be reserved for devices that do not (or should not) utilize DHCP such as printers, servers, and router addresses. The remaining addresses in each subnet will be divided between a pair of DHCP servers for redundancy. For example, the Marketing subnet in Building 1 will have two DHCP scopes: the first DHCP server will be configured with 10.1.12.21–10.1.12.137, and the second server will receive 10.1.12.138–10.1.12.254. Therefore, if the first DHCP server fails, the second server will have its own block of unique address for every subnet.

| **NOTE** | DHCP scopes are typically split in this fashion because the DHCP protocol currently does not specify a mechanism for server-to-server communication. For example, if the scopes did overlap and one of the servers failed, the second server would have no way of knowing what new leases were issued while it was down. Therefore, it might try to issue the same IP address again and create a duplicate IP address problem. Future enhancements to the DHCP standards (as well as proprietary DHCP implementations) can be used to avoid this problem. See Chapter 11 for more information on using DHCP. |

IPX Addressing

Although Happy Homes expects most new applications to be IP based, it currently makes extensive use of Novell servers and the IPX protocol. For consistency, the design recommends that the IPX network numbers should be based on the IP subnet values. IPX network numbers are 32 bits in length, the same as a full IP address. Therefore, IP subnets can be converted from the usual dotted quad notation to an eight-character hex value suitable for use as an IPX network number. For example, the Sales VLAN in Building 1 uses IP subnet 10.1.11.0. By converting each of these four decimal values into their hex equivalents, the corresponding IPX network number would be 0x0A010B00.

| **TIP** | For IPX internal network numbers on NetWare servers, the full IP address assigned to the server's NIC can be converted to hex. |

Table 17-3 presents the IPX addresses along with the corresponding IP subnet values.

Table 17-3 *IPX Network Addresses*

Use	Building	VLAN	IPX Network	Subnet
Management	1	10	0A010A00	10.1.10.0
Sales	1	11	0A010B00	10.1.11.0
Marketing	1	12	0A010C00	10.1.12.0
Engineering	1	13	0A010D00	10.1.13.0
Finance	1	14	0A010E00	10.1.14.0
Management	2	20	0A021400	10.2.20.0
Sales	2	21	0A021500	10.2.21.0
Marketing	2	22	0A021600	10.2.22.0
Engineering	2	23	0A021700	10.2.23.0
Finance	2	24	0A021800	10.2.24.0
Server Farm	N/A	100	0A646400	10.100.100.0
Backbone	250	250	0AFAFA00	10.250.250.0

VTP

To maximize the Layer 2-orientation of this design, the proposal calls for the use of VTP server mode. However, to avoid some of the scalability issues of VTP, each building will use a unique VTP domain. Two mechanisms will be used to partition the VTP traffic:

- The removal of VLAN 1 from the backbone
- Separate VTP domain names

Because the backbone utilizes LANE as a trunking technology, VLAN 1 can be removed from the core of the network by simply not creating a "default" ELAN that maps to VLAN 1 (note that VLAN 1 cannot be removed from Ethernet trunks). Because VTP traffic must be carried in VLAN 1, this action prevents VTP information from propagating between buildings. However, it is not advisable to rely only on this technique—if someone accidentally enabled VLAN 1 on the backbone, it could seriously corrupt the VTP information as discussed in the "VLAN Table Deletion" section of Chapter 12, "VLAN Trunking Protocol."

To prevent this sort of VTP database corruption between buildings, separate VTP domains should be employed (however, note that using anything other than VTP transparent mode still allows VLAN corruption to occur within a single building). Because Catalysts only exchange VTP information if their VTP domain names match, this creates an effective barrier for VTP. Design 1 calls for Building 1 to use the domain Happy-B1, whereas Building 2 uses Happy-B2.

By creating a VTP barrier, the use of unique VTP domain names in each building also modifies the Catalyst behavior to create a Layer 3 barrier at the edge of every building. Keep this technique in mind when you create your own campus designs.

Trunks

To enhance the stability and scalability of the network, Design 1 calls for several optimizations on trunk links. First, it recommends that manual configuration be used to override all speed, duplex, and trunk state negotiation protocols. Relying on autonegotiation of 10/100 Ethernet speed and duplex can lead to many frustrating hours of troubleshooting and network downtime. To avoid these issues, important trunk and server links should be hard-coded. End-station ports generally continue to use speed and duplex autonegotiation protocols to maximize freedom of movement in PC hardware deployment. Similarly, the trunk links have hard-coded trunk state information. By not relying on DISL and DTP negotiation, network stability can be improved.

Second, the design recommends that the trunk links be pruned of unnecessary VLANs. Because this can constrict unnecessary broadcast flooding, it can also be an important optimization in Layer 2-oriented networks. For example, broadcasts and multicasts for VLANs 22–24 are not flooded to Cat-B2-3A because it only participates in VLANs 20 and 21 (the management and sales departments VLANs). The need for pruning becomes even greater in very flat networks without the Layer 3 barriers of scalability that automatically reduce broadcast and multicast flooding.

Load Balancing

Because of the Layer 2-orientation of Design 1, Spanning Tree load balancing must be employed. As discussed in Chapter 7, the Root Bridge placement form of Spanning Tree load balancing is both effective and simple to configure and maintain. That is, if your topology supports it. One of the advantages of having the Layer 2 triangles employed by this design is that it easily facilitates this form of load balancing. For example, by making Cat-B1-0A the Root Bridge for VLAN 21, traffic in the B1_Sales VLAN automatically uses the left-hand riser link. Design 1 calls for the A MDF devices (Cat-B1-0A and Cat-B2-0A) to act as the Root Bridge for the traffic for the odd-numbered VLANS, whereas the B devices (Cat-B1-0B and Cat-B2-0B) handle the even-numbered VLANs.

To create a cohesive load balancing scheme, the Spanning Tree Root Bridge placement should be coordinated with HSRP. This can be done by using the HSRP **priority** command to alternate the active HSRP peer for odd and even VLANs.

Spanning Tree

In addition to Root Bridge placement, several other Spanning Tree parameters should be tuned in Design 1. Because the Layer 3 barrier in Design 1 limits Layer 2 connectivity to small triangles, the largest number of bridges that can exist between two end stations is three hops. For example, if the link between Cat-B1-1A and Cat-B1-0B failed, traffic flowing between an end station connected to Cat-B1-1A and the RSM in Cat-B1-0B would have to cross three Layer 2 switches (Cat-B1-1A, Cat-B1-0A, and Cat-B1-0B). This is illustrated in Figure 17-4 (note that the Catalyst backplane is being counted as a link here).

Figure 17-4 *Path from an End User to the RSM in Cat-B1-0B after a Link Failure*

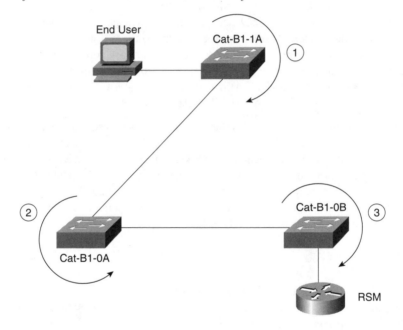

Therefore, the Spanning Tree Max Age and Forward Delay parameters can be safely reduced to 12 and 9 seconds, respectively (assuming the default Hello Time of 2 seconds). The safest and simplest way to accomplish this is to use the **set spantree root** macro to automatically modify the appropriate Spanning Tree parameters. As a result, convergence time can be reduced from a default of 30–50 seconds to 18–30 seconds.

To further speed Spanning Tree convergence, UplinkFast, BackboneFast, and PortFast can be implemented. UplinkFast is only configured on the IDF switches and can reduce failover of uplinks to less than 3 seconds. BackboneFast, if in use, must be enabled on every switch in a Layer 2 domain and can reduce convergence time of indirect failures to 18 seconds (given the Forward Delay of 9 seconds specified in the previous paragraph). Although PortFast is not helpful in the failure of trunk links, it can be a useful enhancement to allow end stations more immediate access to the network and reduce the impact of Spanning Tree Topology Change Notifications (see Chapter 6, "Understanding Spanning Tree," and Chapter 7 for more information on TCNs).

Configurations

This section presents sample configurations used for Design 1. Rather than include all of the configurations, you see an example of each type of device. First, you see an IDF/access layer switch. Next, you see coverage of the various components of an MDF/distribution layer switch: the Supervisor, the RSM module, and the LANE module. This section concludes with discussion of a configuration for one of the ATM switches in the core.

IDF Supervisor Configuration

Because Catalyst configurations are far less readable than IOS-based router configurations, two sections are devoted to coverage of Catalyst Supervisors. First, you see the interactive output of the necessary configuration steps. This allows you to focus only on the commands necessary for a typical MLS design. Second, you see the full Supervisor configuration. However, because Catalysts show *all* commands in the configuration listing (unlike the routers that only list *non-default* commands), these listings can be rather lengthy.

NOTE   Cisco is working on a feature that will only show non-default configuration commands. This should be available in the future.

Configuring an IDF Supervisor: Cat-B2-1A

The first floor switch in Building 2 (Cat-B2-1A) is a representative example of an IDF switch. To begin configuring this device, first assign a name as in Example 17-1.

Example 17-1   *Catalyst Name Configuration*

```
Console> (enable) set system name Cat-B2-1A
System name set.
Cat-B2-1A> (enable)
```

Early releases of code also required the **set prompt** command to include the name in the display prompt. However, starting in 4.X Catalyst images, this step is done automatically.

Next, create the VTP domain and add the appropriate VLANs as in Example 17-2.

Example 17-2   *VTP Configuration*

```
Cat-B2-1A> (enable) set vtp domain Happy-B2
VTP domain Happy-B2 modified
Cat-B2-1A> (enable) set vtp mode server
VTP domain Happy-B2 modified
Cat-B2-1A> (enable) set vlan 20 name B2_Management
Vlan 20 configuration successful
Cat-B2-1A> (enable) set vlan 21 name B2_Sales
Vlan 21 configuration successful
Cat-B2-1A> (enable) set vlan 22 name B2_Marketing
Vlan 22 configuration successful
Cat-B2-1A> (enable) set vlan 23 name B2_Engineering
Vlan 23 configuration successful
Cat-B2-1A> (enable) set vlan 24 name B2_Finance
Vlan 24 configuration successful
Cat-B2-1A> (enable) set vlan 250 name Backbone
Vlan 250 configuration successful
Cat-B2-1A> (enable)
```

Because Design 1 uses VTP server mode, the domain name must be set before the VLANs can be added. Although VTP defaults to server mode, the second command ensures that the default setting has not been changed.

Next, assign an IP address to the SC0 logical interface as in Example 17-3.

Example 17-3   *Catalyst Supervisor IP Address Configuration*

```
Cat-B2-1A> (enable) set interface sc0 20 10.2.20.9 255.255.255.0
Interface sc0 vlan set, IP address and netmask set.
Cat-B2-1A> (enable) set ip route default 10.2.20.1
Route added.
Cat-B2-1A> (enable)
```

Notice that SC0 is assigned to VLAN 20, the management VLAN for Building 2. Next, the **set ip route** command is used to provide a single default gateway for the Catalyst. 10.2.20.1 uses HSRP on the routers to provide redundancy (see the RSM section later).

Example 17-4 shows how to configure the Spanning-Tree Protocol for the IDF switch.

Example 17-4   *Spanning Tree Configuration*

```
Cat-B2-1A> (enable) set spantree portfast 3/1-24,4/1-24,5/1-24,6/1-24,7/1-24 enable

Warning: Spantree port fast start should only be enabled on ports connected
to a single host.  Connecting hubs, concentrators, switches, bridges, etc. to
a fast start port can cause temporary Spanning Tree loops.  Use with caution.

Spantree ports 3/1-24,4/1-24,5/1-24,6/1-24,7/1-24 fast start enabled.
Cat-B2-1A> (enable)
Cat-B2-1A> (enable) set spantree backbonefast enable
Backbonefast enabled for all VLANs
Cat-B2-1A> (enable)
Cat-B2-0B> (enable) set spantree uplinkfast enable
VLANs 1-1005 bridge priority set to 49152.
The port cost and portvlancost of all ports set to above 3000.
Station update rate set to 15 packets/100ms.
uplinkfast all-protocols field set to off.
uplinkfast enabled for bridge.
Cat-B2-1A> (enable)
```

The first command (**set spantree portfast**) enables PortFast on all of the end-user ports. Notice that trunk links are not included (you can set PortFast on trunk ports and it will be ignored, but it is best to avoid this because it can lead to administrative confusion). Next, BackboneFast is enabled (**set spantree backbonefast enable**) to improve STP convergence time associated with an indirect failure. As discussed in Chapter 7, this command must be enabled on every Catalyst in a Layer 2 domain. The last command (**set spantree uplinkfast enable**) enables UplinkFast. Unlike BackboneFast, UplinkFast should only be enabled on leaf-node IDF switches. You can also see that enabling UplinkFast automatically modifies several Spanning Tree parameters to reinforce this leaf-node behavior. First, it increases the Bridge Priority to 49,152 so that the current bridge does not become the Root Bridge (unless there are no other bridges available). Second, the Path Cost is increased to greater than 3000 to encourage downstream bridges to use some other path to the Root Bridge (however, if no path is available, this bridge handles the traffic normally).

Next, configure the trunk links as in Example 17-5.

Example 17-5   *Port Name and Trunk Configuration*

```
Cat-B2-1A> (enable) set port name 1/1 Gigabit link to Cat-B2-0A
Port 1/1 name set.
Cat-B2-1A> (enable) set port name 1/2 Spare gigabit port
Port 1/2 name set.
Cat-B2-1A> (enable) set port name 2/1 Gigabit link to Cat-B2-0B
Port 2/1 name set.
Cat-B2-1A> (enable) set port name 2/2 Spare gigabit port
Port 2/2 name set.
Cat-B2-1A> (enable)
Cat-B2-1A> (enable)
Cat-B2-1A> (enable) set trunk 1/1 on isl
Port(s) 1/1 trunk mode set to on.
Port(s) 1/1 trunk type set to isl.
Cat-B2-1A> (enable) clear trunk 1/1 2-19,25-1005
Removing Vlan(s) 2-19,25-1005 from allowed list.
Port 1/1 allowed vlans modified to 1,20-24.
Cat-B2-1A> (enable)
Cat-B2-1A> (enable) set trunk 2/1 on isl
Port(s) 2/1 trunk mode set to on.
Port(s) 2/1 trunk type set to isl.
Cat-B2-1A> (enable) clear trunk 2/1 2-19,25-1005
Removing Vlan(s) 2-19,25-1005 from allowed list.
Port 2/1 allowed vlans modified to 1,20-24.
Cat-B2-1A> (enable)
```

The first four commands assign a name to the trunk ports, useful information when trying to troubleshoot and maintain the network. Next, the 1/1 and 2/1 ports are forced into ISL trunking mode with the **set trunk** command. If you know that a port is going to be a trunk, it is best to hard-code the trunking state rather than rely on the **auto** and **negotiate** settings (these mechanisms have been known to fail and also require that the VTP domain names match). Finally, the **clear trunk** command is used to remove unnecessary VLANs from the 1/1 and 1/2 links. This sort of pruning can significantly improve the scalability of your network.

The code in Example 17-6 sets up passwords in the form of SNMP community strings and login passwords.

Example 17-6   *SNMP and Password Configuration*

```
Cat-B2-1A> (enable) set snmp community read-only lesspublic
SNMP read-only community string set to 'lesspublic'.
Cat-B2-1A> (enable) set snmp community read-write moreprivate
SNMP read-write community string set to 'moreprivate'.
Cat-B2-1A> (enable) set snmp community read-write-all mostprivate
SNMP read-write-all community string set to 'mostprivate'.
Cat-B2-1A> (enable)
Cat-B2-1A> (enable) set password
Enter old password:
Enter new password:
Retype new password:
Password changed.
Cat-B2-1A> (enable)
Cat-B2-1A> (enable) set enablepass
Enter old password:
Enter new password:
Retype new password:
Password changed.
Cat-B2-1A> (enable)
```

Because SNMP is enabled by default with widely known community strings ("public", "private", and "secret"), you should always modify the SNMP community strings. Do not forget to modify all three. (Most devices only use two community strings, one for reading and one for writing. Catalysts have a third community string that also allows the community strings themselves to be modified.) Finally, because community strings are not encrypted (either in the configuration or as they travel through the network), it is best to make them different than the console/Telnet login passwords.

The bottom section of the Example 17-6 sets both the user and privileged passwords. Unlike Cisco routers that do not allow any remote access until passwords have been configured, Catalysts allow full access by default. Therefore, always remember to change the passwords.

Next, you need to configure a variety of management commands as in Example 17-7.

Example 17-7 *Banner, Contact Information, and DNS Configuration*

```
Cat-B2-1A> (enable)
Cat-B2-1A> (enable) set banner motd ~PRIVATE NETWORK -- HACKERS WILL BE SHOT!!~
MOTD banner set
Cat-B2-1A> (enable) set system location Building 2 First Floor
System location set.
Cat-B2-1A> (enable) set system contact Joe x111
System contact set.
Cat-B2-1A> (enable)
Cat-B2-1A> (enable) set ip dns enable
DNS is enabled
Cat-B2-1A> (enable) set ip dns domain happy.com
Default DNS domain name set to happy.com
Cat-B2-1A> (enable) set ip dns server 10.100.100.42
10.100.100.42 added to DNS server table as primary server.
Cat-B2-1A> (enable) set ip dns server 10.100.100.68
10.100.100.68 added to DNS server table as backup server.
Cat-B2-1A> (enable)
```

Although none of the commands in Example 17-7 are essential for Catalyst operation, they can all be useful when maintaining a network over the long term.

Example 17-8 creates an IP permit list to limit Telnet access to the device.

Example 17-8 *IP Permit List to Limit Telnet Access to the Catalyst*

```
Cat-B2-1A> (enable) set ip permit enable
IP permit list enabled.
WARNING!! IP permit list has no entries.
Cat-B2-1A> (enable) set ip permit 10.100.100.0 255.255.255.0
10.100.100.0 with mask 255.255.255.0 added to IP permit list.
Cat-B2-1A> (enable)
```

Because Design 1 calls for Supervisor IIIs with NetFlow Feature Cards (NFFCs), useful IDF features such as IGMP Snooping (to reduce multicast flooding) and Protocol Filtering (to reduce broadcast flooding) can be enabled as in Example 17-9.

Example 17-9 *Enabling IGMP Snooping and Protocol Filtering*

```
Cat-B2-1A> (enable) set igmp enable
IGMP feature for IP multicast enabled
Cat-B2-1A> (enable)
Cat-B2-1A> (enable) set protocolfilter enable
Protocol filtering enabled on this switch.
Cat-B2-1A> (enable)
```

Next, you need to provide a variety of SNMP traps as in Example 17-10.

Example 17-10 *SNMP Trap Configuration*

```
Cat-B2-1A> (enable) set snmp trap 10.100.100.21 trapped
SNMP trap receiver added.
Cat-B2-1A> (enable) set snmp trap enable module
SNMP module traps enabled.
Cat-B2-1A> (enable) set snmp trap enable chassis
SNMP chassis alarm traps enabled.
Cat-B2-1A> (enable) set snmp trap enable bridge
SNMP bridge traps enabled.
Cat-B2-1A> (enable) set snmp trap enable auth
SNMP authentication traps enabled.
Cat-B2-1A> (enable) set snmp trap enable stpx
SNMP STPX  traps enabled.
Cat-B2-1A> (enable) set snmp trap enable config
SNMP CONFIG traps enabled.
Cat-B2-1A> (enable) set port trap 1/1 enable
Port 1/1 up/down trap enabled.
Cat-B2-1A> (enable) set port trap 2/1 enable
Port 2/1 up/down trap enabled.
Cat-B2-1A> (enable)
```

Enabling SNMP traps cause the Catalyst to report to 10.100.100.21 information it detects related to issues such as Spanning Tree changes, device resets, and hardware failures. Link up/down traps are enabled for the important uplink ports (because of the potential volume of data, it is almost always best *not* to enable this on end-station ports).

Finally, the commands in Example 17-11 configure the Catalyst to send Syslog information to the network management station.

Example 17-11 *Syslog Configuration*

```
Cat-B2-1A> (enable) set logging server enable
System logging messages will be sent to the configured syslog servers.
Cat-B2-1A> (enable) set logging server 10.100.100.21
10.100.100.21 added to System logging server table.
Cat-B2-1A> (enable)
```

Full IDF Supervisor Listing: Cat-B2-1A

Example 17-12 presents the full configuration file that results for Cat-B2-1A after the previous sequence of configuration steps is completed.

Example 17-12 *Full Catalyst Configuration for Cat-B2-1A*

```
begin
!
set password $1$FMFQ$HfZR5DUszVHIRhrz4h6V70
set enablepass $1$FMFQ$HfZR5DUszVHIRhrz4h6V70
set prompt Cat-B2-1A>
set length 24 default
set logout 20
set banner motd ^CPRIVATE NETWORK -- HACKERS WILL BE SHOT!!^C
!
#system
set system baud  9600
set system modem disable
set system name  Cat-B2-1A
set system location Building 2 First Floor
set system contact  Joe x111
!
#snmp
set snmp community read-only       lesspublic
set snmp community read-write      moreprivate
set snmp community read-write-all mostprivate
set snmp rmon disable
set snmp trap enable  module
set snmp trap enable  chassis
set snmp trap enable  bridge
set snmp trap disable repeater
set snmp trap disable vtp
set snmp trap enable  auth
set snmp trap disable ippermit
set snmp trap disable vmps
set snmp trap disable entity
set snmp trap enable  config
set snmp trap enable  stpx
set snmp trap disable syslog
set snmp extendedrmon vlanmode disable
set snmp extendedrmon vlanagent disable
set snmp extendedrmon enable
set snmp trap 10.100.100.21    trapped
!
#ip
set interface sc0 20 10.2.20.9 255.255.255.0 10.2.20.255

set interface sc0 up
set interface sl0 0.0.0.0 0.0.0.0
set interface sl0 up
set arp agingtime 1200
set ip redirect    enable
set ip unreachable    enable
set ip fragmentation enable
set ip route 0.0.0.0          10.2.20.1     1
set ip alias default         0.0.0.0
!
#Command alias
```

Example 17-12   *Full Catalyst Configuration for Cat-B2-1A (Continued)*

```
!
#vmps
set vmps server retry 3
set vmps server reconfirminterval 60
set vmps tftpserver 0.0.0.0 vmps-config-database.1
set vmps state disable


!
#dns
set ip dns server 10.100.100.42 primary
set ip dns server 10.100.100.68
set ip dns enable
set ip dns domain happy.com
!
#tacacs+
set tacacs attempts 3
set tacacs directedrequest disable
set tacacs timeout 5
!
#authentication
set authentication login tacacs disable console
set authentication login tacacs disable telnet
set authentication enable tacacs disable console
set authentication enable tacacs disable telnet
set authentication login local enable console
set authentication login local enable telnet
set authentication enable local enable console
set authentication enable local enable telnet
!
#bridge
set bridge ipx snaptoether     8023raw
set bridge ipx 8022toether     8023
set bridge ipx 8023rawtofddi snap
!
#vtp
set vtp domain Happy-B2
set vtp mode server
set vtp v2 disable
set vtp pruning disable
set vtp pruneeligible 2-1000
clear vtp pruneeligible 1001-1005
set vlan 1 name default type ethernet mtu 1500 said 100001 state active
set vlan 20 name B2_Management type ethernet mtu 1500 said 100020 state active
set vlan 21 name B2_Sales type ethernet mtu 1500 said 100021 state active
set vlan 22 name B2_Marketing type ethernet mtu 1500 said 100022 state active
set vlan 23 name B2_Engineering type ethernet mtu 1500 said 100023 state active
set vlan 24 name B2_Finance type ethernet mtu 1500 said 100024 state active
set vlan 250 name Backbone type ethernet mtu 1500 said 100250 state active
set vlan 1002 name fddi-default type fddi mtu 1500 said 101002 state active
```

continues

Example 17-12 *Full Catalyst Configuration for Cat-B2-1A (Continued)*

```
set vlan 1004 name fddinet-default type fddinet mtu 1500 said 101004
  state active bridge 0x0 stp ieee
set vlan 1005 name trnet-default type trbrf mtu 1500 said 101005
  state active bridge 0x0 stp ibm
set vlan 1003 name token-ring-default type trcrf mtu 1500 said 101003
  state active parent 0 ring 0x0 mode srb aremaxhop 0 stemaxhop 0
set interface sc0 20 10.2.20.9 255.255.255.0 10.2.20.255


!
#spantree
#uplinkfast groups
set spantree uplinkfast enable
#backbonefast
set spantree backbonefast enable
set spantree enable  all
#vlan 1
set spantree fwddelay 15    1
set spantree hello    2     1
set spantree maxage   20    1
set spantree priority 32768 1
#vlan 20
set spantree fwddelay 15    20
set spantree hello    2     20
set spantree maxage   20    20
set spantree priority 32768 20
#vlan 21
set spantree fwddelay 15    21
set spantree hello    2     21
set spantree maxage   20    21
set spantree priority 32768 21
#vlan 22
set spantree fwddelay 15    22
set spantree hello    2     22
set spantree maxage   20    22
set spantree priority 32768 22
#vlan 23
set spantree fwddelay 15    23
set spantree hello    2     23
set spantree maxage   20    23
set spantree priority 32768 23
#vlan 24
set spantree fwddelay 15    24
set spantree hello    2     24
set spantree maxage   20    24
set spantree priority 32768 24
#vlan 250
set spantree fwddelay 15    250
set spantree hello    2     250
set spantree maxage   20    250
set spantree priority 32768 250
#vlan 1003
```

Example 17-12   *Full Catalyst Configuration for Cat-B2-1A (Continued)*

```
set spantree fwddelay 15    1003
set spantree hello    2     1003
set spantree maxage   20    1003
set spantree priority 32768 1003
set spantree portstate 1003 block 0
set spantree portcost 1003 62
set spantree portpri  1003 4
set spantree portfast 1003 disable
#vlan 1005
set spantree fwddelay 15    1005
set spantree hello    2     1005
set spantree maxage   20    1005
set spantree priority 32768 1005
set spantree multicast-address 1005 ieee
!
#cgmp
set cgmp disable
set cgmp leave disable
!
#syslog
set logging console enable
set logging server enable
set logging server 10.100.100.21
set logging level cdp 2 default
set logging level mcast 2 default
set logging level dtp 5 default
set logging level dvlan 2 default
set logging level earl 2 default
set logging level fddi 2 default
set logging level ip 2 default
set logging level pruning 2 default
set logging level snmp 2 default
set logging level spantree 2 default
set logging level sys 5 default
set logging level tac 2 default
set logging level tcp 2 default
set logging level telnet 2 default
set logging level tftp 2 default
set logging level vtp 2 default
set logging level vmps 2 default
set logging level kernel 2 default
set logging level filesys 2 default
set logging level drip 2 default
set logging level pagp 5 default
set logging level mgmt 5 default
set logging level mls 5 default
set logging level protfilt 2 default
set logging level security 2 default
set logging server facility LOCAL7
```

continues

Example 17-12 *Full Catalyst Configuration for Cat-B2-1A (Continued)*

```
set logging server severity 4
set logging buffer 500
set logging timestamp disable
!
#ntp
set ntp broadcastclient disable
set ntp broadcastdelay 3000
set ntp client disable
clear timezone
set summertime disable
!
#set boot command
set boot config-register 0x10f
set boot system flash bootflash:sup.bin
!
#permit list
set ip permit enable
set ip permit 10.100.100.0 255.255.255.0
!
#drip
set tokenring reduction enable
set tokenring distrib-crf disable
!
#igmp
set igmp enable
!
#protocolfilter
set protocolfilter enable
!
#mls
set mls enable
set mls flow destination
set mls agingtime 256
set mls agingtime fast 0 0
set mls nde disable
!
#standby ports
set standbyports enable
!
#module 1 : 2-port 1000BaseX Supervisor
set module name    1
set vlan 1     1/1-2
set port enable     1/1-2
set port level      1/1-2  normal
set port trap       1/1    enable
set port trap       1/2    disable
set port name       1/1    Gigabit link to Cat-B2-0A
set port name       1/2    Spare gigabit port
set port security   1/1-2  disable
set port broadcast  1/1-2  100%
set port membership 1/1-2  static
set port protocol 1/1-2 ip on
```

Example 17-12   *Full Catalyst Configuration for Cat-B2-1A (Continued)*

```
set port protocol 1/1-2 ipx auto
set cdp enable    1/1-2
set cdp interval 1/1-2 60
clear trunk 1/1  2-19,25-1005
set trunk 1/1  on isl 1,20-24
set trunk 1/2  auto isl 1-1005
set spantree portfast    1/1-2 disable
set spantree portcost    1/1-2  4
set spantree portpri     1/1-2  32
set spantree portvlanpri 1/1  0
set spantree portvlanpri 1/2  0
set spantree portvlancost 1/1  cost 3
set spantree portvlancost 1/2  cost 3
!
#module 2 : 2-port 1000BaseX Supervisor
set module name    2
set vlan 1    2/1-2
set port enable    2/1-2
set port level     2/1-2  normal
set port trap      2/1    enable
set port trap      2/2    disable
set port name      1/1    Gigabit link to Cat-B2-0B
set port name      1/2    Spare gigabit port
set port security  2/1-2  disable
set port broadcast 2/1-2  100%
set port membership 2/1-2  static
set port protocol 2/1-2 ip on
set port protocol 2/1-2 ipx auto
set cdp enable    2/1-2
set cdp interval 2/1-2 60
clear trunk 2/1  2-19,25-1005
set trunk 2/1  on isl 1,20-24
set trunk 2/2  auto isl 1-1005
set spantree portfast    2/1-2 disable
set spantree portcost    2/1-2  4
set spantree portpri     2/1-2  32
set spantree portvlanpri 2/1  0
set spantree portvlanpri 2/2  0
set spantree portvlancost 2/1  cost 3
set spantree portvlancost 2/2  cost 3
!
#module 3 : 24-port 10/100BaseTX Ethernet
set module name    3
set module enable  3
set vlan 23    3/1-24
set port enable    3/1-24
set port level     3/1-24  normal
set port speed     3/1-24  auto
set port trap      3/1-24  disable
set port name      3/1-24
```

continues

Example 17-12 *Full Catalyst Configuration for Cat-B2-1A (Continued)*

```
set port security    3/1-24  disable
set port broadcast   3/1-24  0
set port membership 3/1-24   static
set port protocol 3/1-24 ip on
set port protocol 3/1-24 ipx auto
set cdp enable    3/1-24
set cdp interval 3/1-24 60
set spantree portfast    3/1-24 enable
set spantree portcost    3/1-24  100
set spantree portpri     3/1-24  32
!
#module 4 : 24-port 10/100BaseTX Ethernet
set module name    4
set module enable  4
set vlan 23     4/1-24
set port enable    4/1-24
set port level     4/1-24   normal
set port speed     4/1-24   auto
set port trap      4/1-24   disable
set port name      4/1-24
set port security    4/1-24  disable
set port broadcast   4/1-24  0
set port membership 4/1-24   static
set port protocol 4/1-24 ip on
set port protocol 4/1-24 ipx auto
set cdp enable    4/1-24
set cdp interval 4/1-24 60
set spantree portfast    4/1-24 enable
set spantree portcost    4/1-24  100
set spantree portpri     4/1-24  32
!
#module 5 : 24-port 10/100BaseTX Ethernet
set module name    5
set module enable  5
set vlan 23     5/1-24
set port enable    5/1-24
set port level     5/1-24   normal
set port speed     5/1-24   auto
set port trap      5/1-24   disable
set port name      5/1-24
set port security    5/1-24  disable
set port broadcast   5/1-24  0
set port membership 5/1-24   static
set port protocol 5/1-24 ip on
set port protocol 5/1-24 ipx auto
set cdp enable    5/1-24
set cdp interval 5/1-24 60
set spantree portfast    5/1-24 enable
set spantree portcost    5/1-24  100
set spantree portpri     5/1-24  32
!
#module 6 : 24-port 10/100BaseTX Ethernet
```

Example 17-12 *Full Catalyst Configuration for Cat-B2-1A (Continued)*

```
set module name    6
set module enable  6
set vlan 23     6/1-24
set port enable      6/1-24
set port level       6/1-24  normal
set port speed       6/1-24  auto
set port trap        6/1-24  disable
set port name        5/1-24
set port security    6/1-24  disable
set port broadcast  6/1-24  0
set port membership 6/1-24  static
set port protocol 6/1-24 ip on
set port protocol 6/1-24 ipx auto
set cdp enable     6/1-24
set cdp interval 6/1-24 60
set spantree portfast     6/1-24 enable
set spantree portcost     6/1-24  100
set spantree portpri      6/1-24  32
!
#module 7 : 24-port 10/100BaseTX Ethernet
set module name    7
set module enable  7
set vlan 23     7/1-24
set port enable      7/1-24
set port level       7/1-24  normal
set port speed       7/1-24  auto
set port trap        7/1-24  disable
set port name        5/1-24
set port security    7/1-24  disable
set port broadcast  7/1-24  0
set port membership 7/1-24  static
set port protocol 7/1-24 ip on
set port protocol 7/1-24 ipx auto
set cdp enable     7/1-24
set cdp interval 7/1-24 60
set spantree portfast     7/1-24 enable
set spantree portcost     7/1-24  100
set spantree portpri      7/1-24  32
!
#module 8 empty
!
#module 9 empty
!
#switch port analyzer
!set span 1 1/1 both inpkts disable
set span disable
!
#cam
set cam agingtime 1,20-24,250,1003,1005 300
end
```

MDF Supervisor Configuration

The second switch in Building 2 (Cat-B2-0B) is a representative example of an MDF/ distribution layer switch. As with the IDF/access layer switch, the Supervisor configuration is presented in two sections: one showing the interactive configuration steps and another showing the resulting complete listing.

Configuring an MDF Supervisor: Cat-B2-0B

As with the IDF switch, the name, VTP, and SC0 parameters are configured as in Example 17-13.

Example 17-13   *Configuring the Catalyst Name, VTP, and IP Address Parameters*

```
Console> (enable) set system name Cat-B2-0B
System name set.
Cat-B2-0B> (enable) set vtp domain Happy-B2
VTP domain Happy-B2 modified
Cat-B2-0B> (enable) set vtp mode server
VTP domain Happy-B2 modified
Cat-B2-0B> (enable)
Cat-B2-0B> (enable) set interface sc0 20 10.2.20.8 255.255.255.0
Interface sc0 vlan set, IP address and netmask set.
Cat-B2-0B> (enable) set ip route default 10.2.20.1
Route added.
Cat-B2-0B> (enable)
```

Notice that because VTP server mode is in use, the VLANs do not need to be manually added to this switch. In fact, assuming that the Supervisor contained an empty configuration, Cat-B2-0B would have also automatically learned the VTP domain name (making the **set vtp domain Happy-B2** command optional). Because all of the devices in Building 2 share a single management VLAN, Cat-B2-0B receives an IP address for the same IP subnet and uses the same default gateway address.

Next, you need to modify the Spanning Tree parameters as in Example 17-14.

Example 17-14 *Spanning Tree Configuration*

```
Cat-B2-0B> (enable) set spantree root 20 dia 3 hello 2
VLAN 20 bridge priority set to 8192.
VLAN 20 bridge max aging time set to 12.
VLAN 20 bridge hello time set to 2.
VLAN 20 bridge forward delay set to 9.
Cat-B2-0B> (enable)
Cat-B2-0B> (enable) set spantree root secondary 21 dia 3 hello 2
VLAN 21 bridge priority set to 16384.
VLAN 21 bridge max aging time set to 12.
VLAN 21 bridge hello time set to 2.
VLAN 21 bridge forward delay set to 9.
Cat-B2-0B> (enable)
Cat-B2-0B> (enable) set spantree root 22 dia 3 hello 2
VLAN 22 bridge priority set to 8192.
VLAN 22 bridge max aging time set to 12.
VLAN 22 bridge hello time set to 2.
VLAN 22 bridge forward delay set to 9.
Switch is now the root switch for active VLAN 22.
Cat-B2-0B> (enable)
Cat-B2-0B> (enable) set spantree root secondary 23 dia 3 hello 2
VLAN 23 bridge priority set to 16384.
VLAN 23 bridge max aging time set to 12.
VLAN 23 bridge hello time set to 2.
VLAN 23 bridge forward delay set to 9.
Cat-B2-0B> (enable)
Cat-B2-0B> (enable) set spantree root 24 dia 3 hello 2
VLAN 24 bridge priority set to 8192.
VLAN 24 bridge max aging time set to 12.
VLAN 24 bridge hello time set to 2.
VLAN 24 bridge forward delay set to 9.
Switch is now the root switch for active VLAN 24.
Cat-B2-0B> (enable)
Cat-B2-0B> (enable) set spantree root secondary 250 dia 3 hello 2
VLAN 250 bridge priority set to 16384.
VLAN 250 bridge max aging time set to 12.
VLAN 250 bridge hello time set to 2.
VLAN 250 bridge forward delay set to 9.
Switch is now the root switch for active VLAN 24.
Cat-B2-0B> (enable)
Cat-B2-0B> (enable)
Cat-B2-0B> (enable) set spantree portfast 6/1-12 enable

Warning: Spantree port fast start should only be enabled on ports connected
to a single host.  Connecting hubs, concentrators, switches, bridges, etc. to
a fast start port can cause temporary Spanning Tree loops.  Use with caution.

Spantree ports 6/1-12 fast start enabled.
Cat-B2-0B> (enable)
Cat-B2-0B> (enable) set spantree backbonefast enable
Backbonefast enabled for all VLANs
Cat-B2-0B> (enable)
```

To implement load balancing, the MDF switches require more Spanning Tree configuration than the IDF switches. The first six **set spantree root** commands configure Cat-B1-0B's portion of the Root Bridge placement for Building 2 (one command is required for each of the six VLANs in use). Notice that Cat-B2-0B is configured as the primary Root Bridge for the even-numbered VLANs (20, 22, and 24) and the secondary Root Bridge for the odd-numbered VLANs (21 and 23). Cat-B2-0A would have the opposite configuration for VLANs 20–24 (primary for odd VLANs and secondary for even VLANs). For VLAN 250, the backbone VLAN, Cat-B1-0A is configured as the primary Root Bridge (not shown here) with Cat-B2-0B as the secondary. This allows Cat-B2-0B to take over as the Root Bridge for the core in the event that connectivity is lost to Building 1.

PortFast is configured for all the ports on module six. In the event that some of the Building 2 servers are connected here using fault-tolerant NICs that toggle link state (most fault-tolerant NICs do not do this), this allows the NICs to quickly bring up the backup ports without waiting through the Spanning Tree Listening and Learning states.

The last command enables BackboneFast (as discussed earlier, it must be enabled on all switches to work correctly). Finally, notice that UplinkFast is not enabled on the MDF switches. Doing so disturbs the Root Bridge placement carefully implemented with the earlier **set spantree root** command.

Example 17-15 shows how to configure the trunk ports.

Example 17-15   *Port and Trunk Configuration*

```
Cat-B2-0B> (enable) set port name 5/1 Gigabit link to Cat-B2-1A
Port 5/1 name set.
Cat-B2-0B> (enable) set port name 5/2 Gigabit link to Cat-B2-2A
Port 5/2 name set.
Cat-B2-0B> (enable) set port name 5/3 Gigabit link to Cat-B2-0A
Port 5/3 name set.
Cat-B2-0B> (enable)
Cat-B2-0B> (enable) set port speed 1/1 100
Port(s) 1/1 speed set to 100Mbps.
Cat-B2-0B> (enable) set port duplex 1/1 full
Port(s) 1/1 set to full-duplex.
Cat-B2-0B> (enable) set port name 1/1 Link to Cat-B2-3A
Port 1/1 name set.
Cat-B2-0B> (enable)
Cat-B2-0B> (enable) set trunk 1/1 on isl
Port(s) 1/1 trunk mode set to on.
Port(s) 1/1 trunk type set to isl.
Cat-B2-0B> (enable) clear trunk 1/1 2-19,22-1005
Removing Vlan(s) 2-19,22-1005 from allowed list.
Port 1/1 allowed vlans modified to 1,20-21.
Cat-B2-0B> (enable)
Cat-B2-0B> (enable) set trunk 5/1 on isl
Port(s) 5/1 trunk mode set to on.
Port(s) 5/1 trunk type set to isl.
Cat-B2-0B> (enable) clear trunk 5/1 2-19,25-1005
```

Example 17-15 *Port and Trunk Configuration (Continued)*

```
Removing Vlan(s) 2-19,25-1005 from allowed list.
Port 5/1 allowed vlans modified to 1,20-24.
Cat-B2-0B> (enable)
Cat-B2-0B> (enable) set trunk 5/2 on isl
Port(s) 5/2 trunk mode set to on.
Port(s) 5/2 trunk type set to isl.
Cat-B2-0B> (enable) clear trunk 5/2 2-19,25-1005
Removing Vlan(s) 2-19,25-1005 from allowed list.
Port 5/2 allowed vlans modified to 1,20-24.
Cat-B2-0B> (enable) set trunk 5/3 on isl
Port(s) 5/3 trunk mode set to on.
Port(s) 5/3 trunk type set to isl.
Cat-B2-0B> (enable) clear trunk 5/2 2-19,25-1005
Removing Vlan(s) 2-19,25-1005 from allowed list.
Port 5/3 allowed vlans modified to 1,20-24.
Cat-B2-0B> (enable)
```

As with the IDF switch, the ports are labeled with names and hard-coded to be ISL trunks. The 10/100 Supervisor connection to Cat-B2-3A is also hard-coded to 100 Mbps and full-duplex. The Gigabit Ethernet links to Cat-B2-1A and Cat-B2-2A do not require this step because the 3-port Gigabit Ethernet Catalyst 5000 module are fixed at 1000 Mbps and full-duplex.

The **clear trunk** command manually prunes VLANs from the trunk links. Because the Catalyst on the third floor will only contain ports in the Sales VLAN, all VLANs except 20 and 21 have been removed from the 1/1 uplink. Happy Homes is less certain about the location of employees on the first two floors of Building 2. Although the immediate plans call for engineering to be located on the first floor and for finance and marketing to share the second floor, the company knows that there will be a large amount of movement between these floors for the next two years. As a result, both Cat-B2-1A and Cat-B2-2A will be configured with all four end-user VLANs. However, other VLANs (2–19 and 25–1005) have still been pruned.

TIP   When manually pruning VLANs, be careful not to prune the Management VLAN. If you do, Telnet, SNMP, and other IP-based communication with Supervisor are not possible. If you are using VLAN 1 for the Management VLAN, this is not an issue because VLAN 1 cannot be cleared from a trunk link.

It is important to notice that the backbone VLAN, VLAN 250, has been excluded from every link within the building, including the link between the two MDF switches (Port 5/3 on Cat-B2-0B). In other words, the only port configured for VLAN 250 on the four MDF switches should be the ATM link into the campus core. By doing this, it guarantees a loop-free core with more deterministic and faster converging traffic flows as discussed in the section "Make Layer 2 Cores Loop Free" in Chapter 15.

TIP	When using a Layer 2 core, be sure to remove the core VLAN from all links within each distribution block.

The commands in Example 17-16 complete the configuration and are almost identical to the IDF configuration discussed with Examples 17-6 through 17-11.

Example 17-16 *Configuring Passwords, Banner, System Information, DNS, IP Permit List, IGMP Snooping, SNMP, and Syslog*

```
Cat-B2-0B> (enable)
Cat-B2-0B> (enable) set password
Enter old password:
Enter new password:
Retype new password:
Password changed.
Cat-B2-0B> (enable)
Cat-B2-0B> (enable) set enablepass
Enter old password:
Enter new password:
Retype new password:
Password changed.
Cat-B2-0B> (enable)
Cat-B2-0B> (enable)
Cat-B2-0B> (enable) set banner motd ~PRIVATE NETWORK -- HACKERS WILL BE SHOT!!~
MOTD banner set
Cat-B2-0B> (enable) set system location Building 2 MDF
System location set.
Cat-B2-0B> (enable) set system contact Joe x111
System contact set.
Cat-B2-0B> (enable)
Cat-B2-0B> (enable) set ip dns enable
DNS is enabled
Cat-B2-0B> (enable) set ip dns domain happy.com
Default DNS domain name set to happy.com
Cat-B2-0B> (enable) set ip dns server 10.100.100.42
10.100.100.42 added to DNS server table as primary server.
Cat-B2-0B> (enable) set ip dns server 10.100.100.68
10.100.100.68 added to DNS server table as backup server.
Cat-B2-0B> (enable)
Cat-B2-0B> (enable) set ip permit enable
IP permit list enabled.
WARNING!! IP permit list has no entries.
Cat-B2-0B> (enable) set ip permit 10.100.100.0 255.255.255.0
10.100.100.0 with mask 255.255.255.0 added to IP permit list.
Cat-B2-0B> (enable)
Cat-B2-0B> (enable)
Cat-B2-0B> (enable) set igmp enable
IGMP feature for IP multicast enabled
Cat-B2-0B> (enable)
```

Example 17-16   *Configuring Passwords, Banner, System Information, DNS, IP Permit List, IGMP Snooping, SNMP, and Syslog (Continued)*

```
Cat-B2-0B> (enable)
Cat-B2-0B> (enable) set snmp community read-only lesspublic
SNMP read-only community string set to 'lesspublic'.
Cat-B2-0B> (enable) set snmp community read-write moreprivate
SNMP read-write community string set to 'moreprivate'.
Cat-B2-0B> (enable) set snmp community read-write-all mostprivate
SNMP read-write-all community string set to 'mostprivate'.
Cat-B2-0B> (enable)
Cat-B2-0B> (enable) set snmp trap 10.100.100.21 trapped
SNMP trap receiver added.
Cat-B2-0B> (enable) set snmp trap enable module
SNMP module traps enabled.
Cat-B2-0B> (enable) set snmp trap enable chassis
SNMP chassis alarm traps enabled.
Cat-B2-0B> (enable) set snmp trap enable bridge
SNMP bridge traps enabled.
Cat-B2-0B> (enable) set snmp trap enable auth
SNMP authentication traps enabled.
Cat-B2-0B> (enable) set snmp trap enable stpx
SNMP STPX  traps enabled.
Cat-B2-0B> (enable) set snmp trap enable config
SNMP CONFIG traps enabled.
Cat-B2-0B> (enable) set port trap 1/1 enable
Port 1/1 up/down trap enabled.
Cat-B2-0B> (enable) set port trap 5/1 enable
Port 5/1 up/down trap enabled.
Cat-B2-0B> (enable) set port trap 5/2 enable
Port 5/2 up/down trap enabled.
Cat-B2-0B> (enable)
Cat-B2-0B> (enable)
Cat-B2-0B> (enable) set logging server enable
System logging messages will be sent to the configured syslog servers.
Cat-B2-0B> (enable) set logging server 10.100.100.21
10.100.100.21 added to System logging server table.
Cat-B2-0B> (enable)
Cat-B2-0B> (enable)
```

The only significant difference between Examples 17-6 through 17-11 and Example 17-16 is that Protocol Filtering is not enabled.

Full MDF Supervisor Listing: Cat-B2-0B

Example 17-17 presents the full configuration listing for the Cat-B2-0B MDF switch configured in Examples 17-13 through 17-16.

Example 17-17 *Full Catalyst Configuration for Cat-B2-0B*

```
begin
!
set password $1$FMFQ$HfZR5DUszVHIRhrz4h6V70
set enablepass $1$FMFQ$HfZR5DUszVHIRhrz4h6V70
set prompt Cat-B2-0B>
set length 24 default
set logout 20
set banner motd ^CPRIVATE NETWORK -- HACKERS WILL BE SHOT!!^C
!
#system
set system baud  9600
set system modem disable
set system name  Cat-B2-0B
set system location Building 2 MDF
set system contact  Joe x111
!
#snmp
set snmp community read-only       lesspublic
set snmp community read-write      moreprivate
set snmp community read-write-all mostprivate
set snmp rmon disable
set snmp trap enable  module
set snmp trap enable  chassis
set snmp trap enable  bridge
set snmp trap disable repeater
set snmp trap disable vtp
set snmp trap enable  auth
set snmp trap disable ippermit
set snmp trap disable vmps
set snmp trap disable entity
set snmp trap enable  config
set snmp trap enable  stpx
set snmp trap disable syslog
set snmp extendedrmon vlanmode disable
set snmp extendedrmon vlanagent disable
set snmp extendedrmon enable
set snmp trap 10.100.100.21    trapped
!
#ip
set interface sc0 20 10.2.20.8 255.255.255.0 10.2.20.255

set interface sc0 up
set interface sl0 0.0.0.0 0.0.0.0
set interface sl0 up
set arp agingtime 1200
set ip redirect    enable
set ip unreachable    enable
set ip fragmentation enable
set ip route 0.0.0.0          10.2.20.1     1
set ip alias default          0.0.0.0
!
#Command alias
```

Example 17-17   *Full Catalyst Configuration for Cat-B2-0B (Continued)*

```
!
#vmps
set vmps server retry 3
set vmps server reconfirminterval 60
set vmps tftpserver 0.0.0.0 vmps-config-database.1
set vmps state disable
!
#dns
set ip dns server 10.100.100.42 primary
set ip dns server 10.100.100.68
set ip dns enable
set ip dns domain happy.com
!
#tacacs+
set tacacs attempts 3
set tacacs directedrequest disable
set tacacs timeout 5
!
#authentication
set authentication login tacacs disable console
set authentication login tacacs disable telnet
set authentication enable tacacs disable console
set authentication enable tacacs disable telnet
set authentication login local enable console
set authentication login local enable telnet
set authentication enable local enable console
set authentication enable local enable telnet
!
#bridge
set bridge ipx snaptoether    8023raw
set bridge ipx 8022toether    8023
set bridge ipx 8023rawtofddi snap
!
#vtp
set vtp domain Happy-B2
set vtp mode server
set vtp v2 disable
set vtp pruning disable
set vtp pruneeligible 2-1000
clear vtp pruneeligible 1001-1005
set vlan 1 name default type ethernet mtu 1500 said 100001 state active
set vlan 20 name B2_Management type ethernet mtu 1500 said 100020 state active
set vlan 21 name B2_Sales type ethernet mtu 1500 said 100021 state active
set vlan 22 name B2_Marketing type ethernet mtu 1500 said 100022 state active
set vlan 23 name B2_Engineering type ethernet mtu 1500 said 100023 state active
set vlan 24 name B2_Finance type ethernet mtu 1500 said 100024 state active
set vlan 250 name Backbone type ethernet mtu 1500 said 100250 state active
set vlan 1002 name fddi-default type fddi mtu 1500 said 101002 state active
set vlan 1004 name fddinet-default type fddinet mtu 1500 said 101004
```

continues

Example 17-17 *Full Catalyst Configuration for Cat-B2-0B (Continued)*

```
   state active bridge 0x0 stp ieee
set vlan 1005 name trnet-default type trbrf mtu 1500 said 101005
   state active bridge 0x0 stp ibm
set vlan 1003 name token-ring-default type trcrf mtu 1500 said 101003
   state active parent 0 ring 0x0 mode srb aremaxhop 0 stemaxhop 0
set interface sc0 20 10.2.20.8 255.255.255.0 10.2.20.255
!
#spantree
#uplinkfast groups
set spantree uplinkfast disable
#backbonefast
set spantree backbonefast enable
set spantree enable  all
#vlan 1
set spantree fwddelay 15   1
set spantree hello   2    1
set spantree maxage   20   1
set spantree priority 32768 1
#vlan 20
set spantree fwddelay 9     20
set spantree hello   2    20
set spantree maxage   12   20
set spantree priority 8192  20
#vlan 21
set spantree fwddelay 9     21
set spantree hello   2    21
set spantree maxage   12   21
set spantree priority 16384 21
#vlan 22
set spantree fwddelay 9     22
set spantree hello   2    22
set spantree maxage   12   22
set spantree priority 8192  22
#vlan 23
set spantree fwddelay 9     23
set spantree hello   2    23
set spantree maxage   12   23
set spantree priority 16384 23
#vlan 24
set spantree fwddelay 9     24
set spantree hello   2    24
set spantree maxage   12   24
set spantree priority 8192  24
#vlan 250
set spantree fwddelay 9     250
set spantree hello   2    250
set spantree maxage   12   250
set spantree priority 8192  250
#vlan 1003
set spantree fwddelay 15    1003
set spantree hello   2    1003
set spantree maxage   20   1003
```

Example 17-17   *Full Catalyst Configuration for Cat-B2-0B (Continued)*

```
set spantree priority 32768 1003
set spantree portstate 1003 block 0
set spantree portcost 1003 62
set spantree portpri  1003 4
set spantree portfast 1003 disable
#vlan 1005
set spantree fwddelay 15    1005
set spantree hello     2    1005
set spantree maxage    20   1005
set spantree priority 32768 1005
set spantree multicast-address 1005 ieee
!
#cgmp
set cgmp disable
set cgmp leave disable
!
#syslog
set logging console enable
set logging server enable
set logging server 10.100.100.21
set logging level cdp 2 default
set logging level mcast 2 default
set logging level dtp 5 default
set logging level dvlan 2 default
set logging level earl 2 default
set logging level fddi 2 default
set logging level ip 2 default
set logging level pruning 2 default
set logging level snmp 2 default
set logging level spantree 2 default
set logging level sys 5 default
set logging level tac 2 default
set logging level tcp 2 default
set logging level telnet 2 default
set logging level tftp 2 default
set logging level vtp 2 default
set logging level vmps 2 default
set logging level kernel 2 default
set logging level filesys 2 default
set logging level drip 2 default
set logging level pagp 5 default
set logging level mgmt 5 default
set logging level mls 5 default
set logging level protfilt 2 default
set logging level security 2 default
set logging server facility LOCAL7
set logging server severity 4
set logging buffer 500
set logging timestamp disable
```

continues

Example 17-17 *Full Catalyst Configuration for Cat-B2-0B (Continued)*

```
!
#ntp
set ntp broadcastclient disable
set ntp broadcastdelay 3000
set ntp client disable
clear timezone
set summertime disable
!
#set boot command
set boot config-register 0x10f
set boot system flash bootflash:sup.bin
!
#permit list
set ip permit enable
set ip permit 10.100.100.0 255.255.255.0
!
#drip
set tokenring reduction enable
set tokenring distrib-crf disable
!
#igmp
set igmp enable
!
#protocolfilter
set protocolfilter disable
!
#mls
set mls enable
set mls flow destination
set mls agingtime 256
set mls agingtime fast 0 0
set mls nde disable
!
#standby ports
set standbyports enable
!
#module 1 : 2-port 10/100BaseTX Supervisor
set module name    1
set vlan 1     1/1-2
set port channel 1/1-2 off
set port channel 1/1-2 auto
set port enable      1/1-2
set port level       1/1-2  normal
set port speed       1/1    100
set port speed       1/2    auto
set port trap        1/1    enable
set port trap        1/2    disable
set port name        1/1    Link to Cat-B2-3A
set port name        1/2
set port security    1/1-2  disable
set port broadcast   1/1-2  100%
set port membership 1/1-2   static
```

Example 17-17 *Full Catalyst Configuration for Cat-B2-0B (Continued)*

```
set port protocol 1/1-2 ip on
set port protocol 1/1-2 ipx auto
set cdp enable   1/1-2
set cdp interval 1/1-2 60
clear trunk 1/1  2-19,22-1005
set trunk 1/1  on isl 1,20-21
set trunk 1/2  auto isl 1-1005
set spantree portfast    1/1-2 disable
set spantree portcost    1/1-2  100
set spantree portpri     1/1-2  32
set spantree portvlanpri 1/1  0
set spantree portvlanpri 1/2  0
set spantree portvlancost 1/1  cost 99
set spantree portvlancost 1/2  cost 99
!
#module 2 : 2-port 10/100BaseTX Supervisor
set module name    2
set vlan 1    2/1-2
set port channel 2/1-2 off
set port channel 2/1-2 auto
set port enable    2/1-2
set port level     2/1-2  normal
set port speed     2/1-2  auto
set port trap      2/1-2  disable
set port name      2/1-2
set port security  2/1-2  disable
set port broadcast 2/1-2  100%
set port membership 2/1-2  static
set port protocol 2/1-2 ip on
set port protocol 2/1-2 ipx auto
set cdp enable   2/1-2
set cdp interval 2/1-2 60
set trunk 2/1  auto isl 1-1005
set trunk 2/2  auto isl 1-1005
set spantree portfast    2/1-2 disable
set spantree portcost    2/1-2  100
set spantree portpri     2/1-2  32
set spantree portvlanpri 2/1  0
set spantree portvlanpri 2/2  0
set spantree portvlancost 2/1  cost 99
set spantree portvlancost 2/2  cost 99
!
#module 3 : 2-port MM OC-12 Dual-Phy ATM
set module name    3
set port level     3/1  normal
set port name      3/1-2
set cdp enable   3/1
set cdp interval 3/1 60
set trunk 3/1  on lane 1-1005
set spantree portcost    3/1  14
```

continues

Example 17-17 *Full Catalyst Configuration for Cat-B2-0B (Continued)*

```
set spantree portpri     3/1  32
set spantree portvlanpri 3/1  0
set spantree portvlancost 3/1  cost 13
!
#module 4 : 1-port Route Switch
set module name    4
set port level       4/1   normal
set port trap        4/1   disable
set port name        4/1
set cdp enable   4/1
set cdp interval 4/1 60
set trunk 4/1  on isl 1-1005
set spantree portcost    4/1   5
set spantree portpri     4/1   32
set spantree portvlanpri 4/1   0
set spantree portvlancost 4/1  cost 4
!
#module 5 : 3-port 1000BaseX Ethernet
set module name    5
set module enable  5
set vlan 1     5/1-3
set port enable      5/1-3
set port level       5/1-3   normal
set port duplex      5/1-3   full
set port trap        5/1-2   enable
set port trap        5/3     disable
set port name        5/1     Gigabit link to Cat-B2-1A
set port name        5/2     Gigabit link to Cat-B2-2A
set port name        5/3     Spare gigabit port
set port security    5/1-3   disable
set port broadcast   5/1-3   100%
set port membership 5/1-3    static
set port protocol 5/1-3 ip on
set port protocol 5/1-3 ipx auto
set port negotiation 5/1-3 enable
set port flowcontrol send     5/1-3 desired
set port flowcontrol receive 5/1-3 off
set cdp enable   5/1-3
set cdp interval 5/1-3 60
clear trunk 5/1  2-19,25-1005
set trunk 5/1  on isl 1,20-24
clear trunk 5/2  2-19,25-1005
set trunk 5/2  on isl 1,20-24
set trunk 5/3  auto isl 1-1005
set spantree portfast    5/1-3 disable
set spantree portcost    5/1-3  4
set spantree portpri     5/1-3  32
set spantree portvlanpri 5/1  0
set spantree portvlanpri 5/2  0
set spantree portvlanpri 5/3  0
set spantree portvlancost 5/1  cost 3
set spantree portvlancost 5/2  cost 3
```

Example 17-17   *Full Catalyst Configuration for Cat-B2-0B (Continued)*

```
set spantree portvlancost 5/3  cost 3
!
#module 6 : 12-port 10/100BaseTX Ethernet
set module name    6
set module enable  6
set vlan 1    6/1-12
set port channel 6/1-4 off
set port channel 6/5-8 off
set port channel 6/9-12 off
set port channel 6/1-4 auto
set port channel 6/5-8 auto
set port channel 6/9-12 auto
set port enable      6/1-12
set port level       6/1-12  normal
set port speed       6/1-12  auto
set port trap        6/1-12  disable
set port name        6/1-12
set port security    6/1-12  disable
set port broadcast   6/1-12  0
set port membership 6/1-12   static
set port protocol 6/1-12 ip on
set port protocol 6/1-12 ipx auto
set cdp enable       6/1-12
set cdp interval 6/1-12 60
set trunk 6/1   auto isl 1-1005
set trunk 6/2   auto isl 1-1005
set trunk 6/3   auto isl 1-1005
set trunk 6/4   auto isl 1-1005
set trunk 6/5   auto isl 1-1005
set trunk 6/6   auto isl 1-1005
set trunk 6/7   auto isl 1-1005
set trunk 6/8   auto isl 1-1005
set trunk 6/9   auto isl 1-1005
set trunk 6/10 auto isl 1-1005
set trunk 6/11 auto isl 1-1005
set trunk 6/12 auto isl 1-1005
set spantree portfast     6/1-12 disable
set spantree portcost     6/1-12  100
set spantree portpri      6/1-12  32
set spantree portvlanpri 6/1  0
set spantree portvlanpri 6/2  0
set spantree portvlanpri 6/3  0
set spantree portvlanpri 6/4  0
set spantree portvlanpri 6/5  0
set spantree portvlanpri 6/6  0
set spantree portvlanpri 6/7  0
set spantree portvlanpri 6/8  0
set spantree portvlanpri 6/9  0
set spantree portvlanpri 6/10 0
```

continues

Example 17-17 *Full Catalyst Configuration for Cat-B2-0B (Continued)*

```
set spantree portvlanpri 6/11 0
set spantree portvlanpri 6/12 0
set spantree portvlancost 6/1  cost 99
set spantree portvlancost 6/2  cost 99
set spantree portvlancost 6/3  cost 99
set spantree portvlancost 6/4  cost 99
set spantree portvlancost 6/5  cost 99
set spantree portvlancost 6/6  cost 99
set spantree portvlancost 6/7  cost 99
set spantree portvlancost 6/8  cost 99
set spantree portvlancost 6/9  cost 99
set spantree portvlancost 6/10 cost 99
set spantree portvlancost 6/11 cost 99
set spantree portvlancost 6/12 cost 99
!
#module 7 empty
!
#module 8 empty
!
#module 9 empty
!
#module 10 empty
!
#module 11 empty
!
#module 12 empty
!
#module 13 empty
!
#switch port analyzer
!set span 1 1/1 both inpkts disable
set span disable
!
#cam
set cam agingtime 1,20-24,250,1003,1005 300
end
```

MDF RSM Configuration: Cat-B2-0B

To provide high-performance Layer 3 switching between each building and the campus backbone, the MDF/distribution layer switches are configured for MLS.

First, notice that no commands were required to enable MLS on the Supervisor in the previous section. As discussed in Chapter 11, a Supervisor located in the same chassis with an RSM requires no configuration to support MLS. However, if the design called for an external router-on-a-stick, the Supervisor would need to be configured with the IP address of the router.

Although using an RSM does eliminate the need for MLS configuration on the Supervisor, MLS must still be enabled on the RSM itself. Example 17-18 shows the required commands to enable MLS on the RSM.

Example 17-18 *Full RSM Configuration for Cat-B2-0B*

```
!
service timestamps log datetime localtime
service password-encryption
!
hostname Cat-B2-0B-RSM
!
enable secret 5 $1$JiA8$oFVSrScIZX2BnqDV/W9m11
!
ip domain-name happy.com
ip name-server 10.100.100.42
ip name-server 10.100.100.68
!
ipx routing 00e0.4fb3.68a0
mls rp ip
clock timezone EST -5
clock summer-time EDT recurring
!
interface Vlan20
 ip address 10.2.20.3 255.255.255.0
 ip helper-address 10.100.100.33
 ip helper-address 10.100.100.81
 no ip redirects
 mls rp vtp-domain Happy-B2
 mls rp management-interface
 mls rp ip
 ipx network 0A021400
 standby 20 priority 110
 standby 20 preempt
 standby 20 ip 10.2.20.1
 standby 20 track Vlan250 15
!
interface Vlan21
 ip address 10.2.21.3 255.255.255.0
 ip helper-address 10.100.100.33
 ip helper-address 10.100.100.81
 no ip redirects
 mls rp ip
 ipx network 0A021500
 standby 21 priority 100
 standby 21 preempt
 standby 21 ip 10.2.21.1
 standby 21 track Vlan250 15
!
interface Vlan22
 ip address 10.2.22.3 255.255.255.0
 ip helper-address 10.100.100.33
 ip helper-address 10.100.100.81
 no ip redirects
 mls rp ip
 ipx network 0A021600
```

continues

Example 17-18 *Full RSM Configuration for Cat-B2-0B (Continued)*

```
 standby 22 priority 110
 standby 22 preempt
 standby 22 ip 10.2.22.1
 standby 22 track Vlan250 15
!
interface Vlan23
 ip address 10.2.23.3 255.255.255.0
 ip helper-address 10.100.100.33
 ip helper-address 10.100.100.81
 no ip redirects
 mls rp ip
 ipx network 0A021700
 standby 23 priority 100
 standby 23 preempt
 standby 23 ip 10.2.23.1
 standby 23 track Vlan250 15
!
interface Vlan24
 ip address 10.2.24.3 255.255.255.0
 ip helper-address 10.100.100.33
 ip helper-address 10.100.100.81
 no ip redirects
 mls rp ip
 ipx network 0A021800
 standby 24 priority 110
 standby 24 preempt
 standby 24 ip 10.2.24.1
 standby 24 track Vlan250 15
!
interface Vlan250
 ip address 10.250.250.4 255.255.255.0
 no ip redirects
 mls rp ip
 ipx network 0AFAFA00
!
router eigrp 131
 passive-interface Vlan20
 passive-interface Vlan21
 passive-interface Vlan22
 passive-interface Vlan23
 passive-interface Vlan24
 network 10.0.0.0
!
no ip classless
no ip forward-protocol udp netbios-ns
no ip forward-protocol udp netbios-dgm
!
logging 10.100.100.21
access-list 1 permit 10.100.100.0 0.0.0.255
!
snmp-server community lesspublic RO
snmp-server community moreprivate RW
```

Example 17-18 *Full RSM Configuration for Cat-B2-0B (Continued)*

```
snmp-server host 10.100.100.21 trapped
snmp-server location Building 2 MDF
snmp-server contact Joe x111
snmp-server enable traps config
banner motd ^CPRIVATE NETWORK -- HACKERS WILL BE SHOT!!^C
!
line con 0
 password 7 055A545C
line aux 0
 password 7 055A545C
line vty 0 4
 access-class 1 in
 password 7 055A545C
 login
!
end
```

Each VLAN interface has been configured with a separate HSRP group for default gateway redundancy with Cat-2B-0A. Because Happy Homes will require NetWare and IPX services for the foreseeable future, the RSM has been configured with IPX network addresses (notice that IPX automatically locates a new gateway when the primary fails [although a reboot might be required] and therefore does not require the support of a feature such as HSRP).

Each interface is also configured with a pair of **ip helper-address** commands to forward DHCP traffic to the Server Farm. If desired, a single **ip helper-address** could have been specified using the server farm subnet's broadcast address (10.100.100.255). Also notice the two **no ip forward-protocol udp** statements. These prevent the flooding of chatty NetBIOS over TCP/IP name resolution traffic, a potentially important enhancement in networks with large amounts of Microsoft-based end stations.

EIGRP has been configured as the IP routing protocol (IPX uses IPX RIP by default). Because EIGRP includes interfaces on a classful basis, the **passive-interface** command has been used to keep routing traffic off the IDF segments. Although this is not going to save much update traffic with a protocol such as EIGRP (in this case, it only prevents EIGRP hello packets from being sent), it prevents a large number of unnecessary EIGRP neighbor relationships (by default, there is one for every pair of routers in every VLAN). By reducing these peering relationships, you can improve the performance and stability of the routing protocol.

TIP Reducing unnecessary peering can be especially useful in the Catalyst 8500s where excessive control plane traffic can overwhelm the CPU. However, it is an important optimization for all VLAN-based router platforms.

The RSM has also been configured with many of the same management features as Catalyst Supervisors, including the following:

- SNMP community strings
- SNMP host and location information
- SNMP traps
- A message-of-the-day banner
- Passwords
- A VTY access-class to limit Telnet access from segments other than the Server Farm
- DNS
- Syslog logging
- Timestamps of logging information

MDF LANE Module Configuration: Cat-B2-0B

As you probably gathered from Chapter 9, "Trunking with LAN Emulation," the theory of LANE and ATM is fairly complex. However, a large part of that complexity is designed to make ATM as plug-and-play as possible. As a result, configuring most of the LANE components becomes a trivial exercise. For instance, the Example 17-19 shows the code for the LANE module in Cat-B2-0B.

Example 17-19 *Full LANE Module Configuration for Cat-B2-0B*

```
!
hostname Cat-B2-0B-LANE
!
!
interface ATM0
 atm preferred phy B
 atm pvc 1 0 5 qsaal
 atm pvc 2 0 16 ilmi
!
interface ATM0.250 multipoint
 lane server-bus ethernet Backbone
 lane client ethernet 250 Backbone
!
!
line con 0
line vty 0 4
 no login
!
end
```

Only five lines differ from the default configuration:

- The LANE module has been named with the **hostname** command.

- A multipoint subinterface was created for the Backbone ELAN.

- The LAN Emulation Server (LES) and Broadcast and Unknown Server (BUS) are created with the **lane server-bus** command.

- A LAN Emulation Client (LEC) is created with the **lane client** command.

- PHY B (PHY is short for Physical) is selected as the preferred port (the reason why is discussed in the next section).

LS1010 Configuration: LS1010-A

In general, ATM switches that fully support protocols such as ILMI and PNNI require virtually no configuration. However, because this design calls for the LS1010s to act as the LAN Emulation Configuration Servers (LECSs), the configuration is somewhat more involved. Example 17-20 shows the configuration for LS1010-A.

Example 17-20 *Full ATM Switch Configuration for LS1010-A*

```
!
no service pad
service password-encryption
!
hostname LS1010-A
!
enable secret 5 $1$JiA8$oFVSrScIZX2BnqDV/W9m11
!
ip domain-name happy.com
ip name-server 10.100.100.42
ip name-server 10.100.100.68
!
clock timezone EST -5
clock summer-time EDT recurring
!
!
atm lecs-address-default 47.0091.8100.0000.0010.11be.ac01.0010.11be.ac05.00 1
atm lecs-address-default 47.0091.8100.0000.0010.2962.e801.0010.2962.e805.00 2
atm address 47.0091.8100.0000.0010.11be.ac01.0010.11be.ac01.00
atm router pnni
 node 1 level 56 lowest
   redistribute atm-static
!
!
lane database Happy
```

continues

Example 17-20 *Full ATM Switch Configuration for LS1010-A (Continued)*

```
     name Backbone server-atm-address 47.009181000000000102962E801.001029075031.05
     name Backbone server-atm-address 47.009181000000001011BEAC01.00102941D031.05
     name Backbone server-atm-address 47.009181000000001011BEAC01.001029075031.05
     name Backbone server-atm-address 47.009181000000000102962E801.00102941D031.05
 !
 interface ATM0/0/0
  description OC-12 link to Cat-B1-0A
 !
 interface ATM0/1/0
  description OC-12 link to Cat-B1-0B
 !
 interface ATM1/0/0
  description OC-12 link to Cat-B2-0A
 !
 interface ATM1/1/0
  description OC-12 link to Cat-B2-0B
 !
 interface ATM2/0/0
  no ip address
  atm maxvp-number 0
  lane config auto-config-atm-address
  lane config database Happy
 !
 interface ATM2/0/0.1 multipoint
  description In band management channel to Backbone ELAN
  ip address 10.250.250.201 255.255.255.0
  lane client ethernet Backbone
 !
 interface Ethernet2/0/0
  description Out of band management channel to Bldb 1 Mtg VLAN
  ip address 10.1.10.201 255.255.255.0
 !
 interface ATM3/0/0
 !
  description OC-12 link to LS1010-B
 interface ATM3/1/0
 !
  description OC-12 spare
 no ip classless
 !
 logging 10.100.100.21
 !
 snmp-server community public RO
 snmp-server community private RW
 snmp-server host 10.100.100.21 trapped
 snmp-server location Backbone
 snmp-server contact Joe x111
 banner motd ^CPRIVATE NETWORK -- HACKERS WILL BE SHOT!!^C
 !
 line con 0
  password 7 055A545C
```

Example 17-20 *Full ATM Switch Configuration for LS1010-A (Continued)*

```
line aux 0
 password 7 055A545C
line vty 0 4
 password 7 055A545C
 login
!
end
```

Both of the LS1010s require four configuration items to support LANE under Design 1:

- The addresses of the LECSs (in this case, the LS1010s themselves) must be configured with the **atm lecs-address-default** command. Because the design calls for SSRP, both ATM switches are configured with two LECS addresses. See Chapter 9 for more information on SSRP.

- The LECS database. Again because of SSRP, there are two LES/BUS devices in use. Because both LES/BUSs are using dual-PHY connections to different ATM switches, a total of four different LES addresses are possible and must all be included in the database.

- The configuration on logical interface atm 2/0/0 (the ATM Switch Processor [ASP] itself) of the **lane config auto-config-atm-address** and **lane config database** commands to start the LECS process.

- The configuration on the logical subinterface atm 2/0/0.1 of a LANE client to provide an in-band management channel for the ATM switch.

In addition to the in-band management channel provided by the LEC located on interface atm 2/0/0.1, an additional connection is provided for occasions where the ATM network is down. One way to accomplish this is to provide a modem on the AUX port of the ASP. However, in campus networks, it is often more effective to utilize the ASP's Ethernet management port. In this case, the port is configured with an IP address on the Building 1 Management VLAN and then connected to a 10/100 port on Cat-B1-0B.

The order of the statements in the LECS database deserves special notice. Figure 17-5 shows a detailed view of the ATM links specified in Design 1.

Figure 17-5 *Detailed View of ATM Links*

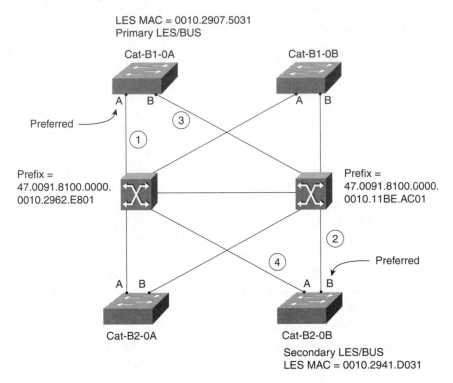

Recall from Chapter 9 that careful planning of the order of LECS database can avoid unnecessary backtracking. Because Cat-B1-0A is the primary LES/BUS and is configured with PHY A as its preferred port, the combination of LS1010-A's prefix and Cat-B1-0A's ESI is listed first in the database. If this port fails, it takes 10 or more seconds for Cat-B1-0A's PHY B to become active, making it a poor choice for the secondary LES. Because Cat-B2-0B's preferred port, PHY B, should already be fully active, it is more efficient as a secondary LES address. If Cat-B2-0B's PHY B fails, the tertiary LES address can be Cat-B1-0A's PHY B. As a last resort, Cat-B2-0B's PHY A is used. For more information on this issue, see the "Dual-PHY" section of Chapter 9.

Finally, the LS1010 is configured with many of the same management options as earlier devices: SNMP, passwords, logging, a banner, and DNS.

Design Alternatives

Although an endless variety of design alternatives exist, several are common enough to deserve special mention. One popular design alternative involves pruning the IDF VLANs from the link that connects the MDFs together. This effectively converts the Layer 2 triangles discussed in this design into the Layer 2 V's used in Design 2 (a Catalyst 8500-based design). It is exactly this sort of minor change in a campus topology that can have a dramatic impact on Spanning Tree and the overall design. For details on how this affects the network, refer to Design 2 (from a Spanning Tree and load balancing perspective, this modification to Design 1 makes it equivalent to Design 2).

In addition, network designers wanting to fully utilize the Layer 2 features of their networks might want to implement Dynamic VLANs and VMPS. Given the Layer 2-orientation of MLS and the approach presented in Design 1, this enhancement is fairly simple to configure. For more information on Dynamic VLANs and VMPS, see Chapter 12.

Furthermore, VTP pruning can be used to automate the removal of VLANs from trunk links. This prevents the need for the manual pruning via the **clear trunk** command as discussed earlier.

Also, when implementing a design that maintains any sort of Layer 2 loops, you should at least consider implementing a loop-free topology within the management VLAN. As discussed in Chapter 15, loops in the management VLAN can quickly lead to collapse of the entire network. Although one of the great benefits of creating a Layer 3 barrier is that it isolates this failure to a single building (and it further helps by making the Layer 2 domains small enough that loops are unlikely to form), some form of looping is always a possibility when using Layer 2 technology.

In another common change, many organizations like to make trunk and server links high priority using the **set port level** command.

Finally, the servers can be directly connected to the ATM core by supplying them with ATM NICs. However, one of the downsides to this approach is the question of how to handle default gateway routing from the servers to the routers located in the MDF switches. For example, if the servers are configured with a default address of 10.250.250.4, the address of the interface VLAN 250 on Cat-B2-0B's RSM, all traffic is directed to Building 2. Traffic destined for Building 1 would therefore incur an additional routing hop and cross the backbone twice (unless ICMP redirects were supported). Another problem with using default gateways is the issue of redundancy. Although HSRP can be configured, it exacerbates the previous issue by disabling ICMP redirects on the router. In general, the best solution is to run a routing protocol on your servers (also requiring you to migrate the RSMs in this design from EIGRP to something like OSPF).

Design 2: Maximizing Layer 3 with Catalyst 8500 Switching Routers

This section presents Design 2, an approach that relies on Catalyst 8500-style hardware-based routing (in other words, the 8500 is a switching router). Figure 17-6 illustrates Design 2.

Figure 17-6 *Design 2 Network Diagram*

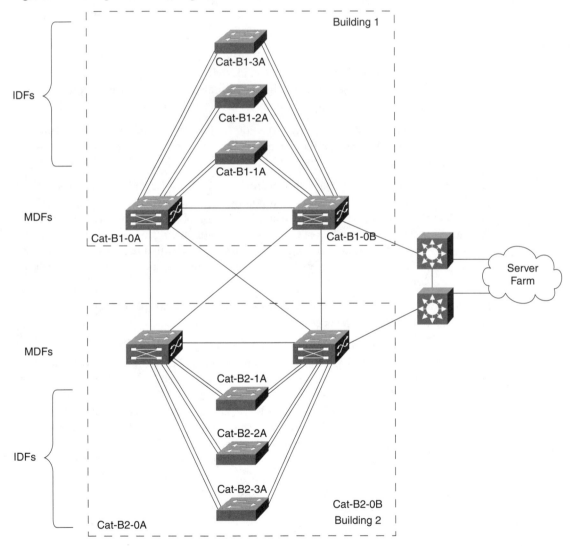

Several differences from the physical layout used in Design 1 are important. First, the ATM core has been replaced with Gigabit Ethernet. Second, the Building 2 third floor has been replaced with a Catalyst 5509. However, both designs are similar in that a pair of redundant MDF devices is used in each basement with two riser links going to each IDF.

Design Discussion

Whereas Design 1 sought to blend Layer 2 and Layer 3 technology, Design 2 follows an approach that maximizes the Layer 3 content in the MDF/distribution layer switches. In doing so, this somewhat subtle change has a dramatic impact on the rest of the design.

The most important change created by this design is that all IDF VLANs are terminated at the MDF switch. In other words, users connected to different IDFs always fall in different VLANs. As discussed in Chapter 11, although it is possible to have a limited number of VLANs traverse a Catalyst 8500 using IRB, this is not a technique that you want to use many times throughout your campus (it is appropriate for one or two special-case VLANs). In other words, this style of Layer 3 switching is best used as a fast version of a normal routing.

The second most important change, a simplification of Spanning Tree, is discussed in the next section.

Spanning Tree

Although some view the loss of IDF-to-IDF VLANs as a downside to the approach taken in Design 2, it is important to offset this with the simplifications that hardware-based routing make possible. One of the most important simplifications involves the area of Layer 2 loops and the Spanning-Tree Protocol. In fact, hardware-based routing has completely eliminated the Layer 2 loops between the IDF and MDF switches. Whereas Design 1 used Layer 2 triangles, this design uses Layer 2 V's.

NOTE	As was stressed in the discussion of Design 1, MLS can be used to build loop-free Layer 2 V's. However, it is important to realize that switching routers such as the 8500 do this *by default*, whereas MLS (and routing switches) require you to manually prune certain VLANs from selected links. See the earlier section "Trunks" for more information.

Because this design removes all Layer 2 loops (at least the ones that are intentionally formed), some organizations have decided to completely disable Spanning Tree when using this approach. However, because it does not prevent unintentional loops on a single IDF switch (generally as the result of a cabling mistake), other network designers want to maintain a Spanning Tree security blanket on their IDF switches. However, it is important to recognize that even in the cases where Spanning Tree remains enabled (as it is in Design 2), the operation of the Spanning-Tree Protocol is dramatically simplified for a variety of reasons.

First, Root Bridge placement becomes a non-issue. Each IDF switch is not aware of any other switches and naturally elects itself as the Root Bridge.

TIP	It can still be a good idea to lower the Bridge Priority in case someone plugs in another bridge some day.

In addition, Spanning Tree load balancing is not required (or, for that matter, possible).

Also, features such as UplinkFast and BackboneFast are no longer necessary for fast convergence.

Finally, the Spanning Tree network diameter has been reduced to the IDF switch itself. As a result, the Max Age and Forward Delay times can be aggressively tuned without concern. For example, Design 2 specifies a Max Age of 10 seconds and a Forward Delay of 7 seconds. Although somewhat more aggressive values can be used, these were chosen as a conservative compromise. As a result, failover performance where a loop exists is between 14 and 20 seconds. However, because the topology is loop free at Layer 2, there should be no Blocking ports during normal operation. As a result, *IDF uplink failover performance is governed by HSRP, not Spanning Tree.* Also as a result, the network can recover from uplink failures in as little as one second (assuming that the HSRP parameters are lowered).

TIP	The Spanning-Tree Protocol does not affect failover performance in this network.

VLAN Design

Although the concept of a VLAN begins to blur (or fade) in this design, the IDF switches are configured with the same end user VLAN *names* as used in Design 1. However, notice that all of the VLANs use essentially the same numbers throughout this version of the design. The management VLAN in all switches is always VLAN 1 (even though they are different IP subnets). Similarly, the first end-user VLAN on an IDF switch is VLAN 2. If more than one VLAN is required on a given IDF switch, VLANs 3 and greater can be created.

Notice that this brings a completely different approach to user mobility than Design 1. Design 1 attempted to place all users in the same community of interest located within a single building in the same VLAN. In the case of Design 2, that is no longer possible without enabling IRB on the Catalyst 8500. Here, it is expected that users in the same community of interest may very well fall into different subnets. However, because DHCP is in use, IP addressing is transparent to the users. Furthermore, because the available Layer 3 bandwidth is so high with 8500 technology, the use of routing (Layer 3 switching) does not impair the network's performance.

NOTE	Note that a similar case for Layer 3 performance can be made for the Catalyst 6000/6500. See Chapter 18 for more detail.

IP and IPX Addresses

Because Design 2 is less flat than Design 1, it requires more IP subnets (and IPX networks). For example, every link through the core is a separate subnet. Furthermore, *every IDF uses a separate subnet as a management VLAN* (remember, all VLAN terminate at the MDF switches). To avoid using an excessive number of address space, variable length subnet masking (VLSM) has been specified in Design 2.

Although in reality this is not a concern for most organizations using the Class A network such as network 10.0.0.0, it provides another benefit by making the subnets appear similar to the subnets used in Design 1. For example, whereas Design 1 uses a single backbone subnet of 10.250.250.0/24, Design 2 uses multiple 10.250.250.0/29 subnets. Just as Design 1 uses 10.1.10.0/24 and 10.2.20.0/24 for management VLANs, Design 2 uses multiple smaller subnets of 10.1.10.0/29 and 10.2.20.0/29.

As a result, Design 2 uses two subnet masks:

- /24 (255.255.255.0) for end-user segments
- /29 (255.255.255.248) for management VLANs, loopback addresses, and backbone links

Although it is possible to further optimize the address space utilization by using a /30 mask (255.255.255.252) for loopback interfaces and backbone links, a common mask was chosen for simplicity (furthermore, this one-bit optimization quickly reaches a point of diminishing returns when working with a Class A address!). Table 17-4 shows the IP subnets along with the corresponding IPX network numbers.

Table 17-4   *IP Subnets and IPX Networks for Design 2*

Use	Description	Bldg	VLAN	Subnet	Mask	IPX Net
B1_Mgt	Cat-B1-1A SC0	1	1	10.1.10.8	/29	0A010A08
B1_Mgt	Cat-B1-2A SC0	1	1	10.1.10.16	/29	0A010A10
B1_Mgt	Cat-B1-3A SC0	1	1	10.1.10.24	/29	0A010A18
B1_Sales	End-user segment	1	2	10.1.11.0	/24	0A010B00
B1_Mkting	End-user segment	1	3	10.1.12.0	/24	0A010C00
B1_Eng	End-user segment	1	2	10.1.13.0	/24	0A010D00

continues

Table 17-4 *IP Subnets and IPX Networks for Design 2 (Continued)*

Use	Description	Bldg	VLAN	Subnet	Mask	IPX Net
B1_Finance	End-user segment	1	2	10.1.14.0	/24	0A010E00
B2_Mgt	Cat-B2-1A SC0	2	1	10.2.20.8	/29	0A021408
B2_Mgt	Cat-B2-2A SC0	2	1	10.2.20.16	/29	0A021410
B2_Mgt	Cat-B2-3A SC0	2	1	10.2.20.24	/29	0A021418
B2_Sales	End-user segment	2	2	10.2.21.0	/24	0A021500
B2_Mkting	End-user segment	2	3	10.2.22.0	/24	0A021600
B2_Eng	End-user segment	2	2	10.2.23.0	/24	0A021700
B2_Finance	End-user segment	2	2	10.2.24.0	/24	0A021800
Svr. Farm	Server Farm segment	Backbone	100	10.100.100.0	/24	0A646400
Loopback	Cat-B1-0A	Backbone	N/A	10.200.200.8	/29	0AC8C808
Loopback	Cat-B1-0B	Backbone	N/A	10.200.200.16	/29	0AC8C810
Loopback	Cat-B2-0A	Backbone	N/A	10.200.200.24	/29	0AC8C818
Loopback	Cat-B2-0B	Backbone	N/A	10.200.200.32	/29	0AC8C820
Backbone	Cat-B1-0A to Cat-B1-0B	Backbone	N/A	10.250.250.8	/29	0AFAFA08
Backbone	Cat-B1-0A to Cat-B2-0B	Backbone	N/A	10.250.250.16	/29	0AFAFA10
Backbone	Cat-B1-0A to Cat-B2-0A	Backbone	N/A	10.250.250.24	/29	0AFAFA18
Backbone	Cat-B1-0B to Cat-B2-0B	Backbone	N/A	10.250.250.32	/29	0AFAFA20
Backbone	Cat-B1-0B to Cat-B2-0A	Backbone	N/A	10.250.250.40	/29	0AFAFA28
Backbone	Cat-B2-0A to Cat-B2-0B	Backbone	N/A	10.250.250.48	/29	0AFAFA30

VTP

Given the Layer 3 nature of Design 2, VTP server mode has little meaning (8500s do not propagate VTP frames). Therefore, Design 2 calls for VTP transparent mode. Although not a requirement, the design also calls for a VTP domain name of Happy (unlike server and client modes, transparent mode does not require a VTP domain name).

As a result, each IDF switch must be individually configured with the list of VLANs it must handle. However, this is rarely a significant issue because each IDF switch usually only handles a small number of VLANs.

TIP   If the VLAN configuration tasks are a concern (or, for that matter any other configuration task), consider using tools such as Perl and Expect. Both run on a wide variety of UNIX platforms as well as Windows NT.

Trunks

> To present an alternative approach, Design 2 uses Fast EtherChannel links between the MDF and IDF switches. To provide adequate bandwidth in the core, Gigabit Ethernet links are used.

Server Farm

> This design calls for a separate Server Farm building (a third building at the corporate headquarters campus will be used). The Server Farm could have easily been placed in Building 1 as it was with Design 1, however, an alternate approach was used for variety.

Configurations

> This section presents the configurations for Design 2. As with Design 1, you see only one example of each type of device. First, you see configurations for and discussion of a Catalyst 5509 IDF switch, followed by configurations for and discussion of a Catalyst 8540 MDF switch.

IDF Supervisor Configuration

> As with Design 1, this section is broken into two sections:

- The interactive configuration output
- The full configuration listing

Configuring an IDF Supervisor: Cat-B2-1A

As with the IDF switch in Design 1, begin by configuring the device VTP domain names as in Example 17-21.

Example 17-21   *System Name and VTP Configuration*

```
Console> (enable) set system name Cat-B2-1A
System name set.
Cat-B2-1A> (enable) set vtp domain Happy
VTP domain Happy modified
Cat-B2-1A> (enable)
```

Unlike Design 1, this design utilizes VTP transparent mode and requires only a single end-user VLAN for Cat-B2-1A as shown in Example 17-22.

Example 17-22   *VTP and VLAN Configuration*

```
Cat-B2-1A> (enable) set vtp mode transparent
VTP domain Happy modified
Cat-B2-1A> (enable)
Cat-B2-1A> (enable) set vlan 2 name Engineering
Vlan 2 configuration successful
Cat-B2-1A> (enable)
```

The SC0 interface also uses a different configuration under Design 2. First, the IP address and netmask are obviously different. Second, SC0 is left in VLAN 1, the default. Third, Design 2 calls for two default gateway addresses to be specified with the **ip route** command (this feature was first supported in Version 4.1 of Catalyst 5000 code). This can simplify the overall configuration and maintenance of the network by not requiring a separate HSRP group to be maintained for each management subnet/VLAN. Example 17-23 demonstrates these steps.

Example 17-23   *IP Configuration*

```
Cat-B2-1A> (enable) set interface sc0 1 10.2.20.11 255.255.255.248
Interface sc0 vlan set, IP address and netmask set.
Cat-B2-1A> (enable) set ip route default 10.2.20.9
Route added.
Cat-B2-1A> (enable) set ip route default 10.2.20.10
Route added.
Cat-B2-1A> (enable)
```

Next, configure the Spanning Tree parameters as in Example 17-24.

Example 17-24   *Spanning Tree Configuration*

```
Cat-B2-1A> (enable) set spantree root 1 dia 2 hello 2
VLAN 1 bridge priority set to 8192.
VLAN 1 bridge max aging time set to 10.
VLAN 1 bridge hello time set to 2.
VLAN 1 bridge forward delay set to 7.
Switch is now the root switch for active VLAN 1.
Cat-B2-1A> (enable)
Cat-B2-1A> (enable) set spantree root 2 dia 2 hello 2
VLAN 2 bridge priority set to 8192.
VLAN 2 bridge max aging time set to 10.
VLAN 2 bridge hello time set to 2.
VLAN 2 bridge forward delay set to 7.
Switch is now the root switch for active VLAN 2.
Cat-B2-1A> (enable)
Cat-B2-1A> (enable) set spantree portfast 4/1-24,5/1-24,6/1-24,7/1-24,
   8/1-24 enable
Warning: Spantree port fast start should only be enabled on ports connected
to a single host.  Connecting hubs, concentrators, switches, bridges, etc. to
a fast start port can cause temporary Spanning Tree loops.  Use with caution.
Spantree ports 4/1-24,5/1-24,6/1-24,7/1-24,8/1-24 fast start enabled.
Cat-B2-1A> (enable)
```

The first two commands (**set spantree root**) lower the Max Age and Forward Delay timers to 10 and 7 seconds, respectively. For consistency, this also forces the IDF switch to be the Root Bridge. (Although this is useful in the event that other switches or bridges have been cascaded off the IDF switch, in most situations this has no impact on the actual topology under Design 2.) Finally, PortFast is enabled on all of the end-user ports in slots 4–8.

Next, the trunk ports are configured as in Example 17-25.

Example 17-25   *Port and Trunk Configuration*

```
Cat-B2-1A> (enable)
Cat-B2-1A> (enable) set port name 3/1-4 FEC link to Cat-B2-0A
Port 3/1-4 name set.
Cat-B2-1A> (enable) set port name 3/5-8 FEC link to Cat-B2-0B
Port 3/5-8 name set.
Cat-B2-1A> (enable)
B2-MDF-02> (enable) set port channel 3/1-4 on
Port(s) 3/1-4 channel mode set to on.
B2-MDF-02> (enable) set port channel 3/5-8 on
Port(s) 3/5-8 channel mode set to on.
Cat-B2-1A> (enable)
Cat-B2-1A> (enable) set trunk 3/1 on isl
Port(s) 3/1-4 trunk mode set to on.
Port(s) 3/1-4 trunk type set to isl.
Cat-B2-1A> (enable)
Cat-B2-1A> (enable) set trunk 3/5 on isl
Port(s) 3/5-8 trunk mode set to on.
Port(s) 3/5-8 trunk type set to isl.
Cat-B2-1A> (enable)
```

As mentioned earlier, Design 2 uses Fast EtherChannel links from Cat-B2-1A and Cat-B2-2A to the MDF switches. For stability, these are hard-coded to the port channel **on** state. The resulting EtherChannel bundles are also hard-coded as ISL trunks. Also notice that although the **set trunk** command is only applied to a single port, the Catalyst automatically applies it to every port in the EtherChannel bundle.

The commands in Example 17-26 are very similar to those used in Example 17-16 of Design 1.

Example 17-26 *Configuring SNMP, Password, Banner, System Information, DNS, IP Permit List, IGMP Snooping, Protocol Filtering, SNMP, and Syslog*

```
Cat-B2-1A> (enable) set snmp community read-only lesspublic
SNMP read-only community string set to 'lesspublic'.
Cat-B2-1A> (enable) set snmp community read-write moreprivate
SNMP read-write community string set to 'moreprivate'.
Cat-B2-1A> (enable) set snmp community read-write-all mostprivate
SNMP read-write-all community string set to 'mostprivate'.
Cat-B2-1A> (enable)
Cat-B2-1A> (enable) set password
Enter old password:
Enter new password:
Retype new password:
Password changed.
Cat-B2-1A> (enable)
Cat-B2-1A> (enable) set enablepass
Enter old password:
Enter new password:
Retype new password:
Password changed.
Cat-B2-1A> (enable)
Cat-B2-1A> (enable)
Cat-B2-1A> (enable) set banner motd ~PRIVATE NETWORK -- HACKERS WILL BE SHOT!!~
MOTD banner set
Cat-B2-1A> (enable) set system location Building 2 First Floor
System location set.
Cat-B2-1A> (enable) set system contact Joe x111
System contact set.
Cat-B2-1A> (enable)
Cat-B2-1A> (enable) set ip dns enable
DNS is enabled
Cat-B2-1A> (enable) set ip dns domain happy.com
Default DNS domain name set to happy.com
Cat-B2-1A> (enable) set ip dns server 10.100.100.42
10.100.100.42 added to DNS server table as primary server.
Cat-B2-1A> (enable) set ip dns server 10.100.100.68
10.100.100.68 added to DNS server table as backup server.
Cat-B2-1A> (enable)
Cat-B2-1A> (enable) set ip permit enable
IP permit list enabled.
WARNING!! IP permit list has no entries.
Cat-B2-1A> (enable) set ip permit 10.100.100.0 255.255.255.0
10.100.100.0 with mask 255.255.255.0 added to IP permit list.
Cat-B2-1A> (enable)
Cat-B2-1A> (enable)
Cat-B2-1A> (enable) set igmp enable
IGMP feature for IP multicast enabled
Cat-B2-1A> (enable)
Cat-B2-1A> (enable) set protocolfilter enable
Protocol filtering enabled on this switch.
Cat-B2-1A> (enable)
Cat-B2-1A> (enable)
Cat-B2-1A> (enable) set snmp trap 10.100.100.21 trapped
```

Example 17-26   *Configuring SNMP, Password, Banner, System Information, DNS, IP Permit List, IGMP Snooping, Protocol Filtering, SNMP, and Syslog (Continued)*

```
SNMP trap receiver added.
Cat-B2-1A> (enable) set snmp trap enable module
SNMP module traps enabled.
Cat-B2-1A> (enable) set snmp trap enable chassis
SNMP chassis alarm traps enabled.
Cat-B2-1A> (enable) set snmp trap enable bridge
SNMP bridge traps enabled.
Cat-B2-1A> (enable) set snmp trap enable auth
SNMP authentication traps enabled.
Cat-B2-1A> (enable) set snmp trap enable stpx
SNMP STPX  traps enabled.
Cat-B2-1A> (enable) set snmp trap enable config
SNMP CONFIG traps enabled.
Cat-B2-1A> (enable) set port trap 3/1-8 enable
Port 3/1-8 up/down trap enabled.
Cat-B2-1A> (enable)
Cat-B2-1A> (enable)
Cat-B2-1A> (enable) set logging server enable
System logging messages will be sent to the configured syslog servers.
Cat-B2-1A> (enable) set logging server 10.100.100.21
10.100.100.21 added to System logging server table.
Cat-B2-1A> (enable)
Cat-B2-1A> (enable)
```

Full IDF Supervisor Listing: Cat-B2-1A

Example 17-27 presents the configuration code that results from the previous sequence of configuration steps.

Example 17-27   *Full Catalyst Configuration*

```
begin
!
set password $1$FMFQ$HfZR5DUszVHIRhrz4h6V70
set enablepass $1$FMFQ$HfZR5DUszVHIRhrz4h6V70
set prompt Cat-B2-1A>
set length 24 default
set logout 20
set banner motd ^CPRIVATE NETWORK -- HACKERS WILL BE SHOT!!^C
!
#system
set system baud  9600
set system modem disable
set system name  Cat-B2-1A
set system location Building 2 First Floor
set system contact  Joe x111
!
```

continues

Example 17-27 *Full Catalyst Configuration (Continued)*

```
#snmp
set snmp community read-only       lesspublic
set snmp community read-write      moreprivate
set snmp community read-write-all mostprivate
set snmp rmon disable
set snmp trap enable   module
set snmp trap enable   chassis
set snmp trap enable   bridge
set snmp trap disable repeater
set snmp trap disable vtp
set snmp trap enable   auth
set snmp trap disable ippermit
set snmp trap disable vmps
set snmp trap disable entity
set snmp trap enable   config
set snmp trap enable   stpx
set snmp trap disable syslog
set snmp extendedrmon vlanmode disable
set snmp extendedrmon vlanagent disable
set snmp extendedrmon enable
set snmp trap 10.100.100.21    trapped
!
#ip
set interface sc0 1 10.2.20.11 255.255.255.248 10.2.10.2.20.15

set interface sc0 up
set interface sl0 0.0.0.0 0.0.0.0
set interface sl0 up
set arp agingtime 1200
set ip redirect    enable
set ip unreachable    enable
set ip fragmentation enable
set ip route 0.0.0.0          10.2.20.9     1
set ip route 0.0.0.0          10.2.20.10    1
set ip alias default          0.0.0.0
!
#Command alias
!
#vmps
set vmps server retry 3
set vmps server reconfirminterval 60
set vmps tftpserver 0.0.0.0 vmps-config-database.1
set vmps state disable
!
#dns
set ip dns server 10.100.100.42 primary
set ip dns server 10.100.100.68
set ip dns enable
set ip dns domain happy.com
!
 #tacacs+
set tacacs attempts 3
set tacacs directedrequest disable
```

Example 17-27 *Full Catalyst Configuration (Continued)*

```
set tacacs timeout 5
!
#authentication
set authentication login tacacs disable console
set authentication login tacacs disable telnet
set authentication enable tacacs disable console
set authentication enable tacacs disable telnet
set authentication login local enable console
set authentication login local enable telnet
set authentication enable local enable console
set authentication enable local enable telnet
!
#bridge
set bridge ipx snaptoether    8023raw
set bridge ipx 8022toether    8023
set bridge ipx 8023rawtofddi snap
!
#vtp
set vtp domain Happy
set vtp mode transparent
set vtp v2 disable
set vtp pruning disable
set vtp pruneeligible 2-1000
clear vtp pruneeligible 1001-1005
set vlan 1 name default type ethernet mtu 1500 said 100001 state active
set vlan 2 name Engineering type ethernet mtu 1500 said 100002 state active
set vlan 1002 name fddi-default type fddi mtu 1500 said 101002 state active
set vlan 1004 name fddinet-default type fddinet mtu 1500 said 101004
   state active bridge 0x0 stp ieee
set vlan 1005 name trnet-default type trbrf mtu 1500 said 101005
   state active bridge 0x0 stp ibm
set vlan 1003 name token-ring-default type trcrf mtu 1500 said 101003
   state active parent 0 ring 0x0 mode srb aremaxhop 0 stemaxhop 0
!
#spantree
#uplinkfast groups
set spantree uplinkfast disable
#backbonefast
set spantree backbonefast disable
set spantree enable  all
#vlan 1
set spantree fwddelay 7      1
set spantree hello    2      1
set spantree maxage   10     1
set spantree priority 8192   1
#vlan 2
set spantree fwddelay 7      2
set spantree hello    2      2
set spantree maxage   10     2
set spantree priority 8192   2
#vlan 1003
```

continues

Example 17-27 *Full Catalyst Configuration (Continued)*

```
set spantree fwddelay 15     1003
set spantree hello     2     1003
set spantree maxage    20    1003
set spantree priority 32768 1003
set spantree portstate 1003 block 0
set spantree portcost 1003 62
set spantree portpri  1003 4
set spantree portfast 1003 disable
#vlan 1005
set spantree fwddelay 15     1005
set spantree hello     2     1005
set spantree maxage    20    1005
set spantree priority 32768 1005
set spantree multicast-address 1005 ieee
!
#cgmp
set cgmp disable
set cgmp leave disable
!
#syslog
set logging console enable
set logging server enable
set logging server 10.100.100.21
set logging level cdp 2 default
set logging level mcast 2 default
set logging level dtp 5 default
set logging level dvlan 2 default
set logging level earl 2 default
set logging level fddi 2 default
set logging level ip 2 default
set logging level pruning 2 default
set logging level snmp 2 default
set logging level spantree 2 default
set logging level sys 5 default
set logging level tac 2 default
set logging level tcp 2 default
set logging level telnet 2 default
set logging level tftp 2 default
set logging level vtp 2 default
set logging level vmps 2 default
set logging level kernel 2 default
set logging level filesys 2 default
set logging level drip 2 default
set logging level pagp 5 default
set logging level mgmt 5 default
set logging level mls 5 default
set logging level protfilt 2 default
set logging level security 2 default
set logging server facility LOCAL7
set logging server severity 4
set logging buffer 500
set logging timestamp disable
```

Example 17-27   *Full Catalyst Configuration (Continued)*

```
!
#ntp
set ntp broadcastclient disable
set ntp broadcastdelay 3000
set ntp client disable
clear timezone
set summertime disable
!
#set boot command
set boot config-register 0x10f
set boot system flash bootflash:sup.bin
!
#permit list
set ip permit enable
set ip permit 10.100.100.0 255.255.255.0
!
#drip
set tokenring reduction enable
set tokenring distrib-crf disable
!
#igmp
set igmp enable
!
#protocolfilter
set protocolfilter enable
!
#mls
set mls enable
set mls flow destination
set mls agingtime 256
set mls agingtime fast 0 0
set mls nde disable
!
#standby ports
set standbyports enable
!
#module 1 : 2-port 10/100BaseTX Supervisor
set module name    1
set vlan 1     1/1-2
set port channel 1/1-2 off
set port channel 1/1-2 auto
set port enable       1/1-2
set port level        1/1-2  normal
set port speed        1/1-2  auto
set port trap         1/1-2  disable
set port name         1/1-2
set port security  1/1-2  disable
set port broadcast 1/1-2  100%
set port membership 1/1-2  static
set port protocol 1/1-2 ip on
```

continues

Example 17-27   *Full Catalyst Configuration (Continued)*

```
set port protocol 1/1-2 ipx auto
set cdp enable   1/1-2
set cdp interval 1/1-2 60
set trunk 1/1  auto isl 1-1005
set trunk 1/2  auto isl 1-1005
set spantree portfast    1/1-2 disable
set spantree portcost    1/1-2  100
set spantree portpri     1/1-2  32
set spantree portvlanpri 1/1  0
set spantree portvlanpri 1/2  0
set spantree portvlancost 1/1  cost 99
set spantree portvlancost 1/2  cost 99
!
#module 2 : 2-port 10/100BaseTX Supervisor
set module name    2
set vlan 1     2/1-2
set port channel 2/1-2 off
set port channel 2/1-2 auto
set port enable    2/1-2
set port level     2/1-2  normal
set port speed     2/1-2  auto
set port trap      2/1-2  disable
set port name      2/1-2
set port security  2/1-2  disable
set port broadcast 2/1-2  100%
set port membership 2/1-2  static
set port protocol 2/1-2 ip on
set port protocol 2/1-2 ipx auto
set cdp enable   2/1-2
set cdp interval 2/1-2 60
set trunk 2/1  auto isl 1-1005
set trunk 2/2  auto isl 1-1005
set spantree portfast    2/1-2 disable
set spantree portcost    2/1-2  100
set spantree portpri     2/1-2  32
set spantree portvlanpri 2/1  0
set spantree portvlanpri 2/2  0
set spantree portvlancost 2/1  cost 99
set spantree portvlancost 2/2  cost 99
!
#module 3 : 12-port 10/100BaseTX Ethernet
set module name    3
set module enable  3
set vlan 1     3/1-12
set port channel 3/1-4 off
set port channel 3/5-8 off
set port channel 3/9-12 off
set port channel 3/1-4 on
set port channel 3/5-8 on
set port channel 3/9-12 auto
set port enable    3/1-12
set port level     3/1-12  normal
set port speed     3/1-12  100
```

Example 17-27 *Full Catalyst Configuration (Continued)*

```
set port duplex      3/1-12  full
set port trap        3/1-8   enable
set port trap        3/9-12  disable
set port name        3/1     FEC link to Cat-B2-0A
set port name        3/2     FEC link to Cat-B2-0A
set port name        3/3     FEC link to Cat-B2-0A
set port name        3/4     FEC link to Cat-B2-0A
set port name        3/5     FEC link to Cat-B2-0B
set port name        3/6     FEC link to Cat-B2-0B
set port name        3/7     FEC link to Cat-B2-0B
set port name        3/8     FEC link to Cat-B2-0B
set port name        3/9-12
set port security    3/1-12  disable
set port broadcast   3/1-12  0
set port membership 3/1-12   static
set port protocol 3/1-12 ip on
set port protocol 3/1-12 ipx auto
set cdp enable       3/1-12
set cdp interval 3/1-12 60
set trunk 3/1   on isl 1-1005
set trunk 3/2   on isl 1-1005
set trunk 3/3   on isl 1-1005
set trunk 3/4   on isl 1-1005
set trunk 3/5   on isl 1-1005
set trunk 3/6   on isl 1-1005
set trunk 3/7   on isl 1-1005
set trunk 3/8   on isl 1-1005
set trunk 3/9   auto isl 1-1005
set trunk 3/10 auto isl 1-1005
set trunk 3/11 auto isl 1-1005
set trunk 3/12 auto isl 1-1005
set spantree portfast    3/1-12 disable
set spantree portcost    3/1-12  19
set spantree portpri     3/1-12  32
set spantree portvlanpri 3/1  0
set spantree portvlanpri 3/2  0
set spantree portvlanpri 3/3  0
set spantree portvlanpri 3/4  0
set spantree portvlanpri 3/5  0
set spantree portvlanpri 3/6  0
set spantree portvlanpri 3/7  0
set spantree portvlanpri 3/8  0
set spantree portvlanpri 3/9  0
set spantree portvlanpri 3/10 0
set spantree portvlanpri 3/11 0
set spantree portvlanpri 3/12 0
set spantree portvlancost 3/1   cost 18
set spantree portvlancost 3/2   cost 18
set spantree portvlancost 3/3   cost 18
set spantree portvlancost 3/4   cost 18
set spantree portvlancost 3/5   cost 18
```

continues

Example 17-27 *Full Catalyst Configuration (Continued)*

```
set spantree portvlancost 3/6  cost 18
set spantree portvlancost 3/7  cost 18
set spantree portvlancost 3/8  cost 18
set spantree portvlancost 3/9  cost 18
set spantree portvlancost 3/10 cost 18
set spantree portvlancost 3/11 cost 18
set spantree portvlancost 3/12 cost 18
!
#module 5 : 24-port 10/100BaseTX Ethernet
set module name    5
set module enable  5
set vlan 2     5/1-24
set port enable     5/1-24
set port level      5/1-24  normal
set port speed      5/1-24  auto
set port trap       5/1-24  disable
set port name       5/1-24
set port security   5/1-24  disable
set port broadcast  5/1-24  0
set port membership 5/1-24  static
set port protocol 5/1-24 ip on
set port protocol 5/1-24 ipx auto
set cdp enable    5/1-24
set cdp interval 5/1-24 60
set spantree portfast    5/1-24 enable
set spantree portcost    5/1-24  100
set spantree portpri     5/1-24  32
!
#module 6 : 24-port 10/100BaseTX Ethernet
set module name    6
set module enable  6
set vlan 2     6/1-24
set port enable     6/1-24
set port level      6/1-24  normal
set port speed      6/1-24  auto
set port trap       6/1-24  disable
set port name       6/1-24
set port security   6/1-24  disable
set port broadcast  6/1-24  0
set port membership 6/1-24  static
set port protocol 6/1-24 ip on
set port protocol 6/1-24 ipx auto
set cdp enable    6/1-24
set cdp interval 6/1-24 60
set spantree portfast    6/1-24 enable
set spantree portcost    6/1-24  100
set spantree portpri     6/1-24  32
!
#module 7 : 24-port 10/100BaseTX Ethernet
set module name    7
set module enable  7
set vlan 2     7/1-24
```

Example 17-27   *Full Catalyst Configuration (Continued)*

```
set port enable       7/1-24
set port level        7/1-24  normal
set port speed        7/1-24  auto
set port trap         7/1-24  disable
set port name         7/1-24
set port security     7/1-24  disable
set port broadcast  7/1-24  0
set port membership 7/1-24  static
set port protocol 7/1-24 ip on
set port protocol 7/1-24 ipx auto
set cdp enable      7/1-24
set cdp interval 7/1-24 60
set spantree portfast    7/1-24 enable
set spantree portcost    7/1-24  100
set spantree portpri     7/1-24  32
!
#module 8 : 24-port 10/100BaseTX Ethernet
set module name     8
set module enable  8
set vlan 2     8/1-24
set port enable       8/1-24
set port level        8/1-24  normal
set port speed        8/1-24  auto
set port trap         8/1-24  disable
set port name         8/1-24
set port security     8/1-24  disable
set port broadcast  8/1-24  0
set port membership 8/1-24  static
set port protocol 8/1-24 ip on
set port protocol 8/1-24 ipx auto
set cdp enable      8/1-24
set cdp interval 8/1-24 60
set spantree portfast    8/1-24 enable
set spantree portcost    8/1-24  100
set spantree portpri     8/1-24  32
!
#module 9 empty
!
#switch port analyzer
!set span 1 1/1 both inpkts disable
set span disable
!
#cam
set cam agingtime 1,2,1003,1005 300
end
```

MDF Configuration: Cat-B2-0B

Example 17-28 presents the full configuration listing for Cat-B2-0B, an 8540 MDF switch. The chassis contains a 16-port 100BaseFX module in slot 0 and 2-port Gigabit Ethernet modules in slots 1 and 2. Because IOS-based router configurations are shorter (they only list non-default commands) and easier to read than XDI/CatOS-based Catalyst images, this section does not show a separate listing of the interactive command output.

Example 17-28 *Full Catalyst 8540 Configuration*

```
!
no service pad
service timestamps log datetime localtime
service password-encryption
!
hostname Cat-B2-0B
!
logging buffered 4096 debugging
logging console informational
enable secret 5 $1$C3lJ$qVaCyxa7mpq2OXMzTHY7h1
!
clock timezone EST -5
clock summer-time EDT recurring
redundancy
 main-cpu
  no sync config startup
  sync config running
facility-alarm core-temperature major 53
facility-alarm core-temperature minor 45
ip subnet-zero
ip domain-name happy.com
ip name-server 10.100.100.42
ip name-server 10.100.100.68
ipx routing 0090.2149.2400
!
!
interface Loopback0
 ip address 10.200.200.33 255.255.255.248
 no ip directed-broadcast
!
interface Port-channel1
 description Link to Cat-B2-1A
 no ip address
 no ip directed-broadcast
 hold-queue 300 in
!
interface Port-channel1.1
 description Mgt VLAN: Cat-B2-1A SC0
 encapsulation isl 1
 ip address 10.2.20.9 255.255.255.248
 no ip redirects
 no ip directed-broadcast
!
```

Example 17-28   *Full Catalyst 8540 Configuration (Continued)*

```
 interface Port-channel1.2
  description User VLAN: Engineering
  encapsulation isl 2
  ip address 10.2.23.4 255.255.255.0
  ip helper-address 10.100.100.81
  ip helper-address 10.100.100.33
  no ip redirects
  no ip directed-broadcast
 ipx network 0A021700
 standby 1 priority 100
 standby 1 preempt
 standby 1 ip 10.2.23.1
 standby 1 track GigabitEthernet1/0/0 7
 standby 1 track GigabitEthernet1/0/1 7
 standby 1 track GigabitEthernet2/0/0 7
 standby 2 priority 110
 standby 2 preempt
 standby 2 ip 10.2.23.2
 standby 2 track GigabitEthernet1/0/0 7
 standby 2 track GigabitEthernet1/0/1 7
 standby 2 track GigabitEthernet2/0/0 7
!
interface Port-channel2
 description Link to Cat-B2-2A
 no ip address
 no ip directed-broadcast
 hold-queue 300 in
!
interface Port-channel2.1
 description Mgt VLAN: Cat-B2-2A SC0
 encapsulation isl 1
 ip address 10.2.20.17 255.255.255.248
 no ip redirects
 no ip directed-broadcast
!
interface Port-channel2.2
 description User VLAN: Finance
 encapsulation isl 2
 ip address 10.2.24.4 255.255.255.0
 ip helper-address 10.100.100.81
 ip helper-address 10.100.100.33
 no ip redirects
 no ip directed-broadcast
 ipx network 0A021800
 standby 1 priority 100
 standby 1 preempt
 standby 1 ip 10.2.24.1
 standby 1 track GigabitEthernet1/0/0 7
 standby 1 track GigabitEthernet1/0/1 7
 standby 1 track GigabitEthernet2/0/0 7
```

continues

Example 17-28 *Full Catalyst 8540 Configuration (Continued)*

```
 standby 2 priority 110
 standby 2 preempt
 standby 2 ip 10.2.24.2
 standby 2 track GigabitEthernet1/0/0 7
 standby 2 track GigabitEthernet1/0/1 7
 standby 2 track GigabitEthernet2/0/0 7
!
interface Port-channel2.3
 description User VLAN: Mkting
 encapsulation isl 3
 ip address 10.2.22.4 255.255.255.0
 ip helper-address 10.100.100.81
 ip helper-address 10.100.100.33
 no ip redirects
 no ip directed-broadcast
 ipx network 0A021600
 standby 1 priority 100
 standby 1 preempt
 standby 1 ip 10.2.22.1
 standby 1 track GigabitEthernet1/0/0 7
 standby 1 track GigabitEthernet1/0/1 7
 standby 1 track GigabitEthernet2/0/0 7
 standby 2 priority 110
 standby 2 preempt
 standby 2 ip 10.2.22.2
 standby 2 track GigabitEthernet1/0/0 7
 standby 2 track GigabitEthernet1/0/1 7
 standby 2 track GigabitEthernet2/0/0 7
!
interface Port-channel3
 description Link to Cat-B2-3A
 no ip address
 no ip directed-broadcast
 hold-queue 300 in
!
interface Port-channel3.1
 description Mgt VLAN: Cat-B2-3A SC0
 encapsulation isl 1
 ip address 10.2.20.25 255.255.255.248
 no ip redirects
 no ip directed-broadcast
!
interface Port-channel3.2
 description User VLAN: Sales
 encapsulation isl 2
 ip address 10.2.21.4 255.255.255.0
 ip helper-address 10.100.100.81
 ip helper-address 10.100.100.33
 no ip redirects
 no ip directed-broadcast
 ipx network 0A021500
 standby 1 priority 100
```

Example 17-28   *Full Catalyst 8540 Configuration (Continued)*

```
 standby 1 preempt
 standby 1 ip 10.2.21.1
 standby 1 track GigabitEthernet1/0/0 7
 standby 1 track GigabitEthernet1/0/1 7
 standby 1 track GigabitEthernet2/0/0 7
 standby 2 priority 110
 standby 2 preempt
 standby 2 ip 10.2.21.2
 standby 2 track GigabitEthernet1/0/0 7
 standby 2 track GigabitEthernet1/0/1 7
 standby 2 track GigabitEthernet2/0/0 7
!
interface FastEthernet0/0/0
 no ip address
 no ip directed-broadcast
 channel-group 1
!
interface FastEthernet0/0/1
 no ip address
 no ip directed-broadcast
 channel-group 1
!
interface FastEthernet0/0/2
 no ip address
 no ip directed-broadcast
 channel-group 1
!
interface FastEthernet0/0/3
 no ip address
 no ip directed-broadcast
 channel-group 1
!
interface FastEthernet0/0/4
 no ip address
 no ip directed-broadcast
 channel-group 2
!
interface FastEthernet0/0/5
 no ip address
 no ip directed-broadcast
 channel-group 2
!
interface FastEthernet0/0/6
 no ip address
 no ip directed-broadcast
 channel-group 2
!
interface FastEthernet0/0/7
 no ip address
 no ip directed-broadcast
```

continues

Example 17-28 *Full Catalyst 8540 Configuration (Continued)*

```
 channel-group 2
!
interface FastEthernet0/0/8
 no ip address
 no ip directed-broadcast
 channel-group 3
!
interface FastEthernet0/0/9
 no ip address
 no ip directed-broadcast
 channel-group 3
!
interface FastEthernet0/0/10
 no ip address
 no ip directed-broadcast
 channel-group 3
!
interface FastEthernet0/0/11
 no ip address
 no ip directed-broadcast
 channel-group 3
!
interface FastEthernet0/0/12
 no ip address
 no ip directed-broadcast
 shutdown
!
interface FastEthernet0/0/13
 no ip address
 no ip directed-broadcast
 shutdown
!
interface FastEthernet0/0/14
 no ip address
 no ip directed-broadcast
 shutdown
!
interface FastEthernet0/0/15
 no ip address
 no ip directed-broadcast
 shutdown
!
interface GigabitEthernet1/0/0
 description Gigabit link: Cat-B1-0A to Cat-B2-0B
 ip address 10.250.250.18 255.255.255.248
 no ip directed-broadcast
 ipx network 0AFAFA10
 no negotiation auto
!
interface GigabitEthernet1/0/1
 description Gigabit link: Cat-B1-0B to Cat-B2-0B
 ip address 10.250.250.34 255.255.255.248
```

Example 17-28   *Full Catalyst 8540 Configuration (Continued)*

```
 no ip directed-broadcast
 ipx network 0AFAFA20
 no negotiation auto
!
interface GigabitEthernet2/0/0
 description Gigabit link: Cat-B2-0A to Cat-B2-0B
 ip address 10.250.250.50 255.255.255.248
 no ip directed-broadcast
 ipx network 0AFAFA30
 no negotiation auto
!
interface GigabitEthernet2/0/1
 description Gigabit link: Server Farm
 ip address 10.100.100.4 255.255.255.0
 no ip redirects
 no ip directed-broadcast
 ipx network 0A646400
 no negotiation auto
!
interface Ethernet0
 no ip address
 no ip directed-broadcast
!
router eigrp 131
 passive-interface Port-channel1.1
 passive-interface Port-channel1.2
 passive-interface Port-channel2.1
 passive-interface Port-channel2.2
 passive-interface Port-channel2.3
 passive-interface Port-channel3.1
 passive-interface Port-channel3.2
 network 10.0.0.0
!
ip classless
no ip forward-protocol udp netbios-ns
no ip forward-protocol udp netbios-dgm
!
logging 10.100.100.21
access-list 1 permit 10.100.100.0 0.0.0.255
snmp-server community lesspublic RO
snmp-server community moreprivate RW
snmp-server host 10.100.100.21 trapped
snmp-server location Building 2 MDF
snmp-server contact Joe x111
snmp-server enable traps config
banner motd ^CPRIVATE NETWORK -- HACKERS WILL BE SHOT!!^C
!
!
line con 0
 password 7 055A545C
```

continues

Example 17-28 *Full Catalyst 8540 Configuration (Continued)*

```
 transport input none
line aux 0
 password 7 055A545C
line vty 0 4
 access-class 1 in
 password 7 055A545C
 login
 !
end
```

Three logical port-channel interfaces are configured to handle the links to the three IDF switches. Because the EtherChannels are using ISL encapsulation to trunk multiple VLANs to the IDFs, each port-channel is then configured with multiple subinterfaces, one for each IDF VLAN. For example, interface port-channel 2 is used to connect to Cat-B2-2A on the second floor. Subinterface port-channel 2.1 is created for the management VLAN, 2.2 for the Finance VLAN, and 2.3 for the Marketing VLAN. Each subinterface is configured with an **encapsulation isl** statement and the appropriate IP and IPX Layer 3 information.

The subinterfaces supporting end-user traffic are also configured with two HSRP groups. As explained in Chapter 11, HSRP load balancing should be employed in designs where a single end-user VLAN is used on each IDF and there are no Layer 2 loops (making Spanning Tree load balancing impossible). To enable HSRP load balancing, a technique called Multigroup HSRP (MHSRP) is used. Under MHSRP, two (or more) HSRP groups are created for every subnet. By having each MDF device be the active HSRP peer for one of the two HSRP groups, load balancing can be achieved. For example, Design 2 calls for two HSRP groups per end-user subnet (as mentioned earlier, the management VLANs use multiple default gateways instead). The first HSRP group uses .1 in the fourth octet of the IP address, and the second group uses .2. By making Cat-B2-0A the active peer for the first group and Cat-B2-0B the active peer for the second group, both router ports can be active at the same time.

NOTE   Note that the recommendation to use MHSRP is predicated upon the fact that a single VLAN is being used on the IDF switches (as discussed in Chapter 11, this is often done to facilitate ease of network management). If you are using multiple VLANs on the IDFs, you can simply alternate active HSRP peers between the VLANs. See Chapter 11 for more information and configuration examples.

The catch with this approach is finding some technique to have half of the end stations use the .1 default gateway address and the other half use .2. Chapter 11 suggests using DHCP for this purpose. For example, Happy Homes is planning to deploy two DHCP servers (from the **ip helper-address** statements, we can determine that the IP addresses are 10.100.100.33 and 10.100.100.81). All leases issued by the first DHCP server, 10.100.100.33, specify .1 as the default gateway. On the other hand, all leases issued by the second DHCP server, 10.100.100.81, specify .2 as a default gateway. To help ensure a fairly random distribution of leases between two DHCP, the order of the **ip helper-address** statements can be inverted between the two MDF switches. For example, the configuration for Cat-B2-0B shows 10.100.100.81 as the first **ip helper-address** on every end-user subinterface. On the other MDF switch, Cat-B2-0A, 10.100.100.33 should be listed first.

Further down in the configuration, the actual Fast Ethernet ports are shown. Notice that these do not contain any direct configuration statements (the entire configuration is done on the logical port-channel interface). The only statement added to each interface is a **channel-group** command that includes the physical interface in the appropriate logical port-channel interface.

Because the Gigabit Ethernet interfaces are not using EtherChannel, the configuration is placed directly on the interface itself. Each interface receives an IP address and an IPX network statement. Because these interfaces do not connect to any end stations, HSRP and IP helper addresses are not necessary.

The remaining configuration commands set up the same management features discussed in the earlier configurations.

Design Alternatives

As with Design 1, hundreds of permutations are possible for Design 2. This section briefly discusses some of the more common alternatives.

First, as shown in Figure 17-5, Design 2 calls for a pair of 8500s for the server farm. Figure 17-7 illustrates a potential layout for the server farm under Design 2.

Figure 17-7 *Detail of Server Farm for Design 2*

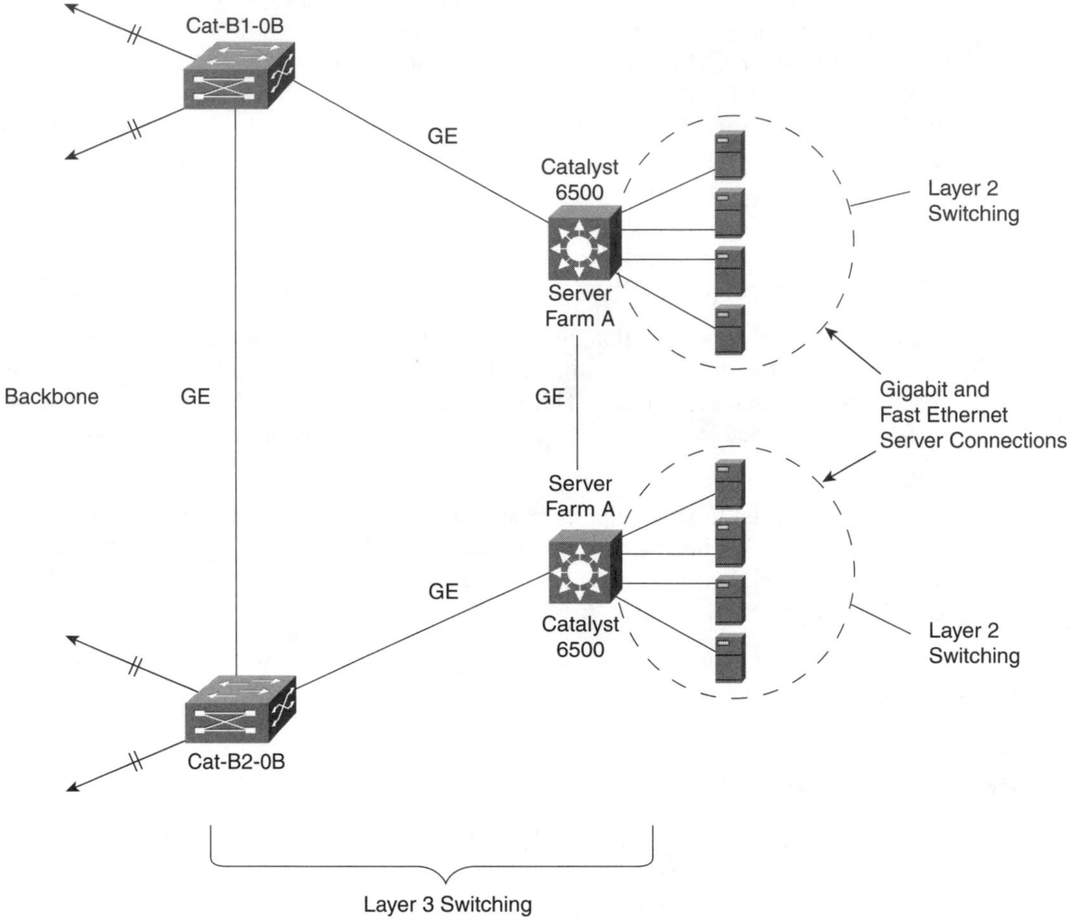

In this plan, a pair of Catalyst 6500 switches are directly connected to the backbone via Cat-B1-0B and Cat-B2-0B. By using the Catalyst 6500's MSFC Native IOS Mode, you can leverage the capability of these devices to simultaneous behave as both routing switches and switching routers (see Chapter 18 for more information on this capability). This gives you the flexibility to provide Layer 2 connectivity within the server farm while also utilizing Layer 3 to reach the backbone. In essence, the server farm becomes a miniature version of one of the buildings, but all contained within a pair of devices (the 6500s are acting like MDF and IDF devices at the same time).

As an alternative, some organizations have used the design shown in Figure 17-8.

Figure 17-8 *Layer 2 Server Farm Design*

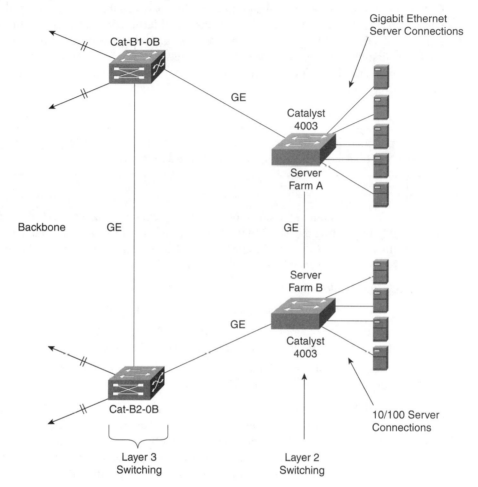

In this example, the Layer 2 Catalysts (in this case, 4003s) have been directly connected to the existing 8540s, Cat-B1-0B and Cat-B2-0B. The advantage of this approach is that it saves the expense of two Layer 3 switches and potentially removes one router hop from the typical end-user data path.

Unfortunately, this design is susceptible to the same default gateway issues discussed earlier in association with directly connecting servers to the LANE cloud in Design 1. As a result, it can actually add router hops by unnecessarily forwarding traffic to the wrong building. (You can run HSRP, but all traffic is directed to the active peer. MHSRP can be used, but it is generally less effective with servers than end users because of their extremely high bandwidth consumption.) If you do implement this design, consider running a routing protocol on your servers.

However, potentially the most serious problem involves IP addressing and link failures. Consider the case of where the Gigabit Ethernet link between the 4000s fails—both 8500s continue trying to send *all* traffic destined to the server farm subnet out their rightmost port. For example, Cat-B2-0B still tries to reach servers connected to Server Farm A by sending the traffic first to Server Farm B. And if the link between Server Farm B and Server Farm A is down, the traffic obviously never reaches its destination. This is a classic case of the discontinuous subnet problem.

TIP	Look for potential discontinuous subnets in your network. This can be especially important in mission-critical areas of your network such as a server farm.

Probably the most common modification to Design 2 entails using a Layer 2 core rather than directly connecting the MDF switches to each other with a full or partial mesh of Gigabit Ethernet links. Although the approach used in Design 2 is fine for smaller networks, a Layer 2 core is more scalable for several reasons:

- It is easier to add distribution blocks.
- It is easier to upgrade access bandwidth to one building block (simply upgrade the links to the Layer 2 core versus upgrading all the meshed bandwidth).
- Routing protocol peering is reduced from the distribution layer to the core.

The most common implementation is to use a pair of Layer 2 switches for redundancy (however, be careful to remove all Layer 2 loops in the core).

A third potential modification to Design 2 involves VLAN numbering. Notice that Design 2 uses the pattern-based VLAN numbering scheme discussed in Chapter 15. Because designs with a strong Layer 3 switching component effectively nullify the concept of VLANs being globally-unique broadcast domains, this approach is appropriate for designs such as Design 2. However, some organizations prefer to maintain globally-unique VLAN numbers even when utilizing Layer 3 switching. In this case, every subnet is mapped to a unique VLAN number. See Chapter 15 for more information on pattern-based versus globally-unique VLAN numbering schemes.

Finally, another option is to deploy Gigabit EtherChannel within the core and server farm. By offering considerably more available bandwidth, this can provide additional room for growth with the Happy Homes campus.

Summary

This chapter has sought to enhance the many concepts and commands covered earlier in this book by looking at real-world issues, problems, and designs. Two out of hundreds of possible solutions were considered. Although both designs have their advantages and disadvantages, neither design represents the right answer. Table 17-5 summarizes some of the more important differences discussed earlier.

Table 17-5   *Differences Between Design 1 and Design 2*

Characteristic	Design 1	Design 2
Layer 3 switch	Routing switches (MLS).	Switching routers (8500s).
Layer 3 vs. Layer 2	More Layer 2-oriented.	More Layer 3-oriented.
IDF VLANs	The same VLAN can traverse several IDF switches.	Every IDF switch should use different VLANs/subnets.
Spanning Tree	Triangles.	Running, but no (intentional) loops.
Load balancing	Spanning Tree.	MHRSP.

Catalyst 6000 Technology

This chapter covers the following key topics:

- **Catalyst 6000 Layer 2 Characteristics**—Discusses the base Catalyst 6000 and 6500 configuration.

- **MSM Layer 3 Switching**—The Multilayer Switch Module (MSM) is a router-on-a-stick configuration that provides ASIC-based routing for IP, IPX, and multicast traffic. This section discusses how to configure, use, and deploy these devices.

- **MSFC Hybrid Mode Layer 3 Switching**—The Multilayer Switch Feature Card (MSFC) Hybrid Mode is an implementation of Multilayer Switching (MLS) on the Catalyst 6000 platform. It is very similar to using MLS with a Route Switch Module (RSM) on a Catalyst 5000 (only much faster). This section looks at how to configure and implement this technology.

- **MSFC Native IOS Mode Layer 3 Switching**—The MSFC Native IOS Mode brings the effectiveness of Cisco's IOS in Layer 2/switched networks to new heights. By allowing the Catalyst 6000 to run a full copy of Cisco's traditional router software for both Layer 3 *and* Layer 2 processing, this represents an exciting and powerful tool for campus designs and implementations.

| NOTE | The term MSFC is used in this chapter to refer to both the MSFC *and* the Policy Feature Card (PFC). Note that currently the MSFC cannot be purchased without an accompanying PFC. On the other hand, a PFC *can* be purchased and used without an MSFC. This configuration supports QoS and access list functionality (but *not* Layer 3 switching). |

CHAPTER 18

Layer 3 Switching and the Catalyst 6000/6500s

The Catalyst 6000 family represents a significant step forward in switching technology while retaining a strong foundation in existing and proven Cisco designs. As this chapter discusses, the Catalyst 6000s and 6500s can act as faster versions of Layer 2 Catalyst 5000s. For shops starved for Gigabit Ethernet bandwidth and port density, this can be extremely useful. However, it is the Layer 3 switching capabilities of the Catalyst 6000s that set them apart from other switches and is the primary focus of this chapter.

Because of these powerful new features, the Catalyst 6000s are intentionally discussed in the last chapter of this book. In essence, the 6000s draw on material learned in virtually every prior chapter of this book but also add exciting new capabilities. For example, Chapter 4, "Configuring the Catalyst," discussed the XDI/CatOS Catalyst user interface of **set**, **clear**, and **show** commands. In one configuration, Catalyst 6000s use all of these commands and concepts. However, by taking advantage of the Catalyst 6000 *Native IOS Mode*, you can instantly convert your box into a full-fledged Cisco router (an entirely new, but familiar, user interface)! Similarly, the Catalyst 6000 can be used to implement most of the Layer 3 switching designs discussed in Chapter 11, "Layer 3 Switching." However, it goes beyond these features by offering a completely new approach to Layer 3 switch configuration and management—the previously mentioned Native IOS Mode. The Native IOS mode builds on the material discussed in Chapter 14, "Campus Design Models," and Chapter 15, "Campus Design Implementation," by supporting more flexible Layer 3 switching designs.

Catalyst 6000 Layer 2 Characteristics

In many respects, Catalyst 6000s can be viewed as bigger versions of Catalyst 5000s. This is especially true when Catalyst 6000s are configured to run the traditional Catalyst XDI/CatOS images. In this case, Catalyst 6000s use exactly the same user interface discussed in Chapter 4. Virtually every feature discussed throughout the book is supported using the same configuration steps on both products. In short, Layer 2 Catalyst 6000s look completely familiar to anyone who has configured a Catalyst 4000 or 5000.

NOTE   Recall from earlier chapters that XDI is the name of the UNIX-like kernel originally used to build early Catalyst devices.

Although Layer 2 Catalyst 6000s offer the same look and feel as Catalyst 5000s, they obviously offer increased capacity and throughput. For example, whereas the Catalyst 5000s use a 1.2-Gbps backplane and the 5500s use a 3.6-Gbps crossbar backplane, the 6000s use a 16-Gbps backplane (most vendors have started measuring switch capacity on a full-duplex basis, resulting in a backplane capacity rating of 32 Gbps for the 6000s). In addition to the 16-Gbps backplane, Catalyst 6500s also provide a 256-Gbps crossbar matrix (although initial Supervisor configurations do not utilize this capacity). Obviously, the 6000s and 6500s provide a dramatic increase in available Layer 2 switching throughput and Gigabit Ethernet port densities.

Because of the similarity between Layer 2 Catalyst and other Catalyst platforms discussed in detail throughout this book, this chapter does not dwell on their details.

TIP   The Catalyst 5000 Supervisor III uses an RJ-45 style console port that is pinned out in the exact opposite of the console port found on Cisco 2500 (and other) routers, creating widespread confusion when it initially shipped. The Catalyst 6000 Supervisor also uses an RJ-45 connector. However, to maintain backward compatibility with *both* the 2500 routers and the Catalyst 5000 Supervisor III, the Catalyst 6000 features a switch to select the pinout you prefer. When set to the *in* position, it uses the same console cable as a 2500 (that is, a rolled cable). When set to the *out* position, it uses the same cable as a Catalyst 5000 Supervisor III (a straight-through cable). To adjust the setting of this switch, use a paper clip (it is recessed behind a small hole in the faceplate).

MSM Layer 3 Switching

The initial Layer 3 switching engine for the Catalyst 6000 family consisted of the Multi-layer Switch Model (MSM). Based on Catalyst 8510 technology, the MSM provides a router-on-a-stick configuration integrated into the Catalyst 6000 chassis. Therefore, the MSM brings the power of the 8510 to the Catalyst 6000 family (namely IP and IPX routing at approximately 5 million packets per second [mpps]).

NOTE   The MSM contains a faster CPU that is currently used in the 8510.

From a configuration standpoint, the MSM connects to the Catalyst 6000 backplane via four Gigabit Ethernet interfaces. These interfaces are labeled as GigabitEthernet 0/0/0, 1/0/0, 3/0/0, and 4/0/0. Note that 2/0/0 is not used and that these numbers do not refer to the slot where the MSM is installed (they are always locally significant). Figure 18-1 illustrates the Catalyst 6000 backplane connections.

Figure 18-1 *Conceptual Diagram of the MSM*

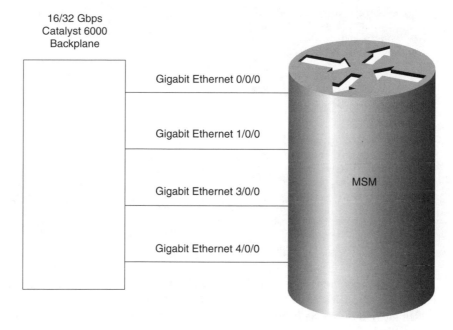

The MSM supports two primary types of inter-VLAN router configurations:

- Using each of the Ethernet interfaces as a separate router port
- Grouping all four of the Gigabit Ethernet interfaces into a single EtherChannel bundle

One important point to note is that both options require that configuration commands be entered on both the Layer 2 Supervisor *and* the Layer 3 MSM. The Supervisor configuration is used to assign the MSM interfaces to VLANs or to an EtherChannel bundle, whereas the MSM configuration is used to actually configure the routing process.

TIP   The MSM requires a coordinated configuration on both the Catalyst 6000 Supervisor and the MSM itself.

Using each of the Gigabit Ethernet interfaces as a separate router port is the simplest of the two configuration types. For example, the partial configuration shown in Example 18-1 configures the interfaces to handle routing for VLANs 1–4.

Example 18-1   *Using the MSM Interfaces as Unique Router Ports*

```
interface GigabitEthernet0/0/0
 ip address 10.0.1.1 255.255.255.0
 no ip redirects
 no ip directed-broadcast
!
interface GigabitEthernet1/0/0
 ip address 10.0.2.1 255.255.255.0
 no ip redirects
 no ip directed-broadcast
!
interface GigabitEthernet3/0/0
 ip address 10.0.3.1 255.255.255.0
 no ip redirects
 no ip directed-broadcast
!
interface GigabitEthernet4/0/0
 ip address 10.0.4.1 255.255.255.0
 no ip redirects
 no ip directed-broadcast
```

This configuration is conceptually identical to the router-on-a-stick configuration discussed in the "One-Link-per-VLAN" section of Chapter 11. Each interface is configured with a single VLAN and an IP address. Example 18-2 shows the corresponding Supervisor configuration that is used to assign each MSM interface to a separate VLAN.

Example 18-2   *Supervisor Configuration for Unique Router Ports*

```
Cat6000 (enable) set vlan 1 7/1
VLAN  Mod/Ports
----  ----------------------
1     1/1-2
      2/1-2
      3/3-24
      4/3-24
      5/1-2,5/5-8
      7/1-4

Cat6000 (enable) set vlan 2 7/2
VLAN 2 modified.
VLAN 1 modified.
VLAN  Mod/Ports
----  ----------------------
2     1/1-2
      5/7
      7/1-4

Cat6000 (enable) set vlan 3 7/3
Vlan 3 configuration successful
VLAN 3 modified.
VLAN 2 modified.
```

Example 18-2   *Supervisor Configuration for Unique Router Ports (Continued)*

```
VLAN   Mod/Ports
----   --------------------
3      1/1-2
       5/7
       7/1-4


Cat6000 (enable) set vlan 4 7/4
Vlan 4 configuration successful
VLAN 4 modified.
VLAN 3 modified.
VLAN   Mod/Ports
----   --------------------
4      1/1-2
       5/7
       7/1-4
```

This assigns each MSM router interface to a separate Layer 2 VLAN. Note that Example 18-2 assumes the MSM is located in Slot 7.

Although the configuration in Example 18-1 and Example 18-2 correctly provides routing services, you can obtain a much more flexible configuration by grouping all four of the Gigabit Ethernet interfaces into a single EtherChannel bundle. By doing so, certain VLANs are not tied to specific Gigabit Ethernet ASICs onboard the MSM, allowing for a more even distribution of traffic.

To create an EtherChannel bundle on the MSM, simply follow the steps outlined in the "EtherChannel" section of Chapter 11:

Step 1   Create one subinterface for each VLAN using the **interface port-channel** *port-channel.subinterface-number* command.

Step 2   Configure each subinterface. At a minimum, this consists of assigning a VLAN with the **encapsulation isl** *vlan-identifier* command and an IP and/or IPX address (802.10 can also be used). (It is possible to configure bridging but not recommended—see the "Integration between Routing and Bridging" section of Chapter 11.)

Step 3   Assign all four Gigabit Ethernet interfaces to the Port-channel interface using the **channel-group** *channel-number* command.

NOTE   Although generally not useful, it is possible to create more than one Port-channel interface and assign different Gigabit Ethernet interfaces to each.

For instance, Example 18-3 displays the complete configuration from an MSM that has been configured with a single EtherChannel interface to the Catalyst 6000 backplane.

Example 18-3 *A Complete MSM Configuration Using EtherChannel*

```
no service pad
service timestamps debug uptime
service timestamps log uptime
no service password-encryption
!
hostname MSM
!
!
ip subnet-zero
ipx routing 0050.730f.6a0c
!
!
interface Port-channel1
 no ip address
 no ip directed-broadcast
 hold-queue 300 in
!
interface Port-channel1.1
 encapsulation isl 1
 ip address 10.0.1.2 255.255.255.0
 no ip redirects
 no ip directed-broadcast
 ipx encapsulation NOVELL-ETHER
 ipx network A000100
 standby 1 timers 1 3
 standby 1 priority 200
 standby 1 preempt
 standby 1 ip 10.0.1.1
!
interface Port-channel1.2
 encapsulation isl 2
 ip address 10.0.2.2 255.255.255.0
 no ip redirects
 no ip directed-broadcast
 ipx encapsulation NOVELL-ETHER
 ipx network A000200
 standby 2 timers 1 3
 standby 2 priority 100
 standby 2 preempt
 standby 2 ip 10.0.2.1
!
interface Port-channel1.3
 encapsulation isl 3
 ip address 10.0.3.1 255.255.255.0
 no ip redirects
 no ip directed-broadcast
 ipx encapsulation NOVELL-ETHER
 ipx network A000300
!
interface GigabitEthernet0/0/0
```

Example 18-3   *A Complete MSM Configuration Using EtherChannel (Continued)*

```
 no ip address
 no ip directed-broadcast
 no negotiation auto
 channel-group 1
!
interface GigabitEthernet1/0/0
 no ip address
 no ip directed-broadcast
 no negotiation auto
 channel-group 1
!
interface GigabitEthernet3/0/0
 no ip address
 no ip directed-broadcast
 no negotiation auto
 channel-group 1
!
interface GigabitEthernet4/0/0
 no ip address
 no ip directed-broadcast
 no negotiation auto
 channel-group 1
!
router eigrp 1
 passive-interface Port-channel1.1
 passive-interface Port-channel1.2
 network 10.0.0.0
!
ip classless
!
!
line con 0
 transport input none
line aux 0
line vty 0 4
 no login
!
no scheduler allocate
end
```

Example 18-3 configures three subinterfaces on the EtherChannel interface: one each for VLAN 100, VLAN 101, and VLAN 102. All four of the Gigabit Ethernet interfaces have been included in the channel to provide a single high-speed pipe to the rest of the Catalyst.

To create the EtherChannel on the Layer 2 Supervisor, the commands shown in Example 18-4 are required.

Example 18-4 *Supervisor Configuration for Unique Router Ports*

```
Cat6000> (enable) set port channel 7/1-4 on
     Ports 7/1-4 channel mode set to on.
Cat6000> (enable) set trunk 7/1 nonegotiate isl
     Port(s) 7/1 trunk mode set to nonegotiate.
     Port(s) 7/1 trunk type set to isl.
```

These two commands first assign all four MSM interfaces to a single EtherChannel
interface and then enable ISL trunking across the entire bundle. (Although the **trunk**
command is only entered for Port 7/1, it is automatically applied to all four ports.)

NOTE   Notice that the MSM, being derived from 8500 technology, functions under the switching
router form of Layer 3 switching discussed in Chapter 11.

MSFC Hybrid Mode Layer 3 Switching

The second phase of Layer 3 switching for the Catalyst 6000 family introduced the Hybrid
Mode for the Multilayer Switch Feature Card (MSFC). This introduced the Multilayer
Switching (MLS) style Layer 3 switching to the Catalyst 6000 platform.

This section discusses the hardware used by the MSFC Hybrid Mode as well as
configuration concepts and syntax. This section also discusses the advantages and
disadvantages of this approach.

MSFC Hybrid Mode Hardware

From a hardware perspective, the MSFC is extremely similar to the Route Switch Feature
Card (RSFC) that is available for the Catalyst 5000s. The MSFC installs as a pair of
daughter cards to the Catalyst 6000 Supervisor. After installation, the Supervisor consists
of three components:

- The Supervisor itself (also referred to as a Switch Processor [SP])

- The PFC—An MLS SP engine very similar to the Catalyst 5000 NetFlow Feature
  Card (NFFC).

- The MSFC—A Route Processor (RP) engine.

Figure 18-2 illustrates these three components.

Figure 18-2 *MSFC Components*

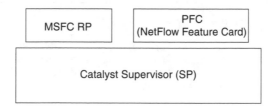

The Supervisor/SP contains a RISC CPU and the ASICs necessary to perform the duties of a Layer 2 switch. The PFC uses technology similar to the NFFC discussed in the "MLS" section of Chapter 11. Functioning as a flexible pattern matching and rewrite engine, it can be used to provide a wide range of high-speed features such as Layer 3 switching, Quality/ Class of Service (QoS/CoS), multicast support, and security filtering. From a Layer 3 switching perspective, it provides the MLS-SE shortcut services discussed in Chapter 11. (Technically speaking, the PFC replaces the Layer 2 forwarding ASIC on the Supervisor and also assumes these duties.) The MSFC daughter card is derived from the NPE-200 used in the Cisco 7200 routers. Being a high-performance and feature-rich router, it handles the MLS-RP end of the MLS scheme and routes the first packet in every IP and IPX flow. It can also be used to provide software-based routing for other protocols such as AppleTalk and DECnet (expect forwarding rates of approximately 125,000–150,000 pps).

In short, the MSFC Hybrid Mode offers the equivalent of a souped up Catalyst 5000 Route Switch Module (RSM) and NFFC in a single-slot solution.

MSFC Hybrid Mode Configuration Concepts

Configuring the MSFC Hybrid Mode is virtually identical to RSM-based MLS configurations discussed in the "Configuring MLS" section of Chapter 11. It uses the same **interface vlan** *vlan_number* concepts for its configuration. Routing protocols and other features use the same RSM-like commands.

The MSFC RP is also similar to the RSM in that it uses a full IOS image, thereby creating the same split personality seen in the RSM sections of Chapter 11. When connected to the console port of the Catalyst Supervisor, you are presented with the usual **set**, **clear**, and **show** commands available in all Catalysts using the XDI/CatOS interface. However, by using the **session** command, you create a virtual connection to the MSFC RP. This instantly transforms you from the world of Catalyst XDI/CatOS to the realm of router IOS.

Recall from Chapter 11 that the **session** command requires a parameter consisting of the router's slot number. In the case of the RSM, this can easily be determined by visual inspection. In the case of the MSFC RP, which operates as a daughter card in Slot 1 and/or Slot 2, the numbering scheme is less obvious because it uses a virtual slot number. One way to determine the appropriate slot is to use the **show module** command as seen in Example 18-5.

Example 18-5   *Using the* **show module** *Command to Determine the MSFC RP Virtual Slot Number*

```
Cat6000 (enable) show module
Mod Slot Ports Module-Type            Model               Status
--- ---- ----- ---------------------- ------------------- --------
1   1    2     1000BaseX Supervisor   WS-X6K-SUP1-2GE     ok
15  1    1     Multilayer Switch Feature WS-F6001-RSFC    ok
3   3    24    100BaseFX MM Ethernet  WS-X6224-100FX-MT   ok
4   4    24    100BaseFX MM Ethernet  WS-X6224-100FX-MT   ok
5   5    8     1000BaseX Ethernet     WS-X6408-GBIC       ok
6   6    48    10/100BaseTX (RJ-45)   WS-X6248-RJ-45      ok

Mod Module-Name          Serial-Num
--- -------------------- -----------
1                        SAD03070893
15                       3024158973
3                        SAD03080262
4                        SAD03080421
5                        SAD03040595
6                        SAD03142742

Mod MAC-Address(es)                            Hw    Fw        Sw
--- ------------------------------------------ ----- --------- -----------------
1   00-50-54-6c-a9-e6 to 00-50-54-6c-a9-e7 1.4   5.1(1)    4.2(0.24)DAY35
    00-50-54-6c-a9-e4 to 00-50-54-6c-a9-e5
    00-50-3e-05-58-00 to 00-50-3e-05-5b-ff
15  00-50-73-ff-ab-00 to 00-50-73-ff-ab-ff 0.305 12.0(2.6)T 12.0(2.6)TW6(0.14)
3   00-50-54-6c-a5-34 to 00-50-54-6c-a5-4b 1.2   4.2(0.24)V 4.2(0.24)DAY35
4   00-50-54-6c-a4-74 to 00-50-54-6c-a4-8b 1.2   4.2(0.24)V 4.2(0.24)DAY35
5   00-50-f0-a8-44-64 to 00-50-f0-a8-44-6b 1.4   4.2(0.24)V 4.2(0.24)DAY35
6   00-50-f0-aa-58-38 to 00-50-f0-aa-58-67 1.0   4.2(0.24)V 4.2(0.24)DAY35

Mod Sub-Type              Sub-Model           Sub-Serial  Sub-Hw
--- --------------------- ------------------- ----------- ------
1   L3 Switching Engine   WS-F6K-PFC          SAD03152173 0.205
Cat6000 (enable)
```

Notice that the second line (marked in bold type) under the uppermost headers in Example 18-5 lists the MSFC RP as a **Multilayer Switch Feature WS-F6001-RSFC** in Slot 15.

NOTE   Example 18-5 shows the output of a 6009/6509 containing a single Supervisor in Slot 1. An MSFC physically located in Slot 2 uses a virtual slot number of 16. A 6006/6506 also uses Slots 15 and 16.

Therefore, by entering the command **session 15**, you are connected to the MSFC RP where you can enter router commands.

TIP Although the numbering pattern is fairly simple, use the **show module** command to determine and remember the virtual slot numbers used by MSFC RP modules.

Configuring MLS with MSFC Hybrid Mode

As with the RSM and Catalyst 5000 Supervisor MLS configurations, the Layer 2 Catalyst Supervisor has MLS processing enabled by default (in fact, it currently cannot be disabled on a Catalyst 6000). Also similar to MLS on the 5000s, the MSFC RP is *not* configured to provide MLS service by default. To add MLS to an already functioning MSFC RP router configuration, complete the following four-step process:

Step 1 Globally enable MLS on the RP with the **mls rp ip** command. (You can also use **mls rp ipx** for the IPX protocol.)

Step 2 Configure a VLAN Trunking Protocol (VTP) domain for each VLAN interface using the **mls rp vtp-domain** *domain_name* command.

Step 3 Enable MLS on each VLAN interface using the **mls rp ip** or **mls rp ipx** commands.

Step 4 Select one or more router interfaces to send MLSP packets using the **mls rp management-interface** command.

NOTE   Chapter 11 presented this list as a five-step list because it included a step (Step 3) to configure non-trunk links on external routers. Because this is not necessary for integrated routers such as the MSFC RP, this step has been omitted here.

For example, the configuration displayed in Example 18-6 enables MLS for VLANs 1 through 3 on an MSFC RP (both IP and IPX are configured)

Example 18-6 *A Complete MSFC RP Configuration for MLS*

```
no service pad
service timestamps debug uptime
service timestamps log uptime
no service password-encryption
!
hostname MSFC-RP
!
boot system flash bootflash:c6msfc-js-mz.120-2.6.TW6.0.14.bin
!
!
ip subnet-zero
!
ip cef
ipx routing 0000.2100.0000
mls rp ip
mls rp ipx
!
!
 interface Vlan1
 ip address 10.0.1.2 255.255.255.0
 no ip redirects
 no ip directed-broadcast
 no ip route-cache cef
 ipx network A000100
 mls rp vtp-domain Skinner
 mls rp management-interface
 mls rp ip
 mls rp ipx
 standby 1 timers 1 3
 standby 1 priority 200 preempt
 standby 1 ip 10.0.1.1
 !
interface Vlan2
 ip address 10.0.2.2 255.255.255.0
 no ip redirects
 no ip directed-broadcast
 no ip route-cache cef
 ipx network A000200
 mls rp vtp-domain Skinner
 mls rp ip
 mls rp ipx
 standby 2 timers 1 3
 standby 2 priority 100 preempt
 standby 2 ip 10.0.2.1
 !
interface Vlan3
 ip address 10.0.3.1 255.255.255.0
 no ip directed-broadcast
 no ip route-cache cef
 ipx network A000300
 mls rp vtp-domain Skinner
```

Example 18-6   *A Complete MSFC RP Configuration for MLS (Continued)*

```
 mls rp ip
 mls rp ipx
 !
router eigrp 1
 passive-interface Vlan1
 passive-interface Vlan2
 network 10.0.0.0
 !
ip classless
no ip http server
 !
 !
line con 0
 transport input none
line vty 0 4
 login
 !
end
```

Note that the configuration in Example 18-6 is functionally equivalent to the MSM configuration shown in Example 18-3.

Example 18-7 shows the results of **show mls rp** on the MSFC RP.

Example 18-7   *Output of* **show mls rp** *on MSFC RP*

```
MSFC-RP# show mls rp
ip multilayer switching is globally enabled
ipx multilayer switching is globally enabled
ipx mls inbound acl overide is globally disabled
mls id is 0000.2100.0000
mls ip address 127.0.0.12
mls ip flow mask is destination
mls ipx flow mask is destination
number of domains configured for mls 1

vlan domain name: Skinner
    current ip flow mask: destination
    ip current/next global purge: false/false
    ip current/next purge count: 0/0
    current ipx flow mask: destination
    ipx current/next global purge: false/false
    ipx current/next purge count: 0/0
    current sequence number: 1507018760
    current/maximum retry count: 10/10
    current domain state: change
    domain uptime: 00:08:32
    keepalive timer not running
```

continues

Example 18-7 *Output of* **show mls rp** *on MSFC RP (Continued)*

```
retry timer expires in 1 seconds
change timer not running
fcp subblock count = 3

1 management interface(s) currently defined:
    vlan 1 on Vlan1

2 mac-vlan(s) configured for multi-layer switching

2 mac-vlan(s) enabled for ip multi-layer switching:

    mac 0050.73ff.ab38
      vlan id(s)
      1    2

2 mac-vlan(s) enabled for ipx multi-layer switching:

    mac 0050.73ff.ab38
      vlan id(s)
      1    2

router currently aware of following 0 switch(es):
    no switch id's currently exists in domain
```

The first section of Example 18-7 shows useful information such as whether IP and IPX MLS are enabled and the currently active flow masks. The next section documents aspects of the MultiLayer Switching Protocol (MLSP) such as the VTP domain name and MLSP sequence number.

Example 18-8 displays the output of **show mls** on the Catalyst SP.

Example 18-8 *Output of* **show mls** *on the Catalyst 6000 Supervisor*

```
Cat6000 (enable) show mls
Total packets switched = 5683
Total Active MLS entries = 87
IP Multilayer switching aging time = 256 seconds
IP Multilayer switching fast aging time = 0 seconds, packet threshold = 0
IP Current flow mask is Destination flow
Active IP MLS entries = 55
Netflow Data Export version: 8
Netflow Data Export disabled
Netflow Data Export port/host is not configured.
Total packets exported = 0

IP MLS-RP IP    MLS-RP ID    XTAG MLS-RP MAC         Vlans
--------------  -----------  ---- ----------------   ----------------
127.0.0.12      15           1    00-50-73-ff-ab-38  1,2,3


IPX Multilayer switching aging time = 256 seconds
```

Example 18-8   *Output of* **show mls** *on the Catalyst 6000 Supervisor (Continued)*

```
IPX flow mask is Destination flow
IPX max hop is 255
Active IPX MLS entries = 0

IPX MLS-RP IP   MLS-RP ID   XTAG MLS-RP MAC        Vlans
-------------- ------------ ---- ---------------- ----------------
127.0.0.12      15          1    00-50-73-ff-ab-38 1,2
```

Example 18-8 shows some of the statistics collected from the NFFC/PFC. For example, the total number of packets Layer 3 switched using MLS is shown on the first line. The second line displays the total number of active shortcut entries in the NFFC/PFC cache. The output also displays information on aging, flow masks, NetFlow Data Export, and IP/IPX MLS-RPs.

For more information on configuring MLS, see the "MLS" section of Chapter 11.

The Advantages and Disadvantages of MSFC Hybrid Mode

The MSFC Hybrid Mode is a very powerful feature because it combines the benefits of an RSM-like router with the Gigabit-speed Layer 3 switching of the NFFC/PFC.

Recall from Chapters 11, 14, and 15 that the RSM's most appealing feature is its very tight integration of Layer 2 and Layer 3 technology. As ports are assigned to Layer 2 VLANs on the Catalyst Supervisor, the RSM automatically places them in the appropriate Layer 3 virtual interface. This scheme is considerably more flexible and scalable than the IRB approach to Layer 2/3 integration used by router platforms such as the Catalyst 8500s (at least from a configuration and management standpoint). Because the MSFC RP functions under the same model as the RSM, it also inherits all of these benefits.

Although the tight Layer 2/3 integration of the RSM is extremely useful when creating large-scale campus networks, its software-based approach to routing can create significant bottlenecks for Gigabit-speed traffic. This is where the NFFC/PFC comes in. By providing standards-compliant, hardware-assisted Layer 3 switching capabilities, it can turbo charge the RSM or the MSFC RP. By doing so, you lose almost none of the RSM's benefits. The resulting collaboration of software and hardware creates an extremely fast yet scalable Layer 3 switching architecture.

Although many organizations have considered MLS to be nothing short of a revolution in Layer 3 switching technology, there is one downside: It requires two separate configurations using two separate user interfaces. The Layer 3 configuration must be maintained on the MSFC RP using the traditional Cisco IOS interface. On the other hand, the Layer 2 configuration must be maintained on the Catalyst Supervisor using the XDI/CatOS interface. In fact, it is the split personality nature of this approach that earns it the designation of Hybrid Mode.

Because the MSFC Hybrid Mode uses a potentially confusing mixture of two user interfaces, many organizations have asked for a way to capture the benefits of this approach to Layer 3 switching while having to deal with only a single user interface. Fortunately, this is where the MSFC Native IOS Mode comes in.

MSFC Native IOS Mode Layer 3 Switching

The MSFC Native IOS Mode approach to Layer 3 switching represents a unique and virtually ideal blend of Layer 2 and Layer 3 technology. It is the result of approximately six years of integration between Cisco routing and Catalyst switching (Cisco acquired Crescendo Communications, Inc. in the fall of 1993). Essentially, Native IOS Mode creates an environment where Catalyst 6000 switches can be completely configured and managed through the familiar and powerful IOS user interface.

The Benefits of Native IOS Mode

Chapters 11, 14, and 15 discussed the differences and unique benefits of the routing switch (MLS) and switching router (Catalyst 8500) approaches to Layer 3 switching. Table 18-1 summarizes the primary advantages and disadvantages of each.

Table 18-1 *Primary Advantages and Disadvantages of MLS and 8500s*

Technique	Primary Advantages	Primary Disadvantages
MLS	Tight integration of Layer 2 and 3.	Allows Layer 2 VLANs to transit the switch by default—can lead to excessively flat networks.
		Requires the use of two separate user interfaces (IOS and XDI/CatOS).
Catalyst 8500s	Uses the familiar IOS user interface.	Integrating Layer 2 and Layer 3 generally requires the use of Integrated Routing and Bridging (IRB), a technique that can be difficult to manage in large networks.
	Offers powerful integration features with ATM.	Too Layer 3 oriented for some campus networks.
		Doesn't understand VLANs.

Although both approaches can be very effective in the appropriate design (MLS in Layer 2-oriented designs and 8500s in Layer 3-oriented designs), both suffer from some drawbacks (although some argue that most of these downsides are not a big deal).

Native IOS Mode is uniquely positioned in between the MLS and Catalyst 8500 approaches to Layer 3 switching. As such, it captures the Ethernet-based benefits of both while completely avoiding the downsides of both. As a result, the Native IOS Mode offers the following advantages:

- It provides an extremely useful metaphor for configuring and integrating Layer 2 and Layer 3 technology. These capabilities are discussed in detail later in the chapter.

- Because it uses a single user interface, organizations can avoid the confusion and training costs associated with supporting two interfaces.

- Because it uses the IOS interface, most network personnel can use the Native IOS Mode technology with minimal training.

- Because of the integrated user interface, organizations can more readily see and visualize their logical topology. Therefore, people are less likely to mistakenly create flat earth networks and campus-wide VLANs.

- Although it is based internally on the same MLS technology used in the Hybrid Mode, the end user is insulated from having to configure MLS directly.

- It understands and has full support for VLANs. (Although the Catalyst 6000 ASICs support Dynamic VLANs and VMPS, this feature is currently not supported on the platform because of its anticipated use as a backbone switch where all ports are hard-coded into each VLAN.)

- It maintains almost all of the Layer 2 features of the XDI/CatOS Catalysts such as VTP, DTP/DISL, and PAgP.

- These capabilities allow the Native IOS Mode MSFC to function as either a routing switch (as with MLS) or a switching router (as with 8500s). Although this can create confusion for those trying to discuss and explain such concepts, it creates an extremely powerful and flexible approach to Layer 3 switching.

- Because the differences between the Hybrid Mode and Native IOS Mode consist only of software, it is easy to convert the box between the two as an organization's needs change (it's merely a matter of changing the images on flash).

Most importantly, the Native IOS Mode allows you to achieve all of these benefits while retaining the speed of the Hybrid Mode (first generation speeds will be approximately 15 mpps).

NOTE   Note that the Catalyst 6000s and Native IOS Mode do not have the Catalyst 8500's ATM switching and ATM-to-Ethernet integration capabilities.

MSFC Native IOS Mode Operating Concepts

As discussed earlier in the chapter, using an MSFC results in there being two CPUs onboard the Catalyst 6000's Supervisor. One is the 150 Mhz R4700 used by the Layer 2-oriented Supervisor itself (when using a Catalyst 6000 Supervisor without an MSFC daughter card, this is the only CPU). This is referred to as the *SP CPU*. The second CPU is the 200 Mhz R5000 located on the RP (essentially an NPE-200 from a 7200 router).

Under the Hybrid Mode discussed in the previous section, the SP CPU runs an XDI/CatOS image and is used to control the Layer 2 side of the box, whereas the RP CPU runs the router IOS and is used to provide Layer 3 services. The key to the Native IOS Mode is that *both CPUs run full IOS software*. And no, this is not some warmed-over XDI/CatOS code made to look like IOS—the executable images used by both CPUs use the full-blown IOS kernel.

From a physical standpoint, the RJ-45 console port on the front of the Catalyst 6000 Supervisor is obviously connected to the SP CPUs hardware. However, during the 6000's boot cycle, control is passed to the RP CPU. Therefore, in Native IOS Mode, the RP acts as the primary CPU, and the SP acts as the secondary. All human interaction is done directly through the RP CPU. As commands are entered that affect the Layer 2/SP side of the device, commands are passed over an internal bus from the RP to the SP.

Also notice that for performance reasons, both CPUs are fully functioning (the SP CPU is not sitting completely idle). The SP CPU concentrates on port-level management (such as link up/down) and Layer 2 protocols such as Spanning Tree, VTP, and DTP. The RP CPU performs duties such as routing the first packet in every IP or IPX flow (or all packets for protocols that are not supported by the NFFC/PFC), running routing protocols, CDP, and PAgP.

The two CPUs boot from two different binary image files. First, the SP CPU takes control and loads an image from flash memory. Then, it passes control to the RP image (along with passing control of the console port) so that it can boot another image and take over as the primary CPU for the entire device.

MSFC Native IOS Mode Configuration Concepts

The unique and unified user interface of the Native IOS Mode is what sets it apart. Before digging into specific commands, this section takes a look at several concepts that underlie the configuration process.

Nonvolatile RAM

As with all Cisco devices, there must be some place to store the configuration while the device is powered down. Almost all Cisco devices use Nonvolatile RAM (NVRAM) for this purpose. However, the Native IOS Mode MSFC is somewhat unique in that it maintains two sets of NVRAM configurations:

- The VLAN database
- The local switch configuration

Although it might appear strange at first to have two different sorts of NVRAM information, it makes complete sense upon closer inspection. Consider that each NVRAM repository is storing a different type of information. The VLAN database contains information that is global to the entire network. As information is added to this list, it should be immediately (or almost immediately) saved and shared through the entire VTP domain. (Assume that the current switch is a VTP server; for more information, see Chapter 12, "VLAN Trunking Protocol.") Also, as VTP advertisements are received from other devices, they should immediately be saved (recall that the definition of a VTP server requires that *all* VLANs be saved to NVRAM). On the other hand, the switch configuration is locally significant. Furthermore, these normal IOS configuration statements are only supposed to be saved when the user enters the **copy run start** or **write memory** commands. After all, one of the benefits to the IOS is that you can make all the changes you want and return to the exact place you started from by merely rebooting the box (assuming that you did not save the new configuration).

Therefore, rather than trying to interleave the two sets of data, two completely different stores are maintained. The VLAN database holds globally significant information that gets saved right away (as it would under the XDI/CatOS interface). The switch configuration stores locally significant information only when the user enters some form of a save command.

Configuration Modes

The split in NVRAM storage also corresponds to two different configuration modes:

- VLAN database configuration mode
- Normal IOS configuration mode

VLAN Database Configuration Mode

The VLAN database configuration mode is used to control VTP information. Not only can it be used to set the VTP mode to server, client, or transparent, it provides a mechanism to add, modify, and delete VLANs. Example 18-9 shows some basic VLAN database commands from the online help system.

Example 18-9   *Using the VLAN Database Configuration Mode*

```
NativeMode# vlan database
NativeMode(vlan)# ?
VLAN database editing buffer manipulation commands:
  abort  Exit mode without applying the changes
  apply  Apply current changes and bump revision number
  exit   Apply changes, bump revision number, and exit mode
  no     Negate a command or set its defaults
  reset  Abandon current changes and reread current database
  show   Show database information
  vlan   Add, delete, or modify values assoicated with a single VLAN
  vtp    Perform VTP adminsitrative functions.

NativeMode(vlan)# exit
APPLY completed.
Exiting....
NativeMode#
```

To use the VLAN database configuration mode, enter the **vlan database** command from the EXEC prompt. This places you in the VLAN database mode and modifies the prompt to indicate this (the prompt now consists of the RP's name and the word **vlan** in parentheses). As shown by the online help in Example 18-9, the **vtp** command can be used to control the VTP configuration of a device. For example, **set vtp client** and **set vtp transparent** change a Catalyst to client and transparent modes, respectively. The device can be returned to the default of server mode with the command **set vtp server**. The command **set vtp domain Skinner** changes the VTP domain name to Skinner. There are other commands to control VTP features such as passwords, pruning, and version 2 support.

The **vlan** command shown in Example 18-9 can be used to add, delete, or modify VLANs. For example, the command **vlan 2 name Marketing** creates VLAN 2. Then, issuing the command **vlan 2 name Finance** changes the VLAN's name from Marketing to Finance. Entering **no vlan 2** removes VLAN 2 altogether. When creating or modifying VLANs, additional parameters can be specified to control attributes such as MTU and media type. Example 18-10 shows a list from the online help screen.

Example 18-10   *Online Help Listing of Available VLAN Parameters*

```
NativeMode(vlan)# vlan 3 ?
  are       Maximum number of All Route Explorer hops for this VLAN
  backupcrf Backup CRF mode of the VLAN
  bridge    Bridging characteristics of the VLAN
  media     Media type of the VLAN
  mtu       VLAN Maximum Transmission Unit
  name      Ascii name of the VLAN
  parent    ID number of the Parent VLAN of FDDI or Token Ring type VLANs
  ring      Ring number of FDDI or Token Ring type VLANs
  said      IEEE 802.10 SAID
  state     Operational state of the VLAN
  ste       Maximum number of Spanning Tree Explorer hops for this VLAN
  stp       Spanning tree characteristics of the VLAN
  tb-vlan1  ID number of the first translational VLAN for this VLAN (or zero
            if none)
  tb-vlan2  ID number of the second translational VLAN for this VLAN (or zero
            if none)
  <cr>
NativeMode(vlan)# vlan 3
```

After making changes, you can **apply** them. At this point, the changes are saved to the VLAN database section of NVRAM (therefore, VLAN changes made under Native IOS Mode are not as immediate as those made under the XDI/CatOS interface). The **exit** command can be used to first apply the changes to the database and then return to the EXEC mode.

Normal IOS Configuration Mode

Contrary to VLAN database mode, the normal IOS configuration mode should be familiar to all users of traditional Cisco router platforms. To enter this mode, use the **configure terminal** command. From there, the usual **interface** *interface-type interface-number*, **router** *protocol*, and **line** *line-type number* submodes can be used to configure the routing characteristics of the device. To exit the normal IOS configuration mode, enter the **exit** command to move one level at a time up towards the EXEC mode. To jump straight from a submode to EXEC mode, use the **end** command or press **Ctrl-Z**. In Normal IOS configuration mode, commands are applied to the running configuration as soon as you press the Enter key. However, commands are only saved to NVRAM when you enter **copy run start** or **write mem**.

Native IOS Mode Interface Types

Much of the appeal of the Native IOS Mode centers around the way in which it handles the various types of ports that exist in the typical campus network. Rather than relying on IRB to mix Layer 2 and Layer 3 in the same device (as mentioned earlier, IRB can be confusing and difficult to configure and manage), Native IOS Mode has a unique approach that is powerful, flexible, and intuitive.

In all, there are two primary types of interfaces under the Native IOS Mode:

- Routed interfaces
- Switched interfaces (also called switchport interfaces)

These two primary types can be further subdivided into the following four interface types:

- Routed Physical Interfaces
- Routed SVI Interfaces
- Access Switchport Interfaces
- Trunk Switchport Interfaces

Each of these is discussed in the following sections.

Routed Physical Interfaces

Like all Cisco IOS devices, interfaces default to being routed. In this configuration, every port receives its own IP and/or IPX address. Notice that each of these must fall on a unique IP subnet or IPX network. For example, if you try to assign 10.0.1.2 to interface 5/2 when interface 5/1 has already been assigned 10.0.1.1, you receive the following message:

```
10.0.1.0 overlaps with FastEthernet5/1
```

TIP   The Native IOS Mode and the XDI/CatOS user interfaces use the terms interface and port differently. In Native IOS Mode, Layer 3 external connections are called interfaces, and Layer 2 connections are referred to as ports (actually, switchports). Under XDI/CatOS, the term interface is used to only refer to the management entities such as SC0, SL0, and ME1 (in the case of SC0 and SL0, these are logical ports that you cannot see and touch; in the case of ME1, it is a physical port, but it cannot be used for end-user traffic). XDI/CatOS uses the term port to refer to all external points of connection (these are ports you can physically touch). This chapter uses the terms interface and port interchangeably.

Also notice that the Native IOS Mode software numbers interfaces starting from 1, not 0 (in other words, the first interface is 1/1, not 0/0). Although this is different than other IOS devices, it is consistent with the rest of the Catalyst platform.

In a similar fashion, you receive the following error message if you try to assign both interfaces to the same IPX network number:

```
%IPX network 0A000100 already exists on interface FastEthernet5/1
```

NOTE   Note that this behavior is the same throughout Cisco's entire router product line. It is not some strange thing cooked up just for the Catalyst 6000 Native IOS Mode.

Access Switchport Interfaces

To place several interfaces in the same IP subnet or IPX network, a common practice in virtually all campus networks, you need to convert the port from a routed interface to a switched interface. To do so, simply enter the **switchport** command on the appropriate interface. For example, the code shown in Example 18-11 does this for interfaces 5/1 and 5/2.

Example 18-11   *Placing Two Interfaces in the Same VLAN (Default = VLAN 1)*

```
NativeMode# configure terminal
NativeMode(Config)# interface FastEthernet5/1
NativeMode(Config-if)# switchport
NativeMode(Config-if)# interface FastEthernet5/2
NativeMode(Config-if)# switchport
NativeMode(Config-if)# end
NativeMode#
```

Switchports automatically default to VLAN 1 (although this assignment is not made until after the **switchport** command has been entered). To alter this assignment, you can use additional **switchport** commands. First, decide if you want the interface to be an access port (one VLAN) or a trunk port (multiple VLANs using ISL or 802.1Q). This section looks at access ports (trunk ports are discussed later). To create an access port, first enter the **switchport mode access** command on the interface. Then enter **switchport access vlan** *vlan-identifier* to assign a VLAN. For example, Example 18-12 assigns 5/1 and 5/2 to VLAN 2.

Example 18-12   *Creating Access Port in VLAN 2*

```
NativeMode# configure terminal
NativeMode(Config)# interface FastEthernet5/1
NativeMode(Config-if)# switchport mode access
NativeMode(Config-if)# switchport access vlan 2
NativeMode(Config-if)# interface FastEthernet5/2
NativeMode(Config-if)# switchport mode access
NativeMode(Config-if)# switchport access vlan 2
NativeMode(Config-if)# end
NativeMode#
```

However, trying to assign an IP address to 5/1 or 5/2 at this point does not work. If you try this, the RP outputs the following message:

```
% IP addresses may not be configured on L2 links.
```

If you think about it, this makes complete sense—these two interfaces have been converted to Layer 2 ports that do not directly receive Layer 3 IP and IPX addresses. This is the same restriction placed on other Layer 2 ports. For example, you cannot apply IP addresses to ports in the XDI/CatOS Catalyst configuration. Also, when using bridging on IOS-based Cisco routers, you cannot assign Layer 3 addresses to the same interface that contains a bridge-group (the software lets you make the assignment, but the interface is now *routing* that protocol, not *bridging* it; see Chapter 11 for more information on bridge-groups).

Routed SVI Interfaces

To assign an IP address to 5/1 and 5/2, you need a separate interface that can act as the routed interface on behalf of both switchports. This is where the Switch Virtual Interface (SVI) comes in. SVIs use names like interface VLAN 1 and interface VLAN 2. These interfaces receive the Layer 3 information for each VLAN. As switchports are added and removed from various VLANs, they automatically participate in the Layer 3 environment created by the appropriate SVI.

NOTE   Notice that this is the same as the RSM. In fact, it is this automatic linkage between Layer 3 SVI VLAN interfaces and Layer 2 switchports that makes the Native IOS Mode such an attractive vehicle for configuring campus networks.

To create an SVI, simply enter the **interface VLAN** *vlan-identifier* command. This places you in interface mode for that VLAN (the prompt changes to **RP_Name(Config-if)#**) where you can configure the appropriate Layer 3 information. For example, Example 18-13 creates and configures VLANs 1 and 2 with IP and IPX addresses.

Example 18-13   *Creating Two SVI Interfaces*

```
NativeMode# config t
NativeMode(Config)# interface vlan 1
NativeMode(Config-if)# ip address 10.0.1.1 255.255.255.0
NativeMode(Config-if)# ipx network 0A000100
NativeMode(Config-if)# interface vlan 2
NativeMode(Config-if)# ip address 10.0.2.1 255.255.255.0
NativeMode(Config-if)# ipx network 0A000200
NativeMode(Config-if)# end
NativeMode#
```

NOTE   Although all ports are assigned to VLAN 1 by default, the VLAN 1 SVI does not exist by default. To assign Layer 3 attributes to VLAN 1, you must create this SVI.

Trunk Switchport Interfaces

Finally, trunk interfaces can be created to carry multiple VLANs using ISL or 802.1Q encapsulations. To apply trunking to a switchport, simply enter the **switchport trunk encapsulation** [**dot1q** | **isl** | **negotiate**] command. Several other **switchport trunk** parameters can be used to tune the behavior of the trunk. The **native** parameter can be used to set the 802.1Q native VLAN (this VLAN is sent untagged). The **allowed** parameter can be used to control the VLANs that are forwarded out that interface. Similarly, the **pruning** parameter can be used to control VTP pruning on the link.

For example, the code in Example 18-14 makes Port 5/10 an ISL trunk for VLANs 1—10.

Example 18-14   *Creating a Trunk*

```
NativeMode# configure terminal
NativeMode(Config)# interface FastEthernet5/10
NativeMode(Config-if)# switchport
NativeMode(Config-if)# switchport trunk encapsulation isl
NativeMode(Config-if)# switchport trunk allowed vlan remove 11-1000
NativeMode(Config-if)# end
NativeMode#
```

Therefore, in total, the MSFC Native IOS Mode uses four port/interface types as summarized in Table 18-2.

Table 18-2   *MSFC Native IOS Mode Port/Interface Types*

Port/Interface Type	Use	Sample Configuration Commands
Routed Physical Interface	Used to configure interfaces functioning as fully routed port. Conceptually, these interfaces are similar to ones found on traditional Cisco router platforms.	**interface GigabitEthernet1/1** **ip address 10.0.1.1 255.255.255.0** **ipx network FEEDFACE**
Routed SVI Interface	Acts as the single routed interface for the collection of all switchports assigned to a given VLAN.	**interface Vlan1** **ip address 10.0.1.1 255.255.255.0** **ipx network FEEDFACE**
Access Switchport Interface	Used to configure a Layer 2 port that belongs to one VLAN.	**interface GigabitEthernet1/1** **switchport** **switchport access vlan 1** **switchport mode access**
Trunk Switchport Interface	Used to configure a Layer 2 port that belongs to multiple VLANs.	**interface GigabitEthernet1/1** **switchport** **switchport trunk**

Native IOS Mode Configuration

Figure 18-3 extends the discussion in the previous section to present a conceptual diagram of the Catalyst 6000 Native IOS Mode.

Figure 18-3 *Conceptual Diagram of the MSFC Native IOS Mode*

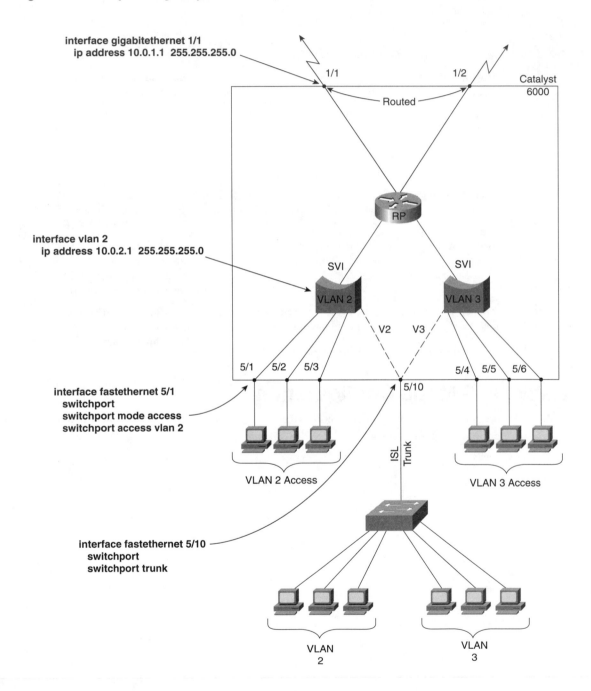

In Figure 18-3, the Gigabit Ethernet ports on the Supervisor (1/1 and 1/2) have been configured as fully routed interfaces. Slot 5 contains a Fast Ethernet line card. Ports 5/1–5/3 have been configured as Layer 2 switchports in VLAN 2. Ports 5/4–5/6 have been configured as switchports in VLAN 3. Port 5/10 has been configured as an 802.1Q trunk. Summarized configuration examples are also illustrated in the figure. As shown in Figure 18-3, the Native IOS mode centers around the concept of a virtual router. Physically routed ports such as Gigabit Ethernet 1/1 and 1/2 directly connect to the virtual router. In the case of switchports, they connect to the router via an SVI. The SVI acts as a logical bridge/switch for the traffic within that VLAN. It is also assigned the Layer 3 characteristics of that VLAN for the purpose of connecting to the virtual router. Trunk links use the magic of ISL and 802.1Q encapsulation to simultaneously connect to multiple VLANs and SVIs.

The sections that follow walk step-by-step through a complete MSFC Native IOS Mode configuration that is similar to the MSM and MSFC configurations shown in Example 18-2 and Example 18-4.

The steps for completing the MSFC Native IOS Mode configuration are as follows:

Step 1   Assign a name to the router

Step 2   Configure VTP

Step 3   Create the VLANs

Step 4   Configure the Gigabit Ethernet uplinks as routed interfaces

Step 5   Configure the VLAN 2 switchports

Step 6   Configure the VLAN 3 switchports

Step 7   Configure a trunk switchport

Step 8   Configure the SVI interfaces

Step 9   Configure routing

Figure 18-4 illustrates the resulting configuration.

Figure 18-4 *Conceptual Diagram for Configuration Example*

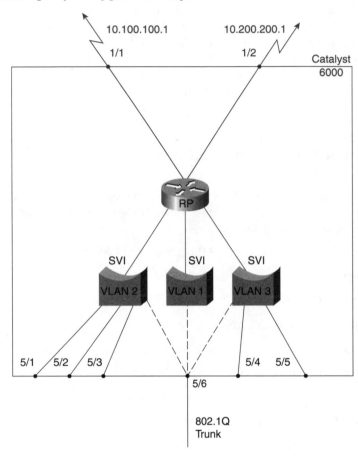

Step 1: Assign a Name to the Router

Using the commands shown in Example 18-15, assign a name to the Catalyst Supervisor.

Example 18-15 *Assigning a Name to the Catalyst*

```
Router> en
Router# configure terminal
Enter configuration commands, one per line.  End with CNTL/Z.
Router(config)# hostname NativeMode
NativeMode(config)# end
NativeMode#
```

Step 2: Configure VTP

Configure VTP to place the Catalyst in VTP transparent mode and to use a VTP domain of Skinner as displayed in Example 18-16.

Example 18-16   *Configuring VTP*

```
NativeMode#
NativeMode# vlan database
NativeMode(vlan)# vtp transparent
Setting device to VTP TRANSPARENT mode.
NativeMode(vlan)# vtp domain Skinner
Changing VTP domain name from Null to Skinner
```

Step 3: Create the VLANs

Create VLANs 2 and 3 in the VLAN database (VLAN 1 exists by default). Use the **exit** command to apply the VLAN and VTP changes and return to EXEC mode. This is shown in Example 18-17.

Example 18-17   *Creating Two New VLANs*

```
NativeMode(vlan)# vlan 2 name Marketing
VLAN 2 added:
    Name: Marketing
NativeMode(vlan)#
NativeMode(vlan)# vlan 3 name Engineering
VLAN 3 added:
    Name: Engineering
NativeMode(vlan)# exit
APPLY completed.
Exiting....
NativeMode#
```

TIP   The **apply** command can be used to apply the VTP and VLAN changes without leaving the **vlan database** mode.

Step 4: Configure the Gigabit Ethernet Uplinks As Routed Interfaces

The Gigabit Ethernet uplinks 1/1 and 1/2 are used to connect to the remainder of the network. To maximize Layer 3 hierarchy and scalability, these ports function as routed interfaces. Enter the commands shown in Example 18-18 to complete this task.

Example 18-18   *Configuring the Uplink Ports as Routed Interfaces*

```
NativeMode# configure terminal
NativeMode(config)# interface gigabitEthernet 1/1
NativeMode(config-if)# ip address 10.100.100.1 255.255.255.0
NativeMode(config-if)# no shutdown
NativeMode(config-if)#
NativeMode(config-if)# interface gigabitethernet 1/2
NativeMode(config-if)# ip address 10.200.200.1 255.255.255.0
NativeMode(config-if)# no shutdown
NativeMode(config-if)#
```

Step 5: Configure the VLAN 2 Switchports

Ports 5/1–5/3 are used as access ports for server connections in VLAN 2. Example 18-19 illustrates these steps.

Example 18-19   *Configuring the Access Ports in VLAN 2*

```
NativeMode(config)# interface fastethernet 5/1
NativeMode(config-if)# switchport
NativeMode(config-if)# switchport mode access
NativeMode(config-if)# switchport access vlan 2
NativeMode(config-if)# interface fastethernet 5/2
NativeMode(config-if)# switchport
NativeMode(config-if)# switchport mode access
NativeMode(config-if)# switchport access vlan 2
NativeMode(config-if)# interface fastethernet 5/3
NativeMode(config-if)# switchport
NativeMode(config-if)# switchport mode access
NativeMode(config-if)# switchport access vlan 2
```

TIP   When creating similar configurations across many different ports, use the **interface range** command discussed in the "Useful Native IOS Mode Commands" section later in this chapter.

Step 6: Configure the VLAN 3 Switchports

Ports 5/4 and 5/5 are used as access ports for servers in VLAN 3. The commands shown in Example 18-20 can be used to provide this.

Example 18-20   *Configuring the Access Ports in VLAN 3*

```
NativeMode(config-if)# interface fastethernet 5/4
NativeMode(config-if)# switchport
NativeMode(config-if)# switchport mode access
NativeMode(config-if)# switchport access vlan 3
NativeMode(config-if)# interface fastethernet 5/5
NativeMode(config-if)# switchport
NativeMode(config-if)# switchport mode access
NativeMode(config-if)# switchport access vlan 3
```

Step 7: Configure a Trunk Switchport

Port 5/7 is used to carry all three VLANs to Cat-B, a Layer 2 Catalyst. The trunk
uses 802.1Q encapsulation with VLAN 1 acting as the native VLAN. The commands in
Example 18-21 can be used for this configuration.

Example 18-21   *Configuring a Trunk Switchport*

```
NativeMode(config-if)# interface fastethernet 5/6
NativeMode(config-if)# switchport
NativeMode(config-if)# switchport mode trunk
NativeMode(config-if)# switchport trunk encapsulation dot1q
NativeMode(config-if)# switchport trunk native vlan 1
```

Step 8: Configure the SVI Interfaces

The MSFC requires three SVI interfaces to provide routing services for all three VLANs.
As in Example 18-3 and Example 18-6, this configuration uses HSRP on VLANs 1 and 2.
All three are configured with IPX network numbers. This is illustrated in Example 18-22.

Example 18-22   *Configuring the SVI Interfaces*

```
NativeMode(config)# interface vlan 1
NativeMode(config-if)# ip address 10.0.1.2 255.255.255.0
NativeMode(config-if)# ipx network 0A000100
NativeMode(config-if)# standby 1 timers 1 3
NativeMode(config-if)# standby 1 priority 200 preempt
NativeMode(config-if)# standby 1 ip 10.0.1.1
NativeMode(config-if)# interface vlan 2
NativeMode(config-if)# ip address 10.0.2.2 255.255.255.0
NativeMode(config-if)# ipx network 0A000200
NativeMode(config-if)# standby 2 timers 1 3
NativeMode(config-if)# standby 2 priority 100 preempt
NativeMode(config-if)# standby 2 ip 10.0.2.1
NativeMode(config-if)# interface vlan 3
NativeMode(config-if)# ip address 10.0.3.1 255.255.255.0
NativeMode(config-if)# ipx network 0A000300
```

Step 9: Configure Routing

The commands shown in Example 18-23 can be used to configure the MSFC with EIGRP as an IP routing protocol (IPX uses IPX RIP by default).

Example 18-23   *Configuring EIGRP as a Routing Protocol*

```
NativeMode(config)# router eigrp 1
NativeMode(config-router)# passive-interface vlan 1
NativeMode(config-router)# passive-interface vlan 2
NativeMode(config-router)# end
NativeMode#
```

Useful Native IOS Mode Commands

One of the benefits of the Native IOS Mode is that it implements most of the Layer 2 features found in XDI/CatOS platforms such as the Catalyst 5000. Fortunately, the IOS command-line interface (CLI) has been enhanced to include much of the information previously only found under XDI/CatOS. This section briefly displays and discusses some of the more important enhancements.

Probably the most important enhancement involves the **interface range** command. Without this feature, it would be necessary to individually configure hundreds of ports in a fully populated switch. Fortunately, this feature allows you to configure multiple interfaces at the same time as shown in Example 18-24.

Example 18-24   *Configuring EIGRP as a Routing Protocol*

```
NativeMode(config)# interface range 5/1-5, 6/1-24, 7/1-48
NativeMode(config-if)# switchport mode access
NativeMode(config-if)# switchport access vlan 2
NativeMode(config-if)# end
NativeMode#
```

This assigns 77 ports to VLAN 2 in one step, a huge time saver! In short, Example 18-24 is equivalent to the **set vlan 2 5/1-5,6/1-24,7/1-48** command on XDI/CatOS-based Catalysts. Notice that **interface range** commands do not directly appear in the configuration. Instead, the results of Example 18-24 will appear in the output of **show running-config** on each of the separate 77 interfaces it references.

TIP   Be sure to use the **interface range** command when configuring Native IOS Mode devices.

Users accustomed to the **show port** and **show trunk** XDI/CatOS commands will find familiar ground in the enhancements to the **show interface** syntax. For example, the XDI/CatOS command **show trunk** has been ported to the **show interface trunk** command as shown in Example 18-25.

Example 18-25   *The* **show interface trunk** *Command*

```
NativeMode# show interfaces trunk

Port        Mode            Encapsulation  Status      Native vlan
Fa5/6       on              802.1q         trunking    1

Port        Vlans allowed on trunk
Fa5/6       1-1005

Port        Vlans allowed and active in management domain
Fa5/6       1-1005

Port        Vlans in Spanning Tree forwarding state and not pruned
Fa5/6       none
NativeMode#
```

Many of the **show port** XDI/CatOS commands have also been ported. For example, Example 18-26 displays information on counters with the **show interface counters** command.

Example 18-26   *The* **show interface counters** *Command*

```
NativeMode# show interfaces counters module 1

Port             InOctets    InUcastPkts    InMcastPkts    InBcastPkts
Gi1/1            1093847         284764           5739           8576
Gi1/2                  0              0              0              0

Port            OutOctets   OutUcastPkts   OutMcastPkts   OutBcastPkts
Gi1/1             876643         198578           4657           7765
Gi1/2                  0              0              0              0
NativeMode#
```

Notice that Example 18-26 uses the **module** *module-number* argument to filter the output to only show information for module 1. This option exists on most of the new switching-oriented **show interface** commands.

TIP

Also use the powerful Output Modifier feature introduced in IOS 12.0. Simply terminate any **show** command with a pipe symbol (|) and specify a pattern to match (regular expressions are supported!). There are options to include and exclude lines (including an option to output all text found after the first match). The slash (/) key can also be used to search for text.

Example 18-27 displays the output of the **errors** option to **show interfaces counters**.

Example 18-27   *The* **show interfaces counters errors** *Command*

```
NativeMode# show interfaces counters errors module 1

Port        Align-Err    FCS-Err   Xmit-Err    Rcv-Err UnderSize
Gi1/1            0          0          0          0          0
Gi1/2            0          0          0          0          0

Port        Single-Col Multi-Col  Late-Col Excess-Col Carri-Sen    Runts    Giants
Gi1/1            0          0          0          0          0          0          0
Gi1/2            0          0          0          0          0          0          0
NativeMode#
```

The **show interfaces counters trunk** command can be used to show the number of frames transmitted and received on trunk ports. Encapsulation errors are also included (use this information to check for ISL/802.1Q encapsulation mismatches).

The **show vlan** command has also been ported to the Native IOS Mode. In fact, as shown in Example 18-28, it is almost identical to the XDI/CatOS version of this command.

Example 18-28   *The* **show vlan** *Command*

```
NativeMode# show vlan
VLAN Name                             Status    Ports
---- -------------------------------- --------- -------------------------------
1    default                          active    Fa5/6
2    Martketing                       active    Fa5/1, Fa5/2, Fa5/3, Fa5/6
3    Engineering                      active    Fa5/5, Fa5/6
1002 fddi-default                     active    Fa5/6
1003 token-ring-default               active    Fa5/6
1004 fddinet-default                  active    Fa5/6
1005 trnet-default                    active    Fa5/6

VLAN Type  SAID       MTU   Parent RingNo BridgeNo Stp  BrdgMode Trans1 Trans2
---- ----- ---------- ----- ------ ------ -------- ---- -------- ------ ------
1    enet  100001     1500  -      -      -        -    -        0      0
2    enet  100002     1500  -      -      -        -    -        0      0
3    enet  100003     1500  -      -      -        -    -        0      0
1002 fddi  101002     1500  -      0      -        -    -        0      0
1003 tr    101003     1500  -      0      -        -    srb      0      0
1004 fdnet 101004     1500  -      -      -        ieee -        0      0
1005 trnet 101005     1500  -      -      -        ibm  -        0      0
NativeMode#
```

Review Questions

This section includes a variety of questions on the topic of campus design implementation. By completing these, you can test your mastery of the material included in this chapter as well as help prepare yourself for the CCIE written and lab tests.

1 In what sort of situation would a Catalyst 6000/6500 using XDI/CatOS software and no MSFC daughter-card be useful?

2 What Layer 3 switching configuration is used by the MSM?

3 The MSM connects to the Catalyst 6000 backplane via what type of interfaces?

4 How can ten VLANs be configured on the MSM?

5 What are the advantages and disadvantages of the MSFC Hybrid Mode?

6 Under the Native IOS Mode, how are switchports configured with Layer 3 information like IP addresses?

7 Is a Catalyst 6000 running Native IOS Mode software more of a routing switch or a switching router?

Appendix

Answers to End of Chapter Exercises

Answers to Chapter 1 Review Questions

1 What is the pps rate for a 100BaseX network? Calculate it for the minimum and maximum frame sizes.

Because all of the bit time values are one tenth that of 10 Mbps Ethernet, the pps for 100 Mbps Ethernet is 10 times the 10 Mbps pps values. So Fast Ethernet supports up to 148,800 pps for 64 byte frames and 8,120 pps for 1518 byte frames.

2 What are the implications of mixing half-duplex and full-duplex devices? How do you do it?

You need to ensure that your full-duplex devices attach to full-duplex hubs. Otherwise, the full-duplex devices need to run in half-duplex mode. Always attach full duplex together and half duplex together.

Another issue concerns bandwidth. The full-duplex devices effectively have 200 Mbps bandwidth, whereas the half-duplex run 100 Mbps. In fact, the half duplex might be even less than 100 Mbps if the device attaches to a shared hub. Therefore, communications between the full-duplex and half-duplex device is limited by the bandwidth of the half-duplex attachment.

3 In the opening section on Fast Ethernet, we discussed the download time for a typical medical image over a shared legacy Ethernet system. What is an approximate download time for the image over a half-duplex 100BaseX system? Over a full-duplex 100BaseX system?

The medical file size was 100 Megabytes. If the system is half duplex, it might be running on a shared hub. Assume that the station has an effective shared bandwidth, then, of 20 Mbps. In reality, it might be less or more. Then the transfer time is about 40 seconds. 100 MB×8/20 Mbps=40 seconds.

Full-duplex operations can provide 100 Mbps bandwidth in the receive direction. Therefore, the approximate transfer time is 100 MB×8/100 Mbps=8 seconds.

Both models assume that the servers can generate traffic at that rate.

4 What disadvantages are there in having an entire network running in 100BaseX full-duplex mode?

One disadvantage can be cost. Every full-duplex device needs to attach to its own dedicated switch port. You cannot have multiple full-duplex devices attached to the same port. If you have many devices, you need many ports, which equates to increased cost.

Another disadvantage can be congestion at the servers. As you increase the number of devices operating in full-duplex mode, higher amounts of bandwidth hit your servers. This amount can greatly exceed the bandwidth capacity of the server connection.

5 Can a Class II repeater ever attach to a Class I repeater? Why or why not?

You should not attach a Class I repeater to a Class II repeater because this violates the latency rules of Fast Ethernet. When you have a Class I repeater, there can be only one repeater.

6 What is the smallest Gigabit Ethernet frame size that does not need carrier extension?

The need for the carrier extension bytes is driven by the slotTime. Gigabit Ethernet uses a slot time for 4096 bits. This equates to 512 bytes. Therefore, any frames of 512 bytes or larger do not need carrier extension, whereas all frames less than 512 MUST have carrier extension.

Answers to Chapter 2 Review Questions

Refer to the network setup in Figure 2-15 to answer Questions 1 and 2.

Figure 2-15 *Graphic for Review Questions 1 and 2*

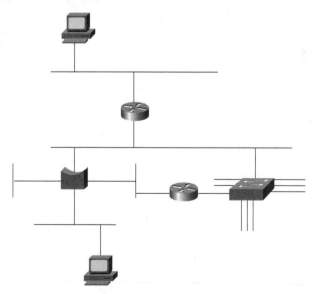

1   Examine Figure 2-15. How many broadcast and collision domains are there?

There are 14 collision domains. Each port on a bridge, router, and switch define a new broadcast domain. You cannot easily tell how many broadcast domains exist in the network due to the presence of the switch. A switch can create one or many broadcast domains, depending upon how you configure it. If the switch is configured as one broadcast domain, there are two broadcast domains. This is not a recommended solution, because both sides of the router attached to the switch and bridge belong to the same broadcast domain. This is not good. On the other hand, the switch can have many broadcast domains defined.

2   In Figure 2-15, how many Layer 2 and Layer 3 address pairs are used to transmit between Stations 1 and 2?

For Station 1 to communicate with Station 2, two Layer 2 address pairs are needed. One MAC pair is used on the top segment, and the other on the other side of the router. However, only one Layer 3 address pair is needed end to end.

Refer to the network setup in Figure 2-16 to answer Question 3.

Figure 2-16   *Graphic for Review Question 3*

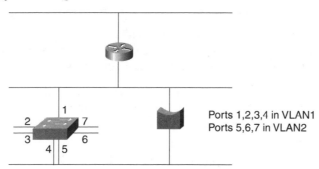

Ports 1,2,3,4 in VLAN1
Ports 5,6,7 in VLAN2

3   What is the problem with the network in Figure 2-16?

Two issues in this network need attention. The most critical problem is that two ports on the Catalyst, which belong to different VLANs, attach to a standard bridge. This merges the two VLANs into a common broadcast domain and defeats the purpose of the Catalyst having two or more broadcast domains.

An additional issue involves Spanning Tree. Although Spanning Tree is not discussed until Chapters 6 and 7, a loop exists in VLAN 1. This might be intentional for resiliency and can be controlled by Spanning Tree. But if unintentional, it can force your network to transmit frames over a less desirable path than you might expect.

4   If you attach a multiport repeater (hub) to a bridge port, how many broadcast domains are seen on the hub?

Legacy hubs have all ports in the same collision and broadcast domains, regardless of the internetworking device they attach to.

5   Can a legacy bridge belong to more than one broadcast domain?

Generally, all ports on a legacy bridge belong to the same broadcast domain.

Answers to Chapter 3 Review Questions

1   If a RIF is present in a source-routed frame, does a source-route switch ever examine the MAC address of a frame?

No, the switch passes the frame to the bridge without looking at the destination MAC address.

2   To how many VLANs can a TrBRF belong?

A TrBRF belongs to only one VLAN

3   The transparent-bridge learning process adds entries to the bridging table based on the source address. Source addresses are never multicast addresses. Yet when examining the Catalyst bridge table, it is possible to see multicast. Why?

Some multicast addresses are identified as system addresses. For example, and frames with 01-00-0C-CC-CC-CC are directed to the Supervisor module. It is also possible to force some multicast addresses out administrator defined interfaces. This overrides the normal flooding processes.

4   Two Cisco routers attach to a Catalyst. On one router you type **show cdp neighbor**. You expect to see the other router listed because cdp announces on a multicast address 01-00-0c-cc-cc-cc, which is flooded by bridges. But you see only the Catalyst as a neighbor. Suspecting that the other router isn't generating cdp announcements, you enter **show cdp neighbor** on the Catalyst. You see both routers listed verifying that both routers are generating announcements. Why didn't you see the second router from the first router? (Hint: neither router can see the other.)

CDP announcements use 01-00-0C-CC-CC-CC as the destination address. The Catalyst receives these announcements and terminates them in the Supervisor module. It does not forward them to other interfaces. Careful examination of the router's cdp neighbor display will show only one neighbor, the Catalyst since it generates cdp announcements.

Answers to Chapter 4 Review Questions

1 What happens if you replace the active Supervisor module?

If you replace the active module, the standby becomes the active Supervisor module. If the configuration files differ between the two, the now active Supervisor updates the configuration on the replacement module. Likewise, if any software images differ, the now active module updates the replacement unit.

2 If your redundant Supervisor engines are running software version 4.1, the uplink ports on the standby engine are disabled until it becomes the active supervisor. What strategies might you need to employ to ensure that failover works for the uplinks?

Referring to Figure A-1, if you connect the uplink ports from the active supervisor module on Cat-A to the active supervisor on Cat-B, everything works well until one of the supervisors fail. The now active uplinks on the standby module of Cat-A are connected to the inactive uplinks on the standby module of Cat-B. Connectivity might be lost, Spanning Tree reconverges. Therefore, you might want to cross connect modules as in Figure A-2 or Figure A-3. The strategy of Figure A-2 enables only one link to be active at a time, whereas the strategy of Figure A-3 allows two links to be active at a time. Another alternative is to not use the Supervisor ports for uplinks, but use them for host connections instead.

Figure A-1 *Uplink Strategies for Failover*

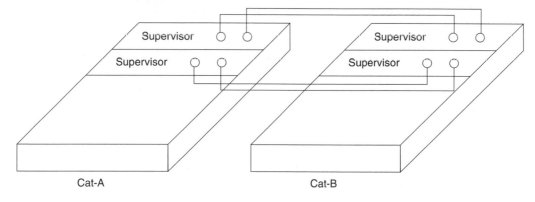

Figure A-2 *Cross Connect Strategy 1*

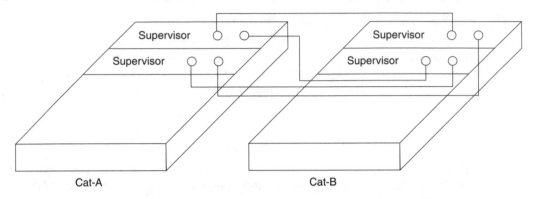

Figure A-3 *Cross Connect Strategy 2*

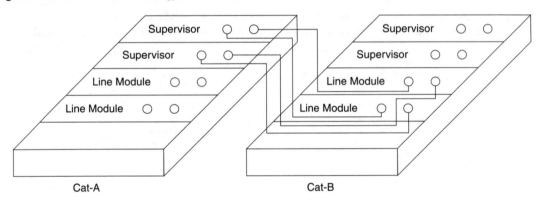

3 Table 4-4 shows how to recall and edit a command from the history buffer. How would you recall and edit the following command so that you move the ports from VLAN 3 to VLAN 4?

```
set vlan 3 2/1-10,3/12-21,6/1,5,7
```

You cannot simply use the edit **^3^4** because this changes not just the VLAN, but the port list too. Ports 3/12-21 become 4/12-21. Rather, you could use the command **^vlan 3^vlan 4** and be more specific about the string you are modifying. This changes only the VLAN assignment without modifying the port values.

4   What happens if you configure the Supervisor console port as sl0, and then you directly attach a PC with a terminal emulator through the PC serial port?

The PC cannot attach to the console, because the Catalyst expects SLIP-based IP connections through the interface. The sl0 configuration means that you access the Catalyst console port by treating the serial line as an IP device. When you attach a PC through the serial port and do not use the IP mode, the PC does not attempt to use its IP stack to build the connection.

5   The Catalyst 5500 supports LS 1010 ATM modules in the last 5 slots of the chassis. Slot 13 of the 5500 is reserved for the LS1010 ATM Switch Processor (ASP). Can you use the **session** command to configure the ASP?

No, you cannot use the **session** command. This command only works to attach to modules through the Catalysts switching bus, not the ATM bus. To configure the ASP, you need to attach a console to the ASP's console port. Use IOS commands to configure the ASP and line modules.

6   The command-line interface has a default line length of 24 lines. How can you confirm this?

Example 4-6 in Chapter 4 shows the configuration file for a Catalyst 5000 family device. Note the configuration command **set length 24 default**, which sets the screen length.

Answers to Chapter 5 Review Questions

1   Early in this chapter, it was mentioned that you can determine the extent of a broadcast domain in a switched network without configuration files. How do you do it?

You can use a brute force approach where you systematically attach a traffic source on a port on a switch configured to generate broadcasts. With a network analyzer, you then check every port in the system to observe where the broadcast appeared. Every port where the broadcast is seen is a member of the same VLAN as the source. Then, you can move the source to a port not mapped in the first step and repeat the process until all ports are mapped.

2   Two Catalysts interconnect stations as shown in Figure 5-22. Station A cannot communicate with Station B. Why not? Example 5-8 provides additional information for the system.

Figure 5-22 *Figure for Review Question 2*

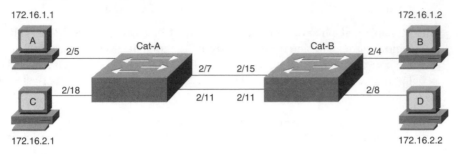

Example 5-8 *Cat-A and Cat-B Configurations*

```
Cat-A >t                         active
 (enable) show vlan
VLAN Name                              Status     Mod/Ports, Vlans
---- -------------------------------- ---------  ---------------------------
1    default                          active     1/1-2
                                                 2/1-8
2    vlan2                            active     2/9-24
1002 fddi-default                     active
1003 token-ring-default               active
1004 fddinet-default                  active
1005 trnet-default                    active


Cat-B> (enable) show vlan
VLAN Name                              Status     Mod/Ports, Vlans
---- -------------------------------- ---------  ---------------------------
1    default                          active     1/1-2
                                                 2/9-24
2    vlan2                            active     2/1-8
1002 fddi-default                     active
1003 token-ring-default               active
1004 fddinet-default                  active
1005 trnet-default
```

Although Station A and B addresses belong to the same logical network, A and B attach to different VLANs. This makes it very difficult for them to talk to each other. Layer 2 switches do not forward traffic between VLANs, and no router exists in the system to interconnect the VLANs. Therefore, they cannot communicate with each other.

3 Again referring to Figure 5-22 and Example 5-8, can Station C communicate with Station D?

No. Although Stations C and D belong to the same logical network and the same VLAN, there is no connectivity between the switches for VLAN 2. Note that, on Cat-A, one inter-switch port belongs to VLAN 1 and the other to VLAN 2. But for Cat-B, neither of the inter-switch ports belong to VLAN 2. This prevents any VLAN 2 traffic from passing between the Catalysts.

4 Are there any Spanning Tree issues in Figure 5-22?

There are no loops in the network, but VLANs 1 and 2 in Cat-A are merged into one broadcast domain through the VLAN 1 virtual bridge in Cat-B. See Chapters 6 and 7 for a discussion of Spanning Tree.

5 Draw a logical representation of Figure 5-22 of the way the network actually exists as opposed to what was probably intended.

Figure A-4 presents a logical representation of the network in Figure 5-22.

Figure A-4 *Logical Representation of the Network in Figure 5-22*

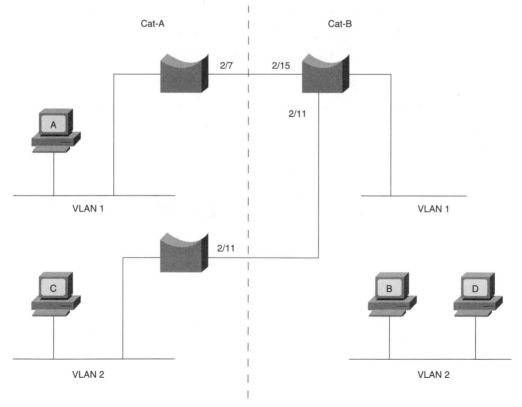

6 Is there ever a time when you would bridge between VLANs?

You might need to enable bridging between VLANs on a router whenever you have non-routable protocols such as LAT or NetBeui. In this case, you need to route all other protocols and bridge only the nonroutable protocols. Be careful of Spanning Tree topology issues though, because the router participates in Spanning Tree along with the Catalysts.

7 List the three components of dynamic VLANs using VMPS.

- A Catalyst system using VMPS has the following components:
- VMPS server
- VMPS client
- TFTP server with a configuration text file.

Answers to Chapter 6 Review Questions

1 Summarize the three-step process that STP uses to initially converge on an active topology.

The three-step process is as follows:

Step 1 Elect a single Root Bridge for the entire bridged network.

Step 2 Elect one Root Port for every non-Root Bridge.

Step 3 Elect one Designated Port for every segment.

2 How many of the following items does the network shown in Figure 6-24 contain: Root Bridges, Root Ports, Designated Ports? Assume all devices are operational.

Figure 6-24 *Sample Network of Four Switches and 400 Users*

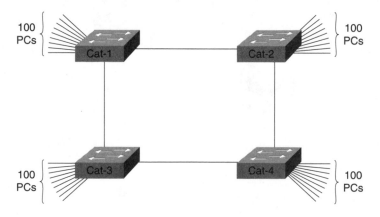

The network in Figure 6-24 contains the following: One Root Bridge, three Root Ports, and 404 Designated Ports (one per segment, including the 400 segments connected to end users).

3   When running the Spanning-Tree Protocol, every bridge port saves a copy of the best information it has heard. How do bridges decide what constitutes the best information?

Bridges use a four-step decision sequence:

Step 1   Lowest Root BID

Step 2   Lowest Path Cost to Root Bridge

Step 3   Lowest Sender BID

Step 4   Lowest Port ID

The bridge uses this decision sequence to compare all BPDUs received from other bridges as well as the BPDU that would be sent on that port. A copy of the best (lowest) BPDU is saved.

4   Why are Topology Change Notification BPDUs important? Describe the TCN process.

Topology Change Notification BPDUs play an important role in that they help bridges relearn MAC addresses more quickly after a change in the active STP topology. A bridge that detects a topology change sends a TCN BPDU out its Root Port. The Designated Port for this segment acknowledges the TCN BPDU with the TCA flag in the next Configuration BPDU it sends. This bridge also propagates the TCN BPDU out its Root Port. This process continues until the BPDU reaches the Root Bridge. The Root Bridge then sets the TC flag in all Configuration BPDUs sent for twice the Forward Delay period. As other bridges receive the TC flag, they shorten the bridge table aging period to Forward Delay seconds.

5   How are Root Path Cost values calculated?

Root Path Cost is the cumulative cost of the entire path to the Root Bridge. It is calculated by adding a port's Path Cost value to the BPDUs *received* on that port.

6   Assume that you install a new bridge and it contains the lowest BID in the network. Further assume that this devices is running experimental Beta code that contains a severe memory leak and, as a result, reboots every 10 minutes. What effect does this have on the network?

STP is a preemptive protocol that constantly seeks the Root Bridge with the lowest BID. Therefore, in this network, the new bridge wins the Root War, and the entire active topology converges on this bridge every ten minutes. Where links change state during this convergence process, temporary outages of 30–50 seconds occur. When the bridge fails several minutes later, the network converges on the next most attractive Root Bridge and creates another partial network outage for 30–50 seconds.

In short, the network experiences partial outages every time the new bridge restarts *and* fails.

7 When using the **show spantree** command, why might the timer values shown on the line that begins with Root Max Age differ from the values shown on the Bridge Max Age line?

The values shown in the Root Max Age line are the timer values advertised in the Configuration BPDUs sent by the current Root Bridge. All bridges adopt these values. On the other hand, every bridge shows its locally-configured values in the Bridge Max Age line.

8 Label the port types (RP=Root Port, DP=Designated Port, NDP=non-Designated Port) and the STP states (F=Forwarding, B=Blocking) in Figure 6-25. The Bridge IDs are labeled. All links are Fast Ethernet.

Figure 6-25 *Sample Network*

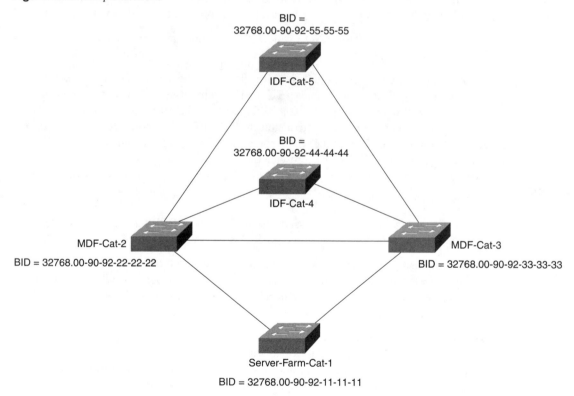

Figure A-5 provides the solution for Question 8.

Figure A-5 *Solution to Question 8.*

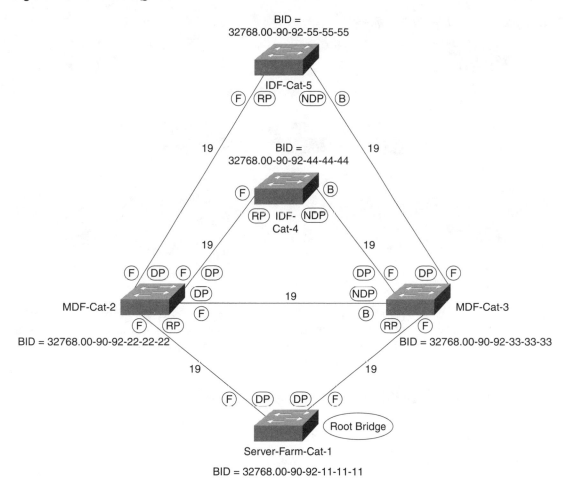

Svr_Farm-Cat-1 becomes the Root Bridge because it has the lowest BID. MDF-Cat-2 and MDF-Cat-3 elect Root Ports based on the lowest Root Cost Path (19 versus 38). IDF-Cat-4 and IDF-Cat-5 have two equal-cost paths (38) to the Root Bridge. Therefore, to elect a Root Port, they have to use Sender BID as a tie breaker. Because MDF-Cat-2 has a lower Sender BID than MDF-Cat-3, both IDF Cats select the link connecting to MDF-Cat-2 as the Root Port. Designated Port elections are all based on Root Path Cost.

9 What happens to the network in Figure 6-26 if Cat-4 fails?

Figure 6-26 *Cat-4 Connects Two Groups of Switches*

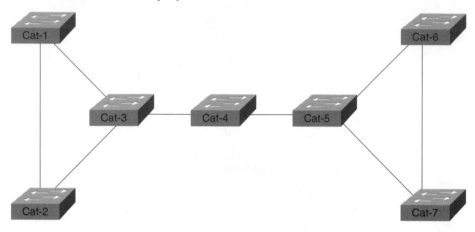

The network is partitioned into two halves. Each half elects its own Root Bridge. There is a partial outage of approximately 50 seconds. After the Root Bridges have been established, connectivity resumes within the two halves, but the two halves cannot communicate.

Answers to Chapter 6 Hands-On Lab

Build a network that resembles Figure 6-27.

Figure 6-27 *Hands-On Lab Diagram*

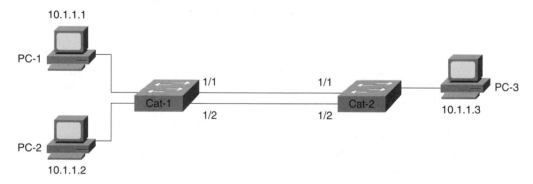

Using only VLAN 1, complete the following steps:

1 Start a continuous ping (tip: under Microsoft Windows, use the **ping -t** *ip_address* command) between PC-1 and PC-3. Break the link connecting PC-3 to Cat-2. After reconnecting the link, how long does it take for the pings to resume?

It takes 30-35 seconds. Some people might observe a period of approximately 50 seconds. This is most often due to a feature called PAgP that runs on Etherchannel-capable ports by default. Disable PAgP with the **set port channel 2/1-4 off** command and repeat the measurements. Note that some hardware requires that you specify a different range of ports than **2/1-4**.

2 Start a continuous ping between PC-1 and PC-2. As in Step 1, break the link between PC-3 and Cat-2. Does this affect the traffic between PC-1 and PC-2?

No. Because the traffic was not using this link, no disruption to traffic between PC-1 and PC-2 occurs (in other words, don't fall trap to the notion that every change in the Spanning Tree disrupts the entire network).

3 Use the **show spantree** command on Cat-1 and Cat-2. What bridge is acting as the Root Bridge? Make a note of the state of all ports.

The Root Bridge is the Catalyst where the Designated Root field matches the Bridge ID MAC ADDR field. Notice that the Designated Root Cost equals zero and the Designated Root Port equals 1/0.

All ports should be in the Forwarding state except the 1/2 port on the non-Root Bridge.

4 Why is the 1/2 port on the non-Root Bridge Blocking? How did the Catalyst know to block this port?

Recall that STP always refers back to the same four-step decision sequence. Assume Cat-1 is the Root Bridge (if you have Cat-2 as the Root Bridge, just reverse the Cat-1 and Cat-2 names in the following discussion). In this case, both bridges are in agreement that Cat-1 is the Root Bridge, causing Root Path Cost to be considered next. However, because both 1/1 and 1/2 have a Root Path Cost of 19, Cat-2 must consider the Sender BID field next. Because Cat-1's BID is listed in BPDUs received on both 1/1 and 1/2, there is once again a tie. This causes Port ID to be evaluated next. Because 1/1 has a lower Port ID (0x8001) than port 1/2 (0x8002), port 1/1 is preferred. This places 1/1 in the Forwarding state and 1/2 in the Blocking state.

5 Start a continuous ping between PC-1 and PC-3. Break the 1/1 link connecting Cat-1 and Cat-2. How long before the traffic starts using the 1/2 link?

It takes about 30-35 seconds. If you observe a period of approximately 50 seconds, disable PAgP with the **set port channel 1/1-2 off** command and repeat the measurements. Note that some hardware requires that you specify a different range of ports than **1/1-2**.

6   Reconnect the 1/1 link from Step 2. What happens? Why?

The traffic stops once again for 30-35 seconds! This surprises many people—you just fixed the network but STP still blocked traffic for approximately 30 seconds. As soon as the 1/1 link is reconnected, BPDUs start flowing from the Root Bridge to the non-Root Bridge. As soon as the non-Root Bridge sees a lower BPDU arrive on port 1/1, it realizes that port 1/2 is no longer a valid Root Port. Therefore, port 1/2 is immediately put into the Blocking state, but port 1/1 must still spend 15 seconds in the Listening state and 15 second in the Learning state (assuming default timer values). After 30 seconds, port 1/1 takes over as the Root Port.

7   With the continuous ping from Step 3 still running, break the 1/2 link connecting Cat-1 and Cat-2. What effect does this have?

No effect. As with Question 2, there is no disruption because the traffic is not using this link.

Answers to Chapter 7 Review Questions

1   Label the port types (RP=Root Port, DP=Designated Port, NDP=non-Designated Port) and the STP states (F=Forwarding, B=Blocking) in Figure 7-30. The Bridge IDs are labeled. All links are Fast Ethernet. Assume that there is only a single VLAN and that the **portvlanpri** command has not been used.

Figure 7-30   *Two Back-to-Back Catalysts with Crossed Links*

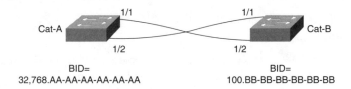

Figure A-6 provides the labels requested in Question 1 for Figure 7-30.

Figure A-6 *Two Back-to-Back Catalysts with Crossed Links*

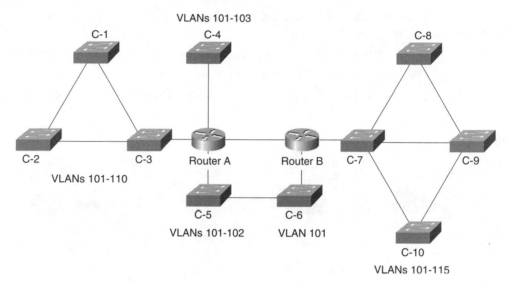

Cat-B becomes the Root Bridge because it has the lower BID. Cat-A therefore needs to select a single Root Port. In the previous examples of back-to-back switches, the links did not cross and Port 1/1 became the Root Port because of the lower Port ID (0x8001).

In this case, the crossed links force you to think about the fact that it is the *received* Port ID that influences the Cat-A, *not Cat-A's local Port ID values.* Although Cat-A:Port-1/2 has the higher *local* value, it is *receiving the lower value.* As a result, Port-1/2 becomes the Root Port. Understanding this issue is critical to effectively use **portvlanpri** load balancing.

2 When do bridges generate Configuration BPDUs?

Bridges generate Configuration BPDUs in the following instances:

- Every Hello Time seconds on all ports of the Root Bridge (unless there is a Physical-Layer loop).

- When a non-Root Bridge receives a Configuration BPDU on its Root Port, it sends an updated version of this BPDU out every Designated Port.

- When a Designated Port hears a less attractive BPDU from a neighboring bridge.

3 When do bridges generate Topology Change Notification BPDUs?

Bridges generate Topology Change Notification BPDUs in the following instances:

- A bridge port is put into the Forwarding state and the bridge has at least one Designated Port.
- A port in the Forwarding or Learning states transitions to the Blocking state.
- A non-Root Bridge receives a TCN (from a downstream bridge) on a Designated Port.

4 How many Spanning Tree domains are shown in Figure 7-31? Assume that all of the switches are using ISL trunks and PVST Spanning Tree.

Figure 7-31 *Multiple Spanning Tree Domains*

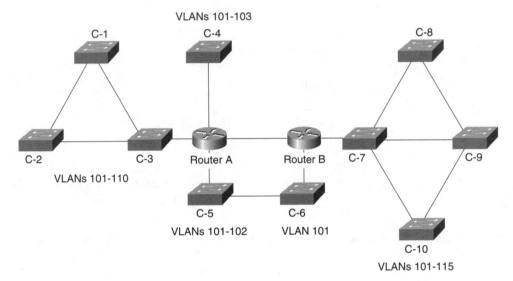

10+3+2+15=30.

Although the same numbers are used for all of the VLANs, the routers break the network into four Layer-2 pockets (Cat-1 through Cat-3, Cat-4, Cat-5 through Cat-6, and Cat-7 through Cat-10). The VLANs in each Layer-2 pocket then form a separate STP domain.

One of the tricks in this layout is to notice that Cat-5 and Cat-6 form a single Layer-2 domain containing two, not three VLANs. Because of the backdoor links between the two switches, the routers do not break this into separate Layer-2 pockets.

5 When is the Root Bridge placement form of STP load balancing most effective? What command(s) are used to implement this approach?

When traffic patterns are well defined and clearly understood. In hierarchical networks such as those adhering to the multilayer design model discussed in Chapters 14 and 15, Root

Bridge placement is an extremely effective form of STP load balancing. Simply collocate the Root Bridge with the corresponding default gateway router for that VLAN (see Chapters 14 and 15 for information). For non-hierarchical, flat-earth networks, load balancing usually requires different VLANs to have server farms in different physical locations.

When placing Root Bridges, either the **set spantree priority** or the **set spantree root** commands can be used.

6   When is the Port Priority form of STP load balancing useful? What command(s) are used to implement this approach? What makes this technique so confusing?

This form of load balancing is rarely useful. It can only be used with back-to-back switches. It should only be used in early versions of code or when connecting to non-Cisco devices. The **set spantree portvlanpri** command is used to implement this feature. This technique can be very confusing because it requires that the **set spantree portvlanpri** command be entered on the *upstream* switch.

7   When is the Bridge Priority form of STP load balancing useful? What command(s) are used to implement this approach? What makes this technique so confusing?

The Bridge Priority form of STP load balancing can be useful if you are using pre-3.1 code and cannot use Root Bridge placement (because of traffic patterns) or **portvlanpri** (because the switches are not back-to-back). If you are using 3.1+ code, **portvlancost** is generally a better choice. The **set spantree priority** command is used to implement this approach. This technique can be confusing for several reasons:

- The Bridge Priority values must be adjusted on devices that are upstream of where the load balancing takes place.

- The Bridge Priority values must not be adjusted too low or your Root Bridge placement is disrupted.

- It can be difficult to remember why each Bridge Priority was set.

8   When is the **portvlancost** form of load balancing useful? What is the full syntax of the **portvlancost** command? What is the one confusing aspect of this technique?

The **portvlancost** form of load balancing is useful in almost all situations. It is the most flexible form of STP load balancing. The full syntax of the **portvlancost** command is:

```
set spantree portvlancost mod_num/port_num [cost cost_value] [preferred_vlans]
```
One confusing aspect to this command is that it only allows two cost values to be set for each port. One value is set with the **portcost** command and the other is set with the **portvlancost** command.

9   What technology should be used in place of **portvlanpri**?

EtherChannel.

10 What are the components that the default value of Max Age is designed to account for? There is no need to specify the exact formula, just the major components captured in the formula.

The default Max Age value of 20 seconds is designed to take two factors into account: End-to-end BPDU propagation delay and Message Age Overestimate.

11 What are the components that the default value of Forwarding Delay is designed to account for? There is no need to specify the exact formula, just the major components captured in the formula.

The default Forward Delay value of 15 seconds is designed to take four factors into account: End-to-End BPDU Propagation Delay, Message Age Overestimate, Maximum Transmission Halt Delay, and Maximum Frame Lifetime.

The last two factors (Maximum Transmission Halt Delay and Maximum Frame Lifetime) could be simplified into a single factor called "time for traffic to die out in the old topology."

12 What are the main considerations when lowering the Hello Time from the default of two seconds to one second?

Lowering the Hello Time value can allow you to improve convergence time by lowering Max Age or Forward Delay (you have to do this separately) but also doubles the load that STP places on your network. Notice that load here refers to both the load of Configuration BPDU traffic and, more importantly, Spanning Tree CPU load on the switches themselves.

13 Where should PortFast be utilized? What does it change about the STP algorithm?

In general, PortFast should only be used on end-station ports. It allows a port to immediately move into the Forwarding state when it initializes. Other than that, the processing is the same. When using redundant NICs that toggle link state, it can also be useful for links to servers.

14 Where should UplinkFast be utilized? In addition to altering the local bridging table to reflect the new Root Port after a failover situation, what other issue must UplinkFast address?

UplinkFast should only be utilized in leaf-node, wiring closet switches. After a failover, UplinkFast must generate dummy multicast packets to update bridging tables throughout the network in addition to updating its own bridging table.

15 Where should BackboneFast be utilized?

To work correctly, BackboneFast must be enabled on every switch in a given Layer 2 domain.

16 Where is PVST+ useful?

PVST+ is useful when you are trying to connect traditional PVST Catalyst devices with 801.Q switches that only support a single instance of the Spanning-Tree Protocol.

17 Can MST regions be connected to PVST regions?

MST and PVST regions cannot be connected through trunk links (MST switches only support 802.1Q trunks, and PVST switches only support ISL trunks). However, the two types of switches can be connected through access (non-trunk) links (although this is rarely useful).

18 Can you disable STP on a per-port basis?

STP cannot be disabled on a per-port basis on Layer 2 Catalyst equipment such as the 4000s, 5000s, and 6000s. In fact, some Layer 3 Catalyst switches (Sup III with NFFC) require that STP be disabled for the entire device (all VLANs).

19 Why is it important to use a separate management VLAN?

It is important to use a separate management VLAN to prevent CPU overload. If the CPU does overload as a result of excessive broadcast or multicast traffic, the Spanning Tree information can become out-of-date. When this occurs, it becomes possible that a bridging loop could open. If this loop forms in the management VLAN, remaining CPU resources are quickly and completely exhausted. This can spread throughout the network and create a network-wide outage.

20 What happens if UplinkFast sends the fake multicast frames to the usual Cisco multicast address of 01-00-0C-CC-CC-CC?

If UplinkFast sends the dummy frames to the usual Cisco multicast address of 01-00-0C-CC-CC-CC, older, non-UplinkFast-aware Cisco Layer-2 devices do not flood the frames. Therefore, this does not update bridging tables through the network.

Chapter 7 Hands-On Lab

Criteria for Chapter 7 Hands-on Lab

The hands-on lab in Chapter 7 asks you to complete an STP design for the network shown in Figure 7-32 which shows a three building campus.

Figure 7-32 *A Three-Building Campus Design*

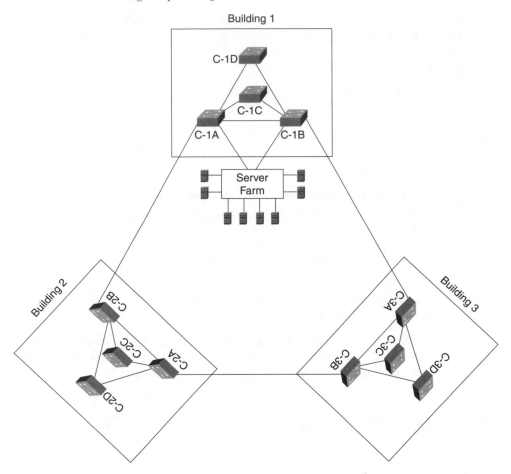

Each building contains two MDF switches (A and B) and two IDF switches (C and D). The number of IDF switches in each building is expected to grow dramatically in the near future. The server farm has its own switch that connects to Cat-1A and Cat-1B. The network contains 20 VLANs. Assume that each server can be connected to a single VLAN (for example, the SAP server can be connected to the Finance VLAN). Assume that all links are Fast Ethernet except the ring of links between the MDF switches, which are Gigabit Ethernet.

Be sure to address the following items: STP timers, Root Bridges, Load Balancing, failover performance, and traffic flows. Diagram the primary and backup topologies for your design.

Solution to Chapter 7 Hands-on Lab

The solution that follows is one of many possible solutions to this lab.

The Root Bridges are best located on Cat-1A and Cat-1B at the entrance to the server farm. Cat-1A can be the Root Bridge for the odd-numbered VLANs and Cat-1B can be the Root Bridge for the even-numbered VLANs.

Because of the danger associated with STP timer tuning, this strategy is avoided here. Instead, UplinkFast can be configured on all of the IDF switches to reduce wiring closet failover to 2–3 seconds. BackboneFast can be configured on all of the switches to improve the convergence time after an indirect failure.

Figure A-7 shows the odd-numbered VLANs. Cat-1A is the Root Bridge. Only forwarding links are shown. The port state information is shown for Building 1 (the other building would follow the same pattern).

Figure A-7 *Primary Topology for Odd VLANs; Backup Topology for Even VLANs*

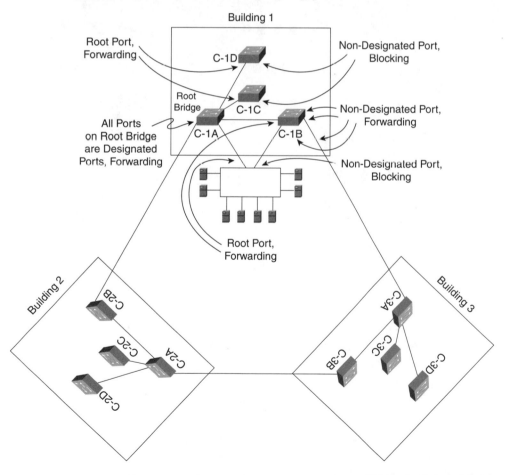

Figure A-8 shows the same information for the even-numbered VLANs. Cat-1B is the Root Bridge.

Figure A-8 *Primary Topology for Even VLANs; Backup Topology for Odd VLANs*

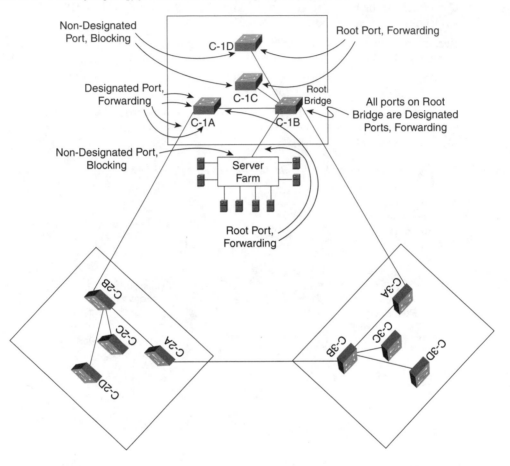

Cat-1A is the backup Root Bridge for the even VLANs and Cat-2B is the backup Root Bridge for the odd VLANs. Therefore, the backup topology for the odd VLANs is the same as Figure A-7c, whereas the backup topology for the even VLANs is the same as Figure A-7b.

Answers to Chapter 8 Review Questions

1   What happens in a traffic loading situation for EtherChannel when two servers pass files between each other?

All of the traffic between the servers crosses the same segment. This happens because the servers use the same MAC address for all of the frames. The ECB performs an **X-OR** on the MAC addresses and comes up with the same result every time.

2   If you have access to equipment, attempt to configure a two-segment EtherChannel where one end is set to transport only VLANs 1–10 and the other end of the segment is set to transport all VLANs. What gets established?

Nothing. Both ends of an EtherChannel must be configured to pass the same set of VLANs on all interfaces.

3   In Figure 8-13, the configuration shows an 802.1Q encapsulation for VLAN 200 on a router. How would you add VLAN 300 to the trunk?

Add the statement **encapsulation dot1q 300** to another subinterface.

4   Configure a Catalyst trunk to transport VLAN 200 and VLAN 300 with 802.1Q. Repeat the exercise with ISL.

Typical configuration statements are as follows:

```
set trunk 1/1 on dot1q
clear trunk 1/1 201-299
clear trunk 1/1 301-1005
clear trunk 1/1 2-199
```

This method is a little awkward in that it allows all VLANs and then removes the disallowed VLANs.

To do the ISL trunk, you could follow the same process, except that the first command would say **set trunk 1/1 on isl.**

Answers to Chapter 9 Review Questions

1   What are the three layers of the ATM stack? What does each do?

Refer back to Figure 9-3 in Chapter 9. The three layers are as follows:

- **AAL**—Slice & dice
- **ATM**—Build headers
- **Physical**—Ship cells

2   What is the difference between ATM and SONET?

ATM is a cloud technology that deals with cells. SONET is a point-to-point technology that is used to carry cells.

3   What is the difference between a Catalyst with two LANE modules and a two-port ATM switch?

As an edge device, the Catalyst only switches frames between ports; the LS1010, as an ATM switch, only switches cells. See Figure 9-8 in Chapter 9.

4   What is the difference between a VPI, a VCI, and an NSAP? When is each used?

VPI and VCI values are two parts of the address placed in the header of every cell (both PVCs and SVCs). NSAPs are only used to build the SVC. After the SVC is built, the VPI/VCI values are used to switch cells along the VC.

5   Assume you attached an ATM network analyzer to an ATM cloud consisting of one LS1010 ATM switch and two Catalysts with LANE modules. What types of cells could you capture to observe VPI and VCI values? What type of cells could you capture to observe NSAP addresses?

All cells contain VPI/VCI values, but NSAP addresses can only be observed in cells that carry signaling messages (such as a UNI 4.0 call SETUP message).

6   What are the three sections of an NSAP address? What does each part represent?

The following list outlines the three sections of an NSAP address and what each represents.

- **Prefix**—What ATM switch?
- **ESI**—What devices on the ATM switch?
- **Selector Byte**—What software component in the end station?

7   How do Catalysts automatically generate ESI and selector byte values for use with LANE?

The following list shows how Catalysts automatically generate ESI and selector byte values for use with LANE.

- LEC = MAC . **
- LES = MAC + 1 . **
- BUS = MAC + 2 . **
- LECS = MAC + 3 . 00

8   What is the five-step initialization process used by LANE Clients to join an ELAN?

The five-step initialization process used by LANE Clients to join an ELAN is as follows:

Step 1   Client contacts LECS (Bouncer).

Step 2   Client contacts LES (Bartender).

Step 3   LES contacts Client.

Step 4   Client contacts BUS (Gossip).

Step 5   BUS contacts Client.

9 What are the names of the six types of circuits used by LANE? What type of traffic does each carry?

The following list outlines the names of the six types of circuits used by LANE and what type of traffic each carries.

- **Configuration Direct**—Requests to join ELAN and NSAP of LES
- **Control Direct**—LE_ARPs
- **Control Distribute**—LE_ARPs that need to be flooded to all Proxy Clients
- **Multicast Send**—Broadcast, multicast, and unknown unicast traffic that needs to be flooded to all Clients
- **Multicast Forward**—Broadcast, multicast, and unknown unicast traffic that is being flooded
- **Data Direct**—End-user data from LEC to LEC

10 What is the difference between an IP ARP and an LE_ARP?

IP ARPs are used to request the MAC address associated with an IP address.

LE_ARPs are used to request the NSAP address associated with a MAC address.

11 In a network that needs to trunk two VLANs between two Catalysts, how many LECs are required? How many LECSs? How many LESs? How many BUSs?

- **LECs = 4**—One per Client per ELAN
- **LECSs = 1**—One per LANE network
- **LESs = 2**—One per ELAN
- **BUSs = 2**—One per ELAN

12 If the network in Question 11 grows to ten Catalysts and ten VLANs, how many LECs, LECSs, LESs and BUSs are required? Assume that every Catalyst has ports assigned to every VLAN.

- LECs = 100
- LECSs = 1
- LESs = 10
- BUSs = 10

13 Trace the data path in Figure 9-26 from an Ethernet-attached node in VLAN 1 on Cat-A to an Ethernet-attached node in VLAN 2 on Cat-B. Why is this inefficient?

Figure 9-26 *A Complete LANE Network*

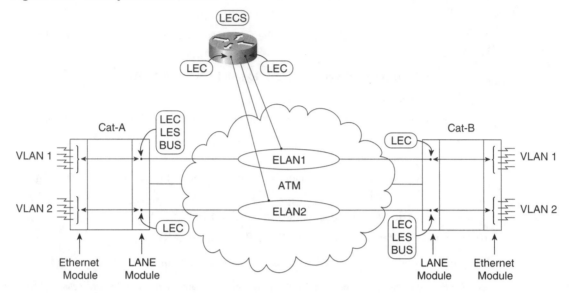

The traffic travels through the ELAN1 to the router where it is routed to ELAN2. It then travels across ELAN2 to reach the node on Cat-B. This is inefficient because: 1) the router might not be as fast as the ATM network and 2) the router was required to reassemble the cells back into a complete packet before the routing decision could be made. After the packet is routed, it has to again be segmented into cells.

Solution to Chapter 9 Hands-On Lab

The hands-on lab in Chapter 9 asks you to build a network that resembles Figure 9-29.

Figure 9-29 *Hands-On Lab Diagram*

Table 9-6 shows the LANE components that should be configured on each device.

Table 9-6   *LANE Components to Be Configured*

Device	VLAN1/ELAN1	VLAN2/ELAN2	VLAN3/ELAN3
LEC-A	LEC, LES/BUS	LEC	LEC
LEC-B	LEC	LEC, LES/BUS	LEC
Router	LEC	LEC	LEC, LES/BUS
LS1010	LEC	LEC	LEC

The LS1010 is the LECS.

Configure IP addresses on the SC0 interfaces of both Catalysts, the router subinterfaces, and the LS1010 subinterfaces (use interface atm 2/0/0 or 13/0/0 for the LS1010). Configure HSRP between the ATM router and an RSM located in LEC-A. Table 9-7 provides IP addresses that can be used.

Table 9-7 *IP Addresses for Hands-On Lab*

Device	VLAN1/ELAN1	VLAN2/ELAN2	VLAN3/ELAN3
LEC-A SC0	10.1.1.1		
LEC-A RSM	10.1.1.252	10.1.2.252	10.1.3.252
LEC-B SC0	10.1.1.2		
Router	10.1.1.253	10.1.2.253	10.1.3.253
LS1010	10.1.1.110	10.1.2.110	10.1.3.110
HSRP Address	10.1.1.254	10.1.2.254	10.1.3.254

When you are done building the network, perform the following tasks:

- Test connectivity to all devices.
- Turn on **debug lane client all** and ping another device on the network (you might need to clear the Data Direct if it already exists). Log the results.
- With **debug lane client all** still running, issue **shut** and **no shut** commands on the atm major interface. Log the results.
- Examine the output of the **show lane client**, **show lane config**, **show lane server**, **show lane bus**, and **show lane database** commands.
- Add SSRP to allow server redundancy.
- If you have multiple ATM switches, add dual-PHY support (don't forget to update your SSRP configurations).

Sample Configurations for Hands-On Lab

Examples A-1–A-5 provide some sample configurations for LEC-A, LEC-B, LS1010, the router, and Cat-A RSM for the hands-on lab. Although your configuration might differ slightly, these examples provide some guidelines to point you in the right direction.

LEC-A

Example A-1 provides a sample configuration for LEC-A.

Example A-1 *Sample Configuration for LEC-A for Hands-On Lab*

```
hostname LEC-A
!
interface ATM0
 atm preferred phy A
 atm pvc 1 0 5 qsaal
 atm pvc 2 0 16 ilmi
!
interface ATM0.1 multipoint
 lane server-bus ethernet ELAN1
 lane client ethernet 1 ELAN1
!
interface ATM0.2 multipoint
 lane client ethernet 2 ELAN2
!
interface ATM0.3 multipoint
 lane client ethernet 3 ELAN3
!
line con 0
line vty 0 4
 no login
!
end
```

LEC-B

Example A-2 provides a sample configuration for LEC-B.

Example A-2 *Sample Configuration for LEC-B for Hands-On Lab*

```
hostname LEC-B
!
interface ATM0
 atm preferred phy A
 atm pvc 1 0 5 qsaal
 atm pvc 2 0 16 ilmi
!
interface ATM0.1 multipoint
 lane client ethernet 1 ELAN1
!
interface ATM0.2 multipoint
 lane server-bus ethernet ELAN2
 lane client ethernet 2 ELAN2
!
interface ATM0.3 multipoint
 lane client ethernet 3 ELAN3
```

continues

Example A-2 *Sample Configuration for LEC-B for Hands-On Lab (Continued)*

```
!
!
line con 0
line vty 0 4
 no login
!
end
```

LS1010

Example A-3 provides a sample configuration for LS1010.

Example A-3 *Sample Configuration for LS1010 for Hands-On Lab*

```
hostname LS1010
!
atm lecs-address-default 47.0091.8100.0000.0010.2962.e801.0010.2962.e805.00 1
atm address 47.0091.8100.0000.0010.2962.e801.0010.2962.e801.00
atm router pnni
 node 1 level 56 lowest
  redistribute atm-static
!
!
lane database Test_Db
  name ELAN1 server-atm-address 47.00918100000000102962E801.00102962E431.01
  name ELAN2 server-atm-address 47.00918100000000102962E801.00102941D031.02
  name ELAN3 server-atm-address 47.00918100000000102962E801.001014310819.03
!
!
interface ATM13/0/0
 no ip address
 atm maxvp-number 0
 lane config auto-config-atm-address
 lane config database Test_Db
!
interface ATM13/0/0.1 multipoint
 ip address 10.1.1.110 255.255.255.0
 lane client ethernet ELAN1
!
interface ATM13/0/0.2 multipoint
 ip address 10.1.2.110 255.255.255.0
 lane client ethernet ELAN2
!
interface ATM13/0/0.3 multipoint
 ip address 10.1.3.110 255.255.255.0
 lane client ethernet ELAN3
!
interface Ethernet13/0/0
 no ip address
!
no ip classless
```

Example A-3 *Sample Configuration for LS1010 for Hands-On Lab (Continued)*

```
!
line con 0
line aux 0
line vty 0 4
 login
!
end
```

Router

Example A-4 provides a sample configuration for the router.

Example A-4 *Sample Configuration for Router for Hands-On Lab*

```
!
hostname Router
!
interface FastEthernet2/0
 no ip address
 shutdown
!
interface ATM3/0
 no ip address
 atm pvc 1 0 5 qsaal
 atm pvc 2 0 16 ilmi
!
interface ATM3/0.1 multipoint
 ip address 10.1.1.253 255.255.255.0
 no ip redirects
 lane client ethernet ELAN1
 standby 1  preempt
 standby 1 ip 10.1.1.254
!
interface ATM3/0.2 multipoint
 ip address 10.1.2.253 255.255.255.0
 no ip redirects
 lane client ethernet ELAN2
 standby 2 priority 101
 standby 2 preempt
 standby 2 ip 10.1.2.254
!
interface ATM3/0.3 multipoint
 ip address 10.1.3.253 255.255.255.0
 no ip redirects
 lane server-bus ethernet ELAN3
 lane client ethernet ELAN3
 standby 3  preempt
 standby 3 ip 10.1.3.254
!
```

continues

Example A-4 *Sample Configuration for Router for Hands-On Lab (Continued)*

```
router rip
 network 10.0.0.0
!
ip classless
!
!
line con 0
line aux 0
line vty 0 4
 login
!
end
```

Cat-A-RSM

Example A-5 provides a sample configuration for Cat-A-RSM.

Example A-5 *Sample Configuration for Cat-A-RSM for Hands-On Lab*

```
hostname Cat-A-RSM
!
interface Vlan1
 ip address 10.1.1.252 255.255.255.0
 no ip redirects
 standby 1 priority 101
 standby 1 preempt
 standby 1 ip 10.1.1.254
!
interface Vlan2
 ip address 10.1.2.252 255.255.255.0
 no ip redirects
 standby preempt
 standby 2 ip 10.1.2.254
!
interface Vlan3
 ip address 10.1.3.252 255.255.255.0
 no ip redirects
 standby 3 priority 101
 standby 3 preempt
 standby 3 ip 10.1.3.254
!
router rip
 network 10.0.0.0
!
no ip classless
!
line con 0
line aux 0
line vty 0 4
 login
!
end
```

Answers to Chapter 10 Review Questions

1   A network administrator observes that the MPC cannot develop a shortcut. An ATM analyzer attached to the network shows that the MPC never issues a shortcut request, even though the 10 frames per second threshold is crossed. Why doesn't the MPC issue a shortcut request? The **show mpoa client** command displays as shown in Example 10-20.

Example 10-20   *Client Output for Review Question*

```
Cat-C#sh mpoa clientMPC Name: mpc2, Interface: ATM1/0, State: UpMPC
actual operating address: 47.009181000000009092BF7401.0090AB16A80D.00Shortcut-
Setup
Count: 10, Shortcut-Setup Time: 1Lane clients bound to MPC mpc2:
```

The MPC cannot issue a shortcut request because it cannot establish a relationship with an MPS. This results from the absence of an LEC to MPC binding. Notice in the last line of the output that no LANE clients are bound to mpc2. Assuming that a valid LEC exists, you can fix this with the **lane client mpoa client** command.

2   When might the ingress and egress MPS reside in the same router?

The ingress and egress MPS might reside in the same router whenever the ingress and egress MPCs are only one router hop away along the default path. That router can then service both the ingress and egress roles.

3   What creates the association of an MPC with a VLAN?

Because an LEC must be associated with an MPC in a Catalyst, the VLAN associated with the LEC also associates the MPC to the VLAN.

4   Example 10-6 has the following configuration statement in it: **lane client ethernet elan_name**. Where is the VLAN reference?

This is from an MPS configuration that resides on a router. The router does not associate VLANs like a Catalyst does. Only Catalyst client interfaces need a VLAN reference to bridge the VLAN to the ELAN. The router associates only with an ELAN.

The following lines appear in both Example 10-14 and Example 10-15: **lane client ethernet 21 elan1** and **lane client ethernet 22 elan2**. Is there any problem with this? Could they both say **ethernet 21**? The values 21 and 22 combine those VLAN numbers to the correct ELANs (1 and 2). Both ELANs define different broadcast domains and support different IP subnetworks. Conventionally then, the VLAN numbers differ. However, the two VLAN numbers could be the same because they are isolated by a router. If, however, they were not isolated by a router, the VLAN values could not be the same because they would be bridged together merging the broadcast domains.

5   If a frame must pass through three routers to get from an ingress LEC to an egress LEC, do all three routers need to be configured as an MPS?

No. Only the ingress and egress routers need to be configured as an MPS. However, any other intermediate routers in the default path must have at least an NHS configured. Further, the NHS must be able to source and receive traffic through LECs.

6   Can you configure both an MPC and an MPS in a router?

Yes. The router may have both concurrently. You can elect to do this when the router functions as an intermediate router or as an ingress/egress router, while at the same time serving local Ethernet or other LAN connections as an MPC.

Answers to Chapter 11 Review Questions

1   What is the difference between routing and Layer 3 switching?

In one sense, nothing. In another sense, the term routing implies that the forwarding is software-based where the term Layer 3 switching implies that hardware-based forwarding is used. In both cases, general-purpose CPUs are used to handle control plane functions (such as routing protocols and configuration).

2   Can the router-on-a-stick approach to inter-VLAN routing also support inter-VLAN bridging?

Yes. Simply configure a bridge-group on multiple subinterfaces. Example A-6 bridges protocols other than IP, IPX, and AppleTalk between VLANs 1 and 2.

Example A-6   *Router-on-a-Stick Configuration That Routes IP, IPX, and AppleTalk but Bridges Other Protocols*

```
interface FastEthernet1/0
no ip address
!
interface FastEthernet1/0.1
 encapsulation isl 1
 ip address 10.1.1.1 255.255.255.0
 bridge-group 1
!
interface FastEthernet1/0.2
 encapsulation isl 2
 ip address 10.1.2.1 255.255.255.0
 ipx network 2
 bridge-group 1
!
interface FastEthernet1/0.3
 encapsulation isl 3
 ip address 10.1.3.1 255.255.255.0
 appletalk cable-range 300-310 304.101
 appletalk zone ZonedOut
 ipx network 3
!
bridge 1 protocol ieee
```

3   How can the RSM be especially useful in remote office designs?

It can be fitted with WAN interfaces if you use the VIP adapter.

4   What are the strengths of the RSM approach to Layer 3 switching?

Its unique capability to both bridge and route traffic in the same platform. For example, it is much easier to mix lots of ports that both bridge and route IP traffic using the RSM (and MLS) than it is to use IRB on IOS-based devices. See the section "MLS versus 8500s" for more information.

5   Does MLS eliminate the need for a router?

No. Because MLS is a routing switch Layer 3 switching technique, it relies on caching information learned from the actions of a real router. The router must therefore be present to handle the first packet of every flow and perform the actual access list processing.

6   Does MLS require a router that runs the router-based NetFlow mechanism?

No. Other than the fact that MLS and NetFlow on the routers can both be used for detailed data collection, the two mechanisms are completely separate. A router doing MLS processing does not need to be running router NetFlow.

7   In MLS, does the router create the shortcut entry and download it to the Layer 3 CAM table located in the Catalyst's NFFC or MSFC?

No. Many people are of the opinion that MLS is simply a router running router NetFlow that learns a flow and then ships the results of this flow to a Catalyst. This is not the case. First, if it were the case, the flow would probably be over before the information could be learned by the Catalyst. Second, the NFFC learns the cache information totally by itself. It only needs to know the MAC address and VLAN information of the router (it learns this via MLSP).

8   What is a flow mask?

A flow mask is used to set the granularity with which MLS creates flows and builds shortcut entries. There are three flow masks: destination, source-destination, and full. See the section "Access Lists and Flow Masks" for more information.

9   How does the Catalyst 8500 make routing decisions?

It uses a general-purpose CPU to build a routing table and then a CEF table that gets downloaded to the line cards. The line cards use ASICs to perform lookups in the CEF table and make forwarding decisions. See the section "Switching Routers" for more information.

10   What are the two routing options offered for the Catalyst 6000 family? From a conceptual standpoint, how do they differ?

The MSM and the MSFC. The MSM is a switching router style of platform (it is based on 8510 technology). The MSFC uses MLS (however, it contains both the MLS-SE and MLS-RP on the same card).

11 What is MHSRP? How is it useful?

MHSRP stands for Multigroup Hot Standby Router Protocol. It is a technique that creates two (or more) shared IP addresses for the same IP subnet. It is most useful for load balancing default gateway traffic.

12 What is the difference between CRB and IRB?

Although both features allow a particular protocol to be routed and bridged on the same device, CRB does not let the bridged and routed halves communicate with each other. IRB solves this by introducing the BVI, a single routed interface that all of the bridged interfaces can use to communicate with routed interfaces in that device.

13 When is IRB useful?

When you want to have multiple interfaces assigned to the same IP subnet (or IPX network, AppleTalk cable range, and so on), but also want to have other interfaces that are on different IP subnets. The interfaces on the same subnet communicate through bridging. All of these interfaces as a group use routing to talk to the interfaces using separate subnets.

14 What are some of the dangers associated with mixing bridging and routing?

In a general sense, mixing the two technologies can lead to scalability problems. Specifically, it merges multiple Spanning Trees into a single tree. This can create Spanning Tree instability and defeat load balancing. It can lead to excessive broadcast radiation. It can make troubleshooting difficult. In general, it is advisable to create hard Layer 3 barriers in the network to avoid these issues.

15 What is the benefit of using the IEEE and DEC Spanning-Tree Protocols at the same time? Where should each be run?

Both protocols can be used to avoid the Broken Subnet Problem. IEEE must be run on the Layer 2 Catalysts (they only support this variation of the Spanning-Tree Protocol). The IOS-based routers therefore need to run the DEC or VLAN-Bridge versions.

Answers to Chapter 12 Review Questions

Refer to Figure 12-17 for all review questions.

Figure 12-17   *For Review Questions 1–9*

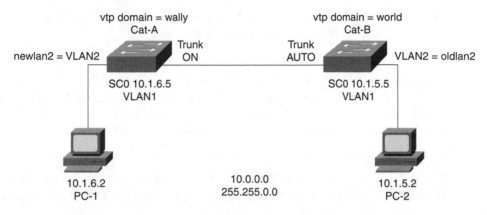

1   In what mode is the link between the two Catalysts?

The link is not a trunk because Cat-A is set to ON and Cat-B set to AUTO. Although this normally forces a link into trunk mode, the two ends belong to different domains preventing the establishment of a trunk. You must set both ends to *ON* or *nonegotiate*. The link is, therefore, an access link.

2   Change both ends of the trunk to *ON*. Can PC-1 **ping** PC-2?

Yes, both are in the same VLAN and the same subnet.

3   Can Cat-A ping Cat-B?

Yes, SC0 for both Catalysts belong to the same VLAN and the same subnet.

4   Can Cat-B ping PC-2?

Even though SC0 and PC-2 belong to the same subnet, they belong to different VLANs. Therefore, they cannot ping each other.

5   VLAN 2 used to be called *oldlan2*. An administrator at Cat-A renames VLAN 2 to *newlan2*. Does Cat-B know about the new name, newlan2?

Cat-B does not know about newlan2 because the two Catalysts are in different VTP domains. The only way for Cat-B to learn about newlan2 is to manually configure it somewhere in the VTP domain *world*.

6   **clear config all** on Cat-B. Reenter the IP address on SC0. Can Cat-B **ping** Cat-A?

After clearing the configuration of Cat-B and resetting the IP address on SC0, the two Catalysts can **ping** each other because they are in the same VLAN and subnet.

7 Can PC-2 **ping** PC-1?

PC-2 cannot **ping** PC-1 because they are now in different VLANs. Clearing the configuration of Cat-B, set all ports to VLAN 1.

8 Does Cat-B know about newlan2?

Assuming that Cat-B did not receive a VTP update from another Catalyst in a different VTP domain, Cat-B now belongs to domain *wally*. The link between the two Catalysts should be a trunk, because Cat-A is set to ON and Cat-B is set to AUTO. This allows Cat-B to receive the VTP updates from Cat-A and, therefore, to learn about newlan2.

9 Can Cat-B remove newlan2?

Yes. If it is set up as either a VTP Server or transparent mode, it can remove newlan2. Because this follows a **clear config all**, the Catalyst is by default set to a VTP server.

Answers to Chapter 13 Review Questions

1 IGMP version 2 includes an explicit leave message for hosts to transmit whenever they no longer want to receive a multicast stream. Why, then, does version 2 include the query message?

The query message remains in version 2 for three reasons. One reason is for backwards compatibility with version 1. Another reason is to enable the router to be absolutely sure that no hosts exist that intend to receive the stream. It is possible that a leave or join message can be lost from a collision or other physical layer event causing the router to erroneously believe that it should terminate the stream. The query message, then, is an insurance policy. A third reason for retaining the query message is to support the query router selection process. Only one router per segment can be a query router. In version 2, the router with the lowest IP address becomes the query router.

2 Why doesn't a Catalyst normally learn multicast addresses?

The Catalyst, a bridge, learns source addresses. Multicast addresses never appear in the source address field of a frame.

3 What Layer 2, Layer 3, and IGMP information does a multicast device transmit for a membership report?

A membership includes the following:

- The Layer 2 header uses the sources unicast address in the source field and the calculated multicast MAC address in the destination field.

- The Layer 3 header uses the source's IP address and the multicast group address for the destination.

The IGMP membership report uses the group multicast address.

4   Assume that you have a switched network with devices running IGMP version 1 and the switches/routers have CGMP enabled. One of the multicast devices surfs the Web looking for a particular multicast stream. The user first connects to group 1 and finds it isn't the group that he wants. So he tries group 2, and then group 3, until he finally finds what he wants in group 4. Meanwhile, another user belongs to groups 1, 2, and 3. What happens to this user's link?

The user's link continues to carry traffic from all four multicast groups until there are no members in the broadcast domain for those groups. CGMP and IGMP version 1 cannot remove a user from a multicast stream until there are no more active members of the group. This stems from the implicit leave function of IGMP version 1. This can create a bandwidth problem for the user because he might have four multicast streams hitting his interface.

Answers to Chapter 14 Review Questions

1   What are some of the unique requirements of an IDF switch?

Cost and port density are the two most important considerations. Other considerations include redundancy options and ease of management.

2   What are some of the unique requirements of an MDF switch?

The key requirements are high availability and throughput, especially Layer 3 throughput. Routing capabilities (such as supporting a wide variety of robust routing protocols) is also important.

3   Describe the access/distribution/core terminology.

Access layer devices are used for end-station connections (through horizontal cabling). They also connect to distribution devices through vertical cabling. In a campus network, the term access device is essentially a synonym for IDF device.

Distribution devices are used to provide a central point of connectivity for an entire building (or portion of a large building). They are equivalent to MDF devices.

The core layer is used to link distribution devices.

4   Why is routing an important part of any large network design?

Routing has many advantages in a properly designed campus network:

- Scalability
- Broadcast and multicast control
- Optimal and flexible path selection
- Load balancing
- Fast convergence

- Hierarchy and summarized addressing
- Policy and access lists
- Value-added features such as DHCP relay

5   What networks work best with the router and hub model?

Networks work best with the router and hub model if they have limited bandwidth requirements and mostly use departmental servers that keep the traffic on the local segment.

6   What are the benefits of the campus-wide VLANs model?

The main advantage of the campus-wide VLAN approach to network design is that it allows a direct, Layer 2 path from end users to servers. This is an attempt to avoid the slowness of software-based routers. This design can also be useful for networks that design lots of flexibility in subnet and VLAN assignments. For example, members of the Finance group can all be assigned to the same VLAN even if they are located in different buildings or locations within the campus. This can then simplify VLAN and security assignments.

7   What are the downsides of the campus-wide VLANs model?

- Management and troubleshooting can be very difficult.
- Spanning Tree can be very difficult to optimize, manage, and control.
- Trunks allow a problem in one VLAN to starve out all VLANs.
- To achieve stability, it often requires all redundancy to be eliminated.
- It is highly dependent upon the 80/20 rule, something that no longer holds true in most networks.
- It is based on the assumption that routers are slow, something that is no longer true.

8   Describe the concept of a distribution block.

A distribution block is a self-contained unit of devices and associated VLANs, subnets, and connectivity. The MDF and IDF switches in distribution blocks form triangles of connectivity. Because routing is configured in MDF devices, a Layer 3 barrier is created between each distribution block and the campus core, increasing the network's scalability.

9   Why is it important to have modularity in a network?

There are many advantages to building modularity into the network:

- Scalability is improved because new modules can be easily added.
- The network becomes easier to understand, troubleshoot, and maintain.
- It is easier to use cookie cutter configurations.
- It is easier to handle migrations.
- It is easier to provide redundancy and load balancing.
- It is easier to provide fast failover performance.

- It is much easier to substitute different technologies at various places within the network. For example, the core can easily use Fast Ethernet, Gigabit Ethernet, ATM, Tag Switching, or Packet Over SONET.

10 What are the concerns that arise when using a Layer 2 core versus a Layer 3 core?

Layer 2 cores are not as scalable as Layer 3 cores. Tuning Spanning Tree and load balancing in a Layer 2 core can be tricky. In many cases, physical loops should be removed to improve failover performance.

11 How should a server farm be implemented in the multilayer model?

As another distribution block off of the core. Workgroup servers can attach to MDF or IDF switches (depending on what users they serve).

Solution to Chapter 14 Hands-On Lab

Design two campus networks that meet the following requirements. The first design should employ the campus-wide VLANs model using Catalyst 5509 switches. The second design should implement the multilayer model by using Catalyst 8540 MDF switches and Catalyst 5509 IDF switches. Here are the requirements:

- The campus contains three buildings.
- Each building has four floors.
- Each floor has one IDF switch.
- Each building has two MDF switches in the basement.
- Each IDF has redundant links (one two each MDF switch).
- The MDF switches are fully meshed with Gigabit Ethernet links (in other words, the core does not use a third layer of switches).
- Each IDF switch should have a unique management VLAN where SC0 can be assigned.
- In the campus-wide VLANs design, assume there are 12 VLANs and that every IDF switch participates in every VLAN.
- In the multilayer design, assume that every IDF switch only participates in a single end-user VLAN (for administrative simplicity).

How many VLANs are required under both designs?

Figure A-9 illustrates a potential design utilizing the campus-wide VLANs model. Because the design is less modular than the multilayer model, this design is usually less scalable and harder to maintain. Each building is contained within a single distribution block.

Figure A-9 *Campus-Wide VLANs Design*

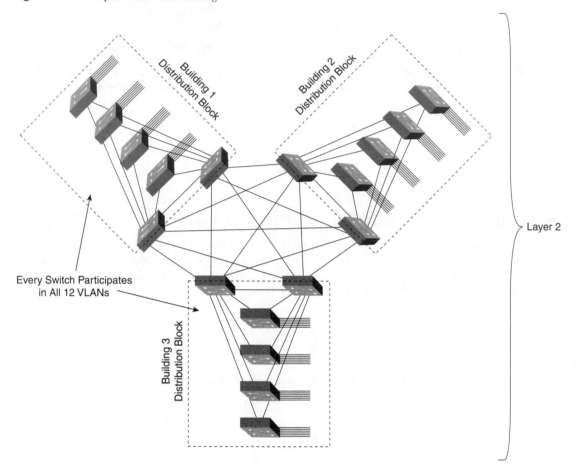

Figure A-10 illustrates a campus design built around the multilayer model. Each distribution block is a self-contained unit. The switching router form of Layer 3 switches are used in the distribution Layer 3. To maximize the potential scalability of the network, a Layer 3 core is used.

Figure A-10 *Multilayer Design Using Switching Routers*

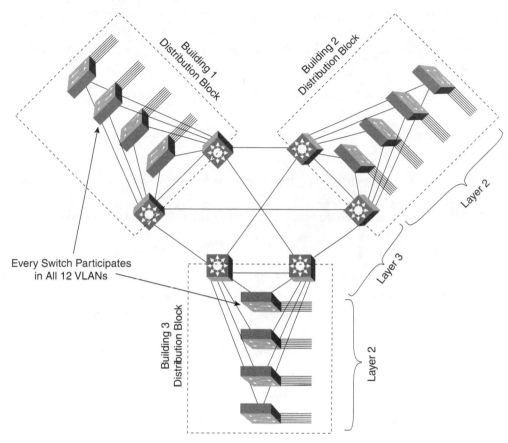

Answers to Chapter 15 Review Questions

    1   This chapter mentioned many advantages to using the multilayer model. List as many as possible.

The advantages of using the multilayer model are as follows:

- Modularity
- Scalability
- Ease of maintenance and troubleshooting
- Improved multicast support

- Deterministic traffic flows

- It is a media-independent design (for example, the core can use either Ethernet or ATM)

- It is very resilient and offers fast failover via intelligent Layer 3 routing protocols

- It provides a high degree of control

2   This chapter also mentioned many disadvantages to using campus-wide VLANs. List as many as possible.

The disadvantages of using campus-wide VLANs are as follows:

- A lack of hierarchy

- Spanning Tree and other problems can quickly spread and cripple the entire network

- Spanning Tree load balancing can be extremely difficult if not impossible to implement

- Troubleshooting is difficult

- It is difficult to expand the network

- Connecting multiple VLANs to multiple servers through mutli-VLAN NICs like LANE, ISL, and 802.1Q often results in low performance and can overwhelm the servers with broadcast traffic from many VLANs

- They often require that redundancy be eliminated to achieve stability

3   List some of the issues concerning management VLAN design.

Some of the issues concerning management VLAN design are as follows:

- Always have separate management and end-user VLANs

- Having loop-free management VLANs can improve stability

4   What are some factors to be considered when determining where to place Root Bridges?

- Place in the paths of high-bandwidth data flows

- Use devices that can carry the aggregate load presented to Root Bridges

- Use a stable device

- Use centralized Root Bridges to facilitate network simplicity

- Use distributed Root Bridges to increase aggregate throughput at the expense of a more complex network design

5 List five techniques that are available for campus load balancing.

Five techniques that are available for campus load balancing include:

- The Spanning-Tree Protocol
- HSRP
- IP Routing
- ATM
- EtherChannel

6 What is the primary difference between using routing switches (MLS) and switching routers in MDF/distribution layer devices?

The primary difference between routing switches and switching routers concerns their handling of Layer 2 and Layer 3 functions. Routing switches are, first and foremost, Layer 2 devices that have been enhanced with a variety of Layer 3 functionality. However, they continue to maintain a strong Layer 2 orientation. As a result, they do not automatically create any Layer 3 barriers in the network (this must be done through manual pruning of VLANs from trunk links). On the other hand, switching routers such as the Catalyst 8500s are essentially high-speed versions of traditional Cisco routers. Therefore, they require no special configuration to partition the network into separate Layer 2 domains (creating a more scalable design).

Note that both types of Layer 3 switches can be used to create essentially identical designs. The distinctions being made here reflect the *default* behavior of these devices and should be kept in mind when designing and building a campus network.

7 What are the pros and cons of using ATM?

Table A-1 lists the pros and cons of using ATM.

Table A-1 *ATM Pros and Cons*

Pros	Cons
High available bandwidth	Complexity
Sophisticated bandwidth sharing	Cost
QoS	Ethernet is growing in sophistication and in its capability to handle features previously only supported by ATM (such as COS/QoS)
Support for timing-critical applications such as voice and video	Many new voice and video applications do not require ATM service
Distance	
Interoperability	

Answers to Chapter 18 Review Questions

1   In what sort of situation would a Catalyst 6000/6500 using XDI/CatOS software and no MSFC daughter-card be useful?

In cases where very high Layer 2 bandwidth is required. For example, it is a good fit for Gigabit Ethernet backbone switching and server farm applications.

2   What Layer 3 switching configuration is used by the MSM?

Router-on-a-stick.

3   The MSM connects to the Catalyst 6000 backplane via what type of interfaces?

Four Gigabit Ethernet interfaces.

4   How can ten VLANs be configured on the MSM?

Although the four Gigabit Ethernet interfaces can be used as individual interfaces, they are generally more useful when grouped into a single Gigabit EtherChannel bundle (referred to as a Port-channel interface in the IOS configuration). By creating subinterfaces on the Port-channel interface, a large number of VLANs can be configured (although, as discussed in Chapters 14 and 15, using a huge number of VLANs is generally a bad idea from a design and maintenance standpoint).

5   What are the advantages and disadvantages of the MSFC Hybrid Mode?

The advantages of the MSFC Hybrid Mode include the following:

- High-speed Layer 3 switching
- Capability to support features such as IGMP Snooping and QoS/COS
- Retains the tight integration between Layer 2 and Layer 3 featured by the RSM (specifically, Layer 2 ports are automatically assigned to the correct Layer 3 VLAN)
- Uses a single slot

The one noteworthy disadvantage of the MSFC Hybrid Mode is the requirement for two user interfaces (IOS on the RP for Layer 3 and XDI/CatOS on the SP for Layer 2)

6   Under the Native IOS Mode, how are switchports configured with Layer 3 information like IP addresses?

Layer 3 information is configured on an SVI VLAN interface, not on the switchport directly.

7 Is a Catalyst 6000 running Native IOS Mode software more of a routing switch or a switching router?

The flexibility of the Native IOS Mode interface allows the Catalyst 6000 to function as either type of device. Because it is based on switching hardware, it has a wide variety of Layer 2 features and functions. However, because both CPUs are running full IOS images, it inherits the attributes shared by virtually all Cisco routers. By configuring most of the ports as switchports, the box takes on a very routing switch-like feel. However, if you leave the interfaces at their default (where every interface is a routed port), the box looks like a switching router. At some point, the difference doesn't matter and the discussion drops off into a meaningless debate of semantics. Don't let the flexibility of the MSFC Native IOS Mode leave you in a situation of brain lock. Instead, simply take advantage of its benefits.

INDEX

Symbols

! (bang), 90–91
? (question mark), accessing help system, 93

Numerics

5/3/1 rule, 40
10BaseT, Manchester encoding, 14
12-port EtherChannel, 309–310
24-port EtherChannel, 309–310
80/20 rule, 45, 605
100BaseFX, 18
100BaseT2, 17–18
100BaseT4, 17
100BaseTX, 17
100BaseX, 19–20, 23–24
802.10 encapsulation, 326–328
1000BaseCX Gigabit Ethernet, 29
1000BaseLX Gigabit Ethernet, 28
1000BaseSX Gigabit Ethernet, 28
1000BaseT, 29
1900/2800 series (Catalyst), configuring, 109
3000 series, configuring, 109
5000 series (Catalyst)
    CLI, 89–90
    configuring, 84–89
8500s
    CEF (Cisco Express Forwarding), 502–503
    comparing to MLS (Catalyst 5000), 506–512
    design scenario, 774
        IDF Supervisor configuration, 779–791
        IP addressing, 777
        MDF Supervisor configuration, 792–797
        server farms, 779
        Spanning Tree, 775–776
        trunks, 779
        VLAN design, 776
        VTP, 778
    EtherChannel, 506
    HSRP, load balancing, 676
    Layer 3 switching, 503–505, 774–799
    MDF switches, 626–628
    MLS, 628–629

practical applications, 679
restricting SPT, 664
See also switching routers

A

AAL (ATM Adaption Layer), 351
access layer closets, 612
    See also distribution layer
access links, 302–303
    EtherChannel, 307–312
    scalability, 303
access lists
    Layer 3, 615
    legacy networks, 127
    MLS, 478–482
access methods
    Catalyst, 88
    CSMA/CD, 6–7
access switchport interfaces, 828–829
accessing
    Catalyst 5000s
        via Telnet, 87–88
        via TFTP, 88
        via console, 86
    help system (Catalyst), 92–93
activating Catalyst permit lists, 87
active peers (HSRP), placement, 516–518
active topologies
    convergence, 209–210
    load balancing, 235
    Spanning Tree, 192–195
        manual Root Bridge placement, 195–196
        programming Root Bridge priority, 197–198
adaptive cut-through switching, 61, 63
adding NSAP to ATM switches, 395
addressing
    ATM (Asynchronous Transfer Mode)
        hard-coded addresses, 403
        NSAPs, 356–358, 388–389
        VPI/VCI addresses, 355–356, 358

C

E

F

G

M

N

O

P

Q

R

V

W

X

CCIE Professional Development

Cisco CCIE Fundamentals: Network Design and Case Studies
Cisco Systems, Inc.

1-57870-066-3 • AVAILABLE NOW

This two-part reference is a compilation of design tips and configuration examples assembled by Cisco Systems. The design guide portion of this book supports the network administrator who designs and implements routers and switch-based networks, and the case studies supplement the design guide material with real-world configurations. Begin the process of mastering the technologies and protocols necessary to become an effective CCIE.

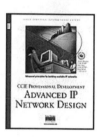

Advanced IP Network Design

Alvaro Retana, CCIE; Don Slice, CCIE; and Russ White, CCIE

1-57870-097-3 • AVAILABLE NOW

Network engineers and managers can use these case studies, which highlight various network design goals, to explore issues including protocol choice, network stability, and growth. This book also includes theoretical discussion on advanced design topics.

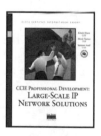

Large-Scale IP Network Solutions

Khalid Raza, CCIE; and Mark Turner

1-57870-084-1 • AVAILABLE NOW

Network engineers can find solutions as their IP networks grow in size and complexity. Examine all the major IP protocols in-depth and learn about scalability, migration planning, network management, and security for large-scale networks.

Routing TCP/IP, Volume I

Jeff Doyle, CCIE

1-57870-041-8 • AVAILABLE NOW

This book takes the reader from a basic understanding of routers and routing protocols through a detailed examination of each of the IP interior routing protocols. Learn techniques for designing networks that maximize the efficiency of the protocol being used. Exercises and review questions provide core study for the CCIE Routing and Switching exam.

www.ciscopress.com

Cisco Career Certifications

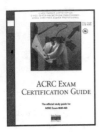

ACRC Exam Certification Guide

Clare Gough, CCIE

0-7357-0075-3 • **AVAILABLE NOW   CCNP/CCDP**

Scenario-based learning and exercises help you master ACRC exam topics, including standard and extended access lists, queuing, scalable routing protocols, route redistribution and summarization, dial-on-demand routing, dial backup, and the integration of bridging with a routed network.

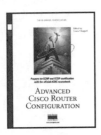

Advanced Cisco Router Configuration

Cisco Systems, Inc., edited by Laura Chappell

1-57870-074-4 • **AVAILABLE NOW**

Based on the actual Cisco ACRC course, this book provides a thorough treatment of advanced network deployment issues. Learn to apply effective configuration techniques for solid network implementation and management as you prepare for CCNP and CCDP certifications. This book also includes chapter-ending tests for self-assessment.

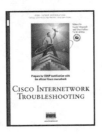

Cisco Internetwork Troubleshooting

Edited by Laura Chappell

1-57870-092-2 • **AVAILABLE NOW   CCNP**

Based on the actual Cisco CIT course, this book covers troubleshooting methodology, routing and routed protocol troubleshooting, campus switch and VLAN troubleshooting, and Frame Relay and ISDN BRI problems. Master standard problem-solving using network troubleshooting tools and Cisco diagnostic tools as you prepare for CCNP certification.

Cisco Internetwork Design

Mathew Birkner, CCIE

1-57870-171-6 • November 1999 • **AVAILABLE NOW   CCDP**

Recommended and approved by Cisco Systems as official study material for CCDP candidates, this book is an in-depth and direct extension of the CID course taught by Cisco-approved training centers. This books contains case studies and exercises that foster an understanding of the application of the concepts, covering design issues for LANs, WANs, SNA, TCP/IP, and desktop protocols.

www.ciscopress.com

Cisco Press Solutions

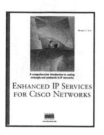

Enhanced IP Services for Cisco Networks
Donald C. Lee, CCIE

1-57870-106-6 • AVAILABLE NOW

This is a guide to improving your network's capabilities by understanding the new enabling and advanced Cisco IOS services that build more scalable, intelligent, and secure networks. Learn the technical details necessary to deploy Quality of Service, VPN technologies, IPsec, the IOS firewall and IOS Intrusion Detection. These services will allow you to extend the network to new frontiers securely, protect your network from attacks, and increase the sophistication of network services.

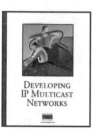

Developing IP Multicast Networks, Volume 1
Beau Williamson, CCIE

1-57870-077-9 • AVAILABLE NOW

This book provides a solid foundation of IP multicast concepts and explains how to design and deploy the networks that will support appplications such as audio and video conferencing, distance-learning, and data replication. Includes an in-depth discussion of the PIM protocol used in Cisco routers and detailed coverage of the rules that control the creation and maintenance of Cisco mroute state entries.

OpenCable Architecture
Michael Adams

1-57870-135-X • AVAILABLE NOW

Whether you're a television, data communications, or telecommunications professional, or simply an interested business person, this book will help you understand the technical and business issues surrounding interactive television services. It will also provide you with an inside look at the combined efforts of the cable, data, and consumer electronics industries' efforts to develop those new services.

Designing Network Security
Merike Kaeo

1-57870-043-4 • AVAILABLE NOW

Designing Network Security is a practical guide designed to help you understand the fundamentals of securing your corporate infrastructure. This book takes a comprehensive look at underlying security technologies, the process of creating a security policy, and the practical requirements necessary to implement a corporate security policy.

CISCO SYSTEMS

CISCO PRESS

www.ciscopress.com

Cisco Press Solutions

OSPF Network Design Solutions

Thomas M. Thomas II

1-57870-046-9 • AVAILABLE NOW

This comprehensive guide presents a detailed, applied look into the workings of the popular Open Shortest Path First protocol, demonstrating how to dramatically increase network performance and security, and how to most easily maintain large-scale networks. OSPF is thoroughly explained through exhaustive coverage of network design, deployment, management, and troubleshooting.

Top-Down Network Design

Priscilla Oppenheimer

1-57870-069-8 • AVAILABLE NOW

Building reliable, secure, and manageable networks is every network professional's goal. This practical guide teaches you a systematic method for network design that can be applied to campus LANs, remote-access networks, WAN links, and large-scale internetworks. Learn how to analyze business and technical requirements, examine traffic flow and Quality of Service requirements, and select protocols and technologies based on performance goals.

Internetworking SNA with Cisco Solutions

George Sackett and Nancy Sackett

1-57870-083-3 • AVAILABLE NOW

This comprehensive guide presents a practical approach to integrating SNA and TCP/IP networks. It provides readers with an understanding of internetworking terms, networking architectures, protocols, and implementations for internetworking SNA with Cisco routers.

For the latest on Cisco Press resources and Certification and

Training guides, or for information on publishing opportunities, visit

www.ciscopress.com.

CISCO SYSTEMS

CISCO PRESS

Cisco Press books are available at your local bookstore, computer store, and online booksellers.